THE URBAN PATTERN

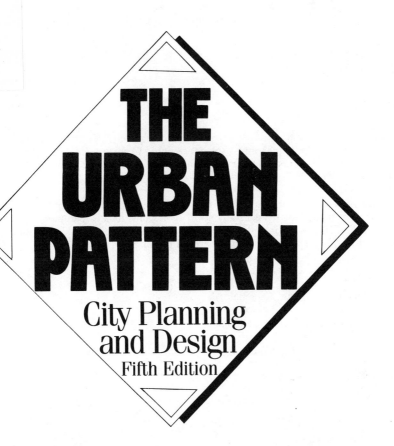

THE URBAN PATTERN

City Planning and Design

Fifth Edition

ARTHUR B. GALLION, FAIA
SIMON EISNER, APA, AICP

VNR VAN NOSTRAND REINHOLD COMPANY
_____ *New York*

Copyright © 1986 by Van Nostrand Reinhold Company Inc.
Library of Congress Catalog Card Number 85–7381
ISBN 0–442–22731–0

Printed in the United States of America

Designed by Paul Chevannes

Van Nostrand Reinhold Company Inc.
115 Fifth Avenue
New York, New York 10003

Van Nostrand Reinhold Company Limited
Molly Millars Lane
Wokingham, Berkshire RG11 2PY, England

Van Nostrand Reinhold
480 La Trobe Street
Melbourne, Victoria 3000, Australia

Macmillan of Canada
Division of Canada Publishing Corporation
164 Commander Boulevard
Agincourt, Ontario M1S 3C7, Canada

16 15 14 13 12 11 10 9 8 7 6 5 4 3 2 1

Library of Congress Cataloging in Publication Data

Gallion, Arthur B.
  The urban pattern.

  Bibliography: p.
  Includes index.
  1. City planning.   I. Eisner, Simon.   II. Title.
NA9031.G3   1985   711′.4   85–7381
ISBN 0–442–22731–0

CONTENTS

Part III
THE PLANNING PROCESS

Part IV
PLANNING FOR THE FUTURE

Part V
IMPLEMENTATION

Part VI
NEW HORIZONS

To Arthur B. Gallion 1902–1978

Arthur Gallion loved and respected the people of this world. He traveled to many lands and observed the basic goodness of all he met. As an educator, he devoted much of his life to the betterment of young seekers of knowledge. He expressed concern for honesty on the part of those who determine the character of the environment. His enthusiasm and critical dialogues inspired and motivated all who knew him.

Development of this Fifth Edition of *The Urban Pattern* without the creative contributions of Arthur Gallion has been a lonely task.

Simon Eisner

If you can look into the seeds of time,
And say which grains will grow and which will not,
Speak then to me. . . .

Shakespeare

PREFACE

No one can fail to observe that, despite the marvels of human inventive genius and the material comforts enjoyed by many, the spiritual and cultural lives of many people in the modern world are still impoverished. All the thought and money that have been devoted to planning have not substantially improved the total environment. The authors of this book do not presume that planning will solve all of the ills of the urban community or that planning by itself will be adequate to preserve or conserve our natural resources. Without creative planning and active implementation, however, we will not be able to begin to achieve an environment conducive to the good life to which we aspire.

The fifth edition of *The Urban Pattern* has been designed for students and for persons active in professional offices. We hope that the book and the concepts contained herein will encourage readers to fulfill their professional potential and expand their abilities to better serve the public they represent, consistent with the highest ethical standards. The reorganization and additions to the book are a response to the changes that have taken place in recent years in the urban design profession and should be of interest to both novice and professional.

The current thrust for comprehensiveness by the planning profession, in response to numerous rulings and decisions by the courts, has broadened the horizons and responsibilities of persons in or entering the field.

No longer concerned only with land use regulation, professionals must now be increasingly involved in related fields. The "comprehensive planner" must bring together many related individuals in the complicated and often conflicting interests of urban living.

The fifth edition of *The Urban Pattern* responds to many of these new opportunities and concerns. It focuses on areas where innovation and experimentation affect the public and private sectors, notably the crisis in housing availability. It also examines growth management regulations, which some communities require as they begin to feel the stress of growth without the substantial economic base required to support the needs and demands of new residents.

The environment within and around urban areas is also discussed, with respect to the increasing concern for health and security in those urban areas subject to careless treatment of resources. Environmental impact studies are cited as the current method of determining the extent of potential problems and the efforts essential to mitigate them. The role of geography in determining the location and nature of urban centers is explored as well.

The problems confronting the increasing number of aging persons are of paramount importance to planners both in the United States and abroad. Materials dealing with housing programs for the elderly in many nations are included. Planning for public health is also touched upon.

Policy planning, the current emphasis of many university programs in urban planning, is reviewed with reference to the policy statement of the American Planning Association.

Materials dealing with areas of exposure to dangerous natural phenomena have been expanded.

The chapter dealing with implementation has been greatly expanded as well, and now includes the role of zoning, land subdivision, capital improvements, and the installation and maintenance of the infrastructure.

The planning process is delineated and the various persons and groups involved are cited. The relationship between the public and private sectors is described, and the potential struggles between the regulators and regulated are illustrated. Additional examples of new towns and national capitals are part of the expanded chapter dealing with these important communities in all parts of the world. Additional material on art in the cities, urban design, and historical preservation is included.

The authors are grateful to the many persons and organizations who have contributed to the expanded contents of this fifth edition of *The Urban Pattern* and to the many who were responsible for prior contributions. Their thought and writings have given depth and richness to this book.

We also extend our thanks to the many who contributed to the text by their suggestions and editing of the material. Special thanks to the staff of Van Nostrand Reinhold, whose courtesy, encouragement, and consideration added to the pleasure of preparing this updated manuscript.

Simon Eisner, AICP, APA

PART 1

THE CITY IS BORN

The People, Yes, Out of what is their
change from chaos to order and
chaos again?
Carl Sandburg

CHAPTER 1

THE DAWN OF URBANIZATION

The simplest definition of urbanism or an urban area might be: the confederation or union of neighboring clans resorting to a center used as a common meeting place for worship, protection, and the like; hence, the political or sovereign body formed by such a community.

An urban area can also be defined as a composite of cells, neighborhoods, or communities where people work together for the common good. The types of urban areas can vary as greatly as the variety of activities performed there: the means of production and the kinds of goods, trade, transportation, the delivery of goods and services, or a combination of all of these activities.

A third definition says that urban areas are those locations where there is opportunity for a diversified living environment and diverse life-styles. People live, work, and enjoy themselves in social and cultural relationships provided by the proximities of an urban area.

Urban areas can be simple or complex. They can have a rural flavor or that of an industrial workshop. They can be peaceful or filled with all types of conflict. They can be small and easy to maintain, or gargantuan and filled with strife and economic problems.

3

FROM THE CAVE TO THE VILLAGE

Contrary to popular belief, urbanism did not begin when people left the cave. It probably started in the caves themselves, where the people gathered for protection against the elements or for defense against rival tribes. Lewis Mumford states:

> Though permanent villages date only from the Neolithic times, the habit of resorting to caves for the collective performance of magical ceremonies seems to date back to an earlier period; and whole communities, living in caves and the hollowed-out walls of rock, have survived in widely scattered areas down to the present. The outline of the city as both an outward form and inward pattern of life might be found in such ancient assemblages.[1]

These places of communal living gave way to the village. The village was a byproduct of the development of agriculture in areas where there was an adequate water supply and fertile soil. Many of these earliest villages arose adjacent to what is now the Mediterranean Sea and the Nile, Tigris, and Euphrates rivers. Mumford holds that the so-called urban areas thus newly created and their rural hinterlands were part of an interlaced whole essential to the sustenance of human and animal life, which in turn promoted agricultural production.

Many early villages were located on sites that offered some natural protection, sites such as elevated terrain, islands, and peninsulas. Otherwise artificial defenses had to be built, and villages would be surrounded by barricades or moats, for example. One of the earliest known villages was built on pilings in a Swiss lake.

People have always been gregarious beings. They have sought companionship and devised group activities and entertainment. The village was also an appropriate sanctuary for the altar of their deity, a meeting place for assembly, and a center for trade. As the environment became increasingly populated, urbanization resulted.

As communities have taken on added functions and have grown, the care of fertile land has become to some extent ignored. Lands still used for agriculture have been infused with so many artificial fertilizers that the soil has become the vehicle for these chemicals. These fertilizers are the main nutrients for fruit and vegetable crops rather than the soil's natural nutrients. Concern for the protection of fertile soils has been slow to develop, but increasing attention is now being focused on conservation worldwide. Sometimes the concern is expressed locally as well. Some Indian communities, for example, opposed urban development on their reservations, favoring instead the protection of their land and culture despite the greater cash return that may result from urbanization.

---

1. "The Natural History of Urbanization," in *Man's Role in Changing the Face of the Earth,* ed. William L. Thomas, Jr. (Chicago, Illinois, University of Chicago Press, 1956).

Cliff dwellings—Mesa Verde National Park, Colorado. *Located in the four corners area, where Colorado, Utah, New Mexico, and Arizona are joined, this ancient American Indian community has left cave dwellings, including multistory buildings, that reveal their form of civilization.*

The large community, as opposed to the village, came about as the result of the growth of crops and the breeding of stock on a more permanent basis than before. The production of hard grains that could be stored from year to year offered stability, since it provided insurance against starvation. Urban areas became known for the type of food they could conserve—wheat and rye in the European areas, rice in the Orient. The ability to preserve food made it possible to diversify into other activities.

With the development of a diversified economy not totally dependent upon food production, it became possible to attract people into a labor pool, thus providing employment in a variety of forms. This in turn brought about the enlargement of villages or hamlets into towns and cities, which operated on different political and economic bases than had been possible in the simpler forms.

Newly created cities retained many of the physical and social characteristics of the earlier urban areas. Even today the food supply of many agricultural centers is located in the fields that surround them. Urban centers like these have had little reason to grow beyond the limited size that their basic needs have dictated.

While many changes have taken place in some rural areas, great parts of the world's developing countries still live primitively as far as their economy and standards of living are concerned. The natives wrest what food they can from poor land, constantly remaining on the verge of starvation. Recent events in Ethiopia are a horrifying illustration of this condition.

The People's Republic of China made its greatest step forward when it freed itself from the danger of famine. The primary planning goal in that nation is still a large-scale commitment to agriculture. A tremendous amount of manpower has been allocated to that end because of the current lack of mechanical equipment.

THE NATURE OF CITIES

The word *city* implies a concentration of people in a given geographic area who support themselves on a fairly permanent basis from the economic activities of that area. The city can be a center of industry, trade, education, government, or involve all these activities. This diversity of opportunity attracts people from rural areas to the cities.

Thus we find that cities tend to become big if their economic base is broad. The smaller cities are usually satellites that depend on larger cities to sustain their economic life. For example, central cities have multiple functions, whereas the suburban "bedroom" communities surrounding them mainly serve the purpose of housing the more affluent members of the work force.

Cities have circulation systems that unite the different areas and provide routes for bringing commodities from the farms and elsewhere to the city's distribution centers. In large cities, multiple kinds of transportation and transit are often available.

Cities have many obvious faults when it comes to their services to people. They can be overcrowded, contain large amounts of substandard housing, be centers of unemployment, and have corrupt governments. Taxation tends to be high and services less than adequate. However, even with all of these faults, cities are here to stay. The charge to planners at all levels, public and private, is to find ways to make these essential elements in our social system work better, more efficiently, and thus to make our cities more desirable places in which to live.

CHAPTER 2

LOCATION AND TYPES OF URBANISM

THE INFLUENCE OF GEOGRAPHY

Historically, natural factors played an important part in the development and growth of urban areas. The danger of fire and flood, extreme climatic conditions, the possibility of earthquakes and volcanic eruptions, lack of natural resources or fertile soils—all influenced decisions either to settle in a given area or to move to a more favorable site. The larger early urban areas, with some exceptions, are found where the climate is relatively moderate. Few of any great size are located north of the sixtieth or south of the forty-fifth parallels. This does not mean that there are no great temperature extremes within these boundaries. The torrid Sahara Desert and the frigid winter of parts of Canada, the United States, and the Soviet Union lie within this so-called temperate zone. However, the climate is habitable for major parts of the year so that life can exist or even flourish.

Geographic studies indicate that urban areas seldom form where the topography is steep. Some cities are located at high altitudes, but the slope of the land is relatively level. For example, Denver, Colorado, and Mexico City are more than 5,000 feet above sea level, but the terrain at these sites is relatively flat. It is only recently, with the invention of earthmoving equipment like the bulldozer, that steep areas have been leveled to permit urban development.

8

The accessibility of other important places usually determines the location of larger cities. Thus most of the largest cities of the world can be found on or near major waterways. New York, Seattle, Boston, Rio de Janeiro, and Chicago illustrate this principle. Some of these cities serve as transportation terminals while others, like Chicago and Kansas City, are crossing points for networks of internal transportation. The geographic study of cities also takes into account the relationship among people, types of housing, population densities and concentration, rates of growth, and the impact of growth upon the land and all other resources.

Impact on the Natural Environment

Urbanism brings about many changes in the surrounding environment. Buildings occupying formerly open land, pavements on streets, and smoke from factories can alter the climate. Sometimes the unintended change is dramatic. The construction of a simple irrigation canal from the Colorado River to the fertile Imperial Valley of California brought about the formation of the Salton Sea in 1905 after a heavy rainfall in the upper reaches of the river. Thus a body of water about forty miles long and ten miles wide exists today where in 1904 there was only desert land.

Recent ventures into the Alaskan wilderness may have long-term adverse effects on the cycles of human and animal life there. Where once a perfect balance in nature existed, today the advance of "southern civilization" has replaced the dogsled with the gasoline-powered automobile. The once-limited paths and roads that did not disturb the permafrost have been replaced by trenches cut by the many heavy vehicles. The migration pattern of the caribou and other large animals may be disrupted by the hundreds of miles of the oil pipeline. Each incident may not be critical to the survival of the Alaskan Eskimos—or Inuit, as they prefer to be called—but the sum of these changes may cause change as great as those that created the Sahara Desert.

The future presents all humanity—not just those living in urban areas—with the problem of coping with the consequences of technological change. The use and disposal of nuclear power and wastes, the filling of the skies and waters with pollutants, even the artificial inducing of rain with iodides: such elements may not only change the microclimate, but they may also ultimately affect the habitability of our planet.

POLITICAL AND SOCIAL ORGANIZATION

Society has been forged in the crucible of natural forces. Because communities are part of nature, people have suffered from many of the evils they have inflicted on the environment. They have faced the necessity to improve economic security, correct social maladjustments, discard mass superstitions, or resist seizure of power by autocrats bent upon personal glory and self-aggrandizement. The conflicts have created varying degrees of pressure upon humankind under a variety of circumstances.

The village brought something new to the lives of primitive people. It introduced the need for mutual responsibility and cooperation. Various social and political organizations emerged as a direct result.

People did not adjust easily to the self-discipline that community life requires. Personal rivalry flared within the village, and the most powerful individual assumed the role of tribal leader. Rivalry between villages often resulted in armed conflict. Several villages might come under the domination of the victorious tribe with that tribe's leader rising to the position of ruler. In time, empires were created and rulers took the titles of king and emperor.

What distinguishes the early city from the primitive village is its higher degree of political and social organization. The more sophisticated social structure allows people to live together in relative peace. Social, economic, and political organization are essential to the growth and development of a city. The history of China, from the time of the Qin Dynasty (221–206 B.C.) to the present, vividly illustrates this progression.

As a result of the more advanced social structure, bold aesthetic changes took place. Temples and other structures of the ruling group became permanent. Tremendous amounts of energy were expended to produce great edifices, such as palaces and cathedrals, which became a source of pride to the public and the seat of power for its rulers. In the meantime, most of the people lived in mud huts or worse where none of the basic amenities existed or even basic needs were met. Such situations still exist in many parts of the world today, where great numbers of people live in slums, *favellas,* and *barrios,* many of which are in or adjacent to urban areas.

EVOLUTION OF PHYSICAL FORM

Sensitive to the surge between oppression and justice, the physical form of cities has been shaped by the economic, social, and political forces of society. The degree to which freedom or slavery has dominated human life, the manner in which war has been waged, the instruments of destruction and defense, the tools for peaceful pursuits and the way they have been used, the consideration, neglect, or disdain people have shown their fellows, all account for the kind of cities people have built for themselves. The effect of these factors on urban development in the past may help guide us in charting future enterprises in city building.

Historians have attempted to isolate and codify the variations in the patterns of cities, but, their development almost precludes such classification. Adjectives like *organic* and *inorganic, irregular* and *geometrical, magical* and *mystical, formal* and *informal, medieval* and *classic*, often obscure rather than clarify the distinctions, or they describe a form without the substance.

Two basic urban forms are discernible in the past: the walled town and the open city. Within these basic forms a wide variety of patterns was woven, each form and design shaped by the character of society at the time.

Neither the presence nor the absence of a particular form affixed upon a people or a period is a conclusive expression of that society. It is rather the manner in which the forms have been manipulated and the purpose for which they have been devised that give significance to the physical patterns of cities. Within these various patterns similar social, economic, and political habits and customs may be found.

Few cities in which great cultures thrived began with a plan. They developed by a process of accretion—the growth was irregular, responsive to changes in the habits of people, and dynamic in character. They began as free cities settled voluntarily. Their external form, their physical pattern, was introduced according to the structure of the land itself or the manner in which the land was apportioned among the inhabitants. Colonial cities founded by great states were given a formal pattern determined in advance by a ruling authority. Privileged landowners divided their land for allocation to settlers, the plots being generally identical in form and character.

With the ebb and flow of civilization irregular and geometrical patterns have been grafted one upon the other. Villages that grew into cities because of geographic, economic, or social advantages may show evidence of geometrical patterns superimposed upon original irregular ones, or an informal and irregular system may have been grafted onto a city with an original gridiron pattern. Cities have been subjected to the process of continuous remodeling through the ages, and the variety of their forms is the result of the particular force or forces that were dominant during the successive periods of their history. The motives of city builders, from emperors to modern developers, are reflected in the designs they have stamped upon their portions of a city.

We are accustomed to measuring a civilization by the monuments it produces. Certain cultural characteristics are revealed by these structures, but it is not enough to observe the monuments alone. If the characteristics of a civilization are to be discerned, attention cannot be confined to the rulers; the affairs of the people must be observed. The city is not the palace, the temple, or a collection of art objects. The city means all of the people who inhabit it, the entire collection of the houses the people live in, the places in which they work, the streets they traverse, and the shops and markets in which they trade. To separate the palace from the dwellings of the populace is like removing a phrase from its context. When related to the lives of the people, the palace may provide quite a different interpretation than when observed as an isolated monument.

More than the great and impressive structures, the common dwellings of the people mark the culture of cities. Civilization is not measured by creations and inventions alone; rather it is measured by the extent to which the people share the benefits these make possible. Progress is not properly gauged by the comparison of an aboriginal village with a modern city; it is more accurately appraised by the degree to which the people participate in the advantages of each. Standards of quality are relative, and it is the contrast between the environment of the privileged and that of the poor that provides the yardstick to measure the freedom and happiness enjoyed by the people in any given period.

Historically there is a lag between moments of great social ideals and the structures that reflect them. Institutions of social and political justice or oppression gather momentum that carries beyond the zenith of their influence. The substance of these institutions, the freedom they have nurtured or denied, may have altered or vanished by the time the physical structure of the urban environment they engendered is finally completed. Frequently the powerful human forces that produced a city have begun to change or disappear, but the physical form of the city has never been modified. An environment that emerged from a society of high ideals may then become the dramatic scene of its decline.

Stability, a status quo of human institutions, in the sense of a consistency of human conduct over a more or less long period, does not long endure. Civilization has not remained static for any protracted period. Humanity must continuously have new cultural food upon which to nourish, or it decays. During periods when social and political institutions were molded to the welfare of the people, they provided the very climate of freedom that permitted humanity to forge and wield the tools of oppression, inequality, and injustice. We observe these trends in early villages, in ancient cities, in medieval cities, during the baroque period, and there is evidence of their presence in our cities of today.

TYPES OF URBAN COMMUNITIES

From earliest times, each urban community has fulfilled a special purpose in the social and economic structure. They have all had particular functions to perform, some singular and others multiple. Thus can be found the following types:

The Crossroad. This is the simplest form of community, expanding or contracting as traders travel from one area to another. It is a place for rest, food, and the exchange of merchandise and of ideas. The location can be at some transportation terminal, like a river or a seaport.

The Primary Agricultural Community. This is the service area for rural activities. Essentials for agricultural activities are acquired here, and here the harvest is brought for shipment to processors and ultimately to its consumers.

The Commercial City. The business ventures, the exchanges, the dealings in commodities take place here. A wide range of goods is available for the consumer to select from.

The Industrial City. Raw or partly processed materials are turned into finished goods here, for shipment to the marketplaces of the world.

The Transportation City. Such a city is located at the center of the transportation web, where goods are brought from far-off places to be distributed to other far-off places.

The Recreational City. Because of their climate or other special offerings, such cities attract large numbers of people for other than business-related or work-related purposes. Examples include health resorts, gambling centers, sports, and scenic areas.

Educational Cities. A major educational institution or group of institutions constitute the primary functions of the urban area. Examples of such places are Claremont, California; Davis, California; and Princeton, New Jersey.

Mining Communities. Here the extraction of minerals forms the economic base. Diamond-mining communities in South Africa are of this type, as are towns in coal-mining areas.

Retirement Communities. These include cities where the principal export capital comes from income and pensions. The communities in the Sun Belt of the United States are examples.

Governmental Centers. Centers of governmental activity, where the principal employer is the government.

Combination (Regional) Cities. A few cities perform all or many of the above functions. They are therefore larger and more complex than any of the individual types of communities.

CITIES OF ANCIENT LANDS

Early civilization spread along the fertile valleys where food, water, and transportation possibilities were at hand. A series of great and small empires rose, waged wars, and fell. Supremacy shifted from one kingdom to another, each adding its contribution to the evolution of the civilized world. One characteristic was shared by every one of these civilizations. All possessions of the kingdom, the land, and its benefits were subject to the will of the ruling monarchs and their appointed emissaries. The rulers were generally considered deities, and their representatives brought the orders of a god to be carried out.

Egypt and Others

In Egypt the lives of the people were dedicated to the pharaoh. The towns they built in the third millennium B.C., erected upon the reigning pharaoh's order, housed the slaves and artisans engaged in building the great pyramids—the tombs of royalty and nobility. Resembling huge barracks, the cells of sun-dried brick were crowded about common courtyards. Narrow lanes served as open drainage sewers as well as common passageways. Walls surrounded the towns. Ancient Egypt was large and mighty enough to be fearless, so these walls were probably built primarily

Mohenjo-Daro. *Excavations at Mohenjo-Daro in the Indus Valley have revealed the remains of a large city built about 3000 B.C. It is apparent that a relatively advanced civilization flourished in this city. Houses ranged in size from two rooms to mansions with numerous rooms. The map shows the archaeologist's assumption that a major street ran in the north-south (First Street) and east-west (East Street) directions. Areas shown in black have been excavated and indicate the intricate plan of narrow roads. Buildings were of masonry, streets were paved, and considerable evidence of sewer drainage from dwellings has been uncovered. The principal buildings excavated are a public bath and a monastery.*

for protection against seasonal floods rather than against invading enemy armies.

Concurrent with the building of the pyramids, permanent towns of sun-baked brick arose along the Indus Valley. In Mohenjo-Daro and Harrapa the streets were arranged in a regular pattern and, as in Egypt, the dwellings were compactly built about interior courts. Building heights were established in proportion to the width of streets, one and two stories predominating. Sanitation was of a relatively high order; a system of underground sewers extended through the towns, and there is evidence that disposal lines were connected to the dwellings. But all trace of the civilization that produced these cities has apparently vanished, and it remains a matter of conjecture whether the peoples who occupied them influenced the city building of the Near East in subsequent centuries.

In the second millennium B.C. Egyptian pharaohs built temple cities on the banks of the Nile. Monumental avenues, colossal temple plazas, and tombs cut from rock remain as mute testimony to the luxurious life of the nobility in Memphis, Thebes, and Tel-el-Amarna. But few snatches

King Solomon's temple and citadel, Jerusalem, c. 900 B.C. *The splendor of the temples and palaces of the kings contrasts with the congested dwellings of the populace. (Restoration by Dr. John Wesley Kelchner.)*

of recorded history remain to describe the city of the people. Time and the elements have washed away the clay huts and "tenements" in which the people dwelled. The dramatic Avenue of the Sphinxes in Thebes and the broad temple enclosure (a third of a mile wide and a half-mile long) in Tel-el-Amarna tell a vivid story of powerful aristocrats, while historians must piece together fragmentary remains of people's homes to conclude that slums spread about the towns.

A series of empires rose in Mesopotamia, and once-humble villages along the valley of the Tigris and Euphrates rivers became monumental cities of the kings. Each was heavily fortified to resist the siege of many enemies. The stately palace-temple dominated the city, and the people lived in the dual shadows of slavery and superstitious religion. Economic hardship added to their burden. A skilled artisan in ancient Sumeria could obtain housing for 5 or 6 percent of his income, but the poorest dwelling cost unskilled workers as much as 30 and 40 percent of their subsistence allowance.[1]

Out of the slums of thriving imperial cities were carved triumphal avenues connecting magnificent city gates. King Sennacherib built his temples and palaces in seventh-century Nineveh. The Greek historian Herodotus described the vivid spectacle of the processional avenues, great walls, monumental gates, and hanging gardens of Nebuchadnezzar's palace in Babylon during the sixth and fifth centuries B.C. He also told that behind the avenues were the narrow streets lined with the three- and four-story dwellings of the populace. Laid in a regular pattern at right angles to each other, the houses of the people were crowded together.

Seeking to improve the lot of the common people, King Hammurabi of Babylon in approximately 1800 B.C. set up a system of laws, among the greatest in the Ancient World. Now called the Hammurabi Code, among other things it set out regulations governing the building of structures, their first recorded appearance. Harsh punishment was meted out to irresponsible builders. For example, if the wall of a building should fall and kill the occupant's son, the life of the builder's son would be sacrificed in retaliation.

Cities of the Aegean

A more enlightened society appears to have arisen in the islands of the Aegean Sea. The reigning kings were apparently not deified as they were in eastern lands. In contrast to the austere detachment of royal palaces in Mesopotamia, the palaces here served as the centers of Aegean life and culture.

---

1. Albert Bemis and John Burchard, *The Evolving House*, Vol. 1 of *A History of the Home* (Cambridge, Mass., MIT Press, 1933–36).

Knossos. *Knossos was the capital of the mythological King Minos of Crete, considered the founder of the Minoan civilization that flourished over 3,000 years ago. Knossos was one of the greatest cities of the ancient world; its population at the height of its splendor was in the range of 100,000. One of the earliest and largest communities, it was famous for great beauty and grandeur. Because of the natural protection offered by its site, Knossos was not surrounded by walls. The people enjoyed free access to the sea and entered into trade with other lands. On the mainland of Greece, however, cities needed the protection of ramparts; the cities of Tiryns and Mycenae were heavily fortified.*
Source: Knossos, CHR Mathiouvoussis, Athens, 1974.

These early cities of the Aegean were irregular in form. Meandering streets followed the rugged topography of the sites. The streets were narrow lanes but they were paved with stone. Excavations have revealed highly developed systems of water supply, sanitation, and drainage for the palace and many of the houses. Most dwellings were one story in height and, although densely built, the towns did not reach the great size and congestion that were apparent in cities of the Near East.

Beijing and Lukang

Beijing was founded in the eight century B.C. in approximately its present location. The capital of the People's Republic of China, it is located in the northern part of the North China Plain. It has an area of more than 16,000 square kilometers and a population of over 8 million people. Geo-

A Forbidden City
B Imperial City
C Tartar City
D Chinese City

Beijing (Peking). *Within each of the cells surrounded by streets in the sketch is a maze of narrow minor roads, also laid out in rectilinear form.*

graphically, Beijing occupies about the same position in China that New York does in North America, both being near the fortieth parallel and enjoying the same climatic conditions in the spring and fall. Unlike New York, however, Beijing does not have direct access to an important river or to the seacoast. The present city plan originated in the eleventh century A.D. The Grand Canal, which at one time provided access to the sea, no longer serves that purpose.

Beijing today retains the same general layout it had in the Ming Dynasty (1368–1644), square and symmetrical. In the center of the city is the group of palaces called the Forbidden City—so named because the common people were forbidden to enter there. To the south of the Forbidden City is the Imperial Palace, Tiananmen, with a circumference of nine kilometers. A square twenty-kilometer area outside the Imperial City is the "Inner City"; it was constructed in 1397. The rectangular part of the city to the south is the Outer (or Chinese) City.

The Inner City is crisscrossed with main streets intersected by lanes called *hutongs*. These *hutongs* are traditionally the homesites for many artists and artisans, as well as the sites of shops that serve local residents with their everyday needs.

Lukang, the old port town in Changua County, was where the Chinese people and culture first appeared on Taiwan.[2] With the silting up of its harbor, the shipping of rice, hemp, and deerskin from the port ceased. Today's Lukang, whose name means "deer-port," is a town of 70,000 people with a total area of about 15,000 acres. It is a backwater town, but it has one quality few other places in Taiwan can boast of: a human and intimate scale.

Crooked streets characterize Lukang. It is an easily walkable community, with visible signs of old China frequently evident, such as the ancient temples and the shops in which artisans worked and musicians performed. The commercial area is located along the line of the main street, as are the two major temples. Beyond the residential section is the agricultural area with its large farmhouses and fish ponds. Small factories are also located outside of the town.

The north-south and east-west streets that divided the ancient town into blocks performed the function of social control. Each block was surrounded by walls that formed a self-contained area. Traditional Chinese architecture expressed the belief that people and the space they occupy were meant to be in harmony. This concept is crucial to understanding the Chinese city.

---

2. Nien-Ting Chang, "Lukang, an Old Port Town in Taiwan," unpublished paper, UCLA.

CHAPTER 3

THE CLASSIC CITY

THE GREEKS

On the mainland of Greece the shepherds from the north mingled with the Aegean peoples of the rising city-states and gradually were absorbed within that culture. The wealthy landowning noble class rose to power, and during the eighth century B.C. this group appropriated much of the influence previously exercised by the kings. The palace citadel disappeared, and temples dedicated to the gods of the Greeks replaced them upon the elevated section of the cities, the acropolis. The nobles assumed the power of kings, dominated the cities, and oppressed the peasant classes. A merchant middle class emerged. Feuds between this new economic group and the city-dwelling nobles forced the selection of a common leader of the popular classes and in the seventh century the Tyrants of Athens came into power by usurping the existing legal authority.

Although they were themselves of the noble class, the tyrants maintained their leadership by the support of the common people. The large estates of the nobles were redistributed among the people, and a strong landholding farmer class developed. Under the successive leadership of Solon, Pisistratus, and Clisthenes, the principle of law as a basis of social conduct evolved. The political organization of the community was given a new form: a government of laws determined by the people.

20

The Acropolis, Athens. *The temple, rather than the palace of the rulers, domi-nated the ancient Hellenic city. Among its other uses, it added a meeting place for political assembly of the people—the* pnyx—*to the urban pattern. As the power of kings diminished and democracy expanded, the houses of the people and the community facilities established for their use assumed greater impor-tance in the city plan. (Trans World Airways photo)*

During the fifth century B.C., with the inspired leadership of Pericles, democracy and a high order of morality took root among the Athenian citizenship. Political education was extended by way of free speech and assembly. Magistrates were elected to execute the laws, and public ser-vice was vested with dignity. Sovereignty of the people was assured and protected by a body of laws to which all agreed and all were subject. The deep sense of individual responsibility was expressed in the vow taken by all male Athenian citizens:

I will not dishonor these sacred arms; I will not abandon my comrade in battle; I will fight for my gods and my hearth singlehanded or with my companions. I will not leave my country smaller, but I will leave it greater and stronger than I received it. I will obey the commands which the mag-istrates in their wisdom shall give me. I will submit to the existing laws and to those that the people shall unanimously make; if anyone shall attempt to overthrow these laws or disobey them, I will not suffer it, but will fight for them, whether singlehanded or with my fellows. I will respect the worship of my fathers.

Athenian Democracy

Inspired by the political genius of Pericles, the democracy of Athens in the fourth century B.C. could be said to have acquired a soul. It required wise citizenship to retain this quality, and philosophers like Socrates strove to cultivate the requisite wisdom and intelligence. Although Socrates sometimes disapproved of the laws and thought some of them bad, he insisted upon the obligation of the citizenry to abide by them until they were revised. Although Demosthenes came somewhat later, esteem for the law was perhaps best expressed in the words of that great orator:

> The whole life of men, whether they inhabit a great city or a small, is ordered by nature and the laws. Whilst nature is lawless and varies with individuals, the laws are a common possession, controlled, identical for all. . . . They desire the just, the beautiful, the useful. It is that which they seek; once discovered it is that which is created into a principle equal for all and unvarying; it is that which is called law.

The Athenian democracy of the fifth century B.C. has been described this way:

> . . . as the exercise of sovereignty by free and equal citizens under the aegis of law. The law, which protects the citizens one against the other, defends also the rights of the individual against the power of the State and the interests of the State against the excesses of individualism. Before the last years of the fifth century there is no sign that liberty has degenerated into anarchy or license, nor is the principle of equality carried so far as to entail the denial of the existence of mental inequalities.[1]

Democracy in the Age of Pericles produced that inherent dignity of the individual born of free speech, a sense of unity with one's fellowman, and a full opportunity for participation in affairs of the community. The Athenian citizen experienced the exhilaration of freedom and accepted the challenge of responsibility it thrust upon him with honor and with pride. The discovery of freedom gave impetus to the search for truth as honest men desire it. Philosophy was nurtured, and there were no depths that the wise and intelligent were afraid to plumb. Reason was encouraged, logic invited, and science investigated. There was no truth that might be discovered and remain undisclosed. Inspired by this atmosphere and its freedom of the spirit, it is no wonder great philosophy was born; only in freedom can such greatness appear and be cultivated. This was the culture that produced Socrates, Plato, and Aristotle.

---

1. Gustave Glotz, *The Greek City and its Institutions* (London: Routledge & Kegan Paul, 1929).

The affinity between freedom and spiritual values was symbolized in the temples built upon the acropolis. In them was reflected the exalted stature of democratic man. Some four centuries later another philosopher, this one from Bethlehem, was to recreate the spiritual values demonstrated by the Greeks at the height of their democracy.

The Humble City

During the early years of Athenian democracy, the Greek city was a maze of wandering unpaved lanes, lacking in drainage and sanitation. Water was carried from local wells. Waste was disposed of in the streets. There were no palaces and, with the exception of the temples, public buildings were few and simple. The common assembly place was the *pnyx*, an open-air podium where the citizens met to consider and discuss affairs of state. The agora or marketplace, the center of urban activity, was irregular in form. There was little distinction between the dwellings of the well-to-do citizen and his less privileged fellow men. The few rooms that comprised the house were grouped about an interior court behind a windowless facade that faced one of the randomly placed streets. Most towns were surrounded by protective walls.

For the Greek citizen the temple was the symbol of his democratic way of life, the equality of men. Upon the temples he lavished all his creative energies, and in them we find a refinement of line and beauty of form that expressed the dignity and humility of the Athenian. In later and less happy days Demosthenes reflected upon this period. "These edifices," he said,

> which their administrations have given us, their decorations of our temples and the offerings deposited in them, are so numerous that all efforts of posterity cannot exceed them. Then in private life, so exemplary was their moderation, their adherence to the ancient manners so scrupulously exact, that, if any of you discovered the house of Aristides or Miltiades, or any of the illustrious men of those times, he must know that it was not distinguished by the least extraordinary splendor.[2]

Hippodamus

It was natural that an atmosphere of philosophical inquiry should impel a search for order in the city. It was a topic that engaged the attention of teacher-philosophers and politicians alike. In the latter part of the fifth century B.C. an architect from Miletus by the name of Hippodamus advanced positive theories of the art and science of city planning. He has

---

2. Ibid., p. 302.

been credited with the origination of the gridiron street system. This is not entirely accurate, however. A semblance of geometrical form had been present in early towns of Egypt, Mesopotamia, and the Indus Valley, and a formal rectangular pattern was used in part in the rebuilding of some earlier Greek cities after their destruction by the Persians in the sixth century. Hippodamus nevertheless vigorously applied the gridiron pattern to obtain a rational arrangement of buildings and circulation.

The city plan was conceived as a design to serve all the people. The individual dwelling was the common denominator. Blocks were shaped to provide appropriate orientation for the dwellings within them. The functional uses of buildings and public spaces were recognized in the arrangement of streets. They provided for the circulation of people and vehicles without interference with the orientation of dwellings or the assembly of people in the marketplace.

Superimposing the rigid geometrical form of the Hippodamian street system upon the rugged topography of the sites occupied by most Greek cities created numerous streets so steep they could be negotiated only with steps. Since the movement of people was almost entirely on foot, this did not present the problem it might assume today, although there were probably some puffing Grecians who reached the top of a long climb to attend a political meeting in the assembly hall. The principal traffic streets, however, were placed to allow the circulation of the few horse-drawn vehicles that entered the town.

PUBLIC SPACE IN GREEK CITIES

The expanding affairs of government required appropriate facilities. The agora was the center of business and political life, and about it were lined the shops and market booths. Accessible from the agora square, but not facing upon it, were the assembly hall *(ecclesiasteron)*, council hall *(bouleuterion)*, and council chamber *(prytaneum)*.

The agora was usually located in the approximate center of the town plan, with the major east-west and north-south streets leading to it. It was designed to accommodate all the citizens who would have business in the marketplace or would attend public functions in the adjacent public buildings. The open space enclosed by the agora occupied about 5 percent of the city area, the dimensions being approximately one-fifth of the width and breadth of the town itself.

The agora was geometrical in form. Square or rectangular open spaces were surrounded by colonnaded porticoes sheltering the buildings about the square. This arrangement was meant to avoid interference between the movement of people across the open space and those who assembled for trade and business in the market. Streets generally terminated at the

A	Acropolis
B	Agora
C	Stoa
D	Theseum
E	Prytaneum
F	Areopagus
G	Pnyx
H	Theater of Dionysus

Ancient Athens.

agora rather than crossing it, the open space being reserved primarily for pedestrian traffic and circulation.

Common open space in Greek cities was largely confined to enclosures in public buildings. Because the city was small in area, the citydweller was never far from the open countryside around the town. Olive groves flourished outside the walls, and it was here that the philosophers founded the academy and the lyceum. In these quiet groves they met their pupils and set the pattern for later institutions of higher learning. From such academies came the world's first university, the Library of Alexandria in Egypt.

Evidence of attention to building regulations is recorded in the chronicles of various Athenian writers. There is reference to laws restricting buildings from encroachment upon the streets and prohibitions against the projection of upper floors beyond the first floor walls. These are forerunners of the present-day notions of "rights-of-way." Windows were not permitted to open directly upon the street, and water drains were not allowed to empty into the street. Though primitive when judged by the standards acceptable today, the early Greek town plans demonstrated a conscious effort to improve the environment for the whole people, the final test of genuine civic responsibility.

A Agora

B Temple of Athene Polias

C Theater

D Stadium

Priene and Miletus. *These cities demonstrate the Hippodamian plan as it developed toward the end of the Hellenic period. The agora occupies the approximate geographical center of the town. About it are the temple shrines, public buildings, and shops. The dwelling blocks are planned to provide the appropriate orientation of houses. Recreation and entertainment facilities are provided in the gymnasium, stadium, and theater. The contours of the site indicate that some of the streets were very steep, steps being frequently required, but the main streets connecting the gates and the agora were generally placed so that beasts of burden and carts could traverse them readily.*

A Agora

B Theater

C Stadium

D Port

It was in the cities founded by the city-states on the shores of the Mediterranean that the planning theories of Hippodamus found their fullest expression. It is recorded that Hippodamus himself planned Piraeus, the port city of Athens, as well as Thurii and Rhodes. The old established cities were remodeled in parts, the agora assuming a more orderly form as new buildings were erected for public affairs, but the newer cities had the benefit of planning prior to their settlement. Although they were founded by a mother city-state, they enjoyed a degree of political autonomy, becoming a part of the confederation of Greek cities that comprised the Athenian "empire."

PRIVATE SPACE: THE DWELLINGS

In their houses the Greeks sought quiet privacy. Most of the social contacts and all business affairs were carried on outside the homes. Small merchants frequently had shops adjacent to their houses, but business and politics were generally conducted in and adjacent to the agora. Sports and recreation were concentrated in the gymnasium, drama and festivals in the theater. Feasts and other celebrations seldom took place in the private dwelling. A small altar was usual in the home, but religious exercises and worship occurred in the temple precincts. Consequently the house was unpretentious in its appointments and, as previously mentioned, there was little distinction among the dwellings in the town. A display of affluence was not consistent with the tenets of Greek democracy in the fifth century.

Early houses were enclosed about a central hearth. A hole in the roof allowed the smoke to escape and also permitted the collection of rainwater in the cistern. Terra-cotta braziers supplemented the hearth as a source of heat in the larger houses. In late Hellenic towns sanitation was improved by the paving of streets and the installation of underground drains beneath dwellings. The town maintained reservoirs, but there was no water distribution system. With the improvement of drainage, however, an increasing number of homes appeared with private baths. Sanitary disposal of sewage was apparently not provided for, and the portable latrine and private cesspool continued in use.

Care in planning the dwelling was not less because of its simplicity. On the contrary, as the center of family life, the proper arrangement of rooms in relation to the site received attention from builders and philosophers alike.

The climate created an emphasis upon the orientation of the dwelling. The maximum amount of sunshine inside the dwelling was desirable in the winter months, and heat could be conserved if the rooms were shielded from the cold north winds. Conversely, the heat of summer was relieved when the direct rays of the sun were excluded. These criteria were satisfied in the plan of the Greek house.

The principal rooms faced to the south, opening upon the private courtyard. A colonnade projecting from the rooms was tall enough to permit the warming low rays of the winter sun to enter, while it sheltered them from the high hot rays of the summer sun. The north wall of the house was punctured with only a few small windows. This type of plan was used in practically all dwellings in the town, whether the street entrance was on the north, south, east, or west.

Chroniclers of the period referred to the importance of proper orientation. Aristotle wrote, "For the well-being and health . . . the homesteads should be airy in summer and sunny in winter. A homestead possessing these qualities would be longer than it is deep; and the main front would face south." According to Xenophon in his *Memorabilia,* Socrates applied the following reasoning to the dwelling arrangement:

> When one builds a house must he not see to it that it be as pleasant and convenient as possible? And pleasant is to be cool in summer, but warm in winter. In those houses, then, that look toward the south, the winter sun shines down into the *paestades* [court portico] while in summer, passing high above our heads and over our roofs, it throws them in shadow.

The effect of these criteria was a planning system that sprang from the elements of the individual unit—the home—applied uniformly throughout the town plan. This consistent treatment is unique in urban planning; we do not find it recurring for 2,400 years, when a similar relation between the dwelling and the site was recognized in the vast housing program in Europe following the First World War.

THE SIZE OF CITIES

In the fifth and fourth centuries B.C. the citizen population of Athens was some 40,000; when slaves and foreigners were included, total population jumped to between 100,000 and 150,000. Most Greek cities, however, were relatively small. Only about three towns exceeded 10,000 persons during the thriving Hellenic period. Hippodamus theorized that this was an appropriate size for cities, and Plato later concluded the range should be between 5,000 and 10,000. It was customary to dispatch about 10,000 people from the mother city-state to settle a colonial town. The descriptions of the glorious metropolis with its teeming millions is undoubtedly an exaggeration of the actual number who dwelt in urban communities in ancient times. The metropolis as we know it today is of comparatively recent origin.

A number of factors influenced the size of a city and the population it could support. The food and water supply was a primary consideration. The tools for cultivating the soil, the means for transporting the products, and the source and methods for distributing the water supply established limits on the urban population that could be accommodated in a single group. As long as people were dependent upon the primitive hand plow, the horse cart, and gravity flow of water, it was not feasible to gather in great numbers and maintain adequate standards of urban hygiene. Hellenic towns relied primarily on local watercourses, wells, and springs, but supplemental supply was sometimes available through conduits from more remote sources in higher surrounding hills.

THE GREEK CITY'S DECLINE

It cannot be assumed that political affairs always ran smoothly in the Age of Pericles. The teachings of the Sophists were disturbing some of the well-established customs. In addition, a little man by the name of Socrates subjected many of the prevailing habits to severe questioning. He insisted upon inquiry and the application of reason to the activities of men. He raised questions about the existence of the gods. He desired that the individual should cultivate an insight into truth, that he should become neither stronger than the state nor subservient to it.

There were some good democrats who believed Socrates was wrong in raising these questions; they had suffered from uprisings of the oligarchy and feared lest the faith in democracy be weakened. They brought charges against Socrates for heresy and for subverting the youth of Athens. There were those who loved this wise man whose only ambition was the quest for truth. They appealed to him to flee his accusers as was the custom, but Socrates would not. He had suggested changes in the habits of men that would improve their lot, and if these were unlawful he would remain to face the consequences of the people's judgment as expressed in the law. Found guilty, he was sentenced to die, and in 399 B.C. he drank the poison hemlock.

The lesson of Socrates has been repeated in history. The institutions of men must change or decay, grow or wither. Socrates showed a way for men to command their destiny by seeking truth. He strove to improve the institutions that they might better serve the people, and for this his fellowmen found him guilty of treason. Greater confidence in the strength of democracy would not have caused him to be so accused; greater confidence might have saved democracy itself.

During the fourth century B.C. there was evidence of growing indifference toward the responsibility of government. Accustomed to liberty, the people were taking it for granted, and they were inclined to allow affairs to run themselves. Freedom guaranteed by democracy was coming to mean that "the people has the right to do what it pleases." In the words of Demosthenes, some people were "even building private houses whose magnificence surpasses that of certain public buildings."

Well-to-do citizens spent more of their time in their country villas, whereas the common people found the difficulty of earning a living more absorbing than participation in public affairs. The middle class was disappearing, and a wide gap was growing between those with money and those without it. Plato and Aristotle saw a degeneration of the democracy of Pericles. They perceived a growing abuse of individual liberty and became increasingly critical of democracy itself. Other philosophers were gripped with cynicism while maintaining the fight for democracy.

Glotz describes the alarming developments of this period:

> . . . in Greece as a whole there existed almost everywhere a glaring contrast between the equality promised by the constitution and the inequality created by social and economic conditions.
>
> The power of money was spreading and corrupting morality. . . . Agriculture was commercialized to such an extent that by progressive eviction of small peasants and the concentration of estates in the same hands the system of large estates was recreated. Rhetoricians, advocates, and artists, who had formerly reckoned it a dishonor to commercialize their talent, now felt no scruples in selling their goods as dearly as possible. Everything could be bought, everything had its price, and wealth was the measure of social values. By gain and by extravagance fortunes were made and unmade with equal rapidity. Those who had money rushed into pleasure-seeking and sought every occasion for gross displays of luxury. The newly rich were cocks of the walk. Men speculated and rushed after money in order to build and furnish magnificent houses, to display fine weapons, to offer to the women of their family and to courtesans jewels, priceless robes, and rare perfumes, to place before eminent guests and fashionable parasites fine wines and dishes prepared by a famous chef, or to commission some popular sculptor to carve their bust.
>
> What happened to public affairs when "love of money left no one the smallest space in which to deal with other things, to such an extent that the mind of each citizen, passionately absorbed in this one purpose, could attend to no other business than the gain of each day" (Plato). Politics also was a business concern; the most honest worked for a class, the others sought for themselves alone the profits of power and barely concealed their venality. We are dealing with a time when "riches and rich men being held in honor virtue and honest men are at a discount," when "no one can become rich quickly if he remains honest" (Plato). Were these merely the capricious outbursts of a philosopher in love with the ideal or of a character in a comedy? Listen to the terrible words uttered before a tribunal: "Those who, citizens by right of birth, hold the opinion that their country extends wherever their interests are, these obviously are people who will desert the public good in order to run after their personal gain, since for them it is not the city which is their country, but their fortune."[3]

---

3. Glotz, op. cit., pp. 311, 312.

The struggle between democracy and oligarchy was renewed, and the Athenian orator Isocrates sums up the growing conflict between the widely separated issues:

> Instead of securing general conditions of well-being by means of mutual understanding, the antisocial spirit has reached such a pitch that the wealthy would rather throw their money into the sea than relieve the lot of the indigent, while the very poorest of the poor would get less from appropriating to their own use the property of the rich than from depriving them of it.

The Hellenistic City

The Peloponnesian Wars weakened Athens financially, and corrupt politicians began to gnaw at the moral fiber of the people. Athens became easy prey for a conqueror and succumbed to the Macedonian armies of Alexander the Great. But the essential qualities of wisdom, logic, and reason, the sensitive, aesthetic character of democratic days, had sunk its roots deep into the soil of Athens. The Greeks were conquered by mighty armies, but their culture dominated the conqueror. Greek influence spread throughout the Mediterranean shores, and the Hellenistic period brought new city building—the planning and architecture patterned after the great works of the Greeks.

Old cities flourished and new cities were founded. Pergamon, Alexandria, Syracuse, and Candahar grew large and populous; the humble quality of the Hellenic city vanished. The city became the scene of luxury, ruddy with the display of empire. Magnificent public buildings—the *odeion*, the treasury, the library, the prison—were added to the agora. The assembly retained its traditional place among these monumental structures, but it remained, as Percy Gardner expressed it in his *The Planning of Hellenistic Cities*, for the citizens "to exercise such functions (a mere show of autonomy) as the real rulers of the country . . . left to them." Baths, *palaestrae*, and stadia were built for entertainment and festivals. Gardens and parks were introduced from the Orient. An entourage of royalty built fine villas in the urban environs, and distinctions in caste grew more apparent.

Small kings, wealthy families, and ambitious foreigners desirous of acclaim within this frame of monumental splendor bestowed generous gifts upon the city. Empty honors were accorded for their beneficence. The great *stoa* at Priene was the gift of a king of Orophernes of Cappadocia. Here, one by the name of Zosimus staged a festive dinner for the whole citizen population of the city in return for receipt of the "dignity of Stephanephorus." According to Pausanias, the bouleuterion at Megalopolis was named after Thersilius who dedicated it, and the donor of the bouleuterion at Elis was one by the name of Lalichmium.[4] Inscriptions bear a quantity of evidence of the surge for popularity through these magnanimous gestures of philanthropy. The genuine character of the Hellenic city was, in the third and second centuries B.C., degenerating into a hollow form of a decaying social structure.

THE ROMANS

In their early migrations to the Italian peninsula, the Greeks had founded cities. Like other peoples on the shores of the Mediterranean, the Romans drew upon the Greek culture planted there. They grafted Hellenic forms upon the irregular patterns of their villages and used these forms for the new towns they founded in the near and far reaches of their broad empire.

The Romans were calculating organizers. They excelled in technical achievement and were skilled engineers and aggresstive city builders. But they lacked the philosophy of the Greeks. Preoccupied with conquest, administration was their prime business, and they devised a political organization that has continued to this day. Intense builders with a flair for gargantuan scale, their works were not graced with the refinement of line and form or the creative spirit of the Athenians. Greek forms were reduced to mechanical formulae that could be readily applied like parts arranged upon graph paper.

With inventive genius the Romans solved technical problems created by the congregation of great numbers of people in cities. They developed water supply and distribution, drainage systems, and methods of heating upon which the health of the masses depended. The great aqueducts for transport of water over tremendous distances and the underground sewers like Cloaca Maxima were feats of engineering skill and prowess. The great highways paved with stone represented the tireless efforts of intense builders.

Monuments and Diversion

The Forum Romanum of the Republic had a human scale. Its proportions and form undoubtedly caused the citizen to feel he was a part of the activity that took place there. Here the individual and his identity were merged with "Rome." The buildings were not so overwhelming in size that they humbled the individual. The common people had their share of hardships, but one can imagine the Gracchi pleading their case in the Senate for an equitable distribution of the land and its benefits. The

---

4. William A. McDonald, *The Political Meeting Places of the Greeks* (Baltimore, Md., Johns Hopkins University Press, 1943).

citizen understood the religion of his temples, and he was proud of the triumphs of the Roman legions abroad. He could participate in the business affairs of the basilica and perhaps engage in the moneylending enterprise carried on there. He felt himself to be one of the actors in this drama as a Greek had been in his assembly and agora.

This citizen of early Rome saw gracious living like that in Pompeii and Herculaneum or the busy life and fashions of Ostia. He observed distinctions in class among the dwellings but took these for granted in a day when a slave economy was all he had thus far witnessed in history. If the citizen was not blessed with wealth, he could nevertheless indulge himself in the various common forms of entertainment the community offered —the gay combat in the colosseum, the drama in the theater, or a festival in the forum.

But the scene changed. World conquest was the ambition of Rome, and the citizen saw great riches flow into his capital. He saw intrigue absorb the military and political leaders, and he saw monuments erected in dedication of great victories, and the triumphant entry of generals from abroad.

The Roman citizen saw emperors crowned and he saw them build new fora that dwarfed his Forum Romanum. He saw each new forum exceed in size the one that preceded it. The Forum of Augustus was greater than the Forum of Julius Caesar; the Forum of Vespasian matched that of Augustus; and the Forum of Trajan was the most magnificent of all. He saw the Palace of Augustus crown the Palatine and the Golden House of Nero span acres.

The Roman citizen saw institutions of pleasure, rather than culture, built to divert attention from social and economic inequities. He saw the huge Colosseum where carnal displays and bloody gladiatorial combats were staged for the excitement of a populace that might otherwise have grown restless. He saw the Circus Maximus, where he could join 150,000 fellow citizens to witness the drama of daring chariot races.

The scale of all these structures, the spaces they enclosed, and the architectural fitments with which they were adorned appalled the Roman citizen. It was not the plan of a city that he saw emerging but a series of ever greater monuments to the glory and deification of his rulers. Even the colonial cities followed the form of the military camp.

Slums and Decay

Diversion was afforded the citizen, but he saw his city grow congested. He saw men, like Crassus, profess to be civic leaders but speculate in the land and build huge tenements. He saw the city crowded with slums to become fuel for disastrous fires. The height of buildings reached six, seven, and eight floors, and Emperor Augustus found it necessary to decree a limit of 70 feet for all tenements. According to the Constantine Regionary Catalog there were 46,602 blocks of apartments and only 1,797 private houses in Rome in the fourth century after Christ.

This Roman citizen saw nobles, the returning heroes, and the rulers move to great estates and comfortable villas in the country. The Empire had grown so broad and so fat no enemy could reach them. Luxury and display were imported from the Orient, and the leaders grew soft. The citydweller lived in slums while the affluent enjoyed leisure in the country. No strong and healthy men with convictions remained to defend the Empire, and Rome gradually merged with the camp of barbarians from the north. Civilization descended into the Dark Ages.

The lesson of Rome and the cities it built is well stated by Henry Smith Williams:

> During the entire ages of Trajan and the Antonines, a succession of virtuous and philosophic emperors followed each other; the world was in peace; the laws were wise and well administered; riches seemed to increase; each succeeding generation raised palaces more splendid, monuments and public edifices more sumptuous, than the preceding; the senatorial families found their revenues increase; the treasury levied greater imposts. But it is not the mass of wealth, it is on its distributions, that the prosperity of states depends; increasing opulence continued to meet the eye, but men became more miserable; the rural population, formerly active, robust, and energetic, were succeeded by a foreign race, while the inhabitants of towns sank in vice and idleness, or perished in want, amidst the riches they had themselves created.[5]

---

5. *The Historian's History of the World* (The Outlook Company, 1904).

CHAPTER 4

THE MEDIEVAL TOWN

OUT OF THE DARK AGES

By the fifth century after Christ the Roman Empire had crumbled under the weight of its own luxury, pomp, and ceremony. Western civilization declined, trade disintegrated, urban populations to a large degree returned to rural life, and cities shrank in size and importance. The period of social and economic confusion and stagnation called the Dark Ages followed.

Barbaric rulers established city-states and formed the nucleus of future nations. The economy was rooted in agriculture, and the rulers parceled their domains among vassal lords who pledged military support. The people were dependent upon the land for their subsistence and entered a state of serfdom under their lords. The feudal system was the new order.

Wars among the rival feudal lords were frequent. Strategic sites were sought for their castles, and within these fortified strongholds the serfs of the surrounding countryside found protection. Through the centuries of the Dark Ages monasteries served as havens of refuge for the oppressed. The church strengthened its position greatly during this period. This influence, combined with the power of the feudal lords, renewed the advantages of communal existence within the protective walls of towns and cities. Invention of the battering ram and catapult increased the danger from enemies, forced the construction of heavier walls, and gave increased impetus for a return to urban life. The countryside was not safe, and fortifications were extended to include the dwellings that clustered about the castle and monastery.

By about the eleventh century the movement to the towns brought a marked revival of trade. Many advantages accrued to the feudal lords— not least because they collected higher taxes and rent for their land in return for protection. Many new towns were founded, and sites of old Roman towns restored. Urban life was encouraged by the lords; they granted charters that secured certain rights and privileges of citizenship to the urban dwellers. This new form of freedom was attractive to those who had lived their lives in serfdom.

In urban areas merchants and craftsmen formed guilds to strengthen their social and economic position. Weavers, butchers, tailors, masons,

A   Market Square
B   Castle
C   Church of Sr. Nazaire

A   Cathedral Plaza
B   Moat

Carcassonne and Noerdlingen. *Medieval cities of the twelfth and thirteenth centuries usually had irregular street patterns and heavy walls. Carcassonne (left) was restored by Viollet-le-Duc in the nineteenth century. In it we see the castle (B) with its own moat and walls, the marketplace (A), and the Church of St. Nazaire (C). The plan of Noerdlingen (right) shows the radial and lateral pattern of irregular roadways, with the church plaza as the principal focal point of the town. The city of the Middle Ages grew within the confines of the walls.*

While the population remained small, there was ample space in the town, but when the number of residents increased, the buildings were packed together more closely and the open spaces filled. Sanitation and water supply did not change, however, and the result was intolerable congestion, lack of hygiene, and pestilence.

millers, metalworkers, carpenters, leatherworkers, glassmakers, all established regulations to control their standards of production, maintain their prices, and protect their trade. A new social order was in the making —a wealthy mercantile class was rising to challenge the power of the feudal lords.

THE PLAN OF THE TOWN

The early medieval town was dominated by the church or monastery and the castle of the lord. The church plaza became the marketplace and, with citizenship bestowed upon the people and merchant and trade guilds established, the town hall and guild hall were built on or adjacent to the market plaza. The commanding position of the cathedral or church gave a singular unity to the town, a unity strengthened by the horizontal envelope of the encircling walls. The castle was surrounded by its own walls as a final protection in the event an enemy penetrated the main fortifications and entered the city.

Distinction between the town and the country was sharp, and this demarcation and the small size of the city provided ready access to the open countryside in times of peace. To aid in the protection of cities, towns were usually sited on irregular terrain, occupying hilltops or islands. The town was designed to fit the topographic features of the area. Circulation and building spaces were molded to these irregular features and naturally assumed an informal character.

The roads radiated generally from the church plaza and market square to the gates, with secondary lateral roadways connecting them. The irregular pattern was probably consciously devised as a means to confuse an enemy in the event he gained entrance to the town. Although the batter-

A   **Cathedral Square**
B   **Market Square**

Montpazier. *During the thirteenth and fourteenth centuries colonial cities were founded by young empires to protect their trade and provide military security. The allocation of sites to settlers was planned and plotted in advance of settlement. The regular plan is a distinct contrast to the informal development of the normal medieval town.*

ing ram and the catapult were instruments for assault upon the heavy fortifications and hot oil poured from the battlements was a means for mass defense, hand-to-hand combat was the principal form of military action. In the maze of wandering streets the advantage rested with the inhabitants against an enemy unfamiliar with the town arrangement.

The entire town was treated with a structural logic that characterized the architectural treatment of the Romanesque and early Gothic buildings. Open spaces—the streets and plaza—developed as integral parts of the sites upon which the buildings were erected. With the exception of a few main roads between the gates and the marketplace, streets were used for pedestrian circulation about the town rather than as traffic arteries as we know them today. Wheeled traffic was generally absent on all but the main roadways.

The monks and artisans were sensitive to the form and materials of the buildings they erected. Under their guidance, care was exercised in the placement of and relation between the structures of the town. Buildings assumed a functional character in both form and location. They were not built to be "picturesque"; that quality emerged from the consideration given to such towns centuries later. Beautiful vistas and lovely contrasts were accidents of form and color resulting from the contours of the land and the ingenious selection of the sites for each structure.

DWELLINGS

In part to conserve heat in the cold climates and also because of the restricted area of the town, houses were built in connected rows along the narrow streets. Open space was reserved behind these rows in which the domestic animals were kept and gardens cultivated. The workshop and kitchen occupied the ground floor. Here the merchants and craftsmen operated their enterprises and produced their goods.

There was little distinction between classes in the population of the early medieval town. The workers and apprentices lived in the homes of their employers. The space for both living and sleeping was on the second floor. Some of the burghers enjoyed separate sleeping rooms, but the accommodations were universally simple and modest in their appointments. The simple plan provided little privacy within the house. The chimney and fireplace replaced the open hearth of the ancient house. Windows were small and covered with crude glass or oiled parchment. Facilities for waste disposal within the dwelling were not usually provided, although some of the houses were equipped with privies. Construction was of masonry or wood frame filled with waddle. As a rule thatch covered the roofs, and the fire hazard eventually caused some towns either to prohibit this type of roofing or to encourage fire-resistant materials by offering special privileges for their use. Streets were usually paved and maintained by the owners of the property facing upon them. This may account in part for their narrow width.

UNIVERSITY AND CHURCH

Meditation and study characterized the monastery. It was extended to research by scholars intent upon the cultivation of professional skills. Monasteries and the guilds combined to form the university, and here were welcomed those who desired to study in withdrawal from the marketplace. Here also were conducted research and training in law, medicine, and the arts. Universities were assisted by the growing wealth of the merchant class. The universities at Bologna and Paris were founded in the twelfth century and those at Cambridge and Salamanca in the thirteenth century. The churches also established hospitals in which the sick could receive care and treatment not previously available to the people.

Life in medieval cities had color, a color visible to all the people. The church provided pageantry and gave drama to the life of every man. It was an institution in which all men could participate, giving inspiration and adding a measure of beauty to the existence of the people. It lifted people above baseness and encouraged better deeds. It offered music, meditation, and meaning. The people—merchants, artisans, and peasants —mingled in the marketplace, the guild hall, and the church; a human scale pervaded the informal environment of the city of the people.

There were innumerable hardships suffered and endured by the people of the Middle Ages, but in the early towns they did not lose the sense of intermingling. Each man had the feeling of being an active citizen in his community. This attribute of the urban environment—a social well-being —was, however, soon to be dissipated in the eras to come.

CHAPTER 5

THE NEOCLASSIC CITY

THE RISE OF MERCANTILISM AND THE CONCENTRATION OF POPULATION

The number of towns increased rapidly during the Middle Ages, but they remained relatively small in population. Many had only a few hundred people, and the larger cities seldom exceeded 50,000 inhabitants. The distance across a town seldom exceeded a mile, the physical size being restricted by the girth of the fortifications, water supply, and sanitation. Water was available at the town fountain. There was no sewage disposal, and all drainage was by way of the streets.

As long as the population remained small, the apparent deficiencies presented no serious problem. Communication between towns was slow, facilities for transport were cumbersome, and the necessity for mutual assistance in times of conflict urgent. The towns were built within ready reach of each other. Most were within a day's journey apart and frequently a round trip to a neighboring town could be made on foot in a single day.

World travel and trade, however, brought a concentration of people to centers situated on main crossroads. During the fourteenth century Florence grew from 45,000 to 90,000 people, Paris from 100,000 to 240,000, and Venice reached 200,000. Successful merchants consolidated their interests in several towns, and moneylending helped their enterprise. Commerce increased between towns and other countries. The danger of military aggression gradually diminished, the roads became safer, and travel increased.

The mercantile economy expanded, and the power of the feudal lords declined. Ownership of the land gradually shifted to a new variety of noblemen, the wealthy merchants. At the same time the church accumulated a vast domain, and consequently two privileged classes emerged— the nobles and the clergy. The guilds declined and serfdom disappeared, but the facilities for processing materials and goods—the mills, ovens, presses—came into the possession of the new noble class. The peasants were required to pay tolls of various sorts for the use of any of these facilities. The feudal economy had been rooted in the land, and the new economy was dominated by the possession and control of money.

Congestion and Slums

The growing population brought about a congestion within the cities not present in earlier days. The traditional height of two stories for dwellings changed to three and four stories. The upper floors projected beyond the first floor; roofs often spanned the width of the street. Open space within the interior blocks of dwellings was built up. Population density increased without change in the systems of water supply or sanitation.

Wheeled traffic increased. The narrow streets became congested, dark, and filth-ridden from refuse thrown from dwelling windows. Provision for elimination of waste remained inadequate. The call of *gare de l'eau* was familiar in France and, contracted to the anglicized "gardo loo," it became equally familar in Edinburgh. Excreta were disposed of in cesspools beneath dwelling floors; there or in the streets it was left in some European cities to ripen for use as fertilizer. Odors from filth in the streets were overcome by keeping windows or shutters closed; ventilation was by way of the chimney only. Because of these conditions, disease spread rapidly in times of epidemic; in the fourteenth century the Black Death, a pestilence of the bubonic plague, took the lives of nearly half the urban population.

During this period the cities reverted to a condition inferior to the days of Rome a thousand years before. The manor house of the nobleman grew spacious while the typical dwelling of the poor remained cramped and moved ever higher into the attic. The first sewer was not installed in London until after the Black Death. Water closets were not introduced until the sixteenth century in Spain, France, and England, and it was early in the seventeenth century before water supply was connected to dwellings in London. Fire hazards were prevalent everywhere. A thirteenth-century London ordinance required that slate or tile roofs replace the usual reed and straw as a precautionary measure. It is interesting to note a similar order that appeared in the American Colonies at a somewhat later date.

> New Amsterdam, 15 December 1657:
> The Director General and Council of New Netherland to All who shall see these presents or hear them read, Greeting! Know ye, that to prevent the misfortunes of conflagrations, the roofs of reeds, the wooden and plastered chimneys have long ago been condemned but nevertheless these orders are obstinately and carelessly neglected by many of the inhabitants. . . . The said Director General and Council have decided it to be necessary, not only to renew their former ordinances, but also to amplify the same to increase the fines. . . .[1]

Overcrowding within the small dwellings of the poorer people further increased the hazards to health and the spread of epidemics. In 1539 an Act of Parliament mentioned that "great mischiefs daily grow and increase by reason of pestering of houses with divers families, harboring of inmates, and converting great houses into tenements, and erection of new houses."

The Appearance of Gunpowder

Gunpowder was introduced in Europe from China in the fourteenth century, and new techniques of warfare appeared as a consequence. The feudal lords had relied upon citizen-soldiers to man the crenellated parapets in time of siege, but the new weapons of attack and defense required larger numbers of soldiers who were better trained and professional. Military engineering became a science. Fortifications were extended, and heavy bastions, moats, and outposts were built. Extension of the area occupied by the fortifications created a "no-man's land," and separation between town and country became more distinct. Open space outside the walls was further removed from the urban dweller. People came to the cities in large numbers to participate in the expanding commercial enterprise and to fill the ranks of professional armies.

THE RENAISSANCE

In fifteenth-century France the kings achieved a semblance of national unity. Elsewhere cities remained provincial dukedoms with wealthy merchant families wielding control. It became the ambition of rulers to display their affluence and power by improving their cities. As in most of

---

1. Quoted in Straus and Wegg, *Housing Comes of Age* (New York, Oxford University Press, 1938).

their intellectual pursuits, they drew upon the classic heritage of Rome for this cultural activity. The noble families of Florence, Venice, Rome, and Lombardy proceeded to embellish those cities; the Medicis, Borgias, and Sforzas built themselves new palaces on which were draped the classic motifs. Although the buildings of the medieval town retained the fortress quality characteristic of the Middle Ages, a formalism was grafted upon them. The basic form did not change, but the structure was decorated with facades made up of classic elements.

The church participated in this movement. The residence of the popes was re-established in Rome, and work on the Vatican Palace was begun. Pope Julius planned to replace the old basilica of St. Peter with a great church that would become the center of Christendom.

Arts and Architecture

Feverish preoccupation with the arts gripped the merchant princes, churchmen, and the kings. The well-rounded man became the ideal. Practice of the arts became a profession. The apprentice system prepared men to work in a variety of artistic fields. An apprentice to a painter would also work in the shop of a goldsmith; a sculptor would study architecture. Versatility was characteristic of the artists. Leonardo da Vinci practiced all the visual arts and became a planner, military engineer, and inventor as well. Kings, merchant nobles, and popes were patrons of the arts and bid heavily for the services of the growing number of practitioners.

The anonymity of the master builders of medieval towns no longer prevailed in the Renaissance. Robert du Luzarches, William of Sens (Canterbury Cathedral), Geoffrey de Noyes (Lincoln Cathedral), Jean-le-Loup, and Henrico di Gambodia (Milan Cathedral) are seldom recorded in the history of medieval town building, whereas a host of individuals received personal recognition in the Renaissance and later periods. The names of Brunelleschi, Alberti, Bramante, Peruzzi, and Sangallo in Italy, and Bullant, de l'Ormé, and Lescot in France, are as well known as their works. Many others achieved world renown; their names were more prominent than the patrons who commissioned their works. Mansart, Bullet, Blondel, Lemercier, de Brosse, Le Nôtre, and Percier in France; Bernini, Longhena, Borromini, Palladio, Michelangelo, and Raphael in Italy; Inigo Jones, Christopher Wren, and the Brothers Adam in England. All these artists enjoyed the confidence and patronage of popes, kings, and merchants.

Monarchy and Monumentalism

Formal plazas of the Renaissance were carved out of the medieval town and given monumental scale and form reminiscent of classical antiquity.

Exterior space was enclosed with formal facades, and the shapes were modeled like sculptural pieces, isolated from the rest of the city.

The monumental character of the classic had returned to the city. Every form had its centerline, and every space its axis. The structural quality of the Middle Ages was replaced by a classic sculptural form, modeled symmetrically. The "barbaric" art of medieval cities was forsaken. With haughty distain Molière called it:

> The rank taste of Gothic monuments,
> These odious monsters of the ignorant centuries,
> Which the torrents of barbarism spewed forth.

The axis and the strong centerline symbolized the growing concentration of power. Kings of France became monarchs, wealthy merchants in Italy became autocratic dukes, large landowners in England became lord barons, and the popes became benevolent partners of all. Louis XIV of France gave voice to the spirit of the times when he shouted his famous words, "L'État, c'est moi."

Out of the cramped medieval town were carved formal squares. The modeling of spatial forms absorbed the attention and skills of designers and planners, and classic elements were ingeniously assembled to form the spaces. Michelangelo created the Campodiglio on the Capitoline Hill in Rome, Bernini designed the huge Piazza of St. Peter's, the Piazza di San Marco in Venice was completed, Rainaldi built the twin churches on the Piazza del Popolo, the Place Royale (now Place des Vosges) and Place des Victoires were built in Paris.

Long-range artillery removed the advantage of the old walls for military defense. Louis XIV ordered Vauban, his military engineer, to redesign the defense system. The engineer tore down the walls and built earthwork ramparts beyond the city. Within the leveled space of the old walls boulevards and promenades were laid. The famous Ringstrasse of Vienna occupied the open space left when the walls of that city were demolished. Cities were opening up, and the city of the Middle Ages was being released from its clutter. Transition from the Renaissance to the baroque was in process.

THE BAROQUE CITY

An air of grandeur permeated the courts of kings. Louis XIV ordered Le Nôtre to design the gardens of Versailles. Here was space of unparalleled proportions, scale of incomprehensible size. Here was the conception of a man who, having achieved domination over the lives of men, confidently set about to become the master of nature. The egotism of rulers

Piazza of St. Peter, Rome. *Originally, a narrow winding street led to St. Peter's. The suddenness with which the visitor was thrust into this magnificent open space made the square seem even more beautiful.*

With Paris in mind, the dictator Mussolini ordered that the path to St. Peter's be opened, and so the medieval buildings that had lined the approaches were removed and the axial avenue from the Castle St. Angelo to St. Peter's came into being.

A Piazza
B Cathedral
C Vatican

Vienna before 1857 (left). Vienna after 1857 (right). *The effectiveness of the old system of walls, moats, and ramparts for military defense was reduced as long-range artillery greatly improved in the late eighteenth and early nineteenth centuries, and the form of the city underwent drastic alterations. The walls and ramparts were leveled, the moats were filled in, and boulevards were built in the open space, as in the famous Ringstrasse encircling the original town of Vienna. These spaces were gradually built up in response to the ruthless speculation of the late nineteenth century, and open space disappeared from the city.*

knew no limitations, nor could it brook a hint of equality; Louis XIV threw the wealthy financier Foucquet into prison for having the temerity to build a château almost as fine as the king's.

In the eighteenth century the baroque city expanded and the dominance of the ruler intensified. The avenues of Versailles focused upon the royal palace, and in Germany the whole cities of Karlsruhe and Mannheim revolved about the palaces and great gardens of the royalty.

Plazas of the seventeenth century had been designed as isolated, enclosed spaces. They were now opened and less confined, as though moved by a desire to recapture the space of the countryside. Design shifted from walled-in architectural forms to an extension and expansion of open space. Jules-Hardouin Mansart, one of the architects of Versailles, designed the Place Vendôme with greater dimensions than any previous square in Paris. The three squares by Here de Corny in Nancy were connected, the continuity of open space emphasized by colonnades and enhanced by a tree-lined avenue.

Versailles. *The centerline and the axis symbolized the mighty power of the monarch. Louis XIV ordered the removal of his palace from the congested city of Paris to the open hunting grounds of Versailles, and he ordered the avenues to radiate from his magnificent palace.*

A Palace

B Gardens

C Town

A Palace
B Gardens
C Town

Karlsruhe. *The entire city of Karlsruhe was designed to revolve about and radiate from the Prince's Palace.*

Probably the most dramatic example of the new surge to penetrate the city with open space was the Place de la Concorde, designed by Jacques-Ange Gabriel during the reign of Louis XV. In this square, space is almost completely released. It flows from the gardens of the Tuileries and the Louvre on one side into the broad avenue of the Champs-Élysées begun by Louis XIV to connect Paris with his palace at Versailles. The scale is further amplified by the River Seine lying along one side. Across the river is the only group of buildings facing this tremendous square.

Another departure in urban design was the Piazza del Popolo in Rome designed by Rainaldi and completed by Valadier. A three-dimensional transition of space was obtained with a series of terraces linking the lower level of the square and the gardens of the Pincio Hill above. Continuity replaced the enclosure of open space as the new direction in civic design.

In England the classic revival came later than elsewhere, the Tudor style having absorbed the Renaissance shock. In reaction against the hazards of overhanging upper stories, a 1619 building ordinance decreed that building walls would henceforth be constructed vertically from foundation to roof. Timed with the onrushing wave of classic formalism, this law aided the introduction of the so-called Italian Style ushered in by Inigo Jones, its leading exponent.

The landowning class had tempered the rise of monarchy in England, and the monumentalism of the "grand plan" did not quite take root there. Christopher Wren attempted it in his plan for rebuilding London after the fire of 1666. He went so far as to place the stock exchange at the symbolic focal point of his plan instead of the traditional palace or cathedral. Even this acknowledgment of the domination of mercantilism in England was not enough to offset disagreement over the necessary reapportionment of property values destroyed in the fire.

Formalism permeated the English Renaissance, but it was expressed in terms of quiet repose rather than striking grandeur. This quality can be observed in the simple curved building forms facing broad open spaces of the Circus and Royal Crescent in Bath designed by John Wood the Younger. The same quality was built into the undulating surfaces and

A   Stock Exchange

B   St. Paul's Cathedral

C   Tower of London

D   London Bridge

E   Old Walls

London (Christopher Wren's plan). *After the Great Fire of 1666 Christopher Wren proposed a monumental plan for the rebuilding of London. He conceded the new power dominant in England by placing the stock exchange as the major focal point. But the plan was not accepted; the necessary adjustment of property boundaries and prices could not be resolved.*

freely curving forms of Lansdowne Crescent, also in Bath. John Nash brought these curving forms overlooking spacious open parks over into his designs for London's Park Crescent and Regent's Park.

Formalism was unobtrusively introduced in the enclosed squares of London during the eighteenth century. They were intended not as impressive plazas but as places for the quiet relaxation of the area's residents. These simple though formal open spaces were created largely by builders who would be classified today as "speculators": they were in the business of subdividing land and building homes. Many are unknown, as in the case of the builder of Lansdowne Crescent, but two builders prominent in London at the time were James Burton and Thomas Cubitt. They and others like them, known and unknown, lent dignity to their profession by the work they performed.

Behind the Facades

The fine rows of formal dwellings and squares in England, the monumental vistas, royal gardens, and palaces of France, the well-modeled piazzas in Italy, all had been built for the upper classes, the wealthy merchants, and the kings. The lot of the people of lesser means had not been substantially improved. It had not been the purpose of the designers and builders of the baroque town to engage in reforms. They were concerned with such improvement of the urban environment that would maintain the prestige and glory of those of exalted position. At the same time, the broad avenues provided more than satisfaction of the vanity and ego in despots, more than delightful promenades for the elegant carriages of the aristocrats; they offered a means with which to impress the populace with the power and discipline of marching armies.

Behind the fine facades of the plazas and wide avenues dwelt the congested urban population. The city lacked sanitation, sewers, water distribution, and drainage. Epidemics and pestilence were frequent, and poverty was appalling. A breach was widening between the aristocracy and the masses. The seventeenth-century fratricidal wars of religion and social restlessness were followed by the stamp of the despotic heel and the courtiers. Oppression brought revolutions in the eighteenth century. The baroque city had unfolded its grand open spaces, and they were overlapping upon the people.

CHAPTER 6

COLONIAL EXPANSION: AMERICA

THE NEW WORLD

Aided by the mariner's compass, courageous explorers in the fifteenth and sixteenth centuries extended the net of colonial empires over the face of the globe. At the same time, oppressed people in Europe looked toward the New World, now North America, for relief from their plight. Many colonies in the Americas were settled by pioneers impelled by a burning desire for freedom, religious and otherwise. Far removed from the mother countries and with a whole great land as an ever-widening frontier to the west, many early settlements did not grow to become permanent fortified towns. Although strong forts were established at some early settlements—San Juan, St. Augustine, New Amsterdam— the barricades thrown up as protection from attack by Indians offered no impediment to the development of villages and towns in the way that fortifications had restricted the growth of European medieval cities. The principal occupation was agriculture; the towns were small and all parts were within walking distance of the countryside about them.

The earliest settlement was sometimes irregular and uneven. The Wall Street district of today's Manhattan retains the pattern of its 1660 settlement as New Amsterdam, and in Boston, streets meander about the Common as they did in colonial days. But most of the towns were allo-

New Amsterdam. *The Dutch settlement of New Amsterdam was built on the tip of what is now known as Manhattan. The streets established in 1660 near the harbor still exist in their original pattern, among them Lower Broadway (called Breedweg by the Dutch), Broad Street, and Wall Street. The almost medieval irregular street plan and the canal are reminiscent of towns in Holland.*

cated in advance for the settlers. The people who ventured across the sea to this new land sought opportunities from which they had been deprived in their homeland, and that meant in part the freedom to work their own land.

Towns in New England reflected the modest character of the Puritan. The center was the meeting house on the common, and each family had its own dwelling, however humble. The environment was one of beauty in simplicity—communities of neighbors. Towns in the South were settled by people just as eager to improve their lot, but they reflected the stamp of the English Crown. Class distinctions, while not so obviously expressed as in England, were retained, and formality characterized the life and pattern of the towns.

Williamsburg

In Williamsburg, Virginia, the quiet and formal repose of an English town was transplanted to the new land. Through the beneficence of John D. Rockefeller, Jr., it was restored as recently as 1926 and presents an accurate impression of the early colonial town. Williamsburg was settled in 1632 as Middle Plantation, and in 1693 the College of William and Mary was granted a charter and located there. It became the capital of the Virginia Colony in 1699.

The surveyor, Theodorick Bland, laid out the city with formal axes

A   Market Square
B   The Capitol
C   Governor's Palace
D   College of William and Mary
E   Bruton Parish Church
F   Duke of Gloucester Street

Williamsburg. *Settled in 1632 as Middle Plantation, the town was renamed Williamsburg and became the capital of Virginia Colony in 1699. It was laid out by the surveyor Theodorick Bland. The main street, Duke of Gloucester Street, was ninety-nine feet wide and extended from the College of William and Mary to the capitol. The land was subdivided in lots about one-half acre in size and held a population of 3,000 to 4,000 people. The spaces are not "grand"; they are of human scale. The quiet formality of the community reflects the English influence.*

adapted from the European aristocratic mode. The Duke of Gloucester Street was the main avenue, extending from the college to the capitol building. A green was placed at right angles to this street and terminated at the palace. The town was subdivided into residence lots of one-half acre each. It was a formal plan, but it neither revolved about monumental features nor was it overpowered by them. A human scale characterized the environment; the town appeared to exist for the people who lived there rather than for the rulers who dominated it.

THE GRIDIRON APPEARS

Philadelphia

Early Philadelphia may have enjoyed this quality of human scale, but it is not apparent in its plans. The City of Brotherly Love was planned for William Penn in 1682 by the surveyor Thomas Holme. It consisted of a rigid gridiron street pattern extending between the Delaware and Schuylkill rivers. Two main streets, Broad and Market, bisected the plan in each direction and intersected at the public square in the center of the town. A square block was allocated for a park in each quadrant.

The plan had little distinction. Penn expected it to be a town of single houses and shade trees. By the middle of the eighteenth century, however, it was common practice to build the houses from lot line to lot line,

A City Square
B Park

Philadelphia. *William Penn commissioned the surveyor Thomas Holme to lay out the city in 1682. A rigid gridiron plan was adopted. Two major streets crossed in the center of the town and formed a public square. A square-block park was placed in each of the four quadrants. Early dwellings were single-family houses. In the middle of the eighteenth century it became a common practice to build dwellings on the side lot lines, resulting in continuous rows of buildings that cut off access to the rear yards. Alleys were then cut through the center of the blocks. These alleys have since become streets.*

Savannah. *Laid out in 1733 by James Oglethorpe, the Savannah plan was a regular pattern of rectangular streets with park squares liberally spotted in alternate blocks. The plan is similar to Philadelphia with a more generous allocation of open spaces.*

and the open spaces were lost within the walls of brick that lined the gridiron streets. Continuous rows of buildings shut off access to the rear of the property, and alleys were cut through the center of the blocks. Then dwellings were built along the alleys, to become the quaint and narrow business and residential streets for which the city is known today.

Savannah

The aristocratic paternalism that characterized the early settlements in the southern colonies was reflected in the plan for Savannah, Georgia. Laid out in 1733 by James Oglethorpe, the plan was a rectilinear street system similar to the gridiron but liberally interspersed with park squares along the avenues. The streets linked these parks and created a continuity of open space when the town was made up of single houses. This pleasing continuity has since been forsaken by the intensive building coverage of the intermediate blocks.

Lansingburgh-on-the-Hudson

Trade and shipping thrived in the North and settlers flocked to the colonies. Landowners opened subdivisions and plotted lots for sale and lease. Rights to pasture and timber on adjacent land were sometimes granted to purchasers of lots in the new towns.

Such a development was Lansingburgh-on-the-Hudson, surveyed by Joseph Blanchard for the landowner Abraham Lansing. This, like many others, was a speculative venture; the plan was a gridiron with a common reserved in the center, as in the New England villages. Profiting from the precedent in Philadelphia, alleys were plotted in the original subdivision.

The gridiron plan adopted for this and similar towns was not only the simplest form to survey; it was also not an unsatisfactory form for the small village. A sense of unity was maintained by the close relation of all dwellings to the town square and to the agricultural land on the outskirts. When this same pattern was extended endlessly, the monotony of the checkerboard lay heavily upon the town.

THE RADIAL PLAN

A small settlement begun in 1649 on the banks of the Severn River in Maryland received the name of Annapolis in 1694. It was the first city in America to adopt diagonal avenues and circles as its basic plan. It was followed by a more dramatic display, the classic plan for Washington, D.C., by Major Pierre Charles L'Enfant.

Washington, D.C.

After much deliberation about an appropriate location for the capital of this new nation, it was decided to avoid existing urban centers such as New York and Philadelphia. Ambitious for the future of their new country, the founding fathers selected a site along the banks of the Potomac River, removed from the commercial environment of established cities. L'Enfant, a young French designer, was commissioned to prepare a plan for the new capital city. With his background in the baroque atmosphere of Paris and inspired by the spirit of the American cause, it was natural that he should conceive of this new city on a grand scale woven into a pattern of geometrical order. Such a plan appealed to the aristocratic tastes of men like Washington and Jefferson, and it was adopted by them in 1791.

Other Examples

Following the example of their capital, a number of American cities wrapped themselves in the radial plan, that system of diagonal streets

Washington, D.C. *The plan by Pierre Charles L'Enfant, approved by Washington and Jefferson, began a series of city planning projects in which diagonal and radial streets were superimposed on the typical gridiron layout. The city was designed as a huge monumental setting for the federal government of a new nation.*

overlaid upon a gridiron pattern. Joseph Ellicott, brother of Andrew Ellicott who surveyed Washington, D.C., planned the city of Buffalo, New
York, in 1804. His plan's diagonal streets crossed a gridiron pattern at
the central square near the lake waterfront.

After the 1805 Detroit, Michigan, fire, Judge Augustus Brevoort
Woodward and Governor William Hull prepared a plan for Detroit in
1807. It was a grand complex elaborated with concentric hexagonal
streets and contained most, if not all, the myriad forms used in Washington, D.C. To implement the plan, owners of property destroyed in the
fire were ceded larger sites conforming to the new layout. New plans in
1831 and 1853 drew away from the original idea and, with the exception
of a few spots like Grand Circus Square, there is little apparent planned
form in the city today.

Among the other cities with diagonal streets were Indianapolis and
Madison. Both these cities were based upon the gridiron, but diagonals
ranged from the center to the four corners of the plan. The center in
Indianapolis was an open circle; in Madison the focal point was the
Wisconsin state capitol building.

NEW YORK CITY

In the midst of this wave of radial planning a significant development
occurred in New York City. In 1800 the city surveyor and architect
Joseph Mangin proposed a plan for extension of the city to the north,
which provided for major north-south streets with squares and plazas
somewhat reminiscent of Washington, D.C. He also suggested a treatment for the waterfront that surrounds Manhattan Island. But Mangin's
plan was not adopted.

Instead, in 1811 an official commission prepared a plan. The commission was composed of three members, two of whom were lawyers and

Detroit. *Plan for Detroit, 1807.*

landowners and the third a surveyor. They proposed a rigid gridiron street system to be laid over the entire island irrespective of the topography and the extensive waterfront. Only one angular street was retained —Broadway. The position of the commission was quite clear: "Straight-sided and right-angled houses," they stated, "are the most cheap to build and the most convenient to live in."[1]

The matter of economy obviously guided the commission in its deliberations and dictated its conclusions. They found that "the price of land is so uncommonly great," and their proposal for retention of open space was indeed frugal. The limit of open area deemed feasible consisted of 69 acres reserved for a military parade ground, 55 acres for a public market, and five small parks.

Assuming that the major traffic would continue to move back and forth between the Hudson and East rivers, the east-west streets, 60 feet in width, were spaced 260 feet apart. This extravagance was offset, however, by economy of streets in the opposite direction; north-south streets, one hundred feet wide, were spaced at distances ranging from 600 to 900 feet.

New York City. *After turning down the 1800 proposal of the city surveyor and architect Joseph Mangin, a commission was appointed in 1811 to arrive at a plan. They proposed a rigid gridiron street pattern laid upon the irregular topography of the city. Open space was not generously allocated: a military parade ground of sixty-nine acres, fifty-five acres for a public market, and five small parks were the only open area provided for in the plan. Despite the "uncommonly great" price of land, explained as the reason for the paucity of open space, the layout of streets can hardly be construed as economical; they occupy only some 30 percent of the land area. This harsh and uncompromising original plan is reflected in the cramped city of today in which open space has all but completely vanished. It was not until the middle of the nineteenth century that the great Central Park was definitely established in the plan. (United Press International photo.)*

---

1. Quoted in Turpin Bannister, *Town Planning in New York State,* American Society of Architectural Historians.

The commission's appraisal of traffic flow was hardly accurate, as the precisely reverse direction in growth it has since taken readily attests. Nor did it reflect particular optimism for the future of this great city. But it is the emphasis on economy on the part of the commission that poses the most pertinent issue, because it bears strong resemblance to that practiced in later and less happy days of urban planning.

It will be recalled that Peter Minuit purchased the entire island of Manhattan from the Indians in 1626. At that time he paid the astounding sum of 24 dollars. When the commission laid out its plan in 1811, most of the land was still devoted to agriculture. Guided by the economy of a surveyor's rod and chain, the island was mapped in a huge checkerboard. The ultimate cost of fitting the topography, "broken by hills and diversified by watercourses," to this pattern of land subdivision was overlooked to be sure. The commission obviously expected the city to continue the growth it was then enjoying; they so mapped it for subdivision and sale. The reservation of 30 percent of the land for streets can possibly be explained by the extensive frontage it provided for the sale of lots. But can the omission of ample open space be construed as economy?

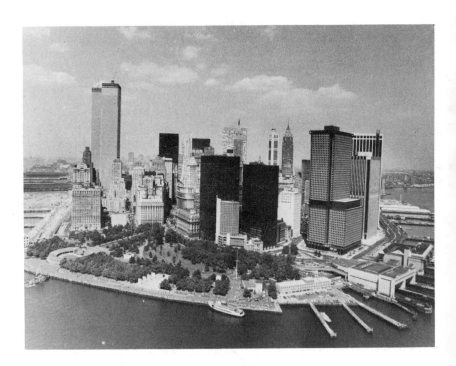

Even if the land had been developed with single-family houses on individual lots, the open space in the commission's plan would have been inadequate in the face of virtually any future growth. Forty-five years later, in 1856, 840 acres were purchased for Central Park, and it cost the city's taxpayers $5,500,000, an astronomical sum at the time.

This kind of "economy" distorts the planning of our cities today. We are obliged to learn and profit from the experience of New York City. Is it economical to avoid the reservation of open space in the name of practical planning, only to find the land value has become so dear we cannot afford the space when the need is urgent? The value of learning from yesterday is to prepare today for a better tomorrow.

There were those who protested the formlessness of the commissioner's plan. Many agreed with Henry R. Aldrich when he claimed its inspiration was "the great facility which it provides for the gambling in land values and ready purchase and sale of building blocks," which has "wrought incalculable mischief." It was an omen of the fate to befall the American city in subsequent years.

PART 2

THE CITY IN TRANSITION

Sir, if you wish to have a just notion of
the magnitude of this city, you must
not be satisfied with seeing its
great streets and squares, but
must survey the innumerable
little lanes and courts.

Samuel Johnson

CHAPTER 7

THE INDUSTRIAL REVOLUTION

FROM HANDCRAFT TO MACHINE

With the nineteenth century came the dawn of the Industrial Revolution, which can properly be called the Machine Age. Until then all goods had been assembled and produced by hand. Shops were modest and generally located in the home of the proprietor. The number of employees was small, and a close relationship existed between worker and employer, for good or ill.

New and important inventions had occurred throughout history. During the Renaissance the uses of gunpowder expanded, the printing press was invented, and the processing of various materials was greatly improved. Simple hand machinery became more efficient. But in 1769 James Watt invented the steam engine and, with it, mechanical power became independent of direct operation by hand. This power was applied to the workplace, and the production of goods grew. With increased production, trade expanded, the shop moved from the home into separate quarters—the factory—and the distance between employee and employer widened.

With the advent of machines driven by independent power a new era was born. In 1776 Adam Smith set forth his theories of laissez-faire capitalism in his *Wealth of Nations*, and his influence is felt to this day.

The number of employees in proportion to owners increased rapidly, and trade unions of workers, in contrast to the medieval guilds of artisans and proprietors, were formed.

The invention of industrial machinery touched off feverish activity; speed of production absorbed the attention of industrial management, and the repetition of operations replaced the variety of individual hand-craft. Each machine had its job, and each man, woman, or child his or her machine. Factories grew in size and the number of workers increased. The factory was like a magnet, drawing about it an ever-increasing belt of workers' dwellings, schools, and shops. With every new device production per worker jumped; the introduction of what can be called mass production made it possible for more people to have more things than had ever been available to them before.

TRANSPORTATION

The industrial system was dependent upon the movement of raw materials to the factory and finished products to the consumers. Thus the development of transportation was crucial to the period.

Before the invention of the steam engine, goods were hauled in wagons and towed on river barges. Beginning in 1761 the inland waterways of America were linked by a system of canals, and in 1807 Fulton built his steamboat, the *Clermont*. In 1825 the first steam railroad to be used for public transportation began operation in England, and a railroad line was laid in the United States in 1829. Industrial production increased and domestic and foreign commerce expanded. Between 1850 and 1880, export trade from the United States leaped from $17 million to $100 million.

In the crowded city, small horsedrawn carriages trundled people about the streets. The *voiture-omnibus,* a larger vehicle capable of holding several passengers, was introduced to Paris in 1819 and was adopted in New York City as the "horse car" in 1831.

Traffic congestion paralleled the increase in population density, and in 1867 an elevated cable car was built in New York City to alleviate the density in the streets. A steam train replaced the cable in 1871, but congestion was hardly diminished. By extending their rails beyond the city, the steam railroads offered some relief to city congestion. Suburbs sprang up along their routes, inviting "commuters" who could afford the time and luxury of escape from the city centers on a daily basis.

The electric street railway that ran on rails replaced the horse car in about 1885, and thenceforth became the principal urban transport until fairly recent times. By 1917 there were 80,000 streetcars and 45,000 miles of track in American cities. In 1895 an electric elevated line was installed in Chicago and, shortly thereafter, in New York and Philadelphia. As a result of this readily available mass transportation, the population moved somewhat away from the center to the periphery of the city, but congestion persisted.

Having failed to untie the knotty problem of traffic and transportation, the electric railway went underground. In 1897 a short line was built in Boston, and the first major subway was started in New York City in 1904. As we are sadly aware today, these developments aided and abetted congestion. The cities spread, population grew, and available transportation only intensified concentration in the urban centers.

When Gottlieb Daimler constructed the first high-speed internal combustion engine in 1885, transportation took a deeper step into the tangle of urban traffic. There were four automobiles registered in the United States in 1895; in 1900 there were 8,000; in 1972, 97,000,000; in 1985, an estimated 125,000,000. The automobile split the city open at the seams, and to this day we are frantically trying to hold it together with patches on a wornout fabric.

It is recorded that Leonardo da Vinci tinkered with a toy flying machine as early as the 1400s, but in the nineteenth century men finally took themselves to the air in gliders and by 1903 the first motor-driven heavier-than-air machine was invented. In 1927 Charles Lindbergh flew the Atlantic Ocean, and in 1938 Howard Hughes flew around the world in three days, nineteen hours, eight minutes, and ten seconds. Today commercial planes travel to every part of the earth, carrying more than 300 passengers at over 600 miles per hour, and soaring into the stratosphere. How long can the city remain congested?

COMMUNICATIONS

Civilization has moved at the rate man has been able to communicate his ideas. In ancient times messages were carried by a runner. With the invention of the printing press the thoughts of men could be recorded for all to see and read. The introduction of a postal service widened the area and types of communications, but their transmission depended upon a carrier on foot or on horseback.

The Industrial Revolution, however, sprang wide the door of man's inventive genius. By 1850 messages were being ticked off on a telegraph key. Then, on March 10, 1876, Alexander Graham Bell sat in his laboratory and spoke into a gadget. His assistant, listening at the other end of a wire, heard the words, ''Mr. Watson, come here, I want you.'' Men could talk to each other on the telephone, and the effect of space and time was drastically altered.

By the end of the first quarter of the twentieth century the miracle of radio not only further changed time and space, it exploded them in the face of civilization, and the adjustment to this fundamental change is still far from complete.

With the development of radio, television, and especially the computer in the latter half of the twentieth century, instantaneous contact and the retrieval and transfer of information are now possible in fractions of a second. Satellites in space make it possible to relay messages, verbal and visual, to all parts of the world in a flash. The long-range social and psychological consequences of all these new systems are yet to be determined.

PUBLIC HEALTH AND SAFETY

Measures for the public health and safety were extended during the nineteenth century. The first system of water supply, by gravity flow, was installed in Boston in 1652. By 1820 pumping systems were in general use, and methods for the disposal and treatment of sewage improved. The heavy building cover on the land reduced the natural drainage of the city, but extensive street paving permitted effective cleaning, and storm sewers augmented the sanitary equipment.

Public thoroughfares in towns of the Middle Ages were dark and foreboding lanes. An occasional oil lamp hanging from a corner building was the only light to guide the stranger through the night. The use of artificial gas for lighting began in London in 1812 and by 1840 was in common use in city streetlamps. Electricity began to replace gas for street lighting when the first central generating plant for the distribution of electricity started operating in 1882.

Electricity illuminated the highway and the residential street. It made the "great white ways" that brighten the city of today, but it also brought the gaudy display of signs and advertising that flash at night and droop hideously by day. With questionable taste they sell the wares of commerce and industry but reduce the city aspect to that of a cheap bazaar.

Services for the health, safety, and convenience of the urban population advanced farther in a period of less than one hundred years than in all previous history. The tremendous progress in this area as opposed to the everyday living and working conditions of the industrial city present a bewildering contrast. Glorification of the industrial system and the fruits of its newborn activity blinded people to the ruin and havoc spreading across the urban community.

Many of the systems of public health and safety that arose in the nineteenth century still are in use. They are obsolete. Their continued use and the consequent difficulties with sewage and solid waste disposal are reflections of some cities' problems, both economic and political.

CITY AND FACTORY TOWN

The steam locomotive extended its rails from the raw products to the factory, and to the cities of consumers all over the land. With its sprawling yards the railroad penetrated the town with a network of tracks. Every amenity of urban life was sacrificed to the requirements of industrial production. The factory with its tentacles of trains and shipping was the heart and nerve center of the city. Railroads and ships joined at the factories, and the waterfront became the industrial core of the city. Port cities on the oceans, lakes, and rivers prospered, drawing to them ships laden with coal and ore to fuel the factories and sending from them shiploads of manufactured goods.

The impact of the Industrial Revolution was first felt in England. The new industrial economy brought with it greater exploitation of the poor and with that the new slums. What could be called mechanical slums, row upon row of crowded workers' houses in the shadow of the factory, were added to the traditional slums. The degraded environment of the factory town hung like a cloud over urban life for the next century and a half. Writing in 1865, Dr. Clifford Allbutt described what he saw in England:

> This is no description of a plague-stricken town in the fifteenth century; it is a faint effort to describe the squalor, the deadliness, and the decay of a mass of huts which lies in the town of Leeds, between York Street on the one side and Marsh Lane on the other; a place of "darkness and cruel habitations" which is within a stone's throw of our parish church and where the fever is bred. These dwellings seem for the most part to belong to landlords who take no interest whatever in their well-being. One block perhaps has fallen years ago by inheritance to a gentleman in Lancashire, Devonshire, or anywhere; another to an old lady; a third, perhaps, to an obscure money-lender. Meanwhile, the rotten doors are falling from their hinges, the plaster drops from the walls, the window frames are stuffed with greasy paper or old rags, damp and dung together fester in the doorways, and a cloud of bitterness hangs over all. To one set of houses, appropriately named Golden Square, there is no admission save by alleys or tunnels, which are only fit to lead to dungeons: so that for perhaps half a century or more the winds of heaven have never blown within its courts.

In the new land across the sea there was a vast source of natural resources and an energetic people inspired by a new-won freedom. The Industrial Revolution, unimpeded by traditions, swept across America. Then the echo of events in Europe was heard. As the American economy shifted from agrarian to industrial, the people and the resources were soon to experience the same throes of exploitation and the same struggle for a decent living environment.

The air of American towns became polluted with smoke and grime

Among the deplorable slums of the nineteenth-century factory town in England, the two-story row house predominated, stretching in long rows with small backyards and narrow streets. The living environment was dreary and monotonous. Crowding on the European continent, however, was even more severe, as indicated in the outline of a tenement block in Vienna. Built to a height of four and five floors, the block typically contained a double row of dwellings, the interior row facing a narrow interior court on both sides. While it has been customary to assume that European slums were more crowded than housing in the New World, the tenement block in New York City does not confirm such a notion. The sketch shows a combination of the "railroad" and the "dumbbell" tenements, many of which remained in use for decades after they were outlawed in 1901.

London

New York

Vienna

from the belching chimneys of the new age. Railroads ate into the core of cities, waterfronts were ruined, soot covered the villages, and sewage flowed into streams and rivers and lined the beaches. Buffalo, Chicago, Detroit, St. Louis, all devoted their splendid sites on lakes and river waterfronts to the industrial plants, the railroads, and the ships of the new factory system. The land was plotted and advertised as "desirable sites for industry."

Floods of immigration from foreign lands created a need for housing and invited the construction of cheaply built tenements. Into them the newcomers crowded, grateful for someplace to live in this country of promise. Industrial growth in the large centers induced the people to remain in cities rather than migrate to the more healthful environment of rural communities, and the inevitable result was the creation of slums.

There was an exception to the concentration in congested cities. A large supply of labor was needed to obtain the raw products for manufacture, and "company towns" sprang up at mining and lumber sites in various parts of the country. They occupy an infamous place in the annals of American town development. Living in deplorable shacks and shanties, the workers' families were subject to the will of a single employer for their livelihood. Shelter, food, and clothing were available only through the mining or lumber company, and only on terms the company prescribed.

The Industrial Revolution and the nineteenth-century city: Stoke-on-Trent, England. *(British Information Service)*

MIDVICTORIAN MEDIOCRITY AND INHUMANITY

There was a depressing consistency about the factory town of the nineteenth century. It bred mediocrity in every aspect of life; mediocrity at best was its characteristic. Peaks of creative inspiration were few and far between. Monotonous order was an inevitable result of rigid organization of people and things. Here and there a pseudo-gaiety pierced the haze, but it was fluffy with gray frills touched more with half-concealed vulgarity than genuine pleasure. The urban environment, when it was not oppressive and filthy, reflected the bawdy can-can rather than the graceful waltz. Vast areas of mean dwellings lay under a pall of smoke; an atmosphere of haze hung over the environment. A film of grime and soot covered all, and the wide range from wealth to poverty meant little more culturally than the difference between glut and endless want. The cultural energy of the city was sapped by the gigantism of industrial development.

Proof of the mediocrity and inhumanity of the age can be found among the few who recognized it. William Morris and John Ruskin cried out against it; Charles Dickens wove it into his classic stories; Octavia Hill fought it with vigorous social work. They saw the dulling of man's crea-

tive spirit. They perceived it in all its shabbiness, poverty, and grime—
the nineteenth-century industrial city.

THE LAST OF THE BAROQUE

In the midst of the orgy of urban expansion, a development of monumental proportions was undertaken in Paris. Sensitive to the restlessness of
the working classes, Napoleon III proposed to open broad avenues
through the slums in which discontent festered. Besides clearing some of
them away in this manner, he was not unmindful of the advantage these
open spaces would provide his soldiers in controlling mob violence.

In 1853 Georges-Eugène Haussmann, a baron and bureaucrat in the
city administration, was selected to take charge of the huge program. The
result was an amazing demonstration of administration and organization.
The entire boulevard system of Paris was planned and executed in a
period of seventeen years and under the most strenuous circumstances.
Haussmann was resisted on the one hand by a city council reluctant to
appropriate the necessary funds, and on the other hand by bourgeois
property owners affected by his broad strokes of planning.

He laid out the new streets in long sweeps that cut through the maze
of winding medieval lanes. With these avenues he connected old plazas
and created new ones. He laid out the radiating avenues across the open
fields from the Place de L'Étoile, the Bois de Boulogne, the monumental
Avenue de L'Opéra, and many other grand boulevards. He was aware of
the need to design for the traffic of a new industrial age, and the broad
avenues opened through the congested districts improved circulation. He
had the conception of scale appropriate for the new city: he saw it as a
complex wanting unification.

The program engineered by Haussmann was stupendous. It transformed Paris and gave that great city much of its color. A series of
masterful projects was executed.

But the tradition of monuments was deeply rooted in the process of
city building. It was not long since the revolution against tyranny, and an
emperor was again the ruler. The tree-lined avenues and vistas were
meant to impress rather than to serve the people.

The time was not ripe for solving the new urban problems. The avenues became continuous streets of ground-floor shops, with dwellings on
the upper floors. There was no separation of land uses, as there had been
in the earlier London residential developments about Bloomsbury that
traffic arteries and shopping streets bypassed. Haussmann's scheme was
gargantuan in scale, but it was too late to become an effective monument
to the ego of a monarch, and too early to solve the planning of the
industrial city. It was the swan song of the baroque city.

Wall **A**	Built by Philip Augustus, Twelfth century	**G**	The Tuilleries
Wall **B**	Built by Charles V, Fourteenth century	**H**	The Champs Élysées
Wall **C**	Built by Louis XIII, Seventeenth century	**J**	The Champs de Mars
Wall **D**	Built by Louis XV, Eighteenth century	**K**	The Île de la Cité
Wall **E**	Built by Napoleon III, Nineteenth century	**L**	The Invalides
F	The Louvre	**M**	The Luxembourg

Paris. *The dark-shaded streets are Haussmann's interpolations on earlier forms.*

Development of Paris

Beginning as a fortified town on the small island in the River Seine, Paris was known as Lutetia by the Romans. At the time of the Norman invasion in the ninth century, the town had expanded beyond the original Île de la Cité and was fortified on both sides of the Seine. The fortifications were extended by Philip Augustus in the twelfth century. The left or south bank was the principal location for churches and colleges, the commercial center lying on the right bank. The kings made their residence on this bank, and in the fourteenth century Charles V built a wall to contain this growing part of the city more adequately. At the east end of the town was the tower known as the Bastille; at the west end, on the banks of the Seine, was the Louvre, which became the royal palace.

The Louvre was extended in the sixteenth century under Henry II, and the Tuileries gardens were created. The power of the monarch was growing. Henry IV built the Place Royal, and in the seventeenth century Louis XIII had the walls expanded to contain the Tuileries gardens.

During the reign of Louis XIV, the Sun King, Paris grew rapidly and court life extended its influence. Vauban reduced the fortified walls, and the ramparts were transformed into promenades, the first of the *Grands Boulevards*. The Tuileries gardens and the Louvre were enlarged, and the initial stage of the Champs Élysées was built into the "suburbs" to the west. The Place des Victoires and Place Vendôme were built. Monumental quais were created along the Seine. Louis XIV, however, built the great palace and gardens of Versailles and moved his court and residence there.

The city expanded further under Louis XV. During his reign the Place Louis XV (now the Place de la Concorde), Rue Royale, and the Church of the Madeleine were built. Streets were widened and new avenues built for fine residences. The Champs de Mars was also established. In the latter part of the eighteenth century a new wall was built to contain the growing city.

After the Revolution the city's industrial development increased. The city outskirts were built up, and a new wall was built in 1840. Under Napoleon III, the huge program of Baron Haussmann was carried out.

Paris underwent remodeling during the reign of each monarch, but the greatest projects in each period were those along the fringes of the city. The great open spaces that distinguish the city today were developed in advance of the city's expansion, and the walls were extended to include them as the city spread about them. The most expansive spaces in today's city, like the Champs Élysées, the Place de l'Étoile, and the boulevards radiating out from them, were laid across open fields. The rapid growth of Paris has spread the city in all its suburbs and absorbed many of the open spaces, created when the walls of 1840 were leveled in the latter part of the nineteenth century.

CHAPTER 8

THE CITY OF CONTRASTS

THE CITY BEAUTIFUL

It was an ironic paradox that out of the smoke, soot, and grime of the industrial cities, the Columbian Exposition of 1893 in Chicago would be called "White City." The fair would be everything the urban environment was not. Cities were cramped, monotonous, and ugly: the fair would be big, broad, and beautiful. The purpose of the exposition was to demonstrate amply the great new industrial empire and to give it pedigree. What more natural way to accomplish this than by clothing it in the robes of classic form, the style of the great days of the past? Was this not an appropriate cloak for a new era when men could produce more than at any time in history? With this new power men could reproduce classic structures that would surpass those of the emperors. This was an easy conclusion in the late nineteenth century, and it was true.

Daniel Burnham, the exposition's chief architect, uttered the magic words that marked the new era: "Make no small plans." The École des Beaux Arts in Paris was the fountainhead for the designers of this period, and plans had to be big to be beautiful. The fair began a tidal wave of "city planning" and it swept across the United States. Every large city planned to become the "City Beautiful." Burnham was commissioned to prepare a plan for San Francisco after the earthquake and fire of 1906.

73

The Commercial Club of Chicago engaged him for the plan of that city in 1909. He produced one for Manila and Baguio in the Philippines, and he was an active member of a commission of architects who revised the plan of Washington, D.C.

Other cities followed suit. Plans were of colossal scale with monumental proportions. Great plazas and broad avenues, generously punctuated with monuments, were almost a civic obsession. Axes shot off in all directions, terminating with proposed buildings that put the visions of past kings to shame. The City Beautiful was the Grand Plan reincarnate.

Civic centers became a popular theme. Nearly every city had its civic center plan—open space landscaped in the traditional fashion, fountains distributed about plaza and garden, public buildings limited in number only by the size and ambition of the city, topped off with a frosted glass dome terminating a long and broad vista.

All this activity was performed in something of a vacuum; an air of haughty detachment, an isolation from the affairs of people and community, pervaded the planning.

A monument or public building blithely placed in the middle of an important traffic artery suggests the characteristic disregard for the ongoing life of the city. It was as though the planners had determined that the people must adjust themselves to the mighty formal arrangement. It did not occur to them that the entire development of a city was essentially derivative of human needs. The civic center concept was one of removal from the life of the community rather than involvement as a functional entity within it. The grandiose buildings were imposing, not inviting. They held the spellbound citizen at arm's length. They did not fit the city, its life, its habits, or its manners; theirs was an air of disdain rather than dignity.

These projected great structures became so expensive that reality stepped in at last. It was recognized that the citizenry could not afford the sums of money they cost. Some grand gestures were made and executed, but on the whole the lavish plans were destined for respectable storage in the archives of a more modest realized city hall. Most of the planning actually executed had to be remodeled later, usually haphazardly, to fit the requirements of traffic and circulation that were ignored in the original conception.

CITY PLANNING: THE COMMERCIAL CITY

The seeds of city planning had nevertheless been planted during this period. Planning organizations sprang up in various parts of the country. A town planning board was established in Hartford, Connecticut, in 1907. In 1909 the first National Conference on City Planning was held. This

Civic center planning. *The 1941 Civic Center Plan for the city of Los Angeles recalls the classicism of the nineteenth-century plans. By the mid-1980s most of the proposed structures had been built about the axial plan established by the dominant tower of the City Hall. The open plaza is now honeycombed with underground parking garages.*

was followed in 1911 with the founding of the National Housing Association. By 1913 there were official planning boards in 18 cities in the country, and in the same year the Massachusetts state legistature was the first to make city planning a mandatory responsibility of local governments, decreeing that all cities with a population of 10,000 or more were required to establish a planning board.

Meanwhile the real city was shoving its sprouts through these well-intentioned but fortuitous efforts. The technical know-how required for industrial production had been learned; industry had now become a commercial process. Financing and distribution were the new emphasis. Selling the rapidly produced merchandise and financing the expanding facilities to produce more were transforming the system into a financial empire. Problems of production solved, industrial management turned its attention to commercial organization, banking, and national and world-wide trade associations. Commodities and their production gave way to tickertape and figures in a set of books. The businessman—the tycoon of commerce—became the main cog of the new era. Statistics, business cycles, bookkeeping, financing, and the stock market were the stock-in-trade of those who strove for success. Trade in commodities rather than the commodities themselves was what counted now. The city began to bristle with buildings, sheltering acres of floor space for the offices of business.

It was apparent that affairs must be operated on a practical basis. Land cost money, buildings cost money, services cost money, and so did time. Cities must work, the ornamental must be discarded, and only the useful could be tolerated. Such demands required the attention of practical men, not dreamers. A "city beautiful" was well and good, but it was far more important that it pay dividends.

To answer these demands there emerged the "city engineer," the practical man who could make surveys and calculations, determine the necessary size of sewer, water, and drainage systems, lay out rail lines, streets, walks, and roadways. These businesslike qualities instilled confidence in civic and business leaders. Businessmen chose such an individual for the responsibility of planning within established budget limitations. City planning became an engineering process engaging practical men free from dreams.

There was merit in this position; the City Beautiful was not frowned upon; it was simply too expensive, costing more than the problems it was intended to solve. Awed by the monumental dreams, impressed by the vision, it was not with disrespect that community leaders set aside the proposals. The great designs had simply lost all connection with the needs of the commercial city growing up in the twentieth century. The City Beautiful was a thing apart, detached, unrelated to the affairs of men. It solved none of the commercial city's problems. Moreover, there was probably some unconscious recoiling from the classic mold into which it would cast the physical environment.

Land took on a new value. First it had been sold as lots; value was later measured in terms of street frontage, a price per front foot. It was now being measured by the square foot. Every square foot of land had monetary value and none could be wasted. The result: building coverage became intense; layer upon layer of floor space was piled upon the land. In the twentieth century, the skyscraper was the dramatic manifestation of the commercial city.

The value attached to every square foot of land for commercial use conflicted with the fine balance between the buildings and open space of classic planning; the classic treatment had made a deep impression. It gave the look of pedigree, which was itself an asset to the business world. In order to capture appearances, remnants of the classic revival were hung upon the facades of buildings. It was a sham, to be sure, but the street thus assumed a stylish front, and the value of land behind the facades was protected. The appearance of dignity was achieved without the loss of a square foot of land.

Monumental Compromise: Washington, D.C.

Washington, D.C., is not a typical American city, but it dramatically displays the contradictions of the twentieth century. The job of government in a great democracy attracted an expanding population to the capital city. With the people came commercial enterprise, and the forces of conflict were set; the commercial city and the classic city were diametrically opposed.

The federal government vigorously attempted to retain the city's original plan. In 1901 the MacMillan Commission was appointed to restore the original character of the L'Enfant plan. Consequently the railroad that had cut across the Mall was removed, and the site for the present Union Station was established. A uniform height limit of future buildings was established. To preserve these and other accomplishments the National Commission of Fine Arts was appointed in 1910 by President Theodore Roosevelt, followed in 1926 by the creation of the National Capital Parks and Planning Commission.

These commissions performed yeoman service to the preservation of the classic city, but that city had changed. A new age had arrived, immature but nonetheless a moving force. Commercialism had descended upon Washington, with all its collection of shops, hotels, office and loft buildings, entertainment and residential development, traffic and transportation. The increased value of land and the consequent intensity of development that had overtaken other cities happened in the capital city as well.

Commercial need and enterprise paid respect to the monumental street system originally laid down by squeezing into this framework the features of the new city. Classic facades were again draped upon building fronts, and behind these fronts formless building space was heaped upon the land, just as in other cities.

The contradiction between the classic and the commercial city was clearly apparent. To protect its character of monumental buildings and planning, the government-building area became a reservation necessarily isolated from the remainder of urban development. With the complex separated in this way, uniform building height and style could be maintained, the choice of site, form, and the use of open space could be easily enforced.

Washington, D.C. The national capital as envisioned in 1941 by the National Capital Parks and Planning Commission. Washington is a city of monumental compromise between the classic and the commercial. The Capitol is near the center. It is encircled (left and counterclockwise) by the House Office Building, Library of Congress, Supreme Court, and Senate Office Building. To the right is Union Station. The Mall extends from the Capitol to the Washington Monument, from which the Reflecting Pool leads to the Lincoln Memorial.

A city of monumental compromise between the classic and the commercial city. The Capitol is near the center of the photograph. It is encircled (left and counterclockwise) by the House Office Building, Library of Congress, Supreme Court, and Senate Office Building. To the right is Union Station. The Mall extends from the Capitol to the Washington Monument, from which the Reflecting Pool leads to the Lincoln Memorial.

The paradox of the city was substantially complete. The plan for the capital of a great democratic government could be executed only by rigidly controlling its form in a preconceived and inflexible mold.

It was falsely assumed that a planning style could be transferred from another age and adapted to a new set of conditions. But great cultures are not recognized because of their similarities to previous periods; rather because of their special stamp, the distinctive qualities they have contributed to the progress of civilization.

The effect of the false premise upon which the plan of Washington, D.C., has evolved is magnified by the design of the structures themselves, the insistence upon classic forms without regard for the required arrangement of interior space. The design of exterior space is equally oblivious to the functional elements of the city. The classic courtyards, their prototypes covered with fine paving or gracious gardens, have in Washington become oil-stained parking lots filled with automobiles. The federal reservation of classic monumentalism is hollow and unnatural; the commercial city, warped into the pattern of its streets, is equally artificial.

THE NEED FOR REGULATION

Laissez-faire took deep root in the affairs of men as the commercial city formed. But soon it became increasingly apparent that if freedom was to avoid license some order must be established. In practical terms this meant the adoption of rules and regulations that placed certain restraints on laissez-faire.

We have observed that regulations over city building were not new in the annals of history. Hammurabi was perhaps the first, in 2000 B.C. The Greeks had building regulations as well. The Romans established height limits for tenements. Towns of the Middle Ages adopted various regulations against fire hazards and projecting upper stories.

The sad condition of housing that developed with the factory system in the nineteenth century eventually forced the enactment of many laws to curb abuses. Regulations for light, air, and lot coverage, though lax in enforcement, were accepted for residential buildings. Restrictions regarding commercial and industrial buildings remained rare, however. Commercial structures were permitted to occupy as much as 100 percent of the lot area for the entire height. Steel construction and elevators pushed buildings even higher. Light and air could penetrate on the street frontage only, and these diminished as buildings rose, floor upon floor, into the air. The advent of the skyscraper had made the need for appropriate regulations more and more apparent.

Regulations increased in number and scope during the early part of the twentieth century. Codes establishing standards of construction and mechanical and electrical installations were adopted to protect the public health and safety. Fireproof construction was required where congestion was most acute. Protection was assured for public rights-of-way.

Mixed land uses—the indiscriminate placement of stores and shops in residential areas—induced premature depreciation of land values and the disruption of residential neighborhoods. The need to exercise some measure of public control over land use had become pressing.

Zoning

There was some precedent for zoning in Europe. When town walls in Germany were leveled in the nineteenth century, building regulations designated "belts" in which apartments and single houses could be built about the periphery of the ramparts. Protection from the encroachment of undesirable land uses had been attempted in America as well. Exclusive residential sections in some Midwestern cities were planned. Access to homes in these areas was by way of prime streets and guarded gates. Block ordinances were framed to restrict improvements to so-called high-class residences. In Boston in 1903 limits were set on building height—125 feet in the central district and 80 feet elsewhere. In 1909 Los Angeles divided the business area into seven industrial districts; the remainder of the city was declared to be residential.

These cases were hardly more than experimental gestures, but the chaotic growth of cities made it imperative that positive steps be taken to bring some order into the urban pattern. It is a fortunate characteristic of human history that when leadership is needed there is usually someone available willing and capable of assuming the responsibility. Such a man was Edward M. Bassett, a New York City attorney. To him goes credit for a public service on behalf of the entire urban population. He undertook a thorough investigation of the power of the people to regulate their own destiny and worked diligently to prepare a legal instrument whereby they could effectively exercise their power to control the use of land in the urban community.

Edward Bassett defined zoning as "the regulation by districts under the police power of the height, bulk, and use of buildings, the use of land, and the density of population." (*Police power* refers to the government's authority to legislate for the protection of the health, safety, and general welfare of citizens.) With this clearcut purpose, the first comprehensive zoning ordinance in the United States was enacted by New York City in 1916. There is no better testimony to the remarkable thoroughness of Edward Bassett and his colleagues than the subsequent history of zoning in the courts. Challenged a number of times in later years, the principle was upheld in every case.

One of these is particularly significant. It confirmed the democratic foundation of zone planning, and established it as an instrument with which the people could attempt to order the destiny of their cities. In *Euclid v. Amber,* Associate Justice George Sutherland of the U.S. Supreme Court said:

> Until recently urban life was comparatively simple; but with the increase and concentration of population, problems have developed, and constantly are developing, which require additional restrictions in respect to the use and occupation of private lands in communities. Regulations, the wisdom, necessity, and validity of which, as applied to existing conditions, are so

New York City. *New York illustrates the contrasts, conflicts, and chaos of modern commercial centers.*

apparent that they are now uniformly sustained, a century ago, or even a half century ago, probably would have been rejected as arbitrary and oppressive.[1]

An instrument had been created to control the use of land in urban areas for the first time. It is a technique that protects the general welfare of the people by protecting that of each individual citizen.

Nothing in the nature of zoning confines it to urban development alone. It is essentially a planning device and as such can be applied in any scale and for any land area that requires public control over its use. It has been applied to counties in a manner similar to that of cities, and it has been adapted as a means to conserve natural resources. For example, in 1929 the state of Wisconsin empowered counties to establish districts comprised of privately owned lands in which agriculture was excluded and forestry and recreational development encouraged for the public good.

Zoning is a vital part of the urban machinery, but it can fail through abuse, misuse, and rigid resistance to changes in the urban pattern essential for the general welfare.

Extension of Public Services

The Industrial Revolution changed the city into a metropolis. The urban population became the multitude, and the supply of basic human wants to this multitude required highly organized services. The need for some form of mass transportation via common carriers, the building and maintenance of roads, adequate water supply, sewage disposal and drainage, sufficient communications capacity, power and light—all vastly expanded in scope. Their impact in turn upon the public health and safety increased accordingly. Thus connected with the public interest, some of these private services were subject to public regulation; others were embraced in public ownership.

Public works to control or harness natural resources for the community at large were not new. We will recall the dikes, reservoirs, and irrigation projects along the Nile of ancient Egypt; the aqueducts, sewers, and roads built by the Romans as public projects. Royalty or the nobility took on this responsibility; it disappeared for a time during the age of Feudalism but returned toward the end of the Middle Ages.

In the early history of this country many of the highways were private toll roads. They were later transferred to public ownership and control. The sewage system and drainage were and remained a public responsibility. Other public services, however, are owned and operated as private

---

1. *Village of Euclid, Ohio, v. Ambler Realty Company,* 272 U.S. 363 (November 22, 1926).

enterprises. Because of their impact upon the common welfare, their continuity and consistency are essential, and they enjoy a monopoly guaranteed by franchise. These, the public utilities, are subject to regulation by public authority.

The airlines, railroads, buses, and other common carriers, the telephone, telegraph, radio, and television are with some exceptions regulated public utilities. The same is true of electric power, illumination, and gas distribution. The supply of water is generally owned by the public, although there are exceptions.

The social control of utilities is an important factor in the future of urban development. The response of the courts is therefore pertinent to our understanding.

In 1876 Chief Justice of the U.S. Supreme Court Morrison Remick Waite set forth the theory of public interest in private property. The case was that of a grain operator who violated a local statute controlling the rates for storage. The court held that the enterprise was "affected with the public interest" because of the dependence of the public upon it and the consequent right of the public to exercise authority over its operations. Justice Waite stated:

> When, therefore, one devotes his property to a use in which the public has an interest, he, in effect, grants to the public an interest in that use, and must submit to be controlled by the public for the common good, to the extent of the interest he has thus created.[2]

Supreme Court Chief Justice William Howard Taft confirmed this position in a later case with this opinion:

> In a sense, the public is concerned about all lawful business because it contributes to the prosperity and well-being of the people. The public may suffer from high prices or strikes in many trades, but the expression "clothed with the public interest" as applied to a business means more than that the public welfare is affected by the continuity or by the price at which a particular kind of business with a public interest, in the sense of Munn v. Illinois and other cases, must be such as to create a peculiarly close relation between the public and those engaged in it, and raise implications of an affirmative obligation on their part to be reasonable in dealing with the public.[3]

It will be observed that any enterprise engaging in public service assumes a dual obligation. First, to supply all the needs of the public implied by the nature of the service; second, to provide the services at a

---

2. *Munn v. Illinois*, 94 U.S. 113 (1876).
3. *Charles Wolff Packing Company v. Court of Industrial Relations of the State of Kansas*, 262 U.S. 522 (1923).

cost reflecting reasonable but not excessive profit. This status of a public utility—a public service for which it enjoys a monopoly—imposes obligations beyond the scope of the usual private enterprise. Public utilities became an integral part of city planning, and successful development of the city is largely dependent upon the effectiveness of their operations.

CHAPTER 9

BETTERMENT OF
LIVING CONDITIONS

The depths to which urban communities sank in the nineteenth century (and in which many still remain) is a shameful blot on the world scene. Constructing tenements solely to gouge rents became a profitable enterprise. Excessive building coverage of the land and the crowding of dwellings within the buildings brought about an almost unbelievable population congestion. The population density in London was 265 persons per acre in 1870. In New York City, which then had only one-third London's population, it was 23 percent higher—326 persons per acre.[1]

Standards of land use were lax. The first law to regulate tenement building was passed in New York in 1867, but only faint improvements were forced upon speculators. Planning persisted at a deplorably low level; the "railroad apartment" was typical of the early tenements, and it had no more evil rival in the world. The usual lot was 25 feet wide, with a depth of 100 feet. The building covered as much as 90 percent of the area. The small space remaining at the rear was used for privies, no sanitation being provided within the building. The tenements were five or six stories high, with four apartments on each floor. Only one room in each dwelling enjoyed light and air; all other rooms had no exterior exposure.

---

1. *American Cyclopedia*, 1875, Vol. XII, p. 382.

The unbearable living conditions imposed on the poor did not go unnoticed. A competition was sponsored in 1879 by the *Plumber and Sanitary Engineer* for a "model" tenement. The result was touched with
irony. The winning plan by architect James E. Ware was the prototype
of the later accursed "dumbbell" plan, which covered 85 percent of the
lot and resorted to a narrow interior light shaft along the property lines.
Despite subsequent legislation outlawing both dumbbell and railroad
buildings, innumerable remained to afflict the city of New York for several decades of the twentieth century.

THE UTOPIANS

The depressed condition of housing for the poor impressed some nineteenth-century industrial leaders who recognized that their present privileged state was connected with the masses of workers on whom they
directly and indirectly depended; they sensed the problems the deplorable conditions of the poor presented to the future of the industrial
economy. As early as 1797 the Society for Bettering the Conditions of
the Poor was formed in England, and efforts to relieve the burdens of the
working classes pierced the haze all through the nineteenth century.
The first half of the century was marked by periodic protests against the
"sordidness, filth, and squalor, embroidered with patches of pompous
and vulgar hideousness." A number of Utopian communities were proposed. One such plan was put forth by Robert Owen.

Owen was the proprietor of a cotton mill at New Lanark in Manchester, England, where he had successfully introduced reforms in the working conditions, hours, and wages for operatives in his plant. Owen saw
beyond even these reforms. In 1816 he set forth an unusual plan for a
cooperative community that combined industry and agriculture. It was
designed to hold about 1,200 people.

Dwellings were grouped about a large open space in which communal
buildings were located. Surrounding the dwellings area were large gardens. This entire area in turn was encircled by a main roadway. On one
side of the compound were factories and workshops. Beyond, on all
sides, was the agricultural belt, to range in size from 1,000 to 1,500 acres.
Owen intended his plan for the use of the unemployed; he assumed that
the community would become self-supporting and thereby reduce the
heavy cost of public relief.

Another Utopian, the English architect J. S. Buckingham, in 1849
published a treatise entitled "National Evils and Practical Remedies," in
which he described his plan for a model town for an "Associated Temperance Community of About 10,000 inhabitants." Buckingham adhered
to the contemporary distinctions of class. He placed the finer houses near

Robert Owen's proposed self-supporting industrial town. *Robert Owen was an English industrialist moved by the deplorable conditions of the ill-housed industrial workers, made worse by increasing unemployment. In 1816 he proposed a plan for a community that, among other things, he believed could become self-supporting and reduce the heavy cost of public relief. Owen further proposed that similar communities be established at appropriate intervals in the countryside. Communal buildings for each were situated in the center of a broad common. About the common were rows of dwellings, and surrounding the dwellings were large gardens. The main road encircled the entire compound, and the factories and workshops were located along the outside boundary of the community. Designed for about 1,200 people, each community was surrounded by an agricultural area of between 1,000 and 1,500 acres to supplement industrial employment.*

the center of his town and the humbler dwellings and workshops of the working class about the periphery.

Some Genuine Changes

Most Utopian proposals were not executed, but they focused attention upon the growing evils of the urban environment. In 1844 the Rochdale Pioneers, a group of English flannel weavers, formed the first consumers' cooperative, and in England the same year the first Royal Commission on Health and Housing was appointed. The first Public Health Act was passed in 1848.

By the middle of the century severe epidemics were spreading over England and the Continent. The wealthy classes could insulate them-

A 1000 houses 20 feet wide   G 120 houses 54 feet wide

B Arcade for workshops   H Schools, baths, dining halls

C 560 houses 28 feet wide   J Public buildings, churches

D Retail shops   K 24 mansions 80 feet wide

E 296 houses 38 feet wide   L Central square

F Winter promenade arcade

J. S. Buckingham's plan of a model town for an associated temperance community of about 10,000 inhabitants. *Proposed in 1849 by the architect J. S. Buckingham, this Utopian plan specified a multitude of features within the community. Buckingham recommended that industries using steam engines be situated at least one-half mile from the town. He also suggested that sites be reserved for "suburban villas" in the agricultural land surrounding the town.*

selves from many undesirable features of urban living, but they were not immune to disease. Spurred by alarm, the rulers of England, France, and Germany caused some model dwellings to be built.

These projects represented two extremes. In the congested urban areas, six- and seven-story tenements were constructed with little improvement in plan and design over previous buildings; they could only decay into more slums with time. At the other extreme, suburbs of single houses were built on the outskirts of the cities. The intention was to encourage home ownership. But the possibility of selling these dwellings at handsome profits removed them from the income group most in need of improved housing. Too expensive for the vast number of low-paid workers, they became no more than middle-class suburbs. There were no solutions in these spurts of activity.

MODEL TOWNS

Recognizing the desirability of good housing for their workers and stimulated by the unexecuted proposals of the Utopians, industrialists undertook to build model communities. One of the earliest of these towns was Bessbrook, built in 1846 for workers in the linen mills near Newry, Ireland. In 1852 Sir Titus Salt built Saltaire near Bradford, England, for some 3,000 workers in his textile mill. Extensive community facilities were introduced in this development. In 1865 the Krupp family began the first of several model villages in Essen, Germany, for workers in their munitions and iron factories.

George Cadbury, the English chocolate manufacturer, moved his plant from Birmingham to a rural site and began the town of Bourneville in 1879. Originally a company town, this community became an autonomous village in about 1900. Today it contains some 2,000 dwellings. In France, another chocolate manufacturer, M. Menier, built a workers' colony at Noisel-sur-Seine near Paris in 1874. Also in France, similar communities were built by the Anzin Mining Company for their workers at Valenciennes, and by M. Schneider et Cie. for the workers at their Creusot Steel Mills near Fontainebleau. Another was developed by the Crespi Cotton Mills near Capriate, Italy, and in 1883 the Van Marken Yeast and Spirit Works put up Agneta Park near Delft, Holland.

In 1886, Lever Brothers, the famous soap manufacturers, built Port Sunlight near Liverpool. Large blocks of the 550-acre site were used as interior gardens and play areas, a forerunner of future planning. Another project foreshadowing subsequent developments was Creswell, built by Percy Houfton in 1895 for his Bolsover Colliery. The community is a hexagon in form, the houses facing inward on the gardens. The cocoa manufacturer Sir Joseph Roundtree commissioned Barry Parker and Raymond Unwin, architects prominent in the emerging new direction of town planning, to build Earswick near York in 1905. This, like Bourneville, was made a community trust.

Port Sunlight, England. *Model town by William Hesketh Lever, 1886. The community was the original site of Lever Brothers, Ltd., the soap manufacturers.*

Some American industrialists sought to improve housing for their workers as well. Among the best known of the community projects is Pullman, Illinois, which was built in 1881 as a permanent town in conjunction with the plant for the manufacture of Pullman sleeping cars.

The model towns of the industrialists were so few that they contributed little to the solution of the real problem of housing in the factory centers. They were flavored with a paternalism similar to the "model" dwellings built by the European rulers at an earlier date. They did demonstrate some planning arrangements from which later communities were to profit, but their rarity emphasized the disparity between the living standards possible for some in the industrial era and the low level to which housing for most had degenerated.

There can be no claim to city planning during this era. The fervor for industrial expansion had blotted out the original plans for cities in America, and only remnants can now be seen. Ambitious proposals remained as diagrams of what might have been. Even the distinction between major and minor arteries established in the early plans, for example, was abandoned in favor of a standard street width of 66 feet.

The gridiron plan of New York City was the early beginning of a sterile urban character that eventually characterized the entire country. The movement westward gripped the early settlers, and with them soon strode the land surveyors. By the time this great trek had moved across the United States the occupied areas of the vast land had been mapped out in a gargantuan gridiron of mile-square sections. The pattern of land division was thoroughly bound in a legal straitjacket of readily recorded deeds. Natural features—rivers, mountains, and valleys—were ignored. Henceforth the grid became the basic pattern of farms, villages, towns, cities, and counties. Desirability of land was measured by its prospects for quick and profitable turnover. Subdivision practices were conveniently designed to enhance these prospects, and the pattern of the future development of cities was fairly sealed in this package of the gridiron plan.

IMPROVEMENT ON THE HORIZON

As the nineteenth century wore on, the British and European governments assumed more and more responsibility for the improvement of the city. Legislation was enacted in Holland to provide for the loan of public funds to "public utility societies" that were engaged in housing, and a similar program was begun in Stockholm, Sweden, in 1879. The British Housing Law of 1890 empowered state and local authorities to condemn land and build dwellings to rent to the working classes. In response to the growing strength of the trade union movement in Germany an 1889 law granted privileges to cooperative housing developments, using funds derived from social insurance inaugurated by Bismarck.

Various measures like these set the stage for the more enlightened era of the next century. Social activism on behalf of decent housing also began, and was to extend into the twentieth century as well. Octavia Hill launched her crusade for the underprivileged in London in the late 1800s —a practical program based on the idea that good and consistent management could improve living conditions even in existing tenements.

In the United States, stirred by the gallant efforts of such crusaders as Jacob Riis, a growing protest developed against the congested tenements of the cities. The hideous railroad and dumbbell tenements on 25-foot lots had spread over New York City, but there were feeble signs of reform. As early as 1871 the Boston Co-operative Company began a modest program of rental housing for city workers, and other model dwellings were attempted.

In 1894 the publication of plans for tenements by the architect Ernest Flagg aroused wide interest. These plans provided broader light courts than the standard practice, reduced the length of interior corridors, and improved the exposure of the rooms. A competition for better housing plans was held by the Improved Housing Council in 1896. Flagg won, with a plan requiring a lot 50 feet wide and a structure that accommodated the same number of apartments per floor as the dumbbell plan. The rooms in each apartment were larger, however, and their daylight exposure and arrangement improved.

With this impetus to improve low-cost housing, the Tenements House Committee of the Charity Organization Society conducted a competition in 1899. Among the design requirements were a maximum lot coverage of 70 percent, large light courts, and a given minimum volume of air per occupant within the dwelling. The winning design was submitted by R. Thomas Short.

The 1899 competition spurred renewed efforts for reform and culminated in the passage of the Tenement House Act of 1901, commonly known as the "New Law," in New York City. The act used the standards set in the competition and established the 50-foot lot as subdivision practice.

Progress became more visible as the twentieth century opened. Several organizations formed with the purpose of building better housing for the low-income worker. One of the most notable was the City and Suburban Homes Company of New York. Starting business in 1896 and assisted by Ernest Flagg, it built some 3,500 apartment units. The company's stated purpose is worthy of note: "to offer to capital a safe and permanent investment and at the same time to supply wage earners improved homes at current prices."

In 1879 the Washington Sanitary Improvement Company was established in Washington, D.C., followed by the Washington Sanitary Housing Company. These two organizations built nearly 1,000 apartments for rental to low-income families in the capital city.

THE MOVEMENT TO THE CITIES

The factory system of the Industrial Revolution brought more and more people to the urban centers. England's rural areas decreased in population from 10,000,000 in 1821 to 9,500,000 in 1936, but cities gained from 4,000,000 to 37,000,000 in the same period. Further changes have occurred since 1936 as rural land has become urbanized. Germany's rural population dropped from 23,000,000 in 1821 to 19,000,000 in 1936, and urban population increased from 2,000,000 to 48,000,000. Between 1800 and 1900 urban population in Europe grew between 300 and 400 percent. At the beginning of the nineteenth century, London had a population of 1,000,000; at the beginning of the twentieth century it was 7,000,000. During the same period Paris grew from 700,000 to 3,000,000, and Berlin from 172,000 to 4,000,000. The industrial metropolis and congestion became synonymous.

The population of the United States was largely agrarian at the beginning of the nineteenth century. Only about 5 percent of the people lived in towns, and these were small communities. In 1790 there were only two cities with a population as large as 25,000. The inauguration of regular steamship service between Europe and America in 1840 helped to feed the factory system with immigrants seeking the freedom of this land. By the middle of the century 20 percent of the total population lived in cities. From that time onward the acceleration was rapid. By 1960 there were almost 179,300,000 people in the United States. By 1980, the population had increased to 226,500,000—a gain of more than 24 percent in twenty years. The latest statistics indicate that in 1983 the population of the U.S. was 234,200,000. Projections to the year 2025 predict that there will be anywhere from 259,673,000 to 356,601,000 U.S. residents.[2]

Population Distribution—Urban and Rural

The 1970 population for urban areas in the United States (the census definition of *urban* includes communities with populations of 2,500 or more) was 149,324,930, compared with 167,050,992 in 1980—an increase of approximately 12 percent. The rural population during the same period

2. *1980 Census of Population. General Population Characteristics. United States Summary.* U.S. Dept. of Commerce, Bureau of the Census.

1300

1600

1800

Bern. *The early medieval town had open space within and about it. With the increase in trade and the rise of mercantilism the city form did not change, but open space was built up. The methods of water supply, drainage, and waste disposal remained the same as more and more people crowded into the city. Bern has continued to grow in population as have other cities; although it extended its boundaries, the process of congestion has increased the intensity of land use. The current congestion has been made bearable only with the vast improvement in water distribution through the public utilities of gas, electricity, and sewage disposal.*

grew from 53,886,996 to 59,494,413—an increase of 10.4 percent.[3] Similar increases in the population of the metropolitan areas, which include large cities and their surrounding areas, have occurred in all parts of the world as people have moved from rural areas, adding to the problems in the already overburdened cities.

Patrick Geddes

Urban speculation and its disintegrating effect upon the living environment of man had aroused the consciousness of some prominent spokesmen during the century. The critical voices of eminent men—John Ruskin, Thomas Carlyle, Lord Shaftesbury, Charles Dickens, Friedrich Engels, and Benjamin Disraeli—brought the issues to the fore with the force of their insight and talent.

---

3. *Statistical Abstracts of the United States,* 1984. U.S. Department of Commerce, Bureau of the Census.

| 1641 | 1812 | Today |

New Haven. *Just as the medieval town became crowded with the increase in trade, the new towns gradually became congested with the development of commercialism. The plan of New Haven shows it as an open residential community until the Industrial Revolution. In the last hundred years, however, the street system has changed only slightly, but the land has been built up until little open space remains.*

Among those who spoke out against the evils at the turn of the century was Patrick Geddes. In 1892 Geddes founded the Outlook Tower in Edinburgh, a center from which he wished to study the whole complex of urban life. He insisted upon a view of all phases of human existence as the base of operations, an integration of physical planning with social and economic improvements.

This principle does not sound unfamiliar today, but it was new when Geddes expressed it. As a contemporary of his said:

> There was a time when it seemed only necessary to shake up into a bottle the German town-extension plan, the Parisian Boulevard and Vista, and the English Garden Village, to produce a mechanical mixture which might be applied indiscriminately and beneficently to every town in this country. Thus it would be "town-planned" according to the most up-to-date notions. Pleasing dream! First shattered by Geddes, emerging from his Outlook Tower in the frozen north, to produce that nightmare of complexity, the Edinburgh Room at the great Town-Planning Exhibition of 1910.

Patrick Geddes gave voice to the necessity for what was later to become regional planning.

The Garden City

Another whose voice rose above the throng was Ebenezer Howard. Disturbed by the depressing ugliness, haphazard growth, and unhealthful conditions of cities, he set forth his ideas in a little book published in 1898 entitled *Tomorrow*. His idea was the garden city.

Howard described a town in which the land would remain in the single ownership of the community. The population would be some 30,000 people in an area of 1,000 acres. The dwellings would be distributed about a large central court, where the public buildings would be located. The shopping center would be on the edge of the town and industries on the outskirts. Surrounding the city would be a permanent belt of agricultural land comprising 5,000 acres.

Unlike the early Utopians, Ebenezer Howard saw his idea become a reality before his death in 1928. The Garden City Association was formed in 1899. In 1903 First Garden City, Limited, a limited dividend society, obtained 4,500 acres of land 34 miles from London and began the city of Letchworth. It contained an agricultural belt of 3,000 acres and was designed for a maximum population of 35,000 at some future date. By 1933 the town had grown to a population of 15,000, had more than 150 shops and 60 industries, and had paid dividends on the invested stock. At a later date a second garden city, Welwyn, was started on a site of 2,400 acres. It was designed for a population of 40,000. In fifteen years it had a population of 10,000 and 50 industries.

Just as Ebenezer Howard planned it, the agricultural belt remained a permanent protection for these cities, not a reserve of land for continued expansion of the urban area, which is usually considered the only good use for vacant land on the periphery of cities. The land increases in value as each community grows and prospers, and the community correspondingly prospers that much more.

There is a difference between the usual joint-stock company and Garden City, Limited, which developed Letchworth. The principal object of the latter is to create a town for the benefit of the community. In so doing, the rights of the shareholders to dividends on their stock are limited (5 percent in Garden City, Limited) and profits earned above the dividends are applied to the benefit of the whole community. The company is in a position of public trustee rather than a private landlord. It has proven a sound but not a speculative investment. Land for all development purposes is leased for a period of ninety-nine years. The town government consists of an urban district council of fifteen members, elected by the residents; five members retire annually and are eligible for re-election or possible replacement.

Another feature distinguishes Letchworth. Development and growth of the garden city are reversed from the practices of the usual speculative city. Aside from the merits of planning in either type of town, zoning in Letchworth determines the use of specific areas, and only those uses are permitted; for example, only factories and workshops are built in the

A Bridge
B Market
  Plaza
C Future
  Market
  Place
D Schools

Margarethen-Hohe, Essen—George Metzendorf, architect. *The village of Margarethen-Hohe was developed in 1912 by the Krupp family for workers in the industrial steel plants in Essen. The community was planned for 2,000–2,500 dwellings (12,000–16,000 population). It illustrates a number of planning features. Surrounded by forest, the principal connection with the city is by way of the bridge (A) on the north boundary. Rather than bisecting the plan in the usual manner, the main traffic street swings around the village and bypasses the market plaza (B). This shopping center and the future principal marketplace (C) are conveniently situated within blocks of dwellings rather than on the periphery. The schools (D) are situated within blocks of dwellings rather than on the traffic roads. The road system is designed to fit the topography of the site but is arranged to avoid through traffic on any but the main roadway. Buildings are generally set back at the road intersections to avoid obstruction of traffic vision at the corners.*

industrial zones and shops in the commercial zones. In the speculative town, on the other hand, any use of a lesser economic character is permitted in its zoning provisions; dwellings are found in industrial and commercial zones, and these mixed uses are largely responsible for the sad state of the urban environment. The overdeveloped center and underdeveloped periphery of the speculative town are absent in Letchworth. Open spaces remain for development as the need arises and for use as provided for in the plan.

Of the 1,500 acres of the town located within the surrounding rural belt, the plan allocated 935 acres for residential use, 170 acres for industry, 60 acres for shopping, and the remainder for parks and roads. There are some 4,000 dwellings in Letchworth, of which the Urban District Council has built 1,300 worker's cottages.

THE COMMON DENOMINATOR

The houses families live in form the common denominator of the city; they are the fiber of the city. The link between family dwellings and city building is so close the two are almost synonymous. Industrial and commercial enterprise strengthen the structure of the city, but it is the community of homes that marks the health, even the civilization, of a people.

Haussmann ripped through the slums of Paris with his boulevards, civic centers were planned for American cities, the impressive garb of classic facades was hung on the streets of the commercial city, and zoning was devised as the legal instrument to lend stability to the urban framework. But housing, the manifestation of the inner structure of civilization and the culture of people, remained as always the "leftover" in the urban plan.

Had zoning come early rather than late, the urban predicament might have been much different. It is not exactly practical to plan a city after it has been built. Planning implies a program before an act, but zoning was adopted after the city had taken shape, and zoning could hardly do more than freeze the mixture. There was no chance to prescribe the ingredients before they had been poured together and well stirred. It was inevitable that housing should become the excrescence of urban land use.

City planning was first an urge to improve the aesthetic pattern of the urban environment. Then zoning made of it a statistical exercise and a marathon of prognostication. These movements were necessary and valuable but they did not improve the environment of the people, and that is the purpose of city planning. Housing has thus become the principal instrument to attain that objective. It brings into focus the social, economic, and aesthetic aims and needs of the urban population. It consequently becomes a political responsibility.

After World War I the housing shortage became a major crisis in Europe. Building inactivity through the war years had left the people of all countries with not only a shortage of dwellings but also with monetary systems that, through inflation and war debt, needed transformation. It was essential that governments take a hand.

Public policy with respect to housing had made considerable progress in European countries during the nineteenth century. The groundwork for public assistance had been laid. Financial aid was available to private enterprise through public utility societies and trade union cooperatives. Local public authorities were empowered to provide housing for the lowest-income families. The exercise of condemnation by public authorities was an accepted instrument to enforce housing improvement, and cities in a number of countries had acquired large areas of vacant land outlying the built-up city.

The housing program was a reminder that standards of living are more than a load of mechanical equipment surrounded by the walls of a building and covered by a mortgage. The family and its dwelling had been engulfed by the tidal wave of the Industrial Revolution. It emerged from World War I as the primary unit of design in city development.

The record of the program is of historic importance. The performance in each country assumed similar characteristics, but each deserves some attention for the remarkable progress it represents in the total pattern.

CHAPTER 10

IMPROVEMENT IN HOUSING

The environment is composed of many elements, both in the natural setting and in the built sector. All of these factors in total are the world in which we live. In addition to the physical there are the social, economic, and political forces that impact upon humans. Combined with the physical, they form the total environment that inspires the responses that take place in the everyday activities of men, women, and children of all ages.

While the material that follows deals to some degree with the progress in housing, the total environment is considered in evaluating the programs initiated by the several nations of the world.

> Housing may be the sleeper environmental issue of the '80s. In the past, environmentalists who advocated slower residential growth were accused of undermining the American dream of owning a single-family home on a quarter-acre lot. Ironically, today that dream is dying, precisely because society has ignored the constraints of natural resources on unplanned home building.[1]

ENGLAND

In response to the Homes for Heroes campaign in England after World War I, the Housing Act of 1919 superseded the 1890 Housing Law. It

---

1. Bruce Stokes, *Sierra Magazine*, September/October 1982.

provided for government subsidies to local authorities for the clearance of slums and the building of low-cost housing. During the twenties and early thirties the purposes of this act were consolidated and extended. Compensation to owners in built-up areas declared ready for clearance was restricted to the market value of the land, and no payment was made for the substandard structures on the site. Standards of occupancy were established to prevent overcrowding of families within dwellings, and local authorities were vested with the police power to order improvements in physically substandard dwellings or their demolition.

The 1890 British housing program had given strong impetus to enactment of the Housing and Town Planning Act of 1909; with subsequent amendments, this became the Town and Country Planning Act of 1932. This was a comprehensive piece of legislation. Local authorities were not only empowered to prepare and enforce plans for the urban area, but, typical of the British pride in their rural countryside, the act also provided for the preservation of rural areas and important buildings. It further implemented the cooperative planning for two or more separate political subdivisions—cities and counties—where they required such treatment as a region.

The Housing Act of 1936 brought the relationships of housing, slums, and city planning into clearer focus. Slum clearance was an important phase of the program. The local authority was required to prepare a plan for redevelopment of blighted areas in which these areas were related to the general plan for the city. Such an area may then have been declared suitable for redevelopment, and the authority was empowered to acquire the land in whole or in part and to arrange for its rebuilding by private enterprise or public authority.

The criteria to be met for this declaration were these: at least 50 working-class houses contained in the area; at least one-third of the dwellings overcrowded or physically unfit, congested, or unsatisfactory for renovation; area located suitably to house, in part, industrial workers; and last, redevelopment necessary to establish adequate standards of low-rent housing.

The effectiveness of the British program was demonstrated by performance. According to the Twentieth Annual Report of the Ministry of Health, there were 3,998,366 dwellings built in England between the end of World War I and 1939. Of this number, 2,455,341 were built by private enterprise, 430,481 by private enterprise with some degree of government assistance, and 1,112,544 by local authorities.

Apartment buildings three to five stories in height were considered necessary to restore ample open spaces in the residential plan, but this was contrary to the traditional dwelling. The cottage-and-garden was the type closest to the heart of the Englishman. The most successful housing developments were consequently those in which this type predominated.

The Satellite Garden Town

Two great projects were undertaken in this period—Becontree, a satellite community for 25,000 families on 2,770 acres near London, and Wythenshawe, adjacent to Manchester.

Sir Ernest Simon called Wythenshawe a satellite garden town to distinguish it from garden cities like Letchworth and Welwyn. The satellite garden town and the garden city have similar characteristics: each is a residential area of low density with not more than 12 families per acre, containing factory and shopping areas, parks, schools, other civic buildings, and protective buffers of permanent agricultural belts on the periphery. A garden city, however, is intended to be a self-contained and self-sustaining community, whereas the satellite garden town is situated close to a large city in which the residents of the town may have their places of work and business.

The city council of Manchester appointed a housing committee in 1926 to consider the possibility of relieving the congested slums in the city with a satellite garden town. An estate of about 2,500 acres in single ownership adjacent to the city on the Mersey River was recommended as the site. It was later increased to 5,500 acres, and after some opposition locally and in Parliament the entire area was incorporated in the city in 1920, most of the land being finally purchased at agricultural value. The architect Barry Parker was invited to prepare the plans for the estate. An agricultural belt of 1,000 acres was reserved, and the original estate grounds were retained as a 250-acre park. A golf course of 100 acres was also provided. Two broad parkways ran through the town that connected it with the city. The residential areas that border these parkways were separated from the roadways by an open space 150 feet wide. Side roads gave access to abutting property; the main road was confined to through traffic with limited access. The residential area was 3,000 acres, with a maximum density of 12 houses per acre; 25,000 houses were planned, with an ultimate population of 100,000.

The land on which Wythenshawe is built remains in the ownership of the city of Manchester. Both the city and private enterprise were allowed to build on the estate. By 1935 a total of about 4,800 dwellings had been completed, of which the city built some 4,600. It was planned that about two-thirds of the residential area would be used for municipal housing and one-third for private housing. About 500 acres were reserved for industrial, commercial, and civic buildings. Both communities are now complete.

S   School
▨   Agricultural Belt
▨   Parks
—   Roads
┅   Railroad
▨   Industry
■   Business

0   1 MILE

Greenbelt ▨
Parks ▨
Parkway ━
Roads —
Railroad ┅
School ○
Shops ●
Shopping Center ●

0   1 MILE

The garden city and the satellite town. *Reflecting the ideas of Ebenezer Howard, the garden city of Letchworth (top, left) was begun near London in 1903; Welwyn (top, right) soon followed. Their initial planning limited the ultimate maximum population. The garden cities were surrounded by agricultural fields, similar to the original proposal by Robert Owen. The satellite towns of Wythenshawe (bottom, right) and Becontree (bottom, left) are similar to the garden cities with the primary exception that the latter are self-contained, each having its own industry, whereas the former are dependent on the larger industrial cities to which they are attached for industrial employment.*

Some criticism was leveled at the Manchester city council for extravagance in purchasing a large tract of land and reserving large areas for permanent open space. Sir Ernest Simon, a staunch spokesman for improved housing, defended the policy of the city by comparing it to the usual procedure of land acquisition:

Let us consider first the question of the bulk purchase of land. The question is whether the City Council has been wise to purchase so large a block of land straight off, or whether it would have been more economical to continue its previous policy of purchasing relatively small plots of land as and when required. It has in fact, since the War [World War I], purchased nearly 2,000 acres at a cost which has been gradually rising, but which must average about £400 an acre. Since then prices have gradually increased. As development has proceeded and as it has become known that the Corporation was in the market for more land, the prices have been put up, and the average price paid for the whole 3,500 acres is perhaps in the neighborhood of about £100 an acre, or a total of say £350,000.

If at Wythenshawe the Corporation had pursued its old policy, first of all developing main roads and main drainage, then gradually buying pieces of land as they were required for housing and became ripe for building, there is not the least doubt that they would have had to pay a similar average price to that paid in the rest of Manchester; that is to say about £400 an acre.

The effect of the bulk purchase, therefore, is that the land has been purchased at an average price of £100 per acre as against an average of £400. So far as the 2,000 acres are concerned which are to be used for municipal housing, nobody denies that this land was needed for housing, and that it would, at some time, have had to be bought for that purpose. The economy through buying in bulk has, therefore, been £300 an acre, of a total of £600,000 for the 2,000 acres. Against this savings must, of course, be set the annual loss in owning the land up to the time of development; say 4 percent for interest charges. This amounts to £8,000 per annum. From this must be deducted the rents receivable from the agricultural land (less cost of management) which would bring the net burden down to a figure of say £6,000 per annum, that is to say, against a total saving of £600,000 there is an annual charge, so long as the land is wholly undeveloped, of £6,000. The period of delay before full development is, of course, uncertain, but if Manchester proceeds with its program of building 3,000 houses a year, most of them being necessarily built at Wythenshawe, the estate will be fully developed in less than ten years. Assuming, however, that twenty years were required, the burden of interest, beginning at £6,000 per annum and gradually falling to nothing, would amount in the whole period to £60,000. The net savings on the housing estate owing to the early purchase would therefore be no less than £540,000.

Let us now turn to consider the 1,500 acres purchased for factories, shops, public buildings, and private enterprise houses. Development is still in its early stages, and no particulars have been published as regards the terms on which this land is being leased for these different purposes. We are informed, however, that the ground rents which are being obtained are such that they represent on the average a capital value of at least £300 per acre above the bare cost of the land. When these 1,500 acres are fully developed there will therefore be a profit on the capitalized value of the land of at least £300 per acre, or £450,000 on the whole area. Against this item also there will be a set-off representing the interest charges during the period of development, which on the assumptions previously made should certainly not exceed £50,000, leaving a net gain of £400,000.

Taking the landlord account as a whole (covering 3,500 acres) we come, therefore, to the following conclusion: that the bulk purchase of 3,500 acres by the Corporation as against the old policy of hand-to-mouth buying of the land required for housing, and not buying any land for other purposes, will, if the estate is fully developed in twenty years or less, show a capital advantage to the Corporation of approximately £1,000,000.

Accusations of extravagance against the City Council for the bulk purchase of land are, therefore, the exact reverse of the truth. The fact is that the City Council has shown a high degree of business foresight in making the purchase, which will ultimately be of great benefit to the ratepayers.

There is only one other aspect of the Wythenshawe development which has been called extravagant: the generous reservation which has been made in the plans for the agricultural belt, parks, parkways, and the preservation of spinneys. Admittedly, the area reserved is an advance on what has previously been done; but the difference between the normal practice of reserving 10 percent of the area for parks, on the one hand, and what has been done at Wythenshawe on the other, is not great. The total expenditure on open spaces in the whole three parishes of Wythenshawe, even if the whole agricultural belt is actually purchased by the City Council, will certainly not reach £200,000; perhaps £50,000 less. But this extra expenditure will make a big difference to the amenity of the estate. Can anybody seriously call this extravagance when it is set off against the £1,000,000 which will be gained on the landlord account?[2]

FRANCE

Cholera epidemics generated some activity in the nineteenth century to correct substandard housing in France, and the threat of mob violence moved Napoleon III to build wide avenues through the slums as a means of control. But it was not until 1894 that serious legislation was enacted. The act passed at that time was similar to the Belgian law of 1889 that made government funds available at low interest rates for houses to be built and sold exclusively to industrial employees. In 1912 the Office Public d'Habitations a Bon Marché (Public Office for Low-Cost Housing), an organization of local authorities, was empowered to loan funds for, and to subsidize, low-cost housing. It was augmented several times later, until the Loucheur Act of 1928 concentrated further upon production of housing for low-income families and expanded financing through public authorities and private enterprise. Nearly half the dwellings pro-

2. Sir E. D. Simon, *The Rebuilding of Manchester* (New York, Longmans Green, 1935).

vided by the Public Office after World War I were concentrated about Paris.

Despite ambitious plans to rebuild the congested slums—the *ilots insalubré*—the housing program in Paris was seriously marred. When the city walls were razed, it was expected that the open space would be reserved and the surrounding slum belt cleared and rebuilt with appropriate planning standards. It was another idle dream. When the fortifications were leveled in 1930 the land was leased to speculative enterprise. In the open space some 20,000 dwellings were crowded into tightly planned tenements eight stories high; the adjacent slums remained.

There were some encouraging developments in the late thirties. The Department of the Seine planned a series of *cité jardins* in the outlying areas of Paris. While literally translated as "garden cities," these developments were designed as satellite garden villages somewhat similar to Wythenshawe in England. In the words of Henri Sellier, Administrator of the Housing Office of the Department of the Seine, the *cité jardins* were planned as "essential elements of the city of Greater Paris."

A blow befell the program. Lack of proper arrangements for transportation meant failure for some of the *cité jardins* and near failure for others. The interesting project at Drancy la Muette remained vacant because transportation was not provided. Chatenay Malabry, planned for 20,000 people, and Plessis Robinson were both partly occupied, but transportation arrangements were not made and neither was successful. All this amply demonstrated the need for cooperation from public utility agencies.

The housing program in France after World War I hardly set a standard to serve as a guide for urban development. The plan for the *cité jardins* about Paris was courageous, but, as indicated, it was not enough for success. Urban development is complex, and provision of the variety of public services required by the residents makes the difference between success and failure.

GERMANY

Certain policies had been well established in Germany prior to World War I. Public utility societies and trade union cooperatives were recognized as effective instruments in the housing field. State financial aid was an accepted method; during the last half of the nineteenth century Bismarck had inaugurated social insurance, and these funds were a source of housing loans for many years. In addition, local governments had assumed responsibility for the housing of government workers and the financing of public utility societies.

During his tenure of office in 1902, the mayor of Frankfurt obtained passage of a law that permitted the city government to pool private property, rearrange it to conform to the city plan, and redistribute such land for redevelopment. The city was further authorized in this process to retain 40 percent of the land without compensation to the owners for streets, parks, and other public uses. Pursuant to this enactment in Frankfurt, numerous German cities adopted a policy of acquiring outlying vacant land on their periphery. The purpose was protection from the speculation and resulting boom in land prices that inevitably accompanied the rapid increase in urban population.

This policy was fully rewarded after World War I when the need for housing, production of which had come to an abrupt halt, became most acute. The cities were then in a position to lease large quantities of these public lands to private and cooperative organizations for the construction of housing without the penalty of excessive land costs. In 70 German towns with more than 50,000 population, more than 6,000 acres of city-owned land were leased between 1926 and the rise of Hitler to power in 1933. Similar policies were adopted in other countries—Austria, Switzerland, Holland, and Denmark; in Czechoslovakia 15,000 acres outlying Prague were made available for housing.

World War I left Germany impoverished. Astronomical inflation demolished the monetary system, an inactive building industry left a serious housing shortage. Intrinsically high financing costs coupled with the inflation rendered it difficult for private enterprise to cope with the housing problem. Although the figures may seem low to Americans, interest on mortgage money had more than doubled, moving from 4 percent to as high as 10 percent. Rents had quadrupled while wages had increased only 50 percent. It became imperative for state and local governments to finance a large part of the housing program.

Property owners had become beneficiaries of the inflation, which had the effect of liquidating all previous mortgages. As a consequence the *Hauszinsteuer* (House Rent Tax) was adopted in 1921. Prewar rents were used as the base for a tax levy ranging from 10 to 50 percent of the rents, and the funds thus derived were used to finance second mortgages at a very low interest rate (generally 1 percent) to compensate for the high cost of first mortgage money. Administered by local government, these funds were loaned to public utility societies and cooperatives for housing. The effectiveness of this policy is evident in the production of some 3,000,000 dwellings between the end of World War I and the rise of Hitler. More than three-quarters of these dwellings received financial aid from the government. The housing problem was not solved, a sufficient supply of dwellings was not provided and the slums remained, but the program represents a remarkable achievement nonetheless for what it did manage to accomplish.

German cities had suffered the same kind of chaotic growth experienced by other cities on the Continent during the nineteenth century. It was obviously necessary to reconsider land utilization and planning if the tremendous housing program was to result in a permanent asset to the communities in which it was built. It is a significant contrast with our experience in the United States. Emergencies have been the excuse to postpone urban planning in our country; in the short-lived German Republic the emergency was considered the sound reason to engage in the most serious planning. Despite the shadows cast over that country by Hitler's subsequent rise to power and Nazism, the housing program of the decade of 1920–30 emerges as an example of an agressive if immature democracy in action.

The pressing demand for new dwellings gave neither the time nor the funds for a real program to clear the slums; this was necessarily postponed until an adequate supply of dwellings could be built. Two effective means were brought into play in the early twenties: the public utility society (limited dividend company), and the cooperative society. The public utility society, though comparable to the limited dividend company in the United States, was eligible to receive the benefits of several forms of subsidy necessary to implement a large supply of new housing. The societies were formed for the purpose of building low-cost housing and, despite careful state supervision, exercised a high degree of initiative and ingenuity in the planning of their projects. The cooperatives, or self-aid societies, were organized largely by trade unions as a means to supply housing for their members. These companies enjoyed privileges similar to public utility societies and assumed the same obligations. The effectiveness of these groups is demonstrated by the extensive operations of the three largest, which built 71,000 dwellings up to 1929. These three, known as Dewog, Gagfah, and Heimat, were among some 4,300 cooperative societies in operation.

In addition to large organizations there were a number of smaller private companies engaged in the program, but they contributed to a much less degree than the above-mentioned organizations. The government created various agencies, under jurisdiction of the several provinces and municipalities, for research in the technical phases of planning, construction, and financing. The results of this research were made available to all private and public organizations in the housing field.

With few exceptions, planning prior to 1925 had been confined to the usual city blocks. Inadequate building regulations had permitted an excessive density for population and building coverage. The first step away from high density in the postwar program was the arrangement of buildings around the perimeter of the usual city block with a concomitant reduction in coverage within the center of the block. Mainly apartment buildings of three and four stories went up, and the "hollow square" thus formed enclosed recreation and service areas for the tenants. Many large-scale developments were placed on tracts of vacant land. Freedom from the subdivision of the gridiron system led to more informal planning, and the row house was adopted where density was not a prerequisite. Main traffic streets were confined to the periphery of the projects, and internal roads were bordered on each side by a row of dwellings. Apartment houses of three and four stories were included along the marginal areas of the site.

Factors similar to today's hygiene planning were considered. Research led to the consideration of orientation. Sunlight in every room was a rule, and the orientation of all buildings to provide east and west exposure became mandatory. The preferable exposure was west light for living rooms and east light for bedrooms. The attention devoted to the proper orientation for all dwellings at this time is reminiscent of the fifth century B.C. in Greece.

The final step was the relation of the buildings to the streets. Buildings in parallel lines along each side of a street did not provide equal privacy for living areas or quiet for sleeping rooms. The new site planning produced uniform orientation for all dwellings but did not give them uniform exposure upon the open spaces surrounding the buildings. Instead, all buildings were placed at right angles to the streets. The space between buildings was thereby free of vehicular traffic, although the walks were designed to permit small trucks access and facilitate the movement of goods and services. This arrangement provided privacy for all living units, safety for play and recreational areas, and uniform orientation for all dwellings.

Recreation space for children and adults, shops, common meeting rooms, and kindergartens were provided in the housing developments. Laundry facilities were placed on the roof of the two-story buildings of early projects, one-half covered washing space and one-half open drying space. The larger apartment buildings continued this until central heating was adopted and central laundries or "washeries" were built in conjunction. Private gardens were provided to the extent that space permitted but were usually confined to the single-family row houses. Some subsistence plots were included in a few of the large developments.

Strict adherence to this plan produced a rigid uniformity that increased during the late twenties, but it served to overcome some of the traditional inhibitions of the gridiron street system. Some later projects developed in 1931 and 1932 demonstrated a degree of liberation from the earlier regimentation. A more plastic and flexible treatment was emerging, but the progress was interrupted by the political domination of Nazism.

Probably the most outstanding example of integrated planning oc-

Possmorweg, Hamburg. *Built in 1927–28 by the architectural firm of Schneider, Elingius, and Schramm, Possmorweg is a variation of the "hollow square" planning characteristic of the early housing program in Germany. The large space of the interior courts was a vast improvement over high land coverage, but orientation of the dwellings was compromised. Under the later direction of the city architect Fritz Schumacher, this type of planning was maintained in Hamburg.*

curred in Frankfurt-am-Main. Ernst May, the chief architect, undertook a comprehensive plan for the entire city in preparation for the housing program. May subscribed to the principle of satellite communities about the periphery of the city. The housing developments were surrounded by permanent open spaces but were planned as part of the city expansion rather than as detached and self-contained garden cities. Frankfurt-am-Main is today considered to be one of the most beautiful cities in Germany.

AUSTRIA

Austria emerged from her period of empire and World War I financially bankrupt. Rampant inflation reduced to a minimum the capacity of private capital to produce housing. Municipal government was forced to take the major role, and Vienna undertook an energetic program. In 1923 the government taxed rents to obtain needed public funds and launched an active program. Approximately a quarter of all revenues from taxes was devoted to housing in 1928.

HOLLAND

At the turn of the century, in 1901, Holland passed an act that required every city with a population of 10,000 or more to prepare a comprehensive town plan in which new areas for housing were to be allocated. Housing standards were to be established by the local authorities, who were responsible for their compliance and could exercise the power of condemnation where necessary. Local authorities were also empowered to build low-cost housing. Government funds were made available to public utility societies at low interest rates.

During and following World War I these powers were extended, and the housing program was accelerated. In the ten years after the war some 500,000 dwellings went up. Because careful attention was directed throughout the program to the needs of the various income levels, it was possible to confine the public housing primarily to the problem of direct slum clearance.

Extensive comprehensive planning was done for many of the large cities following World War II, when urban areas such as Rotterdam were literally destroyed. Rebuilding of that city's town center has resulted in a showplace for the world to enjoy.

SWITZERLAND

The housing situation in Switzerland after World War I did not present as serious a problem as in European countries because of its stable history and its policies of private finance. Nonetheless it too had a housing shortage after 1918, and local governments rendered financial assistance to cooperatives as encouragement to produce an adequate supply. But the advantages of democratic capitalism had always been more evenly distributed in Switzerland than elsewhere, and the excesses suffered in many countries had been absent to a marked degree. The result was that this little country had not sunk to such low depths that drastic social action and fundamental economic alteration were required to restore balance.

SWEDEN

Mature policies of land acquisition by cities in the Scandinavian countries resulted in aggressive participation in the supply of housing by private enterprise via the public utility societies and housing cooperatives. Copenhagen in Denmark, Stockholm in Sweden, and Oslo in Norway made outstanding progress in both urban and rural housing. Standards were maintained at a relatively high level. It is estimated that 10 percent of Stockholm's population lived in housing produced by the cooperative societies alone, and a fifth of the people in Copenhagen and Oslo were accommodated in cooperative and public utility housing.

The Industrial Revolution did not reach Swedish cities until electrical power had been developed as a major power source. As a consequence congestion did not afflict Swedish cities to the extent suffered by other cities on the Continent. Decentralization was feasible—power was brought to the people rather than the people congregating at the source of power. While migration to the cities during the nineteenth century had increased ten- to twenty-fold elsewhere, the increase of population in town and country was stable in Sweden. During the nineteenth century rural population increased from one million to three million, and urban population increased from two million to four million.

The central district of Stockholm contained its share of slums, but they did not constitute the relatively large problem prevailing in continental cities. The principal problem in Sweden was overcrowding within dwellings, undoubtedly due to the rigorous climate and the heating problem it created. More than 40 percent of the families occupied apartments of one and two rooms.

Since Sweden remained neutral during World War I the economy had not only escaped suffering but had fared quite well. A shortage of housing occurred because construction had lagged, but the government was in a satisfactory financial position to render all needed assistance to correct it. From 1917 to 1920 municipalities subsidized public utility societies and cooperative groups that were building low-cost housing to the extent of one-third the cost. In 1920 this subsidy was reduced to 15 percent of the cost because of increased wages and resulting capacity to pay higher rents. With stability generally restored by 1923, the subsidies were discontinued. Interest rates on mortgage money were high, and the State Dwelling Loan Fund was set up to make loans for second mortgages at low interest rates to offset the high first mortgage costs.

It was a tradition in Sweden (prior to current times) for citizens to have the greatest possible freedom from government aid or interference in the housing market. (Younger Swedes today might well find this unbelievable.) This tradition had not only been strengthened by the vigorous and aggressive cooperative movement, but was largely due to it. It became an effective and progressive instrument for the maintenance of democratic procedures and economic freedom. In order to remove itself from housing operations as much as possible, the government created an independent agency in 1929 to administer the Swedish Housing Loan Fund. This agency made low-interest long-term loans to continue the building of housing for low-income families. The successful operation of cooperatives soon obviated any need for these loans, and financial responsibility was shifted to the cooperative societies. By 1934, 10 percent of the people in Stockholm lived in housing developments sponsored by the cooperative societies.

The cooperatives were of two major types. The SKB (*Stockholm Kooperativa Forbundet,* or Stockholm Cooperative Society), which produced various consumer goods, built housing primarily for its member employees. The HSB (*Hyresgasternas Sparkassa och Byggnadsforening,* or Tenant Savings Bank and Building Society) was an organization specifically organized to build dwellings for members of the society, and membership was not restricted to any particular occupation. Careful research in planning was carried on by this society, and the projects it developed introduced advanced techniques in planning, equipment, and community facilities.

Between 1904 and the 1960s, the city of Stockholm purchased 20,000 acres of land surrounding the city. This land was incorporated and planned for "garden suburbs." The city installed streets and utilities and sponsored a program for working families to lease lots and build their own dwellings. Loans were available from the municipality for up to 90 percent of the value of each unit. The loans were in the form of materials purchased by the city, the balance, 10 percent, being the owner's contribution in labor. Standard plans for the dwellings, ranging from 700 square feet to 1,000 square feet in floor area, were prepared by the city, and skilled supervision was provided during construction. It was a popular and successful program, offering an opportunity for low-income families to leave the congested slums.

The rebuilding of cities was aided by the Town Planning Act of 1931, which required all urban communities, regardless of size, to prepare a rebuilding plan. All improvements thereafter were obliged to conform to the plan.

In 1935 encouragement was given to rehousing slum dwellers by means of rent rebates ranging, according to family size, from 30 percent upwards. The municipality advanced loans for other forms of housing improvement, such as joint rehabilitation of substandard buildings by owners of contiguous property. Housing for the aged and for single women was also included within the scope of municipal programs.

The methods employed in Sweden to maintain good housing were varied. Public policy was always flexible enough to be adjusted as changing conditions warranted, and private enterprise, through the cooperatives and housing societies, was courageous and astute in its investments.

THE SOVIET UNION

Since the 1917 Revolution and especially since World War II, planning and housing in the U.S.S.R. have been treated with vigor. The contrast between prerevolutionary Czarist Russia and the Soviet Union is apparent. Vast plans for industrial development were made and many were carried out. New cities were built and portions of old cities rebuilt.

There appears to be a distinction, however, between the tremendous activity and Soviet standards of construction. The latter do not measure up to expectations suggested by the former. A city plan like that proposed for Stalingrad, a linear city, suggests hopeful prospects for the reorganization of the urban pattern. The extensive executed housing developments, on the other hand, are rife with technical inadequacies, and are made up largely of small apartments in multistoried buildings, which offer little to warrant particular attention and leave much to be desired.

It must be said, however, that the quality of the architectural designs appears greatly improved since the 1970s. The buildings nonetheless are even larger than those of earlier planning, seemingly the response to a dedication to bigness for its own sake. The individual apartments continue small, but some flexibility has been provided to satisfy the needs of larger families.

The form of government in the Soviet Union and its economic structure are so different from those of the West that comparisons are ineffective. The political processes, so different from our own, are such an integral part of urban development that experience in planning and its accomplishments cannot be subjected to our reasonable appraisal.

INDIA

The current housing situation in India is alarming. About 10 percent of the population is without adequate shelter. With the population evergrowing and very little overall economic improvement, the future does not appear encouraging for many millions of people. The need to improve these conditions is imperative if India is to remain a civilized nation.

Professor K. P. Bhattacharjee of Jadavpur University cited the following statistics:

> According to a National Building Organization estimate the shortage in 1971 was 15.6 million, of which 3.8 million [are] in urban areas and 11.8 million in rural areas; and by 2000 A.D. there would be a shortage of 40 million houses in urban areas. . . . to wipe out this deficit in ten years at least 4 million houses are to be built in a year; the present rate of construction is 400,000 houses only. In rural areas there would be a deficit of 72 million houses.[3]

He recommended the following national housing policies:

> 1) Increase financial allocation in plan outlay; 2) Set up suitable financial lending intending builders; 3) Prescribe minimum housing standard (in terms of plinth area, materials to be used, and cost) for urban and rural areas; 4) Minimize cost of dwelling units by using indigenous materials and using substitutes for cement and steel; 5) Land price should be kept as low as far as possible and ownership of land should be vested with the Government; land speculation should be discouraged; 6) Public housing investment; 7) Research and development of low cost building materials; 8) Dissemination of technical know-how developed in the research organizations of the nation through training of manpower and demonstration projects.[4]

---

3. Professor K. P. Bhattacharjee, Architect and City Planner, Jadavpur University, Calcutta, India, "Strategy for Housing Development in India during the Decade 1980–1990," paper presented at the thirty-fifth IFHP World Congress, Jerusalem, 1980.
4. Ibid.

PEOPLE'S REPUBLIC OF CHINA

Cities in all underdeveloped countries face the same problem. The People's Republic of China has a history of both rural and urban slums. The shortage of minimal housing is so great that it will take years to meet even basic housing needs. In the cities, a great effort is being made to limit family size to one child. Even in rural areas, where the need for labor is still great, the government has made an effort to limit family size. The government in addition discourages emigration to the cities.

The Chinese consider large cities difficult to manage and poor environments because of high building and population densities. Those who have been to the United States have been quick to cite New York City and its problems as evidence. The relatively undeveloped transportation system still relies heavily on waterways and railroads for long distances and bicycles for short ones. An increase in the number of buses and improved roads has helped, but living near work is still important to the Chinese. And making cities self-sufficient in terms of food supply and consumer goods is also important.

The country is poor but the people do not seem poor. There is none of the squalor usually associated with poverty. People live in what may seem to us cramped quarters with primitive facilities. While the figures cited on the amount of construction since Liberation are impressive, so is the population increase. It is clearly difficult for the nation to keep up with the incredible population growth: less than 550 million at Liberation in 1949 to nearly a billion today. The housing shortage is constantly cited as a major problem.[5]

Financing housing is accomplished through grants from the central government in Beijing (Peking); by grants from the local regional governments; through the profits made by industry or commerce, including agriculture; and finally by individual savings. The latter approach is, in general, discouraged since it places a drain on the efficient utilization of material and labor resources.

Before any building program can be initiated there must be a master plan to ensure efficient development. For example, housing and employment centers must be carefully linked so that employees do not have to travel by bicycle more than 30 minutes from home to work.

Planning in the People's Republic is supposed to take place in consultation with the people. The degree to which this actually transpires is uncertain, for most planning decisions seem to be decided by the central authorities. Joan Robinson describes it in this way:

---

5. U.S. City Planners in China, November and December 1980. Martha M. Davis, Deputy Executive Director, New York Department of City Planning. *Urban Planning Update,* an APA Publication, May 1980.

New housing in Beijing. *This type of housing, in the area once the location of the outer city wall, exemplifies the character of the People's Republic of China, even in some of the rural areas, where the importance of preserving agricultural land is national policy.*

There are several phrases always used in connection with the system of economic planning—"two initiatives, of the top and the bottom"; from the bottom up and from the top down; and leaving leeway, which means allowing room for adjustment as production goes on.[6]

For example, representatives of the province meet with the planning commission in Beijing to review the various programs the province wishes to propose. The planning commission evaluates these programs and assigns priorities and funds for their implementation.

Robinson delineates the various planning bureaucracies:

There are various departments concerned in drawing up a provincial plan. The plan for agriculture gives targets for the major crops and for fisheries and forestry. It is also concerned with promoting mechanization.

6. *Economic Management in China,* monograph, Modern China Series, No. 4, Anglo-Chinese Educational Institute, 1976.

The plan for industry gives all major products in quantities and minor ones as a global sum. It makes allowance for trial production of new items.

There is a plan for communications and transport within the provincial orbit. The plan for commerce covers the volume of purchases of consumer goods to be supplied through the shops and matches the value of sales against total purchasing power.

The plan for capital construction sets out all major projects and the additional productive capacity that they will provide.

There is a plan for the labor force and the wage bill, showing the number of new jobs that will be created.

There are departments concerned with education, culture, and health, dealing with enrollment in schools and colleges and with the medical service, sanitation, and the arts.

The plan covers the distribution of materials and the products of agriculture and industry.

Finally, there is a department concerned with finance, dealing with revenue and expenditure and setting targets for reduction of costs of production. This bureaucracy is performing the functions not only of the civil service in the capitalist countries but also of a large part of private business.[7]

Shanghai

All existing cities with an accumulation of uses and infrastructures that are aged beyond their reasonable life expectancy face great problems in planning for the future because of the enormous cost of rehabilitation and redevelopment. Shanghai is no exception, indeed the problems are inten-sified and multiplied by the conditions that are the result of the extraterritorial rights seized by foreign powers during the nineteenth century.

Shanghai was but a fishing village when Japanese envoys to the Tang Court at Xi'an landed there before the tenth century. Under the Yuan (1260–1378) it became a minor cotton spinning and weaving center. By 1800 it was a flourishing port with a population of approximately 50,000. In the middle of the nineteenth century near the end of the Opium War, the Shanghai garrison surrendered to the British in 1842. From that time until the revolution the city developed as a group of enclaves for foreign interests. These former foreign cities within the city make up the additional complicating aspects of future planning for the most populous city in China.

There were three cities in Shanghai prior to 1949. They were the International Settlement, the French Concession, and the Chinese City. Each had it own government and exercised exclusive jurisdiction within its own

---

7. Ibid.

Shanghai, 1853

boundaries. The history of the growth of Shanghai's three cities can be found in the history of the expanding China trade of the last half of the nineteenth century. The demand of foreign traders that a vast territory with a dense population and strategic locality should not remain closed to the industrialized West led to the opening of Shanghai and other ports in China. The growth of Shanghai and its attainment of the position of key city in China have been due principally to its geographical location as a port of entry to the great and wealthy Yangtze Valley where almost half of China's millions live. During the civil wars and foreign invasions, the two foreign settlements remained undisturbed and came to be islands of safety for the people.[8]

Since each of the elements of the city were distinct entities, the water, sewage, and road systems reflected this separation of authority and were not designed for intercommunity relationships or service. To this day, one of the critical problems facing the city is the coordination of the several communications and servicing systems.

The current population of Shanghai exceeds 11 million. Over 5.4 million of its people live in the congested 58-square-mile urban core. In terms of density this amounts to over 1,450 persons per acre, exceeded only by the population in the most congested square mile of Hong Kong, considered the most densely populated area of any major city in the world.

Faced with almost impossible demands for housing in all parts of the nation, the People's Republic of China had to make do with the limited space and economic resources inherited from prerevolutionary days. However, although much of the old was permitted to remain, 10 industrial towns were constructed in the suburbs around Shanghai. Thirty to seventy kilometers—approximately 18 to 43 miles—away from the central city, these towns have been constructed in keeping with the principles of city planning. They have industrial and residential areas, a road network, commercial centers, greenbelts, railway stations, and social service facilities such as schools, hospitals, clinics, and the like.

Suzhou

The city of Suzhou, located about 75 miles to the east of Shanghai, was settled about 3,000 years ago. It lies astride the Grand Canal, still an important waterway for commercial transport. The master plan for the city contains many interesting details, including the development of a new highway system to be built over some of the canals that have, over the years, silted up or become severely polluted and odorous. However,

---

8. Tsing Tai Chow, master's thesis, University of Southern California, 1950.

enough of the canals are to be retained to continue the role of the city as the "Venice of the Far East." The treatment of the banks of the canals with concrete block facings and dredging will make them not only clean but also handsome.

Major landmarks such as pagodas will be protected by keeping competing high buildings outside the line of vision. Major highways will be constructed to a width of 132 feet. The rights-of-way will be landscaped, and pedestrian and bicycle lanes will be provided.

The plan locates amenities such as storytelling houses, libraries, historical museums, stadiums, stage and movie theaters, as well as many smaller features such as special restaurants and candy shops. The ancient Taoist monastery will be preserved and maintained.

Housing located adjacent to the canals will be regulated as to its relationship to the canal, its architectural style, and the color of its exteriors.

Beijing (Peking)

The master plan for Beijing is more advanced than those being prepared for other cities. It has been submitted to the state for approval. The plan proposes new development in satellites on the least productive land in agricultural surroundings. Industrial plants are proposed in these satellites, located with reference to prevailing wind directions in order to reduce pollution in both the local community and the total city. Housing for the workers in the new industrial plants is located near the industries but separated from them by a greenbelt. Transportation needs are reduced by encouraging walking or bicycle riding to places of employment. Traffic arteries bypass the cities to reduce the amount of internal traffic and the congestion that is so often associated with it.

The Inner City is crisscrossed with main streets that are intersected by *hutongs* (lanes), like a chessboard.

Since the Liberation in 1949, Beijing has undergone many changes. Work to broaden the road around the Forbidden City was started in the 1950s. To ease traffic conditions, the east, west, and north walls of the Imperial City were pulled down and the archways at Tien An Men, Xisi, Dianmen, and Dongsi removed. In recent years, an expressway, the Second Ring Road, was built on the ruins of the old city walls to link the city with its suburbs. Nine overpasses—two triple-decked and seven double-decked—span the expressway. Besides automobile lanes, the expressway has special bicycle lanes for Beijing's some three million bicycles.

Underneath the Second Ring Road is China's first subway, built solely with Chinese materials and technology. Since its first stage was completed in 1969, trains carry some 160,000 passengers a day. The second stage of the project was completed in the early '80s; passengers now number well over 500,000 daily. The circular subway system and the major above-ground roads combine to form a more convenient communication network in the city.

The housing program is integrally related to the new subway system. The high-rise buildings under construction will, when completed, form another type of city wall. Replacing the substandard dwellings in the area, these edifices will have the same visual impact on the city that Tien En Men Square now has: both are dedicated to monumentality.

Located in the heart of Beijing, Tien An Men Square's vast open space of approximately 125 acres can easily accommodate the hundreds of thousands of people who gather here on festivals and holidays and for other celebrations.

HONG KONG

The population of the Crown Colony of Hong Kong, in 1985, was approximately 5.5 million people, 45 percent of whom lived in public or rental housing developed through the activities of the Housing Authority. These 2.4 million people are presently being accommodated in 113 rental and 24 home ownership estates located throughout the territory. Homes are also provided for an additional 130,000 people in temporary housing and 17,000 in cottage areas. Emergency housing is available for 3,400 in transit centers. Another million people will be rehoused by the end of the 1980s.

Present construction of public housing is being maintained at the level of 35,000 units a year, with about 20 percent being for sale. At the end of 1983 work was proceeding on 85 contracts, which will provide 180,000 rental flats, 25,300 home ownership flats, 22 schools, and 18 commercial

Tien An Men Square, Peking.

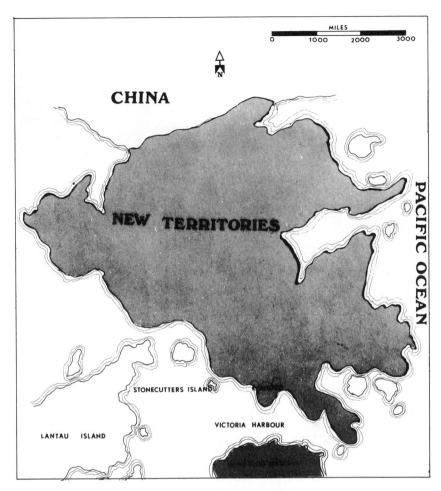

Map of Hong Kong, including Kowloon and the New Territories. *(Courtesy Eno Foundation for Transportation.)*

centers. The land usage is being maximized by building skyscraper blocks up to 36 stories in height, with every effort being made to achieve a pleasant overall environment.

Since the Housing Authority was established in 1973, a total of 38 new rental estates have been opened. A redevelopment program has been steadily carried out in the 12 original resettlement estates since 1972. By redevelopment and other schemes, 250,000 people have been moved out

of their substandard rooms to new estates with modern accommodations.[9]

Population densities are high in parts of the United States, mainly in some of the eastern seaboard cities. But compared with Kowloon (Hong Kong) the densities pale. One portion of Kowloon may be the most densely populated place on earth—4,000 people per acre, approximately 10.5 square feet of land per person.

Lung Hang Estates (left). *A rental housing estate built in the Sha Tin New Town area of the New Territories, which lie between Kowloon and the border of the People's Republic of China.* **Lek Yuen Estates** *(right). Another estate located in the Sha Tin New Town area. The "flags" are actually clothes lines on poles. This means of clothes drying is common throughout the Orient. (Courtesy of Hong Kong Housing Authority)*

Location of housing estates—Hong Kong. *At the end of June, 1984, more than 2.4 million people, or about 45 percent of the population, were living in public housing of various types, including 2,172,400 in 116 public housing estates.*

About half a million people still live in squatter's huts in the territory. These structures have been erected without permission but are tolerated following the 1982 stock-taking exercise. It is the government's aim to clear these structures and rehouse the residents.

---

9. *Hong Kong 1985*, published by the Hong Kong Information Service, Beaconsfield House, Queen's Road, Hong Kong.

Public housing in Hong Kong is managed by the Housing Authority, a statutory body whose executive area, the Housing Department, has a staff of about 6,000. Established in 1973, its purpose was to bring together various departments that had previously been responsible for different facets of the task. Aside from planning and construction, the authority is responsible for controlling squatters and for clearing land required for development. It advises the governor on all matters of housing policy. By the mid-1980s permanent self-contained homes with amenities have been provided for virtually every eligible family in Hong Kong.

Shek Kip Mei. *This housing estate, located in northern Kowloon, was erected after the great fire of 1953, which left more than 50,000 people homeless. It was one of the first public housing estates built to rehouse many of the refugees fleeing the People's Republic of China after the 1949 revolution. The project has served as a stepping stone from the slums and boat dwellings that sprawled over the hills and waterfronts of the Crown Colony as the population of Hong Kong increased from 600,000 in 1945 to over 2,000,000 in 1951. (Courtesy of Hong Kong Housing Authority)*

CHAPTER 11

ENVIRONMENTAL PRACTICES

THE ENVIRONMENT DEFINED

All too often when persons talk about the environment, their discussions are limited to the physical conditions in certain specific and limited areas. While some environmentalists seem seriously concerned about the protection of agriculture, open spaces, and specific animal and plant forms, little thought appears to be directed to the social and economic environments and less than that to the political environment, all of which have a serious impact on the quality of life. As a matter of fact, the social, economic, and political environment determine the quality and growth of the physical environment.

In the face of this the U.S. Supreme Court in 1983 held that "environment means physical conditions, not psychological."

ECOLOGY

Ecology refers to the mutual relations among organisms and between them and their environments and with social studies of the spatial distribution of population in reference to material and social causes and effects.

Studies of the ecological processes and interactions within urban areas and between human settlements and the surrounding natural systems that support them is known as the ecology of urban development. It is concerned with the analysis of the total urban system as well as its various elements.

NATURAL DESTRUCTIVE FORCES

Decisions as to where human habitation should occur have been made without concern for the natural forces that might adversely affect life and development. Some of the natural forces are predictable. We know that there will be actions endangering humans, the unknown being the time when the events will occur. In planning urban communities or parts of communities, the use of known critical areas must be avoided and urbanism should be developed where the risks are minimal. Some of the natural forces to be wary of are:

Flooding. Areas for urbanization should be located outside of flood plains. They should avoid the bottom of steep canyons where flash floods may destroy everything in their path. Areas with high groundwater should be avoided if sewage disposal is to be by septic tanks or cesspools.

Fire. In hilly terrain, great care must be taken to plan urban settlements where good water pressure is available, where access in more than one direction is in place, and where the road grades are not excessive for fire-fighting equipment. In addition, building roofs should be of fireproof or fire-retardant materials. Weeds and brush should be cleared from around the buildings.

Seismic Activity. Many areas of the world are subject to seismic forces as the earth's surface slips and slides. Some locations are in well-defined earthquake zones. Where these faults are defined development immediately adjacent to them should be avoided through the use of zoning ordinance prohibitions. In the vicinity of known faults buildings should be carefully designed and tied to their foundations. Special internal bracing and shear walls should become standard practice to minimize the major danger, that from falling materials and glass.

Landslides. There are many areas in hilly terrain where the earth is unstable and heavy rains or seepage can undermine any development located on the slopes. Not only are the developments located on the unstable soils in danger, but also those that are located below them in the valley areas. Careful study of the soil conditions and the history of past occurrences should guide builders to either avoid these areas or to take structural precautions to prevent slippages.

Extreme Temperatures. Many areas of the world are subject to temperature extremes that must lead to special designs and construction to cope with the forces of nature. Desert areas, where temperatures and availability of water may affect the ability of humans to survive, should be dealt with to avoid enticing the uninitiated to risk their lives in speculative ventures.

Wind. Several well-defined areas are subject to severe windstorms in the form of tornadoes, hurricanes, cyclones, and similar forces. There are no means of preventing these natural phenomena. Even the best of structures are subject to failures under the most trying of conditions. Storm cellars and masonry construction appear to be the best safeguards for human life in these exposed areas.

Volcanoes. The definition of an active volcano indicates the danger of locating anywhere near the slope or foot of the mountain. Developments sometimes many miles away have been obliterated by ash from sudden activity. Pompeii is a vivid example. Here the city was wiped out and rebuilt, subjecting residents to recurrent dangers. Mount St. Helens, an inactive volcano in the United States, blew its top and destroyed many miles of the surrounding countryside as well as filling the air with drifting ash for months. Community development on the island of Maui has been threatened, and homes have been destroyed. Zoning laws should prohibit development that would expose people to loss of life and property.

All of the above-mentioned forces are natural and are to be expected. Planning can only caution urban developers to do what they can to avoid critical areas and to develop urban structures with the most effective materials.

HAZARDS PLANNING: WHOSE RESPONSIBILITY?

It is difficult to predict the occurrence of natural events that result in danger to humans and their property. These events are often the result of a course of action initiated by the people themselves. The potential dangers are thus a consequence of actions taken in the face of known, unstable conditions with the hope and expectation that, if and when catastrophic events occur, those responsible will somehow escape the consequences. However, plans must be made to safeguard human lives in such instances and to care for them after tragedies occur. Wesley Marx, a writer on marine and environmental affairs, states:

> Traditionally, the jurisdiction that has the power to avoid hazardous development through land-use and building controls also happens to be the one with the strongest incentives to risk disaster: the city or county. The local government profits from allowing people to occupy hazardous areas: the property tax base expands. A community in an upper watershed has very little motivation to control land uses—such as mining—whose siltloads can intensify flood hazards in downstream communities.[1]

---

1. "Disaster Planning," *California Tomorrow,* Wesley Marx, Summer 1978.

George Mader, a planning consultant in Portola Valley, California, had this to say on the subject of planning for hazards:

> Land use planning is an important coordinating device for dealing with seismic hazard mitigation. Strides have been made in this field in recent years. We are doing a better job. We still, however, flounder considerably in selling our ideas to decision-makers. Better prediction will improve our own work and our ability to convey critical information to legislators as to the risks involved in taking or not taking mitigation actions.[2]

CONCERN FOR THE TOTAL ENVIRONMENT

The changes that we have allowed to occur to the earth's ecological system clearly demonstrate that the welfare of other people is not uppermost in our minds. We profess to love our children and grandchildren but we are little concerned with the world we are leaving them. Our negligence would not be so deplorable were the damage that we do to our environment less manifest.

Halting efforts are being made in all parts of the world to check the undisciplined exploitation of nature. Sometimes the freedom to abuse continues in the guise of the costs involved in making the changes needed to ameliorate the problems. This is particularly true in the areas of pollution and wasted energy. The long-term effects of our negligence have not been clearly determined.

IMPACT STUDIES

The environment has little to do with the political boundaries established by the individual communities or nations that we find all over the world. To develop a meaningful environmental impact assessment there is need for a broad range, including all of the elements that would be found in the study of at least a region or metropolitan area. Unfortunately the political entity needed to finance and develop the environmental basis for judgment is almost uniformly absent.

At present each community assesses its own area and the overlapping areas that fall into other jurisdictions. The cost of the individual studies can become monumental.

Regional studies should be prepared of all the elements of the environment—physical, social, and economic—and the findings be computerized in both mapped and statistical forms. Such a study was prepared in 1981 for the Coachella Valley in California, covering large portions of the unincorporated area and the seven cities contained in the subregion.

---

2. George Mader, AICP, *California Planner,* March 1980.

ENVIRONMENTAL ASSESSMENT PROCESS FLOW CHART

EIS Required   **No EIS Required**

The lead agency* evaluates proposal to determine if there is a possibility that it may have a significant effect on the environment. Refers to agencies with direct concern.

→ No possible significant effect.

If possible significant effect

Lead agency determines if a project is ministerial and/or exempt.

→ Exempt

Lead agency undertakes initial study to determine if project will have a significant effect.

→ Will not have a significant effect

If significant effect

Lead agency prepares or assigns contract for EIR and submits it to planning department.

Lead agency prepares negative declaration and submits to planning department.

Planning department prepares Environmental Impact Review and submits to the Planning Commission

Planning Commission makes final recommendation

City Council Environmental Assessment

Final decision

*In the majority of cases the planning department is likely to be the lead agency. In some cases, however, the lead agency might be a federal government agency.

Basic data was then available for any projects proposed in any part of the study area. Unfortunately, the political support and the funds needed to keep the data current were lacking, and the monumental project was abandoned.

CHAPTER 12

SEARCH FOR THE GOOD CITY: THE "NEW UTOPIANS"

The population of the world is exploding. The rising flood of urbanization is surging outward from the enter and engulfing the surrounding country-side. Congestion festers within and eats about the edges. Communications are breaking down. Medical science sustains health and prolongs the lifespan. Famine and pestilence are no longer the levelers of excess population in most of the world. Nuclear war may be. If mankind is to live on, the urban pattern he occupies will require major unraveling and reweaving. Much understanding will be required, and the nature of the metropolis will undergo severe examination.

Men in all walks of life have raised their voices against the inequities, the ugliness, and the congestion of the city. John Ruskin and William Morris pleaded for craftsmanship, Charles Dickens portrayed the evils of the workhouses, Edward Bellamy in *Looking Backward* warned and predicted, Patrick Geddes in his Outlook Tower urged a broader vision, Karl Marx threatened, Robert Owen experimented, Ebenezer Howard reasoned, Jacob Riis exposed.

An early utopian expression, mentioned previously in the discussion of the Columbian Exposition of 1891, was the swan song of Victorian grandeur—"The City Beautiful." Absorbed in the monumental splendor of avenue and plaza, Daniel Burnham reflected the fading era with his famous words:

Make no little plans; they have no magic to stir men's blood and probably will not be realized. Make big plans; aim high in hope and work, remembering that a noble, logical diagram once recorded will never die, but long after we are gone will be a living thing, asserting itself with ever-growing insistency. Remember that our sons and grandsons are going to do things that would stagger us. Let your watchword be order and your beacon beauty.[1]

This, however, was not typical. Many other social critics turned the light of their analysis upon the city, tested the forces of disintegration in the laboratories of their keen minds, and some dared to describe cities men could build when they acquired the will.

Nor were they all cries in the wilderness. Housing, the most appalling testimony to neglect in the urban scene, received attention. Planning agencies were formed, zoning and building laws were enacted. But these efforts remained a step behind the improvement of which society was actually capable; they never quite caught up with technological and scientific progress. The overgrown metropolis fed upon its inhabitants, gnawing at the physical, mental, and spiritual fabric of the people. No inhabitant could escape the heavy weight of urban living, regardless of fortune or social status.

The insidious course of urban disintegration had forced an examination of the basic nature of the urban structure, and it was to this task that the new utopians set themselves.

THE SEARCH FOR SPACE

The driving urge has been for release from the cruel congestion that so degrades the individual, a search for space in which man may recapture his identity. This quest lends unity to otherwise apparently divergent views of future urban structure.

The persistent expansion about the periphery of the great cities has removed the countryside farther and farther from the urban population. Abandoning the concentric form of the crowded city, in 1882 the Spaniard Soria y Mata propounded the theory of the linear city—la cuidad linear. He sought to expand the city along the spine of communication—the highway. Housing and industry stretched along the roadway would thus border a continuous artery that linked existing cities. Raymond Unwin, an English housing pioneer, espoused the cause of satellite communities about the periphery of the city, an idea clearly in the tradition of the garden city. Each community would contain 12,000 to 18,000 people and be small enough to require no vehicular transport within it.

---

1. Quoted in Charles Moore, *Daniel Burnham: Architect, Planner of Cities* (Boston, 1921).

The linear city uses the countryside to contain urbanization along the highway. The garden city and satellite town rely upon their relatively small size to maintain a balance between urban development and surrounding open space. Integrating these elements, in 1917 Tony Garnier presented his plans for la cité industrielle—the industrial city. His inspiring idea separated the civic center and residential sections from the factory district with a broad buffer zone, a greenbelt, and the highway and railroad traversed this broad space.

In the latter half of the twentieth century many opportunists have become articulate and persuasive. Congestion has inspired a variety of panaceas and some fantastic proposals have been suggested by otherwise practical men. Among the most popular was the concept of the double- and triple-decked street and the doubling up of families in order to provide shelter for economically displaced persons. High land cost was so firmly rooted in the urban state of mind that its effect was accepted as the normal course of "land economics." Nevertheless the traffic problem had to be solved, and piling layers of street upon each other and increasing density all had the appearance of plausibility. As the roofs of skyscrapers moved upward so did proposals for multiple-level streets.

The idea of double-decked streets stemmed from the New York World's Fair of 1939 where the dramatic proposals by Norman Bel Geddes illustrated the separation of the automobile way and the pedestrian way. These ideas have been adopted in limited form in many cities, with the raised pedestrian "flyway." Urban freeways have been double decked where rights of way were limited, as along the East River in New York and the Alaska Skyway in Seattle.

The doubling up of families, either in individual homes or in backyard garages, has returned to the American scene as the economic plight of elderly people has caused hardships for many. The reduction of lot sizes and the increases in urban densities during the past few years is a fact of life in many cities, even those that have had a history of low-density development.

Beneath, on the surface of the earth, darkness pervaded man's environment. A growing apprehension of the light gripped the people. Man was building so broad and so high that the more there was light the deeper were the shadows.

The metropolis lay heavily upon its inhabitants. The problem of the underprivileged increased, social welfare expanded, and more and more of the tax income was directed to charity, until the advent of "Reaganomics."

The great industrialist Henry Ford said what was in the minds of many people: "Nothing will finally work more effectively to undo the fateful grip which the city has taken upon the people than the destruction of the fictitious land values which the city traditions have set up and maintained."[2] It is rather vexing that he did not suggest how those "fictitious land values" might be "destroyed," but he did point out a major obstacle to the improvement of the urban environment.

All who have protested the congestion and ugliness of the city reveal the anachronism of our industrial age—the inability of society to muster the forces of technological progress in the cause of the improvement and organization of the urban environment. Theories conflict and opinions vary. It is inevitable, and it reflects the enigma of the age. The tremendous advance of science and invention thrusts forward the horns of a dilemma and civilization is perched upon them.

Congestion in the city is not new. It has occurred in all civilizations from the beginning of urbanized existence. The gregarious instincts of man are satisfied by the agglomeration of people. Crowds have a natural attraction. The problem of density does not turn about this issue; it hinges upon the necessity to maintain a balance between enclosed and open space to accommodate the functions of both.

The drama of the city by day and by night will be enhanced when this balance is achieved. There will be room for people to circulate with convenience and pleasure. The ground level will not be reserved solely as conduits for moving vehicles or storage places for them. The spectacle of the city will be a visual experience from all about—from below as well as from above—when interior and exterior space are in balance.

Le Corbusier

In 1922 in Paris, the architect Le Corbusier displayed his vision of *La Ville Contemporaine.* His utopian scheme was a city of magnificent skyscraper towers surrounded by a broad and sweeping open space. The city was a huge park. Sixty-story office buildings accommodating 1,200 people per acre and covering only 5 percent of the ground area were grouped in the heart of the city. The transportation center, railway and airfield, was the hub. Surrounding the skyscrapers was the apartment district, eight-story buildings arranged in zigzag rows with broad open spaces about them, the density of the population 120 persons per acre. Lying about the outskirts were the *cité jardins,* the garden cities of single houses. The city was designed for a population of 3,000,000.

The beautifully delineated plans and succinct reasoning with which they were described created a sensation, and in 1925 Le Corbusier adapted his *Ville Contemporaine* to the Plan Voisin for the center of Paris. The contrast with the old city was dramatic, and the architect

---

2. From "Mr. Ford's Page," *The Dearborn Independent,* Dearborn, Michigan, 1922.

A Railroad Station   **B** City Hall   **C** Concert Hall   **D** Palace

La Ville Radieuse by Le Corbusier. *The plan submitted in the international competition of 1933 for the replanning of Nedre Normalm in Stockholm was an adaptation of Le Corbusier's scheme for continuous staggered rows of high buildings (shown in black) set on piers with broad open space. The plan also makes a distinction between the various types of roadways: the encircling freeway raised above the ground level, the secondary trafficways uninterrupted by the building forms, and the informal system of local traffic and pedestrian ways that likewise circle beneath the buildings, which are open at the ground level. The existing or new proposed low buildings (cross-hatched) are provided settings within landscaped open space.*

hammered at his theme, pointing a finger of scorn at the undesirable population density in Paris—an average of 146 persons per acre, and 213 persons in the overcrowded sections.

Le Corbusier followed this conception with his Ville Radieuse, the Radiant City, one of continuous rows of tall buildings woven in zigzag form across landscaped space. A prolific writer and indefatigable reformist, he prepared his visionary schemes for Algiers, Nemours, Antwerp, and Stockholm. The conception and construction of Brasília were based on his theories. He was enamored of the skyscrapers of America and the energy of the industrial processes. His shock value was tremendous, and those who waved aside his proposals as another wild dream were themselves quite blind to the wilderness that had overtaken the city in which they themselves were trapped.

THE SEARCH FOR FORM

A brutal quality of the great city is the absence of human scale. The sense of community is obscured by the common grayness of the industrial metropolis. Despite the durability of great cities, they are caving in beneath the mammoth weight piled up at the center. As they spiral upward and outward, the people are forsaking the centers for the suburbs. Satellite bedroom communities all over the Western world cling to the economic lifeline of the existing city, and regions of greatest urban settlement have actually become continuous linear cities. But expanding suburbanization is exhausting the space it was intended to preserve and overextending the cities' public facilities and lines of communication.

Movement to the suburbs is essentially motivated by the search for a more desirable environment. The basic yearning for harmony between the individual and community scale is no less reflected in the suburban sprawl about great cities than in the garden city, the greenbelt, the towers of Le Corbusier, or the British New Towns. The contrast between worn-out, secondhand residential districts and neighborhoods in new subdivisions; between shopping centers and stores without parking on traffic-ridden streets; or the advantages of an industrial park over the disorderly factory district: all suggest the same aspirations that appear in the models of the new utopians. The search is for an organic structure for the city of the industrial and scientific age in which we are destined to live. As we move toward an integration of urban components, the form of a regional city begins to emerge.

The International Congress of Modern Architects (CIAM) posited four basic elements of urban biology: (1) sun, (2) space, (3) vegetation, (4) steel and concrete. Le Corbusier, who assumed a leading role in CIAM, organized the Assembly of Constructors for an Architectural Renovation (ASCORAL), and extended the investigation into the character of the city.

ASCORAL set forth the "Three Human Establishments": the farming unit, the radioconcentric city, and the linear industrial city. The farming unit is the space for agriculture and the villages that serve it; the radioconcentric city is exemplified by the existing urban area from which the theory of concentration evolved. The third human establishment—the linear industrial city—is derived from earlier utopians, but it is a new element in Le Corbusier's theories. Leaving the "evils of the sprawling town," the ASCORAL studies move into the country. New industrial communities are placed at intervals along the main arteries of transportation—water, rail, and highway—that connect the existing cities; the latter remain as administrative, commercial, and cultural centers. Factories—called "green" factories because of their proximity to landscaped areas—are placed along the main transportation routes, separated from the residential section by the auto highway and green strips. The residential area includes the horizontal garden town of single houses and a vertical apartment building with its complement of communal facilities. Sports, entertainment, shopping, and office facilities are distributed in this district, and all the facilities of the community are placed within ample open space enhanced with natural verdure.[3]

Thus the image of a regional city unfolds and, with it, the conventions that dominate today's concepts of urban zoning practices are exposed as the stultifying elements they are.

Zoning

Implicit in the planning postulates of the new utopians is the assumption that land zoned for specific uses will be reserved for those uses. This is presumably the reason for planning, and it is apparent that the effective reorganization of the urban structure depends upon acceptance of this assumption. Our present practice of zoning, however, runs quite counter to this; any use is permitted in an industrial zone, while only industry is excluded from a commercial zone, and all types of residential uses are permitted therein. As a consequence the only zone actually reserved for its planned use is the single-family district (a premise disputed in the 1980s). This indiscriminate mixture of land uses is inconsistent with planning, and means by which it may be corrected are essential to the effective relationship between land uses in the future. The distinction between present trends and the theories of the new utopians would appear less sharp if the chaotic mingling of incompatible uses was replaced by the principle that urban land uses shall conform to the classifications for which they are planned and zoned. This is a rather disarming thesis, since it would reveal excessive overzoning and materially alter prevailing attitudes toward zoned uses for which there is inadequate economic support.

THE DENSITY EQUATION

As the future decentralized city form emerges, some land will necessarily be withdrawn from intense use, while the intensity of use for other land will increase. The changes should result from planning decisions rather than fortuitous speculation. Under the system of zoning for public control of land use, the potential capacity of land is thereby a function of community determination. Land value thus created by the community should

---

3. *Les Trois Etablissements Humains*, ASCORAL (Denoel, Paris, 1945).

LA CITÉ INDUSTRIELLE
by Le Corbusier

A   Existing Central City
B   Auto Highway
C   Vertical Residences
D   Community Facilities
E   Horizontal Residences

F   Factories
G   Railroad
H   Service Highway
J   River
K   Industrial Communities

La Cité Industrielle by Le Corbusier. *In 1945, under the leadership of Le Corbusier, ASCORAL shifted attention from the existing urban center to a consideration of the basic organization of urban settlement in this industrial age. The group presented a fusion between the concentric form of the garden city and the ribbon form of the linear city. The principal forms of circulation—water, rail, air, and highway—became the arteries along which self-contained industrial cities were distributed. Although it is assumed that open space surrounding these industrial clusters would be maintained, the greenbelt is here used as a buffer between the various and separate land uses: housing, highway, and factories.*

The basic organization is shown in the left-hand sketch, the passenger highway connecting the great existing cities; between it and the river, rail line, and service highway are the groups of "green factories," located in landscaped areas. Opposite are the housing areas, which contain the administrative, shopping, sports, and educational facilities for the immediate population. The existing metropolis remains the principal administrative, commercial, and cultural center.

The sketch at the center indicates the distribution of these industrial "cities" between the great cities, and the one on the right indicates the separation of traffic forms: the distinction between through traffic and local traffic, and the separation between them. Le Corbusier retains the tall building—the vertical residence—for apartments near the civic center and places the community of single-family homes away from this center in order to permit greater freedom for families.

be retained by the community; by the same token, losses in value imposed by the community should be compensated by the community.[4]

Taxation based on the densities and intensities of the uses permitted by zoning, the sliding scale ascending from low to high, might provide

---

4. See the discussion of compensation and betterment in chapter 35.

for more careful zoning and the better utilization of critical land in both urban and rural areas. It certainly would have an impact on the premature zoning of land with only a long-range speculative prospect and no development plans or infrastructure to serve existing proposals.

The extreme population density to which we have become accustomed is due for critical review. The density equation is compounded by the introduction of factors that serve the mental and spiritual needs of people, the environmental features that enrich the process of living. Such an environment, to be sure, should be the overriding aim of planning in an advanced civilization, but the practical issues compel attention to the density equation.

The balance between floor space occupied by people and the ground space for circulation is among these practical factors. Many cities in the industrial nations must accommodate the transportation vehicles on the streets and provide space for their storage. It might be possible to so regiment people's lives that the freedom of movement afforded by modern motor vehicles could be rigidly curtailed, but the means for such control would hardly be consistent with the doctrine of liberty upon which the West's institutions are founded. The density equation must therefore embrace three practical elements: population in buildings, space for the movement of vehicles on streets, and parking space for the vehicles. A workable urban pattern requires a balance among these elements.

Man has demonstrated a consummate ability to build tremendous structures. The construction of a skyscraper is a remarkable feat, but the high-rise has struck a popular chord by default rather than by design. It is presumed to compensate for high land cost and thus maintain a semblance of economic balance. In reality it induces ever-mounting land prices. Every urban dweller is familiar with the consequences—intolerable congestion.

The attraction of the skyscraper is undeniable. The drama has been eloquently expressed by Le Corbusier. With boundless enthusiasm for the ingenuity, the daring, and the skill of those who made the tall building possible, his desire for the machine, conditioned air, pushbuttons, and swift elevators is like a romance with science. Dreaming of his future city from within the medieval context of the European city, he sees the

> tonic spectacle, stimulating, cheering, radiant, which from each office appears through the transparent glass walls leading into space. Space! That response to the aspiration of the human being, that relaxation for breathing and for the beating heart, that outpouring of self in looking far, from a height, over a vast, infinite, unlimited expanse. Every bit of sun and fresh, pure air furnished mechanically. Do you try to maintain the fraud of hypocritical affirmations, to throw discredit on these radiant facts, to argue, to demand the "good old window," open on the stenches of the city and

A   Industry
B   Main Highway
C   Local Highway
D   Commercial Area
E   Residential Area
F   Schools in Park Area

Urban reorganization. *Searching for an urban form appropriate to the metropolis of the industrial age, the new utopians have produced some principles that may guide a reorganization of the city of tomorrow. These principles merge the common characteristics of the linear and concentric city forms; they accept the physical properties of the neighborhood unit in favor of the basic needs of the family and regain the prospect for identity of the individual parts of the great city now lost within the dreary grayness of the present metropolis. Because the city form must change if it is to survive, and because it must survive as an integral element of the industrial age, the proposals of the new utopians are essential ingredients of urban thought and action.*

Relationship of residential areas to light industrial and commercial areas, as proposed by Ludwig Hilberseimer.

street, the noise, air currents, and the company of flies and mosquitoes? For thirty years I have known the offices of Paris: conversations cut to pieces by the uproar, suffocating atmosphere, the view broken thirty feet away by the wall of houses, dark corners, half-light, etc. . . . Imposters should no longer deny the gains of our period and by their fright prevent changing from one thing to another, keeping the city or cities in general from going their joyously destined way.[5]

5. Le Corbusier, *When The Cathedrals Were White* (New York, Reynal and Hitchcock, 1947).

The towers of Manhattan and the gridiron plan are straight and clear to the European eye, the hygiene of plumbing so inviting, the illuminated brilliance by night so thrilling. It is a fascination not reserved to Europeans alone; Americans find it appealing too. Le Corbusier argues concentration versus congestion. He demonstrates that his city will concentrate the people, conserve the daily hours they consume in horizontal travel, and direct this time into productive effort and leisure. He contends the American skyscraper is too small and proposes a residential population of 6,000,000 on Manhattan, with a density of 400 persons per acre and 88 percent of the ground left free and open. In his City of Tomorrow, the density is 1,200 per acre in 60-story office towers with 95 percent of the land in open space, a "green" city. The concept is magnificent, but it reflects the deception of high buildings, high density, and the actual use of this "open" space.

Structures permitting such densities are not unusual. Several times the density proposed by Le Corbusier are found in the huge apartment buildings of America. The density in his proposed office towers is less than half that of Radio City, and the Empire State Building can accommodate nearly 10,000 people per acre. Concentration is an accomplished fact in the cities of America. The World Trade Center in lower Manhattan exceeds these intensities of use, here presumably compensated by the open space of the adjacent Hudson River. The drama of the high-rise building is heightened by the space about it and the prospect it offers for trees and landscaped gardens. Such space, in which the tensions of the day may be dispelled, has strong appeal in contrast to the cluttered surroundings of the congested city.

But here enters the delusion of high density and open space. When the automobile is reckoned with, a site housing 400 persons per acre becomes not a lovely garden, but a parking lot. And the open space for an office building with a density of 1,200 per acre would be a roof garden atop a three- or four-story garage. The balance of the "open" space is in the streets that carry the cars into and out of these storage places. The "green" space, to which we aspire and which offers much promise, actually becomes a pavement for the vehicles of transportation. Complicating the situation further is the fact that preservation of the air space above the ground could be assured only by restricting all buildings to high-rise; low buildings with high density would continue to cover the ground as it is now covered.

The desirability of low density for a residential environment is obvious; it has been demonstrated in all places and for all people on the face of the earth. Low density does not forestall blight, but with the exception of apartment developments with commodious space and enriched facilities, high density has induced blight. A protest against the density of population that our gigantic buildings can accommodate does not deprecate the ingenuity of the builders, but some questions require deliberation and answer if concentration is to be seen as an organic necessity of the future metropolis, among them: Is every man destined to live in an apartment cubicle in a high-rise building?

The city performs a far greater variety of services today than ever before. Its economic theory and practice are more complex. Yet the same forces that have made this so are those that now render congestion unnecessary. Science, commerce, and industry have intensified the functions of the city. They have also created the instruments to neutralize its effect. The heavy concentration of people is no longer necessary for the conduct of business or for convenient and comfortable living. Methods of transportation, power, and communications invalidate the crowded concentration we unwittingly accept as a necessary evil of urban existence. Crowding of people and buildings is a negation of every contemporary means of communication and transportation at our command. Congestion denies them the chance to serve to their full capacity.

There is stimulation in great distances seen from the skyscraper. Conditioned air has its advantages. The elevator rising a thousand feet a minute offers rapid vertical transit. But do these render the human desire for a house on its land a phenomenon or a whim? Horizontal space means much to the human being. Contact with the earth is not a choice reserved to the agrarian, the tiller of the soil, alone. There is a sense of freedom, human freedom, in traversing the space of the earth under one's own power—on foot. There is a healthy sensation when interior and exterior space merge into unity, with no more visual separation than a crystal sheet of glass. There is mental freedom and a quiet repose in horizontal space.

Because the "economy" of ownership is often a fiction or because the people are frequently tenants does not alter the essential desire for horizontal living space. This is not a question of politics, economics, or social reform. It is a matter of human aims, aspirations, desires, and the mental repose in physical reality. It is not a theory of aesthetics, nor is it romantic nonsense that people desire a home and garden. It is not enough to substitute air-conditioned cells in multistory buildings simply because we have the technical know-how to create them.

It is the fundamental desires that beat in the human breast that must shape the city. The skyscraper holds its head aloft with an air of plausibility; it can absorb high land cost and save utilities and transportation time. But it also can create congestion and high land values that nullify its advantages and remove all choice for another form of habitation from the hope of the urban dweller. If we are concerned with economy, it is not the skyscraper that produces it; the skyscraper is not built because it is economical—it is not so. It is built because the cost of land is extravagant, and continuing this process without restraint only adds fuel to the flames of urban congestion, blight, and disintegration.

ON COMMON GROUND

It is significant that whatever the direction taken in the search for a new urban form and however persistent the trend of decentralization, the idea of the City is not forsaken. The complex and diverse functions are reshaped, regrouped, reorganized, but the constituent elements of the city are not abandoned. The commerce, the industry, the cultural institutions upon which our society depends for its spiritual and material enrichment are retained. That the inherent advantages of the city have been abused, misused, exploited, or simply allowed to lie dormant, does not deny their necessity.

There is a wavering line of continuity springing from the dismal factory town of the nineteenth century through the garden city and the New Towns, the urban "biology" of ASCORAL, and the reorganization of industrial community clusters in the future regional city. The line moves at a tangent to the city we know today, but there is a strong affinity with the decentralization and sprawling suburbs that are drawing the life-blood from the overgrown, overzoned, and congested metropolis. A comparable liberation of space appears in the greenbelt of the New Towns and the London plan by Abercrombie, Frank Lloyd Wright's Broadacre City, and Le Corbusier's towers in green space. It is likewise present in the standards for flexible zoning in modern subdivision practice.

A human scale is recovered in the ideas of the new utopians for a planned integration of land uses. The assumption that the metropolis should absorb an unlimited population is challenged by them, and density standards are related to the organic functions of the city. The natural forces operating the great city are forcing the re-evaluation of form and structure, a development the new utopias anticipated. Advances in transportation and communication can release us from the previously inexorable destiny of large cities. We can have tall and low buildings, open space, and convenient communication, as well as the amenities consistent with good living. All of this will take place when the density equation and the relation between planning and zoning for land use are taken into account.

In the Orient, due to the age of the cities, the design of the buildings, and the life-styles of the people, we find housing densities that have few parallels to those in the United States and Canada. Hong Kong since the 1960s has increased the number of square feet per person from 35 to 50. In China, the current average living space per person is 22 square feet.

A   County Seat Ad-
    ministration

B   Airport

C   Sports

D   Professional Offices

E   Stadium

F   Hotel

G   Sanitarium

H   Small Industry

J   Small Farms

K   Park

L   Motor Inn

M   Industry

N   Merchandising

P   Railroad

R   Orchards

S   Homes and Apart-
    ments

T   Temple and Ceme-
    tery

U   Research

V   Zoo

W   Schools

Area of Plan is Two Square Miles

Broadacres by Frank Lloyd Wright. *Essentially a linear city form, Frank Lloyd Wright's proposal distributes industry, commerce, housing, social facilities, and agriculture along the railroad artery and has access to highways. The unit dominating this plan is the minimum one acre of land for each family rather than the neighborhood unit, although the various neighborhood facilities are provided.*

This density is equivalent to 18 persons in the typical American two-car garage. The plan is to increase the space per person to 54 square feet by 1985, thus allowing only about 7 persons per "garage." This "living space" would not include kitchen or toilet facilities.

Smaller Is Better?

With the cost of land and housing in many of the Western nations soaring out of sight because of the inflation and speculation of the late 1970s and 1980s, the search for an answer to the demand for shelter has initiated the drive to reduce the size of lots and the living space in homes. In the name of providing affordable housing for the people, the theme "smaller is better" is the slogan for the future. Perhaps there will soon be a renewal of the concept that there is something to be gained from overcrowding. No one knows what the consequences of this reversal in direction will be.

CHAPTER 13

REBUILDING OUR CITIES

THE PENALTY FOR NEGLECT

Physical decay has eaten deeply into the urban community. Unchecked obsolescence stretches its withering fingers over the environment and brings degeneration to the city. Irresponsible civic management invites it, and negligent urban housekeeping permits it to spread. It menaces health, breeds crime and delinquency, and brings traffic death and injury. It undermines civic pride, threatens municipal bankruptcy, and gnaws at the human mind and nerves.

Blight casts its sinister shadow across the face of the city. It decays the core of the business and industrial districts, and it disintegrates the outskirts. It is not confined to the slums, but it is most apparent there; it is there that we have failed to maintain the much-vaunted "American standard of living." Harold Buttenheim once said: "We not only need to defend our standard of living, we need to achieve it." [1]

The housing problem remains unsolved, but certain policies have taken shape during the past few decades. The necessity for government to render assistance in some form has been recognized. It has become apparent that private enterprise, unaided, is not able to provide an ade-

---

1. "The American City," *Architectural Forum*, January 1945.

quate supply of satisfactory housing to meet the wide variations in the income levels of all the people. This was made evident by the success of the mortgage insurance program of the Federal Housing Administration. Initiated as a "pump-priming" measure during the Depression of the thirties, it continued to be popular through periods of high economic prosperity. Acceptance of public assistance through public housing for low-wage earners persists as an issue, but the history of housing in Europe and the situation in the United States indicate that the issue revolves around the extent to which public housing shall become an integral part of our economic and social machinery, not whether such a program should be instituted.

Practically every city is vested with the police power to require maintenance of adequate housing standards. Not only has the enforcement of these powers been ineffective but also the nature of the problem has moved beyond the scope of this device. Lack of planning, poor subdivision practices, excessive land values, ineffectual zoning, archaic streets, and inadequate transportation have created a condition of congestion, unplanned and incompatible mixed land uses, and economic distortions that render whole sections of the city in a process of built-in physical decay and social disintegration. The problem has transcended piecemeal treatment for improvement and has reached a stage where large-scale rehabilitation is the only feasible procedure. Such procedure implies the understanding of social and economic problems of the poor as well as the coordination and participation of all forces at the command of the urban population.

Sound business thrives on production and distribution; they create investment opportunities. Speculation travels in its wake, clinging like a leech and eating away its solvency. The effect is evident in the urban pattern. Industrial and commercial growth was expected to continue horizontally and outward from the center. But as speculation set in, land prices boomed, and industrial enterprise eluded the trap by hurdling to the outskirts. Commercial enterprise expanded vertically via the skyscraper or skipped to the expanding market in the suburbs.

What havoc has been wrought by this economic warfare! In its wake lies a mass of industrial, commercial, and residential derelicts, hemmed in by a network of obsolete streets and alleys. It has left land values so inflated they defy self-improvement through normal channels of enterprise. It has heaped a relentless burden of taxation upon the people, and it encourages the persistent exodus of the population to the periphery of cities and beyond.

City government is in partnership with this process. As the city deteriorates the cost of upkeep increases. Lip service is given to local responsibility, but it has been customary for city and state governments to avoid the issue of subsidy by transferring that responsibility to the federal government. The cost of maintaining obsolete cities has exacted heavy demands upon the taxpayer.

The Tax Burden

In the last few decades, many studies have indicated that slum areas do not generate nearly enough tax revenues to support the many services essential to the maintenance of decent communities. In recent times, with the federal government exacting a greater share of the tax dollar for its programs, and with less and less being funneled back into the local communities, the plight of all segments of urban areas has become increasingly difficult. Services are reduced, local taxes are increased, and cities are forced to allow their physical and social structures to decline, especially in those areas that are already blighted.

In the age of "Reaganomics," however, local government can no longer look to the federal government for meaningful financial assistance. As a reaction to the tax burden on property owners, legislation such as Proposition 13 in California and Proposition 2½ in Massachusetts have limited the taxing powers of all levels of local government to the point where many cities are faced with demands for services and are without the funds to provide them.

Tax-limit laws like these extend and increase the problems. They freeze the taxes on older structures at past assessed values and thus reduce available income required to update and rehabilitate obsolescent areas. To circumvent the drastic reductions of city income, special charges are now assessed for such essentials as sewage collection and processing, rubbish collection, and many other services heretofore covered by property taxes. Additional city revenue is obtained by increased development and processing fees that in the past had been nominal.

One essential item not covered in all the discussion of the need for tax limits is the repayment of debts and interest owed for bonds and for the installations of facilities and utilities prior to the enactment of the legislation. This can be a considerable burden upon the capacity of the city to finance, and it could also undermine the capacity to make future improvements that might be subject to bonded indebtedness.

Although concern over the deterioration of cities was confined for a time to social reformers and a few utopians, leadership in all phases of urban enterprise was awakened to the hazards to the people and institutions whose roots are in the city, to its life and its economy. Some persons were stimulated to action by an aversion to public housing serving a single role—as an instrument for rebuilding. They were genuinely disturbed by the downward trend in the physical environment and became convinced that broad steps were necessary to stem the tide. Emotions and reason were mixed among those who, comprehending the social and economic evils rooted in our cities, recoiled at the prospect of saving the financial souls of those allegedly responsible for and profiting from the slums, and those who, confessing the evils, were reluctant to admit the inability of conventional enterprise to cope with them. As these forces moved toward the center, the issues gradually came into clearer focus. In the absence of the concerted willingness or ability on the part of those who own urban property to check disintegration, it fell to the lot of the public through the instrument of government. "The legitimate object of government," said Abraham Lincoln, "is to do for a community of people whatever they need to have done but cannot do at all or cannot do so well for themselves in their separate and individual capacities."

The central problem of urban rebuilding is the cost of land and financing. Measured by any standard of appropriate use the land will cost too much; it will be out of all proportion to the economic value for acceptable redevelopment, and any other terms will make the venture worthless. If we are to restore decency to the urban scene, the excess cost of land must be liquidated—written off the books as a loss. No magic will make it vanish. The cost of rebuilding our cities is the price that must be paid to restore a decent standard of city building. It is the penalty for permitting such congestion that rebuilding is not an economic possibility. Responsibility for this error rests with every community in which it has occurred.

If the processes of rebuilding cities to the standards considered appropriate to the times in which we live are to begin, it will be essential for the people of the communities to understand their vested interest in the structure of their urban environment and what it can mean to themselves and the future of their families. Based upon knowledge and understanding, this interest must be translated to participatory democracy through activities that will be reflected in political action by elected officials.

PUBLIC HOUSING: HISTORY AND REDEVELOPMENT

Recognizing the need for action on the public front, and in anticipation of federal financial assistance, various states enacted legislation during the 1940s to implement urban redevelopment. The Wagner-Ellender-Taft Bill (S1592) was introduced to the Congress of the United States in 1946. Known as the General Housing Bill, it provided a broad legislative base for a national housing and redevelopment program. It failed to pass the Seventy-ninth Congress, and a similar bill, identified as the Taft-Ellender-Wagner Bill (S866), was introduced in the Eightieth Congress. It extended and broadened the private housing program of the Federal Housing Administration, continued the public housing program, and implemented urban redevelopment through loans to local agencies for land acquisition and subsidies to assist in writing off the excess land costs. It provided a basis for a national policy of urban redevelopment but did not receive favorable action during that session of the Congress. During the Eighty-first Congress, however, this position was reversed and the Housing Act of 1949 became law. Since then the act has frequently been amended.

Current Federal Policy

The secretary for Housing and Urban Development (HUD) stated in 1981 that it was national policy for "all Americans to have the opportunity to live in a decent home in a suitable living environment."

To that end the federal government has spent hundreds of billions of dollars during the past thirty years. Yet the American dream has only been approached, not met. The current federal programs deal with an effort to enlist the private sector as partners, with assistance and subsidies going to the builders and owners of housing as a means of making housing affordable to a larger cross-section of the American people. As the current housing stock gets older, it appears that it will require action in line with the scope of the problems. The tasks are monumental.

Obsolescence and Urban Renewal

The accelerated rate of physical deterioration in our cities was among the deficiencies in our national well-being revealed by the decade-long Depression of the thirties. It was then estimated that urban housing was becoming obsolete five times as fast as it was being replaced. Despite the high level of economic prosperity and production after World War II, the President's Advisory Committee on Government Housing Policies and Programs reported in 1953 that slums were still growing at a more rapid rate than they were being cleared and strongly urged that the attack be extended along a wider front. The committee recommended that "the program of federal loans and grants established by Title One of the Housing Act of 1949 should be broadened. It should provide assistance to communities for rehabilitation and conservation of areas worth saving as well as for the clearance and redevelopment of worn-out areas." As a consequence, the Housing Act of 1954 extended the role of the federal government to include rehabilitation and conservation, and the program was expanded from redevelopment to urban renewal.

Fanning out from the center of the city, extensive sections have been caught in the crossfire of traffic, transition, and neglect. Their energy has been sapped and their quality drained away. They are the twilight zones

Urban renewal planning in the 1950s. *Large-scale projects were the norm in the early days of the urban renewal programs. Vast areas considered blighted— usually the neighborhoods inhabited by poor minority groups—were to be swept clean, and a new "fabric" of development placed on the land. The costs in money and inconvenience to the residents were pushed into the background in an effort to renew the structure of the city. The scope of these concepts was so extensive that in most areas local and federal governmental agencies viewed the plans as artists' conceptions without the substance to achieve reality.*

COMMUNITY REDEVELOPMENT PROPOSED PLAN
WATTS AREA

DEPARTMENT OF CITY PLANNING · CITY OF LOS ANGELES

LEGEND

GARDEN APARTMENT - 2 STORY - 12 DWELLING UNITS
DUPLEX RESIDENCE - 2 STORY
ROW TYPE DWELLING - 2 STORY - 5 DWELLING UNITS
APARTMENT - 3 STORY - 64 DWELLING UNITS
GROSS AREA OF PROJECT - 992 ACRES

SCALE 1" = 800'

LEGEND

8-STORY APARTMENT   156 DWELLING UNITS

GARDEN APARTMENT   12 DWELLING UNITS

ROW TYPE APARTMENT   5 DWELLING UNITS

SINGLE FAMILY RESIDENTIAL AREAS

SCHOOL

COMMERCIAL

JEFFERSON AREA

COMMUNITY REDEVELOPMENT

DEPARTMENT OF CITY PLANNING

LOS ANGELES   CALIFORNIA

CHARLES B. BENNETT   DIRECTOR

in the urban pattern. Block after block of old houses and apartments, laced with traffic-filled streets, have been reduced to a dull order of decaying mediocrity or worse. They have not entirely deteriorated into slums but have lost their vitality as residential neighborhoods. Into this urbanized vacuum a haphazard and indiscriminate mixture of commercial uses has been drawn. Overall obsolescence has overtaken these areas but the physical resources—buildings, streets, utilities—might be saved if aggressive planning measures were applied to them.

A prototype for the conservation of such areas was initiated by the Health Department of Baltimore, Maryland, in 1939. A 1942 ordinance empowered the department to enforce the health requirements for housing. Enforcement was applied to whole blocks rather than individual buildings. In 1947, a special court was established to regularly adjudicate alleged violations. With the vigorous support of a Citizens Advisory Committee in 1951, the program enjoyed considerable success in the abatement of nuisances and brought about some remodeling of substandard housing.

Aggressive enforcement of the building codes to maintain housing standards must be pursued, but the limitations of such piecemeal renewal should be recognized. The physical improvement of old buildings is but one aspect of effective renewal, and it may result in the postponement of the planning corrections necessary to improve traffic conditions and alleviate the undesirable mixture of incompatible uses that also contributes to community blight.

Blight

Blight is the critical stage of urban obsolescence. Defining an area as blighted serves as the basis for redevelopment. Its elimination and prevention are justifications for using eminent domain to acquire and assemble sites for private development, for the expenditure of public funds including tax increment moneys, and for the imposition of controls in the project area.

The definitions that follow are based on California's health and safety code, but they can be usefully applied to any city.[2]

Structural blight refers to buildings and structures used for living, commercial, industrial, or other purposes, that are unfit or unsafe to occupy and may cause ill health, transmission of disease, infant mortality, juvenile delinquency, and crime, because of any one or a combination of the following factors:

---

2. "Introduction to Redevelopment," compiled by the Community Redevelopment Agencies Association. The definitions are based on California Health and Safety Code Sections 33030–2, 33320–1, and 33367.

Urban and rural slums: residential blight in barrios in South America. *All too many people are compelled by economic conditions to live in areas such as these in all parts of the world.*

Defective design and character of physical construction;

Faulty interior arrangement and exterior spacing;

High density of population and overcrowding;

Inadequate provision for ventilation, light, sanitation, open spaces, and recreational facilities; and/or

Age, obsolescence, deterioration, dilapidation, mixed character, or shifting of uses.

Economic blight refers to properties that suffer economic dislocation, deterioration, or disuse because of one or more of the following factors:

An economic dislocation, deterioration, or disuse resulting from faulty planning;

The subdividing and sale of lots of irregular form and shape and inadequate size for proper usefulness and development;

The laying out of lots in disregard of the contours and other topographic or physical characteristics of the ground and surrounding conditions;

The existence of inadequate public improvements, public facilities, open spaces, and utilities that cannot be remedied by private or governmental action without redevelopment;

A prevalence of depreciated values, impaired investments, and social and economic maladjustment; and/or

The existence of lots or other areas that are subject to being submerged by water; provided that any ecologically valuable existing features in such areas shall, to the maximum extent feasible, be preserved.

Such conditions must cause a reduction of, or lack of, proper utilization of the area to such an extent that it constitutes a serious physical, social, or economic burden on the community, one that cannot reasonably be expected to be reversed or alleviated by private enterprise acting alone.

The conditions of blight should predominate and injuriously affect the entire project area. Nonblighted properties may be included if their inclusion is necessary for effective redevelopment; they shall not be included for purposes of tax increments without other substantial justification for their inclusion.

Noncontiguous areas should either be blighted or, if not blighted, necessary for effective redevelopment. An unblighted, noncontiguous area is not deemed necessary for effective redevelopment if included only for purposes of tax increments.

The legislative body must make findings of blight and must justify inclusion of nonblighted properties in the ordinance adopting a redevelopment plan. The findings must be supported by substantial evidence in the record. A preponderance of the evidence is not necessary. Evidence need only be substantial enough for the legislative body to make a good-faith finding. If there is no legal challenge to the finding within sixty days after adoption of the ordinance, the existence of blight in the project area is conclusively presumed.

The wasteful neglect of the resources within the broad belt of blight about our city centers has been underscored by the shift in emphasis from redevelopment to renewal. The 1960 Housing Act made provision for pilot rehabilitation projects. Local agencies could purchase individual dwelling units, remodel, and sell them to private owners. Each such project was limited to 50 units or not more than 2 percent of the total units in any renewal project.

The 1949 Housing Act requirement that a project be "predominately housing" reflected the general assumption that the low-cost housing program was being transferred, along with "slum clearance," from the public to the private sector. Public housing had grown in disfavor, and political resistance to its continuation accounts for some of the reluctance to adopt the redevelopment provisions of the act at an earlier date. It was consequently assumed that the redevelopment program would shift the emphasis from public housing as the means by which slums and blight could be overcome. The fact that the physical deterioration is not confined to housing areas alone was overlooked. Such deterioration is the result of the general neglect of the basic standards that guide the building and the maintenance of the whole physical environment. The restriction therefore interfered with a comprehensive approach to redevelopment until 1954 when the Housing Act was amended to permit 10 percent of the federal grants for nonresidential sections of a redevelopment project.

Congress has been slow to acknowledge the responsibility of the government in the total problem of urban blight, persistently inclining to the position that housing is the primary concern. Nevertheless, relaxation from this firm position has been demonstrated. In 1959 the restriction was again modified to permit 20 percent nonresidential uses in redevelopment projects, and it has since been increased to 30 percent. By the mid-1960s concern about the displacement of families from renewal areas and the destruction of socially viable communities led to a new emphasis on rehabilitation rather than wholesale clearance. To expand the effectiveness of the program, use of funds for nonresidential purposes was increased to 35 percent. Rehabilitation demands unusually sensitive planning or it may become a deterrent to genuine improvement; the physical condition of individual buildings is but one of the elements in the creation of a living environment.

However, positive steps taken in the sixties toward a comprehensive attack on the physical decay of the urban community have since been altered. Redevelopment programs were almost completely modified to favor the development of commercial structures. Only a minor effort was directed toward the construction of housing, which was the original intent of the redevelopment legislation passed in 1949. Bunker Hill in Los Angeles is a prime example of this. The original plan proposed mainly residential structures. But the projects constructed since 1980 and those now being constructed are largely for office buildings, hotels, and other cultural and commercial uses. The major proportion of the redevelopment area, once almost totally residential, now has only a small portion of the land devoted to that use.

THE WORKABLE PROGRAM

An innovation in the 1954 Housing Act made local agencies responsible for the development of an action plan for renewal—an overall community program for the removal of slums and blight. Known as the Workable Program, this important requirement deserved a more imaginative title.

"There is no justification for federal assistance except to cities which will face up to the whole process of urban decay and undertake long-range programs." That statement is from the 1953 report of the President's Advisory Committee on Government Housing Policies and Programs. It sums up the challenge to cities laid down by the Workable Program.

The program has been accorded rather casual attention; it entailed planning discipline that is not customarily practiced but that clearly should be almost as a matter of course. It is included here as a possible checklist for urban renewal by responsible public officials and for all who would be interested in an informed approach.[3]

1. *Codes and Ordinances.* Adequate codes and ordinances, vigorously enforced, are all-important means of preventing the occurrence and spread of slums and blight and are one of the most valuable achievements, in the long run, for the entire program. Without adequate codes and enforcement a community may be permitting shoddy construction below minimum levels of health and safety. By enforcing antiquated, restrictive regulations a community is increasing the cost of housing. Codes need periodic review and revision to permit the use of improved building methods and materials.

Two principal types of regulations, essential to every community, establish:

Standards for construction, assuring structural strength, reasonable safety from fire, and proper plumbing, electrical, and heating installations. These include a Building, Plumbing, Electrical, and Fire Prevention Code.

---

3. *Workable Program for Community Improvement,* Housing and Home Finance Agency (Washington, D.C.: Government Printing Office). Revised February 1962.

Bunker Hill—Los Angeles. *Originally planned as a residential community as this plan (a student project) shows, it was intended to replace existing homes close to the center of the city. The plan conformed to the intent of the Housing Act of 1949 that established the purposes of redevelopment for residential uses and supportive services.*

These codes normally apply to all new construction, including alterations and major repairs.

Standards for housing, which prescribe the minimum conditions under which a building, or parts of it, may be lawfully occupied as a dwelling. Housing regulations set standards for occupancy to prevent overcrowding, for basic sanitary facilities, for light and ventilation, for maintenance, and for heating where climatic conditions warrant. These standards should apply to all existing, as well as new, dwellings and dwelling units. They may be enacted as a separate code or may be contained in other codes, ordinances, or regulations. The broad and general nature of many of these standards are more clearly defined and amplified in the construction codes.

While the two types of standards required mention specific codes, they are not intended to limit a community's responsibility to adopt and enforce other codes and regulations necessary to eliminate or prevent conditions of blight in the particular area. For example, regulations may be required for gas installations, air conditioning, air pollution, fire prevention, and other hazards applicable not only to dwellings but to public, commercial, and industrial buildings.

The codes that are adopted and enforced will affect every family and every piece of improved property in the community. It is essential that the regulations developed be workable in the local situation and effective as minimum standards of health and safety.

2.   *Comprehensive Community Plan.* The purpose of community planning is to anticipate the physical environment that will best serve the needs of the people living and working in an urban area, and then to make plans for achieving this environment. It is a continuing process of developing a comprehensive program to guide urban growth and renewal.

A planning program which meets the needs of one community may not be adequate for another; the complexities of a large city call for details and studies not applicable to small communities; and the emphasis on some elements of a plan for a built-up community will vary for a newer, more rapidly growing community. Nevertheless, there are six minimum planning requirements which are the backbone of any program:

The Land Use Plan—projects future community land needs, showing by location and extent, areas to be used for residential, commercial, industrial, and public purposes.

The Thoroughfare Plan—provides a system of major streets, existing and proposed, distinguishing between limited access, primary, and secondary thoroughfares.

The Community Facilities Plan—shows location and type of present and proposed schools, recreation areas, and other significant public facilities.

The Public Improvements Program—identifies and recommends priorities for future public improvements needed to meet objectives established in other plan elements.

The Zoning Ordinance and Map—establish regulations and zone districts which govern the use of land and the location, height, use, and land coverage of buildings.

The Subdivision Regulations—provide standards for land development by requiring adequate lot sizes and arrangement, utilities, and street improvements; guide development to conform with the comprehensive plan.

3. *Neighborhood Analysis.* Only through a thorough, overall examination of the entire community and an analysis of individual neighborhoods can blight be found and measured, its causes diagnosed, and a sound course of treatment prescribed. This process is essential to knowing the magnitude of the job and to planning an all-out attack on existing blight and preventing its spread. It involves the following basic steps:

(a)   Delineation of the residential areas of the community by neighborhoods for study and planning purposes.
(b)   Determination of the location, extent, and intensity of blight in each neighborhood.
(c)   The analysis of each neighborhood in terms of its condition and need for treatment.
(d)   The making of recommendations for programming action required to meet neighborhood needs—code enforcement, public improvements, conservation, reconditioning, clearance, and redevelopment.

Neighborhoods must be analyzed by condition of housing and also in terms of environmental conditions—the pattern of land use, traffic flow and street arrangement, neighborhood facilities and services. The type of treatment needed for any area can be prescribed only after its total deficiencies have been determined and the causes of blight pinned down.

In developing recommendations for programming renewal action, a community can take advantage of its opportunities:

(a)   To remove sore spots of blight affecting surrounding areas.
(b)   To save declining areas and restore them to sound condition by early action.
(c)   To plan renewal in conjunction with schedules for public improvements.
(d)   To take advantage of a market for cleared land.

4. *Administrative Organization.* Each of the other program elements provides the tools for community improvement. Administrative organization is the means of putting the tools to work. No matter how good the tools themselves may be, their ultimate effectiveness will depend on whether the community's administrative machinery works efficiently.

For a community with little previous experience in Workable Program activities, the first task should be that of developing the administrative organization to handle these activities. Communities with previous experience may find that existing administration should be reorganized to meet new objectives.

Take a cold, clear look at the community's administrative machinery to see how it can be organized and put into action to meet the challenge of an effective Workable Program for a broad-scale community improvement:

(a)   Decide on and establish the organization needed.
(b)   Find the right people for the jobs to be done.
(c)   Give them clearcut authority and responsibility.

Program activities cut across organizational lines. Most local government departments and agencies will be involved, directly or indirectly, to some extent. Without coordination of these activities, there will be lost motion, poor timing, and waste of funds.

A total attack on slums and blight and community-wide action for improvement require the strength that comes from overall coordination. Assign the responsibility for coordination to some appropriate local official or interdepartmental committee. This will provide the means of

(a)   Keeping a regular check on progress and timing.

(b)   Achieving balanced action so that all seven elements move forward together.

5.   *Financing.* An effective Workable Program can save a community infinitely more than it costs. Some examples of financial benefits are as follows:

(a)   Protection of property values through enforcement of codes and planning measures.

(b)   Savings resulting from the proper planning of public works.

(c)   Reduction of the drain on municipal services from slum areas which require more fire and police protection, more health and welfare services.

(d)   Increases in tax base through conservation, reconditioning, or redevelopment; through stimulation of new commercial and industrial construction.

As the program gets underway, most communities will find that they need to initiate or increase appropriations for the following types of activities:

(a)   Enforcement of codes.

(b)   Technical assistance for comprehensive planning and neighborhood analyses.

(c)   Administration of zoning and subdivision regulations.

(d)   Overall coordination of the program when this is a full- or part-time assignment.

As definite plans for community facilities, public works, and renewal projects are developed, the community can plan and coordinate its capital outlays expenditures. By projecting them for a five- or six-year period into the future, a sound fiscal program for improvement can be developed. Advance scheduling of expenditures provides the opportunity to market obligations at better terms. Through coordination of urban renewal activities with expenditures for public improvements, a community can make local dollars do double duty.

6.   *Housing for Displaced Families.* As a community goes into action on its Workable Program—enforcing codes, eliminating slums and blight, constructing public improvements—some families will be displaced from housing they now occupy. Many of the families will need substantial assistance in finding suitable relocation housing. Many communities will find that existing local housing will not meet relocation needs. This is often true in regard to the limited number of sales and rental units available to displaced minority group families.

The community must accept the responsibility of providing relocation assistance to all families displaced as a result of governmental action. It must make every effort to assure that these families have the opportunity to relocate in decent, safe, and sanitary housing that is within their means. With the housing resources that exist in the community and with action to augment them, the needs of displaced families can be met—but not without advance preparation and planning.

Those responsible for relocation assistance must work with officials of agencies likely to cause displacement through activities such as:

(a)   Code enforcement.
(b)   Construction of local public improvements, state or federal installations.
(c)   Urban renewal.
(d)   Expressway or street-widening projects.

By determining both immediate and long-range relocation needs in advance of displacement, a community will be in a position to remedy any shortage of housing. There will be opportunity to organize relocation services, to let people know that they are going to have help in finding a new place to live, to work with private housing developers, and to obtain federal relocation aids if they are needed.

Before a family is displaced, suitable relocation housing must be available. Hardships are created and community improvement plans and projects are delayed when a community's relocation responsibilities are neglected.

7.   *Citizen Participation.* There is some degree of citizen participation in any program a community undertakes. It is evident in expressions of support or opposition in newspapers, in meetings, in conferences, at public hearings, at the ballot box. Ultimate success for the other six elements of a Workable Program depends on the kind of citizen participation a community is able to achieve.

Citizen support and concern for community improvement can be a powerful force. Enlist the finest leadership of every sphere of community life and action—industrial, professional, labor, welfare, religious, and educational interests; civic clubs and women's groups. The active support of the business community will be a major asset. Special emphasis should be placed on minority group participation, for minorities are often most adversely affected by lack of housing opportunities.

A basic approach to building the kind of citizen participation a program needs is three-pronged. It must be planned to inform and to involve the following:

(a)   The community as a whole.
(b)   Special-interest groups, enlisting their assistance in solving particular problems.
(c)   Residents of areas to be directly affected by various program activities.

People need to know what is happening to their community, what neighborhoods are going downhill, what is causing blight, what is being done to fight deterioration, and what more can be done. They must have every opportunity to take constructive action.

Each community will know from its own experience what means of enlisting citizen participation have proven most successful; what groups and local leaders can provide effective support; the type of information that will promote the understanding and interest of local citizens. Work to build the kind of participation that is ready to take action and share responsibility in developing and carrying out a Workable Program for Community Improvement which utilizes the full range of private as well as public resources.

Public Action

Aggressive public action against the slums in American cities was initiated in 1933 when the National Recovery Act launched the low-rent housing program of the Public Works Administration. The economy of the nation had collapsed and the times were troubled. There were those who viewed the housing program as a means to improve the standard of housing for the lower-income families in our cities, but the overriding incentive was general economic recovery. A pervasive air of emergency has attended all activities of the federal government since then. The anachronism is apparent. Slums have grown as a natural consequence of neglect. Voices raised in protest have had effect in isolated quarters, but the national disposition has been apathetic. The deterioration of cities has been a process, not a willful act that may be corrected on command. Rebuilding our cities to standards appropriate to our times is also a process and calls for effective action along a broad front. The Workable Program gave articulation to this process as a matter of public policy, and it is not a program that, having begun, will reach an end.

The urgency to produce "results" leads inevitably to compromises in the administration of a public program. Patience is required to wait for cities "to face up to the whole process of urban decay and undertake long-range programs." This is the urgent need, and less-than-adequate planning action at the local level reduces the program to a process of "getting federal money" rather than a process of genuine urban renewal.

The formulation and diligent enforcement of ordinances to maintain adequate housing standards, zoning ordinances, and subdivision regulations that prescribe adequate standards for future building, self-analysis of local deficiencies, and action programs for correction—all require the persistent will of the people of a community. They cannot "go it alone" and federal assistance is necessary, but the Workable Program offers both the means and the opportunity to wait long enough for the treatment to take effect.

In 1965 all housing agencies were consolidated within the Department of Housing and Urban Development, a new post in the president's cabinet. The following year the Demonstration Cities and Metropolitan Development Act introduced the Model Cities Program to coordinate federal programs related to social services, education, open land, employment, and physical development. A galaxy of amendments to the Housing Act was directed to more participation by private enterprise in the production of low-cost housing. Sections 235 and 236 subsidized interest rates on housing loans to reach an equivalent of a one percent rate for both home ownership and apartment rental. With much fanfare, experimental projects were financed by HUD to demonstrate efficient housing prototypes and new construction technology. Begun in 1969, this Operation Breakthrough was elaborately organized, but the practical results were inconclusive.

By 1970 inflation overtook the nation, and federal assistance to low-cost housing was cut back. Revenue sharing was proposed in order to enlarge the initiative of local governments in the allocation of federal aid.

The great cities of America are distinguished by the concentration of huge economic institutions that dominate the affairs of the nation and the vast multitude of people attracted to them in search for survival. While cities such as New York, Chicago, Philadelphia, Boston, and Los Angeles serve the national interest as centers of enterprise, they have themselves become socially and economically unmanageable.

These cities are confronted with uncontrolled physical deterioration, a concentration of low-income families in ghettos, the flight of the affluent population to the suburbs, and the extension of highways to implement that decentralization. In the face of this, the promotion of excessive property values in core areas to compensate for an imbalanced tax base has contributed to a condition of institutional decay.

Revitalization through federally assisted redevelopment has been undertaken with a program of piecemeal "projects" of publicly and privately financed housing. Handicapped by exorbitant costs for site acquisition in congested areas, new developments of high-rise apartments are either alien to the life-style of low-income families or beyond their economic means. The social and economic plight of the underprivileged urban population continues to fester and, on occasion, to explode from intense pressure.

Reflecting the bloated character of very large cities, programs have been instituted to recover community participation in the decision-making process. New York has been divided into areas of common interest in which individuals may relate to government institutions. Los Angeles has attempted to cope with its huge land mass by delineating geographical areas in which citizen committees may participate in planning. The paradox of this urban balkanization is the fact that a city or regional government is necessary to assure a variety of essential urban services and coordinate basic elements of growth and development.

A POSSIBLE SOLUTION

Congestion created high land values and congestion now threatens to destroy them. To ward off this imminent disaster, the protection of land values is a compelling motive for improvement of the environment. Land is a natural resource; it is not a product of men's toil. Value attached to it is essentially a byproduct, a value not of the land itself but of the way in which it may be used. Stable values can be maintained only through social controls cast in the form of laws that prescribe the limits of its use. This has not occurred. Stimulated by the almost anarchic nature of laws governing urban development, speculation has enjoyed a violent career. Inflation bubbles blow up, they burst; land prices quiver but rise again to unprecedented heights. Over 50 years ago, Harland Bartholomew said: "Too often is the American city considered an unlimited speculation in real estate."[4]

Negligence and abuse have sapped some of the vitality of our traditional practices. The public power of eminent domain is summoned to force adjustment, and public funds are drawn upon to aid in purging the economic congestion. Condemnation and public credit now receive general acceptance as necessary instruments for urban rebuilding. These are not measures to be taken as temporary sedatives. The high cost should produce a cure; it is reasonable to expect them to prevent a recurrence of the same ills.

State laws for urban redevelopment provide that land acquired by condemnation may be resold. It is generally provided that the new use to which the land is put shall comply with standards of use which conform to a comprehensive plan for redevelopment.

Public financial assistance for urban rehabilitation serves a dual purpose. It implements rebuilding at standards of land use that will restore a decent environment, and it provides unlimited opportunities for sound and profitable investment by private enterprise. The investment of public funds as subsidies is warranted on the condition that the resulting improvement is permanent, and there must be assurance that the same investment to cure the same ills will not be repeated every generation. It is of vital importance, therefore, to ascertain that the new standards of land use are of a permanent nature.

To determine this, it is necessary to refer to the laws that apply to urban building. A comprehensive plan is not a permanent document, nor

---

4. Introduction to *Urban Land Uses*, Harvard City Planning Series, Cambridge, Mass.: Harvard University Press, 1932.

are the "administrative decisions" that emanate from a planning agency preparing that document. A comprehensive plan is only part of a series of legislative acts controlling the development of cities. An immediate improvement may conform to the new standards administratively determined within the scope of a comprehensive plan, but subsequent use of land will depend entirely upon later revisions and modifications that may emerge. To rely upon administrative policy, no matter how inspired, is to invite inevitable chaos and abuse.

Adequate protection is afforded only by the laws that set the standards, and there is little evidence that reasonable legal standards are yet remotely intended. This raises a question as to the advisability of delivering land, acquired by the public power of condemnation, back to the same abuses that have made it necessary to exercise that power. The question may be elaborated by inquiring if justice is served by taking land from some private owners and selling it to other private interests at a reduced price. The purpose of public funds is to bring land costs down to an economic value for redevelopment at standards of decent land use. To that extent the public interest is served and to that extent it must be protected. To sell land at a subsidized price is to make a gift of public funds as an inducement to engage in urban rebuilding for a profit. Such a policy is somewhat of a distortion of the high purpose for which it is designed.

Thus we come to the central question: Rather than buy land only to sell it at reduced cost, other things aside, thereby creating potential dangers for the future, why should not publicly owned land be leased for redevelopment use?

The suggestion is not new. In 1942 an English Royal Commission reported its recommendations for a reconstruction program. That report said in part:

> We recommend . . . that once any interest in land has passed into public ownership it should be disposed of by way of lease only and not by way of sale, and that the authority should have the power to impose such covenants in the lease as planning requirements make desirable, breach of such covenants to be enforceable by re-entry.[5]

Building on leased land is by no means rare. It is common practice in commercial enterprise and offers no deterrent to sound investment. It need offer no obstruction to the sale of improvements on the land. Nor would tax revenue be affected, since a lease value would return revenue to the city, and the usual taxes could be assessed against the improvement. The objections of the local bureaucracy could be avoided by ob-

---

5. Report of the Expert Committee on Compensation and Betterment presented to Parliament by Minister of Works and Planning, September 1942.

taining the services of competent and established firms in property management.

We are confronted with a situation in which public powers must be called into action to restore the productive enterprise of our cities and the initiative of private enterprise in our urban economy, and, in so doing, create an urban environment consistent with our contemporary capacities and skills. The fact that land values obstruct the path to this goal becomes a matter of concern to the people—a public responsiblity—and the gains made at the expense of the people must be retained by them.

CONTROL OF OBSOLESCENCE—TAXATION

An effective method of controlling the spread of obsolescence is not yet available. The police power to restrain the "nuisance" of blight has limitations. Obsolescence is an obstruction to full production of housing. Normal competitive enterprise does not and cannot cope with it, as the accumulation of huge areas of blighted districts testifies.

When blight sets in, the land is deemed ripe for more intensive land use. As single-family districts, some being the "fine old sections," begin to run down, their only salvation seems to be a change to apartment development. Intensity of land use moves relentlessly from the city center, and the "old" areas are drawn into this ever-widening vortex. The greater density permitted in apartment zoning then swiftly moves to reinforce a claim to higher land values. Thenceforth only multiple-dwelling development can be afforded. Old residences are converted to apartments, and the district declines further. Strip zoning for business use is soon permitted, and unplanned stores are spotted in the neighborhood. After that, "light" industrial uses seep in. The "salvation" of revised zoning is dissipated among unplanned mixed land uses, and the community environment decays.

Pressure is ever present to "save" obsolescent areas by permitting a greater intensity of land use. Indeed, there are a few instances where this usually insidious process has restored to blighted areas a decent standard of residential or commercial development. More normally, the careless mixture of land uses leaves a series of derelicts in its wake. Land values increase rather than decrease as blight eats its way from the central core of the city, and they defy recovery of neighborhood values. Good development retreats from these damaging blows and seeks protection of new and more economical land at a safe distance. Disorderly expansion continues. Self-maintenance is the urgent need—a form of preventive treatment that will build resistance to decay and render major operations less necessary.

Federal, state, county, and city taxes in general are intended to provide for sound governance and the provision of essential public services to protect the health, safety, and public welfare. Certain portions of the funds collected by the federal and state governments have been returned to communities to assist in the financing of many local services, mainly education, transportation, and, in the recent past, public housing and urban renewal. Taxes associated with property, sometimes called *ad valorem* taxes, affect urban development directly. In the mid-1980s much discussion in the federal administration has been directed to the reduction in assistance to local government, especially in revenue sharing, support of education, health, and transportation. Curtailing of this sharing of federal taxes places additional burdens upon the already limited assets of state and local governments. Federal interest in the urban renewal programs has been all but eliminated, with the threat of curtailing the functions of HUD in the process.

The use of public funds to assist—that is, to subsidize—urban development is not a new function of government. However, the extent and direction of both legislative and financial assistance increased immeasurably after the first and second World Wars, when much of Europe was so devastated that it required public assistance to once again become socially and economically viable. In addition, the recessions and Depression that followed the wars highlighted the conditions of the poor, and programs were initiated to construct and reconstruct those areas hardest hit.

One factor has remained consistent over the years. Changes are made in all programs to aid urban areas as different political groups come into power. Some once abandoned as unworkable are revived under a different name, thereby proving that people remember and learn little from experience. The previously mentioned shift in emphasis, from rehousing the poor in areas to be redeveloped to support for super-commercial development, is an example of the pendulum swing in recent years; it is a far cry from the initial intent of the programs.

Taxation in Reverse

Buildings are built to provide space in which to live or conduct business. Taxes are collected to support the public services that make these building ventures possible and profitable. Today taxes are measured by the assessed value of land and buildings. The value of land may increase. The value of physical improvements, on the other hand, depreciates with age and use. At the same time the cost of public services increases as physical deterioration continues. Yet the present assessment of taxation actually works in reverse of this: tax revenue goes down as the cost of urban maintenance goes up.

There is little inducement for an owner to remove obsolete buildings as long as it is possible to derive a profit from them. The present order of real property taxation penalizes new construction and encourages the retention of old buildings until they have reached the last stages of decay. It retards sound real estate development and management, makes unhealthy communities, and adds to the burden of the taxpayer. This trend must be checked and reversed.

Taxation is our traditional instrument for maintaining economic and social equilibrium. Our system of enterprise is intended to give the individual full freedom of choice and initiative; devices employed by government to serve the public welfare should remain consistent with this pattern. It is up to the individual to measure his opportunity for investment; he must determine the extent to which he, in his own interest, will take part in the building of a community. But his interest cannot be served when a system of taxation imposes the penalty of high taxes on new building while it encourages competition from old buildings. Yet that is our current method of ad valorem taxation, and it is inimical to the full use of our productive resources.

It would be productive to look at a common technique used to reduce taxes in business enterprises: the cost of improvements to carry on the business may be deducted from gross income. Applying this principle to real property taxation would establish a logical order: as buildings deteriorate with age, thus contributing to the spread of blight and retarding new building, taxes would increase rather than decrease. Taxation would serve as an effective instrument to encourage expanding production and protect against blight, as well as no doubt adding revenue to the community for public services. This technique would be the more effective because real property taxes are levied primarily by local government and are thereby readily subject to such periodic adjustments as changing local conditions may warrant.

The Economic Life of Buildings

The control of obsolescence has a twofold purpose: the maintenance of a stable economy through continuing full production, and the maintenance of adequate standards through continuous improvement. The FHA program introduced the repayment of loans for urban construction in regular installments over a predetermined period—amortization. This helped to stabilize financing, but more than that it recognizes the vital role of time in our economic machinery. It acknowledges that buildings have an "economic life," a period during which they are economically useful. The wheels of the system are kept turning by the circulation of money, and the time required to pay for buildings marks the frequency of the circulation of money. Unless the demand for building continues to exceed the existing supply, circulation of building money diminishes or ceases. The building industry then slows down or stops.

In *Building Height, Bulk and Form,*[6] George B. Ford pointed out that the average life of skyscrapers was calculated at twenty-five to thirty years. The period of residential financing ranges between fifteen and twenty-five years. Except for commercial dwelling structures that have become a sordid blight, few acceptable buildings remain in use for more than thirty-five years without such major alterations that they become the equivalent of new buildings. The obsolete buildings need to be weeded out of the urban environment.

If the physical life of buildings were linked to their economic life, money would continue to flow into the production of new structures. Improved methods would find normal reception and application. But as long as old and obsolete buildings remain on the market, they suffocate new production. Rundown and wornout buildings sustain themselves too long on no maintenance and low rents. It is that type of competition that must be weeded out. Control of obsolescence would maintain the economic flow of goods and services and therefore a higher level of decency in the urban environment. Taxation could be effectively used to establish this control if the rate were related to the economic life of buildings.

It would be possible to establish a low tax base for new buildings and thereafter increase the tax rate from year to year. During the early life of a building—about ten years—the increase would be moderate. Thereafter it would gradually accelerate for the succeeding fifteen to twenty years. After that the increase would move rapidly upward at such a rate that a major improvement to sustain a profitable income on the building or a complete removal to make way for a new structure more suitable to the market and the community would be induced by the time the age of the structure had reached thirty-five years. A major improvement would cause a building to revert to a proportionately lower tax bracket rather than be penalized by an increased assessment, as occurs with current policy. Standards of construction would be improved because they would benefit from lower taxes rather than be discouraged by the present ad valorem system.[7]

Such a method rejects the traditional supposition that a building may remain as long as it produces revenue satisfactory to its owner. It may seem to be bitter medicine, but the accelerating degeneration of our cities has amply demonstrated that neither the public welfare nor sound private enterprise is served by current methods. The proposal does not presume

---

6. Harvard City Planning Series, Vol. II.

7. This approach to building improvements could be coordinated with some form of taxation on land, such as that referred to in chapter 2.

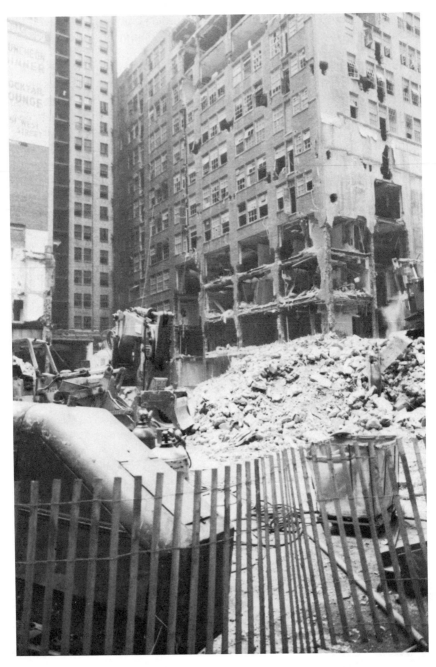

Piecemeal urban redevelopment: New York City. *Making way for a new development on individual parcels of land.*

Changes occur, even in cities where property values are exceedingly high and where redevelopment occurs on a lot-by-lot basis—as in New York.

to solve the broad problem of taxation, but it would put our current tax system in a logical order. Without such a change, the regulations of today offer no prospect for correcting the insidious evil of obsolescence.

No surgeon ever performed an operation without destroying some live tissue. His aim is to save the patient, knowing that time will heal the wounds and restore the living cells. Our economy as well as our social well-being depends upon our capacity to carve out the parasite of decay with the destruction of as little useful tissue as is practically possible. But we cannot continue to rely upon vagaries of chance. In an organized society it must become a matter of law.

It may be alleged that this order of taxation would impose an undue hardship on low-income homeowners who depend upon their dwelling solely as a place to live. The most articulate protests of this nature will undoubtedly come from those who profit most from blighted property, but the criticism has some validity. Nonetheless, every community will have to face, sooner or later, this question: How long can the accumulation of obsolete buildings and "improvements" that deface the environment and eat away at the civic solvency be tolerated? Each community is obliged to address itself to that question and deliberate the problems—all the problems—it poses. Only then will cities begin the long road out of the sordid morass that the anarchy of urban development has wrought.

All things grow obsolete with time and change. That is inevitable. But obsolescence must be brought under control, as weeds are kept out of a prosperous garden. Degeneration of the urban environment is an epidemic feeding upon lack of attention. The absence of public control and effective treatment is like the underwriting of obsolescence by law. It has become a public liability. It is consequently a public responsibility to devise machinery to put its house in order, and to keep it in order by the progressive regulation of obsolescence.

RENEWAL IS FOR PEOPLE

There is little doubt that slum conditions must be eradicated and the families living in them must have decent housing. Blight must be removed and further spread prevented. Rundown business sections need rehabilitation, and industrial areas must be cleaned up. The decay must be carved out. But there are some related issues from which a program of renewal and rehabilitation cannot be dissociated. Bright new projects replace the slums. Buildings rise high and open space appears where there was none before. The apartments all have a view. Efficiency and convenience replace the drudgery of a house and yard; services are well-maintained by management. The great new buildings are quite urbane, the parking garages and traffic circulation ingenious. But as the program progresses there is evidence that money, buildings, and bulldozers are receiving somewhat more attention than people. For what people are these giant developments intended?

Further, are these projects an expression of the environment we really seek? Is the agglomeration of cells in huge building blocks the design for future family life? Have we become incapable of distinguishing between "habitable" and "livable"?

The frequency with which these questions have been asked is reason enough to ponder them. It is the human spirit of the city, rather than land prices, which renewal is presumed to sustain. As the prospects for orderly rebuilding of our cities loom brighter, we cannot be unmindful of its underlying purpose: re-creation of an urban environment in which the functions of the contemporary city can be performed with order. Other advantages will accrue, but we may be guided by Aristotle's advice: "A city should be built to give its inhabitants security and happiness."

Urban renewal is not supposed to be solely for the purpose of restoring stability to real estate values, although this will result. It is not for the purpose of bailing out the investments of landed gentry, since much of the decaying city pays dividends to its absentee owners. It is not intended to recover speculative losses, since the curse of blight has fallen upon the property of those who cannot afford to join the flight to better places. It is not for the purpose of reinforcing government bureaucracy, although the public that these bureaus represent has a heavy stake in the problem. It is not for the purpose of providing employment, although it will create unlimited opportunities for labor in field and factory. Urban renewal is for none of these specifically, but each is a part serving the main objective: building a decent city for people.

Cities are for people. Cities are not objects to be coddled by zealots nor commodities to satisfy speculative greed. The philosophy of escape from the city is a retreat from reality; within this philosophy are the seeds of our own destruction. To deny the place of the city in our industrial age is to invite economic slavery and social suicide. Our proper course is not the destruction of urban life; it is the building of a better one.

John Osman, then vice-president of the Ford Foundation for Adult Education, once stated:

> Building a city is a sacramental act on the part of the whole people. For a city is the physical manifestation of an invisible reality: the soul of its people. Ancient cities were worshipped by their citizens. Americans appear to hate their cities. We do all we can to demean and disgrace them.
>
> But there is an intangible spirit at the heart of a contemporary commercial city that must find its expression in and give purpose to the city building of its people. We should endeavor to make an art out of our town building.
>
> The citizens of a city must discover the character of the city if they are to build an image of its soul. They must understand its nature and its function before they can design it. For the design of a city is not to be found on the drawing board of the city planner. The forms of the city live in its people. They emerge out of the mind and spirit of its citizens. They reside in the very history of "the place." . . .[8]

It is well to think about that counsel as we consider the confused maze of housing "programs" intended to improve the lot of the poor while rebuilding rundown areas in our cities. Civic and political leaders, disenchanted with the public housing programs after World War II, decided private enterprise should clear slums and build decent housing for low-income families. Urban renewal programs failed to take into account the plight of families who, for economic, ethnic, or social reasons, were not eligible for or could not afford the new high-rise apartments that replaced the blight. Where the new buildings were intended for underprivileged

---

8. *Architectural Forum*, August 1957.

families, it was discovered that high-rise cell blocks were incompatible with the living mores of their intended occupants.

The bizarre example of the Pruitt-Igoe public housing development in St. Louis should alert our attention to the human element in the housing equation. Because the development had such an oppressive atmosphere to the low-income occupants for whom it had been planned, less than a quarter of the dwellings were ever occupied. Eventually, in 1972, the government ordered two of the eleven-story towers destroyed by dynamite; the remaining towers were reduced to less than half their original height.

Despite such an incredible experience, housing is seldom designed for compatible living patterns. The drama of high-rise buildings appeals not only to architects and engineers who design them; it also satisfies the land-economists and government officials who consider land prices more than the basic needs of people for a compatible living environment. Urban renewal moves toward apartments designed for upper-income groups who want to return to city life and the amenities it offers, or else accommodations for commercial institutions are promoted to replace the blight.

With the drifting course of government assistance to housing, the fact that many low-income families in the nation cannot afford the cost of decent housing—the property taxes, insurance, and maintenance— has been obscured in the enthusiasm to subsidize the private sector in real estate and development. It is quite possible that when the ambition for large projects attractive to planners, architects, and government officials has abated, public housing may be integrated within neighborhoods where the less economically privileged may find a compatible environment.

It would be well to heed the observations of Paul Gaff, urban affairs editor of the *Chicago Tribune*. Despite new Neanderthal monsters in the heart of the city, such as the Prudential Building, the Marina City Towers, the John Hancock Building, the Standard Oil Building, and the Sears Tower, Chicago "is losing its battle with the suburbs." Confronted with the lethargy of the City Planning Department, privately financed plans by the architectural firm of Skidmore, Owings, and Merrill in 1966 envisioned a restructuring of the look of Chicago and the lakefront, a leviathan "new town in town" on 600 acres along the river for a population of 120,000. But Gaff suggests:

Perhaps it is already too late. . . . The nature of the growth points to a day when the last middle-class white family has fled the city—when only the wealthy remain within their fortified apartment towers along the lake and the rest of Chicago is populated by the poor. This is no doomsday fantasy.

. . . Chicago, which keeps telling itself to "make no little plans," continues to move toward the time when it will have little left to plan for.[9]

The changes that have taken place in the central area of Chicago, and in the core areas of many other large cities, indicate a reversal to the earlier trend of white, middle-class flight to the suburbs. While the "new town in town" program has generally been considered a commercial experiment, there has been a residential revival. Old structures have been rehabilitated and are now occupied by affluent individuals and families seeking the social advantages associated with the business institutions and cultural establishments, as well as places of employment, located nearby.

---

9. *Architectural Forum,* January-February 1974.

CHAPTER 14

LAND AND REAL ESTATE

Land seems to have characteristics associated with it that are not possessed by any other element on earth.

The development of land as real estate in the United States has not been distinguished for its attention to the amenities ofa living environment. Speculation was the moving spirit as the frontiers widened and were pushed forward. This was not a characteristic reserved to enterprising Americans alone. It reflects the desires that caused the people to seek this land, and rather points to a difference between the opportunities open to the people of America as opposed to those of countries elsewhere. Freedom from oppression and tyranny implied certain rights, and among them was the right to a piece of land upon which to build a home. The abuse of the privilege was not a new characteristic of human beings.

During the colonial period the mother country granted land as a just reward due the leaders of colonization. The subdivision and sale of the land so acquired were common practice. When it was not lucrative enough, some of the large land-estates were preserved through the English system of long-term leases rather than sale.

In the latter half of the nineteenth century whole towns were used as a speculative medium, and they sprang up almost at random along the railroads that stretched across the land. Some of these towns have become cities, many have vanished, and others remain as ghosts of the speculative orgy in gold and silver.

In the real estate practice, land is considered a commodity to be bought at the lowest prices and sold at the highest. The sole purpose of the professional's services is to handle property for a fee that belongs to other persons. Land entering the market in large units may be divided into small elements called lots or building sites. Where the land is so subdivided, local laws govern and influence the manner in which the action is to take place; the final sale is to be approved by the state real estate commissioner to assure the buyer that no fraud is involved and that all local laws have been complied with.

REALTOR AND DEVELOPER

Realtors—real estate agents or expeditors—are the middlemen in real estate transactions. In most cases they have no economic interest in the properties they handle, other than in the commission obtained by bringing buyers and sellers together and consummating a transfer of ownership. Sometimes they may indicate what they believe is the fair market price, but in most cases they will recommend using an appraiser. He or she then studies the property's condition and location, and reviews the records for the sale of other property in the vicinity as well as the sales history of the property in question.

Developers play a different role. They acquire large parcels of land, prepare plans for the proposed use of the property, process the plans through the necessary public agencies, and install the utilities and facilities that are required. Only then, either through their own organization or through a separate real estate brokerage, do they place the development on the market, as a whole or in parts that can be absorbed within a reasonable time. Developers take large risks, and in general invest a considerable amount of time and money in a venture before they secure a return for their efforts.

THE SUBURBAN COMMUNITY

Although the history of land speculation has not been the most savory, there were those who chose this medium as an instrument to improve land development. This choice was not motivated by the high purpose of the garden city movement in England, for instance, nor was it prompted by deep concern for the nature of the city or its social and economic welfare. It was rather the natural result of competitive necessity, no doubt prodded by the satisfaction that achievement invariably delivers.

With the dawn of the twentieth century high land costs squeezed the single-family dwelling farther and farther to the outskirts. As the city swelled, the outskirts moved to such distances that the community facilities originally able to serve the whole urban population ceased to be readily accessible. The consequent development of extensive facilities in the suburbs gave them the character of satellite communities. Decentralization was in progress.

Originally, only the land surveyor was involved in the layout of land subdivisions, but in recent times the planner became a more active participant in the development of independent residential communities. One of the earliest large-scale residential subdivisions was a 1,600-acre tract to be known as Riverside, near Chicago. It was designed by Frederick Law Olmsted and Calvert Vaux in 1869. Garden City, Long Island, was another such development; it has since become substantially a self-contained community.

The gridiron street system was typical of real estate development, offering the subdivider the most convenient pattern for surveying and recording deeds. But it offered little in return as a living environment. The exceptions are, therefore, the more noteworthy for the progress in planning they demonstrated.

Roland Park in Baltimore, begun in 1891, was distinguished for singularly high standards of physical development. It was designed for fine residences, but at that time few suburbs were not so intended. Forest Hills in New York's Long Island, started in 1913, was one of the earliest planned residential suburbs. The development company undertook the construction of many of the homes, apartments, and shopping facilities.

After World War I a number of well-planned communities were initiated. Mariemont, a satellite of Cincinnati designed by John Nolen in 1921, was devoted primarily to single-family homes with a density of six or seven units per acre. Apartment clusters were developed in connection with the principal shopping center, an arrangement since then true of much development planning.

About this time two other distinguished developments were begun in widely different sections of the country. River Oaks in Houston, Texas, occupying 1,000 acres, was planned with a full complement of community facilities including a golf course and market center. In 1923 the Palos Verdes Estates south of Los Angeles was planned for a dramatic site overlooking the Pacific Ocean. About one-quarter of the total 3,000-acre area was allocated to schools, parks, houses of worship, libraries, shopping, and a golf course; residential lots of one-half acre to 30 acres occupied the remainder. A few small apartment areas were proposed adjacent to the small shopping centers. One-half of the land adjacent to the centers is in roads and landscaped parkways. The quality of all these developments has remained high as the project has been constructed in accordance with the plan.

Among other notable subdivisions in this country are Shaker Heights in Cleveland, the Country Club District in Kansas City, St. Francis Woods in San Francisco, Nassau Shores, Long Island, and Westwood Village in Los Angeles. Each of these developments marks a high level of planning. There was no serious intention on the part of the subdividers to cope with housing for families of low income in these communities. They were intended for the upper income group and were promoted accordingly.

The contrast between these developments and the average subdivision is made the more apparent when we observe the rank and file of urban expansion. Most of it was not planned; it simply oozed over the edges of the growing metropolis. A minimum of improvements in streets, walks, sewers, water, electricity, and gas distribution was installed. The unaware purchaser was left to foot the bill individually at some later date or the burden was shifted to the urban taxpayer.

Local governments gradually awoke to the havoc being wrought in the suburbs, and legislation was enacted to require subdividers to make certain improvements as a condition of approval. These early regulations were feeble, but they were an acknowledgment that some measure of control was necessary to protect the city for the people who live in it.

Nassau Shores, Long Island. *Nassau Shores, begun in about 1926 on approximately 500 acres, was designed to take advantage of the waterfront location. The area was subdivided in lots twenty by one hundred feet, and it was customary to require two lots for each dwelling.*

THE MOBILE POPULATION

Suburban expansion was encouraged by urban growth, but it did not drain off the excess population from the center of cities. People responded to their natural desire to live near their work, and employment opportunities concentrated in the city center. Then, the nature of these opportunities changed from the prefactory system. Stable industrial employment became uncertain. With expanding commercial enterprise, the tendency to shift from job to job extended to movement from city to city. For practical reasons, mobility of the family offered advantages over fixed tenure.

The urban population thus became transient in character. Freedom to move was not desirable in itself but it was necessary. The rental apartment satisfied this need and became popular. The familiar central city tenement of the nineteenth century remained for the poor, but the new multifamily building was not confined to the low-income family. It achieved a new dignity as a form of urban living. Park Avenue, the Gold Coast, and Nob Hill were as popular among the well-to-do as, for example, New York's Lower East Side was necessary for the immigrant family.

Oddly enough, planning standards did not change with the income groups who found the apartment popular. Lots forty and fifty feet wide were more common than the nineteenth-century twenty-five-foot lot and New York's dumbbell tenement had been outlawed, but the arrangement, size, and number of rooms in "high-class" apartments took up much of the additional lot area. In addition, narrow interior courts and side yards with little or no setbacks at front or rear prevailed as standard practice. Consequently, there was little difference in the amount of open space about the building of the "swank" trade, the "efficiency," apartment building of the middle-income white-collar clerk, or the tenement of the low-income industrial worker.

The city was having growing pains. The industrial economy had thrown out of gear all previous concepts of what a city should be. The traditional dwelling for the average American family had been the single-family house. But the industrial metropolis had engulfed the village of homes. Instead of a place to live, the city became a place to make a living. The family no longer dwelt in its home; it hired apartment space for temporary occupancy. The speculative opportunities for profit in this form of building enterprise were obvious and full advantage was taken of them, but the apartment as a form of investment for capital was not yet fully realized. Adjustment to the new kind of city was, and still is, slow. But there were signs of improvements.

RECENT TRENDS

From 1975 to 1984 the land values in all parts of the country spiraled to new heights. Desert land around Palm Springs, subject to wind and erosion damage, was being sold for over $100 thousand an acre. Foreign capital from many nations was pouring into the land market, not only from the oil-rich Middle East but also from Canada and Europe. This sharp increase reflected inflation as well as a basic housing shortage. In the Los Angeles–Orange County areas of California a modest home sold for more than $100 thousand. Jerry-built homes with less than 1,000 square feet of space were selling in the $60- to $70-thousand range. In some locations the demand was so great that lotteries were held to award homes, which all too often were then bought by speculators seeking to take advantage of the soaring land values.

Professor Robert A. Brady, formerly of the economics department at the University of California at Berkeley, once stated that the depressed economic conditions of the 1930s confirmed the law of physics that holds "everything that goes up will eventually come down." Perhaps we will soon see a repetition of that 1930s phenomenon.

In the meantime these land costs and interest rates are reflected in the cost of housing—whether as rentals or as the price of a home. Because of the high costs, one can readily understand why developers often ask to be allowed to build housing of higher densities than that permitted by comprehensive plans and the zoning ordinances. Such requests are difficult to deny when it is claimed, as it often is, that the proportionately smaller profit and consequent higher cost of low-density housing prevents poor people from purchasing decent homes for themselves.

CHAPTER 15

MODERN TRENDS I:
THE TWENTIES AND THIRTIES

The special attention addressed to the plight of housing in the large urban complexes of the world has led to the formulation of many public programs to help alleviate the horrendous conditions facing residents in the slums and blighted areas. To appreciate the extent of the problem one need only observe housing conditions in the central sectors of such cities as Hong Kong, Tokyo, Manila, Shanghai, Rio de Janeiro, and other intensively urbanized places, to say nothing of conditions in the underdeveloped countries and the rural areas of almost every nation.

The material that follows identifies and traces some of the efforts in the United States, a few of which were begun many years ago by nineteenth-century idealists and benevolent industrialists. It does not by any means cover the wide range of efforts in virtually all modern nations to meet the most pressing of their social responsibilities to the masses of their people who live in conditions that could be described as not fit for animals.

The conditions of shelter are the core of the problem, but the causes are social and economic. Poverty consigns people to these areas. Coupled with lack of education and no opportunity to leave, it creates a situation in which the spirit of the residents becomes dulled to the point of accepting their lot as inevitable.

One of the major gains achieved through the drive for better housing and improved living conditions for the working population has been the concern for site planning and the provision of open space. The green areas required organizations for their maintenance, and apartment rentals or cooperative ownerships were the patterns that emerged. Subsidized developments of single-home parcels where maintenance was the responsibility of the individual occupants were infrequent; when the development consisted of clusters of individual homes, homeowners' associations were created to take care of common areas. The condominiums that developed during the 1970s offered another way of providing for uniform maintenance of grounds and other common-use facilities.

Some twenty-seven million American households, one in three, still rent; in older urban areas, two of three do. Although some rents have not kept pace with inflation, they now exact a higher percentage of renters' incomes than ever before. There have also been some basic shifts in the housing market. Rental housing has been and still is considered hand-me-down housing, left behind in the move to suburbia. During the 1970s, those who could do so moved on to home ownership, leaving behind the poor, the elderly, and single people.

Choosing adequate housing amid a wide range of quality and location poses no problems for the wealthy and only minor ones for the upper middle class. The moderate and lower income groups and the poor, on the other hand, face various problems related to their levels of income and social status. Race restrictions have been legally condemned, but there is still the "gentlemen's agreement" that can close the market to those of a color or religion unlike the majority in a given location.

It was for the moderate and lower income groups that subsidized public housing and rent assistance programs were designed. Many of the programs were designed after the two world wars to rehouse those displaced by the destruction of cities and their subsequent reconstruction. New towns were also built in an effort to reduce the pressures on the overpopulated cities.

These efforts at slum clearance and the rehousing of low-income families in decent, clean facilities started all over the world, particularly after the Second World War. Critics of such programs noted that the former slum dwellers did not progress to join the mainstream of the middle class. Some critics went so far as to state that subsidizing rents created a situation in which the tenants would avoid improving their economic condition in order to remain in the public housing. But other problems existed that were as fundamental as the need for money. There were few educational programs to teach those who had lived in slums how to care for their new facilities; and, more, there was no program to provide for improvement of their economic condition.

WORLD WAR I AND AFTER

During World War I the United States government assumed responsibility for the housing of workers in war industries. Two agencies were created to implement this program: the Housing Division of the Emergency Fleet Corporation and the United States Housing Corporation. The Emergency Fleet Corporation, through loans to shipbuilding companies for the purpose, completed some 9,000 family dwellings and 7,500 single-person accommodations. The United States Housing Corporation planned some 25,000 units in 60 projects, but completed about 6,000 family units in 27 projects, none of which were ready before the war came to an end.

The services of the most talented professionals in architecture and planning were enlisted for the program. Among the large-scale projects were Yorkship Village in Camden, New Jersey, Atlantic Heights in Portsmouth, New Hampshire, Buchman in Chester, Pennsylvania, Union Gar-

Seaside, Bridgeport, Connecticut. *One of the World War I housing developments undertaken by the federal government, Seaside demonstrated the advantages of large-scale planning. It included flats and single-family residences at a density of about seventeen dwellings per acre.*

dens in Wilmington, Delaware, and a number of developments in Bridgeport, Connecticut. It was a statutory requirement that projects built by these war agencies be sold immediately upon the end of the war. To make implementation of this provision easier the projects followed the usual general pattern of subdivision, but differences with previous practice were significant. Both superblocks and common open spaces for recreation were absent, but the layout of residential streets and the design of shopping centers presented a decided contrast with what most people had grown accustomed to in their living environment. Most obviously, all dwelling units were only two rooms in depth, in contrast with the narrow, deep building typical of the usual restricted lot in the ordinary urban subdivision. The planning of these projects exerted a strong influence in the decade following the war.

The Garden Apartment

The architect Andrew J. Thomas, who participated in the war program, was active in the postwar period as well. One of his early projects was a large-scale development built in Long Island City, New York, by the Metropolitan Life Insurance Company. Dwelling units were two rooms deep, with stairways serving two dwellings per floor. The units were grouped in a series of U-shaped buildings that covered about 50 percent of the lot area. The open courts faced the garden. Although they retained the characteristic narrow space between buildings, these buildings were a vast improvement over the small, enclosed light courts of the traditional single lot.

Thomas carried this simple planning technique further in the development of buildings of various forms, still using a basic unit of two and three dwelling units per stair. The essential contrast with previous planning was the relation of the buildings to the streets. Buildings constructed on the basis of the Tenement House Act of 1901 and before were on a single narrow lot and placed at right angles to the street—a narrow front and long depth. This forced all but the dwellings on the street front to face into a small courtyard, lightwell, or narrow rear yard. When the restrictions imposed by the narrow lot were removed, large-scale planning permitted the arrangement of buildings with a broad front and shallow depth. The interior of the lot was opened up and the interior court expanded. The result was dwelling units that faced the street in front and an open court in the rear. Such units were henceforth known as garden apartments.

Henry Wright and Clarence Stein

In 1926 the City Housing Corporation of New York built Sunnyside Gardens on a 10-block site in Long Island. Henry Wright and Clarence Stein,

Metropolitan Project, New York City—*Andrew J. Thomas, architect. This development was one of the earliest large-scale apartment projects in this country. The traditional single lot remains, revealed in the repetition of identical individual buildings repeated on the large site.*

the architects, applied the garden apartment principle in a simple perimeter form surrounding an interior garden.

During this period much speculative building was producing the dreary, monotonous rows of cheap and poorly planned single-family and apartment buildings that still curse so many of our cities. The architects introduced in Sunnyside the row or group house and the two-story apartment—one dwelling above another with separate private entrances. Ground coverage was less than 30 percent of the lot area. They insisted on the potential of the group house to improve the planning both of dwellings and the space about them.

Studies by Henry Wright and Clarence Stein about this time demonstrated the need for a complete analysis of all costs that enter into housing. In practice, planner and architect had been prone to detach their functions from those of management. Wright and Stein made clear that these functions could not be isolated and produce satisfactory housing;

that improvement could not be expected unless plan-analysis was merged with experience in the management and maintenance of housing.

The row or group house was not a revolutionary dwelling type. It was prevalent in all Eastern cities. Baltimore and Philadelphia are famous for their row houses with clean, stone entrance stoops. But the architects went one step further: they demonstrated the superiority of dwellings two rooms in depth rather than the tandem arrangement to which the usual row house had degenerated. They showed how the group house improved land planning, in comparison with detached units and their wasteful and useless side yards. These architects contributed much to the enlightenment in planning that emerged in the 1920s and early 1930s.

Radburn

Inspired by the garden city idea, the City Housing Corporation of New York acquired a vacant site in New Jersey within commuting distance of New York City for the community of Radburn. Henry Wright and Clarence Stein introduced the superblock here, ranging from thirty to fifty acres in size. Through traffic was eliminated in these blocks; traffic

Henry Wright developed his case for the row house with studies like the one for Radburn. The typical block layout with two-story flat buildings facing the street is compared with a revised plan using continuous rows of two-story flat units; the alley is eliminated, garage courts are consolidated at the end of each block, and a park space is gained in the center of the block accessible from all dwellings.

Above is a comparative diagram by Henry Wright illustrating the improvement that a modification in the typical gridiron street and block layout might provide. On the left is the usual street plan, on the right the proposed replanning. With but slight loss of street frontage for subdivision of residential lots (the usual plan has 11,800 lineal feet of streets while the modified plan has 10,720 lineal feet), an interior park is gained and through traffic on all interior streets is eliminated.

streets surrounded rather than traversed the areas. Within them, single-family dwellings were grouped about cul-de-sac (dead-end) roads.

Space was allocated for industry, shopping, and apartments, but green space around the town, typical of the English garden cities, was not incorporated in the plan. The houses were oriented in reverse of the conventional placement on the lot. Kitchens and garages faced the road, living rooms and bedrooms turned toward the garden. Pathways provided uninterrupted pedestrian access to a continuous park strip, which led to large common open spaces within the center of the superblock. Under-passes separated pedestrian walks from traffic roadways. The community earned the name of "The Town of the Motor Age."

Radburn's residential character and street access systems have been a prototype of sound community planning in many nations ever since.

HOUSING AS AN INVESTMENT

Historically, subsidy was a means to encourage the expansion of this country, to push railroads across the land, and to smooth out the peaks and valleys of economic inequalities. It was used whenever necessity dictated. In 1926 it was introduced to housing with passage of the New York Housing Law, which established the State Board of Housing. This act granted the privilege of tax exemption for a twenty-year period to

A Shopping Center
B Apartment Groups
C School
D Park Space

PATH

GARDEN

STREET

Radburn, New Jersey—*Clarence Stein and Henry Wright, planners. The Radburn plan came to be known as the Town of the Motor Age. The cul-de-sac residential streets became service roads rather than trafficways, the house being reversed from the usual plan so that living rooms faced on the rear gardens. Pedestrian paths led to the continuous park space.*

limited-dividend companies engaged in housing within reach of the lower-middle class. The statutory ceiling on rents was $12.50 per room per month in the borough of Manhattan and $11.00 per room elsewhere. Investment in apartment development was encouraged by this legislation. This was significantly higher (proportionately) in today's dollars. Fourteen projects, providing a total of nearly 6,000 dwellings, were undertaken in this program. Among the best known were three cooperative developments of the Amalgamated Clothing Workers, which provided 625 apartments for its members. In addition to the Housing Board projects other limited-dividend and semiphilanthropic developments were undertaken in New York. Phipps Houses, Inc., a veteran housing organization, built 344 apartments in four- and six-story walkup and elevator buildings near Sunnyside Gardens. In 1930 John D. Rockefeller, Jr., built the Paul Laurence Dunbar apartments in Harlem, 513 apartments eventually to be acquired by the tenants. About this time the Julius Rosenwald Foundation built the Michigan Boulevard Gardens on the

Baldwin Hills Village, Los Angeles—*designed by Reginald Johnson, Lewis Wilson, Edwin E. Merrill, and Robert Alexander, architects. An attractive large-scale rental development of the early 1940s, Baldwin Hills Village consists of 627 dwellings in one- and two-story group houses and flats on an outlying eighty-acre tract. The low land price of $2,300 per acre permitted low density—about eight families per acre—and a coverage of only 7.3 percent of the land. An innovative feature of this project is the private patio for about two-thirds of all the dwellings. It will be noticed in the plan that the boulevard along the north (bottom) boundary is separated from the project by a park strip and a service road from which the various garage courts are accessible. Additional parking space is provided by indented parking areas along the service drive and along minor boundary streets. Small playgrounds for children are distributed about the development in addition to the "village green" in the center.*

The aerial view below reveals that the standards of planning and space in Baldwin Hills Village did not influence the later conventional subdivision of land about the periphery.

South Side of Chicago, and the Marshall Field Estate built Marshall Field Apartments on the near north side of the city. In Pittsburgh, Chatham Village, built by the Buhl Foundation, was a two-story group house development planned by Henry Wright.

These projects did not produce speculative profits but were sound investments that served a high social purpose as well. Such a purpose is not nourished by irresponsible interests concerned with quick turnover of capital and unlimited profits, nor does it thrive on exploitation and speculation in land, buildings, and people.

The importance of the period we have been discussing is not the quality of planning as a standard to which we aspire today, but rather as a comparison with the unwholesome planning it replaced and the processes that brought it about. Good planning was demonstrated during the twenties and early thirties to be economical planning. Twenty-five years prior, the typical tenement covered 85 percent of a narrow, deep lot. More than half the rooms either had no light or peered into dingy lightwells. Open space about the dwelling was either the paved traffic street or a shabby refuse-ridden rear yard. The energetic talents of such architects as Ernest Flagg, Grosvenor Atterbury, Andrew Thomas, Henry Wright, Clarence Stein, and Frederick Ackerman served to bring about a vast change in all this. Land coverage was reduced to 50 percent or less, and space was

Chatham Village, Pittsburgh—*Ingham and Boyd, architects. A limited-dividend project built as an investment by the Buhl Foundation, Chatham Village was originally planned to include 300 units within reach of the $2,200–$3,600 per year income group. Henry Wright's plan created a density of about twelve families per acre in two-story group houses. He thus continued to practice and to espouse the cause of the group house on urban land that had not yet reached the increasingly high costs of many other areas.*

planned to enhance the environment and provide room for recreation. Careful planning and better interior arrangement of rooms reduced waste space within buildings and eliminated unnecessary corridors and halls. Attention was given to the appropriate size and use of rooms rather than to the greatest number of people that could be loaded on a given site.

Complete disregard for housing standards and the desire for profit regardless of the exploitation it entailed had produced high density, excessive land coverage, and decidedly bad housing. The theory that these evils were essentially good business was exploded. Good planning was discovered to be an effective instrument to compete with bad planning. When laws were enacted to curb irresponsible building of slums, the road was cleared for good planning with financial benefits as well as the restoration of positive social values.

The period of activity during the twenties and early thirties did not solve our urban housing ills but it did provide a foundation upon which future progress could be continued. Building companies became conscious of the advantages of investment in housing. Large-scale planning opened the opportunity for arranging buildings on land so that all dwellings were well located. As a permanent investment such factors were important, and good planning was becoming good investment. Release from the long, narrow lot permitted greater efficiency in planning, lower land coverage, better dwelling units, more space for light, air, and recreations—and safer investment. Good planning built in permanent value.

Charles F. Lewis, Director of the Buhl Foundation that built and manages Chatham Village in Pittsburgh, said in 1937:

> Capital is frankly challenged by this unusual opportunity for sound and productive use of its funds.
> Essentially this will be an investment and not a speculative use of capital. . . . No less has it been demonstrated by the so-called limited dividend companies, from Boston in 1871 to Pittsburgh in 1934, that limited dividends pay. I refer you specifically to the remarkable success of the City and Suburban Homes Company of New York, founded in 1896 by Mr. R. Fulton Cutting and associates. After years of operation, in 1933 in the midst of the depression, this company could boast assets of nearly $10,000,000, a surplus of more than $1,380,000, and net earnings of from $263,000 to $445,000 per year through four depression years. Its average annual dividend rate, from 1899 to 1939, was 4.65 percent. Or let us take six noncooperative apartment projects built in New York City under the New York State Housing Board. All have been consistent dividend payers in good times and bad. Or let us take, in the city of Washington, the Washington Sanitary Improvement Company, which with assets of nearly $1,500,000 can boast that from 1897 to 1923 it paid an annual dividend of 5 percent, and from then on, straight through the depression, of 6 percent. Or the Washington Sanitary Housing Company which has paid 5 percent per annum without interruption since 1927. While Chatham Village in Pitts-

burgh has not yet published earnings statements, those statements when released will give further evidence of the investment soundness of the large-scale housing enterprise on the limited-dividend basis.[1]

THE GREAT DEPRESSION

On the heels of the building boom during the prosperity decade of the twenties came the Crash of 1929 and the decade of the Depression that followed. Financial credit dried up, building stopped abruptly, and unemployment brought widespread privation to millions of families. As the Depression gained momentum, economic and social chaos followed in its wake. Marginal investments in stocks evaporated into thin air. The flood that had been poured into building investments during the craze of the boom was drained off, and ownership changed hands in rapid succession as the level lowered. Homes on farms and in the cities were foreclosed at an alarming rate. Real estate foreclosures jumped from 68,100 in 1926 to 248,700 in 1932.

The complete state of despair made it imperative for the government to act. President Herbert Hoover called his Conference of Home Building and Home Ownership in 1931. Its analysis revealed many of the problems that beset the nation and laid the groundwork for action that ensued in subsequent years. Some twenty-eight states enacted moratoria on mortgage foreclosures in 1931 and 1932. This device relieved the hysteria but only postponed the solution. The Emergency Relief and Construction Act of 1932 created the Reconstruction Finance Corporation, an agency empowered to loan government funds to bolster the faltering economy.

The tide of national collapse forced the government to assume increasing responsibility for the helpless economy, and, beginning in 1933 with the election of Franklin Delano Roosevelt, the Congress created a series of agencies in rapid succession. These government actions brought into focus a fact that had been almost unwittingly overlooked: the United States had no inventory of the national welfare, the assets and liabilities of a going concern dealing in democratic enterprise. The blessing of abundant natural resources, the accident of favorable geographic location, and the aggressive enterprise of a free people had brought fortune and a position of world leadership to this country. This achievement, accomplished in so brief a history as our own—then less than 200 years—had blinded the people to the corollary of great industrial and financial empires—the social and economic hardships that filter into the lives of many who make up the society. The Great Depression lifted the veil on this scene and disclosed the gap between fortune and stability. It was appar-

---

1. Opportunities for Building Rental Properties, Conference on Local Residential Construction, Chamber of Commerce of United States, Washington, D.C., November 17, 1937.

ent that the country must take stock of its resources in order to measure the future prospects for its enterprise.

The Failure of Planning

The state of the Union was desperate at the beginning of the thirties. At no other time was there a more pressing need for the benefits of city planning than during the years of the Great Depression. Nor could there have been more convincing evidence of its absence. Much lip service had been paid to the cause of planning in previous years, and a small but vocal profession had grown up around this theme. A program for action was imperative, yet cities were unprepared for action when the time was ripe.

There was some encouragement in July 1933 when the Administrator of Public Works appointed the National Planning Board. Prior to this time it was customary for separate offices of the government to collect facts appropriate only for their own domain; it was now provided that these facts should be collated and correlated and thus provide a pattern for appropriate action by the respective agencies. For the first time in the history of this country the advantages of research and analysis of our great natural resources were available for the general welfare.

The National Planning Board became the National Resources Board by executive order of President Roosevelt in June 1934. It was the board's purpose "to prepare and present to the President a program and plan of procedure dealing with the physical, social, governmental, and economic aspects of public policies for the development and use of land, water, and other national resources and such related subjects as may from time to time be referred to the Board by the President." The National Resources Committee succeeded the board in 1935. In July 1939 all these functions were transferred to the National Resources Planning Board, which in its turn was discontinued in 1943. Its functions have since been performed by various committees of Congress.

The work of the National Resources Planning Board and its predecessors was directed at issues of national scope, but they were organized on a regional basis. Probably their most significant activity was to encourage planning at local levels and to offer technical assistance to local planning agencies. Regional, state, and city planning were reviewed and organized, comprehensive reports on the state of natural resources were proposed, plans recommended for appropriate conservation and use, the relative importance of various technological changes and developments were recorded, and valuable data were assembled on urban growth and population.

Despite these gains, considerable resistance to planning was met at the local level. Cities were unprepared when the Depression struck, the few exceptions emphasizing the general absence of plans. Faced with an immediate opportunity to establish permanent improvements in their environment, there was little evidence that the people had concerned themselves with the question of their future urban development.

The issues of emergency planning versus sound planning were confused. By the time cities had become aware of their plight, the economic cost of blight, and the social hazard of slums, there was no time to plan. That would have to wait until the Depression had spent itself and prosperity had returned.

Building and maintaining the city constitutes a complex and a vital problem that requires considerable careful planning. The housing program during the Depression demonstrated the tragic results of its absence. Subdivisions sprawled across the city without a plan for the integration of future urban land use. Such a plan would have become an effective means for improvement of the community welfare. Instead, the public housing program was too frequently interpreted as an opportunity to get rid of some isolated eyesore or festering slum that pricked the civic pride.

Had civic leadership glanced back on the history of city development it would have been abundantly clear that planning can never wait. The course of human affairs marches steadily on, and the direction of its course is determined by the degree of planning that precedes it. When goals are set they can be reached; when they are absent, the urban community drifts like a ship without a compass. Sadly, the goals have not yet been considered, and our cities are still adrift.

Greenbelt Towns

The government did succeed, if moderately, with one of its plans. Beginning in 1935, the Resettlement Administration planned four greenbelt towns. These satellite communities near large cities were inspired by Howard's Garden City idea, but they were not planned as self-contained towns; they were more like dormitory villages, sources of employment for the residents being in the nearby cities. Each was surrounded by a belt of permanent open space, part of which could be farmed or gardened. A full complement of community facilities was included in each town—shopping, schools, and recreation space. Three of these towns were actually built: Greenbelt, Maryland, Greenhills, Ohio, and Greendale, Wisconsin. The fourth, Greenbrook, New Jersey, was not built due to legal entanglements.

Greenbelt, Maryland, a development on a 2,100-acre site about 25 minutes' drive from Washington, D.C., includes 712 dwellings in group houses and 288 in apartments, a total of 1,000 units occupying an area of 250 acres. There are 500 garages. The 16-room elementary school is also used as a community center. The shopping center includes space for a post office, food stores, a drugstore, a dentist's and a doctor's office, a 600-seat theater, and such services as shoe repair, laundry, tailor, barber, and beauty shops. There are a bus terminal, a garage and repair shop, a fire station, and a gas station. The recreation facilities include an athletic field, picnic grounds, and an artificial lake. The superblock is used, each block containing about 120 dwellings with interior play areas. Underpasses provide continuous pedestrian circulation without the need to cross main roads. The commercial and community center, in the approximate center of the plan, reduces to a minimum the walking distance from all dwellings.

1	Water Tower	3	Picnic Center and Lake	6	Rural Homesteads
2	Disposal Plant and In- cinerator	4	Community Center	7	Allotment Gardens
		5	Store Group		

Greenbelt, Maryland.

THE REAL CITY

Almost every individual in the city has a home. Some may be rooms in a boardinghouse or a hotel, others fine houses on large estates. Some are slums. Whether the home is a hovel or a mansion, every person should have one. Dwellings occupy nearly three-quarters of the urban area. The economic equation by which people acquire and maintain a place to live measures the social and physical health of a community. The economics of housing is the base upon which cities rest. It is the foundation on which the social superstructure is built.

If we want to see the real city, we do not confine our view to the great skyscrapers, the shopping promenade, or the park and boulevard. To see the city, we look at the dwellings of the people. We see how people live, their streets of homes, the environment in which they raise their families, the children who will be the fellow-countrymen and neighbors of our children and generations hence.

It is this view that gives us direction toward the city of the future. When we comprehend this aspect of the city, we can more accurately guide the tools with which we shape the urban environment.

CHAPTER 16

MODERN TRENDS II: WORLD WAR II AND AFTER

A NEW ERA BEGINS

Another war came, and a stroke of irony marked the affairs of human conduct. Planning assumed proportions never before conceived in history. With destruction of civilization a grim prospect, the scale of planning was gargantuan, staggering the imagination even now in retrospect. However, all this was planning based on essentially military needs and purposes.

With the ominous spread of Nazi domination in Central Europe and the threat of another world war, in June 1940 Congress enacted the National Defense Bill. Industry turned its attention to the production of war materials, and the Lanham Act authorized funds for housing defense-plant workers. Numerous government agencies entered the housing program. In July 1940, the Office of Housing Coordinator was established to determine and identify areas of acute shortage, and to allocate federal funds to the various agencies.

New construction by FHA-insured private enterprise was stepped up, HOLC assisted the conversion of existing facilities, the low-rent program under USHA was stopped, and 100 percent loans were extended to local housing authorities to build defense housing. The Public Buildings Administration, Defense Homes Corporation, and Maritime Commission

Buckingham, Virginia. *One of the earliest large-scale rental developments undertaken in the FHA program, Buckingham is located just outside Washington, D.C., for white-collar workers in the nation's crowded capital. Designed by Henry Wright, Allen Kamstra, and Albert Lueders, it was planned for 2,000 units on a 100-acre site. The first stage (shown in detail) comprised 622 dwellings on 30 acres. The land cost was twenty-five cents per square foot and permitted low density—about twenty families per acre—with a building coverage of about 20 percent of the land area. Approximately 13 percent of the area is in streets. Dwellings are two-story group houses and flats.*

undertook construction of large-scale permanent government housing, and the Federal Works Agency launched a large program of prefabricated temporary dwellings.

With the attack on Pearl Harbor on December 7, 1941, all the energy of the nation was directed to the successful prosecution of the war. Peacetime and defense housing were supplanted by a vast program of war housing, and huge plants were constructed to build ships, planes, and armaments. It has been estimated that migration of industrial workers to war jobs created a need for the housing of some 9,000,000 families.

In February 1942, all federal housing agencies were consolidated in the National Housing Agency. The National Housing Act was amended to include Title VI, which provided FHA insurance for 90 percent loans amortized over 25 years, for housing built by operative builders for sale or rent to war workers. The need to conserve materials was critical. The floor area of dwellings and the materials used were rigidly restricted. The Lanham Act was amended to provide for the construction of temporary dwellings by the federal government.

More than 800,000 new dwellings were built and about 200,000 existing units converted by private enterprise, for a total estimated cost of

$4 billion. Nearly 550,000 family dwellings and 170,000 dormitory units were built, and 50,000 existing structures converted into family dwellings through the direct operations of the federal government. There were, in addition, about 80,000 stopgap shelters provided in the form of trailers to permit mobility as shifting needs dictated. Building costs, without the conversion of existing units, was some $2,300,000,000.

War work was distributed in all parts of the country, but the most pressing need was in large centers for the tremendous new industrial plants. Individual projects of 4,000 units were built in such places as Willow Run near Detroit; Norfolk, Virginia; Vancouver, Washington; and San Diego and San Francisco, California. The largest single operation was 10,000 dwellings for the Kaiser shipyards at Portland, Oregon.

The influx of great numbers of workers and their families strained every urban service. Housing was not complete without new streets, utilities, parks and playgrounds, theaters, shops and markets, and restaurants. Whole new communities were created in a few months, and war production was sustained.

The war was won. The goal had been clear—the survival of freedom. Planning had guided the production and distribution of goods, materials, food, weapons, and manpower. It was necessary and well done.

Thus ended another paradox in the course of human events. While planning for military purposes was winning a great campaign, planning for the peace to come was abandoned. The National Resources Planning Board died during the conflict, and the very planning process with which our institutions were saved in war was denounced as an enemy of freedom. We have need to learn from yesterday so as to prepare today for a better tomorrow.

RECENT FEDERAL HOUSING PROGRAMS

Some of the most interesting of the federal programs of recent years contained features worth noting. They can be seen as a belated response to conditions that began to be recognized after the war and, rather than bringing about planning, slowly worsened. In the 1980s, even these programs fell largely inactive with the advent of the Reagan administration and its "New Federalism." It is possible that they may in the future become reactivated as conditions and political climate dictate.

Housing and Community Development Act of 1977

Purpose. This act provided for the alleviation of physical and economic distress in areas with population outmigration or a stagnating or declining tax base, through the stimulation of private investment and community revitalization. The money had to be spent on programs that would give maximum benefits to low- or moderate-income families or aid in the prevention or elimination of blight.

The act extended the Community Development Block Grant Program (created by the Housing and Community Development Act of 1974) to assist severely distressed cities and urban counties through neighborhood reclamation. Twenty-five percent of the funds available for action grants was designated for cities under 50,000 population that were not central cities of a standard metropolitan area.

One primary goal of the act was to provide 400,000 units of housing for low- and moderate-income persons in fiscal 1978, including 350,000 new and rehabilitated units under Section 8 of the rental subsidy program and 20,000 units under the state housing finance agencies. The remaining 30,000 units were to be conventional housing. Thirty-five million dollars was set aside for public housing modernization. These funds were targeted primarily for capital projects that would promote energy conservation and correct health and safety code violations. Six hundred and sixty-five million dollars was for public housing operating subsidies. About $13 million of this would defray the exceptionally high utility costs incurred in the winter of 1977.

The community development block grant replaced a consolidation of the previously existing narrow categorical grant programs for aid to urban areas (e.g., open space, water and sewer, beautification, and model cities programs). One hundred million dollars was appropriated for each of the three years (1978, 1979, 1980) for phasing out programs begun under the old categorical grant programs.

Cities could choose how the amount of funds they received under the community development block grant program would be determined: under the old formula or a new one. The old formula weighed population twice, while amount of housing, overcrowding, and poverty were counted once. It favored Western and Southern regions that had growing populations. The new (1977) formula counted age of housing 2.5 times, poverty 1.5 times, and growth lag once. Age of housing refers to pre-1940 housing stock, and growth lag is defined as the extent to which a locality has fallen below the average population growth rate of all metropolitan cities; this formula most benefited older cities, many of which are in the Northwest and Midwest.

Application Requirements. Communities were required to include in their application for block grants a summary of housing as well as community development needs, and a program to improve conditions for low- and moderate-income persons to remain in or return to their community. (The HUD secretary was allowed to waive some application requirements for some small communities where the application did not involve a comprehensive community development program.) Citizen participation was required in the formulation of the block grant proposals.

Section 8. Section 8 is the nation's principal housing program. It provides for government rent subsidies to low-income persons. Eligibility is limited to families with incomes up to 80 percent of the median income of a particular area. The law also requires that at least 30 percent of the families have incomes not exceeding 50 percent of an area's median family income. Participating families are required to contribute not less than 15 percent nor more than 25 percent of their total income to rent, which is not to exceed by more than 10 percent the fair market rent as established by HUD. The government subsidizes the difference between the family's required rental share and the actual rental price.

HUD enters into a forty-year contract with public housing agencies or a thirty-year contract with private developers who provide newly constructed, rehabilitated, or adequate existing housing. Public housing agencies are required to establish 1) tenant selection, 2) procedures for prompt payment of rents and evictions for nonpayment, 3) effective tenant-management relations to ensure safety and adequate project maintenance, and 4) viable home-ownership opportunities.

Section 312 provides 3 percent loans for rehabilitation of residential and business properties to residents of areas designated in an area's community block grant application. There were no new applications for 1978 because $70 million was available in carryover funds. (This program supplements and supports block grant housing rehabilitation efforts.)

Miscellaneous Relevant Items Under Title II. The ceiling on FHA mortgage insurance for mobile homes was increased to $15,000 from $12,500. The authorization for the urban homesteading demonstration program for fiscal 1978 was increased to $15 million from $5 million. The maximum loan or advance credit for home improvements insurable under the Title I property improvements and mobile home loan insurance program was increased to $15,000 from $10,000.

Title I Amendment. The HUD secretary was authorized to make a lump sum payment of a community's grant allotment to allow the community to establish a revolving loan fund at a private financial institution.

The following private housing programs are included in this title because there was evidence that such housing programs could be very successfully implemented in smaller cities.

Neighborhood Housing Services Program. Organizing citizens, city government, and private lenders in a team effort for neighborhood preservation, the Neighborhood Housing Services program offered a revolving loan fund for home improvements in sound but deteriorating neighborhoods. The Urban Reinvestment Task Force, a partnership between the Federal Home Loan Bank Board and the Department of Housing and Urban Development, provided technical assistance to local governments interested in establishing an NHS. Once the program was operational the task force involvement ceased except when additional aid was requested.

Systematic code enforcement programs were used in most NHS programs. Capital improvements of code enforcement were funded by the city. NHS operating costs were funded entirely through local sources and local contributions supplied much of the high risk fund. A local commitment of $25,000 was required from financial institutions to fund the development process.

Neighborhood residents controlled the program. Financial institutions participated in order to protect existing investments in the neighborhood, to lessen redlining allegations, and to increase deposits. Thus, because of a strong city and neighborhood commitment to the area, they perceived less of a risk in investing in it. Local government participated because the program provided the opportunity to leverage public investment in older neighborhoods by stimulating private lending in these areas.

Control was vested in a board of directors of a private, nonprofit corporation that consisted primarily of citizens and financial institutions. Governmental representation was usually limited to one member from the local city government.

Each NHS office was staffed by three persons: a director, an associate director, and a clerical-administrative assistant. Each program developed its own priorities and policies. Although the task force could provide technical assistance in helping to establish operating procedures, important decisions that affected the loan fund were made by the NHS board.

Section 235—Mortgage Subsidy. This program was designed to provide low- and moderate-income families financial assistance in achieving home ownership. The assistance was provided in the form of monthly payments made by the federal government to the mortgagee, whose interest was reduced to as low as 5 percent. The homeowner was required to contribute at least 20 percent of his adjusted gross monthly income to the monthly mortgage payment. To be eligible for assistance payments, a family had to have an adjusted family income that did not exceed 100 percent of the median income for an area, with appropriate adjustments for smaller or larger families.

Section 8-515—Renter Subsidy. This program was administered by the Farmers Home Administration. It provided permanent financing at market or subsidized interest rates to eligible borrowers for building low and moderate income multifamily housing in nonmetropolitan areas. Sponsors could be a public or private entity that met certain criteria. The 515 program was eventually coupled with the Department of Housing and

Urban Development's Section 8 program to obtain greater subsidies for Section 515 tenants. Under the Section 8 program, tenants paid no more than 25 percent of family income toward rent (in special cases, 15 percent). The remainder of the rent was paid through a housing assistance payment by HUD or local Public Housing Agency.

Public Housing. This program was designed to help public agencies provide decent, safe, and sanitary housing for low-income families at affordable rents. HUD provided financial and technical assistance to local housing authorities to help them plan, build, and operate low-rent public housing projects. Federal annual contributions covered the debt service on local authority bonds sold to pay for the development or acquisition of public housing. HUD also granted preliminary loans to the local authority for planning and temporary loans for building low-rent housing.

This program was initially intended to eliminate the slums and blighted areas of urban communities. Displacing the residents of these unfortunate areas became most difficult as there were no facilities for rehousing them at rents they could afford. It then became necessary to build public housing on open land. This angered the residents of nearby homes, and protests were launched against the entire program, ultimately reducing the efforts and eliminating many of the proposed projects such as the ones at Chaves Ravine and Rose Hills in Los Angeles, California, where 5,000 units were not constructed after land was acquired and plans prepared.

PLANNING FOR THE ELDERLY[1]

One of the most pressing problems has always been housing for the elderly. This is a worldwide problem, and many nations have taken steps to meet the need. Both public and private solutions have been suggested.

The requirements of the elderly vary greatly. Some elderly are ambulatory while others are infirm, and a wide range exists in between. Special care may be required in addition to a decent living environment.

The ambulatory aged have numerous resources at their disposal. Many have grown children with whom they could live, but often age and other differences make it impossible for the two generations to live together harmoniously. Some elderly have joined large retirement communities. These serve a limited age group, mostly persons over fifty who have relatively large financial resources.

The housing of healthy ambulatory persons constitutes today's main challenge in planning for the elderly. The infirm in general are confined to institutional care facilities of one type or another. But decent housing

---

1. Based in part on an unpublished paper by Sylvia Stern, UCLA, 1978.

for the ever-increasing number of persons who have contributed to the social and economic well-being of their communities during most of their lives has yet to be accomplished. Our civilization may well be judged by how sympathetically we respond to this segment of the population.

Until the early part of the twentieth century most of the countries of the world relegated the indigent aged to "poor farms." There was no differentiation of their problems from those of the poor. Certainly, little money was spent on resolving the problems of the aged.

The patterns and problems of the aged are similar throughout the industrialized world. The breakup of families for various reasons, whether in rural or urban areas, has left the elderly without any anchor. With the advent of social security, retirement pensions, and welfare programs, families feel even less responsibility for their elders. The elders share this attitude, not wanting to be a burden on their children, opting as far as possible to maintain their independence.

Only after 1920 did there begin to be a recognition of the special needs of the elderly. Since World War II particularly there has been a growing concern for their needs, not the least aspect of which has involved their housing. There is currently, in almost all of the nations of the world, an acceptance of some responsibility of ensuring the welfare of the aging population, especially for that portion of the population that cannot afford decent housing. During the past thirty years national governments have passed considerable legislation on behalf of the housing needs of poor elderly persons.

The United States

In 1950 the first National Conference on Aging was held in Washington, D.C., and the problems of the elderly began to assume national importance. In 1961 President Dwight D. Eisenhower called for another national conference on the subject. Over 2,500 delegates met to define the circumstances, needs, and opportunities of elderly citizens and to find ways to improve their living conditions. The most important conclusion of the 1961 conference will seem obvious: that the problems of housing for the aged are everybody's problem.

In 1976, President Gerald Ford asked Congress to join him in improving government programs servicing the elderly. There was no doubt that the over 11 percent of the total population that constituted the elderly then needed assistance and that the greatest part of the problem was economic. In 1977, six out of ten older Americans had incomes near or below the poverty level. More than 20 percent lived in substandard housing. These same persons were and are faced with inflation and fixed incomes that cannot adjust to the increases in the cost of living.

It seems that the American fascination with bigness runs over into the provision of housing for the elderly. Public or private, the ensemble must be large to be "efficient," even though this so-called efficiency often translates into endless mediocrity. Thus the current public housing facilities for the elderly in the United States, with some exceptions, are in high-rise buildings. These complexes are large enough to make the cost of operating them manageable. The clients are normally persons of the same age bracket and level of health.

Current Housing Programs. The Older Americans Act of 1965 formed the basis of all future housing legislation for the elderly. It established that all older people are entitled to suitable housing independently selected, designed, and located in accordance with their special needs, "and available at costs they can afford."

Section 8 of the Housing and Community Development Act of 1974 discussed earlier offered aid to the elderly in its Section 202 in the form of the Senior Citizen Direct Housing Loan. It provided long-term direct federal construction and permanent mortgage loans at below-market interest rates for the construction or substantial rehabilitation of rental housing for the elderly and handicapped. Section 8 is one of the current programs being funded by HUD.

Foster Homes for the Elderly. A specialized service is provided by the Foster Home Program in Bucks County, Pennsylvania.[2] The program is designed for people over sixty who do not need the skilled care of a nursing home but who cannot or should not live alone. It was begun in 1961 by Peggy O'Neill, who developed the program after trying to cope with the problems of a long waiting list at an overcrowded county home for the aged. Many of those in the home, needing only minimal care and supervision, had been institutionalized unnecessarily.

The Foster Home Program started with a grant from the Pennsylvania Department of Labor and Industry. Originally conceived as a way to provide housing for the elderly in a family setting, the program has become an interim care arrangement as much as a housing arrangement.

Unlike house-sharing programs, the Bucks County program is supported by casework services and backup facilities, which are the primary reasons for its success. Caseworkers help their elderly clients with financial matters, make sure they receive any necessary medical and psychiatric attention, and provide ongoing counseling. Foster home residents who need skilled care and are financially eligible have priority for admission to the county nursing home.

The Bucks County program benefits not only the elderly but also the

---

2. Denise P. Frank and Michael J. Frank, *Planning,* The American Society of Planning Officials, 1978, p. 340.

community at large and foster care providers as well. The elderly benefit because they remain in the community rather than being institutionalized and segregated. Followup contact by caseworkers assures that their arrangements are suitable; a different home is usually found within two weeks if irreconcilable conflicts arise or if the elderly person is being given improper care.

Foster home providers benefit, too. Often these individuals are themselves retired or elderly, perhaps "empty-nesters" who provide adult foster care rather than enter the labor market. In addition to the companionship their role provides them, they receive supplemental income that can help with home maintenance costs and rising taxes. The fact that the providers know that they are not responsible for all their residents' needs helps make the program work. Their contract requires that they provide only room, board, laundry, and basic supervision.

Last, the Foster Home Program has advantages for the community and the agency that provides the care. The county nursing home is free to serve the elderly who genuinely need skilled care. Furthermore, it is much less expensive to shelter a person in a foster home than in a nursing home.

The International Scene [3]

The European experience provides much that is relevant to the United States.

Consumer housing subsidies in the form of housing allowances, rent rebates, and rent differentials have been an integral part of the European solution. They deal directly with the special hardships of the elderly poor by providing accommodation for the elderly not only through new construction, which necessarily is limited, but also by using existing housing.

Housing production subsidies, amounting to roughly two-thirds of total West European housing subsidies, constitute the main financial thrust of government policy. Some form of production subsidy or incentive is considered essential as long as critical housing shortages exist in general. These subsidies also ensure the construction of an adequate supply of cluster housing, designed specifically for the elderly, that is integrated with neighborhoods with a normal cross-section of population. Effective land use planning on the part of the local government has been a further important ingredient in the production approach.

Many areas in Europe of warm climate and beautiful environment have become popular retirement areas, such as the Côt d'Azur. In towns like Nice more than a quarter of the population is of pensionable age. In

---

3. Sylvia Stern, Ibid.

Portugal, Spain, Malta, and Cyprus there are flourishing residential developments aimed specifically at attracting retirees from northern Europe. This multinational migration, which mainly attracts people who have lived most of their lives in cities, has taken similar forms wherever it has emerged despite the cultural differences of the retired individuals. Indications are that the migration will continue and grow for years; the areas involved must prepare themselves for coping with the special health and social needs resulting from the increasing presence of a population no longer young.

Canada. Since 1946 an estimated 90 percent of all new housing produced specifically for Canada's elderly has been built with the assistance provided by the government's National Housing Act.

The majority of these accommodations have been provided in just the past twenty years, reflecting vastly increased allocations of federal funds for housing, and new legislative incentives to stimulate the sponsorship of developments to serve elderly persons and low-income families.

Great Britain. In England the local authority has a statutory duty to review the housing needs of its area from time to time and to provide housing when it is not being provided by private enterprise. Local councils initiate new ideas about housing and often press the Minister of Housing for supporting legislation. For example, the city of Birmingham promoted a private act of Parliament to obtain powers to pay rent allowances to private tenants long before this idea became part of national policy.

In England there are no income limits on admission to public housing projects, thus there are no means tests that can force a tenant to leave subsequently. The words "the working classes" were deleted from the titles and texts of all housing statutes in 1949. The result is that the tenants of the public housing stock represent a much wider spectrum of the population than is the case in the United States.

America can learn some lessons by example from the British. One may be found at Roehampton, a housing estate within the county of London but outside of the central city. The housing is located within the larger estate in small groups of one-story row houses. There are about 20 units for the elderly in each of the complexes. They are situated in a garden environment, close to an elementary school and the area's shopping facilities. The residents enjoy the friendships that can only be established in small groups and are revivified by the variety of the neighborhood that surrounds them.

Near enough to an elementary school to be aware of the activity of children, but not so close as to be disturbed by them, the residents are thus close enough, yet far away enough from activity. They can visit others, and whenever they wish they can return to the quiet of their

Roehampton Estates, London. *Housing for the elderly is in the foreground.*

homes. They find jobs as babysitters so that they can continue to feel they are useful human beings; the conveniently located stores allow them to shop for themselves and give them as well a place for social contact. All of these aspects contribute to a pleasant and fruitful life.

France. In 1971, the French government set up housing allowances for those over sixty-five, or those over sixty unable to work. The purpose was to reduce the rent of a principal home to a level compatible with income. This housing allowance takes the place of the former rental allowance that was subject to the rules of welfare aid. Its purpose was to allow the elderly to remain as long as possible in an independent dwelling adapted to their needs.

Sweden. The Swedish government has an outstanding record, far ahead of other nations, in caring for its elderly. The problem was recognized early and remedies attempted in conjunction with other social problems. Sweden has the most extensively organized social service programs of any of the Scandinavian countries. The stated goal is to permit each person handicapped by age or illness to improve within the limits of his or her capacity in order to lead as independent a life as possible.

Social services account for 40 percent of Sweden's national budget. Total welfare expenditure amounts to about 20 percent of the country's national income. This is a little above the proportion in other Scandinavian countries and considerably higher than in the United States. Roughly 85 percent of the central government's and 75 percent of the local governments' expenditures for social benefits are distributed without a means test.[4]

The Swedes are acutely aware of and responsive to the developing needs of their growing aged population. The national government provides financial support. A person reaching sixty-five is entitled to an old-age pension, a basic benefit paid to all persons. The sum is index-adjusted and rises with the general cost of living. Approximately half of all pensioners receive supplementary housing allowances in addition.

The support given by local authorities to the elderly is wide ranging. Apart from institutional care and old-age centers, where pensioners live in a hotel environment and enjoy various facilities for recreation and occupation, there is an extensive home care system, upon which the Swedes place great emphasis. Pensioners live in their own homes or apartments until they can no longer care for themselves or their quarters. The country has about 10,000 specially trained workers, 3,400 of whom are on the government's payroll, assisting with services that include visiting and nursing in the home and providing recreational and other activities arranged by the municipality or by private organizations. In 1967 a home nursing allowance was introduced for those requiring special attention and care who would otherwise be entitled to institutional care. The same year successful experiments were begun with occupational therapy in the home. Home helpers—called Samaritans—shop and do other household jobs and try to help break through their patients' sense of loneliness and isolation.

There are numerous housing projects for the elderly, many of which are outstanding in design and amenities offered. The vast majority of housing is currently constructed by nonprofit building companies, a trend that developed after World War II in all Scandinavian countries. The Swedish National Housing Board finances 90 percent of all housing construction. It provides financial incentives to nonprofit groups, which are eligible for 100 percent loans as opposed to 85 percent loans for private companies.

People's Republic of China.   The treatment of the elderly in the People's Republic of China follows traditional lines. The elderly are, in the words of one Chinese guide, "our treasures." They live with and are part of the extended family. Since space in the home is so limited (currently at about twenty-two square feet per person) the use of space must be carefully planned. All in the family work, so the elders become the managers of the household and the guardians of the very young children, and the linkage that holds the home together.

---

4. John McRae, "Elderly in the Environment—Northern Europe," University of Florida, Gainesville, 1975.

The Elderly in Rental Apartments

During the 1980s the plight of the elderly residing in apartments significantly worsened. Property owners, faced with higher taxes, mounting maintenance costs, and other economic problems, raised rents to meet their needs. Many rent increases were unreasonable, however. The residents were either on fixed incomes—social security or retirement pensions—which limited their ability to meet the inflated conditions. As the housing market became tighter and the options of the residents fewer, the proportion of their income allocated to rent became excessive to the point that it played havoc with diet and other basic needs. Though there were tenant strikes, there were more often dispossessions: the elderly were evicted from the shelter that they could no longer pay for.

As a result, some communities have restricted the conversion of existing buildings, without limiting the construction of new condominiums. The property owners on occasion have assisted residents in obtaining alternative dwellings; municipal housing agencies also have participated in the relocation process. Once moved, however, the elderly find themselves in unfamiliar environments, with little or no ability to adjust to the changed condition of their lives and to the often less desirable housing that their meager income can afford.

Other than units available to the more affluent, few if any of the housing accommodations for the ambulatory elderly were actually designed for their life requirements. In fact, the majority of available accommodations were constructed years ago as general family units. These are old and in many cases too large for the present occupant or occupants, thus wasteful as well. The facilities and amenities available are not designed to meet the needs of the elderly, are often located too far from the dwelling and, without reasonable means of transportation, too difficult for the residents to utilize conveniently.

THE HIGH-RISE "SOLUTION"

The type of building to be developed for housing varies with economic and physical circumstances, with conditions in the urban areas, and the attitude that obtains in each situation. In America, where early pioneers developed the low-intensity towns, land being almost free for the taking, there developed the notion of the single-family detached home as the dream castle of each and every family. Development within the larger urban centers, like New York, Chicago, Baltimore, and Philadelphia, characteristically concentrated high density close to the core where activities were greatest. Just outside of these burgeoning core areas, densities tended to fall off to the level seemingly desired by the aspirants of greater living space. One has but to cross the Hudson River or head north along

the freeways to find low-density communities where the more affluent
find refuge. The really wealthy formed their own compounds in places
named Bel Air, Shaker Heights, Newport, Beverly Hills, and the like,
where exclusiveness and prestige were the hallmarks of status. No
congestion here.

In the world at large, the pattern of congestion in the older portions
can be observed. British cities are built up with great densities, and they
are matched or exceeded by such places as Shanghai, Calcutta, Hong
Kong, Tokyo, or Manhattan Island, São Paolo, and Paris. Other cities
with smaller populations of approximately one million display the same
form and structure. High-rise buildings with little or no open space are

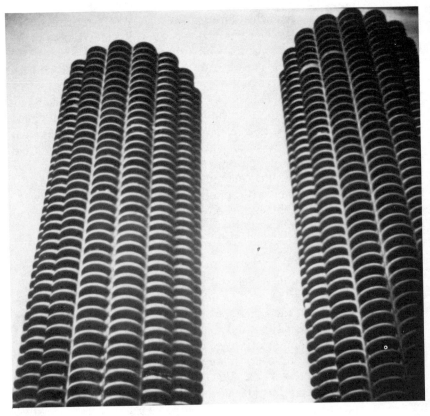

High-rise Marina Towers, Chicago. *High-rise buildings for both residential and commercial uses, where land is scarce and costs are astronomical.*

true for all of them, as are overcrowded streets filled with people and vehicles of all types.

When portions of the older cities have been reconstructed because of war, natural disasters, or reaction against unpleasant and unhealthy conditions prevailing, the forms are more reasonable. However, while providing for some open spaces, the buildings go skyward in order not to reduce the overall densities. The high-rise prevails.

HIGH-RISE BUILDINGS

In general, high-rise residential structure implies more than three stories but more often not fewer than five when economics makes elevators feasible. In practice, however, high-rise has usually meant buildings ranging from ten to fifty stories in height.

Samuel Hurst, former Dean of the School of Architecture at the University of Southern California, stated that high-rise buildings were poor places for family living, especially if the family had small children or animals of any kind. In the Caracas area of Venezuela, public housing was provided in high-rise buildings in the port city of La Guira and residents of the hillside slums were moved into them. After a short period of time the buildings appeared ready for replacement, and the residents moved out and back to the hillsides where they had space, could raise chickens, pigs, and flowers in their small personal gardens. The situation in St. Louis, where the high-rise public housing remained largely uninhabited and was finally physically destroyed, is a classic example of the difficulty people have with the barren sterility of high-rise buildings when they are used to living in personalized if poor housing in close-knit communities.

There is no question but that the more affluent, seeking a maximum of security, find high-rise buildings desirable places to live. Several new buildings along Wilshire Boulevard in the Westwood section of Los Angeles advertised high-rise units, condominiums, for sale in the $11 to $15 million range, and they were being purchased.

RENT CONTROLS AND CONDOMINIUMS

One of the most controversial items in the housing field in all parts of America during the late 1970s and 1980s involved apartment rent controls. Faced with inflation and high interest rates, apartment owners in some cases raised rents to an unconscionable degree. In newer apartments occupied by the more affluent, the raises were absorbed as incomes increased. For the lower middle class and the poor, however, the impact was very different. Those with limited incomes could not meet the increases without being adversely affected in terms of diet and other essentials of survival. Protests began, causing responses that found their way into the halls of city and county governments. One community after another adopted rent control laws, fixing the percentage amount that rents could be raised during a specific period (generally related to the cost of living index). In most cases, however, the vacating of an apartment freed the owner to rent at any rate that appeared appropriate.

The concept of owner-occupied condominium apartments offered the owners of existing apartments a means to be freed from the restraints of rent control. They turned rental units into condominiums and gave tenants the choice of either purchasing the units or vacating them.

The impact of this device on the less economically fortunate, disproportionately the elderly, was devastating. Purchase prices and costs of maintenance went far beyond their limited means. Once again there was pressure on government bodies to adopt regulations that would protect the tenants either from being gouged or being forced to occupy undesirable accommodations.

A true housing crisis was on. New laws were required for dealing with evictions. Families began to double up if at all possible, providing shelter for parents in the homes of children, when and if space was available and personal problems of the different age groups could be overcome.

The crisis was not felt only with apartment space. Many people had purchased mobile homes, locating them on rented small lot-sized spaces or in mobile home parks. But in the 1980s rents for mobile home spaces were, like their apartment counterparts, increased to the point where many occupants could not meet them. Most communities were reluctant to pass any kind of rent-control laws, and few if any did anything other than listen to the complaints of mobile-home occupants.

AFFORDABLE HOUSING

The population of the world is growing with each passing year. It could be assumed that the need for additional housing would be a matter of great concern internationally. As children grow up and greater numbers of families are formed, it might be assumed that the need for additional dwelling units would manifest itself in a building boom in most of the world. However, neither of these is absolutely the case. The gap between the growing need and the evolution of an effective demand constitutes a major gap in the housing market. Effective demand can be defined as the "desire for housing plus the ability to pay for it." With the cost of housing ever increasing in conjunction with economic dislocation of great numbers of families, the demand cannot become effective and the building of housing units falls short of need by a wide margin. Recent statistics indicate that only one-quarter of American households can afford new, single-family housing. A decade ago, almost half the households could.

In the United States, the years leading into the 1980s saw all sorts of experiments. Most attempted to involve the private sector more than before, thus leading away from public housing and into the realm of subsidies to encourage private building for low- and middle-income groups.

HUD's position in the field of housing was weakened in the late 1970s. In the 1980s, for all practical purposes it was virtually eliminated through the efforts of the Reagan administration and the "New Federalism" programs that were espoused. This was described and discussed earlier in the chapter. As with all new programs, new language came into the picture; in this case it was "affordable housing." The application of the term to the housing market was not uniform, since the definition of "affordable" was necessarily vague.

"Affordable housing" was intended to imply housing within the economic reach of the lower-middle income group. The cost for housing in this category runs from 50 to 75 thousand dollars; even in the inflated economy of the 1970s–1980s this priced the units out of many would-be home purchasers' reach, especially with mortgage interest running between 13 and 20 percent. Added to this is the concept of the "variable interest rate" mortgage, which is periodically reviewed for potential increase or decrease in interest. Though the initial rate may be attractively low—lower than the fixed-rate mortgage—home buyers are thus faced with the possibility that the interest rate will change upward and in the worst-case scenario possibly cause them to lose their homes through default.

The housing industry has developed various devices to bring down costs. These include the lowering of standards of all types, extending from the reduction in lot sizes, the elimination of yards, smaller rooms, lower ceilings—these and other practices that ultimately will lead to overcrowding, congestion, conflicts, and potentially the disruption of family life.

It begins to appear that new ideas for providing housing for the many thousands of families with modest incomes will emerge only from a greater degree of local participation, if and when local economic conditions permit. The so-called New Federalism did cut back on social programs, but it provides block grants that may be helpful in building and planning housing, especially in those communities where there is a reasonable concern for the welfare of the residents. The Reagan administration is proposing elimination of block grants as part of their 1985–86 budget.

Local Housing Financing

In the meantime, with federal assistance either limited or unavailable, the states and local communities have been authorized to issue tax-free municipal bonds as a means of securing housing for low- and middle-income families. Funds have also been provided for urban renewal through the issuance of Tax Increment bonds, the amortization coming from both income and property value appreciation.

PART 3

THE PLANNING PROCESS

If we could first know where we are,
and whither we are tending, we
could better judge what to do,
and how to do it.
Abraham Lincoln

CHAPTER 17

THE BASIS OF PLANNING

URBAN ANARCHY

The Greek philosopher Heraclitus once said that the difficulty confronting human society was to combine that degree of liberty without which law is tyranny, with that degree of law without which liberty becomes license. The democracy of Athens, the Magna Carta in England, and the Constitution of the United States were wrought essentially from that same precept. Our society is organized on the basis of a group of laws established to guide the people in their conduct. The overriding purpose is to guarantee and protect liberty and justice for all.

Inspired by this freedom the people of America created a vast domain of commercial and industrial enterprise. And they built great cities.

Today we see these cities scarred by congestion and decay, speculation and ugliness. We see the science and invention of our remarkable age snarled in the tangle of the urban network. At best our cities are mediocre. That mediocrity is a travesty of the productive genius and creative energy of America.

It is not the desire of the people that their cities should be so built. Rather it is their ambition to create fine cities; otherwise the forward strides that have been taken would not even have been attempted. It is the essence of democracy that the people shall be masters of their destiny, that their behavior shall be guided by the precepts of law and order. Yet our cities suffer disorder and confusion as though born of anarchy. The most frantic antidotes of regulation appear inept and futile. The reasons for this state of urban affairs may be apparent upon examination.

Who are the city builders? They are the multitude of city people who invest in urban property and improvements. All the people participate. Some share by their investments of capital in physical improvements for conduct of profitable enterprise; others invest in municipal revenue bonds that pay for public improvements. All participate through their payment of taxes for the public services that make urban investment feasible.

Forty percent of the city area is public property: the streets, parks, schools, and variety of other publicly used elements. Within this area local government may shape the streets, traffic arteries, and open spaces according to the designs of official planners. But the bulk of city building, 60 percent of the total urban area, proceeds parcel by parcel as industry, business, and homeseekers find opportunity for investment.

Those who invest for profit are guided by the market for improvements. Investment in a city implies stability of values. By its nature the city is a permanent institution whose purpose is to shelter the continuing activities of people. An immediate market induces investment, and a continuing market makes of it a sound investment.

Stability in part depends upon the quality of the improvement itself. It also depends upon the quality of other improvements that have preceded and those that will follow. It depends upon the standards at which a community maintains itself, the level of maintenance of existing facilities, and the standards the community demands for future improvements. These determine the difference between environmental degeneration or stability, and upon them rests the difference between speculation and sound urban development.

Physical improvements on private land are not the only factors that affect the health of urban investment. The city functions through the circulation of goods and services. The warp, the infrastructure, of the community pattern is the network of streets, utilities, and transportation. The strength of the urban pattern is measured by the adequacy and convenience of the circulatory system and services; the stability of investment is measured by the level at which the community maintains itself.

Urban growth in some respects is analogous to processes in nature. The soil of fertile and prosperous citizenship is tilled, the seeds of investment are planted, and the garden is cultivated with urban management and maintenance, both public and private. All urban activities and functions are inseparable. The only area in which they may be isolated is that of speculation, and for that reason speculation is damaging.

Speculation—quick turnover for quick profit—contributes in large measure to building a city, but the speculator assumes no responsibility because he is not concerned with the use of the improvement. That responsibility and the obligation for maintaining it are shifted to others when he transfers ownership. The motive of speculation consequently induces inferior quality; it is concerned only with the least possible initial cost and the greatest possible profit.

Speculative improvements are nonetheless an investment in the city. They are investments in which the public participates. Public services must be made available to all property, and the cost of these services is paid by taxes and public utility rates. These costs are determined to a large degree by the quality of the improvements to the elements that comprise the city. High quality resists spotty shifts in urban land use, the wasteful extension and duplication of public and private services and facilities, and holds stable values.

What determines the physical form of the city? It emerges from the initiative and enterprise of many people, acting individually and in groups. They are guided not by some preconceived model of the future city, however brilliant or inspired, but by a set of standards. The real plans for our cities are the standards prescribed by law—the codes and ordinances that regulate the development of urban property.

Laws form an integral part of the whole planning process, and all expression and action of those who design and invest in urban building are within the limits prescribed by law. City building is guided by the maximum quantity and minimum quality legally allowed.

That this process imposes a singular responsibility upon the citizen should be self-evident. It is the obligation of the people to determine the standards they deem appropriate for their community and to translate these standards into effective rules and regulations. It can be fairly stated that this responsibility has not been discharged with the intelligence and devotion demanded of citizenship in a democracy. Our cities bear violent testimony to that fact. If we are to bring improvement to the urban environment it devolves upon the people at large, upon leaders of business, industry, the arts, and in public office, to assume this responsibility with vision, integrity, and an unflinching will to serve the public interest. In the final analysis, only the few reap profitable reward through violation of the general welfare.

Urban development implies a continuing responsibility, all forces associated in the process acting together and interdependently. The degree to which these forces are integrated reflects the aspirations, ambitions, and convictions of a community, and the initiative and responsibility of the citizenship as a whole and in each of its parts. When the forces that contribute to city building are unbalanced, inequities develop and the city declines. The energy is sapped, the city no longer provides a field for sound and continuing business investment, jobs disappear, and the environment degenerates.

Since the laws that apply to the physical development of the city set the standards for that development, it is important to examine the effect of these regulations and the prospects for improvement in them. It is important for those who invest their capital for profitable return and for those who pay the taxes that maintain the community. The cities themselves bear testimony to the ineffective nature of many of our laws and their administration. The legal framework that molds the urban pattern provides some advantages, but implementation appears to have drifted into a state approaching anarchy.

Until recently public contact with city planning has been limited; even today most people have little knowledge about planning practices or limitations, or its significance to their daily living. First contact usually comes when a building permit is sought and either granted or refused. If the permit is granted, the relationship of the individual and planning is a fleeting one and the ignorance continues. If, however, the permit is denied, the citizen may ask why. Informed that the law denies that right because what he wishes to do is inconsistent with the welfare of the community, the citizen may accept this interpretation of the law and leave from the planning office. Or he or she may have the temerity to ask: What law? How does a community come by the right to restrain me from the free exercise of my will in developing property I own? Is this not the confiscation of private property without due process of law and without just compensation, both of which are violations of the Constitution of the United States?[1]

It is in the interest of the people that they be informed on these questions; they are the foundation of planning in democracy.

An Art or a Science?

The discussion of the planning process and the basis for determining decisions dealing with the development of communities has gone on endlessly, with much disparagement of its function in community affairs. Some have called it neither an art nor a science but rather guesswork at best and reaction to pressures at worst.

But forecasting the future is never precise. The best of economists fail to predict the directions that the market will take or what the national economy will do in the future. With the spread of the computer and all other electronic data-generating and gathering devices, the amount of

---

1. Federal Constitution, Fourteenth Amendment, 1869, Section 1: "No State shall make or enforce any law which shall abridge the privileges or immunities of citizens of the United States, nor shall any State deprive any person of life, liberty or property without due process of law, nor deny to any person within its jurisdiction the equal protection of the laws."

existing knowledge can be collected and collated to provide a reasonable statement of where we have been and where we are. Alternative possible projections can be developed that can be of help in determining the path and directions that events in the future might take. It must not be forgotten, however, that even with these tools at our disposal, the unexpected events generated by external forces—a changing of wind direction, a change in political climate—can, for good or evil, change need, timing, economics, or desire for any given planning program.

The debate therefore is academic. Both art and science, along with a lot of intuitive activity, are involved, together with that most precious ingredient—imagination. Thus planning must be understood as an effort to bring orderly development into urban communities and reduce social and economic conflicts that would endanger life and property.

THE EARLIEST PLANNING

The time when land was first allocated to specific uses is, of course, shrouded in prehistoric mystery. The failure of land to respond to cultivation demonstrated that certain land was not adapted to agricultural use but, since there were few ways of passing this information on to others, it was probably necessary for successive users to learn by trial and error that such areas were unfit.

Tribal experience indicated that certain land was suitable for raising crops, other land was better for grazing animals, and some was unproductive. When these experiences were transmitted from generation to generation by word of mouth and custom, we had the first haphazard land use plan. Certainly enforcement was effective; struggle for survival in a not-too-friendly world left the line between life and death too thin for people to cultivate land a second time after it had refused to give them food the first time. Thus land was identified as either agricultural or nonagricultural and, if the latter, it had little value. Since people were few in number and there was much land, nomadic peoples found little need to limit themselves to any single place; they could keep moving on to fruitful areas. Where the land gave bountiful harvest from the plantings, it is believed these nomads settled down and formed the first permanent agrarian communities.

Customs of land use in mankind's earliest days defined the planting and harvesting seasons; then the first descriptions of crop rotation made their appearance, along with the idea of resting the land after a number of years of use. Priests of powerful religions wielded tremendous persuasive powers, and many codes of land use were incorporated in religious doctrines. Some of these are part of religious observations today in certain parts of the world.

The land gave humans many resources other than food. Minerals in the earth provided metals for useful implements of war or peace, the land's stone and wood provided materials for homes and fortifications. The earth itself became a prime building material, as structures were molded into shelters of mud, clay, brick, and so on.

As civilization developed and cities were built as population grew, land took on other values than those attached to agricultural use. The fixed site of the marketplace marked a land use of great value; the land given over to the public open space—the forum—and the commons became important as the centers of the town. Special places were designated for the storage of explosives, for the slaughter of animals, and for the residences of the aristocracy. It did not take rulers long to recognize that the relationship between and among land uses was of paramount importance, that the slaughterhouses had no proper place on the windward side of their palaces. In our present-day cities we have taken far less care in locating smoke- and dust-producing industries. It is true, of course, that protection of a few homes from obnoxious conditions was a far simpler task than controlling industrial development in relation to the mushrooming residential areas that crowd our urban landscape today. Nonetheless, some greater application of this principle might have given us a far less objectionable environment in our urban communities.

HISTORICAL BACKGROUND

While the storage of powder in a convenient place was important to the people's defense, it was soon recognized as a menace when stored too near their homes. With such early concepts of danger and discomfiture began the first official designation of areas within which certain uses were segregated as a matter of protection to the people in a community.

In ancient cities people were themselves regulated as to where they might live. Workers were restricted to areas outside the fortress walls and were called within when required to protect the interests of rulers.

As cities grew in size and power, certain minority groups were restricted to specified areas. These ghettos were always the overcrowded slums and the center of poverty. When disease struck the city the people in these areas suffered most. Limitation of living areas was extended to restrictions on the work the inhabitants might perform and the places they might travel. The regulations, enforced by the government and sanctioned by the public, often carried a penalty of death on violation. The groups thus segregated differed in various periods and in different parts of the world, but history repeatedly records their plight, their misery, and deprivation.

To assume that such conditions are confined to past history or remote places is unrealistic. There remains today considerable regulation over the rights of minority groups; the areas in which they live for social and economic reasons rather than legal ones are not officially named ghettos, but they retain many of the ghetto's historic characteristics.

The first steps toward modern city planning, however, can be traced to the practice of establishing districts within which certain rights were legally curbed, if for different reasons. King Philip of Spain, in outlining the procedure for establishing communities in the New World, instructed his explorers to orient streets in such a manner that they would not be windswept, and to locate slaughtering places for cattle on the outskirts of town so that the odors would not offend the townspeople. The segregation of gunpowder storage houses from the center of Boston was one of America's first recorded acts of zoning. In 1810 certain decrees of Napoleon contained land-use regulations, as did the Prussian codes of 1845.

Most early laws were concerned only with uses considered a menace to life itself. Evidence would be presented in court that a given noxious use was ongoing and had proven itself dangerous, and regulations against it in that area would ideally be forthcoming. The required proof in most instances could be had only after some great loss of life directly traceable to the specific use.

It was considered a critical point in all such legal action at the time that the establishment of dangerous uses could be prevented, but that such laws could not be retroactive. Thus, after repeated tenement house fire disasters in New York City, continued construction of the dangerous buildings was prohibited but little was done to eliminate the danger to the thousands of people who continued to live in "outlawed" firetraps.

Legal Trappings

Legal action on zoning affairs went through two basic stages of development. Initially cases were brought to court that dealt with "nuisance uses." The courts treated these as separate and individual matters, deciding in each specific case whether a use was detrimental to the public health, safety, and welfare. In effect this was simple zoning, legally brought about. As time passed, the courts required more and broader evidence, such that would "indicate the character of a community," before it was willing to rule upon the validity of a use. This call for a larger and more comprehensive view of a community's purpose is now answered in the general plan of land use.

A California ordinance that prohibited a slaughterhouse, hog storage, and the curing of hides in certain areas of the city was upheld in the courts.[2] A Los Angeles ordinance that prohibited the operation of a steam shoddying plant within one hundred feet of a church was upheld in 1895;

---

2. *Ex parte Shrader,* San Francisco (1867).

in this latter case the court passed not only upon the nature of the specific use but the relationship between uses.[3]

The legality of the establishment of fire zones or districts has been upheld in most courts, the structural nature of buildings and their relation to space being admitted as an important factor in determining the uses permitted within a structure. In San Francisco, because of the great number of wooden buildings with party walls, certain districts were established by ordinance within which hand laundries were prohibited; wood fires were burned in the stoves upon which the laundry was boiled and several serious fires resulted. This ordinance was taken to the state supreme court and was held unconstitutional and invalid, not because of the regulation itself but because it was a breach of the Fourteenth Amendment of the Constitution. It was pointed out that the washing of clothes was not opposed to good public morals nor was it subversive of public decency, but the court cited the fact that all of but one of the non-Oriental applicants were issued permits in a similar business in like areas and were permitted to continue in business, whereas the petitioner and two hundred others of his race were denied permits. The court held that the ordinance was not unreasonable, but that its application was arbitrary class legislation discriminating against one group in favor of another. It thus violated the Fourteenth Amendment, and the ordinance was declared to be invalid.[4] The fair administration of a law is an integral part of the provisions of the law in the eyes of the courts.

One of the earliest court decisions in this country upholding an ordinance in the nature of a zoning regulation was made in 1920. In sustaining a town plan before it, the opinion said: "It betters the health and safety of the community; it betters the transportation facilities; and it adds to the appearance and the wholesomeness of the place, and as a consequence it reacts upon the moral and spiritual power of the people who live under such surroundings."[5]

The Use of the Police Power

The power to pass and enforce laws to protect the welfare of all the people, whether they be enacted at a local or a national level, is called the exercise of the police power.[6] In this country the power was retained

---

3. *Ex parte Lacey,* 108 California 326.
4. *Yick Wo v. Hopkins,* 118 U.S. 356 (1895).
5. *Windsor v. Whitney,* 95 Connecticut 357, 363.
6. Police power was expressed in ancient law as: "Due regulation of domestic order of the kingdom where members of the state, like a family, are bound to conform their behavior in good propriety . . . to be good members and an orderly part of the community"; and later: "Police power . . . is the name given to the inherent sovereignty which is the right and duty to exercise when the public policy demands enforcement of such regulations for the general welfare as are necessary for the regulation of economic conditions to provide for adequate community life." *Parker v. Otis,* 130 California 322.

by the sovereign states at the time of formation of the federal government. Only when the national welfare is involved and when the local government is unable to cope with a situation does the state deem it necessary to call for assistance from the federal government. Federal laws, however, do affect the relationships between the states; we have an Interstate Commerce Commission to regulate rates on railroads dealing in interstate commerce, and the national labor laws regulate wages and hours of persons employed in industries that sell their products through interstate commerce. These instances constitute uses of the police power by the federal government.

Some states give the police power to cities and counties by specific legislative acts; others grant this right to communities in their state constitutions. The purpose of the police power is in general always the same, but the manner in which the power is granted differs in the various states. The power to make laws and regulations dealing with the activities of a community's citizens and the property they possess is a key to the planning process and particularly to that phase called *zoning*.

Today it is a widely accepted principle that the source of all power lies in the hands of the majority of the people. This implies that the people of a city or town, through the governing body, have the right to enact laws and regulations that support their ideas of what is best for their community. The distinction between this principle and the exercise of power in the past, whether by a minority or majority, is our recognition that regulations of law today apply to all the people, and no class or element is to be immune. The principal restraint upon law is that it shall not be in conflict with the Constitution of the United States nor the constitution of the state in which it is enacted.

It is necessary that the police power be exercised for a worthy purpose and with definitely stated objectives. In cases where police power is used to regulate or deny the use of property without compensation, it must be clearly shown that the continued use of that property would be inimical to the best interests of the community. A house that is structurally unsound or badly infested with rats may be dangerous to the public in general as well as to the persons living in it, and it is thus subject to being closed under the police power without compensation to the owner. The equity for such actions rests upon the assumption that the people are obligated to maintain their property at standards that will not impose a nuisance on the community and that the necessity to exercise the police power to abate such a nuisance does not warrant compensation to the owners of the affected property.

Taking land for public purpose when the owner does not want to sell is not to be confused with use of the police power: the former is known as the exercise of eminent domain. Condemnation of the property is instituted in the courts, which then establish a fair price based upon testimony from witnesses representing the owner, the community, and impartial appraisers. The principal difference between the police power and the right of eminent domain lies in the matter of compensation to the owner; under the police power the state does not "take" the property from its owner—it regulates the right of use on behalf of the public welfare.

The police power of a community is limited to the area within its political boundaries. Thus state laws may be enforced within any part of the state unless otherwise provided in the laws, the county laws only within the county, and city or township laws only within their limits. Beyond this, cooperation among governmental agencies constitutes the only effective method for coordinated action or regulation. In the state of Texas, however, cities can regulate the subdivision of land in the unincorporated (county) areas within an established area of influence, a distance of five miles beyond their political boundaries. Nonetheless, zoning control in these extended areas is not granted to the cities.

A Sound Idea Corrupted

As with all laws and public regulations, there are those who seek and find ways of circumventing the provisions for their personal gain. Zoning was fair game for those who sought special privilege. Requests were made for special zoning classifications for a highly profitable land use in areas where the general provisions of the law did not provide it. Called *spot zoning,* this soon became so prevalent in some communities that residents or landowners in the vicinity protested the loss of protection that the zoning was supposed to provide.

When the spot zoning process was attacked in the courts, new devices were introduced to provide sanction for the granting of the same special privileges. Amont them was the *variance.* Public officials were required to make a finding that special conditions existed such that the standard features of the ordinance did not apply, and the community could attach conditions to adjust the specific use to its surroundings. Public agencies found it very convenient to invent all types of obtuse reasons for granting variances.

When variances became a recognized problem in local affairs, especially after broad community objection to the abuse of the function, a new device called a *conditional use permit* was invented, which permitted a specific use in a given location where it purportedly was essential to the welfare of the community. Like the variance and the spot zone, the conditional use permit became an instrument for illegal grants of special privilege. It appeared that any profitmaking use could be found to be in the interest of the community if only from the standpoint of tax revenue.

Some communities, under the guise of protecting property values, require extensive and time-consuming reviews of plans that show such details as elevations of buildings as well as the use of the land, denying approval to projects that do not meet the architectural tastes of the reviewing agency. Long delays can become a device to make the applicants change their proposals to conform to the board's judgments of "good taste." Challenging the opinions of these boards in the courts can be a less than satisfying procedure.

Some communities use an unwritten regulatory system. Proposals of all kinds are reviewed and acted upon by the legislators on the basis of their personal prejudices or desire to grant favors. Plans are not comprehensive, nor defined for viewing. Zoning ordinances are without standards, all items before the commission and legislative bodies being decided at meetings that fall far short of being public hearings.

Of course, some people genuinely believe that the elimination or reduction of regulations would free planners, public and private, to do their work without constraint. Without hindrance, their approach to the future would be more open and creative. Local ordinances and regulations dealing with the general health, safety, and welfare would be reduced to the minimum, the sole constraint being that no harm be done to neighbors or community. Failing that, activity would be subject to the consequences of court action for damages (shades of Ayn Rand's *Fountainhead*!). It appears that this process would create a heyday for members of the legal profession as they dealt with people—those who could afford it—who believed they had suffered abuse by their neighbors.

A Means of Growth Management

During the 1970–80 decade many efforts have been initiated to protect the environment. Some of these involved including provisions in zoning ordinances to limit the extent and direction of the growth of cities to a certain number of dwelling units per year. Other provisions protected agricultural land from being depleted by urban expansion into prime areas. In most cases the growth management provisions were a separate part of the comprehensive plan and were supported by separate ordinances rather than by zoning.

In legal actions brought against them, these provisions were described as placing limits on people's freedom of movement and therefore unconstitutional. However, in several important cases the highest courts upheld the right of communities to control their growth as long as the provisions related to the ability of the community to serve and protect the residents.

As a corollary to this, it was argued in recent cases before the U.S. Supreme Court that communities that reserve land for public use or purpose and deny the landowners any use of their property must pay compensation, since for all practical purposes the land was taken from the owner by the act of zoning.

CHANGING INTERPRETATIONS OF THE LAW

Some very significant changes have taken place in the courts' interpretation of laws regulating the use of property. The growth of communities into large cities has necessitated detailed and complicated legislation to govern more and more human behavior. What may be accepted in a small community as an unavoidable nuisance may be viewed as dangerous and contested actively in a metropolis. Thus the keeping of pigs, horses, and chickens would be considered a right in a farm town but would be looked upon with horror on Manhattan Island. The maintenance of open privies in backyards may be accepted practice in nonurban areas with no funds for sewage disposal, whereas the same condition in any large city would have the entire population declaring it a menace to the health and life of all the people.

The dangers of disease, crime, delinquency, fire, and traffic injury are rapidly multiplied as the housing, commerce, and industry of the large city absorb the open space that formerly helped to insulate people against these dangers. The courts have seen the necessity of recognizing these problems. Thus there came into being the concept that people have the right to protect themselves against these and other hazards by planning and zoning an environment that will meet the requirements of safe urban living. Where we have relied in the past upon the police power to prohibit acts that the courts determined to be a violation of a law, today we enact laws that tend to discourage in advance those acts that can be prevented.

Our philosophy of urban conduct is no longer confined to the public health, safety, and general welfare but has extended to the use of the police power for the maintenance of such matters as "public convenience and comfort." The Supreme Court has said: "The police power of a state embraces regulations designed to promote the public convenience or the general prosperity as well as regulations designed to promote the public health, the public morals, or the public safety."[7] Traffic laws that prohibit parking on certain streets are justified on the grounds that they make access to important areas a matter of greater convenience as well as ensure the safety of people. Laws that prohibit dangerous or obnoxious uses from residential areas are considered to protect values from depreciation and, in this manner, protect the general prosperity as well as health and safety.

---

7. *Chicago B. & R. Co. v. Drainage Commissioners*, 200 U.S. 561, 592.

Red Tape

In many areas of the country the planning and zoning processes have become so cumbersome that applicants are strongly dissuaded from participating in development. Some communities require approval by the planning commission, an architectural review board, the legislative body, and sometimes, after vigorous citizen protests, approval by the courts. In some states the referendum on a proposal requires a vote by the electorate before a program can become a reality. The time and money that is involved can become monumental—more than all but the very powerful and wealthy can afford.

Up Zoning—Down Zoning

It has been assumed by much of the public that the only direction for zoning change is to increase the law's permissiveness, to allow those changes that would permit landowners to anticipate greater potential profits from the use of their land. Few legislative bodies have had the temerity to tell owners that their land cannot be used as intensively as had been legislated in the past.

Recent court rulings, however, indicate that, like any other legislative act of government, zoning is subject to modification if required to protect the public health, safety, or welfare. Legislative bodies make judgments based upon data. With new facts before it, a legislative body has an obligation and responsibility to make such modifications and changes as would bring the zoning into a consistent position with the community's long-range comprehensive plan and recognized professional practices.

There is no doubt that persons paying for land on the basis of existing zoning for commercial uses would believe that rezoning for residential uses would be tantamount to taking property without just compensation. However, persons who own residential land make no such complaint, nor do they offer compensation to the community when the legislative body decides to rezone the land for commerce or industry. In each case, there must be careful analysis to be certain that the decision is based on sound planning and zoning principles and that no act of favoritism, prejudice, or discrimination went into the decision process.

In most instances where down zoning has occurred the subject property was not developed for the permitted use. Meanwhile the land around it often developed a pattern indicating that the contested zoning would have been incompatible with its surroundings. If development has already taken place the legislative body may enact a "nonconforming" provision that could include a reasonable amortization period, after which the existing use would have to conform to the surroundings.

Where property owners do not agree with the public action in down zoning their property they will challenge the procedure as being in effect the taking of the property by inverse condemnation, the taking of a substantial property right without just compensation. However, a California court held:

> A zoning action which merely decreases the market value of property does not violate state or federal constitutional provision forbidding uncompensated taking or damaging of property. Accordingly, an inverse condemnation action by property owners, in which it was alleged that plaintiffs purchased property zoned commercial and that thereafter the city rezoned the property to residential so that the property was worth only a fraction of its value under the commercial zoning, did not state a cause of action and the trial court correctly sustained the city's demur without leave to amend.[8]

Administrative or Legislative Acts

The old debates about the applicability of the initiative and referendum provisions to zoning cases, especially in those states where the constitution provides for these remedies to actions taken by the legislative body, seem to have been resolved in a recent case in Colorado.

In the case involving Margolis versus The District Court in and for the County of Arapahoe, the state supreme court found that the zoning decisions by the legislative body were subject to the initiative and referendum provisions of the state constitution. (This was also the finding of the California supreme court in a case involving the city of Claremont.) The opponents to the finding expressed the opinion that this decision would lead to delays in development and would ultimately result in unplanned growth. The court rejected this view, citing the fact that no real problems had occurred in other states where the initiative and referendum processes had been used.

THE PUBLIC WELFARE

The courts were called upon to rule on some mighty problems in the early days of zoning. What was the public welfare? When was public health or life endangered? What was an "obnoxious use"? At what point is the establishment of a district reasonable and at what point does it become only arbitrary? Was it proper for the court to substitute its judgment for that of the legislative body on matters of the "substance" of a zoning ordinance? When can a community permit a use in one area and deny it in another?

A series of court decisions over the years reveals much difference of

---

8. Cal. Jur. 2d. Eminent Domain. #85: Am. Jur. 2d. Eminent Domain. #157 et seq.

opinion, but filtering through them all are sound precedents for the community's right to establish zoning districts and regulate the use of property. The 1913 Hadacheck case in Los Angeles provided one of the basic considerations in all zoning law. Although it preceded recognized zoning statutes, it dealt with the violation of a city ordinance prohibiting the maintenance of brickyards and kilns within a designated residential district of some three square miles. The court ruled that this use of property must cease and desist since the smoke, dust, and fumes emanating from the plant were damaging to the health of the people living nearby. In this case the brickyard was located and operating in the area before it was occupied by residences, but the court did not consider the property right claimed by the owner to be as important as the health and welfare of the people. The claim of discrimination was raised by the owner since brickyards and kilns were permitted in other areas near residential developments, but it was disallowed on the grounds that "it is no objection to the validity of the ordinance that in other districts similarly situated brick kilns are not prohibited. It is for the council to say whether the prohibition should be extended to such other districts." [9]

In 1915 the California city of South Pasadena attempted to restrict the operation of a rock crusher in a high-class residential district. [10] The district was then sparsely developed, whereas similar operations were permitted in other and more heavily populated residential districts. The ordinance was declared void on the grounds that it was unreasonable to prohibit such use in a lightly settled district when the same use was permitted in a densely populated district. The court made much of the fact that the poorer class of homes surrounding the industrial district is entitled to the same protection as the fine homes. In this case, and in others dealing with the mining of natural resources, the courts held that these minerals are only located in certain areas and can only be extracted where they are found. If this activity is denied there would be no material for construction.

A related issue was raised in a case involving rock quarries in the Los Angeles Roscoe area. As each pit's rock supply became exhausted a new site was opened, thus extending the mining area. Eventually it was brought cheek by jowl with the homes of those who had come there for reasons of health in the excellent climate. The expansion of rock-quarrying, it was contended, undermined the value of the climatic resource to the point that the lives of the people were jeopardized. The residents pointed out that the air was filled with dust particles, that the unfenced

---

9. *Ex Parte Hadacheck,* 165 California 416 (1913); *Hadacheck v. Sebastian,* 2390 Supreme Court 394; 60 Law Edition 348.
10. *Matter of Throop,* 169 California 92 (1915).

and abandoned pits were dangerous, and that children had been killed and injured. The community's planning commission upheld the residents' contention, but the city council reversed this stand. The lower courts upheld the legislative body, refusing to substitute its judgment for that of the council on matters of "substance."

The interpretation of the general welfare clause is fundamental to all zoning, and planning rests upon the thesis that regulation of property use will secure numerous benefits to the community. Among others it will lessen congestion on streets, secure greater safety from fire, panic, and similar dangers, promote health by requiring adequate light and air, prevent overcrowding of the land, avoid undue concentrations of population, facilitate the provision of adequate transportation, water supply, sewage disposal, and other basic necessities such as schools, parks, playgrounds, and civic and cultural amenities. Property values are preserved and stabilized, the city's income from taxation will be greater, and the tax rate to supply the required services will be lower. Blight, obsolescence, and slums are discouraged, the city retains a good character and appearance, and an overall improvement of the community reduces the need for and the cost of many social services.

Maintenance of the "general welfare and prosperity" as a reason for imposing race restrictions by means of zoning was termed an illegal use of the police power by the United States Supreme Court. A group of property owners sought to prove that the intrusion of "nonwhite" families into a "white" district caused a loss of property values and thus endangered the prosperity of the community. The court held that the agencies of government could not be used to enforce a law that specifically violated the Fourteenth Amendment of the Constitution. In many other cases the courts have ruled that financial gains or losses are not in themselves sufficient to decide the validity or constitutionality of a law.[11]

Tests of the community's right to prescribe the manner of development within its boundaries engulfed the courts during the 1920s. The newness of zoning law resulted in some phrasing that suggested discrimination to the courts, and decisions were more likely to support the individual against the community welfare, the courts being reluctant to take action which would infringe upon property rights.

As zoning received wider acceptance as a proper use of the police power, a variety of features were incorporated in the ordinances in attempts to dilute their restrictive purpose. There were efforts to use the law as a device to protect the property of the few while permitting the remainder of the city to continue unprotected. Occasionally, in concert

---

11. *Smith v. Collison,* 119 California Appellate 180 (1931). Depreciation in value of property is not fatal to the validity of the ordinance.

with the land speculator, property was zoned for a use that would bring the highest price at the moment; whether the use was commercial, residential, or industrial was of little concern. A weird pattern of spot zoning covered the land like a crazy quilt. Purchasers were informed they could use the vacant land for any purpose they willed, and their neighbors were helpless to protect their investments. Efforts of public officials to maintain conformance with the given character of a neighborhood were hotly contested. "Interim ordinances" were sometimes enacted to forbid encroachments upon "fine" residential districts. Some of these were sustained, but in general the courts found them invalid because of the arbitrary nature of their boundaries; the guarantee of a special area from detrimental uses was viewed as a discriminatory act since the same encroachments were permitted unchecked elsewhere.

Court decisions hammered at a thesis that has since become a cornerstone of zoning: to be valid the law must be both reasonable and fairly applied. The courts were actually leading the way toward the planning of cities; they were directly and indirectly appealing for a comprehensive plan that would provide a foundation for zoning acts and decisions of equity in the shaping and administration of these acts.

Community Character

One of the most important legal decisions in the history of zoning was the Euclid case in 1926. In his ruling, Associate Justice George Sutherland of the Supreme Court pointed out that each community had the right and the responsibility to determine its own character, and that as long as that determination did not disturb the orderly growth of the region or the nation, it was a valid use of the police power.

> Point is raised by the appellees that the Village of Euclid was a mere suburb of Cleveland, and that the industrial development of the latter had extended to the village, and that in the obvious course of things would soon absorb the entire area for industrial enterprise, and that the effect of the ordinance was to divert such natural development or expansion elsewhere, to the consequent loss of increased values to the owners of land within the village. But this village, though physically a suburb of Cleveland, is a separate municipality, with powers of its own and authority to govern itself as it sees fit within the organic laws of its creation and the state and Federal constitutions. The will of its people determines, not that the industrial development shall cease at its boundaries, but that such development shall proceed between fixed lines. If therefore it is proper exercise of the police power to regulate industrial establishments to localities separated from residential sections, it is not easy to find sufficient reason for denying the power because its effect would be to divert an industrial flow from a course which would result in injury to the residential public to another course where such injury would be obviated. This should not exclude the possibil-

ity of cases where the general interest so far outweighs the interest of the
municipality, that the latter should not be allowed to stand in its way.[12]

The decision made it abundantly clear that a community may determine
the nature of development within its boundaries; it may plan and regulate
the use of land as the people of the community may consider it to be in
the public interest.

Justice Sutherland enunciated another principle: a community is
obliged to relate its plans to the area outside its boundaries. Again the
courts anticipate the planning process. Cities are not surrounded by
walls; they are each a part of their region, and each is obliged to plan the
spaces within its boundaries as an integral part of the plan for spaces
outside its boundaries. This suggests, for instance, that a highway plan
prepared without consideration of the routes of major importance within
the regional plan would constitute an improper use of the police power.
A community has both the right to determine its character and the obligation to relate its plan to its regional environs.

Aesthetic Concerns

The drab, uninspired appearance of our cities approaches offensive ugliness. The lack of a long tradition of the arts in society has dulled our
response to the visual plunder in our surroundings. The grace and charm
of a European village, a New England town, the delight of Paris, Venice,
and Vienna, came by way of the manners and morals of the time quite as
much as by craftsmanship. Our values have undoubtedly been contorted
by materialism and the sheer preoccupation with the practical chores of
everyday urban housekeeping. It should not be conceivable in a democratic society with balanced cultural values, but improvement of the aesthetic quality of our cities has actually been attempted through legislative
action.

In the past, legislative bodies have been reluctant to embody aesthetic
considerations in legislation. Judge Swayze of New Jersey specifically
expressed this sentiment:

> No case has been cited, nor are we aware of any case, which holds that a
> man may be deprived of his property because his tastes are not those of his
> neighbor. Esthetic considerations are a matter of luxury and indulgence
> rather than of necessity, and it is necessity alone which justifies the police
> power to take property without compensation.[13]

An early step toward aesthetic control was directed to regulations
against the use of billboards along highways. As the advertising mania

---

12. *Village of Euclid, Ohio v. Ambler Realty Company,* 272 U.S. 365 (1926).
13. *Passaic v. Paterson Bill Posting Co.* 62A, 267 (1905) New Jersey Supreme Court.

spread, the extravagant use of signs and billboards reached intolerable proportions. The police power was invoked when in 1905 the Metropolitan Park Commission of Massachusetts sought to prohibit signs near a parkway. This regulation was held invalid by the court, but restrictions against the wanton blight of the billboard rash gained momentum. In 1935 the same court in Massachusetts supported the use of the police power to regulate signs and billboards.

Although there is precedent for aesthetic control in areas of particular historic importance,[14] the device of architectural control is usually avoided; the prospect of imposing a hierarchy of taste upon a community is approached with caution. However, in a unanimous 1954 opinion of the Supreme Court, Justice William O. Douglas clearly affirmed that a community need not tolerate ugliness and may take legal steps to correct it.

> . . . Public safety, public health, morality, peace and quiet, law and order —these are some of the more conspicuous examples of the traditional application of the police power to municipal affairs. Yet they merely illustrate the scope of the power and do not delimit it. Miserable and disreputable housing conditions may do more than spread disease and crime and immorality. They may also suffocate the spirit by reducing the people who live there to the status of cattle. They may indeed make living an almost insufferable burden. They may also be an ugly sore, a blight on the community which robs it of charm, which makes it a place from which men turn. The misery of housing may despoil a community as an open sewer may ruin a river.
>
> We do not sit to determine whether a particular housing project is or is not desirable. The concept of the public welfare is broad and inclusive. The values it represents are spiritual as well as physical, aesthetic as well as monetary. It is within the power of the legislature to determine that the community should be beautiful as well as healthy, spacious as well as clean, well-balanced as well as carefully patrolled. In the present case, the Congress and its authorized agencies have made determinations that take into account a wide variety of values. It is not for us to reappraise them. If those who govern the District of Columbia decide that the Nation's Capital should be beautiful as well as sanitary, there is nothing in the Fifth Amendment that stands in the way. . . .
>
> . . . In the present case, Congress and its authorized agencies attack the problem of the blighted parts of the community on an area rather than on a structure-by-structure basis. That, too, is opposed by appellants. They maintain that since their building does not imperil health or safety nor contribute to the making of a slum or a blighted area, it cannot be swept into a redevelopment plan by the mere dictum of the Planning Commission or the Commissioners. The particular uses to be made of the land in the project were determined with regard to the needs of the particular commu-

---

14. 333 Mass. 773 and 783 (1955).

nity. The experts concluded that if the community were to be healthy, if it were not to revert again to a blighted or slum area, as though possessed of a congenital disease, the area must be planned as a whole. It was not enough, they believed, to remove existing buildings that were unsanitary or unsightly. It was important to redesign the whole area so as to eliminate the conditions that cause slums—the overcrowding of dwellings, the lack of parks, the lack of adequate streets and alleys, the absence of recreational areas, the lack of light and air, the presence of outmoded street patterns. It was believed that the piecemeal approach, the removal of individual structures that were offensive, would be only a palliative. The entire area needed redesigning so that a balanced, integrated plan could be developed for the region, including not only new homes but also schools, churches, parks, streets and shopping centers. In this way it was hoped that the cycle of decay of the area could be controlled and the birth of future slums prevented. Such diversification in future use is plainly relevant to the maintenance of the desired housing standards and therefore within congressional power. . . .[15]

The decision acknowledged that the appearance of the city stands with other features that involve the public interest. In this case it pertained to conditions that existed and found that the spiritual welfare of the people was imperiled by these conditions, but the point is no less valid. It provides a foundation for legislation that employs the police power to discontinue such conditions. We apparently have yet to establish means by which such conditions may not at the outset be created.

The public can assert its interests directly in two areas. One is in the public domain, since some 40 percent of the city consists of streets, walks, parks, and civic reserves. Herein is a broad and impressive arena for creative treatment of space arrangement, landscaping, street furniture, lighting, signs, and structures. The second area is in the realm of public regulation of three-dimensional volumes related to community design. This involves integrated use of land—open space and landscape—structures, the character of building design, advertising media, and ingress and egress for pedestrians and vehicles. Sensitive attention to the formulation of these regulations may accomplish some effective results without impinging on good taste. In the final analysis, the creation of beauty is the result of a desire that it be produced as well as the talent to produce it, and this demands the cultivation of cultural values.

The importance and validity of aesthetic considerations has been upheld in a case involving the county of Santa Barbara in California. The county zoning ordinance established an amortization period for outdoor advertising structures along its main highway. The outdoor advertisers sued the county, implying that zoning for aesthetic purposes was unconstitutional, that beauty is a matter of personal taste, that outdoor advertising was a legitimate commercial enterprise and therefore must be given

---

15. *Berman v. Parker*, 348 U.S. 26, 75 Sup. Ct. 98, 99 L. Ed. 27 (1954).

the same rights as other commercial uses. The court held that the scenic quality of Santa Barbara county was one of its most important economic assets in attracting tourists and visitors, and as such must be protected for the general welfare. The billboards were therefore ordered to be removed. There was no appeal.

A case involving the Coachella Valley of California, however, turned out somewhat differently. An attempt to restrict the erection of billboards on land held in Indian ownership was rejected, on the grounds that since Indian land was subject only to regulation by the federal government, local laws did not apply.

ENABLING LEGISLATION

The grant of police power by the states to the cities and counties vests these political subdivisions with the power to regulate their affairs and enforce the regulations. It is nevertheless found necessary on occasion for the state to enact legislation for the specific use of that power. Such legislation is in the form of what is generally termed "enabling acts." The purpose may be twofold. It may be for the purpose of affirming state policy in matters of vital interest to the people at any given time and thereby encourage local communities to act; or the special legislation may be for the purpose of removing doubt that the police power was intended for the specific subject of the act. The preamble of all such legislation states the purposes in detail. Such enabling acts are drawn to establish clearly the relation between the use for which the police power is granted and the public health, safety, convenience, and general welfare.

The state sometimes passes zoning enabling acts when cities and counties previously delegated the police power but are reluctant to exercise it until the state has specifically signified that it be so used. These special enabling acts are usually written in greater detail than the general grant of the police power. They define the scope of zoning, the procedure for adoption of the ordinance, the composition of the zoning board and its powers and functions, and the methods for modification or exceptions to the ordinance.

State planning acts are a form of special enabling legislation, although they generally establish a state agency to coordinate planning functions at the state level in addition to setting forth the specifications for local planning activities. Such acts describe the functions of a state planning board and prescribe the process for each city and county to accomplish a complete planning job for itself. These laws usually call for the preparation of a general plan, list the scope of the general plan, and specify the methods for its adoption and enforcement. Power is sometimes given to the local planning commission to levy a special tax for funds to administer the law, but this power is seldom invoked; planning commissions prefer to work within the departmental family of the city government and draw their support from the general tax funds.

Another form of enabling legislation is that which creates new agencies in the state, cities, or counties to cope with problems of a particular nature. Housing and urban redevelopment acts are of this type, local agencies being created with powers conferred upon the city or county to engage in the program prescribed in the state statute.

Just as specific enabling legislation is created at the state level to cover certain fields of urban activity, so special ordinances are drawn at the local level to define in detail the manner in which city charter provisions are to be executed. In cities where there is no "freeholders' charter"[16] the state laws are in effect; in cities having charters that define the exercise of the police power in stricter terms than the state, the local law takes precedence.[17] Thus, if a state speed limit in a school zone is twenty miles per hour and the city law restricts the speed to fifteen miles per hour, the city law is enforceable. If, on the other hand, the city has a limit of twenty-five miles per hour or no regulation at all for those specific areas, the state law is then enforceable. In terms almost identical to the state enabling legislation, city charters often define the functions of a planning commission; as long as all the duties included in the state law are included in terms not less restrictive, the city charter provisions apply.

Too frequently there is no penalty provision for failure to abide by the requirements of state legislation. An example would be the case in which states call for all counties to have planning commissions and many small counties ignore the requirement; there are few ways to compel the local government to conform. However, in some states the local governments are restricted from the benefits of funds appropriated by the state for public improvements until they conform with state laws. There are occasions when funds for the state highway system, for example, are withheld until the counties adopt general plans for highways that show the relationship between the state routes and local roads. But all too often great resources are dissipated without control.

TRANSITION

Since the inception of action against the use of property deemed a menace to health and life, zoning changed considerably. It has passed from regulating land uses for the preservation of property values to the present

---

16. An act of municipal incorporation, provided for in the constitutions of the individual states.

17. *Brougher v. Board of Public Works,* 205 California 426 (1928). A city charter need not follow the procedures of the state zoning enabling act.

position of responsibility not only for protection of the status quo but also for the creation of a better city, better state, and more prosperous nation. It is true that, as zoning becomes a more effective instrument for improvement of the good city, it becomes less like the traditional instrument called "zoning" and more like the act of planning the city, for many factors other than the ones usually identified with zoning enter the scene.

Recently zoning has become a means for both conservation and planning; the narrow concept is extended to the broadest interpretation of the use of the police power for the protection of the public welfare. In these instances zoning law anticipates the future and guides the development of areas through planned uses rather than waiting until the die is cast and merely fixing land uses that already exist. In the cutover areas of Michigan, Wisconsin, and Minnesota, where erosion threatened to rip the growing heart out of the soil and create dust-bowl conditions, legal steps were taken to label as submarginal the worst of the land. In this way use of rural land was discouraged until such time as the topsoil could be replaced and refertilized. Further mining of trees in the areas not entirely destroyed was forbidden. A reforestation program, under the guidance and with the assistance of the federal government, now assures the people of a continuing supply of lumber for future generations. Thus the priceless possession of fertile land will not be wantonly wasted. The Hawaii State Planning Act of 1961 encompasses more than conservation. It provides for urban, agricultural, and conservation land-use classifications, and requires that tax-assessing authorities be guided by these zoned land uses in establishing assessed values for real property.

J. H. Bradley, in his *Autobiography of Earth,* has stated: "The fabric of human life has been woven on earthen looms." We must use every device in our legal system to protect our land and devote it to its highest and best uses for we cannot escape to new frontiers after abusing and ruining what we have. Almost two centuries ago George Washington observed: "Our lands . . . were originally very good; but use and abuse have made them quite otherwise. . . . We ruin the lands that are already cleared, and either cut down more wood, if we have it, or emigrate into Western country." [18]

The use of police power—zoning—to ensure our future seems neither arbitrary nor in contradiction of any freedom assured to the people by the Constitution. [19]

---

18. U.S. Department of Agriculture, *To Hold This Soil,* Publication No. 321 (Washington, D.C.: U.S. Government Printing Office, 1938).

19. U.S. Department of Agriculture, *The Why and How of Rural Zoning* (Washington, D.C.: U.S. Government Printing Office, December 1958).

CHAPTER 18

PUBLIC PLANNING

Public planning is accomplished through the activities of many agencies and authorities. The number of persons involved and the process may vary at different levels of government and with different enabling legislation, but in most parts of the United States the responsibilities are largely similar.

The regulation of private and public affairs essential to the general welfare has come under attack in recent years, and the drive to deregulate has had more than a little success. The best-known efforts are those associated with airlines, oil production, gas extraction, communications, and other activities that impact greatly on the nation's and the people's economic and other welfare. It has had an effect on planning and zoning, in that developers have demanded a freer hand to build without the constraints that often face them. However, even the most vocal opponents realize that many aspects of the very regulatory process they oppose have had material benefits for them and the security of their profitable operations.

ESTABLISHING GUIDELINES

Policy guidelines establish the structure and elements to be considered in planning. At a national level, The President's Urban Policy Report of

244

August 1978 was submitted to the Congress as the first biennial report in accordance with the provisions of the Housing Act as amended in 1977. The report dealt with America's old perception and new realities, changing urban patterns, the need to assist urban residents in distressed areas, presented a new partnership for conserving urban America, and, finally, put forth a national urban policy.

In the chapter defining the policy, President Jimmy Carter stated:

> I think that we stand at the turning point in history. If, a hundred years from now, this nation's experiment in democracy has failed, I suspect that historians will trace that failure to our own era, when a process of decay began in our inner cities and was allowed to spread unchecked throughout our society.
>
> But I do not believe that must happen. I believe that by working together, we can turn the tide, stop the decay, and set into motion a process of growth that by the end of the century can give us cities worthy of the greatest nation on earth.

Needless to say, these policy guidelines have had little or no impact in the years that followed. No such statement of direction has been forthcoming since 1977.

In October 1977 the American Institute of Planners (AIP), devoted to the study and advancement of the art and science of city, regional, state, and national planning,[1] published a series of guidelines. They were intended as a guide to practitioners as well as an educational effort directed toward legislators and the courts. The text was in two parts: (1) planning functions and their role in the decision-making process, and (2) planning goals—areas of major interest to practicing planners. The AIP stated that "the planning process may be, and often is, used within each of these areas (functional planning), as well as for coordination between them (comprehensive planning)."[2]

The areas named were:

Growth management
Economic development
Environmental quality
Energy and other resource conservation and development
Aesthetics and historic preservation
Transportation
Health, education, and welfare
Public safety
Leisure, recreation, and cultural opportunities

---

1. The American Institute of Planners joined with the American Society of Planning Officials in 1978 to become the American Planning Association.
2. Planning Policies, 1977, American Institute of Planners, Washington, D.C.

The AIP recommendations continued:

1. Planning should be widely practiced by the private sector and by all levels and branches of government.
2. Plans should be articulated cogently to private decision makers, the general public, and any others who may be involved.
3. The planning process should provide public and private decision makers and those seeking to influence decision makers with the best possible information, analysis of alternatives, and long range and short range impacts so that issues may be decided in the best interest of the public and conflicts and duplication among public policies may be avoided.
4. The planning process should coordinate functional and comprehensive planning among all levels of government and should integrate planning and programming with the budgetary and legislative processes.
5. The planning process should strive to involve significantly all responsible and affected parties.
6. Public agencies at all levels of government should provide the data needed to adequately support all stages of the planning process —from problem definition through implementation to subsequent program evaluation. The data should be as correct and current as would be cost effective.

The legislation of each state sets forth the objectives of the state government with regard to the contents and practice of planning programs. For instance, the California state law on planning states that "each planning agency shall prepare and the legislative body of each county and city shall adopt a comprehensive general plan for the physical development of the county or city and of any land outside of its boundaries which in the planning agency's judgment bears relation to its planning."[3] Thereafter the elements that are to be included are identified. These may differ in name from those of the AIP, but they are similar in intent. It is in these policy statements of the legislative bodies that the mandate for public planning is established.

Private corporations need no enabling legislation for the internal operation of their programs. The boards of directors must accurately estimate the need for their product or activity and set goals. No large corporation would remain viable for very long without such forecasting.

PLANNING AT STATE AND LOCAL LEVELS

Planning in the United States that deals with state, regional, and local affairs is left to the states and communities to promulgate and implement. Exceptions occur in those areas where the economic support of the na-

---

3. Section 65300, California Laws Related to Conservation and Planning.

tional government is required to meet local needs. There has always been concern that "big brother" be kept out of local affairs. Thus city and regional planning and implementation are often without review by the state or by national planning agencies.

In general, planning can be divided into two major categories: the private sector, and government agencies. The right of the government to regulate the private sector is under constant challenge by those who feel that land ownership includes the right to do with it what one wishes provided the rights of others are not violated. As cities have grown in size and complexity and land has changed hands frequently, some sense of order has needed to be established and accepted, and public regulation is often required.

Public planning takes place at all levels of government. The federal government plans, and its plans affect the everyday lives of people in many ways. In certain areas, especially in land use planning, it has been determined that the federal government does not have the right to regulate other than on federal land. The states in turn usually delegate this authority to local communities for all but state land, either through the state constitution or by the enactment of specific laws. Sometimes planning laws are flexible and permissive, sometimes they are rigid and mandatory.

Communities, cities, and counties enact laws and ordinances that define the areas of planning that they are by state law or local charter allowed to carry out. If a community seeks financial assistance through one of the many federal programs, comprehensive plans must be prepared, detailing land use, circulation, health, housing, energy, safety factors, educational and recreational facilities, means of conservation, and other elements that relate to the social, economic, and physical structure of the community.

In most cases legislative bodies create planning commissions and departments to carry out the mandate of the laws that have been adopted. These bodies in turn are responsible to the legislative body that created them.

ELEMENTS OF THE PROCEDURE

The planning process begins with an in-depth study of the physical, social, economic, and political structure of the community. The study includes material on soil and topographic conditions, hydrology, seismic problems, if any, and air, wind, and temperature conditions. Other factors are also discussed: population growth rates and potentials, employment opportunities, health and welfare conditions, the availability of utilities and public facilities, and a myriad of other data. All of this together identifies the nature and possible choices for future growth and prosperity.

Following the gathering of this basic data the material is analyzed and computerized. In the form of maps, charts, and text, the data is reviewed by the planning agencies and becomes the basis for projections. After internal reviews, the basic data and proposals are presented to the public at regularly scheduled study sessions. These are followed by public hearings before the planning commission and legislative body.

Almost every matter dealing with the use of land requires that the planning commission and, more important, the legislative body hold one or more public hearings prior to the rendering of a decision. In controversial matters, many hearings may be held before a vote is taken to determine the outcome of the issue.

Hearings can be many things. They are often fruitful and productive. But sometimes they are the scene of angry debates. The people may speak and the decision-makers listen but do not hear, having already come to a predetermined conclusion. Sometimes the proponents of a plan are dealt with gently and the opponents challenged in such a way that betrays the prejudice of the legislators. Corruption and hidden economic involvement are not unknown.

When the inputs from the public and the official agencies are digested, and official actions are taken in conformity with local law, the plans become effective and are the basis for future decisions on many facets of planning for the future.

Decisions: A Comment

When decisions are not made by natural forces themselves, such as earthquakes, floods, volcanoes, or similar external factors, they are made by humans. Human forces—decisions—have aided and fashioned the form and substance of our urban communities. Sometimes they have been helped by natural forces and sometimes they have been eliminated. Urbanism in the Nile Valley was conditioned by the annual floods of the Nile River. Pompeii was destroyed by the volcanic actions of Mt. Vesuvius. San Francisco was nearly destroyed by earthquake. Other examples abound in all parts of the world. The recognition of which natural elements are favorable or unfavorable should be a serious determining factor in future courses of action. Urban areas should be built outside flood plains, away from locations subject to seismic or any other potentially catastrophic situations. Yet Pompeii was rebuilt in the same place, and San Francisco is as prone to earthquakes as in the past. A day seldom passes without news of the impact of improper or unwise land use decisions on the welfare of great numbers of people.

Human actions have been just as destructive of urban development as natural ones. The city of Jerusalem had been destroyed time and time again by crusaders and other rampaging armies. Wars, especially recent ones, have made rubble of cities throughout the world.

It is clear that human decisions related to current urban growth and development are (or should be) increasingly involved in dealing with the forces of nature and politics, and are conditioned by logic, reason, sentiment, greed, and outright corruption. The mix of these forces determines the quality of government and its impact on the life-style and welfare of all the residents of that area.

In the modern world, human decisions that affect the public domain are subject to review and determinations by courts of competent jurisdiction. Ultimately controversial issues are subject to review and action by the supreme courts of the lands when constitutional matters are involved.

Some Unwritten Factors

The composition of the decision-making bodies has a great deal to do with the quality of the decisions made. Members of legislative bodies are elected by the residents and citizens of the local communities. In many instances they are interested in the welfare of the entire community, but in some they consider themselves to represent only the particular precinct, ward, or district that elected them. When special-interest groups influence their political behavior to the extent of special deals or projects, the larger community may well be the loser. This holds true as well for agreements with other legislators for projects that will benefit solely their constituency—"pork barrel" projects.

The comprehensive plan and policies associated with it are intended to provide the legislative body with a visible basis for decisions on land use. However, the comprehensive plan is viewed all too often only as a guide, and as such is sometimes ignored as "too general and too idealistic." If the plan gets in the way of their short-term interests, it is amended to make the desired activities possible. In the city of Torrance, California, for example, an application was made for an oil drilling permit in the city's central business district. Both the comprehensive plan and the zoning plan prohibited oil drilling and extraction in the area. Yet the city council approved the permit after stormy hearings, amending both plan and zoning to accommodate the powerful applicant.

In almost every community there is an individual or group of individuals that wields tremendous influence on public decisions, quite often behind the scenes. This group is identified as the local power structure, a basic element in decisions. Input into the process can take place at the country club, the social affair, over the telephone, or by media editorial.

This is not intended to indicate that all influence is evil in intent, but there is no doubt that it is a factor in normal community affairs.

Environmental impact studies and assessments are another device intended to provide legislative bodies with as many facts as possible. But casual observation would indicate that many of these assessments are merely "boiler plate" and are tossed aside with "negative declarations" or merely filed.

One wonders about the number of decision-makers who read and understand the contents of some of these complicated and specialized reports.

PARTICIPANTS IN DECISIONS

Governmental

The Legislative Body. The role of the legislative body is that of decision-maker; ultimately its members determine the character the city shall aspire to achieve. It activates the planning commission, provides finances for its staff, approves its membership, and supports its activities through regard for its recommendations. Except for the relatively narrow limits of administrative determination reserved to the planning commission, decisions on all planning policies rest with the elected representatives of the people. Acting upon recommendations of the commission, the legislative body translates the plan into action. It may also act as a board of appeals on commission decisions, but this function is usually assigned to an administrative committee specifically charged with the responsibility. Policies directing the shape of the city reflect the capacity of the planning commission and the stature of the legislative body.

The Planning Commission. The planning commission is the legal agency of the community through which most planning is performed. In many localities the official family is few in number and the planning commission may not have staff, the engineer or clerk being largely responsible for the preparation of all plans. Large cities, however, usually have well-staffed organizations of qualified personnel.

The commission is a group of private citizens appointed and approved by the area's legislative bodies. The commissioners are community leaders in real estate, banking, the chamber of commerce, or attorneys, architects, doctors, labor representatives, social workers, and so on. It might be assumed that some commissioners, by the nature of their backgrounds and personal interests, would be devoted to the preservation of property values rather than the general community welfare. Although it cannot be denied that such has sometimes been the case, it is not infrequently found that men with experience in the private business of community building are well qualified to serve the public interest and respond accordingly when given positions of genuine public responsibility.

New commissioners are seldom adequately informed about the planning process and its purposes or objectives, and they may require some time for training and to familiarize themselves with the nature of their responsibility. Some communities appoint ex officio members to the planning commission to assist the new commissioners in their tasks. These members may be in the legislature or may be the heads of various departments of the local government—the engineer, the road commissioner, the county surveyor, attorney, the public works officer, and so on. They advise the commission on matters of which they have special knowledge, but they seldom enjoy the privilege of voting upon the proceeding before the commission.

Exclusive of ex officio members, the commission varies between five and nine in number, depending on local charter regulations or state legislation. The frequency of meetings depends upon the extent of the planning program. In some large cities the program is sufficiently active to warrant the establishment of a separate commission to administer the zoning ordinances.

The planning commission usually serves in an advisory capacity to the legislative body, the council, or board of supervisors. These bodies refer matters of planning to the commission for reports and recommendations, which the legislative body may then accept or reject. As a rule the preparation of the comprehensive and other plans for civic development are specified in the enabling legislation that created the commission. In such activities the commission requires no specific instructions from the legislative body. However, these functions require an appropriation of funds for an adequate staff; unless the legislative body is sympathetic to the planning program, it can effectively delay and seriously hamper the commission's performance.

The planning commission recommends plans to the legislative body after it has held public hearings, which then may or may not adopt it. When a plan is adopted it becomes law, governing the actions of all the people in the community as well as local governmental agencies. Because this is so, all public departments are required to refer any plans for specific improvements to the planning commission for review and approval. This coordination avoids the duplication of services and the functioning at cross-purposes that can easily occur in the wide range of urban activities. The coordinating functions are becoming increasingly important as the areas continue to grow.

Rather than use the planning commission, some large cities have a separate zoning administrator and board of appeals. The board is responsible for interpreting the zoning law and creating such variances as unforeseen conditions may warrant. Normally the planning commission prepares the ordinance, and the zoning administrator or local building and safety department enforces it.

Relief from the requirements of the planning policies established by law is provided all citizens if the law deprives them of property without just compensation or it is applied in a discriminatory manner. This relief may be obtained by appeal to the planning commission and the legislative body. In the event that the appeal fails to bring a satisfactory resolution of the case, it may be referred to the courts for decision. It is from such cases that the great fund of judicial opinions on the planning process have emerged.

Because the planning commission is only an advisory body with no legislative powers and with limited administrative authority, some persons have questioned the need for its existence. Rather than a commission, it has been suggested that a competent planning department should report directly to the administrative or executive office and the legislative body. The planning commission, however, plays a vital role as a catalyst for the variety of interests concerned with the objectives and consequences of planning. Providing a forum for deliberation of facts and opinions, the planning commission can serve to resolve issues and offer to the legislative body a well-defined and supported foundation for policy decisions. Some applicants ignore the planning commission's decisions when they are adverse, appealing to the legislative body, where political influence may negate planning logic.

The Planning Department. The planning commission depends for its effectiveness in large part upon the competence of the technical staff in the planning department. Whether the city charter provides for the planning director to report directly to the mayor or to the planning commission, the policies finally adopted by the legislative body are dependent upon the competence, skill, and enlightenment of the staff in the planning department. It is the staff that prepares the comprehensive plan, probably the most important single action affecting the future development of the city, and it is the staff that with legal guidance formulates the provisions of the zoning ordinance and subdivision regulations. Implementing the comprehensive plan, it coordinates with other departments of government with respect to streets and highways; health, education, and recreational facilities; utilities; police and fire protection; and all building and engineering activities. The department is, in many states, required by law to cooperate in the preparation of the city budget for both administrative and capital improvement programs. When the department's staff is endowed with that rare combination of vision, technical skill, and administrative talent, it becomes the heart of urban government.

Zoning Administrator. The amount and variety of improvements applied for in a large community may require an independent administrator for the zoning ordinance, who interprets the zoning ordinance for application in specific cases and may provide relief by variance permits when warranted. The administrator's decisions may be appealed, in sequence, to the planning commission, legislative body, appeals board, or court of competent jurisdiction.

The Appeals Board. As affairs of local government increase in complexity, usually proportionate with the size of communities, the interpretations of zoning ordinances and their variances have encouraged the creation of an appeals board. This agency derives its authority and is created in a way similar to the planning commission. It conducts hearings on appeals of planning commission or zoning administrator decisions and attempts to offer objective attention to appeals that may warrant reconsideration.

Outside Consultants

Outside consultants can bring to the planning commission the advantage of their particular in-depth experience, but their most vital contribution is their freedom from local pressures. They can help supply courage, conviction, and inspiration for the staff and commission. They may function in lieu of a full staff in small communities or serve as expert counsel on planning problems of particular complexity.

It is essential for the consultant to work intimately with the leaders of the community as well as with government agencies and their staffs. This involvement may include participation in public meetings and hearings on various proposals, including the adoption of the general plan, thereby giving greater assurance that the important policy statement would be received favorably by the community. It is equally important that the staff be adequately budgeted to maintain the planning process or employ outside consultants to serve in that capacity.

Consultants frequently represent both the private and the public sectors. However, when the consultant has at one time advised the community on a given matter it would appear less than ethical for him to return at a later date to the same scene and represent a private client's opposition to his original recommendations. Unless, or course, there had been substantial changes in the physical, social, or economic environment.

The Public

Citizen participation is an essential function of the democratic political process. It may be characterized by courteous support or by confrontation and may be extensive or slight. The current emphasis is on the participation of as broad a segment of citizens as possible in the planning process.

To be effective, this participation must be based upon information acquired by study and clear presentation of facts. Recommendations from the public are generally tempered by politicians' understanding of the public's needs, as they try to make reasonable decisions. All too often citizen participation has involved passionate expressions of prejudices for or against a particular proposal, when behind-the-scenes lobbying has already determined the decision-makers' conclusions.

Most if not all of the federal programs that provided financial assistance to local communities call for citizen participation. The effort to determine the nature of the programs locally and thus gain support for them has seldom been successful in spite of some heroic attempts. People tend to become involved defensively; a controversial issue seems to be required to rouse the public. Even then, interest and participation tend to disappear as soon as the issue is resolved.

There is no doubt that the concept of public participation is an excellent one. Citizen involvement in public issues is the best way to obtain effective and responsible government. What must be determined is the best way to achieve it.

The community at large tends not to participate at governmental hearings. The people do not have the information they need about the possible consequences of the proposed action. This lack of involvement prevents the community from manifesting its concern for matters that will directly affect it. Mainly special-interest groups are "the public" in the minds of the legislators.

On the other hand, the wishes of local residents can be made known, especially when they form themselves into a pressure group. They may not have the financial resources of the organized proponents of the plan, but their voting strength gives them power in the community. At times these groups unfortunately take positions of blind opposition to any development, planned or unplanned, good or poor.

The planning profession has made considerable progress in its advisory role, particularly as legislative directives have expanded the programs and broadened the administrative responsibilities of the staff. This position will become more influential, not less so, as the public is informed of the implications of the proposals under consideration. Planners must be open to suggestions made by community members even when these suggestions differ from their point of view. Their task should be to bring together diverse viewpoints for the benefit of the entire community.

The Advocacy Planner. In a sense every proposal presented to a planning commission or legislative body can be considered "advocacy planning" since the plans are intended to serve the special needs of the applicant.

More realistically, the advocacy planner is meant to ensure that those not able to attend public hearings have their interests represented, so that the influential and affluent do not dominate public policy. In recent years this has come to imply the representation of minority groups and the poor. In fact, this seldom occurs. Most cities do not employ anyone whose responsibilities include involvement with these "special interest" groups. A plan's effect on the least mobile, least powerful elements of society is rarely taken into account.

Design centers in some cities have assumed these responsibilities. These are locally established organizations supported by federal funds funneled through an area university. They are usually meant to serve the planning needs of the poorer elements of the community. The design center in San Francisco is supported through the University of California in Berkeley, the one in Kansas City through the University of Kansas.

Lawyers and the Law. The city attorney or the district attorney's office serves as the legal advisor to public agencies. The staff reviews all proposed legislation, prepares codes and ordinances, and represents their agencies in litigations. Their role is generally defensive, their purpose being to keep communities from involvements in costly suits.

Although the decisions of legislative bodies are usually final, the courts become part of the planning process when there are charges of violation of the law, whether state or federal.

The Media. The role of the media is often overlooked. Most people are informed through newspapers, radio, or television. Local news items may deal with planning, especially if it becomes controversial. All too often a commentator or reporter will present his own point of view, making it appear that the opinion is fact. The power of the media to influence final decisions cannot be underestimated. Their views are usually set forth convincingly, are not subject to an immediate counterpresentation, and carry the weight of authority because of who they are.

The Ombudsman. The ombudsman is a mediator, the person or persons who attempt to resolve conflicts before they reach the public arena. Misunderstandings or lack of knowledge are often the basis of conflicts that can frustrate or defeat even the most worthy of programs, and the ombudsman explains the program and finds out where the problems lie. Primarily listeners, they help individuals let off steam and frustration, and frequently direct them to officials who can provide answers—probably their most important function. They are not always included in the staffing of both public and private planning offices, but it would seem they should be.

The Referendum and the Initiative. There are occasions when the general public becomes more deeply concerned than usual with the actions taken or about to be taken by their local legislative bodies. If the actions are sufficiently controversial or if disagreement is widespread, petitions with the public's point of view may then be made up and circulated. The number of registered voters required to sign is stipulated in state law pertaining to the action. The petitions are filed with the local governing body and eventually an election is held in which the legislative action is put to a vote. This is the referendum. If the action or law is voted down, it is no longer valid.

The initiative is simpler. A proposed law is promulgated by the legislative body or by interested citizens and voted upon by the public. If it is approved by the voters it goes into effect.

THE PROFESSIONAL PLANNER

Planners are employed by most public or private organizations to carry out the official policies of the organization. There appears to be more than a suggestion that the planner in municipal government has a role to play in dealings with the community. However, that role invariably gets tangled in several basic conflicts.

Is the planner the representative of the elected public official or officials and, as such, carrying out their policies? Or is the planner's role to initiate programs and seek public understanding and support for them? Does the planner have implicit powers that outrank the elected public official? Can or should he arouse public opinion on an issue that will undermine the authority of the elected official? Can he appear in court as a friend of the court on issues that transcend the traditional, established, politically inspired policies and attitudes? Should the planner merely prepare the plans? Or, in the best interest of the community, should he "sell" them to the public? Should he interpret the desires of one or another lobbying group? Or should the planner be merely an advisor whose advice may be disregarded if it is not consistent with a given segment of community population?

No matter how these conflicts are resolved, whether the planners are involved in the public or private sector, certain professional responsibilities should be understood and adhered to as they make their recommendations to the decision-makers, be they corporate executives or community legislators. These could be called the professional planner's creed.

The Planner's Creed

Planners should be trained and have knowledge of the various aspects of their specialty. They should be willing to listen and learn. They should be objective and as free as possible of prejudices toward people or proposals.

Planners should have an active imagination, be able to portray the future in graphic terms by projecting known trends, practices, and policies.

Planners should have convictions, knowing that weakly presented advice might have an adverse impact upon people. They must be believers in the planning process and the ultimate good that it can do for the orderly development of the community.

Planners must be ethical purists. There should never be a suspicion of favoritism, especially toward one's self, as the basis for a recommendation.

Planners must be communicators, able to provide the decision-makers with clear and concise material upon which to base their judgments. The ability to communicate with the public on all agenda items and proposals is mandatory.

Planners must have respect for those they work for and with as well as the public at large. Being civil and polite at all times marks the successful planner and administrator.

Planners should have courage. Difficult problems are the lot of the profession; without them there might be no need for the planner in the first place. To be able to make a controversial recommendation in a palatable manner is an art essential for a successful program.

Planners are team players. They must understand the policies and the limits within which they operate. When problems arise, they must be able to consult effectively with their peers in the effort to better serve the public.

Planners should understand that in the preparation of a comprehensive plan there must be participation by specialists from allied fields such as engineering, real estate, hydrology, transportation, economics, social sciences, political sciences, and so on. Their expertise can assist in both the preparation and implementation of the plan proposals. Above all, planners should not become dilettantes in all fields and by this lead the community into ill-conceived and ill-considered decisions.

Planners should document all findings and recommendations, keeping full and complete records of all discussions and actions. Telephone messages should be logged along with meetings with applicants, commissioners, and legislators.

In sum, planners must be dedicated to the public's welfare regardless of the sector within which they may work.

The Planner and Social Issues

Developments in the fields of social welfare and the physical environment have intensified the essentially affirmative role of those whose civic and professional responsibility is directed to the public interest. The creative planner is among them.

In recent years the American Planners Association (APA) has consistently expressed a growing concern for the fate of those individuals and groups who have not received an equitable share of the benefits of our affluent society. . . . Since manipulations of the physical environment inevitably affect the distribution of social and economic costs and benefits, virtually all public planning bears strong social welfare implications.

If these developments tend to project the planner into the role of advocate for social well-being, it is hardly a new role. A good city is the intended historical objective of the planner; it should be designed for social well-being. Planners seek to restore cities to a favorable environment for all inhabitants. But such a goal cannot be achieved by remaining in the passive role of "expert technicians." Planning commissioners have an obligation to assert the public interest on all measures embraced in the planning process. Our institutions of higher learning must generate the perception, talent, and capacity for creative contributions to the transformation of the urban structure and instill in their students the commitment to stand for them as advocates.

Among the social welfare issues that directly affect the quality of urban life, housing is a major priority. The professional planner may not be expected to present all the solutions to the housing problem, but he or she must maintain a healthy perspective.

Planners should recognize that juggling statistics of housing production does not produce adequate housing for the underprivileged. They should understand that ethnic discrimination will not disappear, nor will social comfort and compatibility appear, simply by the dispersal of "low-cost" housing in affluent suburbs. They should know that the major financial obstacle to building better housing is the high interest rate on home mortgages, not only the costs of labor or materials. Fundamentally, the planner must understand that as long as landowners may reap the benefit of values created by community prosperity, not only by their own investments, the public will be obliged to deal with unabated rises in land costs in its subsidy of low-cost housing.

The planner should realize that "ghettoization" is not a result of ethnic discrimination alone. People of all groups seek to maintain some vestige of social cohesiveness and economic, religious, and cultural identity: it happens in Scarsdale, Grosse Point, Palm Beach, and Beverly Hills, as well as in Harlem, Watts, and the barrios.

And the planner should recognize that the stain of slums and the blight of physical deterioration must be erased from the face of the city if the human dignity of any people is to be preserved. Toward this goal, the planner must encourage the general public to view problems of the less privileged as community responsibilities to be faced and resolved through the efforts of an informed public, both general and official. Housing, health, culture, and social amenities are interrelated and must be resolved by local agencies run by peers of the community.

THE FUTURE OF PUBLIC PLANNING

While planning has become a more important part of the activities of the private sector, it seems to be subject to a questionable future as an implement of public policy. The full impact of federal actions in deleting or reducing support for planning at state and local levels was accentuated when Section 701 of the Housing Act was done away with. This financial support for local planning was the lodestone of assistance that made it possible for many communities to develop both long-range comprehensive plans and up-to-date zoning and subdivision regulations.

With the severe financial limitations placed upon local government, it is increasingly difficult to employ the staff or consultants to keep the planning programs current, let alone administer the regulations in an effective manner. The future does not necessarily seem bright.

PART 4

PLANNING FOR THE FUTURE

Man's reach should exceed his grasp,
or what's a heaven for?

Robert Browning

CHAPTER 19

THE COMPREHENSIVE PLAN

COMPREHENSIVE PLAN DEFINED

Patrick Geddes promoted the philosophy that called for the integration of natural and social planning and the integration of the natural and social worlds.

All too many persons believe that the comprehensive plan deals only with the use of land and that its most definitive forms are the zoning and subdivision regulations. To be meaningful, the plan must cover a much wider range than that; it must encompass the social, economic, and political elements that guide and implement the life of our communities and those who live within them.

The comprehensive plan must be farsighted, anticipating the needs and desires of the community. It must provide the guidance essential to the preparation of specific plans and the budgeting to accomplish them. In order to be comprehensive it must become the people's plan, supported by them when timely proposals are to be implemented by action agencies.

Neither the master plan nor the general plan is the same thing as the comprehensive plan. The term *master plan* has been applied to almost every scheme for property development, from an individual lot to a large estate, a shopping center, or a city. The term *general plan* identifies long-range, comprehensive planning by or for a government agency as a foun-

263

dation for overall land development policies within specific corporate limits. These terms were interchangeable, but "general plan" was adopted to distinguish it from the varied nongovernmental applications associated with "master plan."

The term *comprehensive plan* was added to the planner's vocabulary in recent years to indicate that current community planning is more than "general." These planning programs now include many social and economic elements that were not included in the earlier days of professional practice. Students graduating from the universities where urban planning degrees are offered frequently are equipped to participate in a variety of programs, many of which have little or nothing to do with the physical planning that formed the basis for the early development of the profession. This should not demean the importance of physical planning; it merely adds a new dimension to it.

Nor should *comprehensive planning* and *a comprehensive plan* be confused. Comprehensive planning may range from the preparation of a series of highly specialized studies to an intensive study of a development plan for an entire area. The comprehensive plan, however, must include a review of the physical structure of a city or planning area; a measurement of development trends; a definition of goals and objectives for future growth and change; proposals to protect and promote health, education, and the general welfare; and specific recommendations, policies, and graphics that delineate the plan and establish standards in support of it.

WHY IT IS NEEDED

After the early adventures in zoning it became increasingly apparent that this use of the police power to safeguard the public welfare could not stand by itself. The courts had upheld the right of a community to exercise the police power in legislating regulations governing the use of land. They had granted that a community has the right to determine its own character. Conservatives such as Justice George Sutherland of the Supreme Court had supported this right, and there was a growing popular acceptance of zoning as a means to protect the interests of a community.

But the courts perceived that if a community was to determine the appropriate uses of its land properly and provide a firm basis for its control as prescribed in zoning ordinances, it needed to appraise the use of all land within its political jurisdiction and give consideration to conditions in areas contiguous to it as well. The courts found good reason for this view. They had observed numerous abuses of the police power. For example, many small districts would be established as a way to prevent the construction of some particular improvement or deny a use deemed undesirable in some existing structure; sometimes a zoning ordinance was intended to create or protect a monopoly.

In order to assure that districts were not arbitrarily or discriminatorily determined, the courts required evidence that the various zones were related to an overall evaluation of land use in the city. There was a growing insistence upon a "comprehensive plan" as a foundation for zoning ordinances; Justice George Sutherland's opinion in the Euclid case clearly expressed this need. Thus the process of the comprehensive plan evolved.

Seeking techniques with which to satisfy the requirement for a comprehensive plan, some communities willfully avoided the issue by employing specious devices. One of these was to zone all land to the least restrictive use with the exception of certain limited "refined" districts. The community could thus allege in court that it had enacted a comprehensive zoning ordinance since every parcel of land in the city was within a zoning district. Although that statement was true, it was not a plan. Another device was to zone all land not specifically zoned for other purposes as a residential district, with the provision for variances from the residential use. In the administration of the ordinance each variation was then interpreted as an act of making the original plan more "precise." Neither of these techniques stood the test for long since they were evasions of the basic principles of planning.

Too frequently zoning practices resolved themselves into a process of "freezing" existing land uses, including all the misuses that had previously established themselves. In some communities, an inventory and classification of all existing land uses were adopted as the "plan" of the city. Travesties on planning, these practices are gradually being replaced by a more enlightened awareness of the advantages of planning to civic growth and development. As a means to provide a pattern for future development of the city, the comprehensive plan has become a generally accepted instrument.

CONTENTS AND FUNCTION

Many states mandate by law that comprehensive integrated plans be prepared and that they be used as the basis for later decisions involving public activity. The 1982 California law is not untypical. It summarizes in a rather brief statement what the contents of the plan shall be and the process that shall be employed in implementing it.

    (a)   Each demonstration county and city shall prepare an integrated general plan which contains the following:
        (1)   Goals, policies, and programs for the physical, social, and economic development of the community;

(2)   Documentation of the data and analysis upon which these goals, policies, and programs are based;

(3)   Assessment of the fiscal capacity of the county or city to implement the plan; and

(4)   An implementation schedule that links the plan to the allocation of public resources, including capital expenditures, the annual budget, and federal and state funding for local programs.

(b)   The planning process developed to prepare the integrated general plan shall include provision for:

(1)   Integration, to the extent possible, of other required planning processes with the general plan process; including, in the case of counties, social services planning;

(2)   To the extent feasible, integration of plans with required regional or county plans, plans and programs of special districts, and with statewide goals and policies;

(3)   Assessment of the potential physical, environmental, social, and economic impacts of alternative plan proposals; and

(4)   Specific mechanisms for involvement of citizens in the planning process.

(c)   The demonstration counties or cities shall record and analyze the cost of development, maintenance, and implementation of the alternative plan.

PURPOSE

The modern city is a complex organism. It is a great human enterprise that should serve the material and spiritual needs of humanity. It is a segment of the land that people have selected as their place to live and to work, to learn and to trade, to play and to pray. It is a mosaic of homes and shops, factories and offices, schools and libraries, theaters and hospitals, parks and religious institutions, meeting places and government centers, fire stations and post offices. These are woven together by a network of streets and transportation routes, water, sanitation, and communication channels, and held together by social bonds and economic conditions.

To arrange all these facilities properly as the city develops is the purpose of the comprehensive plan. The city is a cumbersome affair, at once sensitive to the multitude of small shifts and yet capable of absorbing great shocks. A change in any part affects other parts of this structure. A new home means more traffic on the streets, extra mail in the postman's bag, another customer in the supermarket, more children in the school, more water for the lawn, more picnics in the park. It also means more revenue in taxes. But growth does not always mean strength and prosperity for the community. This rests with the standards a community determines to maintain and the balanced use of its land and resources.

The comprehensive plan is a guide to orderly city development to promote the health, safety, welfare, and convenience of the people of a community.

It organizes and coordinates the complex relationships between urban land uses and many civic activities. It charts a course for growth and change. It expresses the aims and ambitions of a community, delineating the form and character it seeks to achieve. It reflects the policies by which these goals may be reached. It is responsive to appropriate change and for maintaining its essential vitality and is subject to continual review. It directs the physical development of the community and its environs in relation to its social and economic well-being for the fulfillment of the rightful common destiny, according to a "master plan" based on "careful and comprehensive surveys and studies of present conditions and the prospects of future growth of the municipality, and embodying scientific teachings and creative experience." In a word, this is an exercise of the State's inherent authority, antedating the Constitution itself, to have recourse to such measures as may serve the basic common moral and material needs. Planning to this end is as old as government itself—of the very essence of an ordered and civilized society.[1]

THE PLAN AS PROCESS

State legislation usually requires the preparation of a comprehensive plan and sets forth the scope. A passage from the California law reads, in part:

Each commission or planning department shall prepare and the commission shall adopt a comprehensive, long-term general plan for the physical development of the city, county, area, or region, and of any land outside its boundaries which in the commision's judgment bears relation to its planning. The plan may be referred to as the master or general plan and shall be officially certified by the planning commission and the legislative body.[2]

After the comprehensive plan has been adopted by the legislative body:

. . . no road, street, highway, square, park, or other public way, ground or open space shall be acquired by dedication or otherwise, and no street, road, highway or public way shall be closed or abandoned, and no public building or structure shall be constructed or authorized in the area . . . until the location, character, and extent thereof shall be submitted to and shall have been reported on by the planning commission.[3]

Such statements of official policy establish the planning process in our cities, and it is such statements that have been upheld by the courts of our land because they recognize the necessity for a city plan.

Ladislas Segoe described the comprehensive plan in these terms:

The comprehensive city plan or master plan, while it must be thoroughly practical and sound economically, must give expression also to other than

1. *Mansfield & Sweet, Inc. v. Town of West Orange, supra.*
2. State of California, *Laws Relating to Conservation, Planning and Zoning,* 1959.
3. Ibid.

the purely materialistic aspirations of the people of a community. Only then will the plan possess—in addition to its influence toward a more convenient, efficient economical development—the inspirational force that will force civic interest, devotion and loyalty essential for building better cities.

The comprehensive city plan or master plan must therefore be—first, a balanced and otherwise attractive general design best suited to present and probable future needs; second, in scale with the population and economic prospects of the community; and third, in scale with its financial resources, present and prospective. The satisfying of the above criteria calls for the application of scientific as well as artistic effort, in order to produce a city plan of attractive form, pleasing balance and detail, attuned to the economic and social activities of the community. . . .[4]

It is probably more accurate to describe a comprehensive plan as a process rather than as a conclusive statement. It is a pattern for the physical development of the city, a pattern to guide the city builders in locating their investments and measuring the prospect for success. It is a design for the physical, social, economic, and political framework for the city; it welds the sociological, economic, and geographic properties of the city into a structure.

To suggest that the plan is a fluid process may imply that decisions are not represented in it. The plan for a city will be modified as conditions may alter the affairs of people from time to time, but a comprehensive plan represents certain decisions of vital importance to the welfare of the people and their city. It represents a decision as to the number of people the city may build to accommodate; it represents the standards by which the city will be developed. It represents decisions on the appropriate relation between the uses of land and the relation between the land to be developed for residential, commercial, and industrial enterprise. It calls for decisions on the lines of communication that link these areas—the circulation system and the infrastructure required to serve the residents. And it represents decisions on the plan for reservation of open space throughout the city.

These are broad decisions, but they are essential to the formulation of a pattern for city building. It is upon these decisions that the health of urban development rests, for they express the aspirations of a community and set the goals toward which the city may advance.

The comprehensive plan has sometimes been regarded as only a reference guide for the planning commission, being subject neither to formal public hearings nor to official action by the legislative body. This arrangement appears to avoid the cumbersome proceedings that accompany formal action to modify the plan, thus affording maximum flexibility at the

4. Ladislas Segoe, Local Planning Administration, International City Managers' Association, Chicago, 1942, first edition.

discretion of the commission and staff. But it also opens the possibility for personal decision-making in response to special pressures. This status of the plan fails to recognize the essence of the plan itself. Affecting the future of all the people and property in the city, the plan represents the policy that directs future growth and development of the city. It is a public policy for protection of the public welfare and investment in the urban community.

In recent times it has been said that the mapping of proposed future land uses is unnecessary and that the overall set of policies is all that is required to guide the use of land. It is the opinion of others, however, that to do this would leave property owners with no knowledge as to how the policies will be administered on land adjacent to that which they own, and thus endanger the value of their holdings.

Consistency

Assembly Bill 1301, adopted in California in 1974 and still an important legal regulation, requires that zoning be consistent with the comprehensive general plan. It thus establishes these planning policies as the legal criteria for implementation through detailed zoning. This public document is of sufficient importance so that it is subject to public response and discussion and thorough consideration by the legislative body, as well as to adoption as the official plan. It, and subsequent revisions to it, should be adopted by resolution of the legislative body. It serves as the basic frame of reference for all administrative and regulatory measures relating to urban renewal, the capital improvement expenditures. The financial solvency of a city hinges upon a program of public facilities that maintains a balance between expenditure and revenue. The plan aids in weighing this balance. Four basic elements of the comprehensive plan are: (1) plan for land use, (2) plan for circulation, (3) plan for the infrastructure, and (4) capital improvement budgeting. Each of these elements is supported by complete documentary evidence, the social, physical, and economic facts and premises from which they were derived.

Specific Plans

The preparation of specific plans is intended to bridge the gap between the long-range aspects of the comprehensive plan and the immediate requirements of zoning and capital improvement budgeting. The amount of detail involved in the specific plan depends upon the sophistication of the planning system in each community. At least it should show how the comprehensive plan will apply to a specific parcel of land and indicate some of the basic engineering and economics involved in the development process. If an amendment to the comprehensive plan is involved, a detailed plan may be required that includes environmental impact reports to justify the community actions related to the approval of the changes.

ECONOMIC AND SOCIAL CONSIDERATIONS

If the data on the nature of the physical character of the city seem to be complicated, the social and economic facts are even more so. People are not inclined to conceal the manner in which they use the land unless an evasion of the law is involved, but they are reluctant to divulge their ages, incomes, or health; such information is naturally considered to be of a personal nature. To plan for the community welfare, however, it is important to know about the people for whom the plan is intended.

The principal source of economic and social data is the U.S. Census; the elements included have been described earlier. Based upon these data, the Bureau of the Census analyzes the spending habits of the various income groups, indicating the amount each spent for rent, clothes, food, amusement, and other living necessities. However, much of the latter information is given for the whole city and is difficult to relate to the census tracts, the units in which urban statistics are usually tabulated. The exception is housing data, which are listed by blocks in the census and provide a source of information for the land-use survey.

Although most public and private local agencies normally assemble only the information on the social and economic structure of the community in which they are directly interested, the planning agency may obtain and correlate this special information to form an overall picture. Since the various agencies may interpret similar data in different ways, these differences must be resolved by the planners on the basis of the best available known facts.

Care must be taken with the use of these facts. It is a well-known cliché that anything can be proven with statistics; the corollary is that statistics may not prove anything. Thus it is all the more important that they not be misleading. As an illustration, an increase in the number of families and the number of houses built may be nearly the same and therefore indicate no shortage of dwellings. But these "pure" numbers mean little as an evaluation of the housing supply in relation to housing supply and need. The number of families formerly doubled-up, the cost brackets of the new residences, the absence of a normal vacancy factor, and the occupancy of substandard housing facilities are among the statistics to be evaluated with those on the number of families and the housing supply in order for the evaluation of need to be accurate. Such caution and consideration of all related factors are essential for the proper and correct use of statistics.

Availability Of Data

The economic base of urban communities will differ from one geographical area to another, depending upon the nature of the local ecology and environment. Some areas will depend upon the preservation of natural resources, others will depend upon their extraction and exploitation. In general terms the types of activities considered as factors in the economic base include:

industry and agriculture	military
wholesaling and retailing	retirement pensions
services	property income
tourism	insurance and finance
transportation	government

These and many other forms of labor and goods exchange constitute the manner in which residents of a given area support themselves and maintain a reasonable level of community life.

Information on the economic development and prospects of the community is usually available through the chamber of commerce, and these data can be cross-referenced with reports by Dun and Bradstreet and the U.S. Department of Commerce, the U.S. Department of Labor, state employment offices, local agencies and industries, and so on. Trends in industrialization and increases in the working force have a decided effect on the planning process. Data on the earning capacity, the average years of employment, the social security structure, types and diversification of employment, and the income groups represented in the working population are necessary to calculate the purchasing power of the community and the ability to pay rents and taxes. Such information can be traced through the U.S. Department of Labor, the state employment services, and local industries. These statistics are important as a basis for the comprehensive plan.

Other social statistics are available from a wide variety of sources. Data on disease and health can be obtained from the health departments of cities, counties, and states, as well as associations concerned with specific diseases. Local police and probation department files record the location of criminal incidents and the residences of convicted offenders. Foundations, service clubs, veterans' organizations, universities, charitable groups, and other private agencies have valuable data. The birth and death rates, infant mortality rate, marriage and divorce rates, population immigration and emigration, educational level, occupations of the working force, the cultural inclinations—all this is among the data the planning commission must correlate objectively for the best and most workable plan.

General and Family Characteristics: 1980

The Area Neighborhoods	The Area 06-180	Neigh-borhood 001	Neigh-borhood 002	Neigh-borhood 003	Neigh-borhood 004	Neigh-borhood 005	Neigh-borhood 006	Neigh-borhood 007	Neigh-borhood 008	Neigh-borhood 009	Neigh-borhood 010
URBAN AND RURAL											
Total persons	**32 584**	**2 506**	**1 016**	**1 529**	**1 015**	**1 747**	**2 329**	**1 067**	**1 697**	**993**	**1 152**
Urban											
Inside urbanized areas	32 480	2 506	1 016	1 529	1 015	1 747	2 329	1 067	1 697	993	1 152
Outside urbanized areas	32 480	2 506	1 016	1 529	1 015	1 747	2 329	1 067	1 697	993	1 152
Rural	104	—	—	—	—	—	—	—	—	—	—
RACE AND SPANISH ORIGIN											
White	28 963	2 325	938	1 499	58	1 487	1 987	1 017	1 513	944	1 097
Black	1 575	50	28	5	941	45	78	14	144	8	6
Percent of total persons	4.8	2.0	2.8	0.3	92.7	2.6	3.3	1.3	8.5	0.8	0.5
American Indian, Eskimo, and Aleut	184	6	2	6	1	16	12	2	12	7	24
Asian and Pacific islander[1]	786	72	15	15	6	26	79	9	17	17	8
Other	1 076	53	33	4	9	173	173	25	11	17	17
Spanish origin[2]	2 932	260	67	48	22	350	301	59	86	48	43
Percent of total persons	9.0	10.4	6.6	3.1	2.2	20.0	12.9	5.5	5.1	4.8	3.7
AGE											
Total persons	**32 584**	**2 506**	**1 016**	**1 529**	**1 015**	**1 747**	**2 329**	**1 067**	**1 697**	**993**	**1 152**
Under 5 years	1 265	94	38	22	82	104	209	8	39	11	55
5 to 9 years	1 316	138	32	39	93	75	193	12	31	41	49
10 to 14 years	1 577	189	29	69	128	99	136	18	43	46	64
15 to 19 years	1 914	190	49	68	110	137	166	34	47	57	76
20 to 24 years	2 264	150	97	64	85	217	222	34	47	33	64
25 to 29 years	2 205	204	87	44	65	155	276	46	49	27	65
30 to 34 years	1 986	222	47	55	54	122	239	49	28	41	79
35 to 44 years	3 234	291	117	138	108	225	283	68	77	124	138
45 to 54 years	3 795	307	96	241	112	180	226	110	145	128	145
55 to 59 years	2 388	132	58	146	36	110	130	71	150	97	118
60 to 64 years	2 505	165	64	163	40	78	85	102	232	84	81
65 to 74 years	5 122	251	146	337	76	143	120	283	581	165	143
75 to 84 years	2 477	126	106	125	24	80	37	200	198	115	64
85 years and over	536	47	50	18	2	22	7	32	30	24	11

Table columns appear under headings that are cut off at the top edge of the page and cannot be read; eleven data columns are transcribed in left-to-right order.

Under 5 years	604	48	18	10	32	53	94	4	20	4	30
5 to 9 years	642	71	15	22	47	35	89	5	15	25	28
10 to 14 years	801	91	15	27	65	51	68	9	24	23	27
15 to 19 years	959	78	26	36	51	66	82	19	31	28	41
20 to 24 years	1 060	68	49	33	48	104	94	20	26	19	27
25 to 29 years	1 088	96	43	22	44	71	141	26	21	14	37
30 to 34 years	961	106	23	36	28	47	120	18	17	18	38
35 to 44 years	1 677	156	61	74	53	107	133	24	44	65	75
45 to 54 years	2 056	147	49	138	65	97	131	53	87	64	77
55 to 59 years	1 363	78	34	87	21	52	62	43	96	52	68
60 to 64 years	1 413	93	39	84	22	47	45	49	141	43	43
65 to 74 years	2 920	138	102	177	55	84	63	167	313	85	79
75 to 84 years	1 414	75	78	57	17	50	21	117	101	63	31
85 years and over	329	29	40	12	—	13	5	17	16	9	5
Median	49.1	40.1	54.4	55.5	28.5	36.1	30.2	65.9	63.6	54.4	45.0
HOUSEHOLD TYPE AND RELATIONSHIP											
Total persons	**32 584**	**2 506**	**1 016**	**1 529**	**1 015**	**1 747**	**2 329**	**1 067**	**1 697**	**993**	**1 152**
In households	**32 305**	**2 428**	**921**	**1 529**	**1 014**	**1 747**	**2 329**	**1 067**	**1 697**	**993**	**1 152**
Family householder	8 997	664	227	503	246	403	623	280	594	290	340
Nonfamily householder: Male	2 589	162	88	88	16	213	129	171	73	80	69
Female	3 682	140	168	154	49	192	91	221	214	79	91
Spouse	7 455	536	186	456	134	295	495	250	548	263	290
Other relatives	7 716	777	199	272	534	473	847	96	227	196	316
Nonrelatives	1 866	149	53	56	35	171	144	49	41	85	46
Persons per household	2.12	2.51	1.91	2.05	3.26	2.16	2.76	1.59	1.93	2.21	2.30
Persons per family	2.69	2.98	2.70	2.45	3.72	2.91	3.15	2.24	2.30	2.58	2.78
In group quarters	**279**	**78**	**95**	—	**1**	—	—	—	—	—	—
Persons 65 years and over	**8 135**	**424**	**302**	**480**	**102**	**245**	**164**	**515**	**809**	**304**	**218**
In households	**7 882**	**346**	**223**	**480**	**102**	**245**	**164**	**515**	**809**	**304**	**218**
Family householder	2 908	132	59	198	46	84	66	166	354	121	86
Nonfamily householder: Male	515	22	16	28	1	17	7	52	27	22	21
Female	1 808	44	89	73	28	64	23	140	145	49	27
Spouse	2 078	87	44	148	17	51	36	140	258	86	64
Other relatives	417	40	13	28	10	18	29	11	13	14	17
Nonrelatives	156	21	2	5	—	11	3	6	12	12	3
In group quarters	**253**	**78**	**79**	—	—	—	—	—	—	—	—

General and Family Characteristics: 1980—Cont.

The Area Neighborhoods	The Area 06-180	Neigh-borhood 001	Neigh-borhood 002	Neigh-borhood 003	Neigh-borhood 004	Neigh-borhood 005	Neigh-borhood 006	Neigh-borhood 007	Neigh-borhood 008	Neigh-borhood 009	Neigh-borhood 010
PERSONS IN HOUSEHOLDS											
Households	**15 268**	**966**	**483**	**745**	**311**	**808**	**843**	**672**	**881**	**449**	**500**
1 person	5 200	226	221	204	59	310	153	356	259	118	130
2 persons	6 427	378	157	402	82	269	280	267	528	226	213
3 persons	1 740	148	62	73	49	114	185	34	41	48	77
4 persons	1 064	124	25	43	39	59	134	6	25	31	51
5 persons	470	51	13	12	44	31	46	6	18	9	16
6 or more persons	367	39	5	11	38	25	45	3	10	17	13
MARITAL STATUS											
Male, 15 years and over	**13 186**	**1 021**	**373**	**643**	**308**	**731**	**894**	**476**	**691**	**435**	**463**
Single	3 373	306	101	110	120	288	243	102	70	94	107
Now married, except separated	7 874	574	205	470	150	334	533	262	560	277	305
Separated	277	19	10	8	10	18	27	13	8	6	2
Widowed	437	31	19	26	5	12	12	25	22	17	11
Divorced	1 225	91	38	29	23	79	79	74	31	41	38
Female, 15 years and over	**15 240**	**1 064**	**544**	**756**	**404**	**738**	**897**	**553**	**893**	**460**	**521**
Single	2 445	176	110	90	113	178	160	85	72	54	86
Now married, except separated	7 756	570	208	465	147	310	520	258	557	272	297
Separated	407	22	20	16	27	29	28	12	11	13	10
Widowed	2 648	157	135	112	63	111	78	125	176	82	69
Divorced	1 984	139	71	73	54	110	111	73	77	39	59

[1] Excludes "Other Asian and Pacific islander" groups identified in sample tabulations.   [2] Persons of Spanish origin may be of any race.

Sample of 1980 Federal Census of the United States

The Use of Data

The planner can fundamentally be said to be a social scientist. Too frequently the social scientist has been cast in the role of historian of economic facts, reporting past trends and current conditions. The economic aspects of planning have thus been limited to an inventory of data that presents the status quo. Statistical techniques are employed in the projection of population and related fields of importance to planning, but the general effect is a kind of resignation by all concerned to the prospects that these projections imply. If planning means anything, it is the endeavor to direct future growth and development, quite the opposite of drifting with the currents of unregulated trends. The tools of socioeconomic analysis are therefore essential in the effort to find a balance among the basic urban activities. And this balance may require that accepted trends be altered, diverted, or redirected—but this is planning.

The increase in population is a natural phenomenon, and the trend of population growth in cities is a consequence of broad economic and social pressures. But to be effective, urban planning cannot succumb to the weight of statistical evidence. Survival of the urban population is at stake and so is the prospect for building decent cities. Means may be developed to control the number of people who are born, as there have been means to lengthen the lifespan. With the reduction of disease and famine, particularly in the Western world, so-called natural ways of stabilizing the population short of war are meager. However, we have the means, through planning and legislation, to regulate the distribution of the urban population, the amounts of land required for the various functions of an urban community, and the standards for the development of the land. To determine the appropriate allocation of land, both in amount and location, the economic demands must be measured. The physical structure must be arranged to accommodate the facilities required for economic survival, and accommodate them in a manner that will produce good places in which to live and work.

The social scientist carries a heavy responsibility for creative analysis of the relationships between people and their employment opportunities, the production resources, and the commerce and industry needed to support an urban population. The city must be built on a firm economic base or it cannot provide the amenities of a civilized community. The future of cities as desirable social environments will depend on our capacity to integrate physical and economic planning. In 1945 Walter Blucher, then Executive Director of the American Society of Planning Officials, stated:

What is the responsibility of the planning agency for a determination of employment possibilities outside of public works? You may think the planning agency has no such responsibility. I don't see how we can do an effective planning job in any community, however, unless we know what the population of the community will be and what the economic possibilities for that population are.[5]

These words were said over forty years ago. They still apply today.

CHANGING COMMUNITY CHARACTER

With the assembly of the data—that part of the planning process identified as research—we learn the nature of the existing city. This is the knowledge needed for analysis of the city; from it we learn why the city was begun, how it grew, and why it prospered.

The sleepy village of the eighteenth century has apparently little in common with the metropolis of today. There may remain marks of its origin, but the functions may have altered completely. As the city grew in size, as the population increased, and as new enterprises developed, the city's character may have altered. Perhaps the quality of community living deteriorated in the growth from a small, intimate town to the unfriendly metropolitan machine it now seems to be. Much may have been lost in this process, enough to question whether the city can recover the human values by which the true living standards of people are measured.

There are reasons why each city is located where it is; they were important reasons in its history, and they bear upon its future. They may be important as a pattern for continuous development, or they may reveal what changes have overtaken the city and indicate the new directions for which the city must be planned. The reasons for the founding of a city may have multiplied or they may have vanished. There may be entirely new purposes for the city than those that motivated its original settlement.

The changes in urban character reflected in the growth and the deterioration of neighborhood life are illustrated in all our cities. It is apparent in a growing metropolis like Los Angeles. Hardly more than forty years ago this community was renowned for its climate, its recreational opportunities, its beaches, and the grandeur of its mountains. The quality of its living environment and the pleasant mildness of its weather made Los Angeles a haven for travelers from all parts of the world.

The population of Los Angeles was 500,000 in 1920; in 1982 it was more than 3,022,247, and the city had spread over the entire 450 square miles of its area. From its beginning as the center of a predominantly agricultural area, it has developed an important industrial economy. In-

---

5. Walter H. Blucher, Executive Director, American Society of Planning Officials, in *Planning, 1945*, Part 1, Chicago, May 16–17, 1945.

dustrial plants have sprung up with little or no attention to their probable effect on the living conditions of the region and its inhabitants. Water was brought more than 250 miles to supply the growing population. Congestion overtook this city of "open space," blight and slums are taking their toll, and smoke and fumes taint the air.

This story differs only in degree and detail in all our cities; it is the tale of the metropolis. The native advantages of our urban communities have not been respected by the people who built them; in the name of a bigger and more prosperous city, they have been desecrated, and the people are retreating. The people are fleeing the city and it remains neglected, but the same indifference is guiding development on the outskirts. Rather than capitalizing on the native characteristics of a region, exploitation of the urban community is undermining its own investments.

The comprehensive plan of a city or region has two objectives: forestalling the drift into chaos in the yet undeveloped areas of the city, and gradually reconstructing the developed area of the city with particular attention to blighted sections and improved circulation. The present chaotic development of the city is a trend, but this trend can be corrected and redirected to benefit all the people through planning.

The changing nature of the city must be appraised and the natural character defined. Shifts in the emphasis of the urban economy and the services and functions it performs require adjustments in the living habits of the people, the land use, and the transportation, if they are to continue as favorable environments in which to live and work. The comprehensive plan will reflect these adjustments and thereby become a guide for the future growth and development of the community. This demands inquiry into every facet of urban existence. It calls for the coordination of a team of trained decision-makers (both public and private) and enlightened and enthusiastic citizens.

ELEMENTS OF THE PLAN

Knowledge of the physical structure of the city will reveal certain natural uses for the land and existing uses that deserve particular respect in the plan. There may be well-established industrial areas, commercial centers, residential development, a great park, waterways, railroads, and historical and natural features. This knowledge will also indicate some apparent maladjustments in current land use for which corrective measures are obviously necessary. It will also indicate an appropriate relation between industrial and residential areas. With these broad strokes the comprehensive plan is begun.

The city is linked with its neighbor cities and towns and its environs by the highways, railroads, and mass transportation facilities; these form the main arteries of circulation about the city, and they will form the boundaries of the neighborhood units. The freeways, parkways, rapid transit, and railroads will establish the relation between the sources of employment in commerce and industry and the residential neighborhoods.

Laid upon this comprehensive plan will be the reservation of open spaces, the areas adapted for natural parks, or the submarginal lands unsuited for active urban development. In this process the plan begins to take shape. It will reflect the local policies on desirable population density consistent with the character of the city in its residential areas, and it will indicate the standards for the relation of building bulk and open space in these areas and in the commercial districts. Within the broad land use plan and guided by these standards, the precise plans for the various areas of the city may be refined as the time for their development approaches. The schools and playgrounds may be located within the neighborhood units, and requirements for local shopping centers may be determined. Space may be reserved for the freeways and rapid transit rights-of-way. Detailed plans for the improvement of the "downtown" business center may be formulated, and the reconstruction of blighted areas in the central section of the city may be planned and executed. The comprehensive plan will set forth the appropriate use to which the land in the city should be devoted so that the enterprise of city building may have a tangible guide in its determinations for investment.

Teamwork

It takes teamwork to produce a comprehensive plan that contains the inspired will of a people bent upon building a decent and fine city. The decisions emerge from the coordinated teamwork of sociologists and economists, educators and engineers, finance advisors and lawyers, politicians and architects, health authorities and public administrators, and public-spirited businessmen and consumers. It takes boundless enthusiasm and enlightened civic interest, and it takes a competent staff of trained planners to perform the job of coordination and translation.

The preparation of the comprehensive plan, which represents the aims and ambitions of a community in shaping its environment, requires a shift in the usual roles of allied professionals on the planning team: the social scientist must set aside his role as social critic, the economist his role as statistician, the lawyer his role as legalistic obstructionist, the real estate professional his role as supersalesman, the engineer his role as computer expert. These essential participants on the planning team then become creative urban analysts.

Commercial centers and industrial areas may be fairly defined and single-family suburbs readily delineated, but the process becomes complex within the twilight areas of the city which are, in planners' parlance, "transition zones." With public financial assistance, redevelopment in large cities may be planned as components of the city as a whole. Transition areas are older residential sections trapped between chaotic commercial and industrial development and new residential subdivisions. Although blighted areas may have begun, and they may have become the refuge of ethnic minorities, these areas often contain vintage homes and handsome trees that represent the only vestige of urban charm.

It is standard procedure for planners to sweep these transition areas with a broad brush into land use classifications of "R-2, R-3, or R-4," apartments, and a mixture of commercial zoning. With no modification of the original land subdivision, the intrusion of mediocre apartments on single-family lots erodes residential quality and reduces the prospect of neighborhood cohesiveness.

The city is in constant transition. The comprehensive plan delineates the concept of the city the people seek to achieve. Zoning is one of the instruments by which that concept is implemented, but as an instrument of transition it is suffering from atrophy. Conventional zoning regulations are obsolete. Sensitive teamwork to untangle the chaos of urban land uses and shape new instruments of regulation, while guarding the general social well-being, requires, as Jacob Crane observed, "intuition, imagination, and bold action."[6]

PLANNING PLATITUDES

Planning is plagued with platitudes. Some familiar expressions have almost reached the stature of symbols, the mere mention of which presumably is sufficient to convey a significant message. It would be well to examine some of these phrases in order to recognize their meaning.

"Flexibility." We frequently refer to the necessity for "flexibility" in city planning. It is suggested that city plans must be adjustable to changing conditions, that cities grow like "living cells." These are convenient terms and contain much truth. Unfortunately they, too, generally become picturesque phrases. There are some very specific limitations upon their value and application.

A city is more than buildings, streets, utilities, steel, concrete, and glass. Nevertheless these are the materials of which the physical structure is made. They are inert. They have chemical properties, but they are not elastic. Once in place they cannot be shifted about to suit either fancy or "changing conditions." They are static. The width of a street does not pulsate with the intensity of traffic flow, nor can a building flex its beams and columns.

---

6. Jacob Crane, *Urban Planning—Illusion and Reality: A New Philosophy for Planned City Building* (New York: Vantage Press, 1973).

In these important particulars the analogy of city building to a "living organism" is literary confection. The pictorial similarity between a medieval town plan and the cross-section of a tree or the veins in the human arm becomes pure poetry. Lifted out of the rarefied atmosphere of romantic fantasy, "flexibility" means enough space to bring the products of industrial genius into useful service in the city structure.

Cities are inflexible because they are so crowded there is no room for the various elements to "work." They are frozen into congestion, and flexibility will be attained only through the establishment of adequate standards to guide those who participate in building the city.

There comes a moment when decisions must be made. When that moment arrives, there is a degree of finality implied by the act of decision. The structure of the city does not float; it cannot be tugged or pushed about. When a building or other civic improvement is erected, it is there to stay. Flexibility in the plan of a city will be accomplished by standards for city building that preserve enough space for all improvements without overcrowding.

"Trends."   In nearly every kind of business enterprise there is reference to "trends." New conditions, scientific development, and social improvement require adjustments in the conduct of enterprise. They likewise require adjustments in the city. Shifts in the growth of cities prompted by such changes and accompanied by some degree of orderly direction serve as a measure of trends in healthy city development.

But these shifts are confused with quite another sort of change: the urge to escape from the contagious disease of obsolescence and unrestrained speculation. Healthy enterprise shuns association with derelict neighbors; unbridled physical deterioration repels improvement. Shifts in the urban pattern compelled by these desultory forces do not mark trends. They report a rout, a desperate and disorderly retreat. Diagnosing this disease as a trend is to spread the contagion further and ignore or misinterpret the only value that observation of trends can provide: a guide to the natural and appropriate use of land in the growing city.

"Economy."   A familiar slogan. It is also a worthy aim. In practice, however, it has unfortunately been too frequently reduced to a fiction. Expenditures for civic improvements are generally decided upon by their budget appeal, not their adequacy. Patchwork improvements display such an appeal; they appear to be "economical." The question of whether they may actually solve any particular problem is usually overlooked or avoided. Economy may really be, and usually is, quite another matter. We have seen a street-widening prove inadequate almost on the day it was completed. We have seen the immediate need for another improvement added. We have seen the value of adjacent land enhanced with each such piecemeal improvement, and new buildings erected about

it. We have then seen the public forced to pay the added increment of land and building "value" each of these improvements has induced. This process is characteristic of urban "economy," but it is not economical.

"Prematurity." Many times comprehensive plan proposals have been deemed "premature." One must examine the use of this term as it applies to proposals for the future. What is premature in assessing the appropriate relationships between the several uses of the land before they happen? If one were to place a time factor for the development of specific uses then one might say that is too far into the future, but where the time factor is not defined, and in many instances the variables in both economic and social conditions are too many to make accurate predictions, the exact development time is less important than satisfying the questions related to the appropriateness of the use in a compatible location when it will be needed to serve the residents of a community.

Each new or improved utility service introduced to a city crowds some equally needed service. The utility system—sewers, water, gas, electricity—distributes the energy to operate a city of a million people. Yet these vital veins are, with some rare exceptions, buried beneath or suspended above the arteries that carry the stream of daily traffic. The conflict between these services is experienced day in and day out. A utility line breaks down and the repair job stops the circulation of automobiles and other vehicles. These conflicts choke an already congested city and are not economical.

"Efficiency." Another ingrown term. Efficiency obviously has virtue; that virtue is the elimination of waste. In the name of "efficient" planning, however, are examples of the creation of waste. We have observed acres of subdivisions, planned with alleged efficiency, that are actually a waste of urban resources. We have seen the width of a street, the size of a house, or the lot it occupies squeezed to an efficient minimum so low it is reduced to nothing more than a cheap commodity.

In the light of the studies by Sir Raymond Unwin and Henry Wright, efficient planning is more than an obsession to save; it is also a method to improve. Standards are the measurements by which we must be guided rather than remain content with what Elizabeth Denby called "the intellectual pleasure which the architect got from a triumphant arrangement of inadequate space.[7]

ADEQUATE SPACE

It must be clear that space in a city must first and foremost provide for adequacy: it must be ample.

---

7. Elizabeth Denby, *Europe Rehoused* (New York: W. W. Norton, 1938).

The measure of adequacy will be the capacity of the space to receive the buildings of a city without itself being lost completely. It means enough space so that buildings may stand alone or together without violating the sensibilities of those who see and use them. It means that cities will provide space into which the buildings are built rather than a solid mass of buildings through which the fissures we call streets are carved.

The concept of space means relatively constant limitations on population density regardless of the heights that structures may reach. The prospect of squeezing more people into the same space creates instability, not only in land value but also in urban services. It imposes an extravagance on the installation of service facilities. Water, sewers, gas and electric distribution, telephones, streets, walks, transportation, fire, health, educational, and recreational facilities cannot be estimated with any possible degree of efficiency. These services must be installed in sufficient size and quantity to meet unlimited future requirements, or be repeatedly removed, altered, and replaced as the demand fluctuates. Either course is an extravagant venture as city budgets and utility bills attest.

Within a reasonable concept of space in the urban environment is room for the vehicles of transportation to circulate with ease and safety. This means enough room to separate the different types of vehicles and the direction of their travel; room enough to move about on the surface of the earth rather than burrow into the ground with subways. This means the city will no longer be a maze of streets and alleys slicing through a solid bulk of buildings.

This concept means that parking space for the free-moving vehicles of our contemporary age shall be a component part of all floor space provided within or adjacent to buildings, and it means that this integration will bring the relation between open space and building floor area into some degree of balance.

There will be enough room for all the essential utility conduits, a network of vital service arteries so aligned within their respective rights-of-way that interference is avoided at all times.

This concept of space means room enough for people to walk in safety and some degree of beauty; trees would not be unwelcome. Finally it means an environment in which the human spirit can rise above mediocrity; it means relief from the din and the danger that fray the human nerves and dull the human mind.

It may be suggested that the concept of space within the city described above is not a "practical" one. The planning of cities is rather cluttered with bromides, but hardly any is so overworked as "practical." Compromise is the inevitable road to satisfactory human relationships. The capacity to compromise is a requisite to accomplishment. It implies, however, that an objective is clearly defined. The objective of planning is the solution of a problem: in city planning the problem is that of an environment that is rapidly disintegrating under the spell of congestion and ugliness.

DOES IT WORK?

Opinions may vary as to the way in which to arrive at the objective of decent cities, but no purpose is served until some area of agreement can be reached about the nature of the objective itself. Solutions call for ideas. They deal in ideas. Ideas are the tools with which we shape an objective, and they cannot be dismissed only because they may at first appear "impractical." We see about us the results of thus being "practical"; we see these results repeated time and again: more congestion, more traffic problems, more deterioration, more expense, and boundless confusion and bewilderment. If we peer behind this scene, we may well find the reason: the process of planning began with a compromise. The ideas that are the stuff of progress never reach the surface where they may be observed and tested for their validity.

Nor is this approach really practical. The first test of practicality is whether a thing works. Can it be claimed that our cities work? Is traffic congestion practical? Or the crowded business centers? Or the blighted areas and slums? Are the extravagant devices for parking automobiles—overhead and underground—practical? Are the mediocrity of the living and working environment and the obsolete transportation in our cities really practical? Is it practical to spend huge sums on surveys, consultations, and plans, then ignore them all? The urban malady of congestion is like an itch; scratching produces a sensation of relief. But common sense tells us the only practical treatment is a cure, not more irritation.

Must it be considered impractical to propose standards that have as their sole purpose a restoration of permanent values in the urban environment? Ample space for London was denigrated by F. J. Forty, chief planner for the rebuilding program, with the words, "I want it [London] to be the leading place of commerce in the world and not—as some planners suggest—a park."[8] Must this be the interpretation of the need for adequate space within our cities? The original plan proposed for the City of London, a plan that offered little improvement over the city that was destroyed, was commented upon by Donald Tyerman in the *Observer* as "timid rebuilding proposals." He said, "The makers of this plan are not planners but pessimists."[9]

---

8. *Architectural Forum*, September 1944.
9. Ibid. The plan to which Mr. Tyerman referred was that proposed for the mile-square City of London by the Improvement and Town Planning Committee.

We might hark to the words of Lewis Mumford:

> As so often has happened during the last quarter century, the self-styled
> practical men turned out to be the weak, irresponsible dreamers, afraid to
> face unpleasant facts, while those of us who were called dreamers have,
> perhaps, some little right now to be accepted—at least belatedly—as prac-
> tical men. By now history has caught up with our more dire prophecies.
> That is at once the justification of our thinking and the proof of its tragic
> failure to influence our contemporaries.[10]

FAILURES AND MISUSE

The record for successful use of comprehensive plans leaves a great deal
to be desired. Research has indicated some of these reasons for this lack
of success:

lack of sound basis
easy amendment
political disregard
lack of public support
lack of comprehensiveness (warmed-over zoning)
changing local political structure
faulty interpretation
changing economic and social conditions
lack of coordination with other plans
changing external forces (regional, state, national)
lack of periodic review and overall comprehensive amendment
faulty concept of "flexibility"

The importance of the comprehensive plan has been emphasized as
much by the abuses to which it has been subjected as by the uses to
which it has been put. Adoption of a plan has often been treated as a
spurious political gesture; the less specific the plan, the more adaptable
it is to political manipulation. Diagrams of existing land uses have been
accepted as a plan; unrealistic agricultural or single-family zoning has
been adopted for underdeveloped areas to avoid decisions on growth and
development policies. Environmental impact statements for separate developments have become a convenient substitute for planning.

These irresponsible tactics have been politically expedient for incompetent civic leaders and have cast grave doubt on the social and economic
usefulness of planning. The doubts are well founded; much of the planning has not been demonstrably effective in improving the urban environ-

---

10. *Architectural Forum*, May 1945.

ment. City and rural land has become an inviting source for commercial exploitation and speculation. The extension of existing zoning, the legal regulation of land use, has also been misused as a substitute for the comprehensive plan in making decisions about changes in land uses.

Because of the reluctance of local communities to prepare and adopt significant long-range plans for community betterment, some states have found it necessary to require not only that these plans be prepared but also that they contain specific elements, and have further mandated that zoning conform to the plan. Besides the land use and circulation elements, these specific new elements include open space, conservation, noise control, seismic safety, and—for the well-being of all citizens—a housing element subject to state guidelines and review.

The long-range aspects of the plan were the least understood. Some legislators saw the plans as a "pie in the sky" dream of unrealistic academics who do not understand that government in general operated on short-term year-to-year programming. A twenty-year plan (look into the future) was four times more unrealistic than the Russian "five-year plans." If proposals could not be financed under current budgetary allocations, then they were considered pure theory and to be deleted from the plan. This made planning a refinement of the current zoning map and eliminated all of the far-reaching implications of growth and the facilities and utilities that would be required as this growth takes place.

A San Francisco law professor, at the 1981 APA conference, stated that, in his opinion, the best defense a municipality can have is a comprehensive general plan. He also advised cities to develop an economic data base, which they can use to respond to landowners' charges that a planning commission action deprives them of a reasonable return on their land.

Alternatives

As more and more discussion took place in academic and professional forums, alternative approaches were sought to utilize the concepts included in the comprehensive plan but without the techniques that had become rote on the plans produced in the 1960–1970 era. New terms were tried on for size, such as short range, middle range, and long range concept plans; and the direct use of the zoning plan as the land use plan, relating added utilities, facilities, and services on a haphazard demand basis. Other formulas intended to assist a community in keeping its house in order were "invented," all more closely related to the "pay as you go" process. With the national dive toward massive elimination of regulations, the future of all efforts to guide community growth in economically reasonable directions appears in question.

The concept of looking ahead and preparing plans will continue, in some form, represented by the comprehensive general plan, for it is through this process that order is evolved in community development and the services required for urban living. Even in instances where the physical structure of the community is entirely new and the impact of history and tradition are not evident, human instincts and desires will lay a heavy hand on the disposition of the use of land and the manner in which the environment will be impacted upon as the people in the community react to natural forces and opportunities in a given locale.

CHAPTER 20

ELEMENTS OF LAND USE

This we know. The earth does not belong to man; man belongs to the earth. This we know. All things are connected like the blood which unites one family. All things are connected.

Whatever befalls the earth befalls the sons of the earth. Man did not weave the web of life; he is merely a strand in it. Whatever he does to the web, he does to himself.

Great Chief of the Suguamish, Chief Seattle, December 1854

Both economically and legally, past and present, all land has an owner, and title to that land provides for the more or less free use for homes, business, and other purposes. The native Americans, the Indians, thought differently, as Chief Seattle quoted above makes clear. The land was placed here by the Great Spirit, and we cannot sell it because we do not own it. But the belief in ownership is more common and deeply rooted. Even after earthquakes and fires that entirely destroy the structures on the land, titles and descriptions of specific parcels remain, and the titleholder rebuilds on the original site, setting old, often archaic patterns once again upon the land.

With the titles so firmly established on most land, the need for the planning of uses is of paramount importance. It should be self-evident that the use of each individual parcel is inextricably intertwined with the use of all other parcels. And in fact the attempt to create a humanly satisfying environment was recognized by the courts as an important legitimate objective and resulted in support for the development of the first plans for land use.

It is the relationship between the variety of possible uses that becomes

Actual Land Uses[1]

Use	CENTRAL CITIES	
	Per Cent of Total Developed Area	Acres per 100 Persons
Single-family dwellings	31.81	2.19
Two-family dwellings	4.79	0.33
Multifamily dwellings	3.01	0.21
Commercial areas	3.32	0.23
Light industry ⎫		
Heavy industry ⎬	11.30	0.78
Railroad property ⎭		
Parks and playgrounds	6.74	0.46
Public and semipublic property	10.93	0.75
Streets	28.10	1.94
Total	100.00	6.89

[1] Harland Bartholomew, *Land Uses in American Cities*, Harvard University Press, Cambridge, 1955.

Studies by Harland Bartholomew revealed the actual land uses in a number of survey cities. Three types of urban communities were included. The Central Cities are self-contained entities that perform the major social and economic functions of an urbanized area. They include fifty-three cities ranging in population from 1,740 to 821,960. The Satellite Cities are incorporated in and are economically dependent on an adjacent central city. They number thirty-three, ranging in population from 900 to 74,347. The Urban Areas are metropolitan areas that embrace a central city and an urbanized fringe. The eleven urban areas in the survey range in population from 7,150 to 119,825. The study does not include the largest metropolitan areas but presents a fair cross-section of urban land-use characteristics. (Each community is unique, and the land uses in each should reflect its special qualities.)

Land-use allocation varies from location to location, depending upon each community's attitude concerning the type of environment it hopes to create.

the problem of planning. Some are favorable to each other, whereas some are not only detrimental but also dangerous. The plan therefore begins with a definition of land uses and the appropriate location within the topographic, geologic, and geographic structure of the city. Upon these the city pattern should be developed.

Before any plan can be devised, the physical structure of the community must be known and understood—its rivers, its mountains, its plains and prairies, its hills, its climate, the direction of its winds. Is the land suited for agriculture, is it good for grazing? Are there oil or mineral deposits, is it subject to floods, are there natural or historic features to be preserved? The geology, hydrography, meteorology, and geography must be rediscovered beneath the blanket of the built-up city.

SATELLITE CITIES		URBAN AREAS	
Per Cent of Total Developed Area	Acres per 100 Persons	Per Cent of Total Developed Area	Acres per 100 Persons
36.18	3.14	25.05	3.72
3.31	0.29	1.63	0.24
2.49	0.22	1.31	0.20
2.54	0.22	2.65	0.39
		1.87	0.28
12.51	1.09	3.77	0.56
		6.22	0.92
4.37	0.38	4.59	0.68
10.93	0.95	25.30	3.75
27.67	2.40	27.61	4.10
100.00	8.69	100.00	14.84

The following statistics (based on Eisner and Associates studies, 1939–85) indicate the range of percentages found in most urban areas:

Residential	*35 to 39 percent*
Commercial	*4.8 to 5 percent*
Industrial	*10 to 11 percent*
Streets	*20 to 26 percent*
Open space, schools, parks, etc.	*10 to 18 percent*

In evaluating the space requirements for the various land uses in the comprehensive plan, the standards of development—population density and character of the physical environment appropriate to the region—introduce an additional factor: the building bulk and floor space that will occupy the land. This factor may be expressed as a ratio of building floor area to lot area and should be considered in formulating the basic concept of the comprehensive plan (chapter 19), the zoning plan (chapter 28), and commerce and industry (chapter 22).

The constant relationship of nature's three primary elements—land, water, and air—is necessary to the support of human life. One can imagine controlled air conditions, and we know that water can be transported from distant mountain sources to semiarid regions, but the land is where you find it. Perhaps it can be built up, the marshes drained, fertility improved, and water increase its growing yield, but land itself must have the basic capacity for response to man's treatment. We classify it as good or bad according to its ability to provide life for humankind.

INVENTORY AND CLASSIFICATION

Regardless of the high aspirations a people may share for the future of their city or the distant range over which they prepare their plans for its development, the planning process must obviously begin with the city as it exists. It is consequently necessary to know how the land is used and maintain the inventory as a current record. From this inventory the physical characteristics of the city are discernible, those which warrant change or necessitate retention in the comprehensive plan may be determined, and some existing uses may become key controls over the pattern of future land use.

This prospect is particularly marked by the fact that the transition from an existing land use to another classification may span a great number of years. According to Anglo-Saxon law, if land has never been used for a particular purpose, it does not constitute a deprivation of property rights to deny the right to so use it in the future. On the other hand, it is assumed that zoning ordinances must not restrict property to uses considered less liberal than the existing use. The courts have held that zoning may not be retroactive, that existing land uses may not be "zoned out of existence." They must be permitted to continue as nonconforming uses if they are inconsistent with the use the zoning ordinance prescribes.

This may appear to permit the continuation of a nonconforming use that would prove to be a detriment to the surrounding development, like an obnoxious industry in a residential zone. The courts have pointed out that other means are available for relief from such intrusions; proof that a nonconforming use is a nuisance and dangerous to the life and health of the inhabitants and the public welfare may be sufficient reason for the courts to deny a use to continue.

Nonconforming uses may not be renewed if destroyed by fire or act of God. The new structure must then conform to the provisions of the current zoning. In some ordinances a nonconforming structure may be repaired or slightly altered, but it may not be modified to the extent that the space or facilities are enlarged, nor may a different nonconforming use replace that which is removed.

Some zoning ordinances specify a period during which a nonconforming use shall be retired. This time is equivalent to an amortization period with an established date for removal of the structure, the period being related to the years of use already experienced in the structure and the investment in it. In this way property values and human values may be reasonably balanced and intruding uses gradually removed to be replaced by conforming uses. The logic and equity of such a method would seem to impel cities to adopt it in the public interest.

Most cities classify their land in five major categories: (1) open space, (2) agricultural, (3) residential, (4) commercial, and (5) industrial. Each of these broad groups is subdivided into uses ranging from the most to the least obnoxious, from the most to the least restricted, from the most concentrated to the most open. This is generally identified as "step-down" classification as it is applied within each of the broad groups. Thus the general industrial classification contains heavy industry and light industry, expressing the difference between a boiler works and a tin shop, for example. A large department store would be classified in heavy commercial, whereas a neighborhood grocery store would be placed in the lightest commercial zone. Likewise a multistory apartment building would be in the least restricted residential zone, whereas a single-family detached house would be in the restricted area. Open space and agriculture are sometimes one classification.

The number of intermediate steps between the most intense use and the least intense use will vary in different communities as the complexity of the community warrants. In a very large city there may be as many as fifty classes of land use, whereas in a small town there may only be nine. This difference in the number of classifications does not suggest less accuracy in determining the classifications; it indicates that the manner in which the land is used in a small town is less complex than in a large city. The number of classifications should be as few as possible consistent with a complete coverage of the various uses of land and an accurate description of each.

A city should have a record of the way in which the land within its boundaries is used, as well as the quantity of space and structures which comprise it. A periodic inventory of these assets should be undertaken just as a well-organized and well-administered business maintains an inventory of its stock and the value of its stock. During the Depression of the thirties, land-use surveys in a number of cities were conducted under the auspices of the Works Progress Administration (WPA) of the federal government. These data were of immeasurable value to the planning commissions in the respective cities, yet there are few instances in which the records were subsequently maintained.

A continuous record may be maintained by reference to building permits and the tax assessor of the city. Other reference sources are aerial photography; the building and safety department of the city, which records levels of pest infestation, lack of sanitation facilities, and changes in building occupancy and alterations that indicate a change in the use of existing structures; and the local housing authority, from which information may generally be obtained on the physical condition of housing. Banking and lending institutions frequently maintain valid information on new building activity as well.

The record of urban land use is not only for the purpose of ascertaining the condition of the physical structure. It provides the information necessary to observe the rate at which the city is increasing or decreasing its physical plant in the various classifications of land use. It offers a basis for measuring the amount of land to be reserved in zoning for future developments of the city, the quantity of land, and the most appropriate location for the various uses.

The land use inventory is good urban business and should be maintained as a current record. It is not a plan; it is part of the vital data from which plans may be made. The inventory does not in itself reflect quality. A separate evaluation must be prepared dealing with this subject.

LAND USE PLAN

The land use plan is intended as an important means of reaching physical, economic, and social community goals. The plan, through its effects on public and private decisions and investments, can be a powerful influence on the growth rate, character, quality, and pattern of the city's physical environment.

The plan sets forth policies intended to encourage the upgrading and preservation of the existing city and to provide for an orderly, efficient, and logical extension of urban development in the predominantly undeveloped area surrounding the city. A central issue in deciding the future pattern of development is the manner in which future growth is to be accommodated. Already-developed areas can be used more intensively (higher average densities) or undeveloped land can be brought into use. A range of choices exists between these two extremes.

Until recently, many cities have emphasized expansion into new areas rather than the recycling and more intense use of existing areas. However, experience and analysis over the years have brought about a general acceptance of the fact that such an approach toward growth can raise the cost of city services and add to the severity of a number of environmental, social, and economic problems.

Many cities are now attempting to define a "balanced program of expansion and increased utilization. In large measure, each community's proper balance is unique. The balance is a function of the scale of priorities that a community attaches to its goals.

Another important factor affecting the community's choice is the existing pattern of development. The face of the city changes very slowly, and some choices may be feasible only in the long run. For example, an already intensely developed city may have little choice but to expand into new areas. Alternatively, a city "landlocked" by external development or jurisdictions can only accommodate growth internally (San Francisco, for example).

Considerations

Land use considerations can be divided into five parts. The first identifies objectives and principles pertaining to residential, commercial, recreational, educational, and industrial uses and enumerates existing standards for such uses.

The second part focuses on the nature and pattern of development within the existing city boundaries. Descriptive data in this section provide the basis for answering in part questions as to what changes in the pattern of land use are needed and how much growth can be accommodated within the existing area of urban development.

The third part looks in detail at the area of predominantly undeveloped land surrounding the community, the community's "area of influence." Existing uses of land are identified, and factors affecting the land's suitability for future development are discussed. Standards for new development are proposed.

When land is either in agricultural use or can be classified as prime agricultural land, great care must be taken to evaluate the environmental impact when providing for alternate uses that would deprive the public of the foods and fibers (such as flax and hemp) provided by the land. Agricultural land is a world asset that should be protected by careful planning.

The fourth part brings together the analysis and results of the preceding sections and proposes a coordinated, comprehensive land use plan for both the city and its area of influence, including all necessities, facilities, and amenities required to serve the people. This plan is an important element in efforts to manage growth and is based upon current expectations of future growth, the existing pattern of development, and community desires as to how growth can be physically and financially accommodated.

The fifth consideration explores and identifies tools that could be used to implement the proposed plan.

The land use plan establishes the allocation of neighborhood units with

LAND USE

RESIDENTIAL
High Density
Medium Density
Low Density
Hillside Development

COMMERCIAL
General
Professional
Convenience
Transient

INDUSTRIAL

PUBLIC

RECREATIONAL

CIRCULATION & TRANSPORTATION

	EXISTING	PROPOSED
Freeways		
Major Arterials		
Collector Streets		
Interchanges		
Separations		
Pedestrian Overpasses		

COMMUNITY FACILITIES

	EXISTING	PROPOSED
Elementary Schools		
Junior High Schools		
Senior High Schools		
Parks		
Fire Stations		
Public Works		
Cemeteries		

GENERAL PLAN

CITY OF SAN BUENAVENTURA, CALIFORNIA

Planning Consultants Candeub, Fleissig and Ketcham   1964

This Map Has Been Approved By The City Of San Buenaventura
Planning Commission By Resolutions Nos. 2207, 2263 And 7281
Adopted By City Council Resolution No. 5970 'n May 24, 1965

their several facilities, schools, parks, playgrounds, and shopping areas. It is the plan that sets the standards to guide the city builders in their various enterprises, and a complete plan will be more than a single map of the community. It will be a compilation of all the data from which the estimates of required areas were calculated and the standards determined. It will become a reference for all who are engaged in urban development.

This plan will chart the relation of the city to the region and indicate its integration with its satellite communities, and will define the areas and standards for subdivision of new land. This is the plan which forms the foundation for the precise plans for zoning, parks and recreation, schools and other public buildings, the civic center, cultural and sports centers. It is the plan that will guide the community and public utility corporations in the design of utilities—sewers, gas, water, electric distribution, street lighting, and police and fire protection. And this is the plan to which all can refer for guidance in determining their investments in the city.

THE BASIC URBAN UNIT

As the city grows in size, some areas within it assume homogeneous qualities that we have identified as neighborhoods. People who early emigrated to America frequently grouped together with those who spoke their language, shared their particular religious tenets, or came from similar ethnic or racial backgrounds. When some became richer than the rest and enjoyed the greater mobility provided by a fine brace of horses and a carriage and differences in social and economic status became pronounced, they moved their residences to nearby hills and formed more exclusive neighborhoods. Different environmental standards were established, and people who desired and could afford them gathered there to secure these amenities.

Some neighborhoods developed, as in ancient times, more from compulsion than native choice; restrictions of prejudice, limitations of language, or economic pressures often forced the cultivation of neighborhoods identified by distinctions made other than by choice.

As open space in the growing city was built up, some neighborhoods were unable to retain their original identity, the economic level of the people living within them being inadequate to maintain the earlier standard of physical maintenance or community services. Decay set in and slums were on the way toward formation. Residents of formerly exclusive areas moved to new districts beyond the reach of this influence. The metropolis created by the Industrial Revolution completely dissipated whatever urban unity remained from the medieval town and, except for exclusive residential districts that escaped from the sprawling industrial city, the distinctions between neighborhoods gradually merged into a common mediocrity. It was necessary to restore some semblance of human identity to the urban scene; prodded by the social evils that enveloped the factory town, social workers began to function, and developed the settlement house. Probably the settlement house movement, which began in London about 1885, marked the first conscious recognition of the neighborhood as a basic element in the urban structure; the house served as a nucleus for the restoration of human values that had dissolved within the indistinguishable mass of the industrial metropolis.

The dissolution of these values has created among urban dwellers a detachment from each other. Opinions among social scientists differ on the effectiveness of the neighborhood principle as a means to overcome this detachment. Some contend it is imperative to re-establish a "face-to-face" relationship through neighborhood association; others expect that people will seek their friends no matter what distances may separate them even as they remain only chance acquaintances and even strangers with their next-door neighbors; and some oppose the neighborhood with the claim that it leads to a grouping of people that inevitably results in compulsory class distinctions.

These conflicting opinions notwithstanding, it has become a practical necessity to employ the neighborhood unit as a means to restore a recognizable form in the physical organization of the city. However large or small the city may be, there must be a workable unit of human scale with which to weave the urban pattern into a workable whole. Dissolution of human scale has allowed the industrial and commercial metropolis to become socially stagnant and physically flabby. As Benton McKaye said, "Mankind has cleared the jungle and replaced it with a labyrinth."[1]

Neighborhood Unit Defined

The neighborhood unit is not some sociological phenomenon; it embraces no particular theories of social science. It is simply a physical environment in which a mother knows that her child will have no traffic streets to cross on his way to school—a school that is within easy walking distance from home. It is an environment in which the housewife may have an easy walk to a shopping center where she may obtain the daily household goods, and employed persons may find convenient transportation to and from work. It is an environment in which a well-equipped playground is located near the home where the children may play in safety with their friends; the parents may not care to maintain intimate friendships with their neighbors but children are so inclined, and they need the facilities of recreation for the healthy development of their

---

1. Benton McKaye, *The New Exploration: A Philosophy of Regional Planning* (New York: Harcourt, Brace & Co., 1928).

minds and spirit. While the data cited in the following paragraphs are not current, the basic logic is the same today, and the standards will vary with the type of community and the family composition of a specific locale.

The unit measurement for space in urban society is the individual; the common denominator for the arrangement of that space is the family. To satisfy their relatively simple social wants, it is natural for families to seek the advantages that appropriately planned neighborhoods provide. The functions of a neighborhood have been described by C. J. Bushnell as: maintenance, learning, control, and play.[2] One of the earliest authorities to attempt a definition of the neighborhood in fairly specific terms was Clarence A. Perry. Although opinions differ to some degree, the definition he set forth in his 1929 *Regional Survey of New York and Its Environs* is still a valid statement.

Perry described the neighborhood unit as the populated area that would require and support an elementary school. The neighborhood unit would occupy about 160 acres and have a shape that would render it unnecessary for any child to walk a distance of more than one-half mile to school. About 10 percent of the area would be allocated to recreation, and through-traffic arteries would be confined to the surrounding streets, internal streets being limited to service access for residents of the neighborhood. The unit would be served by shopping facilities, churches, a library, and a community center, the latter being located in conjunction with the school.

The neighborhood unit or some equivalent is repeatedly referred to in proposals for urban reorganization. The suggested form varies widely, but the essential characteristics are fairly consistent; Perry was not far off. The suggested population appropriate for a unit has ranged between 3,000 and 12,000 people. In the plans for Chicago in 1942 the range was from 4,000 to 12,000; in Abercrombie and Forshaw's 1944 Greater London Plan, the size was 6,000 to 10,000. Some authorities have expressed a desire for smaller units than a school district, believing the nature of the neighborhood requires a relatively small size—generally 1,000 and not to exceed 1,500 families.

In its report in 1972 on "A Strategy for Building a Better America," the American Institute of Architects adopted the neighborhood unit as the recommended growth unit for future urban growth. The growth unit would range from 500 to 3,000 dwelling units (populations of between 1,700 and 10,000).[3]

---

2. "Community Center Movement as a Moral Force," *International Journal of Ethics,* Vol. 30, April 1920.

3. *American Institute of Architects,* Washington, D.C.

The neighborhood unit—Clarence Stein's conception. *These sketches show Clarence Stein's determinations of the proper design of the neighborhood unit.*

In the upper-right diagram the elementary school is at the center of the unit and within a one-half-mile radius of all residents in the neighborhood. A small shopping center for daily needs is located near the school. Most residential streets are suggested as cul-de-sac or dead-end roads to eliminate through traffic, and park space flows through the neighborhood in a manner reminiscent of the Radburn plan.

The upper-left diagram shows the grouping of three neighborhood units served by a high school and one or two major commercial centers, the radius for walking distance to these facilities being one mile.

Despite the variations the principle of the neighborhood unit runs through all considerations for social, physical, and political organization of the city; it represents a unit of the population with basic common needs for educational, recreational, and other service facilities, and it is the standards for these facilities from which the size and design of the neighborhood emerge.

N. L. Engelhardt, Jr., has presented a comprehensive pattern of the neighborhood as a component of the successively larger segments in a city structure. The unit includes the elementary school, a small shopping district, and a playground. These facilities are grouped near the center so that the walking distance between them and the home does not exceed one-half mile. An elementary school with an enrollment of between 600

Clarence A. Perry's plan. *Perry was one of the first to give some consideration to the physical form of the neighborhood unit. It is substantially the same as in Stein's diagram but suggests that the maximum radius for walking be only one-quarter mile. Accepting the practice that was and still is prevalent, shopping areas are situated at intersecting traffic streets on the outside corners rather than at the center of the unit.*

Reproduced from New York Regional Survey

and 800 pupils will represent a population of about 1,700 families in the neighborhood unit.[4]

Two such units (3,400 families) will support a junior high school with a recreation center in conjunction; the walking distance does not exceed one mile from the center to the most remote home. Four units (6,800 families) will require a senior high school and a larger commercial center. It will also be an appropriate size for a major park and recreation area. This grouping of four neighborhood units forms a community with a population of about 24,000 people. The component parts of this pattern are integrated, and such communities may be arranged in whatever combinations the sources of employment and communications to and from them may require.

Safety Factors

The latter part of the twentieth century has brought with it the age of paranoid fear. We fear walking on our streets, not only at night. We fear living in our homes as we place multiple locking devices on our doors

---

4. N. L. Engelhardt, Jr., "The School-Neighborhood Nucleus," *Architectural Forum,* October 1943.

and windows. We resort to living in securely protected buildings and communities. We construct communities within protective walls and employ security persons to guard us and our possessions. We isolate ourselves from our potential neighbors. We no longer live in a neighborhood other than one described by geography or a geographic symbol. Many of the joys that were derived from knowing and being with people have been lost.

There must be a way to restructure the environment in all of its elements in order to return to the sense of real security that can come only from a rebirth of communications with our neighbors and friends.

As a response to current conditions, however, a number of practical measures must be planned to increase the safety of the local neighborhoods. These include adequate night lighting of the streets, more than just at intersections; neighborhood watches where residents keep watch on their neighbors' properties and report suspicious activities; careful locking of entries to homes to dissuade the casual burglar from easy entry; assurance that police patrolling is adequate, especially during high crime hours. Burglar alarms and special patrols are expensive but may be necessary where a high-value property is at stake.

Protection from bodily injury requires greater concern for the welfare of the people in our neighborhoods. This must be more than a mere dedication to the creed that we are our brothers' keepers and that they deserve our interest in their well-being.

PUBLIC RECREATION

Open space in the city is usually considered as the area for recreation, and appropriately so. However, this space falls into a number of categories. There is space devoted primarily to active playgrounds for children, youth, and adults, and there is also space for adults' more passive relaxation. These spaces are those generally meant in a consideration of recreational facilities. Another classification should not be overlooked: the conservation of natural areas within as well as outside the city. This conservation may take the form of greenbelts to serve as buffers between different land uses—residential and industrial areas—or it may become a reservation of places of particular historic or geographic interest, or it may be space topographically unsuited for the satisfactory development of other urban improvements.

The standards of open space cannot adequately specify the required areas in a city for all these classifications; part of the distinction of cities derives from the way in which the natural site is shaped and planned. The spaces specified for defined recreational uses are not the full measure of adequacy of a recreational program under any circumstances; an abstract area of land in proportion to the population is but a part of the planning for recreation space in the city. It is the distribution of this space that measures the adequacy, not the amount alone.

To suggest that American communities are deficient in recreational facilities is only to repeat what has been often said by many authorities. The reasons for the deficiency are manifold, but one of the most glaring is ill-planned land uses. Our present zoning practices provide extravagant areas for commercial and industrial uses, and the result is an urban pattern riddled with mixed land uses and an absence of stability in residential improvements. Consequently we are faced with two predicaments; either land values render it too expensive to allot adequate open space for recreation, or existing parks are swallowed by commercial and industrial areas, from which the people are trying desperately to escape to a better living environment.

A similar situation prevails with our schools. Because of unfortunate site selection, miscalculated population shifts, or lack of planning at the outset, schools are found languishing in the midst of business and factory areas, stranded between main traffic arteries, or situated in subdivisions too remote to serve the people. Recreation and education are linked with all other phases of urban development, whether they are planned or unplanned. Statistically, parks and playgrounds are deficient in amount, but the maldistribution of available facilities is even more striking. This combination of circumstances makes it imperative to establish true neighborhood units in city planning.

As the machine has produced more and more with less and less manpower, and with the organization of labor, the work period was reduced from sixty hours to the eight-hour day and the six-day week; then, during the 1930s, it was further reduced to forty hours and in some trades to thirty-five hours. Not only has this change made more leisure time available, but the intensified nature of modern production has rendered the necessity for relaxation and recreation the more important.

Uncontrolled spread of blight hastened the flight to the suburbs, the process we usually identify as decentralization, and the absorption of open space within the central areas of our cities was a major factor in creating this blight. The combination of unplanned mixed land uses, physical deterioration, and lack of open space has created a situation that can hardly be cured by the injection of occasional playgrounds into these areas. They will improve the amenities within the hard and bare confines of blighted areas, but such devices will not remedy the condition; replanning and rebuilding will be needed in the great areas of our blighted and congested urban core. This process of rebuilding will necessarily be predicated upon the provision of ample open space, but there is another important and urgent problem of open space that our cities face: the reservation of space within all the subdivisions spreading out across the urban landscape. Standards—adequate standards—of open space are urgently necessary to avoid a repetition of the identical problem presented by the blighted city centers.

Integrated Recreation Systems

There are several excellent examples of the use of a regional stream or flood control channel as the basis for development of park and parkway systems. Several elements of circulation, flood control, and recreation are all planned as a unit and thus provide exceptional opportunities to conserve open space, protect human lives and property, and develop parks and green spaces that provide a community with a skeletal form about which to develop its other land uses. The parkway system in New York State is a fine example. In Arizona, the Indian Bend Wash in the city of Scottsdale is outstanding—linking neighborhood parks, golf courses, and flood control into one multimile strip of green space.

Palm Springs, California, is building a system of parks and open spaces as the spinal column of its proposal for Tahquitz Creek. Decades ago the state of Wisconsin planned and developed a statewide system of integrated park and recreational areas providing lasting quality to the people of that part of the nation.

Neighborhood Recreation

There are three categories of recreation space for which the distribution as well as the amount of land is an important factor. They are identified by different terms in various localities, but the National Recreation Association has classified them as (1) the playlot, (2) the neighborhood playground, and (3) the playfield. Each type fulfills a specific function in the design of neighborhoods and groups of neighborhoods.[5]

The Playlot. The first category, the playlot, is for children of preschool age. In sparsely settled residential districts it is the equivalent of the back yard of homes, and in single-family districts the function is generally fulfilled by the usual open space about the homes. This is usually adequate when the street system is so designed that through traffic is discouraged or eliminated. In densely built apartment districts, however, the playlot assumes an important function.

There should be one playlot available for each group of families, the group ranging from 30 to 60 in number. The size of each lot should range in area from 1,500 to 2,500 square feet, and each should be located within

---

5. George Butler, *Recreation Areas,* for National Recreation Association, 1958.

Relation Between Net Residential Density and the Effective Service Distance of the Neighborhood Recreation Center*

	General Location in California	Average Family Size	Lot Size	Predominant Building Type	Effective Service Distance	Total Net Acres Excluding Streets and Public Uses	Population Within Effective Service Distance
3/8 Mile Radius — Low Density 1, 15–20 persons per net acre, • = 200 people	coastal and valley nonmetropolitan mountain	3.5	7,000 to 10,000 sq. ft.	single-family detached house	1/4 to 3/8 mile	206 ac.	2,500 to 3,000
1/4 Mile Radius — Low Density 2, 20–30 persons per net acre, • = 200 people	coastal and valley metropolitan desert	3.3	5,000 to 7,000 sq. ft.	single-family detached house	1/4 mile	91 ac.	2,000 to 2,500
1/4 Mile Radius — Medium Density, 30–50 persons per net acre, • = 200 people	coastal and valley metropolitan	3.0	varies	duplex, row house, two- and three-story apartments	1/4 mile	91 ac.	3,500 to 4,500
1/8 Mile Radius — High Density, 50–100 persons per net acre, • = 200 people	coastal and valley metropolitan	2.6	varies	multistory apartments	1/8 mile	23 ac.	2,000 to 4,000

* *Recreational Places*, Wayne Williams (New York, Reinhold Publishing Co., 1958).

a clear view of all the dwellings it serves. If a playground is more distant than several blocks or is separated from the residential district by a busy traffic street, the area of the playlots should be increased to 2,000 to 4,000 square feet. Playlots should be equipped with such devices as low swings, slides, sandboxes, jungle gyms, and space for running and circle games; a portion of the lot should be paved.

All equipment should be designed and arranged for small children; authorities have pointed out the fascination of tots for objects like low walls, logs, and other common forms like shallow trenches and small hills. Some form of enclosure—a hedge or fence—about the playlot is advisable, and a pergola and benches for mothers should be included.

Neighborhood Playground. The second category is the neighborhood playground. Designed for children from six to fourteen, this playground is the neighborhood's center of recreation activities. Most authorities contend that a playground should be within one-quarter mile walking distance of the dwelling area it serves; this distance is particularly important in densely built districts, and it should not exceed one-half mile in the most sparsely settled residential areas. A study of five large cities surveyed a total of nearly 35,000 children; of this number two-thirds went to a playground within three blocks of their home and three-quarters lived within four blocks.

The preferable location for a playground is adjacent to a community center or elementary school, where supervised recreation is possible. Below is a schedule of suggested space allowances.[6]

Population	Number of Children	Size in Acres
2,000	450	3.25
3,000	600	4.0
4,000	800	5.0
5,000	1,000	6.0

As a rule a playground for fewer than 200 children is impracticable to operate; more than 1,200 children require two or more separate playgrounds. A minimum size of three acres for a playground is recommended.

The playground should provide an area for apparatus and an open space for informal play. There should be courts for various games such as soccer, softball, tennis, handball, and volleyball. Space is also needed

---

6. Ibid.

Minimal Standards for Public Recreational Areas, City Planning Department, Los Angeles, California*

Nature of Recreation	Operational Agency	Ages Served	Minimum Acres	Service Radius	1 Acre Serves	1 Site Serves	Desirable Features Minimum Facilities
1 Playlot	Group Housing	Pre-school	⅛	1 block	—	136 tots	Housing projects only
2 Neighborhood Playground With Park Facilities	Elementary or junior high school or recreation dept.	5 to 14 and aged persons	Active area—3 / Passive area—2	¼ to ⅜ miles / Same	218 children / 2000 tot. pop.	600–800 children / 3000–10,000 tot. pop.	Space for juvenile tag and athletic games, crafts bldg., table games, rest area and boundary planting
3 District Playground and Park	Senior high school or recreation dept. and park dept.	15-20 and adults	Active area—10 / Passive area—5	¾ to 1½ miles / Same	290 youth / 2,000 to 6,000 pop.	1,000–4,000 youth / 10,000 to 50,000 pop.	Swimming pool, athletic field, all-purpose building, facilities for large group activities
4 Sports Center	Recreation dept.	Youth and adults	30	5-10 miles	Variable	500,000 pop.	Multiple facilities for field games, field house
5 Urban Park	Park dept.	All	30	5 miles	2,000 tot. pop.	50,000 to 100,000 pop.	Shade, lawn and water

6 Regional Park	Park dept.	All	No limit	No limit	Variable	Variable	Outstanding scenic or recr'l attractions
7 Beach	Recreation dept.	All	No limit	No limit	Variable	Variable	Multiple recreation facilities
8 Camp	Recreation dept. or school board	Various	20	No limit	Variable	Variable	Isolated location in primitive area
9 Specialized Park	Park dept.	Various	No limit	No limit	Variable	Variable	Golf course, or other special uses
10 Cultural Site	Semi-public or public	All	No limit	No limit	Variable	Variable	Historical, scientific, or educational interest
11 Miscellaneous Open Spaces	Any government agency	All	No limit	Local	Variable	Variable	Planted strips, squares, public bldg. grounds
12 Preserve or Reservation	Any government agency	All	No limit	Local	Variable	Variable	Protection of primitive or scenic areas

* April 1948.

for the quiet activities such as crafts, dramatics, and storytelling. A wading pool is desirable in warm climates, and a playlot with its facilities should be included in the playground. The lot should be near a shelter and rest area for adults. Lighting for evening use is desirable. Because economy in the operation and maintenance of recreation space in a community is highly important, it is impracticable to substitute a number of small play spaces throughout a residential development. The recommended sizes and design of spaces are more economical and avoid confusion between the various age groups who use the facilities.

The Playfield. The playfield is intended for young people and adults and provides a variety of recreational activities. A single playfield may serve four or five neighborhoods; the walking distance should not exceed one mile, one-half-mile radius being preferred. One acre per 800 population is a desirable space standard, with a minimum size of fifteen acres. Here again the standards vary, some cities holding to a minimum average area of one-half acre per 1,000 population. The space should be designed for the same facilities as a neighborhood playground, with the addition of space for sports like football, baseball, hockey, and archery, should contain a swimming pool, outdoor theater, bandshell, and a recreation building. Night lighting should be provided.

Parks and Other Spaces

The three types of recreation spaces—playlot, neighborhood playground, and playfield—require the greatest attention with regard to their distribution in the community, the adequacy of space allotted to them, and their relation to the traffic arteries, community facilities, and accessibility from the homes. The total space for recreation is not confined to these categories, however. There are, in addition, the large city parks that supply the main facilities for city-wide recreation, organized sports, public golf courses, open-air entertainment, and the zoological and botanical gardens. These parks usually retain or reintroduce natural surroundings to the city and, where the sites are so adapted, they maintain the native wildlife as far as possible. They vary greatly in size, but they are usually of considerable area. Fairmount Park in Philadelphia and Griffith Park in Los Angeles each contain nearly 4,000 acres; Forest Park in St. Louis with its famous outdoor amphitheater has 1,380 acres, Balboa Park in San Diego has 1,100 acres, and Golden Gate Park in San Francisco contains about 1,000 acres. In addition to well-known Central Park, which contains only 840 acres, New York City has five other parks ranging from 1,000 to nearly 2,000 acres each.

Another type closely akin to the large park is the familiar "city" park, which serves as a breather in built-up urban areas. Their frequency depends a great deal upon the degree of population density, five miles apart being an average distance in congested areas and ten miles being a standard in a highly decentralized city like Los Angeles. It is preferable that these parks be not smaller than about thirty acres in size, with a standard of about one acre per 2,000 people as a minimum area. This type of park is somewhat reminiscent of the Boston Commons (forty-four acres), but it is not intended to resemble a village green like the diminutive six-acre public squares located in each quadrant of the original plan by Penn for Philadelphia. Such "squares" are little more than open space upon which some buildings may front. The city park should provide a natural atmosphere that may induce relaxation and some degree of repose.

The broadest reach of open space may be identified as the regional parks or park reserves. They comprise great areas of space, most of which is maintained in its natural state. Cook County Forest Preserve near Chicago is one of the greatest of these spaces devoted to conservation; it contains more than 30,000 acres. Others are the South Mountain Park of 15,000 acres near Phoenix, Arizona, the 10,000-acre reserve near Denver, Colorado, Tilden Regional Parks in Oakland, California, and the Westchester Park System in New York.

The great stretches of open space represented by these reserves or regional parks, and also some of the large city parks, stir the vision of the greenbelts many of these spaces might have become had they been formed as an integral part of the city plan. These parks are frequently the transition between the urban development and the rural countryside, being situated beyond the center of population. They might have been formed as green buffers to separate the different land uses within the city and have been even more accessible to the people than their present locations allow.

There are many recreational spaces of a special nature: cultural centers including the museums and art galleries, beaches, amusement parks, sports centers including athletic fields, swimming pools, and stadiums. There are also the grand sweeps of broad parkways in which recreation areas are developed; the Outer Drive along the lakefront of Chicago is a magnificent illustration of this latter facility.

The overall minimum urban space devoted to the total of the foregoing recreational spaces ranges from about three acres per 1,000 population in the city to a desirable standard of ten acres per thousand persons. It is further recommended that the urban area be planned for a reservation of about 10 percent of the gross area of the city to accommodate the space for an increase in population growth. In the vigorous replanning of London in preparation for the rebuilding program as a result of World War II's devastation, the standard of open space in the outlying areas of the county was seven acres per 1,000 population, while the density of land use within the city boundaries forced a standard of no more than four acres per 1,000 persons.

The absence of open space within our cities may serve as the signal for tomorrow's direction in planning. It will be a sad commentary, indeed, if twenty or thirty years hence our suburbs present the plight of the central city today.

Now is the time to prepare the open space within the growing subdivisions, for we cannot forget that the slums of today were the subdivisions of yesterday. This preparation was implemented by Title VII of the Housing Act of 1961. Identified as a provision for Open Space Land, it made financial assistance available for acquisition of open space in urban areas. Undeveloped or predominately undeveloped land in a comprehensive plan for parks and recreation, conservation of natural resources, and for historic or scenic purposes could be acquired by a city with the benefit of federal grants to meet the partial cost. This program was actively pursued through land acquisition, by dedications as part of the subdivision process, and by grants from state and federal agencies. The Bureau of Land Management reserved a great number of school and park sites adjacent to the city of Las Vegas, Nevada, as a result of cooperation based on a county comprehensive plan.

PUBLIC SCHOOLS

The school board in each community has its policy for extension and the design of the public school plant, but there are a few simple standards that are generally adopted as a key to the allocation of space. These standards link closely with recreational space, since the elementary school is the focal point within the neighborhood unit, and the junior and senior high schools the focal point within the group of neighborhoods we have identified as a community. The open space for recreation should become therefore an integral part of the school location and thereby provide the type of adult supervision and youth leadership necessary to guide the development of young people.

N. L. Engelhardt, Jr., has estimated one-half child of elementary school age (grades one through six) in the average family. The average for families among the low-income group is about 0.7 children, and 0.4 children per family in the high-income group.[7] Since most communities favor elementary schools with an enrollment between 600 and 800 pupils in the first six grades, a neighborhood designed about such a school would have a population of between 1,500 and 1,700 families, or between 5,000 and 6,000 people.

Two such neighborhoods would support a junior high school with en-

---

7. N. L. Engelhardt, Jr., "The School-Neighborhood Nucleus," *Architectural Forum*, October 1943.

Type of Area	Acres per 1,000 Population	SIZE OF SITE (Acres)		Radius of Area Served (miles)
		Ideal	Minimum	
Playgrounds	1.5	4	2	0.5
Neighborhood parks	2.0	10	5	0.5
Playfields	1.5	15	10	1.5
Community parks	3.5	100	40	2.0
District parks	2.0	200	100	3.0
Regional parks and reservations	15.0	500–1,000	varies	10.0

School standards. *Intercounty Regional Planning Commission, Denver, Colorado.*

Urban Land, May 1961, by George Nez, Director, Inter-County Planning Commission, Denver, Colorado.

rollments between 1,000 and 1,200, and four neighborhoods would support a senior high school of about 1,500 enrollment. The walking distance for a junior high school (grades seven through nine) should not exceed one mile, and the senior high school (grades ten through twelve) should be a distance of not more than one and a half miles.

Although the public school system in most communities does not support nursery schools, it would be desirable to establish them by private means. The size recommended by Engelhardt is twenty-five children for each school within a radius not to exceed one-quarter mile from the most distant home served. The average is 0.1 child of nursery school age per family, and a nursery school would serve about 400 families.

It has been considered necessary too frequently in the past to select a school site after the population has arrived and the land has been absorbed for other uses than education or recreation. Consequently standards of adequate area for these facilities have been overshadowed by expedient decisions based upon the cheapest price for such land that might still be available. It is generally agreed, however, that a desirable standard for the three types of schools is: elementary, ten acres; junior high, fifteen acres; and senior high, fifty acres.

New Concepts

In the late 1960s educational authorities tried to solve the problem of school segregation resulting from racially segregated communities. It be-

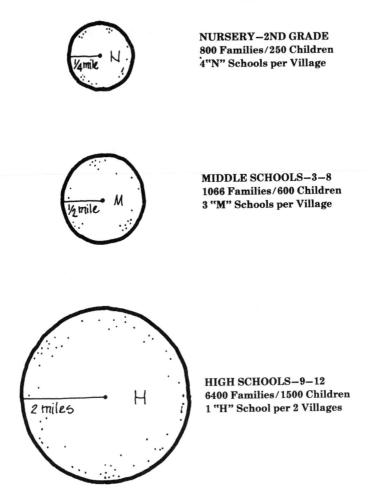

NURSERY—2ND GRADE
800 Families/250 Children
4"N" Schools per Village

MIDDLE SCHOOLS—3—8
1066 Families/600 Children
3 "M" Schools per Village

HIGH SCHOOLS—9—12
6400 Families/1500 Children
1 "H" School per 2 Villages

School service areas.

came clear that busing was not working and that a fresh approach was needed.

One such approach was the "educational park," a concept that emerged from a 1968 study done by the Bureau of Educational Research and Services for Litchfield Park, Arizona, entitled "Design for Lifetime Learning in a Dynamic Social Structure." The park was described as a complex of schools located in a large recreational area. The possibility of reduced educational costs and increasing educational advantages made the idea attractive both to taxpayers and educators.

The system consisted of several related parts, serving different grade and age levels of young people within the community. For the youngest members of the community, a preschool program with facilities closely related to the neighborhood structure was suggested, the parent-child educational center described below. For children in the elementary and junior high age range, facilities are planned at the village level with a cluster of schools on a large single site, bringing students with varying socioeconomic, ethnic, and religious backgrounds together. This new structure is the educational park. High-school educational facilities serve two or three villages.

Parent-Child Educational Center. Each village is composed of three to four neighborhoods. Ideally, a Parent-Child Educational Center should be located in each neighborhood. The facility is intended as a social and recreational activity center for children from infancy through seven years (grades N–2) and their parents. These centers should be located within easy walking distance of the children's homes.

The Educational Park. A village, roughly one square mile in area, containing approximately 8,500 people, could support an Educational Park. The

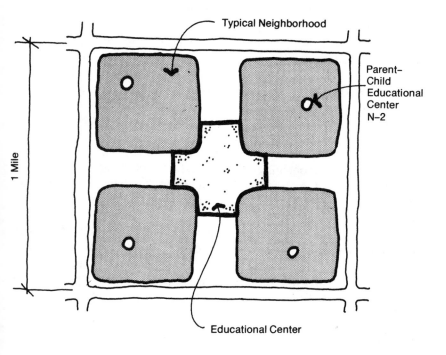

Education within the village.

park would provide a program of education for children of elementary and junior high/high school ages. The park would contain three or four middle schools, providing instruction for children in grades 3–8.

The goals of an Educational Park should be reflected in its shape and organization. An Educational Park's goals will be unique, reflecting the cultural, educational, and social values of a particular community.[8]

The object of the educational park is to create an environment in which learning becomes exciting and rewarding. The use of physical space to complement educational objectives is a principal objective.

During the seventies, in those areas of the country where busing was used to achieve racial balance, the elementary school population fell off as an increasing number of parents sent their children to private or parochial schools.

SITES FOR ESSENTIAL OR CONTROVERSIAL USES

Locational planning for institutional uses can become a crucial problem politically in the decision-making process. While "hot issues" like the determination of a site for a neighborhood shopping center can raise havoc at public hearings, they are like Sunday school picnics compared with hearings that deal with prisons, asylums, hospitals, sewage treatment plants, solid and chemical waste disposal areas, power stations, power transmission lines, and other essentials to protect the health and safety of all urban areas. Even religious institutions become the center of heated discussion and opposition from potential neighbors. Likewise, elementary schools and parks, which serve the children of a neighborhood, find opposition from adjacent property owners. The cry is always the same: put the facility in someone else's back yard. The important factor in all of the problems centers on the attempt to insert these essential functions after the character of a community has been established, by which time the proposed uses are obviously not in conformity with the surroundings.

It is essential, therefore, in the preparation of the comprehensive plan, that these uses be in predetermined locations where potential residents will be aware that they are a part of the community. In addition, the buffering of the uses and the provisions of adequate parking and traffic controls are all essential prerequisites to the construction that will take place.

---

8. Study by the Bureau of Educational Research and Services for Litchfield Park, Arizona, 1968. Published in the General Development Plan for the Salt River Pima-Maricopa Indian Community, June 1970, Eisner & Associates, Consultants.

CHAPTER 21

THE HOUSING ELEMENT

Shelter is one of the most important ingredients in the urban pattern. The many programs developed over the years have seldom resulted in an overall plan for meeting all levels of community need. From the broad scope of the Housing Act of 1949 to the present drastic reductions of federal financial participation, there has been little evidence indicating that those with the greatest need for shelter protection have been provided for. In the past, federal government assistance made some inroads on the solution of the most pressing conditions. In recent years, however, that assistance has diminished greatly and the burdens have fallen on state, county, and city governments, only a few of which have the economic resources or social conscience that are essential.

The major reasons for the lack of adequate shelter for low- and middle-income groups are not only the cost of land but also the facilities that are required to satisfy local laws and ordinances, the inflated costs of construction, and the cost of money itself.

Perhaps the most difficult facet of the comprehensive plan to achieve is the housing element. It requires maximum participation by the private sector in order to accomplish the objectives and to deal with the economic problems associated with those features that involve low- and moderate-income groups; these require extensive subsidy by public agencies, many of which are hard pressed to meet even their everyday financial obligations.

The essence of the housing element is described in the following extract from the California Planning Law. To a great degree it follows other state laws and is consistent with federal regulations.

THE CALIFORNIA PLANNING LAW

Legislative Policy

(a)   The availability of housing is of vital statewide importance, and the early attainment of decent housing and a suitable living environment for every family is a priority of the highest order.
(b)   The early attainment of this goal requires the cooperative participation of government and the private sector in an effort to expand housing opportunities and accommodate the housing needs of all economic levels.
(c)   The provision of housing affordable to low- and moderate-income households requires the cooperation of all levels of government.
(d)   Local and state governments have a responsibility to use the powers vested in them to facilitate the improvement and development of housing to make adequate provision for the housing needs of all economic segments of the community.
(e)   The Legislature recognizes that in carrying out this responsibility, each local government also has the responsibility to consider economic, environmental, and fiscal factors and community goals set forth in the general plan and to cooperate with other local governments and the state in addressing regional housing needs.

Intent
It is the intent of the Legislature in enacting this article:

(a)   To assure that counties and cities recognize their responsibilities in contributing to the attainment of the state housing goal.
(b)   To assure that counties and cities will prepare and implement housing elements which, along with federal and state programs, will move toward attainment of the state housing goal.
(c)   To recognize that each locality is best capable of determining what efforts are required by it to contribute to the attainment of the state housing goal, provided such a determination is compatible with the state housing goal and regional housing needs. To ensure that each local government cooperates with other local governments in order to address regional housing needs.

Housing Element Content
The housing element shall consist of an identification and analysis of existing and projected housing needs and a statement of goals, policies, quantified objectives, and scheduled programs for the preservation, im-

provement, and development of housing. The housing element shall identify adequate sites for housing, including rental housing, factory-built housing, and mobile homes, and shall make adequate provision for the existing and projected needs of all economic segments of the community. The element shall contain all of the following:

(a)   An assessment of housing needs and an inventory of resources and constraints relevant to the meeting of these needs. The assessment and inventory shall include the following:

(1)   Analysis of population and employment trends and documentation of projections and a qualification of the locality's existing and projected housing needs for all income levels. Such existing and projected needs shall include the locality's share of the regional housing need.

(2)   Analysis and documentation of household characteristics, including level of payment compared to ability to pay, housing characteristics, including overcrowding, and housing stock condition.

(3)   An inventory of land suitable for residential development, including vacant sites and sites having potential for redevelopment, and an analysis of the relationship of zoning and public facilities and services to these sites.

(4)   Analysis of potential and actual governmental constraints upon the maintenance, improvement, or development of housing for all income levels, including land use controls, building codes and their enforcement, site improvements, fees and other exactions required of developers, and local processing and permit procedures.

(5)   Analysis of potential and actual nongovernmental constraints upon the maintenance, improvement, or development of housing for all income levels, including the availability of financing, the price of land, and the cost of construction.

(6)   Analysis of any special housing needs, such as those of the handicapped, elderly, large families, farmworkers, and families with female head of household.

(7)   Analysis of opportunities for energy conservation with respect to residential development.

Goals, Objectives, and Policies

A statement of the community's goals, quantified objectives, and policies relative to the maintenance, improvement, and development of housing.

It is recognized that the total housing needs identified pursuant to a subdivision may exceed available resources and the community's ability to satisfy this need within the content of the general plan requirements. Under these circumstances, the quantified objectives need not be identical to the identified existing housing needs, but should establish the maximum number of housing units that can be constructed, rehabilitated, and conserved over a five-year time frame.

Implementation Program

A program which sets forth a five-year schedule of actions the local government is undertaking or intends to undertake to implement the policies and achieve the goals and objectives of the housing element through the administration of land use and development controls, provision of regulatory concessions and incentives, and the utilization of appropriate federal and state financing and subsidy programs when available. In order to make adequate provision for the housing needs of all economic segments of the community, the program shall do all of the following:

(1)   Identify adequate sites which will be made available through appropriate zoning and development standards and with public services and facilities needed to facilitate and encourage the development of a variety of types of housing for all income levels, including rental housing, factory-built housing and mobile homes, in order to meet the community's housing goals.
(2)   Assist in the development of adequate housing to meet the needs of low- and moderate-income households.
(3)   Address and, where appropriate and legally possible, remove governmental constraints to the maintenance, improvement, and development of housing.
(4)   Conserve and improve the condition of the existing affordable housing stock.
(5)   Promote housing opportunities for all persons regardless of race, religion, sex, marital status, ancestry, national origin, or color.

The program shall include an identification of the agencies and officials responsible for the implementation of the various actions and the means by which consistency will be achieved with other general plan elements and community goals. The local government shall make a diligent effort to achieve public participation of all economic segments of the community in the development of the housing element, and the program shall describe this effort.

Regional Housing Needs

While it is the intent that each community take care of its own housing needs for all elements of the housing spectrum, it is obvious that many cannot for a multitude of reasons, sometimes related to the lack of available land or the costs involved in the local scene. In these cases it is sometimes possible to participate with nearby communities where these conditions do not exist. It is also a fact that the community may be removed some distance from places of employment or without a reasonable transportation system, thus making the community unsuitable for that segment of the population that has the greatest need.

It is therefore essential that housing be viewed on a broad area-wide basis, involving the prepartion of a regional plan for the housing element, one that relates housing not only to the needs of people but also to their areas of employment and the availability of a reasonable transportation system.

The California Planning Law contains the following provisions for regional housing needs:

(a)   A locality's share of the regional housing needs includes that share of the housing need of persons at all income levels within the area significantly affected by a jurisdiction's general plan. The distribution of regional housing needs shall, based upon available data, take into consideration market demand for housing, employment opportunities, the availability of suitable sites and public facilities, commuting patterns, type and tenure of housing need, and the housing needs of farmworkers. The distribution shall seek to avoid further impaction of localities with relatively high proportions of lower income households. Based upon data provided by the State Department of Housing and Community Development relative to the statewide need for housing, each council of governments shall determine the existing and projected housing need for its region. The State Department of Housing and Community Development shall ensure that this determination is consistent with the statewide housing need and may revise the determination of the council of governments if necessary to obtain this consistency. Each locality's share shall be determined by the appropriate council of governments consistent with the criteria above with the advice of the department subject to the established procedure.

(b)   For areas with no council of governments, the State Department of Housing and Community Development shall determine housing market areas and define the regional housing need for localities within these areas. Where the department determines that a local government possesses the capability and resources and has agreed to accept the responsibility, with respect to its jurisdiction, for the identification and determination of housing market areas and regional housing needs, the department shall delegate this responsibility to the local governments within these areas.

PERPETUATION OF DISCRIMINATION

The free association of families in "desirable neighborhoods" is not usually looked at as "ghettoization" since those living in the confined area are not forced by law to reside there. In fact, however, the prohibitively expensive rents or prices of homes in some areas have made these communities ghettos, effectively excluding from them those ethnic groups unable to afford the price of housing in the area.

A Supreme Court decision in 1964 held that racial or ethnic agreements based on law could not be enforced in the courts since they violated the Fourteenth Amendment of the Constitution. This decision, however, did not terminate the "gentlemen's agreements" that limited the availability of property to certain ethnic groups.

In order to overcome some of the educational problems derived from ethnic and economic segregation, the Supreme Court held that "separate and equal" educational programs were in fact unequal and thus violated the Fourteenth Amendment. It was obvious that the poorer economic districts, black or white, obtained the poorest of facilities and least qualified teachers.

In the mid-1970s the method developed to solve this problem was to introduce the busing of children from one area to schools in other areas in an effort to produce racial and ethnic balance. In some instances, the children are required to travel a considerable distance from their homes. Protests from both the majority and minority sectors became routine, not only in the South but also in all parts of the country. Obviously, the problem of segregation was not being solved by this effort. In fact greater alienation between whites and racial minorities often resulted.

Similarly a decision in California decreed that the tax funds that support a school system may not be levied on a neighborhood or city basis as the children living in a poor community obtain only meager funds for education under such an arrangement while students from wealthier areas obtain the advantages large amounts of money can buy.

Stratified Communities

Regardless of court decisions, our communities are still highly stratified on the bases of age, color, national origin, and economic status. There are communities where only those people over fifty may reside. We have other locales where only millionaires call the area "home." Recently a project was proposed near Palm Springs, California, where eighteen homes would be located between the greens on a 160-acre golf course. Only 40 acres would be used for the homesites and intended swimming pools and tennis courts. At the other end of the spectrum, as mentioned elsewhere, people are being provided with small homes on parcels of land ever-decreasing in size.

CHAPTER 22

COMMERCE AND INDUSTRY

THE MARKETPLACE

The marketplace has always been the focal point of the city, a center for the exchange of goods. In the most ancient times it was the open space to which farmers and craftsmen brought their products for barter. The development of transportation and money systems implemented the transfer of goods, and the barter system shifted to a form of retail enterprise. Expansion of commerce created a merchant class dealing in the exchange of goods produced by others than themselves. The importance of cities increased as centers of wholesale and retail trade.

As it did with so many other human activities, the industrial system brought more changes in the nature of the marketplace. Not only did the transportation of goods quicken, but also the growing systems of communications accelerated the exchange of goods. The great cities became the trading centers in which world commerce was concentrated. With the growth of urban population the city continued its functions as the center of trade, but emphasis in the great business centers of the city shifted from the commodities being exchanged to the methods and processes for trading in them. Goods are replaced by pieces of paper—documents—that purport to represent them, and transactions for the transfer of commodities are consummated by an exchange of these documents. Negotiations for the sale and payment of good transferred from a merchant in Montevideo to a merchant in Buenos Aires are transacted in a London banking house, or the exchange of grain and meat between the producer on the farm and the consumer in the city next door is arranged through the trading centers of New York or Chicago. The industrial system has introduced to the city a variety of commercial functions never present in the simple marketplace of the ancient town.

Several recognizable types of commercial districts have emerged in the modern city. The most clearcut are the following.

The "downtown" of the large metropolitan city is familiar to every urban dweller. It is the financial and administrative center of its region and, in some cities, it has become the center of business for the nation. New York has its Wall Street, Chicago its LaSalle Street, Paris its Bourse, and London its Exchange district, but every city has its financial center, even though it may serve as a satellite of a greater center. "Downtown" includes the wholesale and retail centers for service to the satellite districts within the city proper or the region. These centers have not been planned; they have simply crept outward and upward within the network of obsolete and confining streets as the fortune of cities and nations fluctuated. The central business district serves a vital and useful purpose as the heart of the city, and its deterioration presents a challenge to business and civic enterprise. Affected by intolerable congestion, noise, fumes, exorbitant land values, and overcrowding, business enterprise shifts restlessly away from the blight eating into the urban core.

A second type of commercial area is the small business district of the satellite community. Dependent upon the metropolitan center for major administrative and wholesale functions, the small commercial center contains the chain retail stores, professional offices, service supply enterprises, motion picture theaters, branch banks, and stock exchanges. In the small, self-contained city, this district will also provide wholesale facilities and include the necessary administrative and transportation centers.

The third type is represented by outlying shopping areas of the city, the community or regional shopping centers. They may overlap with or be the counterpart of the commercial center of the satellite community, but they contain the large-scale service facilities that do not lend themselves to further subdivision and distribution. Among these facilities are large food markets, chain stores of various types, branch banks, telegraph, telephone, and postal district offices, motion picture theaters, branch libraries, and medical and dental offices.

The smallest commercial unit is the neighborhood center. The modern counterpart of the "corner grocery store," the neighborhood shopping center provides the day-by-day commodities for the direct convenience of a limited population. Here, the housewife may perform her regular shopping for the staple goods. It may have an independent grocery store and meat market, television and appliance shop, shoe repair shop, hardware store, a bakery, drug and stationery store, and barber and beauty shop.

Each of the different commercial types are discussed later in this chapter.

The shopping center is just one of many elements that comprise the commercial structure of a city. Legal services, building construction, real estate, and accounting are just a few of the numerous economic activities a city requires. They are as important to the urban pattern as the shopping center, often occupying more total land within a city since they are not usually found in concentrated areas like shopping centers.

Malls are not just another type of shopping area. They are an architectural form wherein the pedestrian shopper is freed from vehicular traffic and where the environment is shaped to encourage shopping and entertain the potential customers.

General business offices are also a part of the commercial structure of a city. Large office complexes in the centers of all of the major cities of the world are occupied by a great variety of businesses and corporation headquarters. Government offices and courts of many types also occupy facilities in or immediately adjacent to business districts. Central city areas that have lost their retail sales attraction are often converted to office or light industrial uses such as garment manufacturing.

The medical center may be one of the exceptions to the scattering usually discerned in other services. The medical center is often located next to a major hospital. It may include rest homes, clinics, and convalescent homes, as well as doctors' offices. Such centers exist in Santa Barbara, California, and El Paso, Texas, and in many communities throughout the United States.

OVERZONING FOR COMMERCE

When communities were small and served a vast outlying area, commercial uses were permitted along both sides of principal traffic routes. A highway passing through the center of a town became the axis for the central business district, and "strip" business developed at random along its route. As the population of the community expanded, additional traffic routes were provided and more business stretched along them. It was then presumed that the highway was the appropriate location for commercial enterprise and, with little further examination of the amount of business a community could support, all existing and proposed street frontage was zoned for commercial use. It is now impossible to classify almost any of these business areas as shopping "centers."

About one-quarter of the streets in our cities are used as main thoroughfares with the property fronting on them zoned for business use. Harland Bartholomew has estimated that some 25 percent of the total area of the average city is occupied by commercial zoning, whereas the area actually used by retail business is only about 3 percent of the total developed area of the city. This contrast gives some measure of the degree to which cities have been overzoned for business development along the traffic arteries.

The gross excess of commercial zoning weighs heavily on the city. Despite the relatively small proportion of commercial zoning actually developed for business, much of this enterprise operates on a marginal basis. The mortality rate is extremely high: between 15 and 25 percent of retail stores go out of business each year. About one-third of all retail stores have a lifespan of a year or less, one-half remain in business no longer than two years, and less than one-quarter remain as long as ten years. The Statistical Abstracts of the United States, 1984 edition, quoted Dun and Bradstreet's statistics, which showed that 118,000 businesses were founded and 16,800 failed in 1981. Robert Dowling, a prominent real estate counselor in New York City, estimated that four or five times as many stores are in business as the need demands.

Inducement to engage in uneconomic ventures is apparently strong, and the impact spreads far beyond the failure of an individual entrepreneur. Unstable business enterprise breeds physical blight; the "shoestring" investments in retail business are analogous to the strip character of zoning. In some cities fully half the property zoned for business is used for residences, and these unplanned mixtures of land uses not only create an undesirable environment but also remove the prospect for consolidation of shopping facilities for convenient access.

Each community has local conditions and practices peculiar to it that will bear upon estimates of the amount of land required, but investigations in a number of cities have shed some light on the relation between population and the business area as a point of departure in developing appropriate standards for the allocation of space for commercial districts. The familiar rule of thumb for commercial development is fifty feet of street frontage for each 100 persons in the area to be served. That the overall amount of space to be devoted to business is an inadequate measure is evident from the observation of cities as well as statistics of land use. The distribution of the space is equally important, if not more vital, to the welfare and service of a city than the total area allocated. The Bartholomew survey disclosed that 44 percent of the total commercial area was in the central business district and 56 percent distributed in the residential neighborhoods.

A survey by the Los Angeles Regional Planning Commission showed a further breakdown in the types of commercial districts.[1] Combined commercial uses amounted to 2.72 acres of land per 1,000 persons throughout the county of Los Angeles. Of this area 1.19 acres was in neighborhood shopping districts, while local or community business districts occupied 0.92 acres; the balance, 0.46 acres per 1,000 persons, was in the satellite commercial centers. An additional 0.15 acres per 1,000 persons was contained in the main "downtown" business center of the city of Los Angeles. These classifications of districts correspond to the four types described at the beginning of this chapter. The Los Angeles County survey included a great variety of communities, ranging from the great metropolitan area of the city of Los Angeles, through the small towns surrounding the city, to semirural areas served by village centers. The 1939 land area devoted to all commercial uses in Los Angeles and three other large urban centers in proportion to the population is shown below:

	Acres per 1,000 Population
Detroit	3.50
San Francisco	1.75
St. Louis	2.15
Los Angeles (City)	3.30

An unpublished study by John H. Riedercorn and F. R. Hearle, prepared for the Rand Corporation, Santa Monica, California, in 1968 indicated the land-use trends in forty-eight large American cities. This study indicated that less than 5 percent of the land was used for commercial purposes.[2]

Observation of the structure of cities as they grow and develop seems to indicate that the pattern of commerce and the use of highway frontages as the locale for retail sales has not changed in the minds of highway frontage property owners. Their logic is that highways are inappropriate locations for residential developments and therefore, per se, they are suitable only for business.

The Skyscraper—Symbol of Big Business

From earliest times people in urban communities placed the temples symbolizing their devotion at the central location of the communities'

---

1. Master Plan of Land Use (Inventory and Classification), Regional Planning Commission, County of Los Angeles, California, 1939, p. 38.
2. *Community Builders Handbook,* Urban Land Institute, Washington, D.C., 1968.

development. It was almost always either the tallest structure or built upon the highest promontory. In small cities it was the religious institution or the city hall, topped with steeple or dome to thus identify the center of local interest. The Parthenon in Athens is an example of how people felt about their most important institution.

In the age of business, the skyscraper represents the symbol of concentrated interest. It rises above its surroundings and gives the urban area an accent, a rallying point about which to cluster activities. These huge structures are the product of the genius of the American architects, engineers, and builders. When constructed in Europe or elsewhere they are called the "American architectural style."

Beginning with the Woolworth Building to the completion of the twin towers of the World Trade Center in New York City more than half a century later, skyscrapers became the identification for the center of large cities. Other examples include the Sears Tower in Chicago, the Bank of America Building in San Francisco, and the many others constructed in Houston, Texas, and elsewhere. In a sense these structures are the symbol of American devotion to "bigness." Architects and engineers vie with each other to devise techniques to build even higher and create intensity of use in the central core of those cities that have achieved the level of economic maturity to accommodate them.

The skyscrapers are a spectacular venture in city building, but like many other manmade spectacular objects they are subject to monumental problems in times of emergency, the simplest of which may be power failure, when elevators fail to operate.

The striving to meet the sky in the central portion of an already established city exaggerates a multitude of problems at the street level, where hordes of people are concentrated in a limited area about these magnificent structures. The ingenuity of the city planners has yet to devise a solution to the problems associated with a limited street system or to develop the services and amenities that should be planned and constructed hand-in-hand with edifices of this stature.

Floor Space

The amount of land area devoted to commercial uses is but a tentative guide for planning. It may, in fact, be deceptive. It omits the primary measure of floor space. Since the inventive genius of man produced the capability to build structures of unlimited heights, the area of land they occupy has been reduced to a relatively insignificant factor in calculating the capacity to accommodate people and their manifold activities. A defect in zoning practice has been the absence of this measurement in allocating space for the various uses in the urban plan. This was illustrated in the Regional Survey of New York and Its Environs of 1931.

That study showed that within the eight-square-mile area between Fifty-ninth Street and the Battery in Manhattan, the average building height was only six stories covering 60 percent of the land, and the average in the Wall Street district was less than eleven stories covering less than 50 percent of the ground area. The lower Manhattan area bristled with the most dramatic display of skyscrapers the world had ever seen, and some of the tallest buildings ever built were held in the palm of midtown Manhattan. Within the relatively limited land area of the great city of New York, the zoning regulations permitted enough floor space to accommodate a business population of 344,000,000 people. Fifteen thousand people could work in the Empire State Building alone. Of course, these numbers pale when compared to current figures.

The significance of floor space to ground area is further illustrated in the floor area ratio provisions of the 1957 Chicago zoning ordinance which permitted floor space ranging from seven to sixteen times the lot area.

Each community has characteristics that form the basis for determining the appropriate relation between population and the space required for the commercial facilities to serve it. In large part it is the restoration of a balance between the open space for the movement of people and the enclosed space they occupy on which the health of city development depends. Although the differences among cities are recognized, Larry Smith and Company has estimated the relative range of floor space for the principal uses in the urban community: [3]

Metropolitan Per Capita Floor Area Requirements for Selected Activities

Activities	Floor Area per Capita (Square Feet)
Retail	20 to 55
Office	2 to 15
Parking (on the ground floor or in structures)	4 to 16
Public	1 to 3.5
Quasipublic	1 to 3.5
Wholesale	5 to 15
Industrial	2 to 15
Residential	200 to 400

Parking

Directly related to the amount of floor space occupied by commercial enterprise is the requirement for vehicular parking to serve it. [4] The future

---

3. Larry Smith, "Space for the CBD's Functions," *Journal of the American Institute of Planners,* February 1961.
4. See chapter 28, "The Zoning Plan."

stability of commercial districts will depend in large measure on the adequacy and convenience of space for automobile parking available to customers, employees, and services. The effects of deficient parking may be measured by the shifts in commercial space to outlying areas of the city.

The automobile is a special breed of locomotion. By far the most uneconomical mode of transportation, it continues to gain in popularity year after year. The phenomenon may be explained in large part by the extended freedom of movement the automobile offers to the driver. Although excessive in physical bulk, this remarkable machine carries few passengers. That excessive bulk clogs the city streets and requires extravagant space for parking. A standing automobile requires 175 square feet of space.

Space for automobile parking is a feature of the shopping center. The requirements vary: some specialty shops are reasonably well served with fewer than five car spaces for each 1,000 square feet of gross floor area, whereas supermarkets may require as many as ten spaces for each 1,000 square feet. An average may be struck at six spaces for each 1,000 square feet in neighborhood centers and eight spaces for each 1,000 square feet in community and regional centers.

It has been estimated that sidewalk space should provide 5 square feet per person. Assuming that there is an average of 100 square feet of building space per occupant and that one-third of the occupants use the sidewalks at one time, it has been estimated that if commercial space in New York City were built to what even the revised zoning ordinance permitted, pedestrians would have less than three and one-half square feet per person in the combined areas of sidewalks and streets.

The enigma compounds. The pedestrian has become a human jumping-jack in the struggle for a place on the sidewalk, and when streets are widened sidewalks are narrowed. Curb parking impedes the traffic lanes and renders the street obsolete as a channel for movement. Land prices exceed any economic value for surface parking, and multideck garages are built. Commercial enterprise in gradually forced to seek other locations in order to conduct business. Mass transportation shows little evidence of correcting the situation. The availability of economical off-street parking is a critical necessity. Chapter 23 contains additional material on parking and its economic impacts.

DOWNTOWN

There is a romance associated with the downtown of almost any city. It represents the tradition that springs from and clings to a place of the beginning. It has been the place where generation after generation has witnessed the vicissitudes of time. It has been the core from which the vitality of the city has found nourishment and energy. It has been the civic center, the place of the city hall, the "big" stores, the theaters. It has been the place people went to when they went to work, and the place they went to when they "went out." It has been the terminus, the hub for railroads, commuting trains, and buses. It has been the headquarters for firms and institutions. It has been the symbol of the life of the city. The central business district and downtown are often synonymous and are used interchangeably. Within this central area of most communities we find businesses, government offices, services, warehousing, and manufacturing. Each operation, in a well-planned city, is in its own segment of the core area, but they all seem to function well together.

A downtown area's strength[5] depends on its ability to remain the employment center of the metropolitan economic region. To help ensure or regain a position of economic dominance, urban centers often look to associations of businesses that are dependent on the center's health. Privately funded central business district associations have frequently been able to help through joint venture planning, by helping develop programs in their respective cities, and by influencing legislation critical to the urban center's well-being.

Urban revitalization does not mean returning to the downtown retail function of twenty or thirty years ago. It means becoming vital to the metropolitan area as a service center, a place to work, a place to visit, and even a place to live. It means involving all government levels in a more efficient and productive manner.

Downtown areas are typically major tax revenue generators, and while their land areas are relatively minute, the assessed valuation of downtown improvements are typically a major portion of those of the entire city. Downtown areas have the in-place infrastructure necessary to support economic growth. And oftentimes it is a city's urban center that forms the image of the state.

States are placing great emphasis on revitalizing their urban centers. State-sponsored special programs for this purpose are increasing. Perhaps the most effective state actions have been enabling legislation that encourages downtown reinvestment. Urban enterprise zones, industrial revenue bonds, grants and low-interest loan programs, tax abatements, and support for public-private venturing are among the legislative milestones passed by state governments. But urban center revitalization remains far from being assured. Inflation coupled with high interest rates is decimating what narrow chance distressed cities have of being competitive.

---

5. Material below is based on the Report on Joint Conference, Eno Foundation for Transportation Board of Directors and Board of Consultants, October 1981.

The structure of the city is undergoing major changes while downtown is slow to respond. Its future is uncertain, not because it is expected to disappear beneath the waves of change, but because of the resistance it poses to change itself—the reluctance of its response to the demands these changes are imposing upon it. Whole districts have deteriorated. Throngs of people mingle in the snarl and ugly tangle of traffic and buildings. It is suffocating under an economic oxygen tent, and breath is coming in shorter and shorter gasps. Choked by obsolescent circulation, people and vehicles have too little room to move. Worn haggard, and with shattered nerves, the urbanite bears testimony to these tensions.

The forces gnawing at downtown are manifold, and the lag in positive response to the competition is hurting. Decentralization of retail shopping to major regional centers has been a natural evolution of urban expansion, and the relative position of the downtown business district is headed for modification. Until the Depression of the thirties, over 90 percent of general merchandise trade was concentrated in the downtown area. In recent years the amount of this trade in shopping centers surpassed that in downtown in all cities with more than a million people. While the rate of this increase spirals ever upward, the dollar volume of trade in the downtown areas has been more than halved.[6]

This trend will not subside automatically nor from natural causes. Aggressive and imaginative attention to and understanding of the function of the downtown area as the heart of the city is necessary.

The central city was once the transportation hub. Except in a few large cities the private automobile is the primary carrier today. The central district is jammed with traffic, but one-half or more of the vehicles that crowd the streets are passing through downtown for destinations beyond. Yet the district, bulging with vehicles, resembles an endless parking lot. A striking image of the central city is Los Angeles, where two-thirds of the downtown area is devoted to streets, alleys, and parking lots. It is not that this allocation of space is disproportionate when compared with modern shopping centers, but the inferior quality of the space, created by the disorderly scattering of buildings among automobile repositories and traffic-ridden streets, is spoiling the district.

Dispersion of the residential population from the environs of the downtown area has altered the economic base. Those who could afford to have escaped to the outskirts, and a ring of slums chokes the central city. The flight to the suburbs has drawn with it a decentralization of consumer retail business. Perhaps more insidious in its effect, however, is the shifting of other traditional downtown activities caught in this centrifugal movement. Restaurants, department stores, theaters, civic and cultural

---

6. Homer Hoyt, *Urban Land*, September 1961.

facilities—museums, art galleries, libraries, auditoriums and sports centers, government offices—and a variety of business firms are moving to new locations along the fingers of commerce stretching outward from the core. These shifts are sporadic, but they seem to be persistent. Consumer shopping naturally seeks proximity to its direct market, but most of the movement is not necessarily induced by improved geographic location nor compatible relationships; it is flight from the congestion of downtown.

The Future

A virtue of the central district is its compact form. The hard core of the center is of relatively limited size, rarely exceeding 160 acres. It thus becomes a natural area for ready access by pedestrian communications. The spearheads of commercial expansion spreading outward overextend these lines of communication and drain the internal energy rather than buttress the economy of the core. Property owners seek to sustain their values, but the incentive to risk capital for improvement by absentee owners lags so long as property yields an acceptable return on the investment. Concerted action is thus slow in forming. Oblique maneuvers, slogans, cleanup campaigns, sidewalk twig planting, reflect a basic pessimism. Enthusiasm will be expressed by a frontal attack, a bold and imaginative plan by business leaders to revitalize the district.

It is possible that major retail commerce may not be equated with the central business district as the functions of downtown evolve. The central area of a great city usually forms into specialized districts—the financial district, theater and hotel district, business and professional offices, the large department stores and shops, and offices of government. These several functions may mingle in a single district of a small city, where they form a fairly compact unit, having their own identification and supporting services.

The future of downtown demands more than piecemeal rehabilitation. The occasional bright new building, replacing some old and wornout structure, is attractive. But the impact of increasing intensity of land use, without change in the street system and parking accommodations, only aggravates an already overburdened circulation system. Business enterprise thus exercises its option to use land more productively, but the public responsibility has not been exercised to update the circulation system and terminal facilities. The "golden noose" draws tighter.

Vehicular and pedestrian circulation are not rehabilitation measures, nor is parking. Rebuilding the broad fringe of slums and blight encircling the city center could attract a multitude of those who have fled to the outskirts. Integrated replanning from within the central district outward, and across the wide twilight zone surrounding it, may restore an enriched quality to this critical area of the city.

CENTRAL BUSINESS DISTRICT

The size and contents of the central business district will be different in each community. Since each urban area of any size has one, the range of the differences will relate to the services that each one performs in the total urban pattern. In a well-planned central business district the types of uses will be in nodes; where the retailing area will be compact and attractive, the financial cluster and general office should be integrated in a "wall street." Banking will be scattered in close relation to the retailing. The wholesaling sector will be distinct and on the periphery as will any manufacturing operations, not interspersed and interfering with the continuity of the retailing. The types and locations of the internal circulation will favor the pedestrian in the heart of the area. Vehicular traffic will be held to the perimeter of the retailing area, and parking facilities integrated with the circulation, not necessarily penetrating into the heart of the retailing area.

Where mass transit serves the central business district it should be closely associated with the heart of the area, making walking distance between terminals and stores short and convenient. When subways are involved they could have station exits into stores, as in Boston and downtown Montreal.

If a major governmental center is also located in the central business district, it should also be in a tightly knit entity on the edge of the district but close enough to the office center to make use of the courts and legal offices an easy relationship.

Cultural facilities such as a major theater district are often an important part of the central business district. It should be closely related to the retail sector and restaurants so that people utilizing the theaters will find themselves in a lively location where there is a feeling of excitement both before and after a performance. When these facilities are located near a civic center, as in Los Angeles, the area is dead at night.

In the past ten years there has been an enormous investment in the central core of many cities, large and small. As the rebuilding of the core area has taken place, many residents who inhabited the area during the years the poorly maintained properties provided shelter were displaced. While there were some efforts to make the transition easy, great numbers of the low- and middle-income families became victims of the changes taking place. In San Francisco the mayor initiated a program whereby 20 percent of a project in the core areas was required to provide housing for

Courtesy Gordon Sommers

Fort Worth, Texas—*Victor Gruen and Associates, architects. This well-known plan for reshaping the central business district of Fort Worth combines the features of the regional shopping center, which are lacking in the downtown of most cities. A circumferential highway system about the district feeds six four-story parking garages. Each garage projects into the central core, and convenient walking distance from the garages to the center encourages the closing of internal streets to serve as pedestrian shopping malls. Service to business establishments is through underground tunnels.*

Northland Center, Detroit—*Victor Gruen and Associates, architects. A major regional center of 1,100,000 square feet in retail space, this development includes a theater, auditorium, and community center. Parking space is available for 10,000 cars, and the center is patronized by as many as 70,000 people per day.*

low- and middle-income families. Other cities are following the same pattern of social responsibility toward their residents.

SHOPPING CENTERS

In the decade between 1940 and 1950 the suburbs surrounding cities increased 35 percent, and the rate of growth between 1950 and 1960 jumped to 50 percent. Following the remarkable increases prior to 1960, the changes that took place in the decade between 1970 and 1980 reflect clearly the population changes that have taken place in various parts of the cities. While the percentage of growth in the United States in this decade increased by 11.4 percent and the metropolitan areas by 10.2 percent, growth in the central city was only 0.2 percent. Further statistics indicate that, not surprisingly, growth outside of the central city increased by 18.2 percent, and nonmetropolitan areas grew by 15.1 percent.

The changes between 1950 and 1980 indicate the shift of urban population away from the central city to the peripheral areas, either just outside of the central city or to more-rural areas.[7]

---

7. *Statistical Abstracts of the United States,* U.S. Bureau of the Census, Department of Commerce, 1984.

Retail enterprise to serve the sprawling residential suburbs gathered in scattered clusters. The corner grocery store was transformed into the neighborhood shopping center. This "new look" suggested a strong contrast with the shabby and congested commercial streets of conventional business districts. Convenient parking without charge was a novel and refreshing experience. Nourished by the volume of new population, the shopping center became popular. The distinguishing feature of the new center is the positive separation between the automobile and pedestrian. Smarting under this new form of competition, the downtown business districts of the large cities and small towns made belated efforts to improve shopping conditions.

Shopping center statistics of the 1960s are still valid in the 1980s. They can be divided into three general categories:[8]

1. *The neighborhood center* is the local source for staples and daily services for a population of between 7,500 and 20,000 people. The average size is about 40,000 square feet of gross floor area, but it may range between 30,000 and 75,000 square feet. The site should be four to ten acres in area. It is usually designed about a supermarket as the principal retail service.

2. *The community center* may serve a population of between 20,000 and 100,000, and extends the services of the neighborhood center by providing a variety store or small department store as the major tenant. The average size is 150,000 square feet of gross floor area with a range of between 100,000 and 300,000 square feet, requiring a site between ten to thirty acres in size.

3. *The regional center* is usually built about one or more major department stores and includes a full complement and range of retail facilities usually found in a balanced small city. It can serve a population from 100,000 to 250,000 people. An average size is about 400,000 square feet of gross floor area, although it may range as high as 1,000,000 square feet. A minimum site of forty acres is required; the largest centers require as many as 100 acres.

Examination of the economic base for retail trade is the initial stage in planning the shopping center, and the techniques of market analysis have come into full play by authorities in their development. The steps in such an analysis follow a logical sequence:

1. The trading area involves an investigation of the population, income levels, places and direction of its growth, the existing and poten-

---

8. *Community Builders Handbook*, Executive Edition, Urban Land Institute (Washington, D.C., 1960).

tial location and volume of trade in competitive establishments. This information will indicate the volume of trade in relation to the site of the new center.

2.   The gross potential sales for the center is derived from estimated expenditures in the trading area. Family income data will disclose the portion devoted to various goods and services—food, furniture, clothing, appliances, drugs, automotive equipment, restaurants, entertainment, miscellaneous merchandise.

3.   The potential net sales volume for a new center is related to the sales volume in existing and potential competitive enterprise in the trading area. This requires informed judgment of the proportion of existing trade that may be attracted to the new location. The sales volume per square foot of retail floor space for the various goods will aid in estimating the gross sales in existing establishments offering comparable goods.

4.   The physical space that can be supported by the net sales from the trading area may be estimated from the average annual sales per square foot of floor space in the several retail facilities.

5.   Anticipated income from the center may be determined by application of the probable rental rates per square foot of retail space, less operating and management costs, taxes, insurance, interest and amortization on the loan for the capital cost for the complete development. The balance represents the net return that may be expected by the developer on his equity investment.

Regional Centers Revisited

Enthusiasm for regional shopping centers has waned. Originally intended to bolster the city, shopping centers have become magnets for decentralization, hastening the decline of the downtown area as a retail center.

One of the major proponents of large-scale shopping centers and the architect of many throughout the United States, Victor Gruen, recently indicated that they are far from what he had envisaged them to be. He had thought that shopping centers could combine retailing with recreational and cultural activities, thereby promoting the revitalization of central city areas. While not accomplishing all the goals initially expected of them, regional shopping centers have nevertheless been built in central core areas in an effort to reestablish their retail function. Urban renewal has often been the vehicle to free land for such centers.

THE MALL

An animated, colorful scene is the attraction of city streets. The gaudy array of signs by day and night conveys a carnival spirit. The kaleidoscopic spectacle is a tasteless, even vulgar, display, but it is the asset of the street. People warm to the crowds and the excitement of variety. Shouting out to the passerby by means of vivid display is a commercial necessity. City streets have become traffic arteries. Capturing and holding the attention of a passing motorist intensifies the pressure on advertising. Business notices must project themselves into the street with a galaxy of illuminated devices. Signs grow in size and novelty in direct ratio to the congestion of traffic. It is a grim, bizarre reality. Design reform could sterilize the city street scene. Neither the shopper-driver nor the shopkeeper can forsake the nervous disorder. The anachronism is obvious. The automobile is not a natural means of locomotion for shopping; the patron of business is essentially a pedestrian, not a motorist.

It is quite possible that much of the distasteful quality of the commer-

City of Miami News Bureau

Lincoln Road Mall, Miami Beach—*Morris Lapidus Associates, architects.*

Model of proposals for Upland town center. *Using the existing commercial facilities and streets, this mall plan for the small city of Upland eliminated the proposed bypass road system and turned the proposed central pedestrian way into a diagonal parking lot for shoppers' automobiles. The community abandoned the plan for the pedestrian mall as a result of shop owners' fears that the inconvenience of walking a few yards from a parking lot to their stores would deter customers.*

cial street would disappear under its own weight if the patron were readily converted from a driver to a pedestrian. The necessity for the raucous display could be replaced by attention to the goods for sale. Again the shopping center makes the case; the automobile is removed from the street, the shopper returns to his natural status of a pedestrian, and the animation of the scene is enhanced. As though it were "proof positive," more dollar volume of business results.

The mall has acquired a magic ring. Contrary to some impressions, it is not accomplished by the simple gesture of closing a street to vehicular traffic. It becomes a complex arrangement of traffic rerouting, parking, service for merchandise delivery and refuse collection, adjustments in utilities, illumination, fire and police protection, and maintenance. Nor is the mall a panacea for the ills that beset downtown. It may become an important element in replanning the central business district, but it is effective only to the extent that the traffic, parking, and general spatial rearrangement are integrated. Not the least element in the program for a revitalized downtown is the spirit with which the property owners and tenants participate. Full cooperation may produce a metamorphosis in downtown and restore it as the heart of the city.

The tragedy of physical and economic neglect that has disfigured so many areas of cities is apparent in the futile and desperate efforts to breathe life into already dead city centers by conversion of traffic streets to pedestrian ways—malls that traverse a desert of vacant stores, empty lots, and outworn advertising signs. The penalty for no planning or bad planning is underscored by this dilemma. In new shopping centers space is reserved for pedestrians separate from automobile parking, and a handsome environment is created free from ugly advertising. The unattractive strip commercial traffic street cannot compete with those advantages. With the deterioration of city centers and in the absence of planning foresight, retail enterprise has been allowed to disperse carelessly to the new shopping centers. The retail function of the city centers further declines until remedies for their recovery are too little and too late.

The Answer?

Some 150 pedestrian malls—including transit malls—have been built in the United States in the last two decades. Most haven't failed outright, but few have lived up to their billing as the salvation of downtown retailing. Just about as many department stores and first-run movie theaters have closed in towns with malls as without, and just as many wig stores, fast-food places, and video-game arcades have opened up.

What's different about the malls is the trees and grass and children's playgrounds—and the ubiquitous Muzak. Now some analysts are questioning whether the park-like atmosphere is conducive to retailing, and some places are going to the other extreme and ripping up their malls. Most, though, are sticking with the mall, while searching for ways to bring it up to date.[9]

Basic to the problems facing street malls is the fact that they are a last-ditch effort to save bankrupt merchants who have done little with their merchandising and less with their investments toward upkeep and modernization. Many street malls in these already deteriorated areas become like flowers at a funeral.

INDUSTRY

Some form of industrial activity is always an essential part of a community's economic structure. However, the term *industry* has many facets.

---

9. Ruth Eckdish Knack, "Pedestrian Malls—20 Years Later," *APA Planning,* December 1982.

Places of employment, research and development centers, electronic assembly plants, heavy industry, factories, and the testing of atomic bombs all come under the heading of "industry." The kind of industry that a community permits within its confines will determine its quality of life.

Industry involves a wide range of activities, varying from the assembly of small premanufactured items into larger elements to the huge steel mills and chemical plants that are the heart of the economic life of many communities. The past behavior of these industries left scars on the areas where they were located. The buildings were most often ugly and dilapidated. The operations were both noisy and contributed to pollution. Their impact was not only on the physical appearance of the area but often adversely affected the health of nearby residents as well.

With the beginnings of planning—as far back as in prerevolutionary Boston where wind conditions were taken into account in the location of slaughtering plants—communities began to be concerned about location. Not until recently have communities become involved in regulation of the appearance of establishments and in the control of both sound and odors and other impacts on the health of people in surrounding areas. Atomic energy plants have been a subject of great concern in the present decade.

In cities such as Santa Barbara, Miami Beach, Palm Springs, and Las Vegas, major industry takes the form of tourism. There are also alternate sources of employment for the residents of these communities in commerce, real estate, and general services but they are usually in some way related to tourism and recreation.

In some communities, educational institutions are the major "industry." They bring financial support to the area through the employment of faculty and service personnel. These people in turn support the shopkeepers and the other institutions that provide housing, food, and other services. One of the purest forms of the educational community is in Davis, California. Once an agricultural college, the University of California at Davis is now a full-fledged university with approximately 17,000 students. Its influence on the surrounding community is enormous.

Industrial Parks

The development of industrial parks has been due to the efforts of specialized industries to become more completely integrated with the home areas of their employees. The development of excellent architecture within a landscaped environment, the maintaining of noiseless, pollution-free operations, and service roads designed not to conflict with the residential area of the community have made the industrial park welcome in many communities, even the most restricted ones.

Typical standards include the establishment of an architectural board of review, minimum setbacks of twenty-five feet with complete landscape treatment of the open areas, provision of adequate enclosed parking and loading spaces, exclusion of any operation that emits smoke or fumes, and the limiting of noise levels. Performance standards for landscaped areas and plant operations are established to ensure that high standards are maintained.

Many cities, however, are substantially developed industrially. These cities afford their residents employment in manufacturing. This does not imply that the bulk of the land area of cities like Gary, Indiana, and South San Francisco is occupied by manufacturing. Even in such industrial cities, usually only about 10 to 15 percent of the land is taken up by manufacturing.

New Orleans is looking to its improved industrial future with the development of the Almonaster-Michoud industrial corridor, which constitutes one of the few remaining large tracts of undeveloped property in the city. This proposed development will be the largest of its kind in the United States, involving approximately 12,000 acres. Many years of planning led to the adoption of an overall master plan for the projected development.

Robert J. Marek discussed the corridor and its problems in a 1982 report:

With all these advantages, why isn't the corridor fully developed?

The answer is relatively simple. First, the corridor lacks proper drainage and sanitary sewer systems and an adequate road network.

Second, a large portion of the potential industrial market has already been won by outlying parishes in the metropolitan area.

To some extent, the corridor has been developing on its own, particularly in those areas where the roadways and drainage are most favorable. The Michoud Assembly Facility . . . covers some 825 acres, and firms like Folger Coffee, Georgia Pacific, TANO Corporation, Siemens-Allis Electronics, and Litton Industries occupy relatively large sites. With its adoption of Mayor Morial's economic development program, however, the city assumed the responsibility of providing infrastructure improvements and committed itself to developing the corridor as a planned industrial park.

As a first step toward fulfilling that commitment, the Morail administration successfully lobbied in 1979 for a state law establishing a 7,000-acre Almonaster-Michoud Industrial District and creating a board of commissioners. The legislation paved the way for a permanent funding source for the district by providing for an ad valorem real property tax of twenty mills. The tax was approved by voters in a citywide referendum last May.

Low Taxes. There is a catch. Proceeds from the tax will amount to only about $165,000 a year initially. That's because of the low assessment values in the New Orleans area, an abundance of tax-exempt land in the district, and—most of all—Louisiana's 10-year industrial exemption program. Tax revenues are not expected to cover significant capital improvements, but rather will be used to staff the industrial district board and provide marketing services, increased sanitation, and security services. As the district develops industrially, land values will increase and the tax will become more important in providing improvements.

Most of the public improvements scheduled by the city and the district board will take place within the 7,000-acre district.[10]

A recent controversy raged over Detroit's "Poletown" neighborhood. General Motors threatened Detroit with the relocation of its Cadillac assembly plant and forced the city to destroy a longstanding ethnic working-class community for a new plant. In an attempt to retain a few thousand industrial jobs, Detroit gave GM twelve years of tax abatements, spent $200 million in public funds for land, and razed more than one thousand houses. This is almost an exaggerated example of reindustrialization, born of Detroit's hard-fought decision to choose economic revival over community preservation.

RESPONSIBILITIES OF COMMERCE AND INDUSTRY

Business plays a major role in the urbanization process. The commerce and industry that make up business not only produce and distribute products important to life, but also provide employment for the millions who reside in urban places. The health of the national economy of all nations depends on the success of the business ventures that are part of their environment.

In addition to its own values, the business community has a responsibility in many aspects of community affairs. These include, beside the payment of fair wages and provision of safe working conditions, keeping the environment free of congestion and the air free of smog, acid rain, and other forms of pollution.

---

10. "Planning," APA publication, March 1982.

CHAPTER 23

CIRCULATION

Managing transportation in cities is almost as old as Western civilization. Julius Caesar, in the early municipal laws of Rome, had considerable regulations as to how wagons should go through the streets of Rome and when they should not, and how they should be restricted during business hours.

Edward P. Morgan,
"Atlantic Dateline" broadcast,
German Marshall Fund of the U.S., 1982

CHANNELS OF MOVEMENT

Since people first charted the fleeting trace of a path across the landscape, routes of travel have been the vital threads in patterns of commerce, cultural exchange, and military conquest. For more than 3,000 years man's mode of transportation was by foot or horseback. Then came the Industrial Revolution and mechanization, steam for rail and water travel, the internal combustion engine for automobile and airplane, and the beginning of space travel. Progressing from the path to the road, the river to the ocean, the rail to the sky, the space for movement of man and his vehicles now occupies more than a quarter of the land in the urban community.

Of all of the products of a remarkable age, none have made more striking progress than the vehicles of transportation. With the variety in modes of travel came increased speed, extended lines of communication, and, most important, unprecedented mobility of countless millions of people.

The impact on the structure of our civilization is appalling. The industrial economy is rooted in large part in the production and circulation of vehicles of transportation. Commercial enterprise in metals, plastics, fuels, rubber, even in insurance, hospitals, and funeral parlors, depends to a large extent upon our capacity to move people and goods. Within our cities we are confronted with a paradox. On the one hand is the struggle to design a circulation system to accommodate vast changes in the speed of transportation; on the other we search desperately for a place for these vehicles to come to a halt. The freedom of movement afforded by the revolution in transportation has reached such an advanced stage of development it is now a major problem to slow down and stop. The automobile is trapped in the network of an archaic street system, but when the circulation routes are improved there must be a place to park at the points of destination. This paradox of conversion speed to pedestrian tempo is dramatized in airplane travel: the time consumed to and from the airport may be greater than a flight of a thousand miles.

In 1847 the Messagèries Nationales coach line in France traveled at six miles an hour and fifty-six miles a day. With the introduction of asphalt in about 1860, the improved roadways brought a further increase in the speed of travel. The Malles-Poste coaches traveled nine to twelve miles an hour and seventy-five miles a day. The automobile has the capacity for speeds several times that of the nineteenth-century horse-drawn coach, but the time consumed by the fits and starts along traffic streets, the search for a place to park, and then the walk to the office reduce the average speed of the commuter to an actually lesser rate.

An even greater issue than the speed of modern transportation is its safety. If urban travel were confined solely to the irritation of a traffic jam, we might withdraw to a point of vantage and view the scene as a farce. But the automobile has indeed become a weapon of murder. Between 1960 and 1982, the yearly accident rate in the U.S. increased from 10,400,000 to 18,121,000. At the same time, deaths increased from 38,600 to 47,300 per year, a national tragedy of major proportions. In California, where the automobile is a way of life (though not necessarily of living), deaths increased from 5,114 in 1970 to 5,860 in 1980.

In addition to the above, deaths involving pedestrians rose from 9,900 in 1970, to 10,300 in 1972, and 8,700 in 1982. Pedestrian slaughter amounted to about 25 percent of the number that died from intervehicle crashes or from other automobile-related deaths, including collisions with trees, telephone poles, and buildings.[1]

Many of these tragedies are due to carelessness, but the tensions generating from the tempo and confusion of the modern city might be relieved through well-ordered street and highway design.

The function of a city's circulation system is to provide for the movement of people and goods. It ranges from the movement of an individual on foot to the daily hordes of commuters entering and leaving the city from distant points. It includes automobiles, buses, trucks, and railroads —on the surface, underground, and overhead—ships, and airplanes. It is the series of routes traversed for a variety of purposes—work, entertainment, shopping, transport of raw materials and manufactured products, education, relaxation, affairs of state, law enforcement. The mixture of these demands for transport, and vehicles to serve them, compounds the equation for the system. It embraces walkways, service lanes, major streets, highways, freeways, the rights-of-way for rail lines, and airway routes. Each of the elements in the circulation system we know today has been inherited from the premachine era. Adjustment to the mechanical vehicle has been an arduous process of wrestling some semblance of order and utility from the archaic layout.

The early surveyors usually laid out towns in gridiron sections one mile square. The major highways followed these section lines in ribbons 100 feet wide. Secondary highways eighty feet in width were aligned along the quarter section lines, and within these squares the interior roads were laid in sixty-feet rights-of-way. The system was adaptable to a regular division of land into lots, and people settled at strategic locations. The pattern continued as the population increased, and later through this network of streets, vehicles of modern transportation poured into the growing cities.

How Shall We Move?

Satellites in outer space make instantaneous audiovisual communication possible on a global scale. Spaceships carry men to the moon, and television is projected into our living rooms from moonwalkers. Yet this same technology only complicates the movement of earthbound persons in cities.

The ever-increasing number of motor vehicles crowd the streets and are trapped in their own self-perpetuating traffic jams. Once associated

---

1. *Statistical Abstracts of the United States,* Department of Commerce, Bureau of Statistics, Washington, D.C., 1984.

with social status and the individual's freedom to move anytime, anywhere, at any speed, the illusion of the automobile has been fleeting.

Traffic congestion in all of the cities of the world has become a headache, in some cities a migraine. The result has been air pollution and dependency on a vanishing resource, petroleum-based fuel. The use of the private automobile as a massive transportation system has provided for maximum individual mobility but at great cost, not only for the user of the vehicles but also in the loss of valuable land devoted to the sprawling communities that dot the landscape of many Western nations.

The expressway or freeway systems were conceived to relieve congestion. But the proliferation of automobiles strains them beyond their capacities. Armed with formulas for measuring "cost-benefit ratios," the limited vision of traffic experts justifies widening streets and adding more expressway lanes and extensive new routes, only to compound the congestion, multiply accidents, and increase injuries and deaths each year. Once expected to delineate the boundaries of neighborhoods, the expressways destroyed them; they became channels of escape from the congested city to the sprawling suburbs.

Automobile manufacture, with related oil, steel, and service enterprises, comprises a major element of the national economy. There are over three times as many new automobiles produced than babies born each year in the United States.

THE ROLE OF THE AUTOMOBILE

"Freedom" in many parts of the Western world has symbolically been the right to own and operate a motor vehicle—be it motorized bicycle, scooter, moped, motorcycle, or automobile. The typical American family owns at least two automobiles and depends on them for the ability to move from home to places of employment, for recreation and other activities. The love for the auto leads one to the opinion that, if possible, the owners would take their vehicles to bed with them, for surely the accelerator has become an integral part of the foot.

Each motor vehicle requires about 4,000 square feet of space in the form of real estate and structures, and the land rent may be as high as $5,000 per year for each car. These costs are paid for in many ways by the consumers as they visit their doctors, the shopping center, the bowling alley, and are added to the mortgage payment, tax bills, and the many other public and private elements of daily living expenses.

The heavily subsidized automobile has become a toy, a weapon, and a means whereby people can express their "macho" image. With the demise of mass-transportation alternatives that are attractive, convenient, and efficient, it has become an essential part of the comprehensive plan to develop streets and highways ranging from the local access ways to our homes to the mechanical marvels exemplified by our freeways and parkways.

Relief from Congestion

As traffic grows, atmospheric pollution spreads across entire urban regions. Streets, expressways, parking lots, and multilevel garages consume valuable land, as exhausts poison precious air. There is not, nor can there be, enough space to accommodate the moving and standing flood of automobiles. In the 1930s Sir Raymond Unwin calculated that all the automobiles that enter New York City would absorb all the space on Manhattan Island. Victor Gruen estimated in the 1960s that nine stories of garage space covering Manhattan would be necessary to store automobiles if everyone entering that island came by car.[2] The Urban Land Institute reported in 1970 that parking for the 150,000 cars entering Pittsburgh's Golden Triangle each day would require 214 garages with 700-car capacity, at a cost of $535,000,000 exclusive of land.[3] These projections may seem preposterous. Yet of the sixty stories in the twin towers of the Marina City apartment complex built in Chicago in the 1960s, nineteen stories are a garage. In the 1980s these factors have increased the cost of parking to astronomical levels, leading to a drive to reduce standards in the face of increases in the number of automobiles.

With city planners spurred by the conviction that relief from traffic congestion would come by way of broader streets, there followed a rash of street-widening projects along the established rights-of-way, and major and secondary highways were designated. Congestion was not relieved, however. More traffic was invited onto these broader streets, slow-moving and short-haul traffic mixed with vehicles destined for more distant points, left turns occurred at all intersections, truck and passenger vehicles vied for parking and loading space along the curbs, vehicular and pedestrian traffic conflicted, unlimited ingress and egress flowed from abutting property into the traffic lanes, frequent intersections impeded movement, and the multitude of commercial distractions along the streets brought chaos to the city.

The profligate waste of resources in materials and land has turned the personal freedom promised by the internal combustion engine into a frantic search for survival at the periphery of cities. Continued decentralization persists without concern for the cost of transportation or the

---

2. Victor Gruen, *The Heart of Our Cities* (New York: Simon and Schuster, 1964).
3. George Prytula, *Community Mobility Systems,* Urban Land Institute, Special Report, 1970.

arrangement of land uses related to economic and functional channels of mass transportation.

Therein lies a crux of the urban planning process: a structure of land uses and distribution of population within a network of mass transportation that can move people and goods with convenience, comfort, and economy. In great cities that evolved before the automobile—London, Paris, Moscow, Saõ Paulo, New York, Chicago, Boston, Philadelphia, San Francisco—the concentration of land uses and the inadequate surface space have forced tunneling underground for subways. Yet building bulk in these cities continues to accelerate, and the equation between the concentration of people and transportation is continuously unbalanced.

If a planned balance between building concentration and transportation service were achieved (and there is no evidence that this is about to happen), the subway would not be desirable. Man is not by nature a subterranean creature; he needs bountiful natural light and air. Since broad rights-of-way are being acquired for vast systems of expressways, comparable channels could be provided for a system of surface transportation within existing city centers, as well as outlying areas.

Such an approach to a desirable system of urban transportation will be expensive; any system of adequate transportation will require vast sums of public financing, as the massive cost of freeways and highways testifies. But it will require much more than public funds; it will require a rare commitment by public and private leaders to the transformation, the reshaping, of the city structure.

Perceptive minds since Ebenezer Howard have recognized the need to restructure the industrial city—now the commercial city—in the image of man himself. Recovery of human scale is at the root of every enlightened concept of the city of our age. Sir Raymond Unwin applied Howard's theory of the self-contained garden city to his own diagrams for the decentralized metropolis. The British New Towns, the planned decentralization of Stockholm, and Tapiola—near Helsinki in Finland—have pursued this same objective.

The urban structure must be designed or redesigned as a series of physically functioning neighborhoods and communities integrated with a circulation system of mass transportation. Whatever the sociological variations, physical facilities for education, worship, trade, recreation, and work are determined by essential human needs. Special services may fit into the basic pattern of facilities that make up the areas of common interest, the neighborhoods and communities.

People are now dependent on automobiles to get to and from homes, schools, stores, and parks. Walking distances are excessive, traffic confrontations too hazardous, and the surroundings are often unpleasant or downright ugly. Poorly located schools and efforts to bring about a socioethnic mix have made the school bus a familiar feature in almost every city and town.

The family car is an anachronism in an industrial system that presumes to glorify "efficiency and economy." The family uses the car for an average of eight to ten trips each day. Most are short hauls to local facilities—shopping, school, house of worship, playground, or friends; they are seldom emergencies. Yet the car is 2,000 pounds of steel, powered with a 250-or-more-horsepower engine, transporting fewer than 1.5 persons per trip (1.1 in the West).

Stable neighborhoods and communities should have local systems of small low-speed minibuses running on frequent convenient schedules; one may recall the "elephant trains" at the 1933 Century of Progress exposition in Chicago, the electric trams in Disneyland parking lots, the free bus systems in modern retirement colonies, moving sidewalks in large airports. With the resulting reduction or elimination of traffic accidents, both pedestrians and bicyclists could discover the joys of a relaxed tempo, as well as economy, in traveling to and from their daily activities. Technology, having successfully created spaceships, with some measure of human ingenuity might even produce a nonpolluting minibus with "piggyback" shopping carts.

Traffic Engineering—A Palliative

Traffic engineering is necessary because the planning of the city circulation system has been neglected.

Because the street plan of cities is insufficient to cope with traffic, various methods have been devised to control the operation of vehicles. It might be more accurate to describe these as measures of control by default, but they are essential to maintain any movement of vehicles through the city streets. The calculation and administration of these are known as "traffic engineering."

Traffic engineers find themselves in the awkward position of attempting to compel the movement of the irresistible force of traffic through the impenetrable obstacle of congestion. Many traffic engineers are repair persons rather than builders, devisers rather than planners, first-aid traffic corpsmen rather than surgeons.

Traffic engineering embraces the host of devices with which the city-dweller is familiar: stop-and-go signs at street intersections, slow-down warnings and speed limits, parking limits and prohibitions, the police whistle, the so-called safety islands at boarding points for buses, the white and yellow lines painted on the pavements to channel moving vehicles and the mechanical divisions sometimes employed for this purpose, and the one-way street. The list of these "solutions" is long, but none has singly or in combination brought any genuine relief of the traffic problem. The devices are more appropriately described as stunts rather than solutions; they are expedient measures to cope with immediate traffic problems in the form of first-aid treatment and offer no real improvement in the capacity of the transportation system to move people.

The automobile travels at a reasonably rapid speed with relative ease, comfort, and convenience. Interruption of the flow of travel conflicts with the effectiveness of the machine as a means for the mass transportation of people, and this interruption also creates hazards to safety. The synchronization of stoplights has improved the continuity of movement, but the effect of these interruptions remains. The average cycle for change of the traffic signal is one minute; cars traveling in one direction are stopped for thirty seconds and move for thirty seconds. The effect is a reduction of 40 percent in the number of cars that could pass a given point if the flow were uninterrupted. In other words, a street intersection controlled by traffic lights can accommodate only two-fifths the number of cars a free flow of traffic will carry.

The conversion of streets from two-way to one-way travel is a familiar system traffic engineers are frequently forced to employ. It is a method for channeling traffic that avoids the conflict of left-hand turns across lanes moving from the opposite direction. But the traffic signal is still necessary to permit the passage of pedestrians, and traffic flow continues to suffer periodic interruptions.

There is a reluctance to design streets for peak loads because of the alleged wasted space during the periods of less intensive use. The alternative is the conversion of six-lane trunk streets to four lanes in the direction of heavy flow and two lanes for the opposite direction during the morning rush, and the reversal of this process for the evening peak. While the painted channel lines are usually the only means for marking these lanes, some cities have mechanical barriers that may be raised and lowered from continuous slots along the channel separations.

Traffic engineers maintain data on the movement of people and vehicles, they measure the service of commercial centers by traffic counts of registered automobiles that park there, they measure the capacity of sidewalks by counts of pedestrians who traverse them; the probable effectiveness of street widening, of new streets and freeways, is estimated by counts of local and through traffic. The need for and effectiveness of traffic signals, prohibitions on left turns and curb parking, and special lanes for traffic flow are calculated by the traffic engineers from the variety of traffic counts and data compiled, and they aid the public transit companies in the routing of mass transportation vehicles.

The traffic engineers maintain a gallant struggle to cope with the imponderable traffic tangles they confront. Until the urban street system is designed for vehicles that traverse it, their devices will remain essential ingredients of our city circulation. It is a choice between two traffic evils: no control and complete chaos, or negative control to avoid paralysis.

PARKING PROBLEMS AND SOLUTIONS

Off-Street

Man's struggle to achieve speed has been successful, and we are confronted with a paradox: inadequate space to slow down and stop. Automobiles, buses, and trucks must have a storage place at both the origin and the destination of their travel routes. And they must have a place to come to temporary rest for the conduct of business or pleasure en route. This is the parking problem.

In the United States as well as in many European countries almost 85 percent of all surface travel in urban areas, except in a few large cities, is by means of the private automobile. The road system on which these vehicles circulate must be a major element in the community's comprehensive plan and must provide for adequate terminal facilities. A component is the accommodation of these vehicles at their destination. The moment when a driver is transformed to a pedestrian plagues the planner. The plan must provide for this.

The horseless carriage inherited the narrow street as a traffic route and the hitching post as a parking place. When the automobile attained its own identity, the number of vehicles burgeoned. They filled the streets, the rate of movement declined, "slot machines" were put on the hitching posts, and curb parking absorbed two street lanes urgently needed for moving vehicles. Although the parking meter produces some revenue for the city, the movement in and out of curb parking seriously interrupts the free flow of traffic along the free lanes. Off-street parking is an urgent need, and methods for both voluntary and mandatory parking have been varied. Parking districts and merchants' associations have been created, but relief from the parking jam in commercial districts remains inadequate.

With the decentralization of commercial facilities, ample parking was a primary prerequisite of the shopping center. This obvious competition forced a recognition of the necessity for off-street parking in built-up central commercial districts. Provisions for off-street parking have been accepted in many zoning ordinances for both residential and commercial areas during recent years. The requirements vary, but none have coped with the situation in central business districts.

The necessity of freeing the streets of standing vehicles is hardly more pressing in the business districts than in the high-density multiple-family apartment districts. Off-street parking is but one important feature for improvement of the total environment. It would aid in achieving a balance between bulk and the capacity of the street system to accommodate the traffic flow.

The requirements for parking space will vary according to the structure of the city and the habits of motor travel. These standards are generally related to the building floor space, and this underscores the issue of excessive zoning and congestion. The issue may be restated by a question of whether it is our intention that cities become gargantuan parking lots partially occupied by buildings. The prospect that mass transportation may offer the solution seems remote; the private automobile is a phenomenon of our age, satisfying a basic instinct for freedom of movement whatever the consequences. The form of cities must be adapted to man's nature and the vehicles he creates. To be effective, cars must have the room to move *and* to stop.

Motorists wish to park as near their destination as possible. Surveys have indicated that they will do this, in many instances at the cost of illegal curb parking. Surveys have also indicated that motorists entering the downtown district for business or shopping do not wish to walk from their parking place a distance of more than 1,000 feet. If we assume the city block to be 600 feet long, it is apparent that those who wish to park for a short time—one-half hour or less—wish to be within 500 to 600 feet of their destination; those who park for about one hour wish to be no farther than about 1,000 feet from their destination, and those who intend to remain for a longer time would wish to be no farther than about 1,200 feet from their destination.

It must be granted that surveys deserve qualification. Consider the environment through which the urbanite must travel; it is little wonder the shopper dislikes to walk in the downtown district or in many other sections of the contemporary metropolis. Ugliness is abhorrent and it repels a human being; it can hardly be expected that people will wish to walk about a business district fraught with every disagreeable feature and lacking convenient shopping and business facilities. When the cities acquire the self-respect that comes with pride in the physical beauty of an environment, the willingness of motorists to walk through these surroundings will probably reveal quite a different set of statistics.

About 80 percent of the parkers in the central business district remain for one hour or less, the number ranging from 60 to 90 percent. When curb parking is permitted, the average time is about thirty minutes because of the preponderance of people who enter the business district for brief periods. Relating these several factors, the parking facilities for the downtown business district could be consolidated in areas ranging between 500 and 1,000 feet in radius from the center of a well-planned group of stores and office buildings. Convenience would be enhanced by the elimination of congestion, discomfort, and the hazards caused by the conflict between pedestrian and vehicular traffic. It is possible that this new element of convenience might encourage pedestrians to walk more and increase business further.

Requirements for parking vary considerably, but experience has divulged some factors that assist in estimating the requirements. The average space per occupant in commercial buildings—office space—is approximately 150 square feet in floor area. If all regular occupants in these business structures were to use private automobiles for their transportation, an area of 150 square feet per person would be required in parking, the equivalent of one square foot of parking for each square foot of building floor space.

This space does not provide for people who patronize the business enterprise, and it may be estimated that an equal number enter the commercial district for this purpose as those who occupy the commercial buildings. In the average city, however, about 50 percent of the people entering the downtown district use the available means for mass transportation—rail or bus. This results in a required space for parking equal to the building floor area, a figure generally confirmed by authorities. Retail shopping imposes a considerably heavier burden on parking space. It is therefore necessary to adjust the required area for parking in central business districts according to the estimated uses to which the land will be put. These estimates will likewise warrant adjustment as mass transportation is improved and becomes capable of adequately moving the largest possible number of people entering and leaving the business district.

More recently, several studies conducted during the 1980s indicated changes considered reasonable for parking standards. Most reduced the number of parking spaces for commercial areas below those incorporated into most zoning ordinances. Where there were nonconcurrent uses, adjustments were made to reduce the number of spaces by a proportional amount, depending on the nature of the uses and the time of their maximum utilization.

Economics

Some of the most valuable land in the central core of urban areas is used for the parking of automobiles. In Los Angeles, a study prepared by the planning department indicated that over two-thirds of the entire area is given over to streets and the parking of motor vehicles. If the streets occupy approximately 25 percent of the central area space, it can be observed that over 41 percent of the land is utilized for the storage of cars. This is in addition to the off-street parking provided within the structure of buildings, since most new development required on-site or nearby parking for both tenants and visitors. The Civic Center Mall is honeycombed with multistory underground parking, and the land about the center is still covered with thousands of vehicles.

One can imagine what the island of Manhattan or the Loop in Chicago would look like if all of the employees and patrons were to bring their automobiles into them. There would be no space for buildings. The cost of parking in Manhattan, however, discourages this practice even though the rapid transit system, extensive as it is, leaves many with concerns about safety and security and rush-hour crushes, causing them to use their automobiles regardless of cost for personal transportation.

The changing size of the motor vehicles will have some impact on the space needed for them in parking areas. A recent study by the Urban Land Institute found that the American automobile owners are questioning the "Queen Marys" that they have been accustomed to as gasoline guzzlers and are turning in increasing numbers to the European answer provided by smaller cars. The study also suggests new requirements for the number of spaces for various types of uses, including shopping centers.

While it may be true that, with the recent affluence of the upper middle class in America, the "Queen Marys" are becoming more prevalent in the sales statistics, the increased sales do not offset the large-scale purchase of small foreign automobiles. Some of the largest of the American manufacturers are in the process, in 1985–86, of placing newly designed small, efficient cars on the market.

The answer to the widespread use of the personal transportation system, with an average of approximately 1.5 persons per vehicle, has not been resolved in most Western nations. With pressures from the freeway and highway builders, it may be a long way into the future before people give up the tremendous, if illusory, freedom that the automobile represents.

Free Parking

One often hears of "free parking"; except for parking in the open wilderness there is no such thing. This freedom is especially scarce in urban areas. Studies will show that even the simplest forms of space required for the storing of a motor vehicle are exceedingly expensive. Parking at residences often requires approximately 400 square feet of space in an enclosed garage, and most communities require garages in residential areas. The cost of the land and structure will add as much as $20,000 to the costs of an apartment unit.

Likewise, free parking on the street is a myth. The cost of the extra land for the parking lanes and the cost of paving and maintenance will have to be borne by the property owner in terms of initial costs and in later taxes to keep the space maintained for use.

Free parking at shopping centers is also anything but free. The valuable commercial land and the paving and maintenance of this area cost a great deal of money, which is passed on to the consumer as part of the cost of everything that he purchases. When parking land is either too expensive or not available, commercial enterprises resort to multistory parking structures as an answer both to serving their patrons and local zoning requirements. Either below ground or above, the cost is roughly equivalent to the construction of additional stories in the building. If underground, the designs must include retaining walls, drainage structures, ventilation, and lighting.

Some merchants and professionals provide for client parking through a validation system in which the business picks up the cost of the space. This forms part of the cost of the service that is rendered and therefore is far from free.

The following article by Dr. Donald C. Shoup, Professor of Urban Planning at the University of California at Los Angeles, examines the cost of free parking.

If you could have either free gasoline for driving to and from work, or free parking at work, which would you choose?

If you are the median U.S. commuter, you drive ten miles round trip to work, and if your car's gasoline consumption is the U.S. average of twenty miles per gallon, you use half a gallon of gas for each round trip to work.[*] If you commute to work twenty-two days a month, you use eleven gallons of gas a month for work trips; at, say, $1.25 a gallon, gasoline for commuting costs you $13.75 a month. Therefore, if you work where the fair market price of parking is more than $13.75 a month, free parking is worth more to you than free gas.

An astonishing number of cars park free at work even in central business districts where parking is most expensive. For example, in 1974, slightly over half the 100,000 cars commuting to downtown Los Angeles parked free, although the market price of parking averaged $35 a month; in 1976, almost half the 140,000 cars commuting to downtown Washington, D.C., parked free, although the market price of parking averaged $50 a month. Nationwide, 90 percent of the labor force commutes to work in private vehicles, and 75 percent of them park free in employer-paid, off-street parking spaces.[**]

---

[*] U.S. Department of Transportation, *Home-to-Work Trips and Travel: Report 4, 1977.* Nationwide Personal Transportation Study (FHWA/PL/81/002), December 1980. Page one of this report provides median commuting distance; average fuel efficiency for the 1977 auto fleet was 10 mpg (report #2, p. 33). Because average fuel efficiency has been increasing since 1977, a figure of 20 mpg seems a conservative estimate for 1982.

[**] Donald C. Shoup and Don H. Pickrell, *Free Parking as a Transportation Problem* (Washington, D.C.: U.S. Department of Transportation, Office of University Research, 1980).

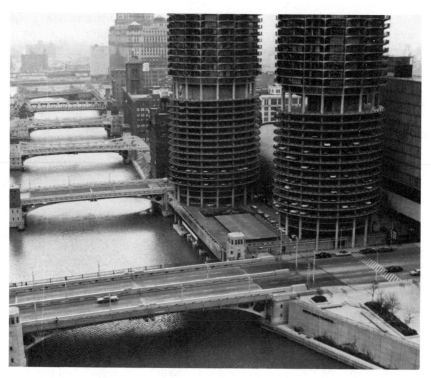

Free parking? The Marina Towers, adjacent to the Chicago River in the city of Chicago, provide in each of the twin towers more than thirteen stories of parking for residents, patrons, and visitors. Located as it is within easy walking distance of the business establishments in the Loop or central business district, the need for an automobile for local transportation should be minimal for the residents of the apartments that tower above the fringes of the core area. One can anticipate, however, that the occupants of the megastructures use their automobiles for transportation to places of employment and to do the daily shopping.

The income tax exemption of free parking at work encourages employers to pay for commuter parking rather than to pay higher salaries. Free parking at work may seem harmless, or even beneficial, but it indirectly pollutes the air, congests traffic, and wastes energy by inviting commuters to drive to work alone.

A tax exemption in lieu of free parking would encourage employers to subsidize people, not cars. If employers pay higher salaries rather than pay for parking, many commuters will do in their self-interest just what they have long been urged to do in the public interest—ride the bus, carpool, bicycle, or walk to work.[4]

---

4. Donald C. Shoup, *Transportation Quarterly* 36:351–64.

Car Pools

Car pools and ride sharing have been promoted in all parts of the United States in an effort to reduce the pressure on central city land for parking and thereby to reduce the costs of new structures in these limited and critical city spaces. Attempts to meet the zoning requirement for parking have resulted in rates that have caused the public to seek an alternative to the use of the individual automobile as the principal means of transportation.

Melody McCutcheon and Jeffrey Hamm in the October 1983 *Traffic Quarterly* described some recent activities in the city of Seattle, Washington. That city used zoning and environmental impact legislation to encourage ride sharing as a factor in approving building permits and zoning requests. The Seattle proposals also included provisions for special parking for ride-sharing vehicles as an incentive to individuals participating in the program. It is still too early to state the degree of success of the program. In 1985 the automobile traffic in the central city seemed as intensive as ever.

THE CIRCULATION PLAN

The circulation plan involves major highways and streets, routes for mass transportation, railroads, airfields, and waterways. It defines the through-traffic arteries, freeways, parkways, and their intersections and interchanges. It charts the course of rail and bus routes about the city and its environs. It is in this plan that all lines of vehicular communications are integrated for the circulation of the people and goods in and about the urban area.

The system of circulation will define the boundaries of neighborhood units. The street system within this broad framework need be determined only to the extent that it impinges on the through-traffic arteries and mass transportation routes. The internal design of the streets could remain unspecified until development is imminent and then be made precise.

As the city develops, the plan will become the reference for improvements and extensions of the circulation system. Precise plans may be made for railroad passenger and freight lines, yards, terminals and stations, air terminals and fields, and internal helicopter connections. Harbor and waterway development may be guided by this plan as improvements are proposed.

The plans for circulation and for land use require integration. They may require occasional modification, but there is no development within one category that can remain unrelated to the other.

"Public" Ownership of Roads

Since approximately one-third of the land in some urban communities is devoted to the road system, it is pertinent to observe how this land came into public ownership. In early times travel over the safest and most easily traversed routes created "public" roadways through usage. Since the basic ownership of all land was the sovereign right of the state, it was normal for the ruler to designate "post" roads and highways to ensure that channels of communication between communities were protected. When ownership was granted to individuals, the head of state provided for a means of access to property, although some passageways remained toll roads until a very late date. In cities the subdivision of land into individual parcels was regulated by decree to maintain certain open spaces for travel and safety against fire.

This practice is reflected in modern subdivision design whereby the state, in granting the right to individuals to subdivide land, requires that the roadways that give access to property be dedicated to public use and be maintained by the city. Streets thus dedicated may either remain as public easements for such time as they are required as streets, or they may be deeded to the city in "fee simple." ("Fee simple" means that the possessor has full ownership of the land. When the right-of-way is no longer needed, the community can sell the land, just as it could with any other property it owns.) When dedicated streets are vacated by the city, the land occupied by them is usually divided on the basis of the original dedication or deed, and title to it returned to the owners of abutting property.

STREET DESIGN

The gridiron street plan formed a pattern of rectangular blocks divided into rectangular lots that were usually very narrow to conserve on utility lines and very deep to conserve on streets. The curvilinear design was then devised to give some semblance of "character" to the subdivision, to subdue the deadly monotony of parallel streets stretching to infinity. The alternative soon developed into a curved grid, a series of parallel curved streets, with no more living amenities than the rectangular grid provided. The more exaggerated of the designs assumed the form of a violently swirling street system in which orientation was completely obscured.

It is customary to maintain the narrowest practicable width for local residential streets that serve only the abutting property. When parking is desired on each side of the street, the right-of-way is between fifty-four and sixty-four feet wide, with a pavement width of thirty-six feet. The paved surface may be as narrow as thirty feet, but this suggests parking on one side only since the traffic lanes should not be less than ten feet wide. Although local streets of narrow width are more economical in their initial cost, the weaving of automobiles about parked cars is a safety hazard to children in the neighborhood.

Economy of street design has been more rationally approached through the effort to reduce the total length of streets rather than their width. Care in site planning brought about an abandoning of the artificial picturesqueness of the arbitrary street system and led to the use of the cul-de-sac and the loop street.

Cul-de-sac and the Loop Street

The cul-de-sac, or dead-end street, came into use to eliminate through traffic in a positive manner. Cul-de-sacs terminate in a circular or hammerhead turnaround. To retain their inherent advantages, they should be short—a maximum length of 450 feet is recommended. The advantages are dissipated in long cul-de-sacs, since they induce accelerated traffic speeds and render access for service and fire protection more complicated. Probably the most renowned example of the cul-de-sac street is in the community of Radburn, New Jersey. The system is fully exploited by the consolidation of open space and the reduction of street crossings, the separation between vehicular and pedestrian circulation being enhanced by the use of pedestrian underpasses beneath the major streets. Although this separation of traffic is desirable, the narrow tunnel shape of the usual pedestrian underpass tends to accumulate refuse and dirt, and presents dangers that may be avoided by convenient pedestrian overpasses above slightly depressed streets.

The loop street is a variation of the cul-de-sac and is employed in substantially the same manner. However, it eliminates the necessity for the turnaround and provides the continuous circulation that is required by some communities to assure no interference with the accessibility of fire protection and other services. While it does not offer complete separation between vehicular and pedestrian traffic, it is as effective as the cul-de-sac in eliminating through traffic. The length of the loop street is not as important as that of the cul-de-sac since the movement of traffic is continuous, but like the cul-de-sac, traffic is normally confined to residents' vehicles or vehicles for service and delivery within the block.

There are some disadvantages in the cul-de-sac and the loop street, but careful planning can reduce these to a minimum. It is sometimes alleged that circulation about a community becomes confusing, although a simple plan can overcome much of this objection. House-numbering and street-naming require attention since they vary from the customary pattern for which the usual systems have been devised.

Highway and Street Standards*

Type of Facility	Function and Design Features	Spacing	R.O.W. Width
Freeways	Provide regional and metropolitan continuity and unity. Limited access; no grade crossings; no traffic stops.	Variable; related to regional pattern of population and industrial centers	200–300 ft.
Expressways	Provide metropolitan and city continuity and unity. Limited access; some channelized grade crossings and signals at major intersections. Parking prohibited.	Variable; generally radial or circumferential	150–200 ft.
Major roads (major arterials)	Provide unity throughout contiguous urban area. Usually form boundaries for neighborhoods. Minor access control; channelized intersections; parking generally prohibited.	1 mile	120–150 ft.
Secondary roads (minor arterials)	Main feeder streets. Signals where needed; stop signs on side streets. Occasionally form boundaries for neighborhoods.	½ mile	80 ft.
Collector streets	Main interior streets. Stop signs on side streets.	¼–½ mile	60–70 ft.
Local streets	Local service streets. Non-conducive to through traffic.	at blocks	50–60 ft.
Cul-de-sac	Streets open at only one end, with provision for a turn-around at the other.	oniy wherever practical	50 ft. (90 ft. dia. turn-around)

* *Urban Land*, May 1961, by George Nez, Director, Inter-County Regional Planning Commission, Denver, Colorado. Standards revised 1979 by William A. Law, Linscott, Law, and Greenspan, Transportation Engineers, Los Angeles, Cal.

Pavement Width	Desirable Maximum Grades	Speed	Other Features
Varies; 15 ft. per lane; 10–14 ft. shoulders both sides of each roadway; 8–60 ft. median strip.	3%	55 mph 88.5 km/h	Depressed, at grade, or elevated. Preferably depressed through urban areas. Require intensive landscaping, service roads, or adequate rear lot building set-back lines (75 ft.) where service roads are not provided.
Varies; 12 ft. per lane; 8–10 ft. shoulders; 8–30 ft. median strip.	4%	50 mph 80.5 km/h	Generally at grade. Requires landscaping and service roads or adequate rear lot building set-back lines (75 ft.) where service roads are not provided.
84 ft. maximum for 4 lanes, parking, and median strip.	4%	35–40 mph 56–64 km/h	Require 5-ft.-wide detached sidewalks in urban areas, planting strips (5–10 ft. wide or more) and adequate building set-back lines (30 ft.) for buildings fronting on street; 60 ft. for buildings backing on street.
60 ft.	5%	35–40 mph 56–64 km/h	Require 5-ft.-wide detached sidewalks, planting strips between sidewalks and curb 5–10 ft. or more, and adequate building set-back lines (30 ft.)
44 ft. (2–12 ft. traffic lanes; 2–10 ft. parking lanes)	5%	30 mph 48 km/h	Require at least 4-ft.-wide detached sidewalks; vertical curbs; planting strips are desirable; building set-back lines 30 ft. from right of way.
36 ft. where street parking is permitted	6%	25 mph 40 km/h	Sidewalks at least 5 ft. in width for densities greater than 1 d.u./acre, and curbs and gutters.
30–36 ft. (75 ft. turn-around)	5%		Should not have a length greater than 500 ft.

Collector Streets and Other Traffic Arteries

The collector street is, as the name suggests, the street into which the local residential streets feed. It may be designed to flow into the secondary or major traffic arteries, in which case the right-of-way is usually sixty feet wide with a pavement thirty-six feet in width. Frequently, however, the collector streets are comparable in traffic load to a secondary highway and must be so designed.

The traffic load from the local residential streets and their collector roadways is carried by the secondary and major highways and, although a difference in function is suggested by this terminology, there is often little real distinction between the traffic they carry. The secondary highway is intended to serve areas intermediate between the major traffic street and thence connect to the major highway. However, major highways have grown so congested that much traffic escapes along the secondary and collector streets, thus rendering each the equivalent of a major traffic artery.

Secondary highways are usually 80 or 86 feet in width of right-of-way with a pavement width of 64 feet; they have four lanes for traffic and two for parking. The major highways are customarily 110 feet in width with a pavement width of about 76 feet, with six lanes for moving traffic and two for parking.

It is gradually becoming apparent that access from abutting property to major and secondary highways must be denied. The movement of traffic cannot be maintained when it is repeatedly interrupted by the ingress or egress of vehicles from side streets. Frontages along these main traffic routes must obtain their service access either from alleys or minor service roads parallel to the highway. A service road is generally twenty-eight feet in width, allowing parking on one side only, and the usual width of alley is twenty feet with parking prohibited. Service roads may be screened from the highways with a planting strip; the highway is thus enhanced while the abutting property is shielded from it, an asset to the development of residential neighborhoods contiguous to highways.

THE REGIONAL HIGHWAY SYSTEM

Following old Indian trails, the winding, twisting, meandering routes between communities became the post roads, the plank roads, and the high roads. These were the trade routes between centers of population and between the rural areas where products were grown and the towns where they were marketed. Like the roads in the center of the early city, they followed the easy way irrespective of property boundaries. As property ownership was formalized the roads served as dividing lines. They represented access to property and a way to and from markets. Most of the important regional links follow, to some extent, these original lines. With the expansion of communities, many of these primitive roadways have been lost in the maze of internal growth. They left their mark, however, as the basis for the orientation of other streets and highways parallel and perpendicular to these original spinal lines.

With the expansion and congestion of cities, the intercommunity roads collapsed under the impact of traffic loads. They carried less and less traffic. Accidents were a byproduct of too many intersections, ill-designed roadbeds and curves, lack of sufficient sight distances, and vertical curves. Widening the roads only intensified the situation by drawing more of the ever-increasing number of vehicles to them. Then the "free-way" introduced the first change in highway design.

The freeway provided a new approach; it released the roadway from old alignments, from abutting property, from intersections at grades, from outmoded design standards, from old right-of-way limitations. The traffic problem remains unsolved, and it is true that at peak hours the freeway can become the longest parking lot in the world. The freeway nonetheless has embraced the salient characteristics of a travelway for free- and fast-moving vehicles. It has yet to find its appropriate relation to the future shape of the evolving modern city.

Freeways

A freeway is essentially a pair of parallel roadways, each of which carries one-way traffic moving in opposite directions, with complete separation from each other and freedom from all cross-traffic. Ingress and egress in either direction flow via accelerating and decelerating lanes. Traffic moves unimpeded by any interruptions from light signals or stop signs. All cross-traffic is carried over or under the freeway, and access from abutting property is closed from the freeway right-of-way.

The freeway appeared on the American scene during the early 1930s with the construction of the Downtown Expressway parallel to the Hudson River in New York City, the Pulaski Skyway from Newark, New Jersey, to New York, and the commencement of the great Chicago Outer Drive. Later developments soon followed in New Jersey, Pennsylvania, New York, Connecticut, Delaware, California, and in the vicinity of Washington, D.C. Many of these early routes were limited in scope, but they were designed for the unimpeded movement of vehicles by the shortest feasible route between points.

The freeway may parallel existing streets or cut across their present pattern. It marks the beginning of a new form of artery that may aid in the solution of the traffic problem and create the huge cells that will ultimately frame groups of neighborhood units as the city grows and is rebuilt. With the freeway a new urban form emerges.

The right-of-way for a freeway is necessarily broad; it must provide adequate space to be depressed or raised without adversely affecting abutting property. Limitations on the width vary with circumstances. Land cost may be one obvious prospect for forcing economy in land area, but another may appear in state laws that restrict the acquisition of property for public improvements to that required for the principal function of the facility.

Such restrictions would limit the right-of-way to the area required only for the traffic lanes and adjacent parkways, the acquisition for contig-

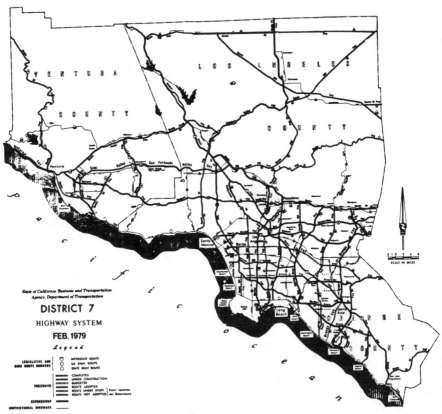

State of California Business and Transportation Agency, Department of Transportation

Map of freeway system, Los Angeles.

uous buffer spaces being considered excessive. To cope with such a situation in New York City, the routes were acquired by the Parks Department as park strips and the trafficways were built within them; the term *parkway* is consequently applied to them. Some states have enacted statutes to permit the acquisition of ample space for the freeway right-of-way; in California a space 150 feet on each side of the centerline of the roadway may be acquired, thus providing for purchase of marginal property to avoid the creation of small remnants of land otherwise unusable for development.

The freeway is usually designed for three lanes of traffic in each direction, rarely more than four. These are intended for the free movement of vehicles, and the greater the number of lanes, the greater is the interference from vehicles weaving between them seeking a satisfactory channel of speed or access to the decelerating lane from which they leave the freeway. Entrance and exit lanes and those for emergency parking should be in addition to the number of channels of clear traffic movement.

Ingress and egress are at infrequent intervals, not less than one-half mile apart and preferably at one-mile distance; this frequency will permit

Courtesy Department of Public Works, Division of Highways, State of California

Four-level intersection—Los Angeles.

adequate stops for bus connections if they are permitted on the freeway system. Lanes should be fifteen feet in width rather than the usual highway standard of twelve feet, and loading and unloading zones must be separated from the clear channels of movement, with transition lanes leading to the stopping places.

The dividing strip between the roads going in opposite directions will vary in width according to the nature of the right-of-way. Some separations are landscaped spaces, but the usual width is between ten and twenty feet. Because the freeway, presently intended for personal automotive vehicles, may someday provide a channel for mass transportation vehicles, an ample dividing strip may one day demonstrate the economy of its original purchase; a minimum of thirty feet and a desirable width of fifty feet should be planned. Oversight, indifference, or lack of vision in planning freeways will cost the people much in money as well as time, confusion, and discouragement; that is demonstrated today in some cities where the freeway and mass transportation plans failed to be integrated.

Safety and efficient flow of traffic have been enhanced by improvements in lighting and directional signs. Lighting for night travel has made great progress, some highways having become ribbons of lighted pavement requiring no headlights for adequate vision and safety. Although not yet fully developed and employed, color may be advantageously used to identify certain lanes for speeds and points of departure from the roadway. The scale of letters and placement of signs that indicate directions, places, and distances are important factors in the design of trafficways for smooth and safe circulation.

TRAFFIC LANES

Traffic hazards arise from excessive speed, but they may also be due to deficiencies in the design of roadways. Separations between traffic traveling in opposite directions and the elimination of intersections are essential. The provision of off-street parking so curb parking may be prohibited is necessary; only one disabled car can reduce a three-lane roadway to a two-lane street and add the hazard of rapid accumulation of vehicles at this bottleneck. Given the free flow of traffic that these improvements offer, the effectiveness of the car depends upon the shape of the roadway over which it travels.

Traffic lanes vary from eight to fifteen feet; this variation is not a fault until it occurs within the same line of travel. The local street may have a width of ten feet and the through-traffic artery may be twelve feet, but the width should be constant for each. Local streets serving residential areas are customarily designed for a lane of ten feet, being four feet wider than the standard American automobile and none too great a separation between two moving vehicles passing at a rate of thirty-five miles per hour. On highways the width is generally twelve feet, increased to thirteen or fourteen feet on the curves.[5] When the freeway is designed for the operation of trucks and buses, a lane fifteen feet wide should be provided.

The width of the lane intended for parking vehicles is usually eight feet; this assumes the wheels will be one foot from the curb and allow three feet between it and a vehicle passing along the centerline of the adjacent moving lane. If the parked vehicle is a truck, it will project into the adjacent lane, creating a sideswiping hazard. It seems more sensible to make no distinction between the width of a lane for parking and one for moving vehicles; in peak hours when curb parking is prohibited, this lane adds a trafficway to the otherwise overcrowded street.

Adjustments to the new character of modern vehicular travel have been slow, and the change in approach to the design of roadways has probably been most apparent at the points of intersection. Traffic circles were the first attempts to merge traffic flow and avoid the conflicts of left turns. While traffic was light, the circle was adequate, but the increase in number of vehicles re-created congestion at these points.

The cloverleaf was the next step toward a solution of traffic interchange, but it has a weakness. Drivers intending to turn left must cross beyond the intersecting street for which they are destined and then make a right turn into a curve that leads back to the cross-street they seek. It is confusing for drivers traveling at a fair rate of speed to find themselves beyond the intersection they want and then to turn right for a left-hand direction. Familiarity with a roadway offsets this sort of confusion, but it is not an assurance of the safest form of traffic artery.

Other types of interchange structures have been designed for the purpose of overcoming the weaknesses of the circle and cloverleaf, and most have incorporated the best features of each. However, all designs assume that slow vehicles remain on the right-hand side of the roadway and, because left-hand turns on level roads are a handicap to speed and safety, movement from the freeway is channeled to the right regardless of the destination of the vehicle. In the General Motors exhibit at the 1939 New York World's Fair, Norman Bel Geddes presented a freeway design in which a driver would turn left from a completely separate left-hand lane. This turn would have the same radius of curvature as the right-hand turn. He observed that the term "slow lane" is a contradiction of the freeway system and that the speed of vehicles would probably be similar in all

---

5. Frank H. Malley, *Location and Function of Urban Freeways, Post-War Patterns of City Growth*, American Transit Association, New York.

**Simple Grade Separation between
Two Highways**

Universal Interchange

Braided or "T" Interchange

Four-Level Interchange

**Simple Interchange of Freeway
with Highway**

Cloverleaf Interchange

Bel Geddes Interchange

Highway interchanges.

lanes. Bel Geddes proposed that the number of through lanes continue undiminished regardless of the left and right turns, and he provided a lane for transition into the left-hand turn as was customary for the right-hand turn. Similarly the transition lanes for entrance to the freeway would be from both left and right sides of the roadway.

The adoption of this logic after fifty years has been rather slow, since it suggests some changes in the engineering that established the habits of drivers who have grown accustomed to the present formula for turning right out of a freeway no matter what direction may be the ultimate destination. It also necessitates some changes in the attitudes of the engineeers who design the highway system. Meanwhile, the knotty problem of the smooth and safe intersection of traffic is met by some rather fantastic combinations of the circle, the universal, and the cloverleaf.

INTERSTATE HIGHWAYS

For many years names like "Santa Fe Trail" and "Lincoln Highway" have lent romance to the roads that cross our vast countryside. The Bureau of Public Roads has supervised the construction of highways and has received federal aid since 1916. Highway planning is currently being performed by the separate states in cooperation with the Bureau of Public Roads. In 1956 the Congress authorized a vast interstate highway program. It was planned to build 36,000 miles of freeways outside urban areas by 1972 as part of the National System of Interstate and Defense Highways. These roads presently connect with thousands of miles of urban freeways.

It had been estimated that passenger car registration would reach 125,000,000 in 1984 and require more than 5,600 miles of urban interstate freeways.[6] However, since the projections of the 1960s were made, U.S. freeway construction has been curtailed due to economically depressed conditions. Bits and pieces are being constructed in the 1980s.

Great highways such as the Pennsylvania Turnpike have been designed for modern motor travel over long distances and at rapid and steady speeds. Uninterrupted by traffic crossings and modeled to the topography of the countryside, these sweeping freeways are unmarred by the stigma of commercial advertising. Roadside restaurants and service stations punctuate the route at convenient intervals. It is now possible to travel from New York City to Chicago and beyond on roadways with limited access rights and few, if any, crossings at grade.

---

6. A report by Wilbur Smith & Associates, Consulting Engineers, for the Automobile Manufacturers Association, 1961.

MOVEMENT OF PEOPLE

In the movement of people about the city every form of mass transportation, except railways and subways, is routed on a street system originally laid out for the easy subdivision of land and in the time when the horse and buggy was the common mode of conveyance. The result is a paradox: the automobile, which has become the principal means of both local and regional travel, receives the most attention in plans for the improvement of urban traffic but is the least efficient form of urban transport. Furthermore, the bus has replaced the streetcar and the electric train, although they were essentially the most efficient forms of rapid transit for the mass movement of people. That the development of effective transit is the most economical as well as the most efficient means for the mass transportation of the urban population may be apparent by comparison of the characteristics of vehicles and the roadways they use.

A typical traffic street with the usual intersections will accommodate 700–800 private-passenger automobiles per lane per hour passing a given point. It will carry about 180 buses per lane per hour. Since it is the movement of people rather than the movement of vehicles with which we are concerned, the capacity of the street must be translated into the number of people these vehicles will transport. Studies have demonstrated that private autos carry an average of 1.5 persons per car. Modern "neoplan" buses will carry about 42 persons seated. Articulated buses will seat 60 persons, and double-decker buses will seat 82. The single lane of the typical trunk street will therefore accommodate about 1,200 passengers per hour in private autos whereas the bus carries 7,200. The capactiy of the bus may be further increased with standing passengers, raising the capacity of the bus to 9,000 per hour.[7]

These figures apply to the capacity of a single lane for each type of vehicle. A proportionate increase in the capacity would occur by the addition of lanes if they could be retained as clear channels. The effect of weaving measurably reduces the efficiency of the street. Surveys have shown that weaving reduces the capacity of the second lane of traffic to 75 percent of the single lane, the capacity of the third lane is 56 percent of the single lane, and that of a fourth lane is only 26 percent of the single lane.[8] Three lanes in one direction with unrestricted weaving have a capacity of only two and one-third lanes of clear channels with no weaving.

Studies by the American Transit Association demonstrate the increase in movement of people by the addition of mass transportation facilities

---

7. *Moving People in the Modern City* (New York: American Transit Association, 1944).
8. Ibid.

on the city streets. A typical city arterial with a pavement width of sixty feet and no curb parking provides three lanes of traffic in each direction. This highway will accommodate about 2,100 private autos in three lanes, assuming reasonable restrictions on weaving, and carry 3,700 passengers per hour. If one lane of autos is replaced by a bus lane, the number of autos is decreased to 1,200 and their passenger load to 3,100, but the bus lane carries 7,200 seated passengers and 9,000 including standees, increasing the total capacity of the route to 9,300 seated and 11,100 including standing passengers.

This study shows that the substitution of a bus lane for a lane of cars on the ordinary arterial will carry two and one-half times the number of people carried by three lanes of cars alone. When standing passengers are included, the capacity of the street is increased to three times the number of people in cars.

A limited-access highway with no crossing materially increases the capacity of private automobiles, but this capacity is not increased proportionately with the speed that cars can reach with uninterrupted flow. Studies show that the theoretical maximum number of vehicles is accommodated at a speed of about thirty-two miles per hour and that the theoretical maximum number of cars is about 2,060 per hour per lane. The practical maximum number of cars that can be carried at this speed, however, is only about 75 percent of this number, or 1,500 cars per hour per lane, the capacity decreasing above and below this critical speed.

A freeway carrying 1,500 cars per hour will move 2,500 people in a single lane as compared with 1,200 passengers on the ordinary city street. The number of seated passengers carried by a bus increases from 7,200 to 10,000 per hour and 13,000 including standees. The free flow of uninterrupted rail lines (either in the form of a subway or an elevated line such as a monorail) further permits the effective use of multiple trains that carry 27,000 seated and 40,000 including standees per hour on a single track, while two tracks in the same direction, with one local and one express train, can increase the total capacity per hour to 70,000 seated and 100,000 or more including standing passengers.[9]

A six-lane freeway—three lanes in each direction—will reduce the capacity per lane for automobiles from 1,500 cars per hour for a single lane to about 2,700 cars for two lanes and 3,500 cars in three lanes. Three lanes will carry about 6,000 passengers per hour in private automobiles compared with one bus lane carrying 7,200 seated and 9,000 including standees. [10] Buses operating on a three-lane freeway would probably also be reduced in efficiency because of the inevitable conflict with automobiles. If the same decrease as applies to automobiles were applied to the

9. Ibid.
10. Ibid.

bus, the latter would still carry 8,000 seated persons and more than 11,000 including standees.

Rapid transit lines or some form of overhead train system (the elevated train or monorail) incorporated in a freeway both require a fairly commodious right-of-way. Because there is a firm reluctance to remove any of the land surface from present or potential use for commercial development in existing urban centers, there is resistance to either of these forms of surface transportation into the heart of the city. Because of the overwhelming congestion on city streets and the inadequacy of rapid transit systems to move the people with convenience, comfort, or speed, the subway was constructed as the natural alternative.

The subway marks the final evidence that the city has succumbed to strangulation by urban congestion. An uninterrupted flow of travel for multiple electric trains is accomplished, but at a cost that exceeds every other form of mass transportation. Only the private automobile exceeds the cost of subways; it is four or five times the cost per passenger mile.

MASS TRANSIT SYSTEMS

The future of mass transit lies in the development of an integrated system that will serve the people who need the service most. The fares must be geared to the income level of its primary users. The aged and lowest-income groups should ride free. The system must be built to take people to places of employment and centers of activity. Most of all the system should be a part of the reconstruction of those portions of the city that have fallen into decay. In this way it would be built into the development itself and people would use it, especially if there were no garages for the storage of automobiles and no off-street or on-street parking permitted other than for brief periods or in cases of emergency.

Every large city in the world has some type of mass transit system. One can imagine what travel would be like in cities such as New York, Paris, and London if mass transit did not exist and automobiles carried no more than 1.25 passengers per unit. In New York City, for example, the streets and the space required for parking would eliminate all sites for buildings. Congestion would be absolute, movement would not be possible.

The subway is a mass transit means that does not impinge on vehicular street movement. There are subway systems in London, Paris, Saõ Paulo, Peking, Hong Kong, San Francisco, New York, Chicago, Montreal, Washington, D.C., and Moscow, as well as in other cities. One may be critical of a system that at times packs people together as if they were inanimate objects, but a better method for moving large numbers of people has yet to be found.

Recent mass transit systems such as the BART system in San Francisco have been criticized because their highly sophisticated mechanisms break down easily. Another criticism has been that these systems do not fulfill their intended purpose of reducing automobile traffic into the central city. Further, critics claim they do not serve poor people, the people who need them the most, as service runs mainly through the affluent areas where personal transportation is more readily available.

How to finance mass rapid transit has been a controversial public issue. Studies all over the world indicate that nearly all systems need heavy subsidy, even if fares are substantially raised.

Support Cost, and Revenue

Statistics have indicated that, for most public transit agencies, 40 percent or less of the cost of operations is generated at the fare box. However, considerable additional revenue is generated from the increases in property taxes by the improvements located adjacent to the transit stations, mainly from increases in both the intensity of uses and the densities of the new housing developments built after or concurrent with the development of the mass transit routes. The funds derived from the tax revenues usually go into the general fund and only thereafter possibly appear as a subsidy for the transit operations.

No great city's public transportation is supported by user fares, with the exception of Hong Kong. Public transportation nevertheless can stand as the hallmark of a great city. When transit systems are designed and constructed after the city has developed, as is usually the case, the costs tend to become exorbitant and the construction disrupts the fabric of the city physically, socially, and economically. Resistance to building becomes great as potential impacts on residential and commercial activities over an extended period of time are contemplated.

During the latter days of President Jimmy Carter's administration massive financial assistance was provided to cities interested in the development of experimental transit systems that would modernize the services in critical locations. The Urban Mass Transit Agency (UMTA) granted funds for development of "people movers" in many cities, discussed later in this chapter.

Subways

Tokyo has the most extensive subway system in the world, some 300 miles reaching from the heart of the city to the suburbs. The system carries more passengers per day than any other with the exception of the Moscow system. It is integrated with the interurban and intercommunity system that leads to all parts of Japan. The trains are modern, color-

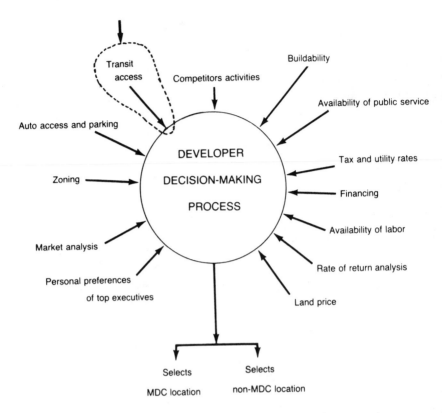

Developer decision-making environment

Developers operate in a complex environment, as exemplified by the diagrammatic description of the many factors that govern their participation in the urban scene.
"Toward a Multinodal Urban Structure," Dr. Mary Jo Huth, Transportation Quarterly, *Eno Foundation, April 1983. Based on research by Jerry B. Schneider, University of Washington.*

coded to make use easy even for the uninitiated foreign traveler. The Hong Kong subway has been in operation since March 1980. Called the Modified Initial System, it is 9.7 miles long with 15 stations, twelve underground and three above ground.[11] Apart from a short overhead section at the Kwun Tong end, construction has mainly been accomplished by bored tunnel with an immersed tube under the harbor.

---

11. Hong Kong Government Information Service Publication, June 1978.

In July 1977, approval was given to extend the Modified Initial System from Prince Edward Station in north Nathan Road to the Tsuen Wan new town in the New Territories. The extension commenced operation in late 1982 and is presently (1985) nearing completion.

The new underground stations are being constructed by the "cut-and-cover" method. They have been designed around the central island platform concept in order to segregate passenger movements in urban areas. Stations are spaced at intervals of about six-tenth of a mile; across the harbor between Admiralty Station and Tsim Sha Tsui, the spacing is 1.5 miles.

"People Movers"

All forms of transportation that carry persons from one location to another can be classified as people movers. However, during the 1970s and 1980s the term took on a different connotation. It meant the introduction of special forms of local transportation, some bordering on the fanciful.

Hong Kong mass transit system.

Moving sidewalks were used at airports to take people to boarding gates. Los Angeles proposed building a system in the central business district; the idea still persists, to the point of funds being allocated to plan the system. Denver has a people-mover system made up of low-slung buses that make boarding from the curb most convenient; the buses go from the capital to the central business district. The Denver program entailed much more than a transportation system; concurrent with the people mover was the major redevelopment of its corridor, designed to the highest standards, resulting in an area of greatest beauty as well as providing for convenient travel. UMTA funded the entire program.

The city of San Bernardino, California, is talking about an overhead system that will connect its two major shopping areas and continue up into the San Bernardino Mountains to serve the resorts located there, especially convenient for skiers during winter months. Disneyland in Anaheim has used a monorail people mover to take people to the main hotel center. Seattle, Washington, built a monorail for the World's Fair held there in the 1960s. This type of people mover has been in use for many years in Germany.

Subway and station, Washington, D. C.

Monorails have captured the imagination of the futurist. Examples, however, indicate that they are no more than a modernized elevated railway, with the same blighting effect on street architecture. The stations occupy large spaces at critical locations. The posts and columns rooted in the street and the heavy structure of the monorail track interrupt the streets and reduce their carrying capacities.

A variety of specially designed transit systems, coupled with the standard bus, streetcar, subway, and elevated railroad, constitute the major efforts by the Urban Mass Transit Agency of the federal government to make local transportation more convenient and, in some cases, safer.

The Multimodal System

The greatest failing of the mass transit system, if it can be called a system, is that it consists of an unintegrated grouping of individual operations, each functioning in its own little world without cross-transfers or transfer points.

Many transit systems need a comprehensive, coordinated plan and program of operation, in which the passengers could move rapidly and conveniently from points of origin to destinations with a maximum of comfort. The program could coordinate trains, subways, buses, helicopters, and ferries into a planned operational system where movement from one form to another could be accomplished at centralized locations.

Multimodal transfer systems are difficult to achieve. They take years to integrate and require political cooperation between cities for the benefit of the whole. The Metro system of Washington, D.C., had eleven separate governmental entities to deal with in discussions of fares and transfers. The system in Paris, France, fared much better; there was a maximum degree of consideration and cooperation among all parties involved.

Transportation Centers. Most multimodal systems will need a central terminal where easy exchange of type of transportation will be possible. During the age of rail transportation, there developed in the world's large cities fine examples of terminal structures, well located to serve the heart of the cities in which they were located. With the near demise of passenger rail service in all but a few parts of the world, these old and sometimes very fine examples of classical architecture have been abandoned, many destroyed. However, those that through chance have remained are now in a position to become the heart of the future multimodal transportation system. They can bring into the critical areas of a community all the elements of the transportation system, including commuter helicopters, trains, buses, subways, and even commuter boats from offshore islands

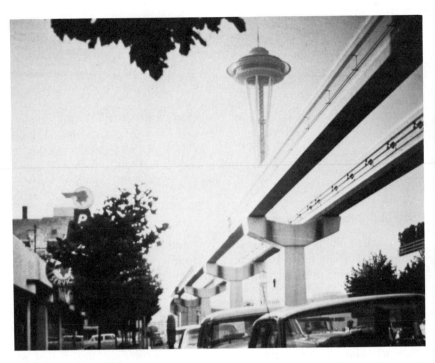

The monorail, Seattle. *The impact that the overhead structure has on the street and the adjacent property is obvious in the photographs.*

Multimodal mass transit. *The neighborhood unit is the common denominator in the urban structure. In this plan, a minibus system serves each neighborhood, circulating to and from the local commercial centers, parks, playgrounds, and schools. An intracity and intercity rail or bus system links the commercial centers with major rapid transit service to central business districts, cultural facilities, airports, railroad lines, and concentrated industrial or other employment centers. Although technically the system would be organized in a general grid, this does not imply a "gridiron" street layout or pattern of land uses. Alignment would be adjusted either to variations in natural terrain or in existing cities, to established and desirable permanent land uses.*

Weaning people from the automobile to mass transit will require both convenient and frequent local transit— the minibus—and parking restrictions in concentrated business and cultural centers. Until most of the urban community recognizes the extravagance of the automobile, and until a convenient mass transportation system is available, massive automobile parking space will be required at rapid transit stations.

In the diagram, solid lines indicate the transit lines; solid spaces, the local and regional commercial centers; cross-hatched areas, the local industrial parks; circles, community, elementary, or high schools; dotted areas, recreation facilities. Dash lines outline neighborhood areas.

as in the Atlantic and Pacific oceans, the Gulf of Mexico, and the Great Lakes.

These reconstituted hubs can then become centers of commerce as well as transportation, reclaiming old areas and encouraging the rehabilitation of both the housing and public services that already exist and are in need of attention.

In the mid-1980s the Los Angeles Rapid Transit District began condemnation proceedings to obtain the neglected Union Railroad station, which is owned jointly by the Southern Pacific, Union Pacific, and Santa Fe railroads. This magnificent structure is located close to the central business district, the historical area adjacent to the plaza, the civic center, and many cultural facilities. It would serve as the multimodal center for the totally integrated transportation system serving the Los Angeles region. The station and the area around it are readily adaptable to serve as the locus of railroad, bus, and helicopter lines, as well as the subway lines that are under serious study. With imagination, this multimodal center could become one of the prime terminal and transfer points for all of the local, interurban, and long distance travel modes. Vast areas for automobile parking could be located within easy walking distance.

Railroads

Builders of the railroads sought level terrain or followed the easy grades along watercourses. Cities sprang up along these routes, and industry developed on the lines of transportation. The passenger station was the entrance to the town, and the center of the city grew about it. Since this hub provided convenient commutation to the suburbs, the commercial district expanded about it.

With the passing of time and the neglect of orderly urban development, industry continued to creep along the railways and waterfronts. The city grew and new railroads entered to help build the metropolis. These lines of transportation were vital to the economic development of the urban area, and industries were accorded preferential sites along the rights-of-way as encouragement to locate in the city. Blocked by spur tracks and sidings, the street system was interrupted, and traffic problems and other hazards were created.

Replacement of the various independent and scattered stations by the so-called union station improved the reception, dispatch, and interchange of passengers and freight, but the city still suffered from the chaotic network of separate rail lines that stretched like tentacles in all directions. Consolidation of the various competing lines was slow because of complicated joint agreements, the abandonment of rights-of-way, the high cost of building new facilities for roads already equipped with terminals, and the necessity for coordination that tended to reduce possibilities for independent expansion. The reduction in the duplication of facilities that would have resulted from such consolidation, however, would have been of immeasurable profit to the city. Simplification of the street system, traffic routes, and grade crossings would alone have vastly improved urban circulation and reduced the hazards and disorderly pattern present.

The shipping of freight comprises a far larger part of railroad business than passenger traffic and presents the more complicated planning problems. Except for some terminal locations, a large part of the freight business is "through shipping"—that is, freight destined for points beyond the city. As the city grew up and spread away from the railroad, the yards remained a no-man's-land within the heart of the urban core. Occupying valuable land and disrupting the circulation system of the city, the yards are generally too cramped for the efficient handling of the tremendous operations involved in the classification, sorting, and redistribution of freights, as well as storage, switching, and the makeup of trains.

Recently, planning studies have been conducted throughout America concerning the potential use of the waste land in the many abandoned classification yards that are so well located in numerous cities. The concepts for reuse range from new commercial centers, produce distribution complexes, and cultural or sports centers to retail and office uses, all to be supported by a partnership between the public and private sectors. Some cities in the eastern U.S. have been giving serious attention to such programs in order to gain the economic advantages that could be secured through this effort.

Rebirth of Rail Transportation.   The adventures of the Japanese with their Bullet Train and the more recent addition of the French "TVG" high-speed system have given rise to the rehabilitation of railroads as a competitor to the automobile and airplane as the means of traveling middle distances in many parts of the world. The efficiency of the Japanese system, its improved travel times and safety, along with its savings in energy and cost, have now been recognized. Consideration is being given to similar experimental lines in the United States, for example in the Los Angeles to San Diego corridor and in the Boston, New York, and Washington, D.C., corridor. As can be expected, opposition from cities along the proposed routes tends to delay some of these proposals.

The Third Dimension: Flight

People's ability to free themselves from the face of the earth created new problems. While the airplane was an experiment, terminal facilities were located as far as possible from people. With millions of people now flying each year, location of the airport in urban centers and rapid delivery of passengers to their destinations are the joint concern of airline operators and the public. Connections from the airport to the destination in the city have become a greater problem than the flying time between cities.

Airport planning is a component part of the comprehensive plan for the city. It requires a complete analysis of the market comparable to what is done for other forms of transportation: the present and potential passenger, cargo, and mail business that may be expected in the community; meteorological data; the present and planned land use within and about the city; the proposed extent of the operators' training program; the local traffic—intercity and state; transcontinental and international air routes; and prospects for development of private airfields.

Air transportation is in a state of flux. The type of equipment continues to change and policies of airline operators are constantly subject to modification with experience. The attitude of the urban population also varies, some desiring complete immunity from proximity to flying fields and lanes, others inclining to support the development of residential communities designed around the airplane as a vehicle for commutation.

The deregulation process, which has had an impact on many of the economic activities in the United States, has had an amazing effect on the airline industry. The number of airline companies has multiplied rapidly and some communities with major airports have been in an uproar over the additional flights, the concern for air safety, and the additional noise and traffic that have been generated. Several of the major airlines, new and old, have gone into bankruptcy while others have ceased to operate, as the current anarchy plagues even the best of carriers. Deregulation may be synonomous with the "antiplanning" approach to the concept of a free market in which anyone can do as he wishes, and cooperation and coordination of activities can be classified as a restraint of trade or conspiracy.

Planning for air transportation must be conceived on a regional scale. Airports are distributed for convenient and rapid connections to the strategic parts of the city, by a variety of means that have not yet been settled. Downtown feeder airports to which light ships may bring passengers into the heart of the city are being considered, and helicopter flights from the major port to landing space in the city center for airmail and commuter service are already in operation. However, many heliports, other than those associated with medical emergencies, have been discontinued because of local conflicts. Air transport is an integral part of the transportation of the city, both passenger and cargo, and must be a component part of the city plan.

Airports. The location of airports and the relationship that these modern-day transportation centers have to the development of urbanization is at a crisis state in many communities. Not only is the safety of millions of passengers at stake, but so are the lives of persons living in the areas surrounding airports.

Examples of the problem exist in all parts of the world. The crash of a plane adjacent to Kennedy some years ago, the 1978 accident in the vicinity of San Diego, and the Chicago tragedy of 1982 are well-known and should make us pay heed to the probability of future occurrences.

The danger of crashes may not be the major problem. Noise from the ever-increasing size and power of the planes has been a major environmental difficulty. Overflights at low levels in the take-off and landing areas have aroused petitions to close airports or to regulate their hours of operation.

The future use of the "dead land" around airports after acquisition and clearance still remains. In the Los Angeles area, some of the land has been turned into a parking lot. This use could be expanded and would be productive if the land was reasonably near the air terminal by shuttle bus. In other areas the possibility of cemeteries or golf courses has been discussed. High-density housing or mobile home developments should be discouraged as a violation of NEPA and common sense.

Harbors

In former times the harbors of the world were the centers of transportation activity, the locale for romance, the heart of developing civilization. It was to ports that ships of many nations brought their goods and passengers. They were the ties to the trade centers, the distribution points for all exchange.

Today in the developed nations the airlines now lead trains and ships in passenger travel. But ships still perform the important function of handling bulk merchandise, and still provide a means of travel for those seeking leisure and recreation. The harbors of the world and the rail lines leading from them must be elements in any planning program. Harbors, unlike airports, cannot be moved from their natural locations. They may be deepened or extended or altered in function from industrial to recreational, but they are always at the water's edge.

The Bicycle

The bicycle, used as a health and pleasure vehicle for many years, has become an important link in the transportation chain. The energy shortage in 1976 caused their widespread purchase. Perhaps their use in urban areas in America has not yet become as important as it has been in many of the European cities, such as in Amsterdam, Holland, but it is approaching this in certain localities. In Davis, California, college students attending the University of California campus use the bicycle as their primary means of movement within the city.

In the People's Republic of China the bicycle is the major means of transportation in cities. While buses serve along major routes, bicyclists are primary occupants of public highways.

The bicycle, like the pedestrian, poses many problems as it competes with the automobile for the use of the streets. The visibility of the bicycle rider going in the same direction as the automobile traffic creates a target. Reactions on the part of both motorist and cyclist are uncertain. Bicycles must move across intersecting streets. Bike lanes adjacent to the curbs often end at parked vehicles, and the bicycle must veer out into the traffic flow. This danger is apparently overcome by prohibiting parking, but there are still the problems of enforcement. Night riding, when the bicycle may not be as visible, may also lead to accidents.

The proper training of bike riders has become as essential as the proper training of automobile drivers. They should be licensed only after passing tests dealing with their safety and that of others.

However, the only truly safe way to deal with the bicyclist is to construct separate roadways paralleling sidewalks. The separation of the pedestrian from the motor vehicle has been a part of the Radburn plan since the 1940s. It is only reasonable to extend this idea to the bicyclist.

THE PEDESTRIAN

People walked on all occasions during urbanization in prehistoric times. The horse, mule, and the like, permitted people to move a little more rapidly. After the wheel came to be used in conjunction with the horse, locomotion became still more rapid. During the mechanical age, steam, electrical energy, and petrochemicals gave the wheel added power. For all practical purposes, motorized vehicles took people off their feet. Briefly stated, industry had produced mechanized mobility for the masses.

Today one seldom goes to the marketplace on foot. In cities where mass transportation is inadequate, the individual automobile is practically indispensable, although in cities like New York it is generally impractical because of limited and expensive parking facilities.

When the automobile is put to rest in a parking lot, people momentarily become pedestrians once again. They are on their feet as they travel the short distances from parking to place of employment, or to the shopping areas that have been designed to make pedestrians' activities convenient and comfortable.

At these shopping areas, unless the car is separated from pedestrian

Bicycle transit—a way of life in China.

Bicycle and pedestrian walk, Tapiola, Finland. *The routes are carefully marked to separate the pedestrian from the cyclist.*

Bicycle and pedestrian parkway in wide setback, Palm Springs, California.

Bicycle transportation means parking must be provided.

travel lanes, people become targets for the automobile. Statistics indicate that more than 300,000 pedestrian accidents occur across American each year, with more than 8,000 fatalities.[12] This latter statistic represents one-sixth of the total national highway death toll.

Improvements. As the accident rates and death tolls have increased, there have been efforts to provide for greater pedestrian safety through better street design, improved lighting of crosswalks, the use of traffic lights, and the slowing of traffic in areas where pedestrian movement is greatest.

The shopping areas themselves have been improved. Almost all of the newly developed major shopping centers are enclosed groupings of stores with a pedestrian safety area in the center. This is not a new concept, but it is newly used in most planned commercial centers. However, in the places between where the automobile is parked and the pedestrian safety areas, it is still open season on pedestrians.

Pedestrian grade separations have been a part of the more sophisticated and costly arterial designs, but they are seldom placed in local areas where people are supposed to do most of their walking. These separations can go over or under the arterial. They were given their best treatment by Clarence Stein and Henry Wright. Here the separation caused the roadway to rise slightly and the underpass to depress about an equal amount. The dangers associated with the overpass, such as vandals throwing objects at moving automobiles, were eliminated, as were the dark, often dirty corridors of the underpass. The midway approach provided safety for the pedestrian as well as visibility in the corners. This type of underpass can be found in many of the new towns in Sweden.

The following recommendations for pedestrian safety were made in an article in the Eno Foundation for Transportation *Traffic Quarterly:*[13]

1.   Pedestrian Midblock Crossing Barriers. At locations where significant numbers of pedestrian accidents result from midblock street crossings, physical barriers along the curbline or in the median of a divided roadway are effective in channelizing these crossings into intersections, where vehicular movements can be controlled by traffic signals or stop signs.

2.   Midblock Crosswalks. Although midblock crossing of streets by pedestrians is generally more hazardous than the use of intersection crosswalks, under certain conditions a marked crosswalk at a midblock location between two widely spaced intersections will reduce pedestrian accidents.

An example would be a midblock location that has a large parking facility one one side of the street and a major pedestrian trip generator on the other side—such as the entrance to a large shopping center, a university

12. David I. Davis and Lawrence A. Pavlinski, *Traffic Quarterly,* Eno Foundation for Transportation, July 1978.

13. July 1978.

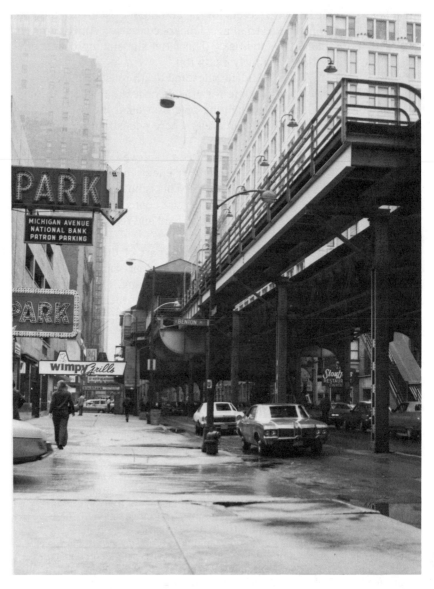

Examples of poor urban sidewalk developments. *The poor planning of sidewalks, where pedestrians should be able to walk comfortably, stems directly from inadequate setbacks and space for people to walk safely.*

campus, or a sports stadium. Rather than erect barriers to force people to walk relatively long distances from the parking area to their destination, a marked crosswalk may be preferable particularly if traffic signals are installed to control vehicular movements.

3.   Diagonal On-Street Parking. On main streets with business frontages, and with only one or two lanes for traffic in each direction, diagonal on-street parking has been found to be hazardous in terms of collisions between motor vehicles. But in terms of pedestrian accidents, such diagonal parking has been found to be safer than parallel parking at the curb. This is because it reduces "dart-out" accidents—the leading type of pedestrian accident—which occur when a person runs between parked cars onto the street.

So while diagonal on-street parking is not recommended on main streets unless they have ample width for vehicles to back out of parking spaces without disturbing the traffic flow, it can sometimes be applied with pedestrian safety benefits on wide residential streets.

INTEGRATION OR DISINTEGRATION

How can these various and diverse characteristics of contemporary vehicles be merged into an effective transportation system?

It is apparent that a change must be made in the present street system, and this change may affect other aspects of land use. The freeway has been hailed as an instrument with which to create a new framework for the community of tomorrow. The freeway can aid in relief of congestion in the central areas of the city, but the rebuilding of these areas to provide ample parking space and an environment as attractive as the outlying areas of the city must be created; otherwise, the freeways may become the arteries that carry the people past the outmoded central districts to the shopping districts that have their stakes in a well-planned, convenient, and pleasant environment of this day.

Adequate parking space, planned open space, and commercial development may be substituted for the futile strip zoning along traffic arteries which themselves will be replaced by the freeways. With replanning, the business district will be removed from traffic congestion and obtain ingress and egress for vehicles and pedestrians. Curb parking may become a thing of the past; with some exceptions the space along the curbs in central areas is less than one-fifth the amount of parking provided in lots and garages, and yet it is all hopelessly inadequate. Traffic flow is reduced about one-half by curb parking on the average street, making it a serious obstruction to traffic movement. The courts have held that streets are for the movement of traffic and not places for storage of vehicles. Since they are separate functions, terminal parking space for cars, the traffic arteries, and the space for circulation of pedestrians with their access to shopping and commercial enterprise, will be planned as separate elements.

There must be a plan for transportation, and this plan must become a guide for each improvement in the city. During the long and arduous period in which the plan is being formulated, first-aid remedies will be necessary. Traffic bandages and tourniquets, splints and casts, will be needed. It is necessary, however, that the distinction between the expedient nature of these measures and permanent solutions be continually recognized. The breakdown represented by traffic congestion must be treated in the most infectious spots to keep the urban traffic stream flowing, but these devices of traffic engineering must not be confused with basic improvements in the street pattern and mass transportation. Too frequently they are interpreted as one and the same, with the result that the prospect of a solution to the urban traffic and transportation dilemma is given up as hopeless. Students of the problem realize that disintegration will eat deeper into the cores of the urban environment and lead gradually to an eventual complete loss of values, unless basic changes are made.

The evidence is already present in cities. We see the decay at its worst in the movement or, to put it more accurately, the retreat of sound business from the blight that has consumed former "high-class" districts. We also see the creation of entirely new business centers, and we see them growing temporarily prosperous at the expense of the older established areas. Finally, we see the first-aid methods being repeatedly used in the vain attempt to revive the dying areas.

CHAPTER 24

CONSERVATION

"... WHERE WE'VE BEEN"

The basic questions regarding environmental management have not changed. Just as past generations have had to define the optimum value and use of environmental resources for themselves and their posterity, so do people today. Just as past generations have had to determine the different functions of the public sector and private enterprise in developing natural resources, so do people today. And, just as population levels, economic development, and technological capability have helped to shape the environmental attitudes of past generations, so too will these factors influence value judgments today.

For the early colonists, environmental values were dominated by the need for survival, both physical and economic. Because in those precarious times when human labor was more scarce than natural resources, it is understandable that they valued these resources less than we do today. The early colonists made little effort to ensure continued yields from virgin forests or to protect wildlife. Nor did they practice methods of farming which preserved or replenished surface soils. Instead, they responded in a resourceful way to both the problems and possibilities posed by a seemingly limitless wilderness.

During the century after 1776 the federal government bought, or was ceded, vast areas of land which were added to the territory of the United States. The midwestern land claims of the original states expanded the new nation's boundaries, and successive events—the Louisiana Purchase

(1803), the Oregon Compromise (1846), the Treaty of Guadalupe Hidalgo (1848), the Gadsden Purchase (1853), and the Alaska Purchase (1867)— added 1.8 billion acres to this young country. The federal government continued the common colonial practice of assigning property rights to new lands by distributing rights through sales, homesteading, and land grants to military veterans, states, local governments, and railroads.

The abundance of land contributed to the uniqueness of America. Instead of the republic of classical antiquity—territorially small, ethnically homogenous, socially conservative, and economically stable—the American republic became big, diverse, exuberant, innovative, and expansive. Slow, planned growth favored by many eastern politicians was replaced by the sprawling, brawling, impatient expansion that characterized the American frontier. America became a republic of hope, opportunity, experimentation, mobility, and personal independence.[1]

"... WHERE WE ARE"

We have become inured to early obsolescence. Goods are plastic-packaged for early discarding. Fashions are outdated as soon as acquired; the trim on automobiles is still shiny when they are replaced by newer models. Commercial prosperity has been geared to the principle of early obsolescence; quantity production substitutes for quality.

Wasteful consumption by an affluent society has become a malady; the passion to consume has been satisfied by the remarkable productivity of an aggressively expanding industrial system. Our appetites have become so gluttonous that the Environmental Protection Agency had to report even in 1970: "The United States, with about 6 percent of the world's population, consumes 40 percent of the total nonreplaceable materials and 40 percent of the world's energy." The oil shortage that surfaced in 1973, dubbed the "energy crisis," exposed only one aspect of the overconsumption that plagues the industrial nations of the world.

The urban environment directly reflects the excesses to which society has become habituated. Commercial enterprise has created gigantic symbols of economic power in urban centers. For more than three decades the 1,250-foot tower of the Empire State Building was the tallest emblem of commercial aggrandizement. But in the sixties, the two 110-story towers of the World Trade Center rose 1,350 feet into the air, while in Chicago the 100-story John Hancock Tower, looming 1,127 feet high, was soon topped by the 1,136-foot Standard Oil Tower, and in 1972, the Chicago Sears Tower triumphed over all competitors with a height of 1,450 feet. The famous architect Eliel Saarinen had pleaded, "Surely the city's form and coherence must not be left at the mercy of commercial

---

1. Council on Environmental Quality, *Environmental Quality—1981: The 12th Annual Report of the Council on Environmental Quality* (Washington, D.C.: U.S. Government Printing Office, 1982), page 3.

speculation,"[2] yet the architect of the World Trade Center, Minoru Ya-masaki, claimed that venture was the "living representation of Man's belief in humanity."[3]

Lower Manhattan seen from the Statue of Liberty, the view of mammoth towers through the trees of Central Park, the silhouette of San Francisco from the Bay, the lakefront skyline of Chicago, are among the dramatic spectacles of urban America. But these are not the views seen by most urban dwellers. Most of the people some of the time and some of the people all of the time experience streets denuded of trees, paved with oil-stained asphalt and concrete, overburdened with buildings and vehicles, strung with wires and glaring advertising signs. Their intimate environment is a jungle of noise, tainted odors, incessant movement, and visual chaos. The refuse of the industrial system, spewed with abandon into rivers, lakes, and the atmosphere, pollutes the water and air nature has bountifully supplied. An economy of planned obsolescence scars the urbanscape.

Psychological and physiological damage is wrought upon the human mind and body. Those who can afford it find refuge in suburbia. Precious open space is devoured, hills are unmercifully bulldozed, and valleys filled to accommodate the burgeoning population. When God created men and women, he admonished them to "replenish the earth and subdue it," but they neglected to distinguish between *subdue* and *destroy*. We have impaired the balance of nature and contaminated our environment.

This, then, is the challenge we confront as we prepare for the twenty-first century. A beginning has been made with our growing awareness of our impact on the environment; these lessons have slowly grown clear as the twentieth century progresses.

Previously unfamiliar words have entered the popular vocabulary. *Environmentalists* protest against the destructive exploitation of natural resources. A new awareness of *ecology* reveals the scope and intricacy of the interlocking relationships between land uses and services required in a manmade environment. Disposal of the waste created by overconsumption and planned obsolescence is a difficult, complex task, and unforeseen scarcities give the term *recycling* a new significance.

Securing food in the city usually means going to the supermarket or the restaurant. Our concept of the creation of clothing is going through racks in a department store. Our understanding of energy resources until recently was limited to the pump at the gas station. We are dependent on the unknown producers of these items, and we would have a difficult time

---

2. Eliel Saarinen, *The City—Its Growth, Its Decay, Its Future* (New York: Reinhold Publishers, 1943).

3. Paul Heyer, *Architects on Architecture* (New York: Walker, 1966), p. 195.

surviving if the real sources ceased to exist. Nevertheless, we encroach upon the best agricultural land and foul the air, giving little thought to the end products of our actions.

The Essential Element

Conservation is not new. In ancient lands flood control was necessary for human survival. Blessed with apparently unlimited land and resources, the United States has been tardy and erratic in conserving its resources. When one resource is depleted, it has been taken for granted that some new technology will certainly replace it. That optimism cannot be applied to land. The amount of land on this earth is fixed, and when the supply, for whatever purpose it may be used, is exhausted, there is no substitute. Land is not yet recognized as the precious natural resource it is, and the civilized concept of limiting speculative gains from land exploitation has not penetrated the American consciousness.

The nineteenth century was rife with disposition of public lands for the ostensible purpose of encouraging economic development. In the early twentieth century the public interest was asserted by the creation of the National Parks and Forest Services. A third (765 million acres) of the land area of the fifty states is still owned by the federal government. Of this federal reserve, 312 million acres have been allocated to specific jurisdictions: the National Parks Service, the Forest Service, the Department of Defense, the Bureau of Indian Affairs, the Bureau of Fisheries and Wildlife, the Bureau of Reclamation, the Department of State, the Atomic Energy Commission, the Tennessee Valley Authority, and the National Aeronautics and Space Administration. To administer the remaining 435 million acres, the Bureau of Land Management was created in 1946. Occupying nearly one-half of the Western states, this precious resource is, in the words of Charles S. Watson, Jr., "the land nobody knows."[4]

Conservation, therefore, implies both the protection of the open lands and resources as well as the preservation of urban areas. Our propensity toward a discard economy and planned obsolescence must be changed. Many states require conservation guidelines in their comprehensive plans. The purpose of these guidelines is to promote the prudent use of our natural resources. Understanding the interconnection of these resources through the activities of man is important to achieving effective conservation.

Implementing land conservation policies through zoning, subdivision ordinances, and growth management will help forestall premature or unwarranted expansion of urbanism into the agricultural areas. The city

---

4. *Sierra Club Bulletin,* September 1973.

zoning ordinance can provide for an agricultural district requiring large minimum lot sizes to protect the integrity of agricultural activity within and surrounding the cities in its area of influence.

THE ROUTE TO SURVIVAL

Many farsighted individuals and groups have fostered the conservation of our natural resources. Proponents succeeded in obtaining presidential support for a National Parks System and the conservation of some of the historical areas of America. For many years European nations have worked to preserve natural landmarks. In recent years, the importance of preserving our soil and forests has received much public attention.

Frequently, however, we think of conservation as applicable only to wilderness areas. While this area is crucial, the protection of our urban environments is equally important. Cities and their hinterlands are an intertwined entity. If we are careless with either, both will fall. We seldom realize the role that rural agricultural land plays in the lives of citydwellers. Without farms and forests the basic necessities of life—food, clothing, and shelter—could not (except for synthetics) be produced.

Earth Ecology and the Biosphere

During the latter days of World War II, people in Los Angeles became aware that the air in their city had become unpleasantly murky. Tests showed that the atmosphere was contaminated. As the contaminants increased it became a favorite laboratory exercise to measure the "parts per million." Sources were traced to oil refineries, industries, incinerators, and automobile exhausts. Their emissions combined with the fog and were intensified by a natural phenomenon of temperature inversion in the southern California basin. The result was "smog."

As industrial garbage was discharged into the air, evidence of similar atmospheric contamination appeared in other cities. People died on one occasion in London. Tokyo experienced near-disasters. Some control measures were gradually and grudgingly adopted by industry. But smog persisted. The automobile was finally declared to be the principal source, and changes in the internal combustion engine and fuel were demanded. New models produced in recent years are required to provide "smog control" devices. Older models are required to have smog checks, and in 1985 the elimination of lead in gasoline was mandated.

Then pollution was discovered in watercourses, streams, rivers, and lakes, a result of the discharge of industrial refuse. Insecticides disrupted agricultural crops. Fish in rivers were poisoned. Fish in Lake Erie were dead. Oil spills threatened wildlife in the sea. Beaches were contaminated. Strip mining for coal laid waste the Appalachian landscape. Disastrous floods followed. Forests were decimated. The effects of a careless "throwaway" society are taking their toll on the natural resources in a rich land. Space in which to safely deposit waste is disappearing. Burial of nuclear waste and excess poison gas threatens areas beyond state and national boundaries.

Ecology suddenly became a cause célèbre in commercial and industrial public relations propaganda. Environmentalists, long concerned with ecology, took up the challenge to preserve natural resources. Legislation could not keep pace with the revelations of abuse to which society had become habituated. "Conservation" became a popular cause. In 1973, 1976, and 1979 the "energy crisis" shocked not only America but the entire Western world. Realization gradually dawned that the continuous squandering of irreplaceable resources has become the Western way of life.

The course of shifting social values is made evident in the observations of the prominent public health engineer Frank Stead. When he began his career in 1931, public health occupied a privileged position: "When we said something was hazardous to health . . . that ended it. Everything else yielded—economics, property rights, everything." Administration of more recent water and air regulations, however, is intended to "balance environmental quality against economic production," the unacceptable concept of "trade-offs" with public health. Stead states the imperative of protecting the

> total biospheric support system, . . . that relatively thin zone at the surface of the earth that contains the land surface only a few hundred feet below the surface and ground waters, and the atmospheric envelope only a few thousand feet above the surface of the earth. Together with solar energy, these are the total resources on which all living things depend.

"The real fact is," he emphasizes, "that we must give first place to the preservation of the biosphere, and within that mandate develop the ability to support an economically productive system to keep our civilization viable." To achieve that, he says, "we will have to make changes far more fundamental than getting rid of the internal combustion engine."[5]

THE COMPREHENSIVE PLAN

With increased commercialism and urbanization, conservation has become a necessary element of the general plan for cities. To preserve the

---

5. Quotations from *Health News,* August 1974. A graduate in public health engineering from Harvard University, Frank Stead instituted the first industrial hygiene program by the Los Angeles County Health Department, and for twenty years was Chief of the Division of Environmental Sanitation, California Department of Public Health. In the early sixties he asserted that by 1980 "the gasoline powered engine must be phased out."

theory of local autonomy, most legislative authority is delegated by state governments to local communities. With public authority thus divided among various local governments, essential conservation measures are beyond the authority of competing local jurisdictions. Although some internal flood control, preservation of watersheds, protection of historic sites, and extraction of minerals may be effectively administered at the local level, the broad conservation measures related to public health and welfare, domestic water supply, fish, plants and game, land and water reclamation, disposal of refuse and sewage, air quality, timber supply, and agriculture extend beyond city boundaries to regional, state, or interstate dimensions. Conservation at the local level has consequently been equated with provisions in the comprehensive plan and zoning ordinances for preservation of parks and recreation areas.

Each city determines the space and distribution of its playgrounds and parks. Rampant land subdivision practices have often failed to provide space for recreation. Planned developments have improved this situation, but cities must require all residential development to allocate land for recreation and schools in accordance with local space standards. In the event that scattered subdivisions are too small to provide a park, prorated payment should be substituted, and the money should be maintained in a revolving fund for acquisition for parks, playgrounds, and school sites as the demand evolves.

The county tax assessor, more than the planning commission and city council, influences the disposition of open space. The office of property tax assessment is required by state law to assess taxes on the basis of "fair market value," and those appraisers determine the values. Regardless of the zoning designation, land that is in the path of development usually acquires a value consistent with that potential development. Land thus taxed cannot be long held off the market for development, nor can the pressure for zoning changes to accommodate "higher economic" use be long resisted by local authorities. Urban sprawl eats into agricultural zones, speculators are rewarded, plans are ignored, and open space disappears.

One tentative remedy is the contract between the state and the landowner to maintain an agricultural use for a specified period (ten years) in return for tax assessments based upon agricultural value.[6] This tax shelter only postpones the inevitable change to urban development, unless the comprehensive plan and zoning ordinance become the recognized reference for land value and tax assessment or, as recommended by the American Institute of Architects,[7] unless public policy provides for the public

---

6. Hawaii State Zoning; Williamson Act in California; Land Conservation and Development Act, 1973, in Oregon.
7. *A Strategy for Building a Better America, 1972.*

to recover that increase in land value that is created not through the productive enterprise of the owner but as the result of public investment and community prosperity.

This policy deserves thorough exploration by civic leaders and authorities on urban law and economics of development. Comprehensive planning of the urban environment is seriously impeded by ineffective land use controls. Their ineffectiveness, according to Robert H. Freilich,

> stems from a supposed constitutional inability to adequately govern the decisions of the private land owner. It is stated to be a constitutional problem limiting the extent of regulatory powers over land use regardless of the political unit which is exercising decision-making authority. The United States has a deep-seated tradition which believes in "absolute" ownership of land. The view that land ownership is "absolute" is, of course, erroneous under American law. All property is held subject to police power, regulations of the State being necessary to preserve the public health, safety, and welfare of the community, a power which is the least limitable and most expansive of all governmental power.[8]

It should be within the power of government to recover that increment of land value that is created by community action through zoning decisions and investment of public funds for capital improvements. Value created by the action of a city council or other governing body in changing a permissible land use from residential to commercial, for example, or the installation of public facilities that enhance the use of property, is unearned by a landowner; it is an increment of value created by public action and should be recovered by the public. Conversely, changes in land use necessary to achieve an improvement of the environment, such as rollback zoning from high to low density of land use, and that result in a reduction of the vested land value, should be accompanied by a compensation to the owner by the public for that increment of lower value. Donald Hagman has referred to the policy as "trading windfalls for wipeouts."[9]

This policy is comparable to the British program of compensation and betterment and, benefiting from the experience in England, both the success and the equity of the policy will depend in large measure on the simplicity of the administrative procedures designed for its implementation. It should be instituted neither as a punitive measure nor as a means to produce revenue. In order to avoid a possible disruption of the land market, it should be implemented in stages.

---

8. Robert H. Freilich and John W. Ragsdale, Jr., *Development Framework Data Report,* Metropolitan Council of Twin City Area, January 1974. See also the *Minnesota Law Review* (58 Minn. L. Rev. 1,009) (1974).

9. "A New Deal: Trading Windfalls for Wipeouts," *Planning,* Association of Planning Officials, September 1974.

Open space in accordance with local standards for parks, playgrounds, and other amenities for built-up districts must be acquired with public funds or special assessment districts. Efforts to preserve open space to enhance the general amenity and enrich the aesthetic quality of a city confront the eternal conflict between the public good and private property rights.

POSSIBILITIES

Buffer Areas

Open space, however, implies more than a street or a neighborhood park or playground. It includes the broad areas of land that separate urban developments from the rural areas. Open space can include regional parks, agricultural land, forested areas, rivers, oceans, lakes, or land masses with dimension adequate to supply breathing requirements in contrast to the congestion of urban development of even the lowest density. Reports indicate that the city of Sochi in the Soviet Union has devoted approximately 70 percent of its land to the protection of open space in the form of forests, parks, recreational areas, and similar uses. The government of Sweden acquired and is holding greenbelts around its major cities to conserve both the quality of urban life and the welfare of the rural hinterland. These greenbelts give form to the urban communities, preserve the air's freshness, and provide areas nearby for the production of foodstuffs.

Cities blessed with hilly terrain within or around them can turn this natural asset into a beautiful urban form, or they can allow it to be chewed up for the homes of status-seekers. We seem to have great difficulty in accepting the fact that the modern city is not the natural habitat of hill dwellers. The site for a medieval castle was not selected for its view, although views of a beautiful countryside were magnificent. The noble's real concern was the observation of approaching enemies, and the compact hill towns that huddled about the castles were built for protection of the inhabitants. Modern city builders generally seek plains and broad valleys for industry, business, transportation, and housing. Lovely hills should be looked at, not cut to ribbons for flatland lots. The undulating ridges and slopes should be preserved. Development should not climb above a 20 percent slope.

Philanthropy rarely extends to gifts of land to enhance the amenities of a city, and political action to restrict development of land for either utility or beauty meets with the claim of "inverse condemnation." But if we intend to halt further destruction of the natural character of our environment, the public and the government must act.

Cherishing the beautiful site of their city along the foothills of the Rocky Mountains, the people of Boulder, Colorado, took action to protect their birthright. Adding to an original 1899 federal grant of 3,000 acres of foothills, donations by enlightened citizens increased their Mountain Parks System. The people of Boulder took the initiative in financing the preservation of open space when potential development threatened the city, as it does other cities. A greenbelt program was approved by referendum in 1967; the people assessed themselves an additional one percent sales and use tax for land acquisition, and the lease or retirement of bonds. A cooperative city-county comprehensive plan encompassed a greenbelt system of parks, recreation, wildlife sanctuaries, and scenic trails. By means of density transfer [10] (compensatory density), open space in planned developments became integral links with the greenbelt. The citizens of Boulder thus have demonstrated that when the people are determined to maintain their environmental assets, they can. Aspen, Colorado, followed suit; so should other cities.

The resolute determination of the people of St. George, Vermont, to maintain the quality of their environment is also instructive. After their population more than tripled in a decade, from 108 in 1960 to 477 in 1970, the people of St. George acted. Recognizing that they must deal with the right to develop land rather than land ownership, St. George required the transfer of development rights for the open space of its lovely environment to the community, to be used for the new village center it planned for the future. [11]

Fearful that "development" would destroy the foothills of the city, Palo Alto, California, undertook a comparative study of open space versus urbanization. The study revealed that the cost of public services for residential development would exceed acquisition cost for preservation as open space. [12] Failing to support a $4 million bond issue for land purchase, the city rezoned the land to minimum lot sizes of ten acres.

The California Office of the Bureau of Land Management has, in cooperation with the city of Palm Springs, prepared plans to preserve a band of desert big horn sheep. By this action, a large open space in mountainous terrain has become a permanent open area to provide a

---

10. The basic density for residential development is four dwelling units per acre. It may increase to six dwelling units per acre with open space thus consolidated to link with the greenbelt.

11. Leonard U. Wilson, "Precedent-Setting Swap in Vermont," *Journal of American Institute of Architects*, March 1974.

12. The professional study was conducted by Livingston and Blayney, Planners, San Francisco, California.

refuge for the endangered species and breathing space for people. Another of the bureau's recent projects is preservation of the great California desert, which was abused by uncontrolled off-road vehicles ranging from motorcycles to dune buggies. Areas are provided for these recreational vehicles, while the more fragile sections are off limits to all but persons on foot or on horseback.

Margins

The most critical areas of our world are the margins, the edges where related conditions require careful planning and decisions to determine the use of land on both sides of a border. In the broadest sense, the relationship between the earth and the space within which it moves requires that we carefully plan our activities not to destroy the protective environment that permits life to continue with a reasonable degree of safety. In more finite situations we have many margins that require special attention and planning if the advantages and disadvantages provided by nature are to be respected.

Perhaps one of the most interesting and challenging margins is where water (oceans, lakes, and streams) meets land. Here, in the past, there has been an almost total disregard of the need for careful planning and nondestructive use. We have placed some of the most obnoxious of industries along the waterfront. We have thrust our sewage and refuse into the waters and polluted them with a reckless abandon. The delightful developments that might have been created at many of these critical and limited areas have been destroyed, as we have literally fouled our nest. In recent years there have been major and costly efforts to restore these margins for recreational uses to the benefit of the residents, not only those close by but also from other regions and the nation as a whole. Los Angeles County began to plan in 1940 for the recovery of its precious ocean frontage. Now, after more than forty years, through local and state funding, a great deal has been acquired for beaches to be enjoyed by the general public.

Another critical margin is that which separates urban areas from the agricultural areas that form the rural environment. In nations where legislative determination through open space zoning for agriculture has been the rule, it is believed to be but a slow-burning fuse to a time bomb that will explode as soon as pressures are placed upon local legislative bodies to change the zoning for more profitable uses for the landowners. Vast areas of productive agricultural land have been converted to urban uses, sometimes—as in the San Jose area of California—by hopscotching and leaving parcels of uneconomically sized agricultural land to wither as they are surrounded by urban development.

Even more dangerous, perhaps, is the unplanned development at the margins of land exposed to great dangers. Some of these dangers are manmade, such as at the edges or upon landfills where dangerous wastes have been disposed of over the years. Developments along the fringes of earthquake faults also constitute an unwarranted ignoring of conditions that could endanger both life and property. Likewise, the edges of areas subject to periodic flooding should be respected.

Many other critical margins provide opportunities for development where conditions could, at one time or another, have significant impact upon humans. These must be defined, understood, and respected in the planning of our urban communities.

Harbors and Seashores

Harbors by their nature have been the locale for industrial and warehousing developments. Unfortunately, these areas of potential open space and scenic attractiveness have become shabby with the neglect often associ-

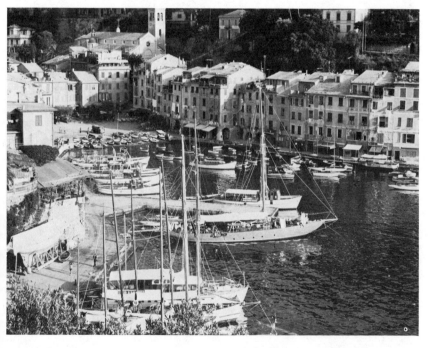

Urban waterfront development—The Harbor, Portofino, Italy. *Serving as seaport on the Mediterranean as well as the town center for a recreational complex, the harbor at Portofino is an attractive, dynamic place for the residents and tourists who gather here at all times of the year.*

San Francisco's waterfront is one of the treasures of the world. The relationship of waterfront areas to the hearts of the cities they serve requires the special concern and planning now being given to the San Francisco area.

ated with the industrial workplace. The visual recreation that should be associated with the activities of the large and small ships and the business of loading and unloading of cargos from far-off places has been overlooked. In some cases, the waterfront has become an unkempt neglected asset. The planned conservation of these limited resources is an essential task for the people of our time.

The seashores and riverfronts are priceless recreational areas wherever they are found in the world. They constitute a limited resource since they are often scattered and in some places inaccessible. The reclaiming of land along these frontages has been a major accomplishment of many European nations as well as America. These special lands have been opened to public use rather than allowing them to remain the private reserve of the few. Millions of people now enjoy swimming, fishing, and boating in the oceans and rivers as a result of state and federal as well as local programs.

Valued Architecture

Many cities have made efforts to preserve buildings that have historical value architecturally. These are the gems of eras past, some showing the flamboyance of their period, others fine detailing and sensitive design. In

NORTH CHINA BASIN AREA

1. CAPITALIZE ON THE AREA'S UNIQUE LOCATION AND ENVIRONMENTAL ATTRIBUTES AND ASSIST IN SATISFYING THE CITY'S HOUSING NEEDS BY CREATING A MIXED INCOME RESIDENTIAL COMMUNITY WITH SUPPORT SERVICES

2. IF NOT NEEDED FOR FUTURE SHIPPING, DEVELOP PIERS 40-46B FOR A PARK AND FULL SERVICE MARINA / SMALL BOAT HARBOR

FERRY BUILDING AREA

1. MAINTAIN THE PHYSICAL PROMINENCE OF THE FERRY BUILDING AND ITS TOWER, RE-ESTABLISH ITS LINKAGE TO MARKET STREET AND ITS FUNCTION AS A TRANSIT CENTER

2. CREATE A MAJOR OPEN SPACE RESOURCE AS A RELIEF TO THE ADJACENT INTENSELY DEVELOPED DOWNTOWN AREA AND PROVIDE MAXIMUM PUBLIC ACCESS TO THE BAY

3. DEVELOP A LIMITED AMOUNT OF COMMERCIAL USES TO GENERATE WEEK-END AND EVENING ACTIVITIES AND REVENUE TO THE PORT

the East, the home of Paul Revere in Boston is but one example of history preserved for future generations to enjoy. In the West, where the structures are relatively young, many of the residences of the 1880s and 1890s are being gathered into centers to form a living museum of the classics of their time.

Architect Philip Johnson once stated that while Europe has its great cathedrals, America has the Grand Central Station. The Supreme Court decision in 1983 that saved the Grand Central Station in New York City from demolition set the stage for the preservation of other fine old structures in many American cities. Even the Pan Am Building that looms above it on Forty-second Street as one looks uptown on Park Avenue has not destroyed the impact that the station has as one views the architecture of the grand facade.

Beautiful natural areas with fine stands of trees, such as the Sequoias in California, are also a part of the natural architecture of our environment; they should be looked upon almost with reverence. While these areas are protected by federal and state laws, encroachment is a constant threat to their survival. A famous man once stated, "When you have seen one of these trees you have seen them all," implying that there was nothing wrong with harvesting some of them for building material.

In the 1970s and 1980s there has been a renaissance of the effort to preserve and restore historical buildings in all parts of the world. The efforts of conservationists have not been limited to natural settings but include as well the classification of buildings worthy of preservation—those that have historical significance even though they may not represent what some purists would call "fine architecture." This is a reflection of the concept that, whereas our historical era is relatively short, it is getting longer each year and, without these evidences of earlier days, we will never have an American past to study and understand.

There must be concerted and continuous effort to preserve our natural and man-made environment if we and our children are to have the pleasure of observing how the world in which we live has developed. We must not turn our backs on our history. We must learn to respect our heritage, for it tells us much about who we are and how we survived to the present.

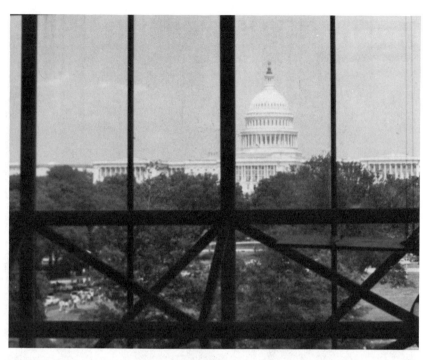

United States Capitol, Washington, D.C.

Four Guardsmen. Sequoia National Park, California. *Courtesy of the National Park Service. U.S. Dept. of the Interior.*

Logging Camp 4. *Wanton destruction of the giant sequoias prior to the designation of the national parks. Courtesy of the National Park Service. U.S. Dept. of the Interior.*

CHAPTER 25

SEISMIC SAFETY

WHEN THE EARTH IS STRAINED TOO FAR [1]

Just what is an earthquake? It is the shaking that occurs when a slowly accumulated strain in the Earth's crust is suddenly released, typically along preexisting fracture lines called faults.

Stress most often builds up in places where parts of the Earth's crust are moving past each other along faults. Scientists believe the crust is actually a number of gigantic plates that are driven by the movement of the underlying convecting mantle. In some places, as along California's San Andreas fault, one plate is slipping horizontally along the edge of another. In others, as along the coast of Peru, one plate is diving beneath another.

Improved zoning is the first and most fundamental step in reducing earthquake damage. The better we get at delineating areas of seismic risk, the better we can decide where to build—not only homes, but schools, hospitals, dams, bridges, high-rise buildings and power plants. Some older buildings can be made more earthquake resistant: houses can be improved, for example, by anchoring the sill to the foundation, adding bracing to supports for floor joists and the load-bearing walls of garages, and strapping the chimney to the house. New buildings can incorporate the latest technology, including shear walls that bend into parallelograms rather than crack when subjected to horizontal force. Gas-, electricity- and water-distribution systems can be made less susceptible to disruption.

---

1. Richard L. Williams, *Smithsonian*, April 1983 and July 1983.

Even knowing that an area will be quake-free for a considerable length of time because it is early in its seismic-gap time period can be an incentive for investment in buildings that need only that much longevity to realize a profit. It may make economic sense to build at a place that has just had an earthquake.

SEISMIC RISKS

A look at a world seismicity map reveals the truly global incidence of earthquakes. Except for Northern Europe, most of the other regions of very low seismicity are largely uninhabited: Greenland, Siberia, Northern Canada, most of Australia, the Amazon basin, the Sahara, and Antarctica.

Most of the great historic architectural styles have occurred in seismic regions, but it does not seem that the architecture that evolved in these areas consciously expresses seismic design principles. The seismic factor has not induced the evolution of indigenous construction forms as sophisticated and effective as the large variety of climatically-determined responses with which we are now familiar.

Much of the explanation for this lies in the fact that the physical characteristics of earthquakes have not been well understood until this century. Prior to this time earthquakes tended to be regarded as acts of God, and proper mitigation measures consisted of prayer rather than architecture and engineering. By the time of the 1906 San Francisco earthquake, the idea that the design of buildings would affect their seismic performance was beginning to be established, and by the 1923 Tokyo earthquake seismic design principles, based primarily on empirical methods, were firmly established. Following the Tokyo disaster the study of earthquake engineering occupied some of the best engineering and geological minds in the world and analytical methods became highly developed.

In the United States research into seismic design was concentrated in California, spurred on by periodic events—Santa Barbara 1925, Long Beach 1933, Kern County 1952—that reminded the public and responsible officials of the seriousness of the problem without, fortunately, providing the impetus of a major disaster.[2]

Two of the most severe earthquakes in the United States did not happen on the West Coast but in the East and Midwest. One was in Charleston, South Carolina, in 1886 and the other was a series of three shocks in New Madrid, Missouri, a small town in the Mississippi River Valley, in 1811 and 1812. The "felt area" was 2 million square miles.

Earthquakes are a national problem. Over 70 million people in the United States live in areas threatened with severe earthquake activity. Another 115 million are exposed to moderate risks. Ground shaking and faulting are not the only hazards connected with earthquakes. Land-

2. Christopher Arnold and Robert Reitherman, *Building Configuration and Seismic Design* (San Mateo, California: Building Systems Development, Inc., 1981).

World seismicity map showing distribution of mid-twentieth-century seismic events.
Christopher Arnold and Robert Reitherman

slides, flooding, and fires that can follow a quake often cause more damage than the quake itself.

Two other activities can take place after an earthquake. First, in locations with a high water table, subsidence resulting from liquefaction, the conversion of earth to a fluid state, can occur. In such areas special foundation structures should be developed to prevent residences from unequal settlement and the fractures that occur. Second, less frequently and only in certain coastal areas, earthquakes can generate a tsunami or the violent wave action often called a tidal wave. In the massive earthquake that struck Japan in 1983, the major damage was the result of the tsunami. Very little can be done to prevent danger to life and property from this type of activity, other than to prevent construction in low-lying areas adjacent to ocean frontal zones.

While new engineering techniques have been developed, especially in Japan, the structures have not as yet been empirically tested with seismic forces of the intensity of those that leveled San Francisco or Tokyo in the early part of this century. Many high-rise buildings, especially in the zones where seismic faults are known to exist, were built without the benefit of the new techniques and safeguards and thus are open to dangers to both life and property. It seems that disregard for the environment allowed public officials to change the regulations related to building heights for the greater profit of a few and risk to the welfare of the many.

The April 1983 earthquakes in Coalinga, California, once again confirmed the danger in codes that permitted structures in critical areas to be built of brick held together with lime mortar and no reinforcement or ties of any type. The miraculous lack of deaths in the midst of structural destruction should serve as a warning of the dangers that could become tragedies of immense proportions, should the same type of seismic action take place in an area of intensive land use and tall buildings or great glass exterior walls—the current fashion in many large cities.

Structural engineers advance the theory that most recent high buildings are adequately designed to withstand a force of eight on the Richter scale. However, they believe that falling glass and masonry would endanger lives outside of the buildings and that most of the interiors would be damaged severely.

THE VALUE OF PARKS

The people of Tokyo learned the value of parks and open spaces at the time of the great earthquake in 1923. They were useful in checking the fires that followed the quakes and also provided space for shelter during the aftermath of the great disaster. After that great earthquake an additional fifty-two small neighborhood parks were planned, laid out in a modern fasion, and opened to the public in a short time.

SEISMIC SAFETY PLANNING

The purpose of seismic safety planning is to protect the health, safety, and general welfare of persons living in areas subject to seismic occurrences. As in all comprehensive planning, it calls for the highest degree of cooperation between the public agencies that would be involved if catastrophic events were to occur and the general public whose safety and welfare would be directly affected. Concerned scientists question the knowledge that planners and civic leaders have about their own communities, and what steps would have to be taken to cut down on injuries, death, and destruction of public and private property.

The following guidelines were developed as part of the Highland Hills Specific Plan for the city of San Bernardino, California, and are based on county standards:[3]

---

3. Prepared by Eisner, Smith and Associates, Planning Consultants, Palm Springs, California, June 1982.

COMMUNITY PLANNING IN EARTHQUAKE PRONE AREA

NATURAL OPEN SPACE

0.6ac.
6-9units

1.6ac.
16-24
units

3.8ac.
38-57units

2.6ac.
26-39
units

8.0ac.
80-120units

6.1ac. 61-92units

2.8ac.

1.8ac.
18-27
units

1.3ac.
13-20
units

4.3ac.
43-65units

7.4ac.
74-111units

28-42
units

.9ac. 59-88units

1.9ac.
19-28
units

IRRIGATED OPEN   SPACE

2.5ac.
25-37
units

2.9ac.
29-44
units

1.3ac.
13-20
units

12.0ac.
120-180units

2.4ac.
24-36
units

3.3ac.
33-50
units

2.1ac.
21-32
units

Recreation
Center

12.1ac.
28 lots

Rec.

2.4ac.
24-36units

8.0ac.
27 lots

Park

7.1ac.
22 lots

SAN ANDREAS FAU

KNOWN FAULT TRA

NORTH   0   200   600   1200

Eisner, Smith and Associates, Palm Springs, California

IMPERIAL COUNTY FAULT MAP

Taken from state geologist's fault map of California.

scale in miles
0 4 8 16 24

Environmental Issues

Objectives	Policies
A. *Seismic Faults* —Minimize risk of seismic damage.	—Prohibit development on the main faults. —Avoid development on faults where possible. —If development straddles a fault ensure no buildings are near the fault. —Provide numerous escape routes from the site. —Specify standards for foundation design.
B. *Liquefaction* —Eliminate the risk of liquefaction.	—Fill over areas prone to liquefaction. —Pump water for irrigation to lower level of water table. —Provide special building foundation design.
C. *Fire Safety* —Minimize fire hazards. —Comply with all city regulations.	—Provide numerous access points to site. —Provide choice of routes to exits (loop street systems). —Landscaped, irrigated greenbelts. —Design streets at 10 percent grade or less. —Minimize 12 percent grades. —Short cul-de-sacs/loop streets where possible.
D. *Flooding* —Eliminate exposure of residential areas to flooding. —Design for containment of 10- and 100-year storms.	—Retain major drainage courses. —Construct debris basin(s) along canyons. —Bridge over major drainage courses to avoid road closures. —Design of curbs, gutters, and culverts to carry 10-year storms in street rights-of-way.
E. *Topography* —Minimize grading. —Respect existing topography and maintain major features. —Balance cut and fill.	—Cluster concept of development using hilltops and valleys. —Preserve hillsides and natural drainage courses where possible. —Blend cut-and-fill slopes with existing topography using contour grading.

Public Facilities Issues

Objectives	*Policies*
F. *Open Space Amenity* —Create a coherent open space system. —Retain natural amenities on the site such as mature trees.	—Retain major drainage courses and existing vegetation. —Cluster concept allows direct visual access to open space for almost all housing units. —Provide community park. —Provide bicycle paths and jogging trails. —Provide recreation amenities in housing area.
G. *Circulation, Access, Traffic Safety* —Provide a coherent circulation system capable of carrying all traffic loads.	—Street system has a simple pattern based on loops and is functionally divided into collectors and local streets.

The outline above indicates the actions that should be considered and implemented prior to a seismic occurrence. The programs essential to dealing with people and property after a major earthquake are still in the study stage. The Seismic Safety Commission of the State of California is deeply involved in the effort to establish the level of coordination essential to care for the needs of residents of an area that has experienced temblors. Funds are being provided by both the federal government and the state to examine the aftermath of earthquakes in both the continental United States and in Japan.

CHAPTER 26

NOISE

Sound is all around us. Some sounds are constant, others intermittent. Some are pleasant, others annoying. Sounds become "noise" when they disturb us, sometimes even causing danger to health and the general welfare. Sounds can be controlled through use of amplifiers or suppressors, natural or electronic.

In the planning of a community it is essential to be aware of the relationship between sound-producing sources and the habitat of people subject to them. This can be accomplished by locating the habitat in an environment free of high intensity sounds, or by providing for acoustical treatment that will reduce the intensity of the sound to a tolerable level.

Some of the principal noise sources in urban development are related to railways running through the heart of a town or city. Freeways have replaced the railroad in the present day. Airplanes, as they approach and take off from airports in major urban centers, cause the greatest threat to health in the areas immediately adjacent to the approaches. Heavy industries, for example foundries, are poor residential neighbors.

All of the worst causes of noise, especially those that result from human decisions, can be tempered. Remedial measures to reduce the impact of existing sources are essential parts of the planning responsibility; good planning for the coming development is crucial.

Highway-related noise can become a violent part of the urban environment. The Chinese city of Shanghai is one of the noisiest in the world. The sound of horns on a variety of motor vehicles, mingling with the sound of bells on the bicycles that compete with pedestrians for the use of limited roadways, results in chaos. Other cities, both in China and in other parts of the world, have regulations prohibiting the use of automobile horns other than in emergencies.

GUIDELINES

The noise element of California state planning law sets forth the following guidelines for all communities in the state. They could well be applied to all cities.

Each county and city shall adopt a noise element, which shall recognize the guidelines adopted by the Office of Noise Control pursuant to the Health and Safety Code, and which quantifies the community noise environment in terms of noise exposure contours for both short- and long-term levels of growth and traffic activity. The noise exposure information shall become a guideline for use in development of the land use element to achieve noise-compatible land use and also to provide baseline levels and noise source identification for local noise ordinance enforcement.

The sources of environmental noise considered in this analysis shall include, but are not limited to, all of the following:

1) Highways and freeways.
2) Primary arterials and major local streets.
3) Passenger and freight on-line railroad operations and ground rapid transit systems.
4) Commercial, general aviation, heliport, helistop, and military airport operations, aircraft overflights, jet engine tests, and all other ground facilities and maintenance functions related to airport operation.
5) Local industrial plants, including, but not limited to, railroad classification yards.
6) Other ground stationary noise sources identified by local agencies as contributing to the community noise environment.

The noise exposure information shall be presented in terms of noise contours expressed in community noise equivalent level (CNEL) or day-night average level (L/dn). CNEL means the average equivalent A-weighted sound level during a twenty-four-hour day, obtained after addition of five decibels to sound levels in the evening from 7 P.M. to 10 P.M. and after addition of ten decibels to sound levels in the night before 7 A.M. and after 10 P.M. L/dn means the average equivalent A-weighted sound level during a twenty-four-hour day, obtained after addition of ten decibels to sound levels in the night before 7 A.M. and after 10 P.M.

The contours shall be shown in minimum increments of five db and shall continue down to sixty db. For areas deemed noise sensitive, including, but not limited to, areas containing schools, hospitals, rest homes, long-term medical or mental care facilities, or any other land-use areas deemed

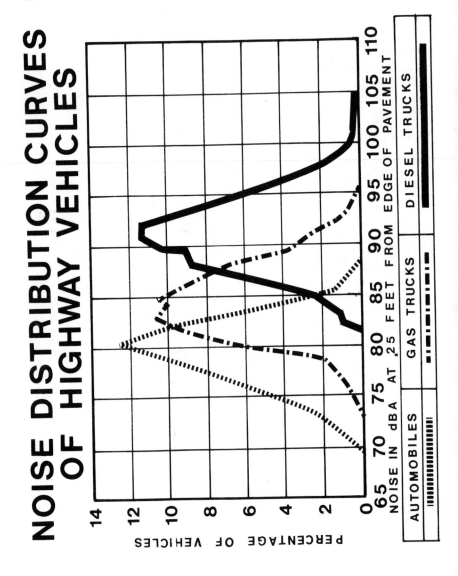

noise sensitive by the local jurisdiction, the noise exposure shall be determined by monitoring.

A part of the noise element shall also include the preparation of a community noise exposure inventory, current and projected, which identifies the number of persons exposed to various levels of noise throughout the community.

The noise element shall also recommend mitigating measures and possible solutions to existing and foreseeable noise problems.

The state, local, or private agency responsible for the construction, maintenance, or operation of those transportation, industrial, or other commercial facilities specified in paragraph (2) shall provide to the local agency producing the general plan, specific data relating to current and projected levels of activity and a detailed methodology for the development of noise contours given this supplied data, or they shall provide noise contours as specified in the foregoing statements.

Freeway Noise Abatement

Where freeways are planned or where they exist in urban areas, high masonry walls are being constructed to reduce the sounds created by large numbers of motor vehicles, especially when the freeways carry trucks and other diesel prime movers.

As in the case of the freeways, many new industrial plants are being designed in a manner that prevents the noises associated with their operations from passing into the outside atmosphere. Some plants, like those in Palo Alto, California, are not only noise free but are set back and landscaped, making them good neighbors in any residential area.

PART 5

IMPLEMENTATION

This is not inflaming or exaggerating
matters, but trying them by those
feelings and affections which nature justifies, and without which
we should be incapable of
discharging the social duties of life, or enjoying
the felicities of it.

Thomas Paine, COMMON SENSE

CHAPTER 27

THE IMPLEMENTATION PROCESS

DEFINITION

Implementation means carrying a plan through to action. Thus the implementation of a proposed plan presumes that the initial political action that made its preparation possible will also make its utilization equally possible. Therefore the first step is the enabling legislation that spells out the responsibilities of the action agencies and the scope of the work to be accomplished. Following this, there must be funding of the activities or construction to permit local personnel to carry out the given goals and objectives.

GOALS AND OBJECTIVES

Sometimes goals and objectives are viewed as similar, but in the implementation process they should be differentiated. The goals are set in the long-range comprehensive plan. The objectives are the short-range action programs to be accomplished when a time limit is placed on one or more elements of the long-range plan, and which involve the preparation of budgets for the physical improvement of the community. These are capital improvements, and they involve those structures or equipment that have a relatively long life, such as public buildings, fire and police vehicles, park equipment, and similar facilities that are costly, must be anticipated in advance, and must be in accordance with the long-term guidelines of the comprehensive plan.

POLITICAL TYPES

Implementation involves participation in several types of political action on administrative, legislative, and citizen-action levels. Laws must be prepared by legal advisors and are subject to public hearings before planning commissions and legislative bodies. Once approved, they enable the development of either social programs or programs of construction for physical improvements. The actions that implement such developments may be described as:

Permissive. The preparation and adoption of laws or ordinances that will permit or encourage the development of plans or programs.

Directive. The actions by the legislative authority that permit the first stages of a program to be initiated and define the scope of the work to be accomplished.

Supportive. The arrangement of the financial programs through the budgeting process to permit the projects or programs to become a reality.

Active. The launching of a social or economic program; the construction of a building; the acquisition of goods and services; the acquisition of land for open space or other essential purposes.

All of the several activities involved in implementation require extensive planning based upon research and analysis of the community's needs and potentials.

THE COMPREHENSIVE PLAN

The most important aspect of the implementation process is that it is based on the comprehensive plan. It fits into the overall structural framework of that document and the carefully analyzed financial capabilities of the community as well.

As the overview of the future of the community, the comprehensive plan must contain a wide range of projects, to be added or subtracted from as time and circumstances warrant. Its very nature implies that it cannot be implemented in total in a short period of time. The plan contemplates changes and additions to accommodate growth, and this implies in turn that the plan should contain a carefully defined program for implementation of those timely parts capable of being financed in the first phase of the growth period.

In the past there has been the implicit common understanding that the state or federal government would offer assistance to meet emergencies when the local communities did not have the resources to accomplish what was essential. Changes in the decade of the 1980s make this assumption subject to reexamination.

When local communities did not have the funds necessary to perform the essentials associated with the mandated portions of the comprehensive plan and/or local attitudes mitigated against federal assistance, all too often they would find a way to comply with the letter of the law but hardly its intent. An "as is" plan would be prepared that merely rounded off the corners of the zoning map and showed existing facilities such as schools and parks and existing streets and highways. By then placing the title "Comprehensive Plan" on the map, the community appeared to abide by the law. Few of these communities ever prepared a report or followed up with the programming of essential improvements.

The Budget

The most important ingredient in the financing of community programs is the preparation of the budget. How much money will be needed? What are the sources for the funds? Will they be derived from local taxes, private sources, from state or federal grants or loans?

Following the estimates of cost and potential sources of income comes the preparation of a phasing scenario in which the projects are arranged in order of importance within the financial schedule.

FEDERAL ASSISTANCE

Since all parts of a nation constitute a federation, whether in the United States or elsewhere in the world, it is understandable that economic and other assistance can be advanced by the central power to its several integral entities when local conditions warrant. The vast differences that exist physically, socially, and psychologically in the several regions make some national concern essential for the less fortunate elements in the federation. Historically, governments have come to the aid of communities in times of emergency or disaster. Sometimes, through foreign aid, this assistance has been advanced to far-off parts of the world. It is thus not surprising that hopes for the abatement of the crisis in housing and community development should include the extension of the hand of the federal government, making changes and improvements possible that strengthen the fiber of the entire federal structure.

While many of the visible portions of the federal assistance programs are in the field of housing and highway construction, it is important to recognize that other aspects of the community physical improvement are also aided. Through incentives and direct financial subsidies to both local communities and private corporations, federal aid makes possible the

Examples of Tools for Implementing the General Plan

Corporate Powers (Acquisition and Development)

- Construction of streets, roads, and water and sewage treatment facilities
- Acquisition and development of parks
- Acquisition of sites for low- and moderate-income housing
- Purchase of development rights and scenic easements
- Establishment of policies governing the timing of improvements to public services
- Creation of development corporations

Others

- Redevelopment
- Intergovernmental coordination
- Public information
- Data management
- Monitoring
- Cooperative arrangements with the private sector

Police Powers (Regulatory)

- Specific plans
- Zoning:

  Open-space zoning
  Environmental hazard zoning
  Inclusionary zoning
  Planned unit development zoning

- Subdivision regulation
- Park dedication requirements
- School dedication requirements
- Review and regulation of public works
- Housing and building regulation
- Code enforcement
- Environmental review procedures
- Design review

California State Guidelines for Implementing the General Plan.[1]

development of sewage treatment plants, water supply systems, and programs involving nuclear, wind, solar, and geothermal energy.

In addition to financial assistance for physical improvements, the federal government grants aid to states—and through the states to the communities—in support of social programs that include education, welfare, and other activities that require funding beyond the abilities of the local entities to provide. Some federal grants of aid are made directly to local communities.

The government's power to tax on a broad national basis provides the economic base for the assistance where great need exists. Legislators in the Congress are always interested in providing programs for their home

---

1. State of California Planning, Zoning and Development Laws, 1982. Office of Planning Research, Sacramento, California.

districts as one means of representing their constituency—and, in the long run, of getting reelected.

Recent Conditions

Many of the federal financial assistance programs that helped local communities to improve their physical conditions have, since 1980, had their budgets either eliminated or reduced materially. Not only did the programs for modernization of water storage, distribution lines, and sewage treatment plants fall by the wayside, but support for other programs dealing with redevelopment and the public health and education were substantially reduced. These were, in most cases, essential and worthwhile as sound expenditures of the revenues collected by the federal government from the very people that the programs served.

FINANCING URBAN RENEWAL

When certain economic conditions became critical in the 1980s, the newly elected administration cut many features dealing with urban renewal out of the budget. The government indicated to local communities that if they desired to continue the rebuilding process, to all intents and purposes they would have to devise means to do it on their own. Various devices were utilized to overcome the financial shortfall resulting from local taxation limitations. Fees, extractions, and charges for services and licenses were all increased to permit the essential services to be provided. Tax increment financing was conceived as a device that would provide an effective means of meeting the challenge of reduced federal activity in the redevelopment programs.

Lyle Alton Stewart, a planning consultant in Oregon, prepared the following description of the techniques involved, based upon his experiences on the west coast of the United States and in Canada and Mexico. The material was prepared to illustrate to the communities he advised how the program would work and what the benefits would be. Regardless of the local political attitudes toward redevelopment, this program is being widely used in small communities as well as in large cities, and is a useful tool wherever implemented.

Tax Increment Financing of Redevelopment Indebtedness[2]

Blighted areas of our urban communities have less dollar worth than do the nonblighted parts. All other factors being equal, the more severe the blight, the less the value. It also follows that a blighted area demands

---

2. Lyle Alton Stewart, Planning Consultant, Medford, Oregon, 1980.

greater services at greater public cost than the area generates in its proportionate share of property taxes. In the private sector this negative relationship of value to cost would be considered as bad economics and programs would be initiated immediately to reverse and correct the problems. In correcting this problem, most people in our society would feel that the private sector is acting responsibly. Should government be any less responsive to these negative relationships?

For decades local governments either ignored the existence of blight within their jurisdictions or were willing to subsidize the added public services required of them. Few communities on their own were able to set aside the funds necessary to rehabilitate or redevelop these deteriorated areas. It was apparent to those close to the problem that adequate funding sources had to be found or created that would allow the problem-solving process to begin.

New Legislation

Some states enacted new legislative conditions that permitted the local communities to utilize devices such as "tax abatement" and tax increment bonding that allowed freezing of taxes in areas where growth or change was anticipated, through natural causes, renewal, or revitalization, to thus permit additional taxes generated by the new uses to be utilized to amortize the bonds issued to pay for the renewal program.

Local government with approved redevelopment (urban renewal) plans were provided with federal loans and grants in amounts related to their population. Communities with 50,000 or less population could receive funding assistance up to three-quarters of the costs of correcting the causes of blight within a given redevelopment project. The maximum federal financial assistance available to communities with a population of more than 50,000 was set at two-thirds of the project's cost.

Based on these funding formulae, local governments in states whose legislatures enacted appropriate enabling legislation were able to evoke the redevelopment process and begin eliminating the physical blight that was placing a heavy burden on their general funds. Even with significant levels of federal financial involvement, local governments—particularly the smaller ones—encountered substantial fiscal difficulty in generating their one-quarter or one-third share.

To further complicate the funding problems facing local government in implementing redevelopment plans, the federal government's passage of the Housing Act of 1974, which created the Community Development Block Grant program, reduced the funds available to local governments to undertake and complete long-term redevelopment projects.

While the CDBG program is of considerable value to local governments, federal funding for classical redevelopment projects of the types undertaken during the fifties and sixties is no longer available. Cities and counties are substantially on their own and dependent on the willingness of their people and respective state legislatures to enact laws that will allow them to generate the requisite funding to undertake meaningful redevelopment activities. State statutes that authorize the use of tax increment financing are one type of such law. Thirty-six percent of the fifty states have such increment enabling laws and several other states are actively trying to enact such laws.

The concept found favor with a majority of members of the California legislature and in 1951 they amended their State Community Redevelopment Law to allow for the division of ad valorem taxes (tax increment) in approved redevelopment projects. Thus another important tool to aid in the financing of redevelopment projects was born.

The state of Oregon was the second to adopt similar legislation. The concept of tax increment financing required an amendment of the state's constitution before their legislature could pass enabling legislation. In 1959 the people of Oregon approved Article IX, Section 1c of the constitution, which reads:

> *Financing redevelopment and urban renewal projects.* The Legislative Assembly may provide that the ad valorem taxes levied by any taxing unit, in which is located all or part of an area included in a redevelopment or renewal project, may be divided so that the taxes levied against any increase in the true cash value, as defined by law, of property in such are obtaining after the effective date of the ordinance or resolution approving the redevelopment or urban renewal plan for such area, shall be used to pay any indebtedness incurred for the redevelopment or urban renewal project. The legislature may enact such laws as may be necessary to carry out the purposes of this section.

Eighteen states currently provide some form of tax increment financing as an integral part of their redevelopment enabling laws. Historically, tax increment financing has been limited for use only in retiring the public indebtedness incurred in implementing redevelopment plans. However, in more recent times, and as a result of local governments' interest in expanding their economic development capability, tax increment financing is being considered as a potential method of financing the needed infrastructure required to attract job-producing businesses and industries. In most states, however, to broaden the use of tax increment financing would require voter approval of state constitutional amendments as well as appropriate action by their legislatures. With a definite public interest in tax limiting measures beginning with Proposition 13 in California, the broadening of the use of tax increment financing is by no means an automatic procedure.

While there are variables in the several state tax increment provisions, the concept as originally conceived by the California legislature is basic to all of them.

When a redevelopment or urban renewal plan—the terms have identical meaning—is officially adopted, the tax assessor for the jurisdiction is required to certify the taxable assessed value, based on the tax roll last equalized, for the property encompassed by the redevelopment plan. This value is usually referred to as the "base year assessed value" or the "frozen assessed value."

All taxing agencies that receive ad valorem tax proceeds from this base year assessed value will continue to receive income based on the equation:

$$\text{Tax Rate} \times \text{Base Assessed Value} = \text{Tax Proceeds}$$

During the period in which the division of ad valorem taxes (tax increment) is operative, the annual tax rate may increase or decrease in any subsequent year but the base assessed value will remain "frozen" throughout the life of the tax increment process.

In the years beyond the base year there usually is an increase in the assessed value of the redevelopment area resulting from a variety of renewal activities implemented. This increase in assessed value (above that of the base year) is referred to as incremental assessed value. The ad valorem taxes (tax increment) realized from this increased assessed value is calculated as follows:

$$\text{Tax Rate} \times \text{Incremental Assessed Value} = \text{Tax Increment Proceeds}$$

These tax increment proceeds are transferred to the agency charged with implementing the redevelopment plan to be used to retire debts incurred in the implementation process. Most state laws limit the agencies' right to receive these annual tax increment proceeds only when there is a legal debt to be serviced or retired. It follows then that an agency, with no indebtedness, cannot collect the proceeds, place them in an interest-bearing account, and use the accumulated fund at some future date. Indebtedness incurred by the agency may be in any legal form including loans, advances, notes, tax allocation bonds, contracts for services, construction contracts, etc.

Most states (including California and Oregon) have included provisions in their enabling laws that require the redevelopment plan or reports on the plan to state a maximum sum of tax increment proceeds to be collected, to estimate the time which the tax increment process will run, and to estimate the impact on the tax rates, taxing bodies, and the taxpayer.

In California, Proposition 13 fixed the tax rate at one percent of the assessed value. As such, the tax increment process has no effect on the tax rate. Prior to Proposition 13, tax increment proceeds that were diverted to the redevelopment agencies were subtracted from the various taxing agency's annual tax income. In Oregon, to generate the tax increment, the tax rate is increased by an amount necessary to produce the tax increment proceeds. Other states have subtle differences, but the Oregon and California procedures are in wide use in the eighteen states that allow tax increment financing.

To illustrate how the tax increment process functions, the following example illustrates the one in Oregon, where the tax increment process was in place for thirteen years (1962–1975). During the thirteen-year period the assessed value increased from a frozen base assessed value of $11.0 million in 1962 to $140 million in 1975—an increase of $129 million. The figure illustrates the continued growth in the project area to fiscal 1984–85, where the assessed value is estimated to reach $275 million. The tax rate in 1962–63 was approximately $23.00 per $1,000 of assessed value. The taxes produced that year and distributed to all applicable taxing agencies was $253,000 ($23 × $11,000). In 1975–76, the last tax increment year, the tax rate was $24.50 per $1,000 of assessed value. The following calculations illustrate how the tax proceeds are distributed. Taxes distributed to all taxing agencies based on the frozen base assessed value of $11.0 million was:

$$\$24.50 \times \$11,000 = \$269,500$$

Tax increment proceeds dedicated to the urban renewal agency were based on an incremental assessed value of $129.0 million ($140.0 million − $11.0 million).

$$\$24.50 \times \$129,000 = \$3,160,500$$

The $3,160,500 in tax increment proceeds for fiscal year 1975–76 was used by the urban renewal agency to retire all outstanding indebtedness in conjunction with implementing the urban renewal plan.

Following is a table that, based on a variety of developer and redeveloper commitments if the blighted conditions were corrected, illustrates the expected annual increase in assessed value and the resulting tax increment flow calculated at one percent per year of the incremental assessed value:

Fiscal Year	Annual Assessed Value Increase	Annual Tax Increment Proceeds
1980–81	0	Base Year
1981–82	$ 11,000,000	$ 110,000
1982–83	22,700,800	227,000
1983–84	35,102,500	351,020
1984–85	48,242,500	482,420
1989–90	229,597,000	2,295,970
1994–95	425,970,000	4,259,700
2000–01	555,350,000	5,553,550
Totals (20 years)		$55,844,060

In this project, the redevelopment plan contains a provision that the maximum tax increment proceeds that will be collected will not exceed $55,200,000. The difference between the plan stated maximum and the total collected amount of $55,844,060 is $644,060. The tax increment process is estimated to be terminated in fiscal year 2000–01 and the surplus $644,060 over the maximum authorized amount of tax increment would be prorated back to the several affected taxing agencies.

It will be observed that in twenty years the redevelopment process is estimated to have stimulated an increase in the assessed value of $555,350,000. The total assessed value of $687,247,510 ($131,897,510 + $555,350,000) then will be available to all of the taxing agencies.

THE SPECIFIC PLAN

A specific plan can best be described as a bridge or link between the comprehensive plan and individual development proposals. Since 1965, California state law has authorized cities and counties to prepare and adopt specific plans. Such plans often combine zoning regulations, capital improvement programs, detailed development standards, and other regulatory elements into one document that can be tailored to meet the needs of the specific area. The size of an area to be included in a specific plan may vary considerably.

Individuals requesting approval of a specific plan on their property would finance its preparation through an agreement with the community. If the community initiated the plan, state law allows reimbursement through an assessment district, a "per unit" or "per acre" fee, or a similar prorated fee based on the benefit received.

The specific plan has several advantages to both the community and developers. For example, processing time for tentative maps, zone

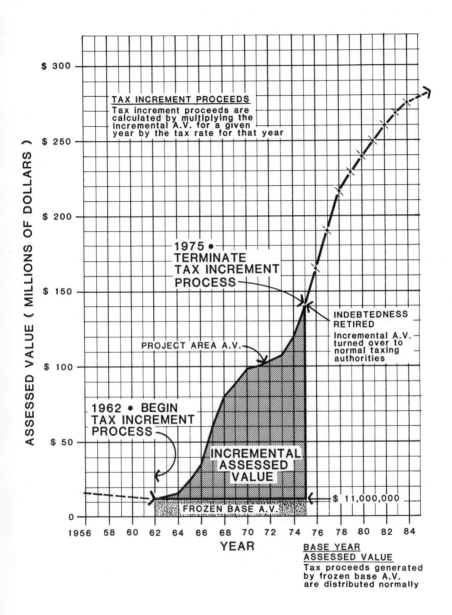

Lyle Alton Stewart, Planning Consultant, AICP, APA

changes, and environmental review can be reduced significantly. In fact, the San Bernardino County ordinance states that:

> Residential projects proposed on a property having an adopted Specific Plan for which an environmental impact report (EIR) has been certified, shall not require additional environmental documentation provided the community Environmental Review Committee finds:
>
> 1. that the certified EIR is sufficiently detailed in scope regarding the proposed project, and
> 2. that the project is consistent with the Specific Plan.
>
> The Environmental Review Committee may issue a Notice of Exemption if the two findings are made.

Also, a developer's uncertainty about whether a project will be approved is lessened since the community, in adopting the specific plan, sets priorities for appropriate land uses, size, and location of public improvements. Thus a developer knows from the outset how best to approach, design, and present a project to take the greatest advantage of the area.

IMPLEMENTATION PROBLEMS

The implementation of a land-use plan requires that government and the private sector have a reasonably similar view of the future. This presupposes that the comprehensive plan has been prepared on a rational basis and decisions have been made without collusion with special-interest groups. If the comprehensive plan is followed up with sound growth management (the timely meeting of people and the facilities that they require), then development can be readily implemented.

However, in many areas of the country long-range planning is still considered only a guide for future growth, to be respected if the politicians see fit and to be disregarded if short-range personal gain is considered paramount. In the latter case development will be uncontrolled, and the decisions on the land use will be made on the basis of momentary advantages to the landowner with little concern for long-term cost of services and inconvenience to residents at large.

Perhaps the most important obstacle to appropriate plan implementation exists in the political process that permits the plan to be amended without sound reason or ignores the plan as though it did not have a definitive role in producing compatible development. A major problem with many plans is that there is no schedule for their development. The past lack of growth management techniques has created plans that are not chronologically and sequentially phased. There was no sound basis for the extension and installation of the infrastructure, and thus there was no indication of where, how, or when the community could implement the plan.

Public Opposition

Objections by citizens' groups often will delay or halt the implementation of portions of a plan. For example, changes in a zone to permit a shopping facility can bring out residents to oppose the facility because it will be incompatible with their concept of their area. Residents of Montecito, California, objected strongly to including such facilities in their hillside areas. They did not mind traveling on narrow streets to obtain convenience items, preferring the travel problems to the danger, as they saw it, of the intrusion of commercial uses and the possibility that these uses might spread to further depreciate their rather pristine properties.

In Arcadia, California, tremendous local opposition was registered to the development of a regional shopping center. Local opposition was overcome when a citywide referendum on the matter indicated that the residents in areas away from the site supported the proposal. The matter was decided on political grounds even though the site was admirably suited for the project insofar as strategic location was concerned. However, the shopping center did present the problem of heavy traffic, so special traffic and aesthetic design features were initiated to protect the area.

CHAPTER 28

THE ZONING PLAN

PRECISE PLANS

The comprehensive plan sets the basic policies for development of the city, the general relation between the various land uses—residential, commercial, and industrial. In brief, it forms the framework of the urban structure. From time to time this general framework is translated into precise plans that specify the zoning for land use, streets and highways, mass transit, recreation and conservation, subdivision expansion, utilities, railways and airports, civic centers, schools, and urban redevelopment. These precise plans interpret the basic policies reflected in the comprehensive plan and serve to adjust it to new situations and conditions as they arise.

The plans serve a dual function. On the one hand, they define the standards for development of the city, the standards of population density, the design of the circulation system, and the amount and location of open space and physical facilities for business and residence. On the other hand, they provide a program for development, establish a basis of timing proposed improvements in the city, the location, design, and installation of utilities, schools, parks, the extension of subdivision development, and the redevelopment of blighted areas. In this way the need for public improvements may be linked with the ability to finance such

438

improvements and maintain a coordinated pace with expansion of private development.

These functions presume continuous attention to the process of urban planning. A comprehensive plan that collects dust in the archives of the city hall is a monument on the grave of lost opportunities in urban improvement. Planning involves an entire process that anticipates the needs of a community, proposes ways and means for the satisfaction of these needs, and relates these proposals to the orderly development of the city through the realization of the comprehensive plan. The precise plans are the action-oriented instruments with which these functions are performed.

ZONING DEFINED

Zoning is the legal regulation of the use of land. It is an application of the police power for the protection of the public health, welfare, and safety. The regulations include provisions for the use of property and limitations on the shape and bulk of buildings that occupy the land. The law comprises two parts: the ordinance in which the regulations are defined, and the zoning map that delineates the districts within which the provisions of the ordinance apply.

For all too many years zoning has been considered planning. The zoning map was seen as the "grand plan" for the community when it fact it was a generalization of existing conditions, freezing them into a format that reflected only the past and frequently thoughtless individual desires of influential property owners supported by their political friends.

The zoning plan is neither a substitute nor an alternative for the comprehensive plan. The latter expresses the basic policies that shape the community character and the general land use, while the former establishes the specific limitations that apply to land use as one of the instruments for achieving the goals set forth in the comprehensive plan. A guide for urban development, the comprehensive plan is usually adopted as a resolution by the legislative body. The zoning plan is adopted as a legal ordinance with penalties associated with violations.

Is It Necessary?

Many people believe that zoning or any public regulation of the use of land is not only unnecessary but unconstitutional. In their opinion zoning has a detrimental effect on the development process. They would substitute the free market process, in which economic forces at any time determine what is the best use for a given parcel of land.

Often cited as an example of a city without zoning is Houston, Texas. Not mentioned, however, are the many land use regulations that affect the free use of land in that city, such as the 10,000 deed restrictions and regulations enforced by residents' associations that cover two-thirds of the city. The deed restrictions are applied in a fragmented manner, and there is the potential for unfortunate changes after the effective period has expired. Nonetheless, the major difference between them and zoning seems to be only that the regulations are applied by a private local body to a local area instead of by official governmental institutions on a city-wide basis.

The question remains improperly posed and unanswered. While there may be no real legal problems at this time in Houston, there may still be tests of the reasonableness of the deed restrictions when they are at a point near termination and the participating property owners start expressing opinions that may not have legal precedent and thus be supportable in a court of law.

Over the years zoning has been an accepted means of regulating the use of land, not only in the United States but also in almost every nation of the world. In some countries the democratic processes involved in the United States are not observed, the government making land use decisions and applying them as it sees fit. Planning in these countries is in many cases arbitrary, expressing only the will of a few in the administration.

Criteria

The validity of the zoning ordinance has been subjected to several court tests; the decisions have generally supported the following criteria:

- The plan (ordinance and map) shall be comprehensive.
- The same regulations shall apply to all districts having similar zone classifications.
- The plan shall demonstrate protection of health, welfare, and safety.
- There shall be neither discrimination nor capricious intent in the plan.
- Administration of the ordinance shall be reasonable and free from arbitrary decisions.

ELEMENTS OF A TYPICAL ZONING ORDINANCE

A. The Text
   Intent and purpose
   Definitions
   Delineation of zones
   Schedules for decisions

PROCEDURES FOR ALTERATIONS

Complications inevitably arise in the administration of zoning, and procedures must be provided to cope with them. These situations may involve natural or manmade conditions of the land, unusual demands not evident when the ordinance was adopted, or developments in which the exacting limitations of zoning do not accommodate reasonable latitude for the adoption of new ideas. Some examples follow.

Density Transfer. In cases where there are reasonably large land-holdings that contain areas where flooding or other potential dangers exist, some zoning ordinances provide for the overall transfer of the permitted densities from the endangered land to safe locations. This process becomes a useful planning device when the endangered land can become a valuable open space or a recreational area during periods of low danger. It is often recommended that the land be either deeded to the community for permanent open space, in which case the owners enjoy a tax benefit, or that it be dedicated as permanent open space, in which case the land remains in private ownership subject to the requirement that it remain open in perpetuity or at least until such time as the dangerous conditions are mitigated to public satisfaction. In the development of the Indian Bend Wash in Scottsdale, Arizona, this technique was used to provide open space without cost either to the community or the property owners. The owner is permitted the same number of dwelling units or commercial intensities on the remaining land that he would have been permitted if the transaction had not taken place.

The Zone Change or Amendment. The most frequent alterations occur when property owners request a change for the classification of their properties from one zoning district to another, usually for the purpose of enjoying greater economic values. Changes on the zoning map should be made only when such changes conform to the comprehensive plan. Otherwise they may, while being beneficial to an individual, be detrimental and costly to the community in terms of their effects on utilities and public facilities.

Amendments to the text of the ordinance are also made quite often. These amendments include changes in terminology; inclusion or deletion of certain uses; changes in standards, either raising or lowering them; and changes in procedures.

Regardless of whether the map or the text is modified, the procedure requires public hearings and discussions prior to any changes becoming effective. The procedure is generally identical with that required for the adoption of the original ordinance.

The Zoning Variance. A variance is a permission granted as relief from some specific and unusual hardship imposed by the strict interpretation of the ordinance. It is a means to adjust the property development standards of the ordinance that, by reason of location, topography, shape, or size, are impossible to comply with. The variance permits a property owner to use his land at the same intensity allowed to others in the same zone; however, it should not allow uses not permitted in the zone. Being readily subject to discriminatory administration and unsound planning, the variance is perhaps the most abused of all zoning procedures. It is not intended to be an alternative to spot zoning or a device to circumvent the intent of the ordinance by a grant of special privilege, nor is it proposed as a means to solve personal problems. The following advice by a high state court in its review of a case involving rezoning brings the issue into clear focus:

We feel impelled to express briefly our view of the proper theory of zoning as relates to the making of changes in an original comprehensive ordinance. We think the theory is that after the enactment of the original ordinance there should be a continuous or periodic study of the development of property uses, the nature of population trends, and the commercial and industrial growth, both actual and prospective. On the basis of each study changes may be made intelligently, systematically, and according to a coordinated plan designed to promote zoning objectives. An examination of the multitude of zoning cases that have reached this court leads us to the conclusion that the common practice of zoning agencies, after the adoption of the original ordinance, is simply to wait until some property owner finds an opportunity to acquire a financial advantage by devoting his property to a use other than that for which it is zoned, and then struggle with the question of whether some excuse can be found for complying with his request for a rezoning. The result has been that in most of the rezoning cases reaching the courts there has actually been spot zoning, and the courts have upheld or invalidated the change according to how flagrant the violation of the true zoning principles has been. It is to be hoped that in the future zoning authorities will give recognition to the fact that an essential feature of zoning is *planning*.[1]

---

1. *Fritts v. City of Ashland*, Court of Appeals of Kentucky, 348 S.W. 2d 712 (June 16, 1961); quoted in *Zoning Digest*, American Society of Planning Officials, October 1961.

Conditional Use Permit. There are occasions when a special use is necessary for the welfare of a community but not permitted within the applicable zone. Permission for such uses may be granted by the conditional use permit. Unlike the variance, evidence of unusual hardship in the development of a property is not required. The permit is for the purpose of meeting a special need of the community based on evidence that the proposed location will serve this special purpose. Protection from adverse effects on abutting property must be assured, and measures for this must be included in the permit. As with the variance, the conditional use permit is not a substitute for rezoning. It is designed to meet a special situation in the public interest; it is not a device by which a new use may be indiscriminately introduced within an established zoning district. The zoning ordinance does not usually provide for a variety of sharply defined uses within a district, and the permit offers a degree of flexibility in adjusting to new demands within the framework of the ordinance.

There remains a difference of opinion on the manner in which a conditional use permit should be granted. Some authorities hold it to be essentially an administrative decision at the discretion of the planning commission. Others contend that it should be subject to approval by the legislative body. It is generally agreed that the ordinance should clearly stipulate the circumstances and indicate the areas under which conditional use permits may be granted as a protection to investors in property.

Administrative Committees. Zoning ordinances contain a variety of provisions, compliance with which may require some form of review and approval. Among these may be the location and size of signs or engineering and architectural design and arrangement. The ordinance may therefore provide for administrative committees vested with the responsibility and authority to pass upon plans subject to these provisions. Such committees are particularly effective when both public officials and lay persons comprise their membership.

ZONING DISTRICTS

In the zoning plan the community is divided into districts in which the land is restricted to certain classified uses. The size, shape, and location of these districts reflect the major uses indicated by the comprehensive plan and should be formed to invite the natural development of neighborhoods. The comprehensive plan may indicate an area to be appropriate for single-family dwellings, whereas the zoning plan may permit a commercial use within specified limits to be developed as a shopping center and contribute to the neighborhood quality of the area. A site for a school and a park may also be provided within such an area. Such developments of the precise plans are refinements of the general plan, their purpose being the creation of balanced community design.

Most zoning ordinances provide for different densities of population in different districts. One residential district may permit only single-family houses with a density of five families per acre, whereas another district may permit "unlimited multiple residential" use in which the density can reach hundreds of people per acre. These variations must be reflected in other precise plans for the city since they affect the provisions of all community facilities and services. The size and location of schools, commercial land use and transportation, police and fire protection, and the size of utility services vary considerably with the number of people to be served.

The land use categories that follow are among the major districts that may appear in the zoning ordinance. Their classification will differ in various communities. Local customs and requirements will determine the definition of each classification.

Open Land

This classification of open land districts, though not included in most ordinances, applies to areas in which the public interest requires the prohibition or restriction of urbanization to protect or enhance the reasonable growth and development of the community. Open land districts may include areas of particular scenic or historic importance, areas too steep to be built upon, areas subject to flooding, and areas where water and sanitary facilities or police and fire protection cannot be provided without excessive cost to the community.

Agricultural

Areas designated as agricultural districts permit the use of land consistent with economically feasible agricultural enterprise, the subdivision of land being governed by the type of agriculture normal to the area. Those about some urban areas may establish minimum lot areas of forty, twenty, ten, five, and two acres, while others include one-acre lots. Uses considered generally permissible include farming, poultry raising, dairying, and cattle and horse grazing. Restricted residential uses may also be permitted, provided the agricultural uses are not adversely affected. Hog raising may be prohibited in some agricultural zones because it is generally interpreted as an obnoxious use. There are usually provisions in the zoning ordinance for exceptions by special permit if an investigation of the particular situation demonstrates no prospect of endangering the general welfare.

Estate

Estate districts are sometimes created with a variety of lot sizes and thus provide property owners the opportunity to establish the character of a residential development of large-sized lots. Such a district can be used to establish a rural quality in some suburban developments. Some agricultural uses are frequently permitted, like poultry raising for domestic consumption or the keeping of saddle horses. This is generally the most restricted residential zone, the minimum lot sizes ranging from 20,000 to 40,000 square feet or more in area. The districts are usually established at the behest of property owners or developers desiring to attract clientele who want reasonably large tracts protected from the infiltration of small-lot subdivision. Other factors sometimes warrant the establishment of estate zones: it may be advisable to limit the population in an area when facilities for sewage disposal are absent or limited, where police and fire protection are not readily available, or community facilities such as schools or commercial districts are remotely situated.

Single Family

In single-family districts land use is restricted to a single dwelling unit per lot. The ordinance establishes a minimum lot area permitted in these zones and frequently specifies the minimum lot width. The standards vary considerably; some cities still permit lot widths of twenty-five feet street frontage, but a width of sixty feet or more is accepted in most communities as the minimum, with a minimum lot area of 6,000 square feet. Such restrictions are not retroactive, and property owners are not obliged to comply with area and lot size regulations enacted subsequent to the recording of subdivisions with lesser restrictions.

The sanctity of the original concept of the single-family home as the residence of a nuclear family is not sustainable. Based on numerous court decisions, it is apparent that a community can regulate what may be placed on a lot and what the population density may be, but not who shall constitute that density of population. In other words, the definition of "family" no longer seems to mean only those people related by blood or marriage.

Two Family

The two-family district classification has been rather generously used in the past to permit the "duplex" type of dwelling, i.e., two dwelling units within a single structure. With the increasing use of density control rather than classification of building type, a provision specifying the density, such as a minimum lot area per dwelling unit, is more equitable than a limitation of two dwellings per lot. Application of a uniform density provision offers a desirable flexibility for lots of varying size, rather than freezing the limitation regardless of the lot area.

Multiple Family

Any residential district in which more than a single one-family dwelling is permitted to occupy a single lot is a multiple-family district. A gradation of dwelling unit densities is usually provided within this classification.

Medium Density

The "medium" permitted in medium-density districts will be quite different in a great city than in a small town. In large cities medium density ranges from twenty to forty dwellings per net acre. It may be prescribed as four times the density of the single-family district. If the minimum single-family lot area is 6,000 square feet, the medium density would then require 1,500 square feet of lot per dwelling. Some communities permit a lot area as low as 1,000 square feet per dwelling in this district.

High Density

High densities ranging from 50 to 150 families per net acre in some districts are not uncommon in large cities, and some laws permit as many as 200 to 300 families per acre. With the increasing congestion of traffic and the growing intensity of the parking problem, zoning ordinances of these high densities are due for a critical review. The classification may be defined as a multiple of the minimum single-family lot size. Assuming a density standard of some fifty dwellings per acre and a minimum lot size for the single-family district of 6,000 square feet, the high-density district would permit about eight times the single-family density, or about 750 square feet of lot area per dwelling unit. Some ordinances further grade these requirements according to the size of the dwelling apartment. Thus 300 square feet of lot area may be permitted for "bachelor" units, 400 square feet for one-bedroom units, 600 square feet for two-bedroom units, and 800 square feet for three-bedroom units.

Mobile Home

The mobility of the population in the United States is demonstrated by the expanding use of the so-called mobile home as a relatively permanent dwelling. It possesses unique characteristics and plays an important role in the housing supply in moderate climates. The essential amenities for this mode of living should be regulated in zoning ordinances. Well-designed mobile-home parks accommodate a density of between six and eight trailer units per acre, or approximately 4,000 square feet of ground space for each unit. The Federal Housing Administration standards and the recommendations of the Mobile Homes Association support the lesser density as the desirable space requirement.

Hotel

The density and lot area requirements for hotel districts are the least restrictive of the residential zones, except in areas where the particular character of the environment warrants special attention to density. Hotels may also be included in the provisions for commercial districts. With the exception of limitations on setbacks for side, rear, and front yards, there has been little control of density, but reconsideration of hotel densities is as urgent as it is with high-density apartment and commercial zones. Recent off-street parking requirements actually determine the number of hotel rooms allowed upon a particular site.

Commercial

The complex structure of the modern urban community has introduced changes affecting the arrangement of commercial facilities, as it has in other land uses. The "mom and pop" grocery store has blossomed into the neighborhood convenience center; the expanding suburbs have forced the decentralization of retail enterprise and the development of the regional shopping center. The density of "downtown" hangs in the balance. Special service facilities, from professional offices to light manufacturing establishments where commodities are also sold across the counter, must be accommodated within the fabric of commercial zoning regulations. Consideration of the relation between these several commercial functions and other land uses must be reflected in the comprehensive plan as a foundation for the zoning plan. Excessive land area and permissible floor space, typical of present zoning, is related to traffic congestion and the parking problem. Transition from the burden of strip zoning for business uses along the major streets to the consolidation of commercial centers will be an arduous task and require a long period of time. The shopping center has confirmed the necessity and provided the impetus for this conversion in the pattern of commercial land use.

Enterprise Zones

Initiated by the federal government, the enterprise zones take on different forms in various parts of the United States. The intent of the zoning is to free the sickly central business areas from generally applicable zoning and to offer tax incentives and subsidies to encourage investments in the revitalization process.

Two questions are most often asked about this subsidized laissez-faire proposal: (1) Who will benefit? Will underfinanced small businesses gain a betterment of their economic plight? (2) Will the redevelopment of the depressed area result in greater employment opportunities for the disadvantaged residents?

Perhaps the most serious unanswered question relates to the propriety of providing a wide range of subsidies for business at a time when public assistance to needy residential families of the unemployed is reduced and children's free lunch programs are curtailed.

Industrial Districts

The classification of an industrial district ranges from the most restricted uses for light industry, in which only electric power may be employed or in which smoke, odors, and sound are rigidly controlled, to the unrestricted heavy industry district, in which any type of manufacturing enterprise or process is permitted. Certain industrial uses which may endanger the public are frequently restricted to specific areas, and still others may require special permits by legislative action in order to conduct business. The manufacture of fireworks or fertilizer or the dumping of refuse and garbage, when allowed, may be confined to areas at least 500 feet from other unrestricted uses, if permitted at all.

The phrase "industrial district" has acquired an unsavory association with rundown hovels in the shadow of the factory. The successful development of the planned industrial district, or industrial park, has therefore been a singular advance. The intensity of land use identified with the crowded workshops of the past is relieved in such a park. A density of some thirty to fifty workers per acre is not uncommon in industrial areas, but in industrial parks it ranges between fifteen and twenty per acre, with areas of heavy industry having less than ten workers per acre. Regulations prescribe restrictions on building height, space between buildings, setbacks from property lines, signs, off-street parking and loading, and landscaping.

The reservation of industrial parks for the exclusive use of industry encourages the planned integration of residential communities, with mutually beneficial results: efficiency in industrial operation and convenience to employment in a desirable residential environment.

In recent ordinances, the manner in which operations are conducted, rather than the type of the industry, is the basis for the classification of an industrial district. The adoption of performance standards may obviate the need for arbitrary distinctions between light and heavy industry and provide a more rational utilization of industrial land. It could also become a means to integrate places of employment and places of residence more closely.

In some regions and states the emission of contaminants from the various types of industries has necessitated the creation of an independent air pollution control agency, but normally performance standards prescribe regulations for control of smoke, odor, glare, vibration, dust, sound, radiation, water or sewer pollution, and moisture. They are enforced through the measurement of the effects of plant operation at prescribed points.

INDUSTRIAL PERFORMANCE STANDARDS

The industry performance standards established in the zoning ordinances of such cities as New York, Chicago, and Denver have been analyzed by the Urban Land Institute and the American Society of Planning Officials. The standards given below are derived from those analyses.

A. Fire and Explosion Hazards

All activities involving inflammable and explosive materials and/or their storage shall be provided with adequate safety devices against the hazard of fire and explosion and adequate fire-fighting and fire-suppression equipment and devices standard in industry. All incineration is prohibited.

B. Radioactivity or Electrical Disturbance

Devices that radiate radio-frequency energy shall be so operated as not to cause interference with any activity carried on beyond the boundary line of the property upon which the device is located. Radio-frequency energy is electromagnetic energy at any frequency in the radio spectrum between 10 kilocycles and 3 million megacycles.

C. Noise

The maximum sound pressure level radiated by any use or facility when measured at the boundary line of the property on which sound is generated shall not exceed the values shown in the following table:

Octave-Band Range in Cycles per Second	Sound Pressure Level in Decibels, 0.0002 cyne/cm²
Below 75	72
75–150	67
151–300	59
301–600	52
601–1200	46
1201–2400	40
2401–4800	34
Above 4800	32

If the noise is not smooth and continuous or is not present between the hours of 10 P.M. and 7 A.M., one or more of the following corrections shall be applied to the above octave-band levels:

	Correction in Decibels
Daytime operation only	+5
Noise source operates less than 20% of any one-hour period	+5
Noise source operates less than 5% of any one-hour period	+10
Noise of impulsive character, such as hammering	−5
Noise of periodic character, such as humming or screeching	−5

The sound pressure level shall be measured with a sound level meter and associate octave band analyzer conforming to standards prescribed by the American Standards Association as set forth in a pamphlet published by the association entitled "American Standard Sound Level Meters for Measurement of Noise and Other Sounds No. Z24.3," published in 1944, and in another pamphlet published by the same association entitled "American Standard Specification for an Octave-Band Filter Set for the Analysis of Noise and Other Sounds No. Z24.10," published in 1953.

D. Vibration

Every use shall be so operated that the ground vibration inherently and recurrently generated is not perceptible, without instruments, at any point on any boundary line of the lot on which the use is located.

E. Smoke

No emission shall be permitted at any point, from any chimney or otherwise, of visible gray smoke of a shade equal to or darker than No. 1 on the Power's Micro-Ringlemann Chart, published by McGraw-Hill Publishing Company, Inc., and copyright 1954 (being a direct facsimile reproduction of the standard Ringlemann Chart as issued by the United States Bureau of Mines), except that visible gray smoke of a shade equal to No. 1 on said chart may be emitted for four minutes in any thirty minutes. These provisions applicable to visible gray smoke shall also apply to visible smoke of a different color but with an apparently equivalent capacity.

F. Emission of Dust, Heat, and Glare

Every use shall be so operated that it does not emit dust, heat, or glare in such quantities or degree as to be readily detectable on any boundary line of the lot on which the use is located.

G. Emission of Odors

No emission shall be permitted of odorous gases or other odorous matter in quantities which exceed those proportions shown in Table III, "Odor Thresholds," in chapter 5 of the *Air Pollution Abatement Manual,* copyright 1951 by Manufacturing Chemists' Association, Inc., Washington, D.C.

H. Outdoor Storage and Waste Disposal

All outdoor storage facilities for fuel, raw materials, and products shall be enclosed by a fence or wall adequate to conceal such facilities from adjacent property. No materials or wastes shall be deposited on a subject lot in such form or manner that they may be transferred off the lot by natural causes or forces. All materials or wastes that might cause pollution due to radiation fumes or dust or that constitute a fire hazard or that may be edible by or otherwise attractive to rodents or insects shall be stored outdoors only in approved closed containers and in specific disposal areas.

I. Special Uses

In some communities land may be subject to special uses, such as drilling for oil and mining for rock or minerals. It is customary to control uses of such a special nature by requiring individual action by the planning commission and the issuance of permits by official action of the city council.

The establishment of cemeteries may also come within this category and be subject to similar control.

The development of nuclear energy has introduced a new element of regional concern. The location of nuclear power plants, as well as performance standards, becomes a matter of state concern. Citizens, as well as wildlife and coastal waters, must be protected from the pollution that can result from the disposal of the plants' waste, and must also be protected from possible ill effects of radioactive material.

HEIGHT AND BULK

One of the most critical problems of zoning is the relationship between buildings and the space around them. The question of space was once predicated on the necessity of preserving adequate light and air for the interior. Sufficient light, air, sound control, and privacy continue to be criteria in measuring adequate space between buildings, but their relative importance has been modified by advances in artificial illumination, sound insulation, and air conditioning. It is possible that the necessity for space in the future will derive far more from the exterior requirements than from the interior demands. The amount of building floor space in relation to exterior circulation—streets, sidewalks, parks—may become the critical factor. The space for vehicular and pedestrian traffic circulation now presents an almost insurmountable problem, and it is compounding annually. The dissipation of exterior space in which the environment may be enriched with landscaping and in which the human scale may be restored is a mounting challenge. This challenge, however, will be best answered in new areas where open land is to be developed or in renewal areas where land is assembled into large plots. The current concern for space to protect light, air, and so on, will still be an important consideration in dealing with old areas divided into small, narrow, individual lots. More than a gesture should be made toward the quantity and shape of the open space.

Over the years there has been a constant effort to increase the distances between buildings and property lines and to devise methods by which setbacks might compensate for increasing building heights. The ground space reserved by these provisions has never been sufficient for its purpose; the setback distances and lot coverage restrictions have rather been token grants of space sacrificed after the land had acquired great value. The initial method of front, side, and rear yard requirements was later augmented by "envelope" provisions to cope with excessive building heights. The modest side yard of five to six feet in residential zones has increased to ten feet for multiple-family districts in some ordinances, with provisions for setbacks above the first or second floors. The space between buildings reserved by these provisions is not adequate for reasonable privacy, but opposition to increasing the space has been adamant. Awareness of the deficiency, however, has induced the subdivision of land into larger lot sizes and the consolidation of small properties. This trend has increased the efficiency of land use and site planning, but successful large-scale developments demonstrate that the conventional regulations have no actual bearing on good planning.

There is an inflexibility in current methods for preserving open space; the minimum standards permitted by law become the maximum standards in practice. The primary issue in the future seems to be the need for regulations directed to a balance between building bulk and exterior space required for circulation, vehicular storage, and the evolution of an urbanscape that satisfies more of the basic material needs of humanity.

The principle of the "floor area ratio" offers some encouragement in this direction. It involves the ratio between the area of building floor space and the area of the lot it occupies. A floor area ratio of two, for example, would permit 100 percent of the lot to be covered by a two-story building or 50 percent of the lot to be covered by a four-story building. Recent applications of the floor area ratio introduce the features of "bonus" or premium space. Chicago adopted such inducements in its revised ordinance of 1957, and they have been proposed in Philadelphia. The first major overhaul of the New York City ordinance since the history-making zoning law of 1916 occurred in 1960. The conventional setback requirements that produced the familiar shapes variously referred to as "cakemold" or "ziggurat" were modified by adoption of the "sky exposure plane" for commercial zones and the "open space ratio" for multifamily residential districts. The effect of these provisions, in combination with the inducements of increased permissible floor space in proportion to the open space reserved at the ground level, is comparable to the floor area ratio method of regulation.

This approach affords a flexibility in the shape of buildings to serve their particular functions and removes the arbitrary limitations on building heights unless such limitations may be desirable for particular purposes. As with other regulations to control the bulk of buildings on the land, the floor area ratio will be effective to the extent that it produces the required balance between enclosed floor space occupied by people and adequate ground space for vehicles and living things, be they human, animal, or plant.

HISTORICAL PRESERVATION

Historical preservation starts with the protection of sites of ancient civilizations, whether in the deserts or the mountainous areas of the world.

Buried in the fields adjacent to Rome are evidences of a great road system, and adjacent to the roads can be found walls and foundations of other types of structures. In North Africa, the remains of an ancient civilization can be observed at Moulay Idriss in Morocco and locations in the many other nations that lie along the Mediterranean rim. Native American Indian artifacts are to be found in many parts of Arizona, and developments are required to devise means for the preservation of vast areas where ancient villages were once located. The ruins at Mesa Verde, Colorado, now a part of a national park, are splendidly preserved remains of a vanished civilization.

These sites require protection from destruction, not to mention modern-day "grave robbers." The need has diverted many developments because extensive investigations and removal of the artifacts discovered caused great delay. Interested citizens have formed associations dedicated to the protection and preservation of these critical areas. Ordinances have been adopted in many communities' zoning areas containing historical remains or where historical buildings constitute a link with the past.

Historical preservation also takes into account the need to protect and preserve rare and endangered species of all forms of wildlife, ranging from whales to fringe-toed lizards.

In urban areas historical preservation deals primarily with two conditions. The first is the historical site or building. Immediately coming to mind are the classical city hall, the fine old colonial mansion, the architecturally exquisite cathedral. These are in many instances isolated structures. The second is the historical area, which may contain a collection of fine structures, be a generously landscaped area with historical significance, a locale where historical events took place such as at Lexington or Concord, or a collection of governmental buildings such as those in Washington, D.C. It may also be a fine example of architectural style in a commercial composition, such as in the Vieux Carré in New Orleans or Tivoli Gardens in Copenhagen.

It would not be appropriate to create a one-building zoning district to preserve the historical site. More appropriate would be the acquisition of the building by either a private institution or by a governmental body, thus establishing not only a permanent future for the structure but also providing funds for essential maintenance.

The historical district can be a zoned area with many regulations to protect the existing buildings, provide for the architectural consistency of new structures, and deal with new building heights and setbacks, signs, and other elements. The buildings may be in separate ownerships, and the owners may take pride in the opportunity they have to participate in a national program as well as possibly enjoy a profit. The regulations can be in the form of restrictive covenants if they are more restrictive than the community zoning, or they can simply be a community action taken by the legislative body.

A national carelessness about our rich natural and cultural heritage has been another byproduct of building for commercial enterprise. The unique grandeur of many natural wonders has been protected through the National Parks Service, but efforts to preserve structures and sites of historical or artistic importance have been severely hampered by economic unfeasibility and social indifference. In some regions significant historic buildings are protected by special government action, and a few have been saved by private philanthropy. The continued maintenance of existing structures, however, is a serious problem. Historically important buildings are often not economically practical, especially since zoning regulations usually permit structures of greater height in bulk in these areas. Professor John J. Castonis of the University of Illinois has proposed that owners of such landmark buildings be allowed to sell the development rights to additional stories (or the bulk that the zoning would permit) to developers of another building on another acceptable site. This would allow the protection of famous and historic buildings without the sacrifice of the property rights that usually preclude preservation.[2]

Several cities followed the lead of New Orleans, which adopted a zoning provision for the protection of the Vieux Carré (French Quarter). The principle involved here is the protection of an area's unity, intended to preserve not only a historical structure, a natural feature, or a site, but also the entire surroundings.

The city of Redlands, California, has acquired some thirty acres of orange groves in order to preserve a portion of its agricultural history in the face of intensive urban pressure. The groves produce crops each year, and the fruit is marketed to provide revenue to compensate for the cost of the grove and its maintenance.

The historical area must have a distinct and desirable character worthy of preservation. The standards for its preservation should assure a continuity of scale and design even if demolition, alteration, renovation, removal, or relocation takes place. A certificate of appropriateness is

---

2. The first application of this proposal is the Heurich House, a Victorian mansion in Washington, D.C., owned and occupied by the Columbia Historical Society. A building ninety feet high could legally occupy the site. The city zoning commission permitted a developer of a high-rise structure on a nearby site to erect a building forty feet higher than the zoning code usually allowed, from which the additional income is to be used for the maintenance of the old building. A similar application is being considered for the Chicago Loop, where many significant buildings of the nineteenth-century Chicago School remain. Report in the *AIA Journal,* American Institute of Architects, March 1974.

often required for any change in occupancy, construction, demolition, removal, or relocation, or any modification of the site that would alter its original form or structure.

Historical preservation commissions are created by the legislative body. The members of the commission must be residents of the special zone. All members must demonstrate knowledge of and interest in the preservation of the area. Santa Barbara, California, always deeply concerned about its early history, has adopted a historical preservation zone to protect the old presidio area where the remains of the city's early days are found. San Diego has also adopted such an ordinance to protect an area containing remnants of its historical heritage.

In 1952 Mr. and Mrs. Henry N. Flynt founded the historic Deerfield district to carry on the tradition of historic preservation in this picturesque western Massachusetts village. It was the last outpost on New England's frontier when it was settled in 1669. Devastated twice, by the Bloody Brook Massacre of 1675 and the Deerfield Massacre of 1704, its resettlement brought agricultural prosperity and a determination never to forget its past. The district maintains twelve house museums, a research library, and an active education program, all devoted to the study of the history of Deerfield, the culture of the Connecticut Valley, and the arts in early American life.

Outside America

Countries outside the United States seem on the whole to be more aware of the need to maintain visible contact with the past through the preservation of structures and areas of historical or cultural importance. This may be so because these countries are so much older than the United States. Some examples of this attempt at preservation follow.

Warsaw, Poland. The Nazis leveled Warsaw in World War II. Damaged areas considered of great historical importance were not replaced with new structures; rather the existing buildings were reconstructed in a manner consistent with the past. The cost of doing this is often far greater than clearance and rebuilding with "modern" structures. However, the value of retaining a taste of the past sometimes seems more important than the cost involved. There can be no doubt of the need to preserve architecturally and historically important buildings, especially if they can be made functionally suitable.

Prague, Czechoslovakia. The government of Czechoslovakia spends more than $200 million a year on restoration in Prague. The Committee to Preserve Old Prague would not let planners tear down the graceful but outmoded main railway station, so a new one was built underneath. In general, Prague's one million inhabitants amble down cobbled lanes

Ascension Cathedral, Red Square, Moscow, U.S.S.R.

Brussels, Belgium. *Town Hall and Guild Houses.*

under spires and buttresses. They pass Hradcany Castle, rising fairytale-like on one of the city's seven hills.

People's Republic of China. In Beijing great concern has been expressed over the past disregard for the preservation of many of the historical and interesting structures in order to make way for new hotels, modern residential structures, and subway routes and stations. An element of major interest is the preservation of the *hutongs,* residential areas built about interior streets and courtyards. A major protest occurred when a street with many fine old buildings was demolished. People, both locally and internationally, requested that the structures be rebuilt to the original style, rather than replaced with modern ones. This protest succeeded. Local Chinese city planners are dedicated to the premise that the city must become a blend of the new and the old in order to retain the worldwide interest it creates because of its character and the quality of its many ancient temples, pagodas, shrines, and hutongs.

Hutongs: *the narrow streets that serve both residential and commercial areas that lie between the main highways serving the large urban areas.*

Government Assistance: The Tax Reform Act of 1976

Since passage of the Tax Reform Act of 1976, federal tax incentives have been responsible for stimulating more than $1.2 billion in private investment in more than 2,500 preservation projects nationwide. Historic buildings listed in the National Register of Historic Places and within registered historic districts in all fifty states have been rehabilitated, including hotels, office buildings, factories and apartment buildings. The benefits have meant more than financial gain for owners and investors. Whole neighborhoods and business districts have been favorably affected by well-timed and well-placed investment in historic buildings.

The Economic Recovery Tax Act, signed into law on August 13, 1981, makes dramatic and sweeping changes that directly benefit investment in real estate. The tax incentives in the new law make rehabilitation of historic buildings a more attractive investment than before. A new 25 percent investment tax credit will replace the existing incentives, together with new depreciation schedules and recapture rules. Along with the National Historic Preservation Act Amendments of 1980, the new law should provide further impetus to encourage capital investment in historic buildings and to spur revitalization of historic business districts and neighborhoods.[3]

---

3. Educational Service/Tax Conference. National Trust for Historic Preservation, Washington, D.C.

SOME COMMON ZONING DEFICIENCIES

Zoning regulations are predicated upon good principles of land control, but many fail to establish standards of urban development that produce good cities. Harland Bartholomew has said:

> Zoning has come about partly through the desire of certain better residential districts to obtain a protection which is difficult, if not impossible, to secure by private initiative, and partly through municipal authorities seeking to curtail the enormous losses brought about by uncontrolled growth. Zoning as now practiced, however, has scarcely succeeded in attaining either of these objectives. Owing to inaccurate and, more particularly, insufficient information, our zoning ordinances have been quite out of scale with actual needs. The same forces of speculation that have warped city growth in the past continue to do so through distortion of zoning ordinances.[4]

Because zoning is a vital instrument, these deficiencies deserve attention. The design of commercial zoning persists in retaining "horse and buggy" features. It is an established community attitude in most areas that all land on highways should be zoned for business. In the early days of the village the road led to the door of the shop. The horse was tied to the hitching post in front and "parked at an angle." This form of curb parking has lingered on while the automobile replaced the horse and buggy, while the number of motor vehicles leaped from 8,000 at the turn of the century to more than 120,000,000 in 1970, and while the electric streetcar and motorbus made the horsecar extinct.

The shopping promenade of yesterday has become the traffic artery of today, but the design of business zoning remains unchanged. Mile after mile of highways are stripped with excessive zoning for commercial use. Strip zoning with its curb parking has become a curse. Through traffic does not mix well with the ready ingress and egress needed for parking and service on shopping streets. Submarginal business enterprises, blighted houses, and acres of weed patches on unimproved lots stretch along streets zoned for business, creating a state of built-in blight. The result is a plan impractical for traffic and undesirable for shopping.

The property protection expected of zoning has been largely confined to single-family dwellings. It is a peculiarity of current zoning that each lesser economic classification is permitted in zones of greater economic intensity. Single-family dwellings are permitted in multiple-dwelling dis-

---

4. Harland Bartholomew, *Urban Land Uses,* Harvard City Planning Series (Cambridge, Mass.: Harvard University Press, 1932).

tricts, and both uses are permitted in commercial districts. Some ordinances still permit all uses in industrial zones. As a result, the only zone restricted to the use for which it is designed is the single-family zone; in this zone only single-family dwellings are permitted. The industrial park is a step forward because it is restricted to industry, but this feature has thus far been infrequently incorporated into zoning ordinances. Mixed land uses are not economically sound. Land occupied by dwellings in an industrial zone reduces the efficiency of service facilities for industrial operations, and the safety and convenience of a residential community are denied to the residents scattered through an industrial district. Zoning and planning will achieve compatibility only when the zoning ordinance restricts uses in each zone to those for which the zone is designated.

The areas of land zoned for their respective uses are usually far in excess of the requirements of the city. The amount of land zoned for commercial use has been estimated at three to ten times the area that will ever be needed in the locations zoned. This not only compels the mixture of incompatible uses but induces the spread of uneconomic commercial enterprise. Submarginal business degenerates into blight and, in turn, creates an unhealthy environment for its more prosperous neighbors. Were land uses restricted to the classifications for which they are zoned, the temptation to retain or seek zoning for uses that cannot be sustained economically would undoubtedly fade.

The tremendous burden of building bulk occupying urban land has contributed to the congestion of people and traffic, the disappearance of space, and ugliness. Zoning regulates the type of use permitted on the land; it also regulates the amount of permissible floor space. The regulations are expressed in terms of setbacks from property lines—front, side, and rear yards—volume envelope, sloping planes from street lines, maximum heights, lot coverage. The building volume resulting from these regulations is the measure of the floor space and population density set by the zoning ordinance. The maximum density permitted by prevailing ordinances is so excessive that open space has disappeared, the streets cannot handle the traffic generated, and there is no room to store vehicles. A final consequence, more difficult to measure but nonetheless vital to the economic health of the community, is the imbalance between the demand for space and the amount of excess space permitted by zoning laws. Neither the total amount of land nor the total amount of permissible floor space can be absorbed for the designated land use. As land development reaches a saturation point, new improvements that exploit the permissible zoning volume drain away the opportunities of less fortunate neighbors to sustain economical business operations. Physical deterioration follows economic blight, and the adverse effects injure both the overbuilt and the underbuilt properties. The potential intensity permitted by the ordinance defeats its purpose as a regulatory measure. Land values are subject to extremes of speculative irresponsibility, and decent standards of open space and site planning occur, if at all, despite the law. Zoning must allow adequate space for dynamic growth, but it must also avoid the excesses that nourish economic and physical blight.

An indiscriminate, unplanned mixture of different land uses can be detrimental to the quality of the physical environment. This is observed in the careless practice of spot zoning—the intrusion of service stations in residential neighborhoods, for example. The convenience of a modest shopping center, however, may enhance a residential neighborhood if it does not lead to undesirable noise, excessive night lighting, and an increase of traffic on residential streets, and if adequate on-site parking and landscaping are components of the plan. With appropriate density control, apartments may not only harmonize with single-family districts but also enrich the appearance of a neighborhood with a variety of form and open space. *Compatibility, rather than similarity of uses, is the key to a harmonious relation between land uses.*

The dull uniformity of mass-produced houses in suburban "cookie-cutter" subdivisions has prompted the effort to achieve visual interest and some degree of individual identification; a variety of setbacks and decorative exterior designs are used to camouflage the similarity in floor plans. These superficial efforts are unpleasant reminders that few custom-built homes have been erected in recent decades. Most homes are produced by a new profession of speculative, large-scale homebuilders. The home, once every man's castle, has been reduced to a piece of merchandise, a commodity for trade.

FLEXIBLE ZONING

It appears that zoning is already adequately flexible. Hardly a day goes by when there is no application for a change in the ordinance regulations or a change in the map to permit uses currently disallowed. The requests for exceptions, variances, conditional use permits, and a variety of other escapes from the rigid enforcement of the law are major items on every planning commission and council agenda. Many of the requests are reasonable and appropriate to the variety of conditions associated with the nature of the land and environment and must be approved, but the vast majority are the result of efforts to gain special privileges and economic advantages beyond the intent and purpose of the law.

But the fact is flexible zoning is necessary. Exploration of methods by which such flexibility may be incorporated has produced the tech-

Incentive concept:

A & B   *Parcels zoned for four units per net acre.*

A1   *Dedicated five acres for flood control and recreation.*

A2   *Forty units permitted on the remaining parcel (five acres) provided the number of units on the residual land is not greater than two times the units allowed on similar acreage of adjacent land.*

Acquisition by deeding of development rights

Compensatory provisions in the zoning ordinance would permit the landowners of property subject to flooding to develop the same number of dwelling units on the land freed from flooding that they might have had on the total ownership if the flood hazard did not exist, with the proviso that the development rights for the area subject to flooding be deeded to the local community.

nique of density control. The monotony of subdivision design that has resulted from the single-family land use classification combined with lot-size regulations is relieved by this method. The zoning classification and prescribed lot size that prevail for a given tract establish the over-all density and maximum number of lots permissible in the subdivision. The density control provision permits the developer to reduce the minimum lot size, providing the maximum number of lots is not exceeded and the balance of the land area is developed for recreation or park space.

The technique identified as "planned development" or "community unit" is another advance in the achievement of zoning flexibility. This permits the planned integration of land uses and, although its application is directed primarily to large developments of raw land in suburban areas, it may be applied to built-up sections of the city. It offers the opportunity to plan for the full range of uses required by a well-balanced community—shopping, parks, schools, and a variety of housing types—uses not generally provided for within the framework of conventional zoning.

Mixed-Use Land Concept

Most of the classical zoning ordinances have consistently advocated the protection of single-family residential areas from intrusion by higher-density residential uses, even more so from commercial and industrial uses. Only in planned unit developments where the homes could be adequately protected from the nonconforming developments and activities associated with them have these been permitted.

The main objection to "unplanned" mixtures of uses remains a valid consideration in the planning of communities, especially in those already built, where there is concern about the conflicts that can and often do arise as a consequence of increased traffic, inadequate streets, lack of parking, noise, and other activities that violate the health, safety, and quiet desired by residents.

On the other hand, where uses are planned in a reasonable relationship to each other, and the problems associated with spot zoning and variances that offer special privilege are dealt with in advance, there can be excellent urban planning opportunities for the careful mixing of uses to provide for the needs of the residents without violating their privacy and safety.

Development Agreements

Over the years the theory that zoning cannot be subject to conditions other than those set forth in the ordinance has been the basis for many court cases, with findings in support of the concept. As mentioned else-where, new devices are always entering the process to make zoning more flexible. In a sense the newly devised development agreements are, fol-lowing approval by the community, a more rigid contract between both the community and the developer.

First, the development agreement does not take the place of any exist-ing law or regulation or any of the approval requirements. It is more like the regulations for a planned unit development used for a complex pro-posal, in which the regulations set forth the basic outlines for the devel-opment.

Second, and most important to the developer, the community agrees not to change its planning and zoning laws applicable to the development for a specific period of time. This assures the developer that he can safely engage in large expenditures for detailed planning and construction dur-ing the valid period of the agreement.

Third, in return for the above guarantee, the community may require, and the developer may agree to, the construction of specific improve-ments, public facilities, and services and develop the land according to a specific schedule. The community may also require other commitments that it otherwise has no right to compel a developer to perform.

Fourth, statutory requirements indicate that a development agree-ment must specify the time during which the city agrees not to change its regulations dealing with the permitted use of the property, the den-sity or intensity of uses, the size of buildings, and the requirement for dedication or reservation of land for public purposes. The agreement may also include other terms and agreements, including a time sched-ule for additional public services and facilities to be provided by the developer.

Fifth, once an agreement has been entered into, the local agency must periodically review the progress made by the developer to comply with the terms of the agreement at least once every twelve months.

Some projects are more subject than others are to development agree-ments. They can provide security to developers of large-scale multi-phased projects, where substantial investments for planning, engineering, and the installation of public facilities are involved.

In addition, the agreements can become a valuable tool in dealing with smaller parcels. This is particularly so where there are many public service problems or where the community seeks to induce the property owners to dedicate land or participate in the construction of new public facilities even though the owner is not ready to develop the property.

The community could also hold out the development agreement as an incentive to encourage a developer to provide low-income housing, extra open space, or other provisions that the community might desire.

PITFALLS

Zoning decisions may often be challenged on the basis of both legislative enactments and constitutional issues. These would include:

Conspiracy, the actions either open or covert, to grant a privilege to a person or organization, either for friendship or financial reward. Contributions to future political campaigns fall into this suspect area.

Antitrust, the denial of equal protection under the law by granting a zoning or other development favor to one party and denying it to another whose property is in a similar situation.

Freedom of speech, the regulation of signs, billboards, certain religious organizations, or certain games and activities that may offend a segment of the populace. Careful treatment in the design of regulations must prevent the appearance of outright prohibition.

Excessive demands for improvement, in the form of fees, licenses, and exactions, especially in those states where other means of securing improvements are not available.

Failure to follow due process, not holding adequate public hearings, providing for appeals, posting public notices in local media, failure to disqualify decision-makers with personal interests in a case, failure to keep adequate records, and illegal conduct of meetings (actions without quorums, for example).

Exclusionary zoning, where a community seeks through zoning to establish such high standards for development that the excessive costs involved in land and improvements will per se exclude all but the most affluent segment of the population from the jurisdiction. The New Jersey Supreme Court, in *Mount Laurel 1* and *Mount Laurel 2,* has ruled that communities shall provide opportunities for the development of a fair share of its housing to be available for low- and moderate-income families.[5] This housing must be provided for in each community and not just in the region.

As the zoning process is reviewed it is possible to conclude that, like much else in the field of public law, it is full of potential for proper use as well as misuse. As indicated, however, it is still one of the better ways in which to implement the comprehensive plan. The flaws become fewer when there is good government and when the ordinance is administered in a reasonable manner.

---

5. *Southern Burlington County NAACP v. Township of Mount Laurel,* 336 A 2d. 713 (N.J. 1975).

In some communities, where attention to details is lax, the legislative body may permit applicants to provide sketchy plans and depend upon the good will of the developer to carry out the proposed program with little if any further approvals. This type of casual approval results in losing control of the actions to be taken at a later date and is considered the contracting away of public power.

CHAPTER 29

SUBDIVISION PRACTICES

The earth is our primary resource. It took hundreds of thousands of years to create the few inches of soil that support humanity. People's greed and neglect have often destroyed what nature took eons to develop. The story of man's improvidence with the land is suggested by Walter Havighurst:

> In 1823 a little Norwegian wanderer, named Cleng Peerson, walked overland from New York to the western territories. At Chicago he turned north. For six days he printed his steps in the blank sands of Lake Michigan. At evening he boiled his kettle at lake's edge. He slept under the soothing drones of water. At the site of Milwaukee (three log huts, one of them empty) he found a tall man, naked to the waist, beside a cabin hung with traps and snowshoes.
>
> "What will I find if I continue north from here?" Cleng Peerson asked.
>
> Solomon Juneau was a fur trader. He knew the great twilight of the forests.
>
> "Woods to the world's end," he replied.
>
> It was literally true. Woods for 600 miles. In that day six-sevenths of Wisconsin was forest. Two-thirds of Minnesota was forest. The upper peninsula of Michigan was all forest. And the forest began beyond Lake Superior, stretching away toward Hudson Bay. A country as big as France and every mile of it mysterious with forest twilight and haunted with the sound of running water. . . . Cedar, hemlock, tamarack and pine. A forest rich and vast enough for the needs of a nation forever.
>
> Try to find that forest now. . . .

468

The timber cruisers came, walked through the country. . . . Behind them came the lumber kings and the great corporations. They logged off the forest in a furious assault. "Come and get it" was the cry of the lumber camp. . . . "Come and get it" was the slogan of the corporations. . . .

How did the big corporations get hold of all the timber? There was the Stone and Timber Act of Congress, designed to safeguard national resources. But the corporations found the loopholes, and they got the timber. . . .

Following the mining of timber came the fires that swept not only the fallen timber but the seeds as well . . . so there was no second growth. Conservation of this forest preserve came fifty years too late.[1]

We have done the same with all of our resources. In our desire to provide a maximum of opportunity and a minimum of regulation, we are prone to pass on a heritage of poverty in natural resources. So often our willingness to protect our resources emerges only after irreparable damage has been done. The control of land subdivision has been similar to that of soil conservation. It is accepted only after most of the urban land has already been butchered into pieces that render our city the unhappy affair we now experience. Carol Aronovicci said: "Wisdom is knowing what to do. Virtue is the doing it." In the subdivision of land, as in many other affairs, our virtue precedes our wisdom and, it might be observed, the "doing" of many subdivisions is without much virtue.

PRIVATE OWNERSHIP: A HISTORY

The history of land ownership commenced when people formed tribes. Living on wild food and game, prehistoric tribes appropriated the territory they occupied. Like the American Indian or the pastoral people of the Asiatic steppes, the primitives guarded their territory from intrusion by other tribes, but equality of use was open to all the members of their own community.

The land belonged to the tribe and not to the individual; in this we detect a precedent for the sovereign states as the true owner of all land. As the tribes grew in size and acquired territory by conquest or peaceful consolidation, they subdivided into villages. A degree of local autonomy was tolerated, but the land remained as community holding.

This ancient tradition of the land vested primarily in the community, with individuals granted rights to its use, has persisted despite the forms it has assumed at different times. Later, it was reflected in the feudal system when land was vested in the king as the head of the state.

The king granted land to his lords for their pledge of military support.

---

1. Walter Havighurst, "The Land and the People," *Land Policy Review,* June 1941.

They in turn allocated rights of land use to their serfs and *villeins,* these rights becoming an integral part of the social and political caste system. As the feudal system dissolved, the privileges of the lords were transformed into a form of ownership, and the landlord was born. In England the system of leasing land estates to tenants reached a stage in which the tenants were assured rights even more firm than those of the landlord-owner; the tenants' intimate association with the land and its use warranted secure protection against unfair eviction and the assurance of full compensation for any improvements they might effect.

The history and nature of land tenure is complicated, varying in different countries at different periods. While the landlord-tenant system prevails in some countries, peasant proprietorship is predominant in others. The concept of land ownership has gradually moved from that of possession—the land as a place to live and to cultivate or capture food for survival—to that of land as property; when it is the latter the land becomes a commodity and is associated with private land ownership.

Because of this identification with ownership it is necessary to recognize the relation between private ownership and community interest. In strict legal terms there is no absolute private right to land in our system. The state alone is vested with that right, which it cedes to the individual possessor only as a strictly defined subordinate right, subject to conditions enacted by the community from time to time. The article on land tenure in *The Encyclopaedia Britannica* is no less accurate for its mention of the British parliament when it says:

> Land tenure, throughout the world, shows that it has pursued one unvarying course; commencing in the community of tribal possession, land has everywhere by degrees been appropriated to the village, to the families, and to the individuals. But in every stage the condition of its enjoyment and use have been absolutely regulated by the community in reference to the general welfare. . . . Those who refuse to admit the right of the state to impose such conditions on private property as it deems for the general benefit, may be dismissed with brevity. Not only do they show entire ignorance of the history of land tenure at all times, but they belie the daily action of the British legislature. Parliament seldom lets a session pass without making some laws which assert the right of the state to take possession of property for private or public benefit, to tax it, and to restrain or regulate the rights of its owners over it. Nor is there any theory of the basis of property which does not tacitly admit that it is subject to the authority of the community.[2]

Land in the United States was originally vested in the crown of the

---

2. *The Encyclopaedia Britannica,* The Werner Company, Chicago, 1893, Vol. 14, p. 259 (American Revision).

country that colonized the area. The English king made grants of land to the trading companies, and they in turn transferred the grants to individuals or groups of settlers. In New England these settlers customarily established compact villages with each family receiving twenty acres. Outside the area of these individual holdings, the land remained in custody of the community for use by all members of the group. In the South, large tracts were granted for agricultural development.

The King of Spain held absolute title to the land in the Spanish colonies. His subjects were dispatched to those areas the crown desired to be populated, and the land was leased for cultivation. The crops were specified, and if for any reason settlers neglected to cultivate the land, they were deported from the colony. Provisional grants of huge estates were made to crown favorites in the western country that later became California, the first in 1784. *Ranchos* like those of José Verdugo in the San Fernando Valley and Manuel Nietos between the Santa Ana and San Gabriel rivers occupied areas of 390,000 acres stretching from the mountains to the sea. These great holdings were roughly measured; the *vara,* the Spanish measurement of distance, was calculated by the distance covered on horseback in a given period of time, and the later problems of untangling disputed claims may well have originated with the relative spryness of some caballero's horse.

Like the Roman *praesidium,* the German *Marktplatz,* and the New England common, the plaza occupied the center of the Spanish colonial pueblos. House lots were grouped about the plaza, with planting fields and public pastureland lying beyond them. This layout historically was intended as protection from attack, but its social advantages were eventually realized and all pueblos and cities founded by the Spanish in North and South America are laid out in this way.

The town of Los Angeles illustrates the typical village plan. The eleven families who were the original settlers were joined by the garrison and the Indians in a gay fiesta to mark its establishment in 1781. (This was probably the first of the supercolossal premieres for which Hollywood later was to become famous.) Each of the settlers was permitted to cultivate fourteen acres of land outside the residential area, and an allowance of stock and equipment was given equally to each family. All had free range for their stock on lands outside the area designated for cultivation.

The first subdivision of the City of Los Angeles was quite simple. It covered an area of four square leagues or about thirty-six square miles centered about the plaza which measured 275 by 180 feet. In accordance with De Neve's instructions, the old plaza lay with its corners to the cardinal points of the compass, the streets extending at right angles so that "no street would be swept by the wind." Upon three sides of the plaza were the house lots, fifty-five feet in width. One-half of the remaining side was reserved for public buildings, the other half was for open space.[3]

After the American Revolution, land formerly held by the crown of England went to the respective states. In order to resolve the conflicting interests of the states, much of it was declared in the public domain by the federal government. The United States thereby became proprietor of the frontier areas. Because the government of the new nation needed revenue for its operation and the expansion of the vast country, settlement was encouraged by the sale of land at nominal prices, and grants were offered in return for development. The Homestead Act was one such instrument, entitling the citizen to 160 acres of land on the condition that he bring it under cultivation within five years. Huge grants were made to the railroads as inducement to extend their rails across the western territories; about 10 percent of the public domain was turned over to them in 1867.

These policies overlooked the possible dissipation of the natural forest and mineral resources that later took place, and it has been subsequently necessary to devote much legislation to the restoration and protection of these domains. In urban communities the abuse of land through speculative excesses has paralleled the dissipation of the natural resources in rural areas.

ZONING

Standards for lot sizes, dimensions, and area are to be found in the zoning ordinance. These standards are different in each zone. They often differ for cities and counties; for example, large-lot zoning has been criticized in many urban areas, but is desired in rural regions where piecemeal urbanization could destroy the potential for economically sound agriculture.

Historically, lots in urban areas tended to be small, as illustrated in many of the early cities of the United States and Europe. San Francisco, with its twenty-five-foot-wide lots, exemplifies the conditions of overcrowding created by this pattern of development. Structures are built next to each other with no open space except the street in front and a small yard at the rear. It was only after earthquakes and fires that community planners realized that little if anything was to be gained by this overcrowding. The standards were thereafter increased to at least double those that had previously existed. The current drive to return to the old standards is based on the exorbitant price of land in most communities

---

3. *El Pueblo,* Security Trust and Savings Bank, Equitable Branch, Los Angeles, California, 1948.

coupled with the desire for greater profits for those participating in the real estate marketplace.

Single-Family Lots

The size of individual homesites varies from the lot 25 feet wide covering an area of 2,500 square feet, to the estate lots where the width may be 250 feet or more and the area extend into acreage. In between these are the so-called standard lots, where the width ranges from 40 feet to 60 feet and the areas from 5,000 to 7,200 square feet. Many suburban communities have minimum standards of 7,500 to 8,000 square feet in order to provide for the openness associated with the village life desired by many middle-class residents.

Zero Lot Line Developments

Zero lot line housing is a potential guide to the solution of dwindling land and resources, increasing housing costs, and the continuing need to conserve energy. By placing residential units on one lot line, the amount of usable space is expanded. The solid lot line wall both provides privacy and is aesthetically pleasing to the residents of the directly adjacent lots. Such projects fulfill the owner's desire for single-family detached housing while maintaining an attractive appearance and conserving resources.

The zero lot line design concept potentially permits greater flexibility in provision for outdoor living, because it doubles the required width of the side yard on one side of the dwelling. This would provide the maximum flexibility in orienting the structure to take advantage of sun and shade. However, care must be taken in the design to protect the adjacent lot's privacy, and the covenants must permit the portion of the structure on the zero side to be maintained. All roof drainage must be on the resident's property.

However, developers seeking to utilize zero lot line procedures are less interested in providing greater amenities than they are in reducing the lot sizes and crowding the land. For instance, in Dade County, Florida, single-family lot areas were reduced from the standard 7,500 square foot requirement to 4,500 square feet. The maximum coverage was increased from 35 to 50 percent of the total lot area. Certain privacy safeguards were introduced by requiring solid walls on critical sides of a structure. To make maximum use of the limited outdoor space, a minimum of 15 percent of the walls of the building had to open onto a patio or garden.

SPECULATION

As our nation grew in size and urban centers became large metropolitan areas, there was increased competition for land for all purposes. Great estates were broken up and sold in parcels of varying size. For the most part, land was still considered a base for some economic or social use. Not until recent years did it become a speculative commodity to be bought and sold for a profit like stocks and bonds and, not infrequently, for a loss.

Some of the wildest exploits in land sales occurred in Florida and California during the early 1920s. Florida land was sold at fantastic prices to people in such places as New York and New England, and much of the land was underwater. When the boom broke, thousands of people found themselves with worthless property and their life savings lost.

Real estate speculation in California involving *los Americanos* and the Spanish *rancheros* was no less fantastic. For example, at one time all land in an area was to be registered in the land office by a specified time or be declared free for claim by anyone desiring it. Various tricks were employed to deceive the Spanish rancheros: some notices were never published or they were "lost"; some were phrased in language not understood by the Spanish landowners; or, as a last resort, owners were terrorized to keep them from the registry office until the deadline passed.

In later days of speculation, land was subdivided and sold in flood areas and on precipitous hillsides; in one example the gridiron plotting of streets rendered the lots useless so that 90 percent of the land has since reverted to the state for failure to pay taxes. A multitude of 25-by-100-foot lots were laid out and sold for "a dollar down and a dollar a week." There were no sewers and no paved streets, and heavy rains washed out roads and water pipes. These subdivisions were not only poor investments for the purchasers; they were also wanton wastes of urban land resources.

As lots in these scattered "wildcat" subdivisions were sold off, the new owners demanded urban services and facilities and transportation, which could not be supported. When the boom died in California, as in Florida, thousands of lots, some improved and some devoid of pavements or utilities, remained as evidence of premature and irresponsible subdivision. Assessment districts, which had been formed to pay for the improvements promised by the subdivider, defaulted on their bonds. The scene was one of economic desperation.

The depths to which abuse of urban land subdivision sank is best illustrated by the contrast with the fine residential suburbs begun during the same period. Such developments as the Palos Verdes Estates near Los Angeles, St. Francis Woods in San Francisco, Roland Park in Baltimore, Forest Hills in New York, River Oaks in Houston, and the Country Club District in Kansas City are among a number in which the best techniques in land division and development were employed.

Escape!

The wanton neglect of the congested centers of our cities has been equaled only by the wastefulness of its sprawling expansion. People are fleeing from the city in search of relief from the ugly evils of congestion in their living and working environment. This does not raise the question of decentralization versus rebuilding. Cities are being continuously re-built, after a fashion, and decentralization is not only coming, it is here. The central problem is to turn the current exodus from a rout into an orderly expansion by way of planning and effective legislation to imple-ment the execution of the plans.

Thus far, expansion has amounted to a scattering of homes over the available outlying countryside. This has provided a means to escape from the outmoded living environment within cities rather than a means to accommodate the growing urban population gracefully. It has not been guided by the foresight of planners, enlightened civic leadership in busi-ness and government, nor wisdom in urban economics and finance. Credit for meeting the demand for better living must go to that aggressive group of patent medicine men of real estate we have identified as "lot hawkers." Only they were prepared for the call, and they made a contri-bution to improved urban living. Of those who could afford to escape, few are not living in some subdivision promoted by the early hawkers or their more recent offspring. The process was chaotic, unplanned, and it created more problems for the future than it solved. But the people were served.

Henry Ford said some years ago, "Plainly, so it seems to some of us, [that] the ultimate solution will be the abolition of the City, its abandon-ment as a blunder. . . . We shall solve the City problem by leaving the City." [4] This reflects the underlying discontent with cities, but can it be a milepost on the way to reaching a decent environment?

People have congregated in cities for their mutual welfare. They are now retreating from the congestion. Commercial and industrial expansion is moving to the outskirts to dodge the incredible land prices in the older areas. Decentralization is on the march, but this is an industrial age and the urban framework forms the basic pattern of our economic and social system. It is in the cities where people find their work. The surge of population to the cities has occurred at a remarkably accelerated rate, but this is not a phenomenon of recent origin.

While exact figures are not available, the changes in industrial activi-ties from 1947 to 1981 are indicated by the following statistics:

---

4. From "Mr. Ford's Page" in the *Dearborn Independent,* Dearborn, Michigan, 1922.

LONDON

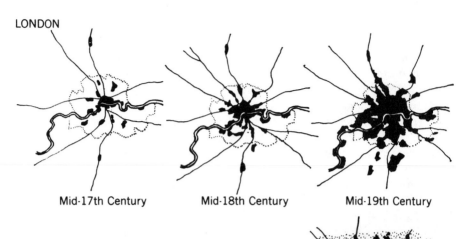

Mid-17th Century   Mid-18th Century   Mid-19th Century

Cities everywhere are growing with disorder along the same pattern, each becoming a metropolis sprawling unplanned over the countryside. These diagrams illustrate the urban explosion since the Industrial Revolution. Rare among such cities, London built a greenbelt to restrict its expansion. This has resulted in the building of numerous New Towns outside of the boundaries of the London city area.

TOKYO

1880   1910   1932   TODAY

PHILADELPHIA

1800   1900   TODAY

CHICAGO

NEW YORK CITY

BARCELONA

ZURICH

- The number of industrial establishments with more than twenty employees grew from 241,000 in 1947 to 360,000 in 1977.
- In 1981 there were approximately 112 million persons in the labor force. This was an increase from 71.5 million in 1960.
- The number of persons employed in manufacturing grew from 18.5 million in 1972 to 21 million in 1981.

During the thirties three-quarters of all industrial jobs were within the major industrial centers, and these centers were confined to only 7 percent of all the counties in the United States. More than one-third of all jobs were in large cities and one-fifth in the peripheral areas and satellite communities contiguous to them.[5]

The urban population of the country was only 3 percent of the total in 1790, and it is almost 70 percent of the total today, having increased nearly 30 percent during the 1950–60 decade. But the great central cities are losing population. This trend has also been evident since the thirties when the suburban districts of metropolitan areas under one million population gained twice as fast as the central cities themselves, with a similar trend in areas over one million. The suburban and satellite areas of Detroit and San Francisco-Oakland increased twice as fast as the central urban districts; the suburban and satellite communities around Chicago, New York, and Pittsburgh gained three times as fast as the central cities; around Philadelphia they gained six times as fast; around St. Louis more than ten times; and around Cleveland nearly eleven times.[6] The trend has advanced to the point where the population in ten of the twelve largest cities, with populations in excess of 700,000 and including the above-named cities, decreased during the 1950–1960 decade; only Los Angeles and Houston showed gains. The people are moving to the suburbs and satellite communities about them, but they seek to retain the advantages of the urban environment. More than three-quarters of the urban population live in the 212 metropolitan areas, and 40 percent of this urban population occupies the sixteen metropolitan areas of more than one million people.

The Statistical Abstracts of the U.S., 1984, indicate that between 1970 and 1980 the population of the U.S. increased by 11.4 percent. Metropolitan areas gained 10.2 percent, the central cities 0.2 percent, the areas outside the central cities 18.2 percent, and the nonmetropolitan areas 15.1 percent.

Spreading at random about the metropolitan countryside, the subdivi-

---

5. Daniel B. Creamer, *Is Industry Decentralizing?* (Philadelphia, Pa.: University of Pennsylvania Press, 1935).
6. Ladislas Segoe, *Population and Industrial Trends*, American Society of Planning Officials, 1935.

sions exact a heavy toll upon the city. Extension of public services—utilities, streets, schools, transportation, police and fire protection—over sparsely occupied sections has heaped a burden upon the city treasury. Financing the urban community has become a lingering illness. Debt hovers over property and improvements until a day when it is either paid in full or foreclosed. It hangs over the city hall and drains the taxpayer. Investments are unplanned; lending institutions compete for loans in the expanding suburbs, mushrooming over the countryside and sapping the strength of the central districts. "Lenders thus find themselves in the unpleasant situation of financing their own funeral."[7] The city invites chaos and awaits the day when the federal government must be summoned to bolster the crumbling local economy. Encouraged by the prospects for cheaper development, uninspired builders surge to the outskirts, create the blight of tomorrow, and retreat to other equally fruitful fields.

Within every city is much land that is either vacant or inefficiently used. The speculative prospect for a future increase in the selling price is a strong inducement to withhold this land from development. The penalty of high real property taxation on improvements is a further deterrent to development. Henry George in 1879 evolved his theory of the single tax on land as a remedy for the situation,[8] and the graded real property tax in Pittsburgh assesses land at twice the value of improvements. Various methods have been proposed to emphasize taxation on land as a means to remove the speculative advantage of withholding land from development and conserve the public facilities and services of a community. Applied to all land, this principle could also discourage speculation in unproductive vacant land in the suburbs.

The role of cities is vital. They provide the range and diversification of employment essential to free existence. Our task is not to destroy the city, but to build a better one.

REGULATIONS

Our conception of land has changed from one of soil cultivated for food and earth mined for minerals and other materials. The change has come about almost imperceptibly but nonetheless surely. Land is still used for the same primary purposes. However, it is not only used for the goods it produces; it is itself treated as goods to be bartered for trade. As such a commodity, trading in urban land is frequently conducted independently of its productive usefulness in the traditional sense. Ostensibly the value

---

7. Miles Colean in a speech before the Mortgage Bankers Association, New York City, 1943.

8. Henry George, *Progress and Poverty*, 1879.

of land is linked with the manner in which it may be used, but possession is quite generally acquired for the purpose of exchanging it as a commodity rather than for its natural productive use.

As a result of this gradual shift in emphasis on land, we have grown unaware of the vital impact that the process of transforming raw acreage into improved urban lots exerts upon the community welfare. It is to assure the protection of the general welfare that subdivision regulations have been devised, with the knowledge that in the final analysis it is the general welfare that protects sound investment.

The questionable practices of the 1920s placed the subdivider of land in an extremely poor light, and the able practitioner was unavoidably identified with the unscrupulous. Reforms were overdue, and the necessity for regulations over the subdivision of urban land was urgent. These controls are based on the principle that the use and development of land constitute a right bestowed by the community upon the individual, and this right may be withdrawn or withheld when and if the individual violates the conditions upon which it is vested in him. The power of eminent domain, the police power, the power to tax real estate, and the power to regulate the use of land are expressions of this principle, and it provides the structure upon which the development of urban land is built.

The California State Subdivision Map Act defines a subdivision as follows: "Any land, or portion thereof, shown on the last preceding tax rolls as a unit or as contiguous units, which is divided for the purposes of sale, either immediate or future, by any subdivider, into five or more parcels within any one year shall be considered to be a subdivision and requires the filing of a map for the approval of the planning commission and legislative body." Such a definition or a similar one is usually contained in state laws that vest the right of police power in cities and counties for the regulation of land subdivision or in planning acts that outline the procedure for preparation of the comprehensive plan.

A definition of a subdivision such as the foregoing does not preclude the sale of a portion of an individual lot; this right is retained by the individual property owner. A parcel of land may be sold in whole or in part at the discretion of the owner without the necessity to follow the subdivision procedures. It is only necessary to inform the county recorder and the tax assessor of the sale so that the official records may be adjusted and taxes reassigned. The regulations applying to the development of individual parcels of land are the zoning laws, the housing laws, health and building codes, and sanitation laws. The division of property falls within the classification of subdivision regulation when (according to a definition like the preceding) a piece of land is divided into at least five separate parcels, each of which is to be separately sold within a period of one year. Many communities regulate the division of property into fewer than five lots through local ordinances. The division of property into substandard-sized parcels will not assure the granting of a building permit on an illegal lot.

There are many interests involved in the subdivision of land, including those of the original owner, the developer, the prospective buyer, and the city as a whole. Ladislas Segoe stated:

> To the land developer the subdividing of land is primarily a matter of profit. He is chiefly interested in realizing as much money as he can from the sale of his land in the shortest possible time. To the community the subdivision of land is a matter of serious public concern. The activities of the developers shape the future of the community and condition in a considerable measure the quality of the living and working conditions of its inhabitants. Where such activities are uncontrolled or inadequately controlled, they also may place an undue burden on the public treasury by reason of excessive cost of public improvements and maintenance, unnecessarily high operating costs of public services, and through the participation of the community in the financing of improvements in premature subdivisions.[9]

One of the first steps taken in some states for the control of subdivisions was the licensing of the subdivider. To obtain a license some education in the principles and practices of land sales was necessary, as well as knowledge of state and local laws pertaining to subdivision. It was generally required by law that the owner employ a licensed engineer to prepare the subdivision map for recording. This was an effort to ensure the accuracy of the subdivision maps and to avoid alteration in the development after it was recorded. In more recent years it has frequently been mandatory to record on the maps any unusual or hazardous conditions, such as the danger of floods in low areas. Such land has not necessarily been precluded from sale, but the purchasers were warned of what they were purchasing. If life was endangered, however, the public body could deny the right to subdivide and sell the land.

Subdivision is the method of transforming a city plan into a reality. The city plan is either realized or it is lost in the subdivision of land. Many of its overall elements are realized at the time the land is developed. Highways are dedicated, streets and alleys are paved, sewer and water lines and electric power are installed, new schools are constructed, transportation lines are extended, and police and fire protection are expanded. The control a community retains over land subdivision is the means by which elements of the comprehensive plan are enforced.

Having sovereign rights over the land within their boundaries, states

---

9. Ladislas Segoe, *Local Planning Administration,* International City Managers' Association, Chicago, 1941, p. 495.

pass laws governing the ownership, transfer, and use of private property, and they vest in cities and counties the right of police power to regulate the subdivision of land. Some states establish the procedures for subdividing land and have real estate commissions that ensure compliance with these procedures. The real estate commission operates in a manner similar to that of a corporation commission that regulates the sale of stocks and bonds. They check the legitimacy of sales organizations, the quality of the lots offered for sale, and ascertain that the required improvements are either installed or assured by a bond posted by the subdivider prior to approval of the subdivision and sale of land.

The design of subdivisions is the responsibility of the local government of the community in which the land is situated. Under the provisions of the comprehensive plan, the local planning agency is generally charged with the responsibility for the administration of the standards for "community design" of subdivisions, the shape and size of lots, the size and length of streets, and the spaces to be reserved for community facilities, schools, and recreation.

In effect, the community reserves an equity in the land and vests in the individual the right to own and use land subject to the requirements for the general welfare of the community. Thus the city may require the subdivider to dedicate certain streets for access to property and it may demand that sewer lines be installed. If this facility is not available, the city may require larger lots to avoid the possibility of water and soil contamination by effluents from cesspools or septic tanks. The city may require service roads where land abuts a principal trafficway to control the ingress and egress to property, and it may require the installation of specific utilities and roads, walks and curbs, street lighting, electric distribution; alternatively, the city may require the subdivider to post a bond to cover the cost of such improvements before the final map of the subdivision is approved. The subdivider may be required to conform with a major highway plan for the community through the proposed grades and alignment of city streets.

The local agency aids the subdivider in planning his land, suggests improved methods of site planning, and recommends to the legislative body exceptions to regulations that may be warranted by peculiar characteristics of the various sites. Material assistance has been rendered by the Federal Housing Administration in the improvement of subdivision design; this federal agency has performed a service in raising the quality of subdivision design in those communities where local laws are ineffectual or no trained planning officials are active.

One of the principal deficiencies in subdivision practice is the difference in standards for improvements that prevail in adjoining communities. These differences are apparent in the strange street alignments, blocked roadways, alternately wide and narrow streets, and differences in type of pavements frequently observable from one community to another. Perhaps less discernible, but more disastrous to the general community welfare and regional development, are the differences in standards for the design and construction of real estate subdivisions. Some communities willfully lower their standards below those of neighboring areas to invite the subdivision and development of land within their boundaries, only to suffer the pain of a degenerated community at some later date. Many cities have made agreements to cooperate in matters of subdivision where the developments are within a certain distance of their respective boundaries. Where regional planning agencies are active, they have coordinated the subdivisions of the various cities within their jurisdiction. Here is a field ripe for significant service and progress.

A way to exercise quantitative control over land subdivision is yet unresolved, but it is urgently needed to restrain excessive and premature expansion of subdivisions. The repetition of the economically disastrous practices of the 1920s, many of which are recurring today, needs to be forestalled, but the method of legally accomplishing this purpose has not been developed. There were suggestions for issuing "certificates of necessity" during the 1920 decade when the effects of wildcat operations became painfully obvious. These certificates were to allow subdivision of land only when the developer could demonstrate the need for developing his property and produce some evidence of bona fide purchasers for it. The certificates never appeared.

The most effective means thus far of coping with excessive subdivision has been the requirement that a subdivider install all utilities and improvements, including streets and walks, in conformance with the standards established by the community. At his expense and prior to sale, the subdivider must thus install all that is needed. This transforms the subdivider from the usual position of a land speculator to that of a land developer. Required to meet the full capital costs of a complete improvement, it is likely that the developer will more thoroughly consider the financial soundness of his development before he ventures willfully upon a highly speculative enterprise.

PROCEDURE

Although procedures vary in different localities, the following steps may serve as a general description of the general sequence from an unimproved site to the development of parcels available for sale:

1. The land is surveyed to ascertain the precise description of its boundaries, the abutting streets, local drainage conditions, contours of the land, and the special features or structures that may occupy the site.

2. Official records are consulted to define the location of special easements or rights-of-way that must be retained in developing the land. There may be a proposed highway passing across the site or easements for sewers or power lines to serve the site or adjoining land. All restrictions on the use of the property must be determined: deed restrictions and zoning, the location of existing sewers or other requirements for sanitation, the height of the water table, the type of soil. The data on orientation and wind directions may affect the layout of streets and building sites. The surrounding land uses, both existing and permitted, require investigation.

3. Schools, parks, playgrounds, and other cultural and social facilities are located, and the availability of transportation and shopping facilities is evaluated in reference to the services they may provide to the residents in the proposed development.

4. The subdivision ordinances are consulted for restrictions that may apply to the size and shape of lots, the width and grade of streets, the setback lines to be observed, and the methods for presentation of the maps required by the local government agency: the planning department, real estate commission, or city engineer.

5. The developer should employ a planner or engineer to prepare the tentative or preliminary plan for the development of the property. This map should show, with reasonable accuracy, the manner in which the land is to be subdivided: the approximate size, shape, and the number of lots, the location of streets, their radii of curvature and grades, the method for providing drainage in all areas, and the utilities to be installed. The zoning and proposed land uses—open space to be reserved or developed for recreation, shopping, or other community facilities—should also be indicated.

6. An estimate is then prepared to show the probable total cost for development of the site and indicate the minimum selling price for the lots to defray the cost of the land, the improvements, and the overhead for subdivision commissions and profits.

7. Before filing the tentative map with the local agency, planning department, or city engineer, it is generally considered good practice to consult with the Federal Housing Administration land planning officials and lending agencies. This is particularly important if approval for mortgage insurance by FHA is expected to be ultimately sought by purchasers of the lots.

8. The tentative map is then filed with the local agency, planning commission, or engineer, and this agency submits it to the various city departments for advice on engineering, health, schools, fire and police protection, and recreation. The suggestions and requirements of each department are coordinated by the planning commission, the specific

conditions being based upon the public health, safety, or the general welfare of the community. On many occasions the planning staff will prepare a revised plan to suggest improvements in the site design or indicate the manner in which the plan may better conform to local conditions and the comprehensive plan for the city.

9. After approval, the developer proceeds with the preparation of the final or precise engineering map for the land. The street improvements and utilities are shown, the lots are staked on the ground, and any minor changes that may be dictated by peculiarities in the site, such as hilly areas, are recorded. The final map is then filed with the city authorities, who check it for conformity with the approved tentative map. If compliance is apparent, the final map is submitted to the local legislative body and the mayor for final approval. It is then officially recorded.

10. Before sale of the land may be undertaken the final recorded map must usually be filed with the state real estate commission and approval of sale obtained from that government agency.

CURRENT TRENDS

The subdivision of land is responding to the techniques of large-scale planning, and the magic words *mass production* and *prefabrication* are having their effect. Jerry-building persists, to be sure, and the city faces a struggle to combat the insidious effect of the cheap products of unprincipled, speculative developers. Pressure to retreat from decent standards is strong, and resistance is difficult in periods when a housing shortage and high costs create social as well as economic problems for citydwellers. In the interest of economy or a greater profit margin, the pressure to reduce standards is ever present, but the necessity for and desirability of such standards is generally recognized. It is in the broader implications of urban expansion that regulations of land subdivision need serious attention.

Conservation of the land is vital, not only to avoid reckless waste of this precious resource but also for the economic and social stability of the community. The sprawl of suburbia is a symptom of the revolt against congestion and exploitation in the central city. The crying need for reexamination of the nature of urbanism in our society is urgent, but the extension of urban facilities ad infinitum to serve the symptom postpones treatment of the malady. A common perhaps national fervor comparable to that which brought the London Plan and New Towns to England after World War II may be necessary to force the search for a pattern of urbanism appropriate to our time. Meanwhile, and without relaxing this search, the uneconomic expansion of suburbia will require some measure of curtailment. The unpleasant reality of deterioration throughout great

SUBDIVISION MAP CHART

Parcel Map
Filing Procedures

Map prepared by or under direction of a registered civil engineer or licensed land surveyor. Procedure for filing and obtaining approvals as provided by city ordinance.

Transmitted after approval to county recorder through clerk of board of supervisors.

County recorder must examine map and accept or reject it for filing within 10 days.

Tentative Map
Filing Procedures 1

Map prepared by or under direction of a registered civil engineer or licensed land surveyor.

Filed with Planning Director

Public Works Director
City Engineer
Building Superintendent

Planning Director

Final Map
Filing Procedures

Map prepared by or under direction of a registered civil engineer or licensed land surveyor following approval or conditional approval of tentative map.

Necessary certificates and acknowledgements obtained.

Map filed with City Clerk (must be filed prior to expiration of tentative map)

Planning Director and City Engineer

If improvements not completed, improvement agreement entered into with local agency as a condition of approval.

Planning Commission

Approves, conditionally approves, or disapproves within 50 days after filing with clerk. (Deemed approved if no action taken within 50 days, but only insofar as map complies with act and city ordinances.)

→ If dissatisfied, subdivider may appeal within 15 days to the City Council

City Council

→ At next regular meeting sets date (within 30 days thereafter) to consider map.

→ Approves, conditionally approves, or disapproves within the 30 day period. (Deemed approved if no action taken within the 30 day period, but only insofar as map complies with act and local ordinances.)

→ Decision of City Council within 10 days. (Deemed approved if no action taken within time limits, but only insofar as map complies with act and city ordinances.)

→ Map approved by City Council within 10 days or at its next regular meeting, if in substantial compliance with previously approved tentative map and conditions, if any, imposed on the tentative map have been met. (Deemed approved if no action taken within 10 day period.)

→ Map transmitted after approval to county records through clerk of board of supervisors.

→ County recorder must examine map and accept or reject for filing within 10 days.

areas of the central city demands attention, but prudent conservation of land is a companion to economy in the cost of government.

The requirement that the land developer assume the cost of street and utility improvements in new subdivisions is accepted practice. Expansion creates the demand for a variety of facilities and services including schools, parks, playgrounds, health, fire and police protection, and highway and utility extensions. It is a public responsibility to assure the provision of these facilities. When the services are required to accommodate an increase in population, the added tax revenue to the community may maintain an economic balance with the cost of the facilities. Imbalance occurs, however, when the municipal facilities are necessarily duplicated to serve the population escaping from the central city, or where expansion is into an area that has no economic support.

The power to withhold permission to subdivide land is one control with which balance may be maintained. Denial of the right to subdivide land, however, is strong medicine, and other means may serve with greater equity and equal effectiveness. Independent of the land's market value, the public improvements and services necessary to development enhance the basic land value. Since this increment of increased value is created by public expenditure, it seems reasonable to assess a pro rata share of the cost against the subdivision.

A policy adopted in a growing number of cities is the requirement that the developer shall provide the new subdivision with a neighborhood park and playground. The policy is based on the premise that recreation space to serve a residential subdivision is in a category similar to public rights-of-way and improvements for streets, sidewalks, service roads, and parkways. Since the size of subdivisions varies, some being too small to require a local recreation area, the subdivider is assessed a charge that is deposited with the city to assure the development of this facility when the demand arises.

PLANNED DEVELOPMENT

The growing acceptance of the principles of community planning is one of the encouraging signs of an improvement in standards. Land in the heart of cities is already subdivided. Improvement in city planning within these huge areas must necessarily emerge with techniques of urban renewal and redevelopment. The major activity has consequently been taking place on the outskirts of the cities and will undoubtedly continue until renewal becomes an effective instrument for rebuilding the central areas.

Attention to the amenities of good community planning is apparent in the standards espoused by such organizations as the Urban Land Institute. The members include some of the pioneers in the development of subdivisions and the planning and building of residential communities. That good planning may also be good business is attested to by the appeal for an improvement in subdivision development by such men and organizations. The mediocre (and worse) product of speculative ventures has succeeded in the past and will continue to succeed as long as it remains a profitable enterprise. As the initiative of creative enterprise in community building produces better standards in the living environment, the speculative ventures will be reduced to a diminishing investment level; by this form of competition and the maintenance of decent standards of land subdivision—land planning—our cities may gradually improve as an environment for the people.

The Community Unit

In the comprehensive plan, the locations of future neighborhood centers —shopping centers, parks, and schools—are only approximately defined within the undeveloped areas of the city. The land use is usually shown by density classifications for residential purposes. The principles of community planning applied to large-scale subdivisions imply a balanced range of dwelling accommodations as well as a full range of community facilities. A provision for planned development, or the "community unit," has been incorporated in zoning ordinances to encourage and facilitate this integration of land uses.

Under this provision an owner or group of owners may produce a complete development plan that, upon approval by the planning commission, may be adopted by the legislative body as the zoning plan for the entire area in lieu of prevailing zoning. This feature affords a flexibility not heretofore available. It implements planning for a diversification of dwelling types, characteristically lacking in conventional zoning, and ensures harmonious density within the plan.

The neighborhood association is a familiar instrument for property owners to secure and maintain common amenities. Membership is usually stipulated in property deeds. The planned unit development embraces this legal instrument as a new level of self-government through cooperative or condominium ownership. The owner of a dwelling—apartment or house—in a cooperative owns shares of stock in the entire development with the right of occupancy in a specific dwelling. The owner of a condominium has title to the dwelling itself and a proportionate interest in the land and exterior facilities. The governing organization in both cases is an association of all owners with responsibility and authority for levying assessments for management and exterior maintenance. The condominium is generally preferred, since owners are financially responsible only for their own dwellings and for a portion of the related common areas and are not liable for obligations incurred by other owners.

The prospects for an improved environment warrant encouragement of this enlightened approach. The cumbersome procedures involved in the modification of conventional zoning fortify entrenched resistance to the flexibility community planning demands. Planned development may be a means to overcome current complications and achieve a variety in urban expansion not previously feasible. It could release the future subdivision of land from the straitjacket in which the built-up city and current subdivision practices are bound; it would provide the amenities and character of an urban environment associated with the central city without its concomitant faults. It may lead to a broader concept of planned decentralization for the metropolitan regions, where the great majority of the population is destined to find itself in the future industrial and scientific age.

Density Control

Conventional residential zoning classifies land uses according to building types—single family or multiple family. This method has its roots in the historical beginning of zoning when "fine" residential sections were protected from the intrusion of undesirable uses. The precedent has lingered while the protection has become a myth. Vast changes in the social and economic structure have completely altered the physical character of the city. The multifamily dwelling is no longer restricted to the "tenement house" class, nor is the single-family dwelling district the sole domain of the privileged class. The apartment and the detached house are not now distinguished by the difference in type of dwelling but rather by the quality of each, the geographic location, and particularly by the preferences of the residents and the composition of the family. Incompatibility revolves about the differences in the density of each type—the relative adequacy of interior and exterior space for comfort, convenience, and safety.

Planned development implements a desirable mix of dwelling accommodations to serve the needs of a balanced range of family sizes and preferences. The quality of the improvements placed upon the land and the level at which they are maintained contribute to the character of a community, but density is the key factor in planning. It establishes the texture of the physical form. It reflects the distinction, for instance, between a community of single-family homes and one of multistory apartments. It is a unit of measure for establishing a balance among all community facilities and circulation.

The term *density* is commonly employed as a measure of the number

Fig. 1   Fig. 3

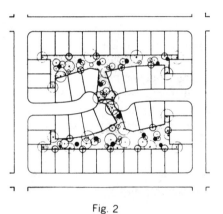

Fig. 2

Density control. *In this illustration Figure 1 represents a typical subdivision of forty-eight lots controlled by the minimum lot size. In Figure 2 relaxation of the minimum lot size as the basic control results in the same number of lots but reduces the area of internal streets, eliminates through traffic, and provides a common open space for all dwellings. It introduces a diversification in streets and an increase of recreation space.*

of dwellings that occupy or may occupy an area of land. *Net density* is identified with the number of dwellings in relation to the land area exclusive of public rights-of-way—the streets and sidewalks, parks and playgrounds, schools and commercial areas—whereas *gross density* usually pertains to the number of dwellings in relation to an area of land including all public rights-of-way and other related land uses. A distinction between these definitions may serve a useful purpose for certain technical measurements and comparisons, but the significant measure for the general texture of the physical form is expressed by gross density.

The pressure of urbanization has intensified the demand for land to accommodate the expanding urban population. Efforts to maintain the traditional single-family dwelling on its individual lot has forced the subdivision of land into increments of inadequate size; the typical "cookie-cutter" subdivision pattern has been inevitable. This, in combination with the pressure to reduce building and site development costs, has resulted in vast areas of mediocre residential tracts about our cities.

Every city will have its districts of single-family detached homes; this traditional form of family dwelling has virtues of particular value. In the very large metropolis these districts may be removed to the distant outskirts, but they should be planned with standards that actually produce the amenities of the detached house on its separate piece of land. In fact, however, in the attempt to preserve the single-family detached dwelling the minimum lot size has been reduced to dimensions that actually nullify the real advantages of this form. The narrow width of sideyards that separate dwellings denies privacy and renders the space wasteful; the conventional street setbacks have lost almost all semblance of usefulness since the automobile converted the street from a promenade to a service roadway. Insistence upon a distinction in zoning between subdivisions of high-density single-family lots and low-density apartment districts has consequently contributed in large measure to the extension of urban sprawl.

The genuine unit for the measurement of adequate planning standards is the individual human being. Family composition and characteristics vary, as do personal desires. Families need space in proportion to their sizes; children need space for active recreation, adults for sports, and the elderly for relaxation. Variations in these requirements may be more than absorbed in the "psychological elbow room" people need and now find wanting in their living environment. A diversification of dwelling types is necessary to satisfy the wide range of desires and family needs in a city. Insistence upon the distinction between a single-family classification of land use and the apartment district has tended to obscure the wide gap that exists between the amount of land per family in these two zoning categories. If the amount of space on the earth were related to the common denominator of the human being, the importance of density rather than the type of dwelling structure or the size of a lot could be employed as the desirable control for residential planning.

It is within the space of this wide gap that conventional subdivision practice and apartment zoning require overhauling. Were a relatively common standard of population density to be adopted as the measure of control for residential development, varied patterns could be woven within the overall texture of the physical form of the city. The apartment and the single house, the tall building and the low building, would then approach equal acceptability as neighbors and as places in which to live.

The interpretation of density control may be extended to mean that the conventional minimum lot size represents an acceptable unit of measurement for the gross density in a community. The number of dwellings that may be placed on an area of land is thereby controlled by this density

With the minimum prevailing lot as the unit of measurement for the overall gross density in the illustration, the site would accommodate as many as 200 dwellings. Adjusting the internal street system to the topography in a typical subdivision plan, with the usual odd lot sizes that result, would produce only 137 individual lots in conformance with the standard regulation (Fig. 1). With the principle of density control applied so that 200 dwellings are permitted, arranging clusters of row (alias "town," "group," "garden," or "patio") houses about cul-de-sac roads results in the allocation of about one-fifth of the site for park development (Fig. 2).

This is the primary community interest served by density control. Other advantages may accrue in the planning of individual dwellings, cul-de-sac roads, attractive plantings along the main circulation roads, and economy in site improvement costs. These costs may be reduced to as much as one-half of those of the conventional subdivision because of economy in grading, paving, drainage, and utilities. The degree to which the consumer of housing shares in these economies will extend the broad social advantages that may also accrue.
(Plans courtesy of Richard Leitch, Architect.)

rather than the minimum lot size per dwelling. This method of control offers flexibility in planning the internal street system and the arrangement of the dwelling units. Efficient planning may also produce economy in development cost. As compensation for these advantages a predetermined proportion of the property would be reserved as open space for community recreation.

CHAPTER 30

DEVELOPMENT ISSUES

PROCEDURE

Before any public or private development can take place the developers must take a number of steps. Among them, they must observe the comprehensive plan as it affects the land, the zoning ordinance and its many regulations, the subdivision laws of both the local community and the state; they must abide by the findings of the environmental review agency, which will determine if the project impacts unfavorably on environment, energy use, or endangered species; they must follow the building code and all of its many components, and, if the site is near the coast, must pass the muster of the critical eye of local and state coastal commissions. Finally, they may have to convince citizens' committees, environmental protection associations, and other groups that are opposed to development on personal or philosophic grounds.

Having cleared all of these steps, the developer is then faced with the costs related to the required procedures and improvements. It is important to recognize that many of the costs now part of the developmental process are due to past excesses in land management and the problems directly related to earlier lack of adequate regulation.

Fees

Some of the fees assessed the subdivider are given in the fee chart that follows. These are determined at the local level and relate to the costs of both materials and manpower at a given time. The data serve only to illustrate the impact of those local government requirements, which are meant to assure the ultimate users of the land that they are not walking into an untenable situation of great expense in the future. Later installation often involves lengthy individual negotiations with a multitude of occupants and a variety of economic situations. In many instances the "after-occupancy" efforts to bring a development up to acceptable levels result in failure and frustration. It is far better to have the improvements included in the original costs so that installations can be done on a mass basis at much less expense.

Typical Fees Related to Land Subdivisions

A. The following fee shall be paid to the community and deposited into the general fund:
  1. Tract No. —— $ 3.00

B. The following fees shall be paid to the planning director and deposited into the general fund:
  1. Tentative land division map, preliminary filing— $ 25.00
  2. Tentative subdivision map, filing— $100.00 plus
  3. Tentative statutory condominium subdivision map, filing— $100.00 plus
     $10.00 per gross acre.
  4. Revised tentative subdivision map, filing— $ 50.00 plus
     $2.50 for any additional lot.
  5. Revised statutory condominium subdivision map, filing— $ 50.00 plus
     $10.00 per additional gross acre.
  6. Tentative parcel map, filing— $ 50.00 plus
  7. Revised tentative parcel map, filing— $ 50.00 plus
  8. Tentative commercial or industrial parcel map, filing— $100.00 plus
     $2.50 per parcel.
  9. Revised tentative commercial or industrial parcel map, filing— $ 50.00 plus
     $2.50 for any additional parcel.
  10. Land projects— $ 50.00
      in addition to regular fee.
  11. Land division unit map, filing— $ 50.00
  12. Reversion to acreage, filing— $100.00
  13. Certificate of compliance, filing— $100.00

C. The following fees shall be paid to the planning director and deposited into the appropriate flood control fund or agency fund providing flood hazard reports:

1. Tentative land divisions map, filing— $100.00 plus $1.50 per lot or parcel.
2. Tentative statutory condominium subdivision map, filing— $100.00 plus
3. Revised tentative land division map filing within one year of the date of approval— No fee
4. Revised tentative land division map filing after one year— $100.00 plus $1.50 per lot or parcel, except that for statutory condominium, the fee shall be $100.00 per gross acre.

D. The following fee shall be paid to the planning director and deposited into the appropriate road fund or gas tax fund:

1. Final subdivision map, filing— $ 30.00

E. The following fees shall be paid to the city and deposited into the appropriate road fund or gas tax fund:

1. Final subdivision map, filing— $100.00 plus $6.00 per lot.
2. Final parcel map, filing— $ 60.00 plus $7.50 per parcel.
3. Final statutory condominium subdivision map, filing— $ 10.00 plus $40.00 per gross acre.
4. Plan checking and field inspection including survey monuments fee shall be 3 percent of the total cost of improvements as estimated by the city engineer and shall be paid as follows:
   a. Filing of map for checking— $ 5.00 per lot
   b. Planned residential development including statutory condominium— $ .25 per linear foot
   c. The remaining portion of the 3 percent shall be paid prior to recording of the final map.
5. Lot revision after checking— $ 6.00 per lot
6. Reversion to acreage— $100.00
7. Recordation of the final map— $ 50.00 for the first sheet plus $2.00 for each sheet thereafter.

COSTS

Aside from the costs related to the processing and installation of certain improvements required by local law, developers are confronted with a multitude of direct costs. These include:

PLANNING AND RESEARCH

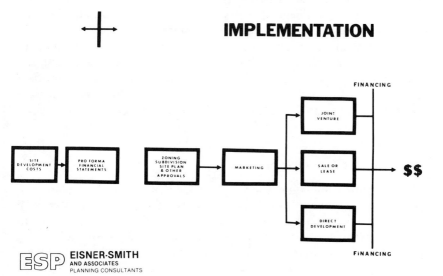

IMPLEMENTATION

The cost of the land
The cost of the money with which to buy the land
The cost of the following improvements:
    Planning and engineering
    Grading of lots and improving the streets
The cost of advertising and sales promotion
The cost of interest on all loans
The cost of bonds for improvements

In many cases the developers do not have funds to pay all the costs. They obtain bonds and pay the interest on these guarantees for the period between the requirement of the posting and the installation of the improvements. Where the project is large there may be several years between obtaining plan approval and the final occupancy permits for potential buyers. Some cities in which intensive building is encouraged have eliminated the usual tax on property entirely. They have substituted a development tax on all new structures. Through these funds they have been able to provide the minimal services new development requires.

Capital Improvement Programs

The investment of public funds in the construction of community improvements is done through capital improvement programs. Each community anticipates its income over a period of years and prepares a budget for the accomplishment of certain essentials to the growth and prosperity of the area over which it has jurisdiction. The types of improvements may include expansion of a sewage treatment plant, extension of trunk sewer or water lines, the development of new parks and recreational areas, and many other projects of this type.

The new growth management plans are making it easier to project future needs, since the plans are under the control of the agencies responsible for implementing the capital improvements.

The location and nature of public improvements such as streets, public buildings, and so on, are a major factor in determining environmental quality. Expenditures for these public improvements should be allocated in accordance with a planned program that balances needs and priorities against available resources and in accordance with the provisions of the comprehensive plan.

Capital improvement planning should not be limited only to those things that require funds from the city budget. Significant programs carried out by other levels of government can have a great effect on the timing, financing, and location of city projects.

THE INFRASTRUCTURE

The infrastructure includes all essential facilities such as water, sewers, streets and highways, public utilities, schools, libraries, parks, police and fire services, and many other facilities related to the protection of the health, safety, and general welfare. Before any property can be offered for sale, there must be a major investment in the infrastructure. The installation of the various elements involves both the public and private sectors identified with a proposed development.

The infrastructure must be in conformity with the comprehensive plan and all other regulations dealing with services to people. All must be related to the density of population proposed or the intensity of the commercial or industrial uses intended for the land.

Many of the elements of the infrastructure are installed prior to the occupancy of the sites. Others can follow when the need arises. Schools must be in place at the time the people and children are on the land. Water, sewers, and other utilities must be available at the time the land is to be occupied. The utilities must be in the streets before paving is done. The timing and sequence of the installation of improvements must be carefully planned. They must be tied into existing lines that have the capacity to accept the additional loading. Offsite connections may become a critical financial problem for the developer.

Although the developer is required to install and pay for most improvements, like all other costs they are passed on to the consumer. If the proposed development is detached from the already urbanized area, the offsite costs are also borne by the developer, but as the in-between spaces are filled the funds collected are returned to the initial activator. In many ways these funds are clear profit since the total cost of the development has already been passed on to the occupants, be they residential, industrial, or commercial.

Beyond the baseline items, there are several other costs. Schools and parks are often assessed against the developer either in the form of demands for land or by in-lieu fees. This cost is, of course, related only to those facilities that serve the people who directly benefit from them. In California, early efforts to secure neighborhood parks were declared illegal on the grounds that the state subdivision law did not list them as improvements; the state law was thereafter amended to include parks. A formula was devised to require the subdivider to allocate either land or in-lieu fees. In addition, in 1977 the state recognized the overcrowded conditions in local schools and adopted legislation to require the allocation of land or in-lieu fees to assist communities in securing temporary buildings and sites for school purposes.

Maintenance

Installation of many of the elements of the infrastructure has generally been established as the responsibility of the persons who develop land. However, the responsibility for the maintenance and replacement of aging elements in the underground and surface systems is almost universally the responsibility of the public agencies called "government." These are elements in general that have to do with the supply of water and gas and the disposal of sewage and solid wastes, among other things.

Very little thought has ever been given to the useful life of these elements of the urban structure, almost with the thought that once in place they live to eternity. Since most urban areas are aged and many facilities outlive their useful life, the economic problems facing communities are often beyond their capability to cope. The condition grows worse and more dangerous to health and safety with each passing year. Aside from the broken pavement and chuckholes on the surface, most of these facilities cannot be seen by the general public, and consequently there is no outcry for improvement. There seems to have been no long-term plan for dealing with the infrastructure that is so essential to urban life.

Obtaining funds for the maintenance of the public domain has rested largely on the general taxpayer and his obligation to pay taxes on his residence or business. Taxpayer revolts in the 1980s have reduced many communities' ability to continue the protection of the physical environment. In the past, efforts to maintain the public ways have been funded by capital grants from the federal and state governments, from taxes that they have collected. But recent programs based on these sources have also been reduced or cut out altogether.

Few people consider the congestion that occurs in the unseen workings of our urban communities. Somewhat like the human body, time and use fills the concealed arteries with rust, metal accumulations caused by electrolysis, and just plain garbage, to the point where the service plants can no longer function efficiently. When bridges fail or roads become unusable, we respond more readily than we do to the failure of water or sewer lines. It has been said that conditions in the city of New York are so bad that it would cost about $40 billion to rebuild the infrastructure, and it would take more than ten years to accomplish the most essential portions of this task. Every large city faces the same problems. While the extent and the costs may not be as great, the ability to perform the tasks is even more difficult financially.

Dr. Pat Choate, author of *America in Ruins,* noted in his comments at a 1983 meeting of the California Infrastructure Task Force that "between $2 and $3 trillion is due to be spent on infrastructure between now and the year 2000." It is far cheaper, he said, to institute timely maintenance procedures on existing structures than to implement new projects.

CHAPTER 31

GROWTH MANAGEMENT

HOW SHALL WE GROW?

It has traditionally been assumed that continuous growth is essential to economic prosperity. But an unpleasant fact of life now becomes apparent: as urban population swells, public welfare and protection absorb increasing segments of city budgets. In the absence of a national or state policy to direct population distribution, individual cities are obliged to make their own decisions about growth and development.

Within the comprehensive plan land uses are designated and population densities distributed; thus the "carrying capacity" of the land in a city is measured. It is useful to know the rate of estimated population increase, through immigration and birth-death figures, in anticipating programs to improve and maintain city services. But it is the comprehensive plan that establishes how many people a city may accommodate and the quality of the environment to be provided for those people. The zoning ordinance translates the land use provisions of the comprehensive plan into specific terms. These instruments of planning policy represent the ultimate "growth policy" of a city. Where they are not so designed and not so implemented, the entire planning process is invalid.

These processes for guiding urban development are invalidated to a large extent by the common assumption that a city must find ways and means to accommodate all the people who may choose to live and work within it, and that regulations of land use that limit density of use are infringements on the "property rights" of landowners. Such allegations nullify the planning process and reflect a serious cultural and economic malady: the conflict between the recognition of land as the precious and rare natural resource it is, and the concept of land as a commodity to be traded as merchandise. The "vested rights" of an owner to use his land as he chooses must be limited to uses that serve the public interest; these are determined by the comprehensive plan and the zoning ordinances derived from it.

The small city of Petaluma in northern California, with a population of some 30,000, illustrates the dilemma. Confronted with inadequate public services, sewers, water supply, and schools to accommodate an unprecedented population growth, the city undertook the unusual measure of restricting further development to 500 dwellings a year. The well-financed Construction Industry Association protested the city ordinance and, in 1974, a federal court judge ruled: "No city can control its population growth numerically."[1]

The issue was drawn between the right of a city to determine its own character and the obligation to accept all the people who may choose to reside there. Petaluma's comprehensive plan of 1962 (when the population was 17,000) provided for growth to an estimated 77,000 by 1985. It also provided a guide for capital improvements of facilities and services in conjunction with expected city revenues.

The Supreme Court, however, reversed the lower court decision, holding that the city had developed a careful timetable for the expansion of city services. It ruled moreover that the city's carefully worked-out plan was predicated on expected tax revenues and so could not be altered.

The legal strife in Petaluma represents the struggle of cities across the land to control their own destiny. A 1972 zoning ordinance in Ramapo, New York, through which the timing and sequence of development could be made consistent with necessary capital improvements for public services, was upheld by the Supreme Court.[2] The issue of exclusionary zoning, however, is not fully resolved, and the equitable distribution of housing for all income levels is a complex issue. An ordinance in Fairfax

---

1. Decision by Judge Lloyd H. Burke, Federal District Court, San Francisco, January 14, 1974.

2. In *Golden v. Planning Board of the Town of Ramapo* (1972), the Court stated: "There is then something inherently suspect in a scheme which apart from its professional purposes, effects a restriction upon the free mobility of a people until sometime in the future when projected facilities are available to meet increased demands. . . . What we will not countenance, then, under any guise, is community efforts at immunization or exclusion. But, far from being exclusionary, the present amendments merely seek, by the implementation of sequential development and timed growth, to provide a balanced cohesive community dedicated to the efficient utilization of land."

County, Virginia, required that 15 percent of all units in multifamily housing be available to low-income families. It was declared unacceptable by the courts, which alleged the provision an illegal "taking" of private property for public purposes.

The impact of growth affects every city, town, and village. Boca Raton, Florida, grew at an alarming rate—from 7,000 in 1960 to 28,000 in 1970—and placed a ceiling on its ultimate growth with a limit of 40,000 dwelling units. Sanbornton, New Hampshire, population 1,000, rezoned to a minimum of six-acre sites to forestall compact development.

The issue of property rights versus public interest is subject to a variety of legal interpretations. Development of Great Salt Meadow in Stratford, Connecticut, was denied by the Environmental Protection Commission. The land was already zoned for industrial use, and the Rykbar Industrial Corporation contended that the action constituted a "taking," claiming $77,700,000 in damages. On the same grounds, disapproval of development of a seventeen-acre site at Fleur de Lac at Lake Tahoe, California, by the Tahoe Regional Planning Agency resulted in a claim for $4,500,000 compensation.

The dilemma is not confined to development of open land. The great concourse of Grand Central Station in New York City, owned by the Penn Central Railroad, was declared a landmark by the New York City Landmarks Protection Commission in 1967. UGP Properties, Inc., had leased the air rights above this historical monument; denied the right to build a fifty-nine-story office building above it, the lessee claimed a "taking" and asked $8 million a year in damages. In 1972, after high-rise apartments near the bay front in San Francisco had obliterated dramatic views for inland dwellers, the city created a forty-foot height limit. It did not apply to the downtown area, where the increasing height of skyscraper office buildings was destroying the scale of the picturesque urban silhouette. Also threatened by high-rise apartments, San Diego set height limitations along its waterfront. The people of Santa Barbara by referendum established a stated limitation on the height of buildings in their charter, simply because they did not want high-rise structures.

How we shall grow to accommodate the new urban population and achieve the civilized quality of the environment toward which we aspire remains a crucial issue confronting cities as we approach the twenty-first century. Violation of the "constitutional right to freedom of movement," alleged in the Petaluma case against the city's restrictive ordinance, is a transparently superficial argument on behalf of those whose interest is the exploitation of land. It reinforces the necessity for distribution of population, but it should not abrogate the city's obligation, as well as its "right," to determine the number of people it shall accommodate and the environment it intends to provide for them.

Premature, scattered, or noncontiguous subdivision of land has perennially plagued city administrations. Agricultural zoning is a common protection, but it is usually a device for postponement rather than planning. It has become common practice for cities to finance extensions of public services—water, sewers, roads, and so on—to encourage urban expansion. These costs are then recovered by the city in whole or in part through taxes on development over ensuing years.

A multitude of other services, however, must immediately be assured to the new residents—schools and fire and police protection among them. Uncontrolled exploitation of land for development about the periphery of large and small cities exceeds the capacity to provide services and maintain desirable open space. People's desire to escape from the oppressive environment of congestion in cities accelerates the trend toward suburban growth. The goal of local administrations must be a balanced use of land and services within the economic capacity of a city to achieve and maintain the quality of the environment.

An enlightened attitude toward the "right" to develop property may emerge as civilized values mature. Meanwhile, this right must be coupled with responsibility to assume the burden of cost it imposes on the public. This would require that landowners and developers accept the obligation for all the costs that may be entailed, including extension of facilities and services. Such a policy does not deny the right to use the property in accordance with the local land use regulations. It is simply a "carry your own weight" policy. Such regulations would act as one means of growth control and take the decision-making power away from the local bureaucracy, which is often arbitrary in its decisions or subject to political pressure.

There is flexibility in the planning process to amend plans and zoning ordinances, but that flexibility cannot be subverted by incompetent, capricious, or corrupt public administrators. Among the most damaging "changing conditions" to which a city is subject is the subordination of public interest to commercial exploitation, the easy zoning changes, casual conditional permits, and a variety of special concessions for private advantage.

A city plan that is a vague diagram or is hardly more than a record of existing land uses transcribed onto a map offers nothing but more of the same; for that there is no need for a plan. In contrast, a plan that embraces innovative and imaginative measures to correct social problems[3] and misuses of land can be a public commitment to progressive change.

---

3. The Sketch Plan prepared by *California Tomorrow*, published in 1971, lists greater political participation, reduction in unemployment, improved educational opportunities, improved access to health service, combating of hunger, and the reduction of crime as social measures that strongly affect the poor of all ethnic groups.

PLANNING

A central concern in plans for accommodating future population growth is determining where new residential development should take place, given the necessity of providing essential public services. While the costs of additional roads, sewer collector lines, and water lines will be borne eventually by new homebuyers, there are other continuing services that must be provided by local governmental units.

For example, current expenditures for such services as police and fire protection, water and wastewater systems operation and maintenance, street maintenance, and solid waste collection amount to a substantial portion of general fund expenditures. The costs of police protection, waste collection, and street maintenance alone amount to about 37 percent of general fund expenditures in El Centro, California. The per capita costs of these services are particularly sensitive to the density of the residential developments, so that a widely dispersed pattern of developments can have a substantial impact on municipal finances and local tax rates.

IMPLEMENTING THE COMPREHENSIVE PLAN

The management of community growth and development is not a new technique. Every step taken since the adoption of the first zoning ordinances has been an effort to direct the structural pattern of a city in a way that would bring about the best, most efficient and desirable living environment for its people. Zoning, however, has not always taken into account the timing and sequence of development and thus has not been effective in indicating where or when services can be provided at levels essential to sound community living.

With the requirement that each community prepare a comprehensive plan for its future growth and development, there was still the lack of an instrument to provide for the phasing and direction of growth other than in a general way. Expansions into new areas are often piecemeal, without the essential studies to determine what the costs of scattered development might be.

Often the zoning of the land reflects decisions made before there was a comprehensive plan and, in most instances, before the decision by the state legislature that zoning must be consistent with the comprehensive plan. In the past, community leaders felt that the plan was a simple guide and therefore had no real meaning in law. In California, this has changed with the adoption of new state laws. The plan is now considered critical in all land use decisions, because it is the only real indication of how a community wants to grow and how it will attain its goals. Until the law was changed there had been a gap in the process; no ties between the comprehensive plan and timing of development existed. Now, however, growth management is to be the vehicle for implementing plan proposals by creating timing and directional guidelines based on the ability of the community to absorb growth.

The growth management program is therefore an outgrowth of efforts by community leaders not so much to stop growth and change as to direct it and limit it to prescribed boundaries based on community capabilities.

The growth management plan is the bridge between planning and development. It is the evaluation system used to determine if the proposals submitted to the community can be accommodated within the fiscal abilities of the community without causing existing residents and commercial and industrial occupants to assume an unreasonable tax burden.

The growth management plan is the best means designed to date to bring about logical implementation of the long-range proposals of the comprehensive plan. Zoning thereafter becomes the legal vehicle that permits development to proceed in those areas where growth management finds it appropriate and timely.

FACTORS AND TECHNIQUES

There must be a well-designed comprehensive plan that establishes the densities and intensities of land uses and gives an indication of the facilities required to meet the needs of the residents. Where facilities and services exist, they would be evaluated in terms of the potential for expanded demands.

If there is a service shortfall there should be a determination of the ability of the individual services to expand to meet new demands, and when this expansion will be possible both physically and financially. Only after the determination of the "when and how" should zoning of the land be approved, which will allow for the development to take place at the densities and purposes set forth in the comprehensive plan.

A number of approaches and techniques have been developed to ensure that future growth occurs in a manner consistent with the community's ability to accommodate new growth. Some are described below.

Zoning. The pace and distribution of growth can be affected by the following types of rezoning:

Downzoning is intended to reduce the ultimate holding capacity of an area, either in terms of the number of residences or the land available for business expansion. The objective is to reduce the pace of population or economic growth to a level consistent with the community's ability to absorb new people and businesses.

Upzoning is intended to increase the ultimate holding capacity of an area and can serve to attract development that might have occurred elsewhere. For example, the upzoning of central areas can help reduce growth pressures on undeveloped lands.

Moratoriums are intended to prevent further development for a relatively brief time in order to allow for the completion of studies and plans, and the implementation of controls directed toward managing and accommodating growth.

Building Quotas. These limit the number of housing units that can be built during a given period of time. They are intended to reduce population growth and to ease the burden of such growth on public facilities and services.

Total Population Densities. Techniques such as downzoning, moratoriums, and so on are used to ensure that a city's total population does not exceed some stipulated maximum. That maximum is set on the basis of the city's ability to provide services affecting the safety and general welfare of its residents.

Land Banking. Land is actually bought by local government and then made available for private development under carefully specified conditions (such as consistency with the comprehensive plan and the provision for some low-income housing), according to a timed-sequenced capital improvements program. This ensures that future growth occurs at a pace compatible with the city's financial resources.

Development Rights Transfer. All landowners receive development rights in proportion to the amount of undeveloped land owned within an area, with no single landowner initially owning enough rights to develop all of the land. Unexecuted rights are bought and sold on the free market (independent of land ownership) and tend to be transferred from rural areas to growth areas.

To develop a specific piece of property to the intensity of use designated on the comprehensive plan, a developer must accumulate sufficient rights.

Timing and Sequencing Controls. These controls are intended to affect the distribution of growth, as well as its pace. A well-known application of such controls occurred in Ramapo, New York. The controls, in conjunction with a master plan and a capital improvements plan, were used to constrain growth around existing developed areas, to prevent hopscotch development into agricultural areas, and to forestall development until necessary public services could be made available at reasonable costs.

Each of these approaches must be evaluated on the basis of a number of legal, economic, and social criteria. The issue of the legality of a particular approach is complicated but tends to revolve around a number of basic questions: Is a regulation related to a "protectable goal" (such as health, safety, or general welfare)? Are equally situated landowners treated equally? Is the regulation "reasonable" in application as well as intent, and not discriminatory in its application? Is the regulation exclusionary or does it restrict free movement? Answers to each of these questions are currently being evaluated through the judicial process.

Economic criteria include the costs of application and administration. For example, land banking involves substantial public money. Also to be considered are the indirect effects of controls. Quotas, downzoning, and population ceilings can increase the costs of housing and may accelerate the rate of growth as developers rush to beat impending deadlines (often at higher cost). Social criteria include issues of equity and exclusion and the political impact of governmental intervention.

SMALL CITIES

The cities of El Centro and Holtville lie within ten miles of each other in a highly productive agricultural area in southeastern California. The problem of growth confronts each of these communities, but in different ways. Both are confronted with the potentials of growth, especially as it may be affected by the development of geothermal resources located in nearby areas. But each has special problems associated with the anticipated growth, and each has its own philosophic approach to dealing with it. El Centro wants to encourage growth. Holtville would discourage it in order to maintain its present rural, low-pressure way of living.

In both cities, most of the land within the city limits has been occupied, and growth must come either by intensifying the uses within the current city or expanding into the agricultural hinterland. El Centro sees no problem in the expansion and annexation program, since the city's major support comes from government and services (the city is the county seat). Holtville, on the other hand, is governed largely by persons sympathetic to the preservation of its agricultural resources. The city sees any invasion into the agricultural area as a reduction of its economic base.

Both communities have utility problems. El Centro's sewage disposal system is operating at capacity. The plant could handle the products of growth if the sewer lines were replaced to prevent seepage into groundwaters. Holtville, however, is not troubled by line capacity, but the treatment plant is underdesigned and there needs to be a complete moratorium on building until plant capacity has been improved to prevent further pollution of local streams and the Salton Sea, a nearby recreational resource.

Water is a problem for Holtville but does not pose any difficulty for El Centro. Other utilities are private or in special districts that can meet even explosive rates of growth that may come into the valley. The potential of the geothermal resources may actually mitigate the energy problem for many years to come.

Thus in the management of growth the entire planning process depended on the abilities of the cities to meet the requirements of health and safety for both the current residents and for those who constitute the element of growth.

Two other cities in California base their growth management plans on entirely different criteria. Both San Juan Capistrano and Rancho Mirage, like many other communities in the world, are deeply concerned about the maintenance of the quality of their environment. They both fear that too-rapid growth may allow some development to slip by without adequate review. Local pressures against increasing the staff that deals with review projects suggest there will be a reduction in the number of applications acceptable at any one time.

As reasonable and logical as the growth management process is, its acceptance by many communities has been limited by the negative stance of potential developers and those landowners whose property might be affected. One of the critical factors in acceptance of the management process is determining the number of residential units that can be absorbed and serviced at any one time. Projects that are already in the "pipeline" pose additional problems. In fairness to the developers who have expended considerable amounts of money to prepare such plans, these individuals are seldom kept from completing their projects, even if they exceed the management allowances.

Since the premise on which most management programs are based is the ability of the community to provide facilities and services for the residents-to-be, the developer should provide funds for additional improvements where needed to accommodate his contribution to the growth of the community. One of the questions this raises is, How can one developer provide for a portion of a school or part of a sewage treatment plant or water supply system? All of these facilities and services must be in place if they are to meet the needs of the proposed addition to the community.

PART 6

NEW HORIZONS

Slowly but surely humanity achieves
what its wise men have dreamed.

Anatole France

CHAPTER 32

URBAN DESIGN

Critics of the concept of urban design say that in fact it does not exist. "Towns are not designed," said one. "They are pasted together, piece by piece." If that is true, it is the result of too many persons being involved in the developmental process and insufficient cooperation among them—time being a major factor.

In recent years several interesting concepts have been put forward to bind individual efforts into a compatible whole. The comprehensive plan with its emphasis on a coordinated, unified system of land use and circulation is at the heart of this effort. The creation of new techniques and acceptance of greater responsibility by the land developer in subdividing property is another important gain. The emphasis on building development in a subdivision has tended to reduce the speculation in vacant land; thus the city may become a place for living rather than a hopscotched checkerboard of partly used real estate. The costly ignoring of concern for the environment—especially in the areas of fire prevention and land erosion—has also made the notion of urban design more acceptable to many people.

PUBLIC INTEREST AND INVOLVEMENT

For many years public interest and control of urban design were limited to the street system and the landscaping of the public portions of the

515

rights-of-way. The question of gridiron or curvilinear streets was discussed at subdivision design meetings, along with street width, street
parking provisions, and curbs and gutters. However, with the beginning
of the design of large communities as part of the new town concepts,
design of the total living environment came to be considered by public
agencies. Architectural and design review boards were created and the
communities became involved, sometimes to excess.

Many large shopping centers have received community approval only
when urban design of the highest quality was the basis for their development. Years of community conflict in Arcadia, California, resulted in
excellent designs by Victor Gruen before the neighbors felt that their
interest had been protected and the city approved the construction.

IMPACT

Urban design has the most effective impact when all of the theories of
serving the residents with open space and amenities are reflected in a
planned unit subdivision developed within the framework of the comprehensive plan. Sound judgment must be applied to the relationships between the permitted number of dwellings and the spaces between them.
The economics of building types, provision for access and parking, and
the responsibility for the maintenance of the open areas are issues that
must be resolved before construction can start.

Building laws not only permit but also have actually forced an enormous bulk to be loaded on the land. Consequently, the city has been
reduced to a network of street pavements lined with facades of unrelated
buildings. Architectural banality and chaos are inevitable. The "right" to
build as one wishes has approached a degree of license; the resulting
ugliness has frequently provoked the panacea of architectural control.

In the name of democracy the proponents of architectural control suggest it will not interfere with free expression. Actually there is little else
it can do. By its nature architectural control sets a form, usually in terms
of some particular style of architecture, and the designer is henceforth
bound by the capricious taste of a select few.

There are designers who produce a higher order of creative work than
others, but should their genius deny the right of self-expression to those
of lesser competence? Rare is the genius in the welter of people who can
capture the sublime in steel, stone, and space. This is clear when we
observe all the buildings of past ages rather than the isolated monuments
alone. If talent to produce appropriate and beautiful buildings is limited,
it is the task of society to raise the level of competence and widen the
cultural horizon, not to remove freedom of expression.

SYMMETRY OR FREEDOM

Democracy in city building is a framework in which the manifold functions of contemporary urban life may be accommodated with freedom of expression. Such freedom in organized society, as we are gradually coming to realize, implies self-discipline and respect for the dignity of others.

The city takes shape over the years through the enterprise of all the people. Moved by their desires, their opportunities, and the evolution of changing conditions, the city is in a continuous state of flux. Therefore its plan must accommodate a variety of forms. Eclecticism cultivated the impression that harmony of form is synonymous with symmetry, and planning assumed a rigid formality. Symmetry about an axis was assumed to produce a grand unity among the forms of the city. City building did not follow those plans, however, and the result was most discouraging if not a little puzzling; it seemed that planning was a futile enterprise, and indeed the form it had acquired was futile.

There was reason for the failure of "grand planning": because buildings were reminiscent of imperial domination over the lives of people, their forms were inimical to the tenets of democracy. Not only is the urge for free expression an integral characteristic of democratic society, it is also a distinct right. There can be no centerline about which the city of democracy is built; it is a fluid, changing form. The rigid symmetry of formal planning is alien. An autocrat may decree a great plan, and he has the power to draft the labor to execute it accordingly; but when that power transfers to the people, a new concept of urban conduct emerges. The people then seek a set of standards we call laws, adopted according to their will as guides in the conduct of their mutual and independent affairs. A new concept of planning also emerges, not less compelling but more plastic and sensitive to the will and expression of individuals in society.

The "grand plan" was conceived by a single mind to be imposed on the future. Thenceforth skill in its execution was not the creative power of the individual to solve a problem, but the ingenuity with which the requirements of a later time could be warped into a precast mold. It was suggestive of a solution before the problem was stated.

That democracy imposes great responsibility on the individual is self-evident; with the privilege of freedom comes responsibility. Harmony in the city of democracy calls for the exercise of individual responsibility and people's mutual respect. Since it was by means counter to democratic processes that a monarch carried out a vast venture like Versailles, so it is contrary to democratic behavior that individuals should ignore the work of others to memorialize their own vanity or expand the contents of their purses. Rivalry for "bigger and better" cities can do no more to open the way to creative civic design than can the stamp of classic planning.

The harmonious integration of various forms is the art of planning space. St. Mark's Piazza in Venice is a dramatic illustration of this. The piazza took five centuries to build. In it we find no sterile symmetry. It was an open space in which throngs of people could congregate. The ornate church of St. Mark's was erected in the eleventh century in the flourishing Byzantine style. The Palace of the Doges, built in the fourteenth and fifteenth centuries, was designed in the Gothic style of that period. It was a colorful building, but the facades were simple rectangles facing the sea and forming one side of the *piazzetta*. The facade leading from the waterfront was set back to frame a view of the church from the canal. Detached from the church, the campanile was a powerful accent in the group arrangement. When the *procuriatie* buildings were built during the late fifteenth and early sixteenth centuries, the Renaissance style was in flower. They were arranged about a long piazza placed at right angles to the piazzetta. Located that the intersection of these two plazas, the campanile was visually linked with the long facades of the *procuriatie vecchie* and library; the tower was not isolated in space like a centerpiece.

There was a variety among the forms, each successive addition to the plaza built in the style of its period. The spaces were intended to harmonize these variations; no part was tacked on to complete an original. The differences in architectural styles enhance the effect of this great plaza; the absence of axial symmetry impresses the observer. The flat facades of the Doges Palace was not imitated elsewhere to conform to a preconceived scheme; the facades of the procuriatie buildings were stretched into an oblong plan at an angle to the piazzetta, and the contrasts in the forms and spaces were emphasized by slanting the buildings in the plan.

The plastic quality of this great plaza is eloquent refutation of the sterile process of symmetrical planning that has frequently been substituted for monumentality in our eclectic period. Forms may be harmoniously integrated by appropriate contrasts—contrasts in form adjusted to accommodate the contrasts in contemporary expression as it evolves in successive periods of culture.

NEW DIMENSIONS

With the abundant labor of slaves ancient cities were built of blocks of stone and wood, their heavy forms refined by sculpturing the structural members. Laying stone upon stone, medieval builders formed soaring arches, flying buttresses, and intricate tracery. During these centuries all construction was wallbearing; all structural stresses were in compression.

The Industrial Revolution brought a violent change. The massive construction of ancient cities was transformed to the lightness of steel in tension. Processed in the crucibles of smelting plants and testing laboratories, materials were refined, their basic qualities extracted and synthesized. A wide range of synthetic materials was mechanically assembled on light structural frames. The dynamism of forces in tension replaced the static forms of compression, and the machine released a new freedom in the organization of space.

With the positive thrusts of railway, highway, and airway, new dimensions penetrated the twentieth-century city. Vehicles of transportation no longer mingled informally in the fashion of the Middle Ages. Seeking channels of uninterrupted directness, moving with uncompromising direction, straight ribbons stretch across level spaces and merge with irregular terrain in graceful sweeping curves. The highway is shaped to the contours of the land. Continuity is uninterrupted by natural obstacles; with almost defiant sureness bridges span chasms and tunnels pierce mountains. Unimpeded continuity is essential and insistent. Almost unnoticed, this new dimension has forced a new scale in city building.

The new scale appears in the Mount Vernon highway, the Westchester County parkways, the New York City highways and parkways, the Outer Drive in Chicago, and the freeways of Los Angeles. More rural than urban, the parkway in combination with clear-channel rapid transit for mass transportation is the salvation of the traffic dilemma in the heart of the city.

Matching the expanse of the parkway is the horizontal span of enclosed floor space. The city of today is a series of horizontal planes, one above the other, and the relatively constant floor heights retain the impression of human scale. Utility and economy are inconsistent with the inflated scale of the poorly conceived imitations of the past; excesses in scale that characterized the baroque city are restrained. Scale is not absent in the volume of floor space enclosed in tall buildings; it has been lost in the congestion of these buildings on the land—the absence of open space as a foil for their size. The skyscraper readily expresses the multiplicity of its floors, but the sense of scale has been destroyed by the oppressive bulk of buildings in proportion to the open space about them. It is toward the restoration of adequate space that the new dimensions of the city are forcing urban development.

The Penetration of Space

A rectilinear street arrangement has generally been interpreted as evidence of conscious planning. That assumption must be qualified by an appraisal of the purpose and functions for which the form was devised.

The Roman city was patterned after the military camp and agricultural and urban land have been subdivided into rectilinear plots; but it does not necessarily follow that the organization of a military camp or a convenient form for legal description and the recording of deeds are keys to the conscious design of cities for the residence and commerce of people. On the other hand, Hippodamus adopted the checkerbòard street arrangement for the purpose of allocating lots that would provide proper orientation of all the dwelling units erected upon them. Vehicular traffic was light, towns were small, and direct communication within them was of no particular import.

The Freeway

Today, the freeway or parkway brooks no interference; freedom of movement is continuous. The futility of the usual network of streets is exposed. Like an irresistible force meeting an immovable object, the freeway meets the gridiron: the city is the battleground. The static form of the right angle meets the dynamic thrust of free form; the tight gridiron of the surveyor versus the swirling twists of our "planned" suburbia. The battle is being waged in a vacuum; chaos prevails in both, the monotony of one, the variety of disorder in the other. The process is one of dividing the land rather than forming spaces, laying out roads and lots rather than planning appropriate and related uses, and allocating parcels as merchandise tagged with a price rather than arranging space for living or business.

Planning circulation about the city implies a twofold purpose: the direct and natural connection between two or more points, and clear direction for those traversing the roadways. The gridiron provides the latter, but it is essentially a devious zigzag route between two points. Complete loss of orientation is the curse of curving roadways, and no amount of picturesqueness can compensate for the confusion it creates.

A test of planning is the order it produces, and the freeway is a new instrument for orderly space arrangement. Its horizontal expanse clearly defines it as an artery with positive direction in contrast to minor roadways. Reliance on signs of nature or the rigid orientation of the gridiron in the old city is supplanted by the positive identification and direct action of the sweeping freeway. A dominant feature of the modern city, it brings time and space into harmony. The parkway is destined to force an orderly development not yet apparent in the cluttered urban environment, or it will sweep the city clean.

Open Space

Just as the freeway has rendered obsolete the corridor and gridiron street, a new relation between buildings and open space was introduced in the great housing developments during the 1920–1930 decade. Parklike open space was incorporated in the eighteenth-century terrace dwellings of the Royal Crescent and Lansdowne Crescent Bath and Regent's Park in London; the squares of Bloomsbury introduced the garden to residential streets. However, these developments were generally confined to the aristocracy, and the amenities were absent from the living environment of the majority of the urban population. During the early twentieth century Hendrik Pieter Berlage in Holland and Otto Wagner in Vienna strove to treat the dwellings of the people as integral parts of civic design, but they retained the corridor street and uniform facades reminiscent of baroque planning.

When the international housing crisis after World War I forced a widespread program of dwelling construction, the new dimensions pierced the archaic armor of the city. Large-scale planning freed from the restrictions of single lots completely altered the relation between dwelling and open space. The corridor street was abandoned, space between building facades was no longer devoted exclusively to vehicular circulation, and building units were arranged in orderly groups within free open space.

Space was designed for use, traffic arteries bypassed residential groups, and internal circulation was by way of service roadways and pedestrian walks. Recreation space was accessible from all dwellings, and buildings were planned so that each dwelling unit enjoyed the same orientation as every other dwelling. For the first time since the building of Hellenic cities a common standard of amenities was applied uniformly to all dwellings in the community plan. There was an affinity between the continuity and breadth of space along the parkway, and the flow of space through the developments of large-scale housing.

The infiltration of space in the center of the city is insistent, although it expresses the anachronism of urban growth. While automobile parking lots expand and slums are cleared, adjacent lots are improved with a greater density than before, and congestion persists round about; one ugly improvement is substituted for another. Nevertheless, space is forcing its way into the heart of the city.

Much land still lies vacant within the city, and more lies fallow on the periphery. No pattern, no plan, and little thought have been directed to the future destiny of this land save for outmoded zoning and ineffective building laws. Should we not profit by experience? The tragic results of chaotic expansion lie all about us, the heavy hand of public debt gropes frantically to support the crumbling environment, and all because we waited too long!

The Future

To pursue this course is to invite the same ills that now plague the central urban areas—and incur the same debt for blight and redevelopment again and again. It is a challenge to invest in the future.

Laws to prevent the abusive use of land are one step. Common sense suggests another: the reservation of space for public use—plan today our program for tomorrow. We will not save by waiting; now is the time for decision. Now is the time, not later, to decide upon the orderly expansion of the urban pattern, or abandon it to the termites of civic decay. If we intend to restore decency to the environment, now is the time to prepare.

The failure of inaction is written in the spectacle of present cities. The success of action is demonstrated in those rare instances when vision triumphed. What would Manhattan do without Central Park, Chicago without Lincoln Park, San Francisco without Golden Gate Park? In contrast, what a price the people have paid to "make" the land for Chicago's lakefront and the Robert Moses parkways in New York! If ample space for public facilities is not reserved now, speculation will grip only more firmly—sink its roots deeper into the nourishment of urban expansion. To delay the day of reckoning will cost the future much too much.

Reservation of open space—greenbelts for recreation, broad thoroughfares, public services—is the least our urban program should include. It would make sense to plan regional park systems as permanent lungs and circulation to protect future expansion. It would make more sense for cities to acquire sections of outlying land as an antidote to the insidious effect of future speculative inflation.

There is need for civic enterprise to provide leadership for urban growth and development rather than remain forever a step behind. Our society requires such leadership—it represents the dominant will of the people. Civic enterprise is the joint participation of private and public initiative; it is neither one nor the other alone. The ultimate goal in our democracy—the general welfare—is approached when both act in unison. And it is then that profit becomes a healthy motive in our economic, social, and political system. This purpose can be well served by preventing urban ills from infecting new development while the cancer is being carved from the old city. Prevention will come by reservation of ample space before the cost renders adequate room too expensive.

THE HABIT OF CONGESTION

Congestion has a strong grip on the megalopolitan city. Excess upon excess of people and building are heaped upon the land. Size is an accretion of ever-increasing population; people are piled in a pyramid expanding at the base in proportion to the accumulation at the center. The heavy burden of building bulk has created a Frankenstein monster of land values, and the result is a paradox.

The value of land is a product of its use. Presumably the use is designed as a service to people, and the value of the land is measured by the income derived from performing that service. When by increasing the intensity of land use the income from it can be increased, the value of the land is likewise increased.

Following this logic with enthusiasm, city building proceeded according to the "highest and best use" to which urban land could be put. Absorbed in the pursuit of this theory, attention to the basic concept of land value as derived from service to people shifted to the concept of land as a speculative commodity, and this is the status of urban land "economics" today.

It is not a new situation. Exploitation of land has been common throughout history. The degree of its effect on the development of cities has been dependent on the extent to which urban growth in any period has been dominated by speculative excess, or implemented by tempered investment.

The novel character of this process today is the self-consuming nature of land economics. The upward spiral of value has created congestion and, seeking to maintain an economic balance, more congestion is the usual antidote. As a result, value is not measured in terms of service to people; on the contrary, the people are now obliged to adjust themselves to congestion in order to maintain land values.

This paradox is at the root of the urban problem, but it is being resolved. Decentralization is gnawing at the values in congested areas, even though the unplanned and disorderly process has the effect of shifting the disease about the urban anatomy rather than curing the malady.

Congestion is a habit hard to break. We see it illustrated in some of the most courageous efforts to release the city from its shackles. The remarkable program of highways directed by Robert Moses in New York City may be fairly compared with achievements of the Roman Empire or Baron Haussmann in Paris. Yet the administrative prowess and engineering skill it represents are unconsciously tangled in the web of congestion.

Struggling to escape from congestion, the smooth freeways loosen themselves from one complicated intersection only to find themselves caught in another. High land cost is a challenge to engineering ingenuity, and the results are triumphs of technical skill, but the capacity to build these structures is sometimes a delusion. The ready escape from congestion offered by the freeways is part of the formula for dissipation of excessive land values, but the highway design is threatened with early obsolescence when it is warped into complicated and extravagant intersections to avoid high land cost. Avoidance of high land cost is inadequate compensation if the civic improvement is crippled rather than a permanent asset to the community. A full statement of the problem cannot omit the necessity for the most direct system of circulation integrated with redevelopment of congested areas.

High-Rise Buildings

Many architects as well as city planners believe that in order for there to be a real urban center there must be a change in the vertical scale of the buildings. The uplifting experience of the cathedral in the medieval town must be restored, a punctuation point that says, Here I am—the city centrum. Few, if any, large cities in the world fail to adhere to this as a principle of urban design. Economic reasons support the desires of the city builders.

Many factors lead to the decision to develop high-rise structures in the urban centers. Most frequently mentioned is the high cost of land, even though the cost of construction sometimes consumes much of the profit provided by the intensified use of the land. In addition, the close relationship to activity or employment centers places the high-rise structure in an excellent competitive position in relation to the scatteration alternative, where land transportation becomes a major factor in the cost. Scarcity of space in already congested areas is also a factor.

Commercial building seems to be able to survive as high-rise structures in the central city and in some of the specially designed outlying centers, since the cost of the space can be written off both in the cost of products or services and in tax savings. On the other hand, high-rise housing structures generally call for rents that can be afforded by relatively few families; in many cases the units are acquired by corporations for their directors or top personnel.

There is no question that good urban design is essential to the development of pleasant urban communities. The real problems associated with the process are that there is either too little coordination of efforts or too little concern with the impact of one design upon others. Too many persons believe that the best urban design is that which has great variety based upon the freedom of the individual. The designation of good design is considered a matter of personal taste, or as being in the eye of the beholder.

CHAPTER 33

ART IN THE CITY

Ideally a good building in itself should really be a work of art architecturally. It should not need another object to make it good. But if you have a first-rate sculpture next to an excellent building —and some rapport or tension between them—this can well lead to an enhancement of the urban surrounding. Good sculpture should be used on city sites with the same discrimination with which sensitive people put paintings and sculpture in their homes.

*Henry Seldis**

COMMUNITY APPEARANCE

Not since the City Beautiful movement at the turn of the century has the planning of cities been accepted as an art. Planning shifted from the

---

* *Henry Moore in America,* Los Angeles County Art Museum (New York: Praeger Publishers, 1973).

province of the landscape architect to engineers and techniques of zoning; planners' attention was diverted to zoning administration and urban management.

Industrial genius created the productive capacity of the world, but it was commercial genius that produced the wealth. The city became a vast commercial enterprise; everything was for sale. The billboard syndrome defaces strip commercial streets in every city, freeway rights-of-way, and most rural highways. Power poles and wires, competing traffic signals, a convulsive mass of distracting color, form, and motion, obscure the identity of individual signs. Every street looks like every other street; in the words of Gertrude Stein, "when one gets there, there is no there there."

It has now become customary to include community appearance as part of a city's comprehensive plan. The refinement of urban form and space, respect for natural topographic features, scenic approaches, views of sea and sky, open space, relationships and identity of structures, have

Street scene, Kowloon, Hong Kong, 1984—community art or anarchy?

Civic art—image of a culture?
Art Institute—Chicago, 1897.

Picasso's *Woman*, Civic Center, Chicago, 1967.

The Opera House, Stockholm.

been skillfully advocated by competent designers.[1] It is perhaps the most nebulous element in the planning process.

But, caught up in the technicalities of urban housekeeping and con-

---

1. Kevin Lynch, *The Image of the City* (Cambridge, Mass.: The Technology Press and Harvard University Press, 1960).

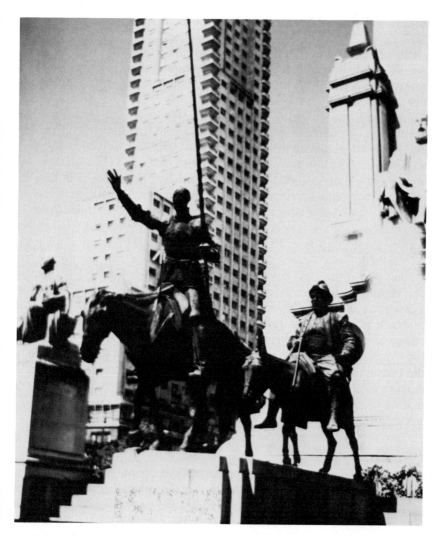

The Central Plaza, Madrid.

fronted with apathy among the urban populace, administrative planners, public officials, and citizens alike have become inured to the ugliness around them and incompetent to make judgments on urban aesthetics.

Public authority has absolute jurisdiction over some 40 percent of the city area: streets, parks, and public facilities. Yet a street will be widened to accommodate more automobiles, even though doing so destroys trees and ruins the visual quality of adjacent property; a school or other public building will be crowded onto an inadequate lot, and acquisition of enough space is alleged to be "uneconomic" because it would cost more. An old city hall will be abandoned and a modern facility built elsewhere without concern for the historical value of the old building or the disruption of the city's sense of identity.

Despite official insensitivity to urban aesthetics, the city may improve or preserve attractive features within the area of its authority—if an alert citizenry and a competent planning staff are vigilant. But the balance—60 percent of the city area—is within the province of private enterprise, and regulation of aesthetic quality by legislative processes is largely ineffectual. Strategic locations may be controlled by regulations of height and bulk, and billboards may be eliminated in time by imposition of amortization zoning. The 1954 Supreme Court decision offers some encouragement, but the courts are generally reluctant to impose judgment on aesthetic issues alone. Subdivision ordinances can require underground power utilities, building setbacks, and open space. The planned unit development introduces the advantages of large-scale planning. But a city can exercise its major influence on aesthetic quality by the degree to which an orderly structure of land uses is planned—the relationship of streets to abutting property and their effectiveness for traffic movement, the elimination of strip commercial zoning (also by amortization zoning), the consolidation of commercial facilities in shopping centers, the maintenance of street trees, the preservation of open space and historic landmarks, the location and intensity of street lighting, and the design of street furniture.

Wall Art

In many communities artists, both amateur and professional, have been encouraged to place their graphic art on the otherwise blank walls of multistory buildings. This is a far cry from the undisciplined graffiti that has covered many structures, especially in outlying areas. New York City subways are an example of the most intensive spray-can art.

LOCATIONAL PLANNING[2]

The arts, like other urban activities, are affected by public regulations dealing with land use and structures. Such regulations were basic to the establishment of zoning as a means of protecting the "sanctity of the home," as they barred all nonresidential uses from residential areas in

---

2. Harvey Perloff, "The Arts in the Economic Life of the City." In *Locational Planning for the Arts*, Simon Eisner (New York: 1979).

particular. Other regulations, not as frequent, restrict the intrusion of residential uses into commercial and industrial areas. The fear of unplanned mixing of residential and nonresidential uses caused many communities to adopt prohibitions against the extension of mixed uses by ordinances establishing exclusive zones. Changes in the concept of the desirable structure of commercial areas have resulted in some reversals of this policy, especially where nonconforming uses had existed on a large scale and where new techniques of urban design overcame prior objectionable conditions. Obviously there must be some changes in the current zoning laws of many cities if, among other things, the artist is to be accommodated in the sections where the mixing of studios and living accommodations is now prohibited.

The creation of artists' enclaves seems particularly appropriate in the postindustrial age we are now entering. When service employment characteristically can be expected to be the mainstay of most cities' economies and the older large cities have to struggle to maintain their economic and financial viability, the arts and cultural activities will inevitably have to be counted on as a significant part of city economies. The artists' enclave may well become an important symbol of the postindustrial city, suggesting the importance of art in its many forms to the economic and residential life of the city.

Some General Needs

Artists have special locational needs. They require large areas of work and storage space, and yet their income is frequently limited. Their hours of work do not necessarily correspond to the normal work patterns of others, often requiring either the close proximity of residence and studio or their fusion. Buyers must be able to come to the studios to acquire the artists' work; the area should therefore be visually attractive, and safe, to lure middle-class potential clients.

What seems ideally suited to these special needs is a single large building in a preferred location or in an area that is revitalizing itself. Where they exist, vacant loft buildings are best because no one is displaced. The building must be substantial and capable of being used for the intended purpose. It probably should be located in or adjacent to an attractive commercial area.

The main problem is economic. The cost of a centrally located building and of the renovations to make it suitable for residences and studios is great, and it must be passed on to the occupants. Unless subsidies are available, the district would be of value only to a limited number of artists. Such rehabilitated structures become increasingly attractive to others, causing impressive increases in property and other values, and

Wall art in urban centers. *End walls of public housing projects are converted into artistic representations that reflect the cultural and ethnic background of the residents.*

many artists soon find themselves unable to afford the enclave. However, where a central city is concerned about losing taxpaying residents—and many larger central cities are experiencing serious declines—it makes good sense for the city to sponsor such enclaves as a way of helping to revitalize the city. It is also appropriate to subsidize at least some portion of artists' rent through federal assistance.[3]

Under such circumstances it would be necessary to define rather carefully who is eligible to receive such assistance. New York City has already begun the task of definition, defining "artist" as one "who is regularly engaged in the fine arts, such as painting and sculpture, or in the performing or creative arts, including choreography and film making, or in the composition of music on a professional basis, and is so certified by the city department of cultural affairs and/or state council on the arts."[4]

Zoning

Zoning ordinances could be amended to define and limit two basic types of artistic activity.

Individual practice. Where individual artists alone are involved, it is possible to accommodate them in residential areas of most cities, provided that two factors are true. First, that their activities are not obnoxious to their neighbors. Involved in this would be such things as the noise factor—practice and rehearsal of musicians, actors, dancers, and the like —or the introduction of unusual amounts of traffic and consequent parking because of a formal or informal school situation. Second, that as a home occupation they may not merchandise products of their art or craft on the premises or formally conduct business there. Any such activity would be disclosed if the artist required a business telephone and therefore a business license from the community wherein he lived.

Group practice. The areas open to any large-scale operation, one with more than one artist or pupil, are those generally in the commercial districts. This is true even though certain districts are reserved for highly specialized types of retail services; examples include the neighborhood, district, and regional shopping centers where areas are specifically designed and limited to retail sales operations. This does not mean that there could not be precincts for artists, especially on second or third floors, which are not desirable for most retail outlets.

The potential economic benefits of this far more flexible approach to zoning and locational planning are significant. It would enable artists to

---

3. Ibid.
4. Ibid.

live and work in many areas. If zoning changes were linked to the restoration and revitalization of the downtown, artists might come to choose it as a location for their special work. This in turn would greatly enhance the center of the city and contribute to it the excitement and creative energy so sorely needed.

The Example of Los Angeles[5]

The problem of locating artists' centers has some special features in Los Angeles. As other cities did, Los Angeles some years ago set up exclusively residential, commercial, and industrial districts. In order to accommodate artists, it became necessary to develop a new zone for mixed occupancies. The zone thus developed permits residences in commercial or industrial structures. In residential zones, the ordinance requires the agreement of the residents of the area.

Certain areas within the city have already attracted groups of artists. These include Venice, Mount Washington, and the several canyons leading from Westwood and Beverly Hills to the San Fernando Valley. Because of the cultural appeal associated with these locations, the artists compete with affluent individuals for homes in limited places.

Commercial and industrial areas seem to offer a better than average potential for the combined occupancy of specific buildings. This is especially true in the Hollywood area. There are no loft buildings as there are in New York, but there are industrial structures that could lend themselves to the development of artistic centers.

In downtown Los Angeles, many of the buildings that once held the garment industry and banking offices are vacant. By renovating the upper floors, one or more of these structures might become centers for the arts. The cost of bringing the buildings into habitable condition as residences might, however, price the accommodations out of the artists' market, and rent subsidies might be required. While at present the attractiveness of being located in the downtown business district of Los Angeles is limited, the restoration and revitalization proposals could fundamentally alter this situation. Downtown Los Angeles could become a significant center in which artists could live and work.

Other communities, among them Winston-Salem, North Carolina, Dallas, Texas, and San Francisco, in the United States, and York and Toronto in Canada, are experimenting with the creation of special districts. In some instances these are supported financially by local industries and institutions.

---

5. Ibid.

NEW UTOPIANS

In the wake of Le Corbusier's polemics, some recent new utopians have become increasingly esoteric. Abstract terminology is drawn upon to support imaginative concepts of urban form. Words acquire their own subtle and occult significance: a "continuum of constant change," "ever-fluid movement," "transiency of life-cycles," "mobility," a "new objectivity." The rhetoric is eloquent; words in the lexicon are employed with enviable conviction. Yet when the terms are converted to delineations of tangible form, they reveal a strong basic similarity to the conventional city. Any alternatives seem even less appealing than existing cities. At one time, a platform is proposed to cover Paris; at another, an urban bridge leaps across the English Channel.[6] Buckminster Fuller proposed a series of "floating neighborhoods" moored in New York City's East River.[7]

In their 1958 plan for the Haupstadt in Berlin, Peter and Alison Smithson were intent upon the theme of "mobility." Pedestrian and vehicular traffic were separated by a network of decks and bridges elevated above the road system. Sinuous "walls of office slabs" to contain the inner city would become as rigidly fixed as any conventional urban structure. In that proposal, as in their 1963 plan for Mehring Platz,[8] the Smithsons feature the motor way rather than a dynamic concept for mass transit that might have been expected to shape the modern city. Bearing strong resemblance to freeways in American cities, the new planning vision appears remarkably conventional and in fact rather old. There is little evidence that the new aesthetic of urban form would be any more adaptable to fluid change than existing cities.

Kenzo Tange and the Metabolists of Japan envision dramatic vertical and horizontal forms linked by automobile highways projecting into Tokyo Bay. The forms are exhilarating, but the fundamental difference between their proposal and the cities we have, and know to be outmoded, is not readily discernible.[9]

---

6. Illustrated in Udo Kuterman, *New Architecture in the World* (New York: Universe Books, 1965). Paris Platform, Yona Friedman; Channel Bridge, Schulze-Fiedlitz and Friedman.

7. The "floating city" was developed under a grant by the Triton Foundation, Cambridge, Massachusetts, 1968.

8. Haupstadt Plan (1958), Peter and Alison Smithson and Sigmonde Wonke. Mehring Platz Plan (1963), Peter and Alison Smithson and Gunter Nitschke. See David Lewis (ed.), *Pedestrian in the City* (New York: D. Van Nostrand, 1966).

9. Illustrated and described in Lewis, ibid.

The Realities

Where among the broad roadways in these theatrical visions is the mass of motor vehicles to be lodged? Where in the incessant movement of traffic can the automobiles stop? That function was featured in the visions of Louis Kahn for Philadelphia in 1956. He glorified the multilevel garage; among images of tall shafts, pyramids, and "tinker-toy" cages, a collection of great cylindrical garages, or "ports," dominated the scene.

The popular acceptance of the idea of the mechanistic beehives designed for a million or more people by the desert mystic Paolo Soleri[10] as recently as the 1970s and George Favre's "cellular agglomerates, clip-on or plug-in cities, grid structures, containers, submarine cities, cities in outer space, megastructures and all the gidgety-gadgety et ceteras"[11]: both of these visions reflect the desperate malaise of a technologically oriented society. The incredible impact of the computer on every aspect of contemporary human existence is evident in a widespread reliance on that ingenious instrument for solutions to problems of the urban environment. It has value as a mechanical tool, but it is gifted with neither a conscience nor ultimate wisdom; it cannot make decisions related to social and economic welfare or the physical form of the city unless the concepts are devised by humans and imparted to its memory system.

Encompassing the full range of human activity, the city is the living image of the culture that spawns it. It reflects the social values, aspirations, and aesthetic sensibilities of the people who create and occupy it. These characteristics will be represented in the comprehensive plan and zoning ordinances, the allocation of land uses, and regulations that accommodate individual and collective participation in city building. A city that functions adequately may not be aesthetically satisfying; but conversely it will not become an art form unless the functional parts work effectively.

In the final analysis, the aesthetic quality of the city is the measure of the cultural values of a community, values identified with the elevation of mind, morals, and taste of a society. Beautiful cities in the world are not only charming because of a colorful history or the patina of age. Cathedrals of Europe were beautiful when the stone was white. Paris and Venice were built to be beautiful, and they show that beautiful cities can grow old gracefully.

The city needs space for the free flow of transportation and movement of people, space in which to create a desirable environment for living and

10. Paolo Soleri, *Arcology: Cities in the Image of Man* (Cambridge, Mass.: MIT Press, 1969).
11. George Favre, "Cities Are for People . . . or Are They?" *Christian Science Monitor,* June 14, 1972.

for work, space in which the functions of the city and the aesthetics of our time may be welded into an inseparable unity. Space in the city will encourage the inventive genius of mankind to fulfill the wants of people and free them from the wanton congestion that renders the city a detestable place in which to live and work.

The urban environment shrieks with the production of science and industry and the commodities of commercial enterprise. The city is like a cave in which a multitude of weird and raucous echoes create a psychological din. Self-discipline in organizing the advantages of our industrial age is lagging, and the citydweller is suffering distraction.

Reams of statistics reveal the habits of the urbanite. They show, for example, the short distance people will walk from their parking place to their shopping destination. This reluctance to walk is interpreted as a significant characteristic of the present-day shopper, but the fact that these statistics also measure the repellent character of the urban environment is overlooked. There is ample evidence of the response of the people to studied civic design and their hunger for open space. The plaza in Rockefeller Center evokes spontaneous response, and the success of planned residential communities and neighborhood shopping centers attests to the good business of adequate space. Statistics may show the characteristics of the urban population, but they may also reveal the deficiencies of the environment that induces those traits; they may tell the story of how rank congestion violates human sensibilities and how abhorrent are slums to the human spirit.

THE CULTURAL VACUUM

City building is neglectful of human feeling; it is a cold, harsh enterprise devoid of the amenities for living. It explains the desire for escape that eclecticism provided, a refuge from reality in which the people could draw the walls of romanticism about themselves. The people did not live a real existence, but the romanticism showed that they could still dream, and it is dreams that will lead civilization out of the darkness—dreams of the future rather than the past.

The significance of freedom is not yet fully grasped; society is not yet adjusted to the democracy of our industrial age. Political rights have been won, and mechanical tools of phenomenal number and variety are at our disposal, but the significance of man's achievement is blurred in its whirling presence. It was entertaining and amusing fiction that Jules Verne wrote in the nineteenth century. Today reality so far surpasses his visionary anecdotes that society is bewildered. There is a strangeness about the powers science has thrust into the hands of man; his capacity to manipulate these powers and the responsibility it bestows cast a spell upon society. When we contemplate their effect upon our social and economic life, the stupendous possibilities are appalling. Imagination pulsates with the vibrating tempo of the modern world.

Evidence of technical progress is all about us. The material benefits of our age are delivered ready-made; gadgets are a part of our daily existence and we take for granted the marvelous developments of science. But the assimilation of these accomplishments into our cultural environment is coming hard. Forging a culture from the technology of our time is a complicated process. Ultimately the adjustment of civilization to the reality of our age will generate the cultural climate in which the creative work of artists flourishes.

Meanwhile we are moving in a cultural vacuum, into which has been drawn the technological progress we misinterpret for culture itself. Mediocrity is the maximum standard bred of materialism. Inured to this standard, we are hardly conscious of its reality and unaware of the cultural potentials present but undeveloped. Their development offers a whole new frontier in our world of progress—the cultural expression of democratic freedom in which the vitality of contemporary art will shape our physical environment. There is resistance to a new aesthetic, but it is more passive than active. The pursuit of material welfare distracts attention from cultural achievement as we bow low before the great god Mammon, but the result is indifference more than a wilful denial. Economic distortions exert more convincing pressures for improvement of the urban environment than does the creative urge for a fine city. The loss of land values to congestion and the economic burden of blight and social maladjustments are more impressive than the aesthetic and spiritual baseness to which the city has degenerated.

UNITY OF PURPOSE

The search for form in the urban environment would stagnate without the imagination of fertile minds. It is the more regrettable that official planning agencies are so timid in their leadership. The aspirations of city people are suffocating. Some cities may have illusions of grandeur, others have ambitions for greatness, but false pride obscures their decadence. We can hardly conclude that the ugliness of our environment is due to a complete absence of civic pride, that nerve-wracking congestion and unhealthful overcrowding answer the natural desire for activity and vitality, and that people have become so inured to their surroundings that they prefer mediocrity to an environment of decency and culture regardless of their social or economic station in life.

What is there to stir the citydweller in the prospect of nothing better than more of the same? The people need to see new plans. Civic leadership needs to emerge with standards of urban development that will convince the people it will be worth the cost to restore decency to their cities. Planning implies a goal to be reached. This, in turn, suggests some unity of purpose. Sorely needed progress is frustrated by disunity and unimaginative leadership. Unity of purpose—a conviction about the form and character we desire for our cities—has been absent. Consequently, planning has wandered aimlessly, frequently promising much but delivering little.

Cities have not yet reached the stage of crowding and congestion that present laws permit, and yet they are already pitifully overcrowded and congested. These legal limits have induced a state of anarchy in city building. Feeble innovations for improvements are not enough. Facelifting will not do the job; it will take a major operation. Our conception of unlimited exploitation in urban property and people will need modification; the relation between the amount of space occupied by buildings and the amount of land about them must be altered. An inspiring projection of the City of Tomorrow by Le Corbusier, a studied group like Rockefeller Center, a well-planned subdivision like River Oaks, and the parkways of New York and Chicago have pointed the way. If we expect our cities to be shaped in their images, however, we must look to the laws that set the standards for that accomplishment.

Cities are breaking down. As they are rebuilt they must conform to standards that ensure they will not break down again. This will require major decisions, and we must be prepared to make them. Unless these decisions are made wisely, it would be far better and more economical to beat a hasty retreat from the congested urban centers and build new communities elsewhere.

We can build better cities when we quit gnawing at the fringe of the urban garment and accept some of the bitter with the sweet. We will replan our cities to provide a rational density of population, and from these plans we will lay a foundation of law that prohibits crowding and congestions of people and buildings. We will plan for such expansion and decentralization as the regions about our cities require, and we will plan for such rebuilding as obsolescence and decay demand. We will go about this as civilized human beings with due consideration for each other, rather than barbarians bent upon destruction or as creatures of greed and deception bent on personal power and profit. We will seek the values in cities Thomas Guthrie described in the early nineteenth century:

> They have been as lamps of life along the pathway of humanity and religion. Within them science has given birth to her noblest discoveries. Behind their walls, freedom has fought her noblest battles. They have stood on the surface of the earth like great breakwaters, rolling back or turning aside the

swelling tide of oppression. Cities, indeed, have been the cradles of human liberty.[12]

The tragic impact of the great city on human welfare aroused the search by the new utopians, and their vision may light the way toward a metamorphosis of the city. Statistics, economic analyses, graphs, and charts urge a popular plea that planning must adopt scientific methods for the direction of future urban growth. The facts are essential; there can be no question about the necessity for full and complete information about our cities. But cities are the creatures of people, built by people for people, and their form is subject to the will of the people. Scientific analysis may indicate trends, but it does not direct action.

Science is an invention—an instrument with which people reach their objectives, the goals they may set for themselves. The force that moves humankind in the selection of these goals is morality, not science; it is a morality rooted deep in their culture and sharpened by their intuitive capacity. People have the power to control their environment; they can mold it to their purposes. They can observe trends, determine their direction, then reverse or shift them to suit their purposes. The course of human events is not some inevitable fate to which the people are destined; it is subject to their will. They can examine the facts and from them they can select their course. This is the power of humans, and it is the purpose of planning. Guided by a high moral sense and acting with freedom, the people can plan their cities of tomorrow. And, in the words of John Ruskin, "let it be as such work that our descendants will thank us for . . . and that men will say, as they look upon the labor and the wrought substance of them, 'See this our fathers did for us.' "

---

12. Thomas Guthrie, "The City, its Sins and Sorrows," *Sunday Magazine,* Scotland, 1857.

CHAPTER 34

REGIONAL CONCEPTS

Many persons, like Lewis Mumford, have contributed to the understanding of the complexities of the planning process. Few have understood as well as he the essential relationships between local and regional planning and the dependence on national policies in the development of civilized communities.

URBAN ECOLOGY

An ecology of natural and human resources is linked inextricably with the ecology of urban resources in the industrial age. In the final decades of the twentieth century, complicated social, economic, and technological phenomena have extended the dimensions of urbanization beyond the concentration of traditional cities. It should be the objective of a civilized society to achieve a harmonious, attractive, convenient, and healthy living environment. The extent to which we meet this challenge will be the test of contemporary society. Thus far, the prospects are not encouraging. Creeping urbanization is engulfing entire regions, reducing the significance of political boundaries between cities and counties to a shambles of legal technicalities.

The growing regional agglomerations along the northern Atlantic and southern Pacific coasts are well known, and no viable mechanism of

542

government has been devised to deal with these massive groupings of people and conflicting overlapping public and private institutions. New public policies are required, fashioned at national and state levels of government, to direct the distribution of population, industry, transportation, and the conservation of resources essential to sustain the structure of the national economy.

REGIONAL PLANNING EFFORTS

Like many other important programs for public improvement, regional planning efforts started with a group of dedicated and concerned private citizens. Observing the many areas where public functions overlapped and wastefully duplicated activities, this group of persons, including Charles H. Whitaker, Benton MacKaye, Clarence Stein, Henry Wright, and a handful of others, among them Lewis Mumford, formed the influential Regional Planning Association of America in 1923, an informal group dedicated to social betterment through planning. At about the same time the RPAA was being formed, another private effort was starting— this one to produce a regional plan for New York and environs. The work was directed by Thomas Adams, a Scotsman who had worked on Letchworth and Welwyn, garden cities outside London.

The efforts of both groups resulted in the preparation of comprehensive reports citing the virtues of regional planning and are, in fact, the basis for some of the efforts that initiated the development of the New York Port Authority, a regional effort affecting both New York and New Jersey.

In the early days of the New Deal, President Franklin Delano Roosevelt proposed and the Congress created the National Resources Board, a federal agency that later became the National Resources Planning Board. The board produced voluminous reports dealing with every aspect of broad-gauge planning. In the final term of President Roosevelt's administration, Congress, alienated by some of the efforts of the board, cut the appropriations that supported it. The president continued its activities out of special funds until the end of his term.

It is difficult to evaluate the byproducts of this effort. While the individual recommendations have little or no application today, the overall recognition of the importance of regional planning has affected many parts of the states and the nation. For instance, the army divided the nation into its own form of regions, the Federal Reserve Board created others, and so on.

The one great regional planning effort supported by President Roosevelt and Congress was the Depression-born TVA. This project achieved

A Lands for City People

B Lands for Priests

C Lands for Princes

Regional planning in ancient times. *While in captivity in the sixth century B.C., the Israelites planned their return to Jerusalem. In Ezekiel 25:45 the prophet had described plans desired by God for the allocation and use of the land upon their return. An area of 10,000 by 25,000 reeds (18 by 45 miles) was to be set aside for the people of the city. The land on both sides of these areas was reserved as princely lands.*

There was no indication of the precise location of the boundaries. It is probable that Ezekiel understood God's wishes were directed more to the area of land needed for the production and distribution of abundant goods than to the exact location surrounding the city of Jerusalem. Perhaps the amount of land allocated to the people was less than that for the priests because Jerusalem was a crossroads for trade routes; people derived considerable wealth from the resulting commercial enterprise in which they were engaged. The princely lands supported the kings, who maintained residences near the Mediterranean and Dead seas as well as in Jerusalem.

the goals that had been set for it, including flood control and the development of electric power in an area badly needing it. At about the same time the Port of New York Authority was created. Its function has been to promote commerce and transportation in the New York metropolitan area and, like the TVA, its activity has affected several states.

A more limited example of regional planning is the Los Angeles County Regional Planning Commission. Created in 1923, it was initially charged with drawing up a master plan for Los Angeles County. The commission's main objective was to develop a network of major and secondary highways. Programs were also initiated in the Midwest and in Canada.

REGIONAL PLANNING

Regional planning offers a marked advantage for contiguous areas sharing common interests. Such matters as air pollution, unified circulation systems, water distribution, and sewage and solid waste disposal cannot be regulated by an individual community. An overriding authority with the power to enforce decrees is needed to deal with these problems.

Why So Little?

The main reason why so little regional planning has been done is that local political entities fear a loss of their power. Another reason is that a regional agency, if it is to have real authority, must have the power to tax. This alone is enough to frighten local communities into opposition. One more taxing body, one more layer of government, seems to add up to additional expenses for what is seen as a superfluous governmental body.

In the early 1970s California tried to establish planning districts. Meetings were held in various areas of the state to determine the districts that had common economic, social, and cultural interests. The result: the local communities resented the initiative that had been taken by the state; the project was a fiasco.

John Friedman, in his "The Concept of a Planning Region," states:

Regional planning in the United States has at various times had reference to different types of activity as well as to different types of area. There was a time, roughly 1933 until the end of World War II, when regional planning meant primarily the development of water resources and the adjacent land resources within a given river basin. The basic planning unit was the watershed and the objective, the fullest possible use of all physical resources for the improvement of living levels within the area. The Tennessee Valley Authority has been the outstanding example of this type of planning, but a number of other river basins have followed suit: the Columbia; the Central Valley of California; the Missouri; the Arkansas; and the Red River. The TVA, however, remains the only authority in full charge of a comprehensive development program.[1]

During the past few years in almost every state there has been created one or more coordinating agencies concerned with aspects of regional planning. These councils of government (COG) are usually voluntary associations with little or no power other than to make an effort at coordination of the individual planning going on in the various member communities.

---

1. John Friedman and William Alonzo, eds., *Regional Development and Planning* (Cambridge, Mass: MIT Press, 1964).

NATIONAL PLANNING

Despite the inability of independent community jurisdictions to cope with air contamination, transportation, sanitation, and water supply, the concept of local control is retained with fanatical fervor. The rule of "divide and conquer" breeds intense rivalry between cities and counties for economic advantage. Competition to capture the maximum tax-productive enterprise justifies irrational land uses, induces the relaxation of development standards to attract business and industry, and favors local politicians bent on perverting the public interest to the benefit of special interests. National planning is needed for the conservation of natural resources, the designation of areas in which the new urbanization would be compatible with related land uses, new industrial and energy development, and transportation by land and air.

The United States

With the possibility for a population increase of 60 million in the United States by 2000 A.D., urban centers will have to accommodate nearly 40 million more people than now occupy the nation's cities, or the equivalent of forty new cities of one million. New forms of urban development will be needed.

Land use planning at state and national levels of government is either faltering or nonexistent. A galaxy of "regulating agencies" struggles within limited and often competing jurisdictions. The annual cost of preparing environmental impact statements by only three of the federal agencies was $16 million and countless man-hours, with few if any national policies by which to measure the validity of these studies.[2] These costs have increased tremendously in the past decade.

Piecemeal planning in 1985 is a costly undertaking. Consolidation of the fragmented budgets for administration of public resources would provide a tidy sum with which to launch a comprehensive national planning program. It will call for a national commitment to the public interest unprecedented in the nation's history. Some measure of the gap between necessity and realization has been illustrated by the fate of Federal Land Use Planning Legislation[3] in the Congress. After strong support by environmentalists, state governors, and the House Committee on the Interior, as late as 1974 the legislation was sidetracked by adverse political manipulation, in what *The New York Times* referred to as "a perversion

---

2. Estimated cost for environmental impact statements by the Atomic Energy Commission was $6 million; Department of Agriculture, $2 million; Department of the Interior, $8 million. *Traffic Quarterly,* Eno Foundation, January 1974.

3. H.R. 10294.

of the democratic process" on a "question of immense national importance." No progress is yet visible at a national level, and with the current
federal attitudes, little immediate change can be anticipated.

Changing Patterns of Land Settlement—Israel

Rural settlement in Israel can be described as a synthesis of European
and traditional/local models imbued with modern social concepts. Two
main patterns have evolved—the collective and the cooperative. A third
intermediate pattern, combining joint production with individual domestic living, has exerted considerable influence on other settlement forms
in spite of its limited numbers. All settlement patterns in Israel adhere to
the principle of agglomeration, but without sacrificing farmyard space.
Adequate room for farmyard activities has encouraged diversification and
facilitated the expansion of production.

The amalgamation of rural settlements into an independent system of
regional cooperation is another common feature of the Israeli village. The
physical plans reflect the tendency to shift to bigger units in order to
achieve economies of scale in supporting services and specific production
lines. The resulting returns, both in economic and social areas, have
generated new sources of employment for the younger generation,
thereby counteracting the universal trend of depopulation that usually
follows the modernization of agriculture.[4]

Current Regional Planning in Israel

The regional development bloc was a concept that evolved in Israel during the 1960s: clusters of cooperative agricultural villages of the three
types mentioned above were established near each other with strong
regional councils to deal with matters of common social and economic
concern. A large urban center served both as an industrial base and
marketing outlet as well as the site of hospitals, high schools, theaters,
and other facilities designed to serve the entire region.

The most successful bloc was established in the Lachish area of the
northern Negev, with a total of twenty-nine villages. At its hub is the
town of Kiryat Gat, where the cotton and sugar beets grown in the region
are processed, heavy equipment is repaired, and other commercial, administrative, social, and industrial services are provided.

An Israeli plan for the southern area of the country is intended for a
population of 900,000 within a total projected population of five million
by the end of the twentieth century. The preliminary surveys have been

---

4. Jacob O. Maos, in *Papers and Proceedings, 35th World Congress, International Federation for Housing and Town Planning,* Jerusalem, 1980.

completed and the regional scheme is now being drawn up. Special attention is devoted to problems of infrastructure. The scheme deals with the siting of urban and rural settlements, improvement of existing settlements, and rural service centers. A special feature is the planning of Bedouin settlements, intended to convert the nomads into settled farmers.

The main water-supply lines have been indicated, as well as the means of storm water interception, and the location of spreading grounds, dams, and other works involved in the water economy. Areas have been indicated for the utilization of natural resources and for basic heavy industries, as well as sites for combined industries, processing raw materials and minerals, major pipelines for conveying crude oil, oil products, natural gas, oil pumping stations, tank farms for oil storage, and sites for plants connected with the processing of oil. Areas have also been sited for national parks and large nature reserves.

After years of intensive study, a route was selected for the Mediterranean-Dead Sea Canal. The canal is more a series of tunnels than an open trench, the usual definition of a canal. The intent of this multipurpose waterway is to bring relatively low-salt water from the Mediterranean Sea to raise the level of the high-salt Dead Sea, or at least to counter the evaporation that has lowered the level of the water in recent years, while at the same time providing for development of electrical energy.

In the course of its meander from the Mediterranean Sea to the Dead Sea it passes some 400 meters below sea level. In the interim areas, water would be drawn off through adits or towers for agricultural use in the Negev Desert, thus making multiple use of the resource.

STATE PLANNING

National planning requires implementation by the individual states, and state plans are slow to emerge. Hawaii is the first state with such a plan.

Hawaii

Planning was initiated in Hawaii with the creation of a planning commission for Honolulu in 1915, and a zoning law was initiated in 1922. The Territorial Planning Agency established in the late thirties became the State Planning Office when Hawaii became a state in 1957. The State Land Use Law of 1961 defined three basic land use zones for all land in the state: urban, agricultural, and conservation. Regulation of land uses within designated urban zones is administered by the county governments, which also maintain a measure of control within agricultural districts. The conservation zone is administered by the state. Zonal boundaries are defined by the State Land Use Commission.

Both planning and land use zoning are aided by several unique advantages. Overlapping governmental jurisdictions are absent. Each island, with a small number of exceptions, is a county, and each county is surrounded by the permanent "bluebelt" of the Pacific Ocean. Each has a city-type government; there are no independently incorporated cities. Authority for property assessment and taxation is vested in the state government, and taxes are assessed in accordance with land use zoning. The Director of State Planning and Economic Development is a member of the governor's cabinet.

Despite this idyllic setting, the people of the island paradise display characteristics similar to those of citizens elsewhere in the nation. Shortly after adoption of the three zoning districts, a fourth zone, rural, was incorporated by the legislature. Within this zone the provision for one-half-acre lots allows for land exploitation, which the legislation was intended to curb. The rural district was omitted from Oahu, where the declining role of agriculture leads to the pressure for urbanization of agricultural land. This trend is progressing at such a rate that urbanization of the entire island seems imminent.

There is little contemporary evidence that urbanization in Hawaii will be more humane than elsewhere. There have been urban slums in Honolulu for generations, although a benevolent climate somewhat tempers the harshness of typical ghettos. It is apparent that the tradition of plantation villages has been forsaken for suburban sprawl, as in other American cities, and the same brutalism is present in the proliferation of ever-taller commercial and residential structures.

The natural beauty of Hawaii has been impaired in the course of accommodating tourists attracted by climate, tropical character, traditions, and the racial blend of the islands' populace. It is not, however, the welcome to brief visitors that presents the major threat. It is the insidious trend toward exploitation of a lovely land for an unlimited increase in permanent population that will inevitably compound the burden of economic support from sources beyond the island shores. How this strong temptation will be controlled is the pressing issue for state and county leadership. In the words of Robert Wenkam, stalwart conservationist: "Treat gently. These are the only Hawaiian Islands we have."[5]

Other States

Issues that prompted state planning in Hawaii are even more critical in states on the mainland. The tangled political boundaries between counties and cities, the desperate competition for tax-productive enterprise, and

---

5. *Hawaii* (Chicago: Rand McNally & Company, 1972).

the rivalry between cities to outstrip their neighbors in population statistics all present formidable obstacles to the prospects for rational and essential planning at state and federal levels of government. Yet these same obstacles render the need for planning even more urgent. State planning and broad classifications of land use zoning are as essential to administration of the public business as the general plan and detailed zoning ordinances are at the city and county levels of government.

The annual flood of 300,000 new residents and the 57,000 acres of land converted to urbanization in Florida demand not only measures like the Environmental Land and Water Act, the Water Management Act, and the Land Conservation and Comprehensive Planning Act that the state adopted in 1972; there must be a comprehensive state land use and zoning plan as the basic reference for administration of the state agencies and county or regional authorities. Without such a definition of land use zoning, the ambitious program to evaluate "developments of regional impact" can only drift ineffectually.[6]

Thwarted by political ineptitude and a California state planning department with no plan,[7] a group of enlightened citizens determined to construct a framework for comprehensive planning for the state. Taking into account all aspects of the state's economy, its social structure, and its physical characteristics, the "California Tomorrow Plan"[8] is a guide to state planning. Adopting land use categories similar to Hawaii's, the plan divides the state into four zones: urban, agriculture, conservation, and regional reserves, administered by regional government authorities. This plan was never officially accepted by the state.

REGIONALISM ON THE LOCAL LEVEL

Jacob Dash had this to say in 1980:

> There is growing recognition at the national and regional planning levels of the close interdependence of town, region and state resulting from the intensified interconnections and rapid communications which govern modern life in the country. The need is steadily growing for combined planning within one regional framework of rural and urban settlements and of the larger towns. This is essential as a means of assisting the people in finding employment and adequate income from their economic assets, to enable them to receive such services as communications, water supply, sewage,

---

6. "Developments of regional impact" are equivalent to "environmental impact statements" and are administered under the Comprehensive Planning Act.

7. Alfred Heller observed that after ten years and an expenditure of $4 million, the State Development Plan Program simply recommended further studies. (Speech at National Forum on Growth with Environmental Quality, Tulsa, Okla., September 25, 1973.)

8. *The California Tomorrow Plan* (Los Altos, California: William Kaufman, 1972).

health and educational services, and benefit from gardens, shopping centers and various communal services.

The planners have realized long since the need, when planning a town, of bearing in mind the public, commercial and employment services the town should also supply to the rural areas in its surroundings. Likewise, the planning of a town must take into consideration the services, supplies and employment that the town's inhabitants can obtain in the rural areas around it. The lines of communications must be planned so as to meet all these requirements, and the whole combined region must be planned as one organic whole.

Present-day planning trends throughout the world are towards reducing the attraction of metropolitan areas and limiting the growth of large cities.[9]

The City and the Region

Cities are the focal points of intensive economic development within most regions. They are intimately related to the hinterland from which the raw materials are imported. They are also, to a large extent, the purchasers of the finished products. No effective planning can be done without a deep concern for the interrelationships that must be protected and conserved. There can be no waste of resources in this partnership, whether land, water, or energy, without the community structure becoming unbalanced and uneconomic. The social consequences result in both areas losing their viability. Sound planning must take into consideration the total environment that makes the city function as the core for the total economic structure.

Recent efforts at metropolitan area planning take into account the importance of both the urbanized core and the surrounding areas, which in some instances are called the "areas of influence." However, it is important to realize that in most cases the power to control the development of areas surrounding a city lies with the county government.

REGIONALISM IS IMPERATIVE

In states where urbanization and industrial concentration infringe heavily upon land resources, state zoning and national policies (planning) for industrial allocation and population distribution are imperative. Yet conservation of agriculture, timber, water, and mineral resources is equally vital in the states that thus far have been saved from excess urbanization. The "energy crisis" of the early seventies emphasizes the urgency of this problem.

The necessity for both federal and state financial assistance to support

---

9. Jacob Dash. Speech at the IFHP Conference (International Federation for Housing and Town Planning), Jerusalem, 1980.

urban functions amply demonstrates that cities and counties cannot "go it alone," however attractive the concept of local autonomy may be. Thus far most states rely on reviews by state agencies or on the preparation of environmental impact statements for approval of various types of development in so-called critical areas. The inevitable increase in population can only compound both the number and extent of these critical areas. It would demonstrate appropriate public responsibility to establish land use zoning regulations both to preserve state resources and to set parameters for economic and urban development. Meanwhile, city and county governments struggle at the administrative level and in the courts to maintain some semblance of environmental equilibrium.

Acknowledging the limitations of independent cities in attempting to cope with the full range of urban ills, some forms of regional authorities have already been created. The San Francisco Bay Conservation and Development Commission was created by the state of California in 1965. The Miami Valley Regional Planning Commission has jurisdiction within the metropolitan area around Dayton, Ohio, and the Twin Cities Metropolitan Council encompasses Minneapolis and St. Paul, Minnesota. The Hackensack Meadowlands Development Commission includes fourteen cities and two counties in New Jersey. The regional government of Dade County, Florida, which has jurisdiction over all local communities, is considered highly effective. Councils of government with limited powers have been created in some areas to conform to the federal requirement for a regional clearinghouse for programs involving federal grants.

Land Acquisition

Acquisition of land within and around cities has been policy and practice in a number of European countries since the turn of the century. The policy has been implemented in Sweden since 1904; some 200 square miles are now owned by the city of Stockholm, a program that made possible the new towns of Farsta and Vallingby. The development of "land banks" in the United States has been confined to New York, Louisiana, and Puerto Rico. The appropriate responsibility for stewardship of the land has been generally abdicated in favor of private interests in land ownership and development. Partially filling the vacuum, nonprofit "trusts" are acquiring or leasing land to remain as open space. The Nature Conservancy has preserved some 377,000 acres in various parts of the country, holding the land until public agencies are financially able to acquire it. The Trust for Public Land (TPL) is directly concerned with preservation of a 672-acre ranch for the city of Los Angeles.

It is a gross irony that state legislatures require cities and counties to make plans and enact zoning ordinances in conformance with them, yet

A development concept for the Toronto region. *In 1965 the provincial government of Ontario initiated a program for regional planning and development, centered about the city of Toronto. The program was under the direction of Dr. Richard S. Thoman between 1967 and 1971.*
(Map from Richard Thoman, "A Checklist for California," Cry California, Fall 1974.)

reject their own responsibility to create plans and land use zoning for the states. The situation is further aggravated in states that require local communities to plan for open space and conservation; in the absence of funds for the necessary land acquisition, communities are confronted with threats of "inverse condemnation" suits as a result of conforming with state laws.

CHAPTER 35

THE NEW TOWNS

An appropriate form for the future city has not yet emerged. Nonetheless, serious attention has been directed to the nature of the modern city in two major areas: the redevelopment of the internal urban structure, and planned decentralization—the new towns. The results are not yet conclusive in either, but our present consideration of the new towns may serve as important experience in shaping our vision of the city of tomorrow.

NEED

Every large city has a planning department; often they are very large ones. The results of their planning may be primarily confined to patchwork efforts dealing with zoning, to beautification of the streets, and, where they exist, the setback areas.

Big cities do not respond to large-scale comprehensive planning since the changes that take place deal for the most part with individual projects involving one or more contiguous properties. One may observe New York City rebuilding itself with the tearing down of a large structure and the replacing of it with a larger one. Nothing can be done about the circulation system as the traffic becomes more congested with each intensification of use. Parking is required for the new uses, but the amounts are never adequate and the costs for the spaces are prohibitive. Chicago and San Francisco suffer the same situations. Planning for the future of the Chicago Loop was an excellent exercise when sponsored by Carson Pierie and Scott. The changes since the completion do not reflect the ambitious plans that were submitted.

The same problems face the cities of the Orient, only in exaggerated form. Shanghai represents the essence of the problems: too many people housed in inadequate shelter. Both the housing and circulation systems, handed down from the past, are based on the political rivalries and antagonisms that were associated with nineteenth-century imperialism. Here we have, today, a city that was three separate entities. Street systems were not coordinated. Separate utility systems served the areas. Transportation was largely by foot. Replanning from a base such as this will take generations, since the rehousing of even a few families means the destruction of existing shelters, as mean as they may be.

The answer to all these problems may well be the almost universal development of new towns on open land where people can be provided with new shelter and opportunities for employment in new locations as the older areas are cleared for renewed uses. It is important to understand the difference between "new towns" and "new cities." Since World War II, there has been a tremendous growth of new cities in the United States. In Los Angeles County, for example, forty-five new cities have appeared since 1940. The county population, which includes both the cities and the unincorporated areas, has increased from 2,785,642 in 1940 to an estimated 7,781,109 in 1985. These new cities are *not* new towns, however. Rather, they are existing clusters of population, in either rural or urban areas, that want to have greater control over their local affairs than was being provided by the county government.

New towns, of which there are very few in the United States, are completely designed and constructed urban complexes. Some are self-sufficient entities while others are satellites to nearby major communities. The distinguishing feature of the new town is that it is designed in advance and is not merely a political "divorce" from an existing urbanized, developed community.

The United States

Creating facilities to accommodate 40 million more urban inhabitants in the United States by the turn of the century cannot be left to chance. Cities will require massive rehabilitation, regrouping of densities, allocation of open space, and effective mass transportation. Left to speculation and exploitation by free enterprise, suburbanization outside corporate city limits seriously impairs the economic viability of the cities. In Europe, decentralization has been planned by government authorities to distribute the population, industry, and commerce in satellite towns, notably around London and Stockholm. As socially responsible attitudes develop in the United States, large American cities will collaborate with county or regional enterprises for the same kind of orderly decentralization of population.

Big cities are swollen and decaying. Some states can accept more population only to their own detriment economically, socially, physically. Florida is already suffering. Oregon chooses not to grow in population. In its plan and land use regulations, each state has to consider its particular attributes. Responsibility devolves upon the federal government to harmonize state policies with the national imperative. There is much land, and, though it is perhaps underdeveloped, it is precious.

A "new cities" program, comparable to the British New Towns or Swedish satellites, may be implemented in the United States though no such program has yet been initiated. Any equivalent of British public development corporations will conflict with the ingrained American assumption that the public role shall be subordinate to the role of free enterprise, which is necessarily contingent on the degree to which financial profit is assured. Free enterprise has thus far been primarily engaged in existing cities and urban expansion where a full range of public facilities and services is available.

In his review of the New Communities Act of 1968, the veteran British New Town proponent Sir Frederic J. Osborn anticipated the administrative problems

> of a Federal department without town-funding experience confronting developers necessarily concerned for profitability but themselves not having staffs adapted to building complete towns, and local municipalities accustomed only to providing public services for adventurous growth rather than cooperating in town design. Some think that good new-town creation is only possible if a public body comparable with our development corporation is entrusted with the land ownership and groundwork, leaving the provision of building mainly to commercial developers. They are probably right.[1]

The record of large land-development companies across the nation does not bode well for their effectiveness in town building. From Cape Coral and Palm Coast in Florida to Adirondack Park in Pennsylvania; Treasure Lake in Georgia to Colonias de Santa Fe in New Mexico; Lake

---

1. "Planning Commentary—U.S.A. on the Way to New Town," *Town and Country Planning*, October-November 1968.

Winnebago near Kansas City to Lake Tahoe in California: the consuming objective has been the rapid sale of land, not the building of cities. "Decisions about where millions of Americans should be encouraged to migrate are left to land speculators while the National, State and Local Governments give up by default the right of the public to say what land use or growth policy should be."[2]

Time is growing short. As the population grows, vigorous redevelopment of existing cities can upgrade the environment and accommodate more people. Based on the assumption that "most of America's expected growth from now until the end of the century will occur within existing metropolitan areas,"[3] the National Task Force of the American Institute of Architects recommended that future urban growth should proceed in neighborhood increments identified as "growth units."[4] The estimated increase in national urban population during that period, however, can hardly be absorbed in existing metropolitan areas without a massive multiplicity of such growth units.

Numerous and extensive land subdivision has occurred on the periphery of the cities of America. Many of these developments have incorporated parks, schools, and shopping centers, but usually they have been random residential tracts without benefit of a plan for decentralization of the cities to which they are attached. The planning and development of complete self-contained towns in North America are rare. Kitimat in British Columbia, planned by Clarence Stein, and Don Mills near Toronto, discussed later in this chapter, are exceptions.

Exploitation of desirable open space proceeds in the guise of "new towns," although most serve as expansion of suburbs for discontented refugees who can afford to escape from the city or own a second home. The growth of suburbia is not confined to ticky-tacky subdivisions for the middle class. Wealthier citizens are in the market for fine, well-planned, and expensive communities with a full complement of commercial and recreational enterprises.[5] These are not independent new towns, however, and the economic and social stratification increases pressures upon low-income families, ethnic minorities, and the elderly.

---

2. Robert Cahn, "Land in Jeopardy," *The Christian Science Monitor*, January 17–January 24, 1973. Reprinted by permission of The Christian Science Monitor, © 1972. The Christian Science Publishing Society. All rights reserved.

3. American Institute of Architects, *A Plan for Urban Growth: Report of the National Policy Task Force*, January 1982, page 3, Item G.

4. American Institute of Architects, National Task Force, *Strategy for Building a Better America*, December 1971; Report of Constraints Conference, May 1972; *Structure for a National Policy*, October 1973.

5. Florida is "blessed" with such high-class developments, like North Palm Beach, and California has its share; Rancho San Bernardo and Laguna California in San Diego County, Laguna Niguel in Orange County, Conejo Village in Ventura County, and Valencia and Westlake Village in Los Angeles County are examples.

The Urban Land Institute defines a "new town" as a

land development project having acreage sufficiently large to encompass land use elements of residence, business, and industry which, when built, provide opportunities for (a) living and working within the community; (b) a full spectrum of housing types and price ranges; (c) permanent open space in passive and active recreation areas with sufficient land on the periphery to protect the identity; (d) strong esthetic controls.[6]

History

Planning new towns is certainly not a novel activity for Americans. Williamsburg was a new town in 1633, Savannah in 1733, Washington in 1791, and Chicago as late as 1833. The "company town" of the nineteenth century was notorious, such as the town of Pullman near Chicago, built for the workers of the Pullman Car Company. Many large and fine residential communities were developed near large cities in the twentieth century, and independent new towns were promoted to serve major industrial enterprises—Gary, Indiana (1906); Kingsport, Tennessee (1910); Kohler, Wisconsin (1913); Tyrone, New Mexico (1915); and Longview, Washington (1923), among them. Radburn, New Jersey, begun in 1928 as the Town of the Motor Age, will be remembered for the greenbelt circulation through the community. In the thirties, the Resettlement Administration communities of Greenbelt, Maryland; Greendale, Wisconsin; and Greenhills, Ohio, were planned after the Radburn prototype.

An ambitious program for a new "city" of Irvine was incorporated in 1972 on a huge singly owned ranch in southern California. Although elaborately planned for a population of nearly 500,000, the community depends on neighboring cities for most urban facilities and services. With an expanding campus for the University of California, an airport, and a large industrial park, the new city emerges as a series of planned real estate developments in a street system for automobiles. Later developments based on changes in the corporation policies seemed to turn the excellent planning of the early stages into a look-alike scheme of the usual large-scale speculative subdivisions, without the originally provided amenities or the careful preservation of open spaces that gave special character to the community.

Reston, Virginia, and Columbia, Maryland, are both new towns begun in the early sixties. Reston, with a population of 75,000, is near Washington, D.C.; Columbia, with a population of 100,000, lies between Baltimore and Washington. Each is a well-planned, privately financed community. Although some industrial-research development is antici-

6. *The Community Builders Handbook*, The Urban Land Institute, Washington, D.C., 1968.

Courtesy Gulf Reston, Inc.

Lake Anne village center. *Aerial view of Reston's first village center, Lake Anne —designed by architects Conklin and Rossant—showing the fifteen-story Heron House apartments; the J-shaped Washington Plaza shopping area; the thirty-acre Lake Anne, with the townhouse clusters, single-family detached and patio homes, and rental and condominium garden apartments that surround the lake.*

pated in both, the principal economic base is the nearby federal government.

In Europe new towns are public ventures of a high order. A city is a political entity of citizens; it is not a private domain, a corporate "company town." Although the city in the United States is, for many, a "fat calf" to be exploited for private gain, accommodation of the growing population will require aggressive public initiative, implemented by the equivalent of the British development corporation to administer public funds for initial investment in land and public facilities. New York set a precedent with the creation of the State Urban Development Corporation in 1968. With some tax support from the state, the corporation was empowered to issue tax-exempt bonds as its major source of funds. Its function was to initiate needed public facilities with emphasis on housing for low-income families. With the power of eminent domain and to deviate from local codes and zoning ordinances where necessary, the corporation used private capital in its developments. Roosevelt Island was a

Reston, Virginia—master plan. *Lines indicate residential areas, which include low-, medium-, and high-density mixtures; cross-hatching includes industrial and "advanced educational" uses; solid areas denote commercial centers; round dots are high schools; the dotted areas, internal recreational space, lakes, and ponds. No permanent surrounding open space was planned.*

major project, financed with federal assistance under the Communities Development Act.

Alert to the need for new urban communities, competent and experienced developers recognize the necessity for public participation in new town building to achieve the full range of housing and urban facilities. "There is absolutely no means whatsoever by which the home-building industry, as it is now constituted in America, can develop the sensibly organized new communities that America needs to accommodate its future growth," said James Rouse, developer of Columbia. "The country needs to enlarge the application of the process by which Columbia was built. It cannot afford to rely on the capacity or the whim of the private developer alone."[7] Philip Klutznick observed the need for public assistance to meet the need for housing and basic facilities of all income groups, and Emmanuel Cartsonis, Director of Planning and Design of Litchfield Park near Phoenix, Arizona, developed for the Goodyear Tire and Rubber Company, asserted the need for federal assistance in site acquisition and low-interest financing for this well-planned and partially developed new community.[8]

7. James Rouse, *Taming Metropolis: How to Manage an Urbanized World* (New York: Doubleday & Company, Inc., Anchor Books, 1967).

8. Shirley Weiss, *New Town Development in the U.S.*, New Towns Research, Center for Urban and Regional Studies (Chapel Hill: University of North Carolina Press, March 1973).

NEW TOWNS INTOWN

Dr. Harvey S. Perloff, former Dean of the School of Architecture and Urban Planning at the University of California at Los Angeles, presented his vision of the New Town Intown in an article published in the *AIP Journal,* May 1966. The following excerpt indicates the premises upon which his ideas are based:

> The heart of the new town idea is the creation of an urban community conceived as an integrated and harmonious whole. Starting from scratch in an open area, the new town can provide the most modern of facilities, whether schools, shopping or parking. The ability to develop through an overall plan makes possible community amenities and aesthetic qualities normally not realized. Because people today have both rising income and expanding leisure time, recreation receives an important role in the new town plan. (Reston, Virginia, for example, has made a golf course, an artificial lake, riding stables and bridle paths, and other recreational facilities the very backbone of the community.) The more advanced new town makes an effort to provide a balance between workplaces and homes. It has a distinctive center with important functional and visual purposes. High-rise apartments as well as low-lying buildings and individual homes help to provide variety as well as a superior design for living.
>
> With adequate imagination and purpose, the essence of all this can be applied to the older parts of the metropolis. Since replanning is much more difficult than starting from scratch, it will require particularly good planning —aimed at the same goals of harmony and balance. It will normally require some strategic rebuilding as well as rehabilitation for continuous improvement according to a plan. An essential element would be a working partnership in planned urban development between the people of the area, a variety of public agencies, and private enterprise. The aim should not be to create communities that are all alike; each should have its own special character, its own focal points, its own attractions.
>
> The New Town Intown concept can greatly help in transforming the physical environment of the city in keeping with social objectives and human resources needs. It cannot solve the human problems of the city, nor even all the physical problems. It can provide a valuable lever for both. If we hope to achieve the objectives of the antipoverty and other social programs, it will be necessary, among other things, to transform the total environment of poverty—the physical aspects as well as the social, economic, and political. It is important to create an environment in which the community as well as the individual family are important.

The New Town Intown concept involves the large-scale rehabilitation, modernization, and redevelopment of the core of the city. It is proposed that the functions of the area be changed to make for a viable living environment that will be attractive and safe for persons of all ages who like to be in the heart of a city where interesting and exciting activities are available. The concept involves recognition that the central city areas are too important to discard. To reconstitute the central core as a total living environment is a challenging idea. To make it an economically sound as well as socially desirable part of the total city is imperative. The changes called for will take time and monumental efforts on the part of both government and the private sector to complete. The old format for the area must be abandoned. Vehicular traffic must be reduced or confined to special locations, the concentration of pollutants must be eliminated, the streets must be well-lighted and protected against vandalism and crime.

Presently, plans are being developed for the rehabilitation of buildings that have been vacated by their former occupants. These buildings, like the warehouses in the SoHo artist district of New York City, can be converted to special uses and bring people with like interests together. The effect of this rehabilitation is to bring economic stability into areas on the verge of collapse.

As a means of coping with the tremendous urban dilemma, the Urban Growth and Community Development Act of 1970 provided federal financial aid until the early 1980s for the New Towns Intown program. Intended to recover a human scale through comprehensive redevelopment of large cities, it provides more flexibility than was embodied in previous redevelopment "projects." The Housing and Urban Development Agency does not make its usual requirement that a site be a minimum of 100 acres, and wholesale condemnation is not necessary. A full range of urban facilities and social amenities may be incorporated to achieve an effective community. Cedar-Riverside in Minneapolis was the first development to be undertaken; Roosevelt Island in New York was the second.

Plans for sweeping redevelopment should open avenues to the essential restructuring of the urban form, to phase out strip commercial zoning and substitute genuine commercial centers, and to readjust land uses to a system of mass transportation without which large cities will continue to strangle themselves in an endless network of streets, highways, and parking facilities. It will take time, in some cities a desperately long time, to achieve the transformation. But it has taken a long and dreary time for cities to reach the current stalemate, and it should be worth the time to recover. It is the public's responsibility to replan cities for the integration of renewal through redevelopment programs, and a combined public and private responsibility to ensure that each new development will serve that purpose.

BRITISH PLANNING POLICY

Throughout the nineteenth century the British were stirred by the woeful impact of the Industrial Revolution on the living environment. Improvement in housing conditions was the focus of concern and action. In 1909 there began a series of legislative steps up the ladder of urban planning.

New Town Intown, Roosevelt Island, New York City—New York State Urban Development Corporation. *A 150-acre site developed for 25 percent housing, 16 percent commercial/industrial, 44 percent open space and public use, 15 percent circulation. Of 5,000 dwelling units, 30 percent are for low income, 25 percent for moderate income, and 45 percent unsubsidized.*

It was a cogent, complete experience in the search for a physical structure to accommodate the people and the functions of urbanization. The Housing and Town Planning Act of 1909 granted powers to local authorities to prepare plans for their respective jurisdictions. To encourage building after World War I the Housing and Town Planning Acts of 1919 for both England and Scotland introduced the policy of joint planning action among several local authorities, and in 1923 the act empowered the local authorities to plan for built-up as well as undeveloped areas. In 1925 planning functions were separated from the field of housing alone for the first time. The Town and Country Planning Acts of 1932 for England, Wales, and Scotland extended the responsibility of local authorities to both urban and rural land and included the preservation of historic buildings and the natural landscape. The powers under these acts were only permissive (i.e., not mandated), and they were conferred on all local authorities. As a consequence, the local authorities were subject to excessive compensation for any claims that might result from the exercise of their powers. These acts, however, with the addition of the Ribbon Development Act of 1935 that regulated the space along the highways, provided the basic framework in Great Britain for the following 15 years.

In 1937 a royal commission was established under the chairmanship of Sir Montague Barlow to inquire into the distribution of industrial population and the social, economic, and strategic disadvantages arising from the concentration of industry and working people in large, built-up communities. The commission report, published in 1940, contained recommendations for redevelopment of congested areas, the dispersal of population from such areas, the creation of balanced industrial employment throughout Great Britain, and the establishment of a national au-, thority to deal with these matters.

In 1941 two new committees were created to study the recommendations of the Barlow report—the Scott Committee on Land Utilization in Rural Areas and the Uthwatt Committee on Compensation and Betterment. From these committees came recommendations for the creation of a central planning authority, measures to ensure state control of development, increased powers of local planning authorities for compulsory purchase (eminent domain), and major revisions in the laws on compensation and betterment.

The Scott and Uthwatt reports led to the adoption of a new series of town planning acts. The first, in 1943, created a new office of Minister of Town and Country Planning for England, Wales, and Scotland, and strengthened the powers of local authorities to control development. The Town and Country Planning Act of 1944 for England and the 1945 act for Scotland gave local authorities power to enforce comprehensive redevelopment of obsolete and war-damaged areas, and implemented the acquisition of land for both open space and a balanced arrangement of land uses. These acts culminated in the Town and Country Planning Act of 1947 for England and Wales and a counterpart for Scotland. The principal features were (a) to establish a framework of land use throughout the country based on development plans by local authorities, approved by the Minister of Town and Country Planning (now the Minister of Housing and Local Government) or the Secretary of State for Scotland; (b) to control all development by making it subject to permission from the local planning authorities; (c) to extend to local authorities all necessary powers to acquire land for planning or development and provide for grants from the central government for these purposes; and (d) to ensure the preservation of buildings of historic interest and the natural character of the landscape. In contrast to prior legislation, this act conferred these powers upon only 188 local authorities in large cities and county boroughs, and rendered their exercise mandatory rather than permissive.[9]

Compensation and Betterment

During the past hundred years the policy of "compensation and betterment" became an accepted procedure in the regulation of land use in Great Britain. The principle that the use of private property is subject to regulation for the community welfare was complemented by a dual provision: just compensation is due to private owners for any restrictions public authorities create that impair the value of land; and, the enhancement of property values that accrue through public planning decisions may be assessed by the local authorities. It was assumed that the public funds expended for compensation to property owners would be balanced by the assessments for the betterments that resulted from land use regulations. The administration of this policy, however, became unduly complicated. Assessments for betterments for improved values were awkward to determine and almost impossible to collect. As a consequence, local authorities had inadequate resources upon which to draw to fulfill their obligations for payment of compensation.

A major task of the Uthwatt Committee was to investigate this entire policy and to make recommendations for improvement. Based on the report of the committee, the 1947 act introduced a comprehensive modification in land policy with the provision that the state shall reserve all rights to the *development* of land; the government was empowered to expropriate all development rights. This sweeping revision, while following the principle of compensation and betterment, was intended to remove the involved processes in the collection of betterments and the determination of appropriate compensation. Owners of property approved for development at the time the legislation was enacted were entitled to compensation for the loss of these rights at land values prevailing in 1947. A central land board was appointed to administer these negotiations, and a fund of £300 million was set aside by the national government for this purpose. As permission was subsequently granted by local planning authorities to develop property, the landowners were required to pay a development charge to the government. This charge was in the amount of the difference between the value of the land for the existing use and the value for the new development approved by the planning authority. Since, under the act, owners who had suffered loss through expropriation of development rights were to have been compen-

---

9. Beverley J. Pooley, *The Evolution of British Planning Legislation* (Ann Arbor, Michigan: University of Michigan Law School, 1960).

sated for this loss, all landowners were subsequently liable for the development charge. A permitted use that resulted in a lesser land value entitled the owner to compensation for the difference, whereas one that would support a land value greater than the existing use entitled the government to charge the owner for this difference.

This remarkable land policy was developed under a coalition government, similar to that under Winston Churchill when he was prime minister. The committee that recommended it included conservative members with a sound knowledge both of British tradition and the problems of land development. The chairman, the Honorable Augustus Uthwatt, was a lord judge of appeal, a high rank in the public affairs of England. But opposition to the entire procedure formed soon after passage of the act and its administration became increasingly cumbersome. In 1951 a Conservative government came into power and, in an act of 1953, abolished this feature. Permission to develop land was still required, but landowners were thereafter free to realize the values on the open market. Sadly, the long tradition embraced in the principle of compensation and betterment as a basic policy for the equitable regulation of land in the implementation of the planning process was ended.

The administration of planning in England has been vested in the public authorities of large localities, the county, and borough councils. Contrary to the practice in the United States, zoning as a means to regulate land use has not prevailed. Local planning authorities are required to prepare a twenty-year development plan, approval of which is required by the government. This plan is reviewed every five years and has the statutory effect of establishing the land use policy by which the authorities are guided in granting permission for development. The power to grant permission is the vehicle for the control of development within the policy set forth in the plan, and this procedure has been retained for the purpose of maintaining flexibility to meet changing conditions.

Although the enlightened landownership policy embraced in the act of 1947 is absent and the experience in Great Britain demonstrated its difficulties, the tradition of responsibility by public authorities may yet offer the prospect for favorable land development in that country. There are planning authorities who believe these difficulties might have been materially altered if the landowners had shared in the increment of increased property value by a development charge fixed at a lower level, such as 75 percent of the difference in value.

This issue will undoubtedly remain alive. It revolves about the relation between the necessary public control of land use and the element of monopoly that such control vests in land values. Any form of public control over land use, whether it may be permission for development from planning authorities as in England, or by zoning regulations as in the United States, conveys to some owners and withholds from others privileges that accrue because of the relative location of land. The maintenance of a balance between the open channels of competition and the effect of monopoly values that sound planning may confer is an unresolved issue in the United States as in Britain. An equitable distribution of all the benefits of planning was the basic purpose of compensation and betterment; the operation of this principle may yet restore an appropriate measure of equity in the conduct of urban affairs.

London Region

England suffered heavy damage to its cities during World War II. One-third of its 13 million dwellings were damaged, and there was practically no new building. With devastation all about them, the people found it necessary to consider plans for reconstruction. The 1944 Town and Country Planning Act had extended financial aid to local authorities for the purchase of land when rebuilding became possible.

A large proportion of the English live in urban communities, but there are only seven large industrial centers. These are agglomerations of urban areas ranging from two to eight million people, and congestion in these cities is acute. Nonetheless it remains the British ideal to live in "cottages." A density of twelve families per acre was suggested by Ebenezer Howard and became the standard density for the garden cities; Sir Raymond Unwin dwelt upon it at length as a desirable standard. It remains today the standard toward which enlightened planners strive.

The destruction of large urban areas impressed many thoughtful people with the possibility of recapturing some open space within their congested urban centers in the large-scale rebuilding that was necessary. The British realized that they should try to cope with the problem of congestion in their cities. Launching the postwar planning program, they began where they were with what they had and sought the way to a new concept of the urban structure.

The elements of the garden city held strong appeal for the British; the characteristics of the village, in contrast with the metropolis, attracted them. Proximity to the beautiful countryside was a natural desire. They prefer the bicycle to the subway. They probably enjoy walking more than motoring. The two successful garden cities, Letchworth and Welwyn, were before them for comparison with the huge and congested cities. The English people have seen the advantages of the small community as a better way of life. They have been justly proud of their delightful rural country, and preservation of the countryside has occupied the aggressive attention of the most influential peers of England.

To the people of Britain, London is their great and noble city, the capital of the Commonwealth, and as colorful as any city in history. It is also synonymous with overcrowding. The County of London covers an area of 117 square miles. In 1944 it had a population of 4 million. At the core of this area is the City of London, one mile square, with 5,000 people. This is the financial and political heart of the British Commonwealth. Fanning out from this center, Greater London had a population of 8 million in an area of 700 square miles. The planning program of 1944, under the direction of Patrick Abercrombie and F. J. Forshaw, was directed toward a dual objective: rebuilding the wartorn city and relieving the intolerable overcrowding and congestion.

The essential elements of the Abercrombie plan for Greater London were the reduction of the population within the congested center, the creation of a greenbelt to contain Greater London, and the movement of industry to an outer ring. This was consistent with the enlightened planning tradition in England, but it demanded courageous conviction and bold decision. A major issue at the outset was the standard of population density to be sought within the overcrowded center. Although some authorities held to a density of about 70 to 75 persons (20 dwellings) per acre as a desirable maximum, the London planners proposed a density of 100 to 150 persons; the inner districts of the county are being redeveloped in this latter range. The density within the inner ring ranges from 70 to 100 persons per acre, and in the suburban ring it is maintained at about 50 persons. About this complex a broad greenbelt ring ranging from five to fifteen miles wide has been reserved. Within this greenbelt the existing towns are permitted to increase within the plotted areas of their jurisdictions, but the balance is reserved for recreation. Beyond the greenbelt and within the Greater London region are the outer ring of villages and small towns separated by open countryside.

The plan encompassed a total area of some 2,600 square miles. The population densities involved a reduction of about 40 percent, or more than 6,000, in the county, and more than 400,000 in the inner urban ring. Some increase was proposed for the suburban ring, but the population of Greater London was reduced by a total of over one million people. This program for the decentralization of vast population resulted in the New Towns Act of 1946.

As in the United States, the structure of urban government in Great Britain was designed for an era when the administration was relatively simple. With the growth of the metropolis and its accretions of urban entities, the governmental organization bears no relation to the real character of a metropolitan area. Legislation was implemented to establish a single authority, the Greater London Council, for the 800 square miles and 8 million people of metropolitan London. Within this council struc-

Legend:
- London Region 1961
- London Region Abercrombie Plan
- County of London
- Inner Ring Abercrombie Plan
- Suburban Ring Abercrombie Plan
- Greater London Conurbation 1961
- Green belt
- Outer Ring
- New Towns

1 – Stevenage
2 – Welwyn
3 – Harlow
4 – Basildon
5 – Hatfield
6 – Hemel – Hempstead
7 – Bracknell
8 – Crawley

N

0   5   10   15
MILES

The London region. *The Greater London plan of 1944, by Patrick J. Abercrombie and F. J. Forshaw, embraced a region of 2,600 square miles. A series of four rings surrounded the County of London. The population within the heavily urbanized areas of the county and the inner ring was to be reduced by some one million people by dispersal within the suburban and outer rings. The urban conurbation (concentration) of the region has extended the boundaries of the suburban ring beyond the limits of the plan and has forced attention to the preservation and expansion of the greenbelt. The regional sphere is also extended to some 4,600 square miles since the plan was conceived, and the total population has grown from 8 million to 10 million.*

The development of the New Towns may not have resulted in the hoped-for population reduction in the city of London. However, no one can deny that these well planned communities have provided residents with a healthful environment in new facilities.

ture there are boroughs, each with a population of about 200,000, that are responsible for all local administration except the functions of metropolitan scope, including planning.

The adoption of the policy that more than a million people had to be removed from the central districts of London was of major consequence. It represented a conviction that the overcrowding within the city must be relieved, that the expansion of the city must be controlled, and that the amenities of urban life could be achieved only by decentralization of employment and residential communities. The New Towns were conceived in the tradition of the garden cities, as self-contained communities with all facilities that make an independent environment. They were not intended to be satellite dormitories connected to the central city. Some were related to the larger orbit of London, however, to make available to the people of the New Towns the special facilities of the central city and, being thus attractively near, to encourage movement from London to release the city for a program of redevelopment.

The New Towns Act provided for the creation of development corporations to plan, build, and manage the New Towns. The corporation obtained sixty-year loans from the Ministry of Housing and Local Government (now the Department of the Environment) to finance the acquisition of land, prepare the plans, and improve the land with all utilities and road systems. The corporation could construct buildings to rent to business and industry, or could lease sites for private development. Lease arrangements were generally for a period of ninety-nine years. Housing could also be built by the corporation and, to ensure adequate housing for industry employees, the corporation did build most of it. Increasing participation by private enterprise has been encouraged. The Minister of Housing and Local Government has general jurisdiction over the program and all plans for development are subject to approval by the ministry. The New Towns Act of 1959 determined to dissolve each corporation when the town was completed and transfer management to a commission for New Towns, made up of members appointed by the Minister of Housing and by local government.

The earliest towns, beginning with Stevenage in 1946, were located in the London region. Eight were so designated, including Welwyn, which was begun in 1920 but taken under the jurisdiction of the New Towns Act. These towns, from eighteen to thirty miles from London, were intended to accommodate the overspill of people and industry to implement the London Plan.

Overspill from large cities has not been the principal reason for building more New Towns. The purpose has shifted to economic support and development on a regional scale. As reported by the Town and Country Planning Association: "The regional aim of new towns is both to assist the restructuring and growth of our major urban regions and to bring the advantages of strong growth points to relatively depressed regions." [10]

Thirty-three towns had been authorized by the end of 1973. Of these, twenty-eight have been built. Today each of these towns houses between 60,000 and 250,000 persons. Thus about 2 million people reside in these planned communities, in both urban and rural settings. By the end of the century it is predicted that the figure will grow to 3.5 million.

This planning at a national level in support of regional development is an important first step toward the redevelopment of congested urban centers and the general improvement of the living and working environment, as well as a rational approach to accommodating a growing national population. [11]

Planned as clusters of neighborhoods around a business and civic center, the New Towns are predominantly made up of row cottages, ranging in density from twelve to fifteen per acre. The neighborhoods have populations of 4,000 to 8,000, each neighborhood has its own schools, recreation facilities, churches, and a small shopping center. There is convenient and efficiently arranged access to industrial areas.

In an effort to overcome the monotony of the standard two-story cottage, some high-rise apartment buildings have been introduced. Commenting on this trend, Dame Evelyn Sharp, Permanent Secretary of the Ministry of Housing and Local Government, said: "The architect likes the occasional high block; whether the new town tenant really does is one of the great debates." [12] The apartment is considered objectionable for the large numbers of families with children; 5 to 15 percent of the apartment buildings are planned for single people and childless couples.

Industrial enterprise, though initially slow to move to the New Towns, became attracted by the efficient operating conditions, the availability of good sites, and the stable employment conditions. The expanding range of industries settling in the New Towns offers a desirable diversification of employment, although skilled and professional workers predominate.

Retail services are arranged in the conventional manner of shopping centers in the United States, with a variety of facilities arranged around a pedestrian mall or plaza. Automobile ownership increased in the New Towns beyond that anticipated in the early plans, and it has been necessary in some towns to build garages to augment shopping center parking. Ownership in the original eight towns within the London ring ranged between 50 percent and 60 percent and has reached 70 percent in Ste-

10. Report by the Association to the House of Commons Sub-Committee of the Expenditure Committee, November 1973.
11. See chapter 17 for a discussion of national and state planning in the United States.
12. *Town and Country Planning,* January 1961.

venage, as compared with 42 percent in Greater London and 46 percent in Wales and England.[13]

An experimental "superbus" system in Stevenage doubled bus travel (from 20 percent to 39 percent) between 1971 and 1972, but the New Towns in Great Britain were not planned for internal mass transit. The London-region towns are connected by rail to London. Only in Runcorn is there provision for an exclusive bus lane along the road system, but Cumbernauld New Town, near Glasgow, was designed for complete separation of pedestrians and motor traffic. Cumbernauld is also unusual in the design of its commercial center.

The New Towns, in the words of Dame Evelyn Sharp, "have been a great experiment and are on their way to being a great success. Mistakes have been made and there are many problems still to resolve. But for thousands of families they are providing living conditions among the best in Britain; and for industry they are providing the conditions for efficiency. They will prove a first-class investment, in money as well as health and productivity."[14]

After twenty-three years of growth and maturity, the New Towns have been highly successful in providing decent housing and a healthful environment for the residents. The number of nations that have adopted the concept provides the best evidence that the New Towns are both self sustaining and supportive of the regional centers (as a result of effective transportation ties).

A 1973 American assessment stated:

> The crowning achievement of British planning is not the new towns themselves, but rather the protection of the bulk of the beautiful landscape around London and other major cities. Along with control of development in new towns and expanded areas designated for growth, all are coordinated with a sensible rapid transit system. The British have found the formula for coordinated regional and national planning and curbing of urban sprawl, which may be ten years away in the United States. There is no *direct* cost for this 610,000-acre greenbelt. It would have been impossible to purchase in full fee at market prices, which is the only permanently successful way to protect the landscape on a significant scale.
>
> The success with the greenbelt is not immediately transferrable to the United States. It is based upon several factors which makes it successful, but which are difficult to transfer . . . [including]:
>
> A concept of government ownership of the incremental value of property derived from public improvements and zoning, where property owners need not be compensated for permanent freezing of land use in open space of existing uses. This would be impossible under current court rulings under

---

13. Report of the United Nations Seminar, London, June 1973, the Office of International Affairs, U.S. Department of Housing and Urban Development, Washington, D.C.

14. *Town and Country Planning,* January 1961.

Town and Country Planning Association

New Towns in Great Britain and Northern Ireland. *Locations of the thirty-three New Towns in the current program are shown on the map of England, Wales, and Scotland. The towns are experiments in the design of an environment in which the human scale predominates. They are self-contained communities seeking a balance between sources of employment, business enterprise, shopping, education, and recreation for those who live in them. They are, however, significant for another important reason: they are essentially an organic element in a broad program of decentralization of the congested urban centers, the London region having received the principal attention.*

Two of the towns related to the London region are shown in diagrammatic plans. Stevenage, begun in 1949, was the first of these towns. The site comprises 6,100 acres, and the original population of 60,000 for which the town was planned has expanded to 80,000.

Stevenage (left)—designed by Clifford Holliday; Crawley (right)—designed by Anthony Minoprio. *The town of Crawley, originally planned for a population of 50,000 on a site of 6,000 acres, will have a population of 70,000. Two existing villages—Three Bridges and Crawley—have been absorbed, and the town center occupies the latter. An industrial area of 264 acres is planned for 8,500 workers. Nine neighborhoods have populations of 4,000 to 7,000, and the density is about twenty-nine persons per acre.*

Each neighborhood in the New Towns has a small subcenter for shopping, a primary school, playfields, and social facilities. The secondary schools serve several neighborhoods; in Crawley they are combined in three separate campuses (S).

The residential neighborhoods are indicated by cross-hatched areas, industrial areas by heavy cross-hatching, and the town center by black. Open space and farmland, forming a greenbelt about the towns, are indicated by dotted areas. A desirable attribute of the New Towns is their relatively small size, designed to encourage pedestrian circulation and maintain close proximity to surrounding open space. The plans indicate an abundance of space flowing throughout the community as separations between the neighborhoods. The preservation of natural wooded areas or unusual topographical characteristics within this space is advantageous, but the proportionate quantity of land reserved for permanent open space may be excessive in view of the surrounding greenbelt, low density, and internal recreation fields. This abundant open space may overextend walking distances, exaggerate the separation between neighborhood cells, and thus tend to nullify the advantages of the modest size of the towns.

the Fourteenth Amendment in the U.S., where freezing of large areas, not subject to natural hazards, in nondevelopment could be challenged as taking without just compensation.[15]

Impact

Since, to some degree, the New Town policies of the British government were intended to reduce the overcrowding of the central cities, especially after the end of World War II, many have wondered about the degree of the success of this program and what its impact might be on the central city and its industrial base. Peter Gripaios responds to this in part in the following excerpts.

Locational Influences

The very concentration of population and economic activity in the London area indicates that at one time it must have been, relatively, a very profitable location. Have there then been changes in this relative profitability such that London firms have been forced to go into liquidation or to move elsewhere? If London can be compared with other cities it does seem likely that this has been the case. There have been net firm losses in many large cities throughout the world and locational factors have been shown to be an important influence. Studies of New York (Hoover and Vernon, 1959; Lichtenberg, 1960; Leone, 1971), Chicago (Moses and Williamson, 1967), Sydney (Logan, 1966), and Glasgow (Firn and Hughes, 1973) indicate that this is particularly true with regard to the decentralization of manufacturing industry.

These studies reveal that firms have been driven out of central areas by lack of room for expansion, difficulties of access, competition from other uses and high factor costs. They have been pulled to peripheral locations as a result of improvements in transportation, technology and communications and by the existence of plentiful supplies of factors of production. Certainly, there can be no doubt that the development of motor transportation has radically altered the pattern of location. Modern road systems and vehicles mean that distance within urban areas is now unimportant and that it does not much matter where factories are located. In addition, the flexibility of road transport has enabled manufacturing firms to capitalize on improvements in production technology. They have been able to utilize space in peripheral locations to build large single-storey plants operating with assembly-line techniques. Finally, improvements in communications have enabled such firms to differentiate their production activities from those requiring face-to-face contacts. As a result, production establishments can be moved to low-cost "greenfield" sites and only small head

---

15. A report by the Office of International Affairs of the Department of Housing and Urban Development on the United Nations Seminar on New Towns in London, June 1973. The report, written by Jack A. Underhill of the Office of New Communities Development, HUD, clearly stipulates that "the material presented does not necessarily represent the views of the Department."

offices maintained in the metropolitan core. Such factors may well have contributed significantly to employment decline in London. Certainly, various questionnaire studies of relocating firms have revealed that shortages of space and skilled labour and access difficulties figure prominently in the relocation decision (Keeble, 1968; South East Joint Planning Team, 1971). Moreover, in the case of London it seems possible that such factors have been reinforced by the spatial policy measures of national and local governments (below) with regard to their effect on the relative profitability of an inner London location.

Does then, the South East London evidence support the contention that the profitability of an inner London location has changed? It is difficult to be certain one way or the other given the simultaneous interaction of various possible influences but it does appear that the evidence is at least consistent with this contention.

(1) One would expect such problems as access difficulties, shortages of space for expansion, high costs and unsuitable buildings to be more serious in the older and more densely populated inner parts of the city. This would in turn suggest that the percentage loss of firms and employment would be higher the more central the location.

(2) Since the studies of other cities have emphasized that the improvements in production, transportation and communications have particularly affected the viability of an inner city location for manufacturing industry, one would expect, ceteris paribus, the loss of jobs and firms to be concentrated in this sector. This was especially true of the loss of jobs in South East London, 90 percent of the jobs lost 1961–71 being in manufacturing industry. The survey of closures indicated that though manufacturing establishments declined more than their service counterparts, service industry nevertheless declined significantly.

(3) Assuming that the cost of land, labour and the cost of obtaining suitable premises in general increases with the centrality of the location, one would expect the direction of firm movements to be outward. It might further be expected that manufacturing firms with (in general) less need to be close to the market and an assumed higher average land/output ratio than service firms would be moving farther afield than the latter. The data on firm movements confirms both expectations. It can be seen that, regarding the total number of firms, most tended to move from South East London to other areas of the capital, outside of the central area, in that such moves accounted for over 40 percent of all moves.

There is no breakdown of movement within Greater London but the fact that there were very few moves (4) to the central area and a large number of moves to beyond the Greater London area indicates, in general, that the movement was certainly outwards. The data, surprisingly, do not show widespread local movement (probably as a result of the bias of the sample towards large firms). In general, the movement of internal relocaters was also outwards—the fourteen internal moves consisting of ten outward, one orbital and three inward moves. The destination of moves differed greatly between manufacturing and service firms. Internal relocations were the most significant in the case of service industry whereas, in manufacturing, moves to elsewhere in Greater London and to the area beyond were most significant, accounting for 42 percent and 37 percent of all moves respectively.

Urban and Regional Policy

There have been two aspects of spatial policy which have affected the London labour market. Regional policy has been aimed to induce firms to move from prosperous to depressed areas and urban planning policy has attempted to move population and jobs from congested areas to new towns. Local government redevelopment schemes have been an additional influence. There can be no doubt that both aspects of policy have to some extent been responsible for part of the job loss. Regional policy tried to stop firms growing in London and encouraged them to move to Development Areas.[16]

"NEW TOWNS" OUTSIDE ENGLAND

The British New Towns are an expression of the national disposition. Whereas most of the people live in the great industrial centers, the English village and the open countryside represent the cherished qualities of an ideal environment. This ideal was given tangible expression by Ebenezer Howard and established as a traditional British objective in the garden city. Urban desires have not followed this firm direction in other places, however. The strong affirmative approach to decentralization represented by the English New Town program has exerted positive influence elsewhere, but the traditional bond with the older cities in most countries is strong. The self-sufficient community as a module for decentralization does not present the same attraction in other countries as it has in Great Britain. As a consequence, the movement of planned decentralization is marked by variations of the British theme.

Gideon Golany, Professor of Urban and Regional Planning at Pennsylvania State College, presented an excellent overview of new towns in both Europe and the Orient in *Cities*.[17] His comments deal with conditions and policies in the many nations that have been experimenting with the development of this effort to improve the housing and environmental conditions of their people. The following material includes excerpts from his intensive studies.

Canada

The community of Don Mills was begun in 1953 by the Don Mills Development Corporation, a private land investment company. Being part of North York, one of the thirteen municipalities in the Toronto metropolitan area, it is not politically independent but represents an approach similar to the New Towns of England. Occupying a site of 2,058 acres, it

---

16. Peter Gripaios, Division of Economics, Plymouth Polytechnic, Devon, England.
17. Nancy Akre, ed. *Cities*. (New York, Cooper Hewitt Museum, 1982.)

was planned as a new industrial community for a population of 25,000. Located one-half mile from a limited-access highway and twenty-five minutes from the Toronto airport, it is served also by two railways that traverse the site. The sponsoring development company has encouraged a wide diversification of industrial enterprise, and the entire town has been developed by private companies. It is distinguished for the high level of architectural quality that prevails.

Perhaps the most significant aspect of this new town is the policy of the development company to seek an economic balance between residential and industrial or commercial development. It is the objective to maintain a ratio of 60 percent in the assessed values of residential development and 40 percent in industrial and commercial development. This policy of a balanced economy in the administration of urban affairs suggests an approach to the regulation of urban growth and development everywhere, not merely in new town developments.

Fundamentally, however:

> Canada has also suffered from a fragmented policy towards new-town planning. The Canadians have had a long history of pioneering settlements and exploration of new areas, but it was not until 1973 that a New Communities Act provided capital and planning and management assistance for new towns. The Act also provided 100 million dollars per year until 1978 for land acquisitions. While the Act aims at many of the same things planners implemented elsewhere—stabilization of population movement and stimulation of economic growth—the Canadian policy has suffered from use as a complement to urban growth strategies rather than as a part of a regional, more comprehensive plan. The Canadian new communities project is still in its infancy and has the potential to become a strong tool in the development of vast uninhabited areas.[18]

Brazil

Around the middle of the twentieth century Copacabana, near Rio de Janeiro, was a seaside paradise. A quarter of a century later, 250,000 people occupy tall buildings in three square miles by the sea. A new city is now planned ten miles away. Barra de Tijuca, occupying seventy-five square miles of open space and mountains stretching along fourteen miles of beach, was planned in 1969 by Lucio Costa, the planner of Brasília. Planned as a series of urban communities of 12,000 separated by green-belts and two large centers for 80,000 to 100,000 people each, the new city is expected to accommodate a population of 2 million. Designed with the flair of architect Oscar Niemeyer, the first center is dominated by

---

18. Ibid.

seventy thirty-four-story apartment towers, six office buildings, and elaborate associated amenities. The grandiose concept of Barra de Tijuca is in the Latin American tradition of dramatic scale.

Aratu was also planned by Lucio Costa. An extension of Salvador in the province of Bahia, it is planned for a population of 1,500,000. Aratu is a neighboring city rather than a satellite community; Salvador itself has a population of less than one million. The land for Aratu, the first completely planned industrial city in Brazil, was purchased by the state and sold at low cost to developers of industry and housing. Tax incentives are also granted for development. The National Housing Bank (NHB), founded in 1964, is the primary source of financing for urban development; several thousand low-income dwellings have been built in Aratu with NHB loans.

NHB funds are obtained by an 8 percent tax on payrolls of all private enterprise in the country. The NHB borrows from this special fund (Fundo de Garantía do Tempo de Servico) at 5 percent interest to finance its urban housing programs, which are directed primarily to housing for families in the slum areas or *favellas*. These families pay from one to ten percent interest on the loans, according to their income.

The unique program has elicited the interest of other countries, but it is not without problems. New outlying housing communities are far from sources of employment. The degree of authoritarian direction concerning the movement of families from the *favellas* to the new and unfamiliar living conditions, some of which include the proverbial high-rise apartments, has aroused resentment. The bank has also been confronted with the not uncommon predicament of many low-income families unable to meet the continuing financial obligations of home ownership.

France[19]

The places of greatest historic interest in Paris, most of the important commercial, financial, educational, and political activity, and the entertainment center are confined to an area of less than ten square miles in the heart of the city. The city, however, covers an area of forty square miles with a population of 3 million. More than 4 million people have settled in surrounding districts. This region of between 7 million and 8 million people occupies 300 square miles. Since an urban population increase of 20 million is anticipated by the turn of the century, a multiplication of housing "colonies" is inadequate. Implementation of an urban

---

19. The data below are from *New Communities in Selected European Countries,* U.S. Department of Housing and Urban Development (Washington, D.C.: U.S. Government Printing Office, April 1974).

policy of planned decentralization in the country has been slow. But the pressure of population and industrial growth has required positive action, and with the passage of the Boscher law in 1970 financial assistance for new towns has become available. Five new towns with populations between 330,000 and 500,000 are planned within a ten- to twelve-mile radius of Paris. Existing villages will be integrated within new town developments here and elsewhere.

> A group of four new towns have been planned about the periphery of Paris . . . some thirty-five or more miles away from the center of the city. These town are either tied into the central city or are to be by mass transit facilities to make possible a wide range of choice to the residents for places of employment.
>
> Many have thought that these new towns would become the locale for the poor of Paris as the central portion of that city was taken over by the wealthy. In the planning, however, it was the policy of the local and state planning groups, that government-assisted housing and the affluent would find facilities to meet their needs . . . sometimes just across the street from each other.
>
> One of the new towns is Evry. It has a centrum called, in the reflection of the Greek civilization, the Agora. In and about this commercial center are found all of the amenities that are desirable to meet the need of the local residents. Beautifully planned and developed, the Agora not only serves but it enriches the residents with cultural facilities. The Agora is an air-conditioned mall arranged for pedestrians.
>
> The residential sections are in the form of microneighborhoods containing clusters of approximately 100 dwellings. In the course of the development, the technicians worked closely with the existing and potential residents, especially in the middle class areas of Paris. These new towns are formed by a mix of existing residential communities with new, sometimes high-rise, structures. The French program is state-planned; private enterprise was enlisted in development. Other satellites are also under construction around Lille [for 150,000], Lyons [for 300,000], Marseilles [for 750,000], and Rouen [for 140,000]. The French new-town satellites are coming into their own as economic entities, and their population will exceed 100,000.[20]

Spain

In Spain, where the same concentration of population in large urban centers exists, a 1970 legislative decree created Urban Urgent Action (ACTUR), a plan for eight new satellite towns ranging in population from 60,000 to 120,000. Three of these are near Barcelona, the principal city of Spain, and the others serve Madrid, Seville, Valencia, and Cádiz.[21]

---

20. Golany, *Cities*.
21. Op. cit. *New Communities* . . .

Sweden

Sweden was the first country in Europe to enact legislation for planning, with the Urban Building Act of 1874. However, the social and economic circumstances there have not compelled attention to planning on a regional scale. The first Town Planning Act of 1907 and the 1931 act were similar to the 1909 and 1932 planning acts in England, but emphasis was placed on site planning and street and building arrangements rather than on regional relationships.

The consumer cooperative movement reflected the direct and pragmatic approach to the solution of economic and social conditions for which the Swedish people have demonstrated capability. The self-help small cottage or Magic-House program initiated in 1927 is another example. One-tenth-acre plots on city-owned land were made available for sixty-year lease and a ground rent of 5 percent of the land value. Prefabricated houses were also made available for erection by the owner, his labor amounting to 10 percent of the cost. The balance of 90 percent was to be repaid to the city in thirty annual installments. This program presented a practical means for families of low income to acquire decent homes as a substitute for substandard tenements in the congested city.

The plan for the decentralization of Stockholm has resulted in two noteworthy developments in urban planning—Vallingby and Farsta. Some 50,000 people with sources of employment in the central city have had to seek dwellings within the suburban districts. This is equivalent to about one-third of the housing in the new suburban developments. These two new communities are therefore related to the general plan of the city. They are served by a subway to the center. It was intended that the usual development of small suburban increments, proven unable to support an adequate community center, be avoided. The Vallingby group was therefore planned for a population of 60,000 that, including the immediate existing suburbs about it, could support a complete shopping and commercial center. The Farsta district, with a surrounding population of 35,000, was planned for the existing number. Industrial sites were reserved within the vicinity of both communities as part of the decentralization program.

These towns are built on publicly owned land. They attest to the wisdom of the policy adopted by the city many years ago to acquire large tracts of land about the periphery of the city. Planning for the greater city of Stockholm was thus implemented and the complete development of these new communities was made possible. The city built some of the housing, and land was leased to cooperatives and other private organizations for additional housing and commercial and industrial development. Open space for recreation was reserved between the towns and

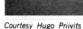

Courtesy Hugo Priivits   FARSTA—Town center   Courtesy Hugo Priivits

Courtesy Hugo Priivits   Courtesy Hugo Priivits
VALLINGBY—Town center   VALLINGBY—Town center
                                              and apartments

Vallingby and Farsta. *Neither Vallingby nor Farsta are, nor were they intended to be, self-contained "new towns." They are integral developments of the general plan for the decentralization of the city of Stockholm. They were planned, however, to support a complete marketplace and business center, to provide industrial employment to complement the employment opportunities in the central city, and to accommodate a diversification of dwelling types to meet the wide range in family composition in a balanced community. When completed, Vallingby will have nearly 500,000 square feet of shops and more than one million square feet in office space, social and welfare facilities, and entertainment. Some 40 percent of the employment has been within the nearby new industrial district.*

Visitors to the new towns in recent years have marveled at the way in which the homes, grounds, and overall living environment have been maintained. Employment opportunities have increased as new firms are lured away from the more intensively developed, older cities. The plight of London is an indication of the decentralization of industry to the open sites in the new towns.

Stockholm, but the relatively convenient proximity (Vallingby seven miles and Farsta six miles) to the central city offers a diversification of employment and the advantages of cultural facilities in the city.

Since these successful towns were founded, Skarholmen-Varherg and Soderby-Salen have also been built around Stockholm, and a dozen relatively small communities are distributed through the southern part of the country.

Denmark

A series of urban concentrations in a linear alignment, known as the Finger Plan, was adopted in 1949, part of the plan for the development of an integrated decentralization of the entire metropolitan region of Copenhagen. It is estimated that the urban population of this region will increase 70 percent, about one million people, by 1980. The Finger Plan was expanded in 1958 with the recommendation for two large urban centers southwest of Copenhagen. Each of these new centers will accommodate 250,000 people, a population considered by the planners to be an optimum size to support all necessary major urban services, provide a desirable diversification of industrial employment, and yet facilitate the convenient circulation of motor vehicles without the congestion that afflicts the larger cities. Although the new communities are intended to have self-sufficient economic bases and their size and facilities would exclude them from the category of satellite towns, a key purpose of the Finger Plan is convenience of communication between the new centers as well as to the central city of Copenhagen. The aim is integration with, rather than isolation from, the metropolitan complex, and this linear structure is therefore dependent upon a rapid and efficient system of rail transportation.[22]

Finland

The policy of planned decentralization is also illustrated in the new town of Tapiola in Finland. Situated on a superb wooded site six miles from Helsinki, the new satellite town is exemplary. Although it is relatively modest in size—a population of 17,000 on 670 acres—Arne Ervi's town plan, chosen by a competition in 1952, reflects the sensitivity and skill of the several architects who participated in its destiny, among them Jorma Jarvi, Keija and Heiki Siren, Viljo Rewell, and Aluis Blomstedt. Residential groups are situated among the forest areas in three neighborhoods of about 6,000 people. Each is provided with convenient shopping centers with indoor and outdoor recreational facilities. Bicycle and pedestrian ways are carefully separated from motor roads. Housing ranges from one- and two-story dwellings and three- and four-story walk-up apartments to eleven-story apartment towers. Dwellings are purchased with the aid of loans at low interest from the State Housing Board.

---

22. Eric Reade, *Journal of the Land Planning Institute,* London, December 1961–January 1962.

An area of light industry provides employment for about half the residents, and a short bus trip to Helsinki extends employment and cultural opportunities. Completed in 1965, Tapiola was carried out by the Housing Foundation, an association of consumer, civil servant, and trade union organizations created in 1951. The town site was purchased by the Family Welfare League before the establishment of the Housing Foundation. With aggressive private initiative, this new town achieved an environment of unique distinction under the direction of Heiki von Hertze, Chief of the Planning Department for the Foundation.

Poland

In Eastern Europe there has been considerable activity, most notably in Poland.

> In Poland, the creation of new towns became an emergency issue after the destruction of Warsaw and other cities during World War II. After 1950, the Polish government built three free-standing new towns, six satellite towns, and forty-four new towns within Warsaw limits. Except for the satellites, the new towns were usually expansions of existing small towns. In their early stages, the new towns were characterized by geometric uniformity and "monumentalization," but the government later shaped new towns as entities of their own and developed the neighborhood as the unit of social focus. Some new towns lacked adequate old centers (such as Tychy) or convenient access (such as Konin), creating difficulties for planners. The government is responsible for assemblage, planning implementation, and operation of the new towns.
>
> In 1972, there were half a million people in the Polish new towns, but population will eventually reach 800,000. A large portion of the Polish new-town population is young married couples with small children who have come from all over the country. In the years just after the war, shortages in urban labor brought many workers from small towns who regarded the new towns as an improvement, although the standard of living was not and is not high.[23]

Soviet Union

The theory of the new towns has been adopted by the Soviet Union. Industries are discouraged from settling in cities that have reached a population of 500,000 or more, but new communities are to become satellites of large cities, to assure proximity to cultural activities. Three population sizes are favored for new towns: 30,000–50,000; 80,000–100,000; and 100,000–300,000. In 1974 plans were made for five new towns of 100,000 for the region around Odessa. Eighteen such towns have

---

23. Golany, *Cities.*

been proposed for the region around Moscow, the first of which is Kryu-kov. The future size of this great urban complex will be limited to 5 million people.

The Russians have employed a number of new-town designs. Some are dormitory towns for commuters, some are self-sustaining with local employment, some are built to sustain rural industry, and some are built to disperse the population for strategic military purposes.

According to Russian sources more than 1,200 new towns have been built in Russia since 1926, housing more than 40 million people, or a quarter of the national population. Between 200 and 250 more new towns are to be built by 1985. A longer-range plan targets twenty-five cities and regional centers for intensive construction of small and medium cities by 1991, each with a population of up to 100,000.

Russian new towns have brought progress and technology to backward regions, have increased industrial production, have succeeded to some extent in population distribution, have supported natural resources exploitation, and have distributed industry.

But because of the immense cost of building new towns, coupled with harsh climatic conditions and the remoteness of many regions, the Soviet approach has had only limited success. Brining population to the east and especially to Siberia has been a major problem, as has the complaint that many of the new towns are created and managed in "company-town" style, the result of planning a new town to serve a single industry.[24]

Israel

Israel faced several unique problems in planning new towns. First, the nation started entirely from scratch, in order to create a homeland for widely dispersed Jewish populations. Second, the geographical area involved is quite small and population must be spread away from the cities to avoid overconcentration on the Sharon (Mediterranean) coast. And third, the nation feels acute defense and geo-political needs, and towns are placed accordingly.

Most of the Israeli development towns are self-supporting communities built from the ground up. All of them were built through government support and planning, and all are considered in the public domain. More than 20 percent of the total population now resides and works within the twenty-eight development towns. There are no specific towns for specific jobs—all are planned for mixed land use and all provide basic social and daily services. Because many current residents came to Israel without any wealth, housing for the development towns is publicly subsidized.[25]

Israel has built many new towns in addition to the reconstruction and expansion of Jerusalem, Haifa, and Tel Aviv. New communities were

---

24. Ibid.
25. Ibid.

developed, some as defense outposts, others as permanent homesites, for immigrants arriving from many parts of the world. Along the coast of the Mediterranean two important centers were constructed in the late 1960s and early 1970s, Ashdot and Askelon. The new town of Eilath was constructed at the northern end of the Gulf of Aqaba.

The government utilized British town planning standards and techniques. Most structures are two or three stories in height and built of masonry materials. The site planning is, for the most part, very good, with adequate open spaces for recreation and outdoor living in the temperate climate.

The decision to establish the new town of Arad was taken by the Israeli government in 1960. During the course of the following two years a team of planners was engaged in developing the physical, demographic, and economic basis of the town; and by the end of 1962 the first settlers arrived.

Arad is situated in the northern Negev east of Beersheba and borders the Judean Desert. It is located on a plateau 600 meters above the Mediterranean and 1,000 meters above the Dead Sea—overlooking these bodies of water from the west. It is located forty-five kilometers from Beersheba and 100 kilometers from Jerusalem. To the Dead Sea and its curative springs one has only to travel twenty-five kilometers—a mere half hour. There are two highways leading to Massada—one by way of Sodom, while the other, originating from within Arad itself, leads to the ancient Roman ramparts only forty-five kilometers to the west.

Ancient Arad, as it is called in the Bible, is located ten kilometers west of the new town. Archaeological excavations exposed an Israelite fortress dating back to the period of the kings of Judaea (seventh century B.C.) and an ancient Canaanite city no less than 5,000 years old.

Today, Arad has a population of 11,500 comprising 3,700 households. Arad was planned during the sixties without the population pressures caused by the fifties' waves of mass immigration. Thus the type of planning errors that characterized and plagued development towns preceding Arad were avoided. The streets are wide, apartments spacious, and the town itself is planned for a projected population of 70,000 inhabitants. Clearly established development priorities favor industrial expansion, high- and low-density housing, commercial growth, and the tourist hotel industry.

The local climate is uniquely suitable for sufferers from asthma and various allergies. From its inception, the town has actively prevented air pollution; the municipality of Arad directs special attention to the preservation of clean, dry, and refreshing air. Even the flora is controlled in order to preserve the air's unique properties.

Egypt

The late president of Egypt Anwar el-Sadat stated that until his administration, "not a single new city has been erected in Egypt since the opening of the Suez Canal." In the short course of his presidency a cluster of new towns was designed and construction started. Most of the efforts were directed to the developments in the delta land of the Nile adjacent to Cairo. Tenth of Ramadan new town lies fifty kilometers from the center of Cairo on the Cairo-Ismailia highway. It has a target population of 500,000, which may be reached before the year 2000. Tenth of Ramadan is to be an industrial city with medium industries. Some major facilities were already constructed and the school, shopping, and cultural facilities for the first unit were completed in 1980. Other communities include Sadat Industrial New Town, located sixty-five kilometers from Cairo adjacent to the Cairo-Alexandria Desert Road. It, like Tenth of Ramadan, is planned for a population of approximately 500,000 by the year 2000 and an ultimate population of one million. El Obour is being planned for a population of over half a million, El Amria for approximately one million. Other new towns are in the planning stages.

The location of the new towns—between Cairo, Alexandria, and the Suez Canal—is intended to relieve the tremendous population concentration in Cairo, Alexandria, and Ismailia.

The housing types, as for example in Tenth of Ramadan, vary from one-story modest accommodations to two-story buildings of a rather handsome character. All are constructed of masonry.

People's Republic of China

Since 1949 more than ten industrial towns have been created in the suburbs around Shanghai. These towns are eighteen to forty-two miles away from the central city. They have been developed in conformity with sound city planning principles and provide for industrial, residential, and commercial areas as well as for greenbelts, railway stations, schools, parks, medical facilities, and other amenities. Some of these communities were built as an extension of existing small enclaves, where the population ranged from 3,000 to 5,000 persons. They have now grown into small industrial complexes with more than 70,000 residents. Ties with the existing central city have been constructed to ensure regional services such as energy and transportation. The open space between the old cities and the new towns is being utilized for intensive agriculture to provide food for the residents, thus narrowing the difference in attitude between city and country residents and workers.

One of the most exciting of the new town policies can be seen in action along the Chinese coastline. Four cities there have been developing new towns in what are called Special Economic Zones: Zuhai, near Portuguese Macau; Shenshen, near British Hong Kong; Shantou (Swatow), and Xiamen (Amoy). There will be an industrial base centered in manufacturing and export centers to attract foreign trade. It is the hope of the Chinese that these centers, while exporting goods, will become the educational institutions for teaching the Chinese people the ways of the Western world. They are or will soon be the leaders in the developing open door policy toward economic dealings with the other nations of the world.

To encourage foreign investments the Chinese government makes the land available free of cost for residential and commercial developments. Much of the capital being invested in the new areas comes from Hong Kong, as many of the people of that community seek better living and working accommodations than those available in that overcrowded Crown Colony.

Hong Kong

With virtually all of the urban land in Hong Kong and Kowloon in use, most new construction must be in the New Territories that border the People's Republic of China. Six new towns have been built in this area and a seventh is planned. The biggest is Tsuen Wan, which is well on its way to full occupancy, with a population of about one million people. Next biggest will be Sha Tin and Tuen Mun, each planned to have a population of about 500,000. The other new towns at Tai Po, Yuen Long, Fanling, Sheung Shui, and Sai Kung (under planning in 1985), will not be as large, but each will become the commercial and administrative hub of its district.

Japan

Japan's major cities are phenomena of congestion.

> In an attempt to deal with what is perhaps the world's most pronounced example of urban congestion, Japan's new-town program calls for satellite towns beyond the greenbelt surrounding large cities. Tsukuba, an academic new town under construction northeast of Tokyo in 1980, plans to accommodate forty-three educational institutions between 100 and 200 thousand people. More than half of the population is slated to live in high-rise buildings at the town's center. Senri, which was constructed to draw off Osaka's swelling population, now has a population of 150,000. In all, there are twenty-seven new towns in Japan, most of them started after 1960. The biggest problem now facing Japanese planners is locating the new towns so that not too much of the sorely needed agricultural land is displaced.[26]

---

26. Ibid.

Tama New Town, constructed just outside of Tokyo, is another excellent example of recent development in Japan. This site contains over 3,000 hectares (7,500 acres) of land on a hilly site. Housing is all in high-rise buildings. Access to central Tokyo is provided by two electric railway lines, both privately operated. Over 14,700 dwelling units were completed by January 1981. The town will ultimately provide housing for 370,000 people at a gross density of approximately fifty persons per acre. This density, when compared with the crowded conditions in the Tokyo metropolitan area, is very low.

Suma New Town, just outside of the city of Kobe, was completed and occupied in 1985. This new town contains 31,420 dwelling units located on 895 hectares (2,237 acres) of land and houses a population of 115,000 people. The goal of this town was to provide good-quality living conditions at a reasonable cost. In addition the planners aimed to provide for a "human-oriented" environment, safe and comfortable to live in. The town provides medical and cultural facilities as well as sports centers and other recreational facilities. The town is comprised of six housing complexes, formed as distinct but integrated neighborhoods. Municipal express trains link the central area and the industrial districts of Kobe.

A plan for the new town of Suzuran-Ko was prepared at the request of the Japanese Ministry of Transport. The proposed site was an area of approximately 2,918 acres located about nine kilometers northwest of downtown Kobe. The site analysis was conducted by means of a computerized system that offered appropriate synthesis for development areas compatible with environmental facts, thus reducing the overall impact of urban structures on the natural environment.

Suzuran-Ko (which means "Lily of the Valley") was intended to provide a variety of residential types totaling 25,945 dwelling units, together with 4,000 dwelling units for a special environmentally and urban-oriented university. The expected total population after ten years of development was to be approximately 100,000 persons, with residential densities ranging from thirty-five families per gross acre to forty-four families per net acre.

Aside from featuring a cluster of nine villages gathered around a 325-acre lake formed by earth removal, Suzuran-Ko was to incorporate a special intercommunity transit system that would support town community centers, a regional park, and marina facilities. This transit system was designed to enable residents to be within five minutes' walking time to all sections of the town. Open space was to represent almost half of the total site area; much of it was to be developed for regional recreational use. The estimated cost for Suzuran-Ko was to be about 570 million yen.

While this hypothetical new town was not built, Suma New Town may

Suzuran-Ko New Town. *The creation of this town involved the movement of 350,000,000 cubic meters of earth to Kobe Bay to achieve the landfill for the creation of the new International Airport, together with the development of the site for Suzuran New Town. The new town will accommodate almost 26,000 dwelling units and all essential services.*

well have become a reality as a result of the intensive study devoted to Suzuran-Ko.

Developing Countries

Developing countries face larger, more comprehensive problems in new-town planning, so perhaps intelligent planning now will yield more effective

New town planning in Japan.
Courtesy Embassy of Japan Information Section, and Cooper Hewitt Museum,
Cities, 1982.

cities than those of the developed world. Venezuela, for example, has
pooled large resources to build new towns, including Cuidad Guyana, a
new center for 300,000 near the center of oil and iron production; Alta
Gracía, built around the petrochemical industry and planning a population
of 330,000; and Cuidad Losada, a satellite of Caracas. Mexico, which is
looked to with increasing frequency as a proving ground for city planning,
showed foresight when in 1959 planners named a Mexico City suburb Satellite City. Critics who chided planners for placing a satellite so far from
the city were silenced, however, when the burgeoning city expanded past
its own satellite a few years ago.[27]

---

27. Ibid.

NEW NATIONAL CAPITALS

The occasion to undertake the building of new cities to serve as government capitals is rare, and those in progress in Brazil and India are unusual both in this respect and in the boldness of their expression of urban form. Such planning is outside the context of towns as they relate to the mammoth problems of metropolitan urban expansion, but these two recent examples warrant attention: Chandigarh in India and Brasília in Brazil.

Brasília

The constitution of the Republic of Brazil in 1889 included a provision for a new capital for that country. The location was not determined until 1955, when a site at the confluence of two rivers some 600 miles from Rio de Janeiro was selected. A development corporation, appointed by the president, assumed charge of the building of the new city, and a competition for the plan was held in 1957. It was won by the Brazilian architect Lucio Costa. The creative talents of Oscar Niemeyer are among those employed for the dramatic architectural forms throughout the city.

The concept is bold—two huge axes in the sign of the cross. The principal multilevel traffic arteries traverse these axes. Separate centers for government, commerce, and entertainment are located along one axis, and the residential districts are distributed about the other. Building of the city has progressed as rapidly as funds are available. Great blocks of tall apartment buildings dominate the residential sections, and the entire theme of the city is a monumental expression of concrete and glass.

The positive conviction, uncompromising courage, and daring forms represented in the new city are inspiring. Perhaps a faint question can be heard through the powerful thrusts of this dynamic place: Is it really for people? Visitors to Brasília in the 1980s have commented on the condition of the buildings, noting that many are in disrepair. The bright, attractive new city has lost much of its glamor. The hopes that *favellas* would not develop on the outskirts are long gone. Workers and the poor flocked to the new city when it was under construction and have remained as evidence of the sad economic plight of many of the people of that lovely country.

Chandigarh

The ancient capital city of the state of Punjab in India was Lahore. When India and Pakistan were partitioned, Lahore was contained within Pakistan. The site of Chandigarh, on the rolling plains near the foothills of the

Brasília—general plan.

Himalayas, was selected for the new capital of the Punjab. Prime Minister Nehru appointed Le Corbusier to serve as advisor to the government for the plan of the new city. In collaboration with Maxwell Fry and Jane Drew of England and P. L. Varma, chief engineer for the state, a master plan was developed in 1951.

A future population of 500,000 was anticipated, but the initial stage of the plan provided for a population of 150,000 on a 9,000-acre site. The plan is a huge gridiron of major roads intersecting at distances of one-half mile in one direction and three-quarters of a mile in the other. These roads define neighborhood sectors, each 240 acres in size and housing about 15,000 people. The commercial and civic center occupies the heart of this great square.

The capital complex is set apart along one boundary of the city on a site of 220 acres. Comprising the palace of ministers or secretariat, the palace of the assembly, the palace of the high court, and the palace of the governor, this complex and the buildings within it were designed by Le Corbusier, who added a symbolic sculptural feature to the group—the Open Hand (representing Buddha's upraised palm).

The plan is no more bold than might be expected from the creative mind of Le Corbusier. Situated on a vast plain in a hot and arid region, it nevertheless evokes positive response from those who view it. The highly disciplined order and the sweeping scale of the entire concept are at once impressive. In this respect it shares an affinity with the tradition of the Mogul Empire which, during the period of Islamic domination in India, executed unsurpassed strokes of bold planning and city building. Yet there is a basic difference between the monumental group of this new capital and the earlier Mogul tradition. Even in a dead Mogul city like Fatepur-sikri, a human scale seems to pervade the paved courts and the varied structures within and about them. This city lived for only fifty years but, stark and empty though it now is, the relation between buildings and space, the light and shade of arcades and sheltered areas, convey a vivid impression that the place was meant for people. Somehow this quality is not present at Chandigarh.

At Chandigarh, the palace of ministers, a tremendous concrete structure 800 feet long and nine stories high, is one-quarter of a mile distant from the high court palace. Perhaps trees may one day provide a welcome canopy of shade within this vast space, but a rich landscape to cover the dimensions of the open space in this complex is hardly indigenous to the region nor reminiscent of the delightful gardens that once graced this country. The great structures are powerful expressions of abstract form and pattern, and the space between them is of mighty proportions. Yet they seem to withhold an invitation for people to share in the experience, and tender no protection from the burning sun. Thus one may ponder the art of planning and await the emergence of Chandigarh as a complete reality to evaluate the grand concept it represents.

Islamabad

When the new nation of Pakistan was formed, changing the status of the former Indian province to a separate state, it became necessary to select a capital. The provincial capital in the ancient city of Lahore was moved to Rawalpindi, located along the foothills of the Himalayas in West Pakistan. The facilities in Rawalpindi proved unsatisfactory to meet the needs of the new nation, and in 1959 a capital development authority was appointed to develop a new capital, Islamabad, nearby. The rigid geometrical plan, by the Greek architectural firm of Doxiadis Associates, is divided into residential sectors or neighborhood units of some 800 acres. Each sector is served by civic facilities, schools, health services, recreation facilities, and mosques. The administration center at the crossing of two main avenues contains the president's house, the secretariat, the assembly, the supreme court, and cultural buildings, with a large enclave for foreign missions. With a great national park and extravagantly monumental public buildings in Muslim tradition, the city of Islamabad should reflect the ambitions of the new nation.

CONCLUSION

New towns the world over vary greatly. At Farsta in Sweden, built upon hilly terrain, the buildings rise excitingly from natural rock formations, providing for a happy marriage with the site upon which they have been built. British New Towns have, for the most part, been constructed on relatively flat or rolling land, where the topography does not add interesting variations. Tapiola in Finland contains a wide variety of building ·

The new national capital, Islamabad.
Courtesy of the Pakistan Embassy.

types, including both high- and low-rise structures, all within heavily forested land and with water as another sort of architectural relief.

As one meditates upon the qualities that charge a city with the human spirit, the images of many places loom in contrast to the remarkable new towns in Brazil and India. Probably none is more heartwarming than that of Paris. The charm of its monumental spaces, the saucy animation of its avenues, the delight in its varied perspectives, seem less to have been planned than to have blossomed.

Perhaps, more than an efficient arrangement of its streets or the abstract shape of its buildings, it takes "the music of men's lives" to give a city character.

Let Gideon Golany, who said it so well, pen the conclusion.

The experience of careful planning and allocation of resources has shown that new towns can be a successful alternative to increasingly cramped cities. In places where nations have been willing to adopt the recommendations of planners and create new towns, such as Great Britain and France, the towns that resulted were not only pleasant places in which to live, but also economic pluses for the area. As world and especially city population expands, the new-town concept will continue to be a sound and feasible option.[28]

---

28. Ibid.

CHAPTER 36

METAMORPHOSIS

SYMBOLS OF PURPOSE

Freedom seems to be a natural need of humans. It has been sought and fought for from time immemorial. Transcending the animal's instinct for self-preservation, the human mind makes a person a social entity. The animal's behavior is conditioned by its environment, whereas people have the capacity to mold their environment to their purpose through their intellect. Purpose, then, lies at the vital core of human conduct.

Material progress marks peaks of civilization, but the culture of a people is measured by relative social values and the purpose that directs human progress. The cultivation of human sensibilities, the shaping of intuitive power, and the spiritual content of social institutions elevate a people to the cultural plane. These processes are nurtured in the soil of freedom wherein people share responsibility for society, and individuals are active collaborators with their compatriots in directing mutual affairs.

The city is a laboratory in which the search for freedom is carried on and experiences are tested. The design of the city is the warp and woof of people's lives; the pattern is woven with the toil of mind and hand guided by a purpose. We cannot dissociate purpose from achievement in evaluating affairs or charting a course toward human welfare. We detect symbols of that purpose in city building; symbols of the dominant will of a tyrant or the common weal of free persons, the rigid formality of ruling authority or the plastic form of liberty, the sumptuous pretension of aristocracy or the false symbol of unity—the pyramid.

Forged with the toil of countless slaves, the pyramid is a symbol of the "unity" of uncontested power wielded by autocratic rulers over the lives of people. The emperors of Rome built great fora, a series of huge projects dedicated to the glory of mighty rulers. Each forum was designed about an axis, the arrangement of structures and spaces dictated by symmetry. Like a symbol of undaunted might, the centerline dominated the cities built by emperors, and when their power waned there were no strong citizens to sustain the same social order.

The monarchs of France built avenues and plazas about the symbolic axis of autocratic power. The liberated space of the baroque city was appropriated by rulers rather than the ruled. Louis XIV built his palace and gardens at Versailles. Aloof from the motley crowd of the city, he transferred his court to these magnificent spaces and ordered the streets to focus upon them. *L'état, C'est Moi*. Louis XV built the Place de la Concorde, and in the center of the formal square he placed a statue of himself. The city was a formless mass of slums on which the bloated forms of palaces and gardens, boulevards and plazas, were grafted. The urban population, with no identity as people, became the crowd. Uniform facades lined the avenues as a frame for royalty. The people receded to the borders of the boulevards and took their places as spectators of the stately display rather than as participants.

The city of Hellenic democracy was planned for the people. The houses were designed for the amenities of living—each dwelling arranged as every other dwelling for appropriate orientation and privacy. The agora was the meeting place for people, and the marketplace and center of urban activity designed as an outdoor area for the mingling of citizens. The axis was incidental; it was not a dominant feature. Hellenic builders composed rectilinear forms with subtle refinement, shifted the scene from major to minor squares, and surrounded them with the continuous rhythm of colonnades. Streets did not bisect and obstruct the open space reserved for public assembly, and sculpture adorned the public square about the periphery of the open space. Size itself was not the aim of Greek city builders. The agora was large enough to accommodate the citizen population; its space was commodious, but the urban population was small. A monumental quality in public spaces was obtained through a juxtaposition of small and large spaces, contrast between the shape of forms, and the rhythm of voids and solids. The distinction between space for the movement across and circulation within the simple rectangular forms produced an order of quiet dignity.

Human scale was the measure of design in the Hellenic city, and it likewise guided the builders of the medieval town. Emerging from the Dark Ages and unprotected by the broad reaches of empire, the feudal town huddled within the confines of its encircling walls. The church provided the new common bond for humanity and, in response to the spiritual need of the people, the cathedral dominated the town but was not set apart from its surroundings. Built against other buildings, it formed an integral part of the enclosing walls of the plaza. Town life centered upon this plaza. It was designed for the mingling of people intent upon exchanging the products of their labor and learning the news of their fellow men. The urban facilities were designed for use, and they were arranged accordingly. Roadways traversed the plaza but left open space free for the movement of people. Fountains served the vital function of water supply and they, like buildings and sculpture, were not isolated within the open space of the public squares.

City design is inextricably woven into the social order of people. The design reveals symbols of the dominant economic, social, political, and spiritual patterns of civilization. The city is a melting pot of cultural forces, and its design is the expression.

ECLECTICISM

In the latter part of the eighteenth century and the early nineteenth century social upheaval burst the bonds of monarchical tyranny; the violent tensions of the Industrial Revolution broke the chain of cultural development. A new freedom was unleashed, but uncertainty as to our cultural direction aroused emotional conflicts. An air of overconfidence concealed the indecision of society. The fancy of personal taste was the new right of every individual and it confused critical judgment. Good taste was absent, and ugliness settled upon the city.

Recoiling from the dread monotony of the industrial city, people sought escape from the ugly reality. They cloaked public edifices with an artificial pomposity and found retreat in dwellings that simulated sumptuous surroundings of a glorified ancestry. As though to insulate themselves from aesthetic degradation, the arts donned the mantle of classic pedigree. A cultural veneer obscured the ugly environment of the "brown decades," and eclecticism engulfed society. Artificial taste flavored parlor conversation on the arts. Art became a commodity to be bought, sold, and collected; it moved from the streets of the people into the salon.

The muralist who once adorned the walls of buildings stepped down from his scaffold, retired to his studio, and painted pictures to be framed and hung in galleries. Works of art were no longer integral with the environment of people. The legends in stained glass of the cathedral were replaced by book printing. Sculptured figures draped in Roman togas were fitted into classic pediments of banks and courthouses. Fountains no longer supplied water for the population; they dripped or spouted solely in memory of some event or person.

Civic design reflected the confusion and uncertainty of aesthetics. Scholars studied the cities of old; they observed the assurance and strong centerline of imperialism and the picturesqueness of the Middle Ages. The past was a vast storehouse of historic forms available for reproduction. New buildings, each with its historic prototype, were assembled about a whole complex of axes shooting off in all directions. Plazas were laced with major and minor axes, streets bisected open spaces at diagonals and right angles, avenues focused on pompous structures, and a galaxy of artificial features, statues, fountains, and formal landscape effects were arbitrarily distributed about these spaces. The variety of symmetrical effects interrupted the flow of traffic; both the utility and the scale of open spaces were lost to the people who traversed them.

The grandiose formality of open spaces was awe-inspiring, and the people were impressed. The grand planning of the world's fairs "took." Like the great Mall in Washington, D.C., generous open spaces were admired but did not invite relaxation and rarely served as gathering places for people. Their formal character was like a picture to be observed rather than partaken of. The delightful quality of our capital city lies in the fine old elm trees that grace the residential streets and the quaint Georgian houses of the eighteenth century. Frederick Law Olmsted, the great landscape architect, strove to design open spaces for people rather than as an abstract feature in the grand plan, and Central Park in New York City is a case in point. While the people might be better served if this huge space had been more adequately distributed, it is nevertheless designed as a natural park for the people to use.

Eclecticism was a masquerade, and a veritable bazaar of planning forms appeared. The face of the city concealed the misshapen bulk behind the masque. Once-functional features occupying a graceful place in the environment of people were now used as decorations on the false face of the city. The shopping street became the main variety show, but there were also special features. Forms of ancient Rome were frozen into civic centers, and plazas were carved out of slums to reveal a railroad station or open a traffic artery. New obstructions were then substituted: interrupting "squares" or "circles" as spots in which to isolate diminutive statues. The entire range of architectural and planning styles from the past was applied to the new city. Tastes were torn asunder in the process of selecting the appropriate garment or applying the right cosmetic. Inspired by the Gothic cathedral, the impressiveness of St.

Peter's, the charm of the colonial meeting house, and the dignity of the Georgian mansion, the choice was not an easy one.

CHANGING ATTITUDES

Persons familiar with the current trends and attitudes toward planning will recognize the changes of attitude when compared with what existed thirty years ago. The changes and the increased sophistication that have taken place on both the governmental and private levels reflect the concern felt for the public welfare and the understanding that planning is a salable commodity. There is a widespread demand for it. This should not imply that there is no longer a conflict between the regulators and the regulated. The battlegrounds usually pertain to the time delays and the costs involved in meeting such regulations as those in the new environmental and growth management procedures.

The restudy of the comprehensive plan lies ahead, as some professionals advance the idea that the plan should be a series of broad policies rather than a detailed map. The generality of this approach may please some, especially legislators, for it seems to provide them with a free hand to determine the consistency of their zoning plans and the prerogatives to make decisions that may be more flexible. We are not sure how the individual landowner will feel when his property is affected by some unpredictable use. Some past "general plans" were so general that the new idea seems but an extension of the approach of having a "no-plan plan."

As the world continues to be more urbanized there will have to be new approaches to solving the many problems associated with employment, housing, health, transportation, education, recreation, and the many other needs of people. Each new step that is taken will require understanding of the impact that it will have on people. Each step will add to the responsibilities of the planning profession and will establish the need for the broadening of the scope of its involvement in community affairs. Real problems must be discerned; by working directly with the affected people, we must find ways to solve them. Democracy in the planning process has little place for an elitist who "knows what is best" for the people.

In order to meet these challenges new tools are already being devised. They include the development of area-wide or regional environmental studies to relieve the pressure on the multiplicity of public agencies that are currently preparing and reviewing individual environmental studies. Data will not only be more extensive, but will also be more readily retrievable for use in the decision-making process.

The wise decisions are all that will still be necessary, based on factual data acquired by the legislators. There will still be a need to differentiate between short-term political or economic gains for the few and the preservation of long-term values and benefits for the general public.

"GENTRIFICATION": A REVERSAL

The renaissance of the central core of cities appears to be underway in some of the most unlikely communities, such as New York City with its troubled economic conditions and Detroit with decay appearing to etch at the core. In San Francisco, with the reconstruction and beautification of Market Street, the central area has assumed a new appearance and new life.

The trend of middle-class emigration appears to have come to a slowdown if not an end. Competition for close-in accommodations where the life of the city can be experienced is becoming an incentive to the redevelopment of older buildings; the rents on formerly abandoned structures are skyrocketing.

The SoHo section of New York City is a prime example of what is happening in many places.

> The experience of SoHo (an abbreviation of South of Houston)[1] in New York, where an art colony was encouraged, is instructive. When the rehabilitated space was offered for rent or lease, the immediate attraction of the project for renters caused rents to skyrocket. Rents originally ranging from 60¢ to $1.60 per square foot escalated in the 1980s to astronomical levels. In addition, there are reports that persons desiring apartments have paid several thousands of dollars as "key money," in order to secure a lease. The people now occupying the facilities are only those who can afford to pay rents at the inflated prices or were able to buy accommodations before the area became glamorous.[2]

An article in *The New York Times Magazine* cites many of the factors leading to the revitalization of the central core areas.[3] The decay that is setting in at suburban locations, the boredom and uniformity of the setting, the lack of cultural opportunities, the time spent getting to work each day, the rising crime rates, the increased cost of land and housing, the added burden of the rising cost of transportation, the threat of gasoline shortages—all this and many other factors make the return to the central city attractive.

As these events take place, the poor and minorities now living in the

---

1. Houston Street is the area's northern boundary.
2. Based on information provided by Ms. Adriana R. Kleinman, AIP, Principal Planner on the staff of the Planning Department of New York City.
3. "The New Elite and Urban Renaissance," Blake Fleetwood, *The New York Times Magazine*, January 14, 1979.

central areas are driven out by the rising cost of living space. There may be a flight to the suburbs as the cost of housing in these outlying areas decreases. The need for places of employment for blue- and white-collar workers will become monumental in these outlying areas. New social and economic problems may surface outside of the areas where they have tended to concentrate in the past.

As the central areas become the haven for the new "gentry," as the *Times* article calls them, the suburbs may have problems that will need much planning attention: economic planning, social planning, and the physical effort to turn the changes in occupancy into advantages for the people who will live there.

CITIES ARE DATED

Eclecticism with its parade of styles beclouded the tradition of city building, concealing the fact that urban forms in all great periods of culture were the contemporary expression of creative workers in their day. Neither order in our cities nor culture in our society can be expected without the creative expression of the contemporary character of our time.

There were undoubtedly accidental effects among the attractive features in cities of old, but we may be reasonably confident that the harmony is not due to the patina of age alone. There is an integrity of character in fine buildings and spaces that commands respect through the years. It is the integrity of creative effort, the quality of being *genuine,* that is the quality that gives harmony and continuity to creative works of all cultures. The process of reproducing the works from another period leaves a cultural void. Eclecticism is the expression of that void in our present stage of civilization.

When we observe the cities of old, we find little evidence of the eclecticism we suffer from today. Cultures developed their own characteristics, and it is by these characteristics that we identify them. When we detect signs of imitation we suspect a decline in civilization or a culture that is not yet mature. Cultures grew, expanded, evolved; just so did the forms of their cities. Changes in the style of buildings were reflected in the forms. A cathedral begun during the Romanesque period was built with heavy walls and small windows, round arches and vaults. Additions during the Gothic period were designed with pointed arches, refined tracery, and flying buttresses. The parts of a building were dated; we identify the time when they were built by the style in which they were built. The quality of thus speaking from the past is one we respect; it tells us of the character of the people; it has meaning for us.

Is it not significant that builders of today assume an opposite view of building design? How often have we observed objection to a design that would "date" a building? This contradiction marks a singular contrast with building of past ages and it is, in truth, the base following of fancy, the fashion of substituting artificial pedigree for creative expression. If we were to follow the tradition of great cultures of the past, we would engage today in the most powerful period of creative contemporary city building the world has ever seen. We have the people, the tools, the science, the industry, and the ingenuity to make the finest cities of all time.

CHAPTER 37

EPILOGUE

Any attempt to project into the future of a city, even if only into the short-range future of ten to twenty years, must attempt to define the variables that could, in the intervening years, affect the course of that city's development. But even before this can be done, existing conditions must be evaluated. So far, cities have not developed comprehensive approaches to solving the problems they face. Responses have only been to emergency situations. Band-Aids have been applied, or the problems have been swept under the municipal rug in the hope that they will go away. There must be a new attempt to understand the effects on cities of the multiple impacts of growth, decay, and economic impoverishment, especially when they occur at the same time.

The real crux in predicting the future lies in whether we have a choice in determining that future, and who the "we" are who will make that choice. Depending on attitudes and economic and political policies, it is possible to imagine many alternative scenarios for the shape of future cities.

Scenario 1: Cities will continue in the direction they are going.

Cities will get older, and they will reflect the serious economic problems that face the nation as a whole. The larger the city, the more complex the economic problems will be that relate to the provision of services protecting the health, safety, and general welfare of its inhabitants.

Scenario 2: Cities will improve in response to enlightened leadership.

Massive allocation of funds will be redirected toward the improvement of the physical/social structure of cities, and people's hope for life in the

605

city will be reborn. Redevelopment and revitalization programs will face up to and meet the housing crisis, and there will be new opportunities and assurances for improved economic futures. With abundant open space and clean air, the city will become the refuge that it should be, bringing light, friendliness, and security.

Scenario 3: Terminalitis

The danger of accidental or planned conflict cannot be discounted lightly. The mass destruction of cities, as well as all other places of human habitation, could occur. It matters little if the neutron bomb will only destroy people while leaving structures intact or if the "regular" megaton nuclear bombs destroy both buildings and people indiscriminately. The end result will be the same: cities without people or cities of brutalized people without the essential life supports that make existence possible.

The remains at Ephesus, Mycenae, Knossos, Tyre, Babylon, Athens, Ancient Rome, Luxor, Machu Picchu, Angkor, and the many other cities born in ancient times remind us of the temporal nature of all human handiwork. If the "terminal scenario" is acted out, archaeologists examining the ruins will wonder how a civilization with the wealth and capabilities and the genius of persons such as Ebenezer Howard, Clarence Stein, Henry Wright, Le Corbusier, Frank Lloyd Wright, and other "philosophers" with concepts of better cities could have come to such an end.

Native American legend has it that "all life is a circle." In the course of history, city after city has come and gone, sometimes as the basis for the rebirth of new and better cities. Some have disappeared due to natural forces, while others have disappeared through human corruption, waste, and abuse of resources. Will this be the fate of twentieth-century cities? Is the life of our cities to be part of a great circle?[1]

COMMUNICATIONS REVOLUTION

In this age, where communications between outer space and the earth could bring people in contact with each other to resolve their problems in peace and harmony, we find instead that person-to-person communications are disrupted by clouds of suspicion and fear. With the radio, television, and other means at our disposal it appears that people have been drawn inward by events close to their habitat. Never before in the history of the earth have people been closer to each other yet farther apart—locally, nationally, and internationally. The very means that could open avenues of cultural pleasure are to a great extent exploiting brutality and violence.

---

1. "The Future of Cities," by Simon Eisner. From *Cities,* published by Cooper Hewitt Museum, 1982.

WISDOM AND KNOWLEDGE

Many years ago T. S. Eliot asked, "Where is the wisdom we have lost in knowledge? Where is the knowledge we have lost in information?" Since then we have moved farther down the same path and can ask, "Where is the information we have lost in data? Where is the data we have lost in computers?"

The new electronic technologies offer exciting possibilities for handling and processing data, but they do not give us the wisdom required to resolve the great dilemmas that confront our civilization. What we must now do is create a world future network, that is, a system that will link up people and institutions all over the world so that they can communicate effectively with each other. Communication is an essential preliminary to collaboration. If we can use the new technology to share our knowledge, our ideas, our dreams on a global scale, we may be able, little by little, to agree on planetary goals and begin to work harmoniously together.

"Communications and the Future" will be a major step in the creation of the world future network that can provide a basis for global wisdom that we desperately need to manage our planet during this period of convulsive change.[2]

CONCLUSION

The patterns of urbanism are much the same the world over. The texture of the fabric that constitutes an urban complex may vary from one country to another, from one area of a nation to another, but the basic elements do not vary. Urban areas, be they large or small, all need places for residences, places for commerce and industry, places for recreation and open space, and places for transportation and communication systems.

As long as there are cities they will, to a greater or lesser degree, depend on the surrounding rural areas for the many ingredients necessary to sustain and support life. Conversion and distribution of goods and the reinforcing of people's efforts in the rural areas are among the responsibilities of urban areas.

Short of catastrophic destruction, the urban places of the world will, in one form or another, continue to exist. The pattern that urbanism will take should, if the people of the future learn from history, result in better, more civilized environments where people can enjoy freedom from fear and corruption. Cities and other urban places should be dedicated to assuring both internal peace of mind and freedom from the aggressive competition that destroys those human values so essential to the survival of an intelligent society.

To these hopes and ideals, *The Urban Pattern* is dedicated.

---

2. Edward Cornish, President, World Future Society General Assembly and Exposition, Washington, D.C., July 1982.

BIBLIOGRAPHY

Part 1

Adams, Thomas. *Outline of Town and City Planning*. New York: Russell Sage Foundation, 1935.

Bemis, Albert, and Buchard, John. *The Evolving House*. Cambridge: M.I.T. Press, 1936.

Bonavia, David, and editors of Time-Life Books. *Peking*. Amsterdam: Time-Life International, 1978.

Bosanquet, R. C. "Greek and Roman Towns." *Town Planning Review,* January–October, 1915.

Breasted, James Henry. *Ancient Times: A History of the Early World*. Boston: Ginn & Co., 1914.

Brion, Marcel. *Pompeii and Herculaneum*. New York: Crown Publishers, 1960.

Chase, Stuart. "The Case Against Home Ownership." *Survey Graphic,* May, 1938.

Childs, Marquis. *The Middle Way*. New Haven: Yale University Press, 1936.

Chow, Tsing Tai. "Shanghai." Master's thesis, University of Southern California, 1950.

Churchill, Henry. *The City Is the People*. New York: Reynal & Hitchcock, 1945.

Davis, K. "The Origin and Growth of Urbanization in the World." *American Journal of Sociology* 60 (5): 429–37.

Giedion, Sigfried. *Space, Time and Architecture*. Cambridge: Harvard University Press, 1954.

Giulio, Gianelli, ed. *World of Ancient Rome*. New York: Putnam, 1967.

Glotz, Gustave. *The Greek City and Its Institutions*. Translated by N. Mallison. London: Routledge & Kegan, 1929.

———. *The Aegean Civilization*. New York: Alfred A. Knopf, 1925.

Green, Constance M. *American Cities in the Growth of the Nation.* New York: John de Graff, 1957.

Hamlin, Talbot. *Architecture Through the Ages.* New York: G. P. Putnam's Sons, 1940.

Hammarstrand, Nils. "Cities Old and New." *Journal of the American Institute of Architects*, 1926.

Hatt, P. K., and Reiss, A. J., Jr. *Cities and Society: The Revised Reader in Urban Sociology.* Glencoe: Free Press, 1957.

Haverfield, Francis J. *Ancient Town Planning.* Oxford: Clarendon Press, 1913.

———. "Town Planning in the Roman World." Town Planning Conference, Transactions, R.I.B.A., London, 1910.

Hilberseimer, Ludwig. *The New City.* Chicago: Paul Theobald, 1944.

Hiorns, Frederick Robert. *Town Building in History.* London: Harrap Ltd., 1956.

Korn, Arthur. *History Builds the Town.* London: Lund Humphries, 1953.

Lavedan, Pierre. *Antiquite, Moyen Age: Histoire de l'Urbanisme,* Vol. 1. Paris, 1926.

Lee, R. H. *The City: Urbanism and Urbanization in Major World Regions.* Philadelphia: J. B. Lippincott, 1955.

Macaulay, Rose, and Roloff, Beny. *Pleasure of Ruins.* Norwich: Thames and Hudson, 1964.

Marinatos, Spyridon. *Crete and Mycenae.* New York: Harry N. Abrams, 1961.

Marshall, Sir John. *Mohenjo-daro and the Indus Civilization.* London: Arthur Probsthain, 1931.

Mathioulakis, C. H. R. *Knossos.* Athens: Mathioulakis and Gouvoussis, 1974.

Mayer, Harold H., and Kohn, Clyde F. *Readings in Urban Geography.* Chicago: University of Chicago Press, 1959.

McDonald, William A. *The Political Meeting Places of the Greeks.* Baltimore: Johns Hopkins University Press, 1943.

Moses, Robert. "What Happened to Haussmann." *Architectural Forum,* July, 1942.

———. *The Condition of Man.* New York: Harcourt, Brace, 1938.

———. *City Development.* New York: Harcourt, Brace, 1945.

———. "The Natural History of Urbanization." In *International Symposium on Man's Role in Changing the Face of the Earth.* Chicago: University of Chicago Press, 1956.

———. *The City in History: Its Origins, Its Transformations, and Its Prospects.* New York: Harcourt, Brace, 1961.

Mumford, Lewis. *Natural History of Urbanization.* Chicago: Chicago University Press, 1956.

Murphy, Raymond E. *The American City: An Urban Geography.* New York: McGraw-Hill, 1966.

National Geographic Society, editors. *Our Continent: A Natural History of North America.* Washington, D.C.: National Geographic Society, 1976.

Nien Ting Chang. "Lu Kaing, An Old Port in Taiwan." Unpublished paper, U.C.L.A., 1974.

Peets, Elbert. "The Genealogy of L'Enfant's Washington." *Journal of the American Institute of Architects,* April–June, 1927.

Pirenne, Henri. *Medieval Cities.* Translated by Frank Halsey. Princeton: Princeton University Press, 1925.

Reich, Hans. *The World From Above.* New York: Hill and Wang, 1966.

Robson, W. A., ed. *Great Cities of the World: Their Government, Politics and Planning.* New York: Macmillan Publishing Co., 1955.

Roseman, Rose. *The Ideal City*. Boston: Boston Book & Art Shop, 1959.
Sandstrom, Gosta E. *Man the Builder*. New York: McGraw-Hill, Inc., 1970.
Seminar Research Bureau. *City in Crisis*. Chestnut Hill: Boston College, 1959.
Sitte, Camille. *The Art of Building Cities*. New York: Reinhold Publishing, 1945.
Smithsonian Institution. *Bureau of Ethnology, 8th Annual Report*. Government Printing Office, 1891.
Stewart, C. A. *Prospect of Cities: Being Studies Towards a History of Town Planning*. London: Longmans, Green & Co., 1952.
Thomas, William L., ed., with the collaboration of Carl O. Sauer, Marston Bates, and Lewis Mumford. *Man's Role in Changing the Face of the Earth*. Chicago: University of Chicago Press, 1956.
Tunnard, C. *The City of Man*. New York: Scribner, 1953.
Vitruvius. *The Ten Books on Architecture*. Cambridge: Harvard University Press, 1914.
Wallbank, T. Walter, and Taylor, Alastair M. *Civilization Past and Present*. Chicago: Scott Foresman & Co., 1942.
Wirth, Louis. "Urbanism as a Way of Life." *American Journal of Sociology* 44 (July 1938).
Wolfe, M. R. *Locational Factors—Suburban Land Development*. Prepared for the Weyerhaeuser Co. in the College of Architecture and Urban Planning. Seattle: University of Washington, July 1961.
Wycherley, R. E. *How the Greeks Built Cities*. New York: Macmillan Publishing Co., 1949.
The Yugoslav Review Magazine. *Yugoslav Cities*. Turishcka Stampa Publishers, 1961.
Yutang, Lin. *Imperial Peking*. New York: Crown Publishers, 1961.

Part 2

Abercrombie, Patrick. *Greater London Plan, 1944*. London: His Majesty's Stationery Office, 1945.
Abrams, Charles. *The Future of Housing*. New York: Harper & Brothers, 1946.
Alm, Ulla. *Cooperative Housing in Sweden*. Stockholm: The Royal Swedish Commission, 1939.
American Institute of Architects. *Reports of Committee on Community Planning*. New York: 1924, 1925, 1926, 1927.
Aronovici, Carol. *Housing the Masses*. New York: John Wiley & Sons, 1939.
Augur, Tracy. "Planning Principles Applied in Wartime." *Architectural Record*, January, 1943.
Bartholomew, Harland. *Urban Land Uses*. (Harvard City Planning Series.) Cambridge: Harvard University Press, 1932.
Bauer, Catherine. *Modern Housing*. Boston: Houghton Mifflin Co., 1934.
Boardman, Philip. *Patrick Geddes: Maker of the Future*. Chapel Hill: University of North Carolina Press, 1944.
Boyd, John Taylor, Jr. "Toward the Reconstruction of New York's Lower East Side." *Architectural Forum*, January, August, 1932.
Burnham, Daniel H., and Bennett, Edward H. *Plan of Chicago*. Edited by Charles Moore. Chicago: Commercial Club, 1909.
Childs, Marquis. *The Middle Way*. New Haven: Yale University Press, 1936.

Community Redevelopment Agency of Sacramento. "Blight Defined." (brochure). Sacramento: 1984.

Dean, John P. *Home Ownership: Is It Sound?* New York: Harper & Brothers, 1945.

DeForest and Veiller. *The Tenement House Problem, Vols. I and II.* New York: Macmillan Publishing Co., 1903.

Denby, Elizabeth. *Europe Rehoused.* New York: W. W. Norton & Co., 1938.

Encyclopaedia Britannica. *Land, Vol. 14.* R. S. Peal Edition. Chicago: The Werner Co., 1893.

Federal Emergency Administration of Public Works. *Homes for Workers.* Housing Division Bulletin No. 3, Washington, D.C., 1937.

Ford, James. *Slums and Housing.* Cambridge: Harvard University Press, 1936.

Forshaw, J. H., and Abercrombie, Patrick. *County of London Plan.* London: Macmillan & Co., 1943.

Fortune Editors. *Housing America.* New York: Harcourt, Brace & Co., 1935.

Geddes, Patrick. "City Deterioration and the Need of City Survey." *The Annals of the American Academy of Political and Social Sciences,* July, 1909.

———. "Talks from My Outlook Tower." *Survey Graphic,* February–April, 1925.

George, Henry. *Progress and Poverty.* Canaan: Phoenix Publishing, 1979.

Gerckens, Laurence C. "American City Planning Since 1900 A.D." 1976–77 edition. Unpublished syllabus. Columbus: Ohio State University.

Gray, George. *Housing and Citizenship.* New York: Reinhold Publishing Corp., 1946.

Graham, John. *Housing in Scandinavia.* Chapel Hill: University of North Carolina Press, 1940.

Hardy, Charles O., assisted by Kucznzki, Robert R. *The Housing Program of the City of Vienna.* Washington, D.C.: The Brookings Institution, 1934.

Hegemann, Werner. *City Planning: Housing, Vol. I, Historical and Sociological.* New York: Architectural Book Publishing Co., 1936.

———. *City Planning: Housing, Vol. II, Political Economy and Civic Art.* New York: Architectural Book Publishing Co., 1938.

———. *City Planning: Housing, Vol. III, A Graphic Review of Civic Art.* New York: Architectural Book Publishing Co., 1938.

Hoagland, Henry. *Real Estate Principles.* New York: McGraw-Hill, 1940.

Home Loan Bank Board. *The Federal Home Loan Bank System.* Washington, D.C.: August, 1947.

Housing and Public Health Committee. *London Housing.* London: London County Council, 1937.

Hoyt, Homer, *100 Years of Land Values in Chicago.* Chicago: University of Chicago Press, 1933.

Johansson, Alf, and Svenson, Waldemar. "Swedish Housing Policy: The Royal Swedish Commission." *Annals of the American Academy of Political and Social Sciences,* May, 1938.

Johnson-Marshall, Percey. *Rebuilding Cities.* Chicago: Aldine Publishing Co., 1966.

Justement, Louis. *New Cities for Old.* New York: McGraw-Hill, 1946.

Le Courbusier. *The City of Tomorrow.* London: The Architectural Press, 1929.

———. *La Ville Radieuse.* Boulogne, 1934.

———. *When the Cathedrals Were White.* New York: Reynal & Hitchcock, 1947.

———. *Concerning Town Planning.* Translated by Clive Entwistle. New Haven: Yale University Press, 1948.

————. *New World of Space*. New York: Reynal & Hitchcock, 1948.

Leven, Maurice, Moulton, Harold G., and Warburton, Clark. *America's Capacity to Consume*. Washington: The Brookings Institution, 1934.

Lohmann, Karl B. *Principles of City Planning*. New York: McGraw-Hill, 1931.

Mader, George. "Seismic Hazard Mitigation." *California Planner*, March, 1980.

Marx, Wesley. "Disaster Planning." *California Tomorrow*, Spring, 1983.

McAllister, Gilbert, and Glen, Elizabeth. *Town and County Planning*. London: Faber & Faber, 1941.

McQuade, Walter. *Cities to Live in and How We Can Make Them Happen*. New York: Macmillan, 1971.

McRae, John. *Elderly in the Environment: Northern Europe*. Gainesville: University Presses of Florida, 1975.

Mumford, Lewis. *The Story of the Utopias*. Magnolia: Peter Smith Publishers, Inc., 1922.

Olmsted, Frederick Law. *Public Parks and the Enlargement of Towns*. New York: Arno, 1980 (reprint of 1870 edition).

Owen, Robert. *New View of Society, 2nd ed.* Fairfield: Augustus M. Kelley, 1977 (reprint of 1816 edition).

Osman, John. "The City as a Sacramental Act." *Architectural Forum*. August, 1957.

Reps, John W. *The Making of Urban America*. Princeton: Princeton University Press, 1965.

Riis, Jacob. *How the Other Half Lives*. New York: Charles Scribner's Sons, 1934.

Robinson, Joan. "Economic Management in China." *Modern China Series*. London: Anglo-Chinese Educational Institute, November, 1976.

Scott, Mel. *Cities Are for People*. Los Angeles: Pacific Southwest Academy, 1942.

Sert, Jose. *Can Our Cities Survive?* Cambridge: Harvard University Press, 1942.

Simon, Sir E. D. *Rebuilding Britain: A Twenty Year Plan*. London: Victor Gollancz, Ltd., 1945.

————. *The Rebuilding of Manchester*. New York: Longmans, Green & Co., 1935.

Smith, Adam. *An Inquiry into the Nature and Causes of the Wealth of Nations*, 2 vols. Edited by R. H. Campbell. New York: Oxford University Press, 1976.

Steffens, Lincoln. *The Shame of the Cities*. New York: Hill & Wang, 1957.

Stein, Clarence. "The Price of Slum Clearance." *Architectural Forum*, February, 1934.

Stern, Sylvia. "Housing for the Elderly." Unpublished paper, U.C.L.A., 1978.

Stokes, Bruce. "Housing, The Environmental Sleeper." *Sierra Magazine*, Sept.–Oct., 1982.

Straus, Nathan. *The Seven Myths of Housing*. New York: Alfred A. Knopf, 1944.

Unwin, Raymond. *Nothing Gained in Overcrowding*. London: Garden Cities and Town Planning Association, 1912.

Weimar, Arthur, and Hoyt, Homer. *Principles of Real Estate*. New York: The Ronald Press Co., 1954.

Wendt, Paul F. *Housing Policy: The Search for Solutions*. Berkeley: University of California Press, 1962.

Winnick, Louis. *American Housing and Its Use: The Demand for Shelter Space*. New York: John Wiley & Sons, 1957.

Wright, Henry. *Rehousing Urban America*. New York: Columbia University Press, 1935.

Part 3

Abrams, Charles. *Revolution in Land*. New York: Harper & Brothers, 1939.

Adams, Thomas. *Outline of Town and City Planning*. New York: Russell Sage Foundation, 1935.

Bauer, C. "The Pattern of Urban and Economic Development." *American Academy of Political Science Annual,* May, 1956.

Bettman, Alfred. "The Decisions of the Supreme Court of the U.S. in the Euclid Village Zoning Case." *University of Cincinnati Law Review,* March, 1927.

———. *City and Regional Papers*. Edited by Arthur C. Comey. Cambridge: Harvard University Press, 1946.

Bogardus, E. S. *Fundamentals of Social Psychology*. New York: D. Appleton–Century Co., 1942.

Bogue, D. J., ed. *Applications of Demography: The Situation in the United States in 1975*. Oxford, Ohio: Scripps Foundation Studies in Population, 1957.

Citizens' Housing and Planning Council of New York. *A Citizen's Guide to Rezoning*. New York: 1959.

Friedmann, John. *"The Good Society."* Los Angeles: U.C.L.A., June, 1976.

Hagman, Donald G. *Urban Planning and Land Development Control Laws*. St. Paul: West Publishing Co., 1975.

Myers, William, Dorward, Robert, and Kline, David. "Social Ecology and Citizen Boards: A Problem for Planners." *A.I.P. Journal,* April, 1977.

Moody, W. D. *Wacker's Manual of the Plan of Chicago*. Chicago: Calumet Publishing Co., 1916.

National Municipal League. *The Citizen Association: How to Organize and Run It*. New York: 1958.

———. *The Citizen Association: How to Win Civic Campaigns,* 2nd ed. New York: 1959.

Scott, Mel. *Cities Are for People*. Los Angeles: Pacific Southwest Academy, 1942.

Siegel, Shirley Adelson. *The Law of Open Space: Legal Aspects of Acquiring or Otherwise Preserving Open Space in the Tri-State New York Metropolitan Region*. New York: Regional Plan Association, 1960.

Walker, Robert Averill. *The Planning Function in Urban Government*. Chicago: University of Chicago Press, 1950.

Webster, Donald H. *Urban Planning and Municipal Public Policy*. New York: Harper and Row, 1958.

———. *Urban Planning and Municipal Policy*. New York: Harper and Row, 1958.

Wood, Robert C. *1400 Governments*. Cambridge: Harvard University Press, 1961.

Part 4

Abrahamson, Julia. *A Neighborhood Finds Itself*. New York: Harper & Row, 1959.

Adams, Thomas. *Design of Residential Areas*. Cambridge: Harvard University Press, 1934.

———. "What Proportion of Public Land and of Private Land Should be Reserved for Open Space." *American City,* June, 1928.

Alterman, Rachelle, and Hill, Morris. "Implementation of Urban Land Use Plans." *A.I.P. Journal*, July, 1978.

American Association of State Highway Officials. *A Policy of Arterial Highways in Urban Areas*. Washington, D.C., 1957.

American Automobile Association. *Parking and Terminal Facilities*. Washington D.C., 1940.

————. *Parking Manual: How to Solve Community Parking Problems*. Washington, D.C., 1946.

————. *Roadside Protection*. Washington, D.C., 1951.

American Public Health Association. *Planning the Neighborhood*. Chicago: Committee on the Hygiene of Housing, Public Administration Service, 1960.

————. *Planning the Home for Occupancy*. Chicago: Committee on the Hygiene of Housing, Public Administration Service, 1950.

American Public Works Association. *Airports: Location, Design, Financing, Zoning, and Control*. Chicago, 1954.

American Society of Planning Officials. "Preliminary Report of Committee on Park and Recreation Standards." In *A.S.P.O. Proceedings*, 1943.

————. "A Program for Tax Abandoned Lands." In *A.S.P.O. Proceedings*, 1942.

————. "A Model State Subdivision Control Act." In *A.S.P.O. Proceedings*, 1947.

Anderson, Nels, and Lindeman, E. C. *Urban Sociology*. New York: Alfred A. Knopf, 1928.

Arnold, Christopher, and Reitherman, Robert. *Building Configuration and Seismic Design—Architecture of Earthquake Resistance*. Menlo Park: Building Systems Development, Inc., 1981.

Automobile Club of Southern California. "California Statutes Relating to Public Acquisition of Off-Street Parking Facilities." Los Angeles: 1958.

Baker, Geoffrey, and Funaro, Bruno. *Parking*. New York: Reinhold Publishing, 1958.

Barnett, Joseph. "Express Highway Planning in Metropolitan Areas." *Transactions of the American Society of Civil Engineers*, Vol. 112, 1947.

Bartley, Ernest A., and Bair, Frederick H. Jr. *Mobile Home Parks and Comprehensive Community Planning*. Studies in Public Administration #19. Public Administration Clearing Service. Miami: University of Florida, 1960.

Basset, Edward M. *Model Laws for the Planning of Cities, Counties and States*. Cambridge: Harvard University Press, 1935.

————. *The Master Plan*. New York: Russell Sage Foundation, 1938.

————. *Zoning*. New York: Russell Sage Foundation, 1940.

Black, H. "Detroit: A Case Study in Industrial Problems of a Central City." *Land Economics*, August, 1958.

Black, Russell Van Nest. *Planning the Small American City*. Chicago: Public Administration Service, 1944.

————. *Building Lines*. Cambridge: Harvard University Press, 1935.

Blumenfeld, H. "Are Land Use Patterns Predictable?" *A.I.P. Journal*, May, 1959.

Breese, G. W. *Industrial Site Selection, Burlington County, N.J.: A Case Study of Existing and Potential Industrial Location*. Princeton: Princeton University Press, 1954.

Brown, Thomas H. "Long Range Aviation Planning in the Northeast." *Traffic Quarterly*, January, 1979.

Buckley, James C. "Comprehensive Transportation and Terminal Planning for Large Urban Centers." *A.I.P. Journal*, Winter, 1947.

Bureau of Public Roads. *Toll Roads and Free Roads*. Washington, D.C.: Department of Agriculture, 1939.

Butler, George. *Introduction to Community Recreation*. New York: McGraw-Hill, 1940.

California Division of Highways. *Los Angeles Regional Transportation Study*. Los Angeles: 1960.

California State Reconstruction and Reemployment Commission. *Forecasting a City's Future*. Sacramento: 1946.

Claudill, Harry M. *My Land is Dying*. New York: E. P. Dutton, 1971.

Central Association of Seattle. "Planning the Future of Seattle's Central Area." A report from the Planning Commission, Seattle, 1959.

Chapin, F. Stuart, Jr. *Urban Land Use Planning*. New York: Harper & Row, 1957.

———. *Shopping Centers: Design and Operation*. New York: Reinhold Publishing, 1951.

Churchill, Henry, and Ittleson, Roslyn. *Neighborhood Design and Control: An Analysis of the Problem of Planned Subdivisions*. New York: National Committee on Housing, 1944.

City of Detroit, City Planning Commission. *Proposed Generalized Land Use Plan*. Detroit: 1947.

Claire, William H. *Study of a Truck Terminal Under A Freeway*. Los Angeles: Community Redevelopment Agency, 1952.

Clawson, Marion. *The Dynamics of Park Demand*. New York: Regional Plan Association, 1960.

———. *Methods of Measuring the Demand For and Value Of Outdoor Recreation*. Washington, D.C.: Resources for the Future, Inc., 1959.

———, Held, R. Burnell, and Stoddard, Charles H. *Land for the Future*. Baltimore: Johns Hopkins University Press, 1960.

Cleveland City Planning Commission. *Downtown Cleveland—1975*. Cleveland, 1959.

Collison, Peter. "British Town Planning and the Neighborhood Idea." *Oxford University Housing Centre Review: 6*.

Contini, Edgardo. *The Renewal of Downtown U.S.A.* Los Angeles: Victor Gruen & Associates, 1956.

Council on Environmental Quality 12th Annual Report. Washington, D.C.: U.S. Government Printing Office, 1982.

County of Los Angeles Regional Planning Commission. "Master Plan of Airports." 1940.

Dahir, James. *The Neighborhood Unit Plan*. New York: Russell Sage Foundation, 1947.

Davis, Harmer E. *How May the Planning, Financing and Construction of Vehicular and Mass Transit Systems in the Modern Metropolitan Area Be Integrated? Part I: A Statement of the General Problem*. Berkeley: University of California, 1955.

De Leuw, Cather & Co. *Report on Parking Facilities for the City of Chicago*. Chicago: 1956.

Denby, Elizabeth. *Europe Rehoused*. New York: W. W. Norton, 1938.

Denver Planning Office. "Lower Downtown Denver." 1958.

Detroit City Plan Commission. *Neighborhood Conservation*. Detroit: Committee for Neighborhood Conservation and Approved Housing, 1956.

Dobriner, William M. *The Suburban Community*. New York: G. P. Putnam's Sons, 1958.

Dowling, Robert. "Neighborhood Shopping Centers." *Architectural Forum*, October, 1943.

Eisner, Simon. "Freeways for the Region." County of Los Angeles Regional Planning Commission, 1943.

Engelhardt, N. L., and Engelhardt, F. *Planning School Building Programs*. New York: Columbia University Press, 1930.

Fawcett, C. B. *A Residential Unit for Town and Country Planning*. London: University of London Press, 1943.

Federal Housing Administration. *Planning Profitable Neighborhoods*. Washington, D.C., 1938.

Foley, Donald L. "The Daily Movement of Population Into Central Business Districts." *American Sociological Review*, October, 1952.

Ford, G. B. *Building Height, Bulk, and Form*. Cambridge: Harvard University Press, 1931.

Ford, Henry. *Ford Ideals: A Selection from "Mr. Ford's Page" in the Dearborn Independent*. Dearborn: The Dearborn Publishing Company, 1922.

Freilich, Robert H. and Ragsdale, John W., Jr. *Development Framework Data Report*. St. Paul: Metropolitan Council of the Twin City Area, 1974.

Garrison, William L., and Marts, Marion E. *Influence of Highway Improvements on Urban Land: A Graphic Summary*. Highway Economic Studies. Seattle: University of Washington, 1958.

Geddes, Norman Bel. *Magic Motorways*. New York: Random House, 1940.

Gruen, Victor, and Smith, Larry. *Shopping Towns U.S.A.* New York: Reinhold Publishing Corp., 1960.

Haar, Charles M. *Land Use Planning*. Boston: Little, Brown & Co., 1959.

Hagman, Donald. "A New Deal: Trading Windfalls for Wipeouts." *Planning*, September, 1974.

Heyer, Paul. *Architects On Architecture*. New York: Walker & Co., 1966.

Hjelte, George. *The Administration of Public Recreation*. New York: Macmillan Publishing Co., 1939.

Horack, F. E. D. Jr., and Nolan, V., Jr. *Land Use Controls*. St. Paul: West Publishing Co., 1955.

Horwood, Edgar M., and Boyce, Ronald R. *Studies of the Central Business District and Urban Freeway Development*. Seattle: University of Washington Press, 1959.

H.U.D. "Historic Preservation Plan, Savannah, GA." 1973.

Hurd, Fred W. "These Traffic Factors Are Involved in Intersection Design." *Traffic Quarterly*, 1953.

Huth, Mary Jo and Schneider, Jerry B. "Toward a MultiModel Structure." *Traffic Quarterly*, April, 1983.

Hyde, D. C. "Fringe Parking." *Traffic Quarterly*, July, 1953.

Ingraham, J. *Modern Traffic Control*. New York: Funk & Wagnalls, 1954.

Isaacs, Reginald R. "Are Neighborhoods Possible?" *Journal of Housing*, July, 1948.

———. "The 'Neighborhood Unit' Is an Instrument for Segregation." *Journal of Housing*, August, 1948.

Jurkat, E. H. "Land Use Analysis and Forecasting in Traffic Planning." *Traffic Quarterly*, April, 1957.

Kaptur, Marcia C. "Neighborhoods and Urban Policy: A View from the White House." *Practical Planner*, September, 1978.

Kelley, Eugene J. "Shopping Centers: Location Controlled Regional Centers." *Traffic Quarterly*, 1956.

Kennedy, G. Donald. *Modern Highways*. Report of Conference Committee on Urban Problems, U.S. Chamber of Commerce, Washington, D.C., 1944.

Knack, Ruth Eckdish. "Malls 20 Years Later." *A.P.A. Planning Magazine*, December, 1982.

Kostka, Vladimir Joseph. *Neighborhood Planning*. Winnipeg: University of Manitoba School of Architecture, 1957.

———. *Planning Residential Subdivisions*. Winnipeg: University of Manitoba School of Architecture, 1954.

Lederman, Alfred, and Trachsel, Alfred. *Creative Playgrounds and Recreation Centers*. New York: Frederick A. Praeger, 1959.

Lewis, David. *The Pedestrian in the City*. New York: D. Van Nostrand Co., 1966.

Lohmann, Karl. *Principles of City Planning*. New York: McGraw-Hill, 1931.

MacElwee, Roy S. *Ports and Terminal Facilities*. New York: McGraw-Hill, 1926.

Mace, Ruth L., ed. *Guidelines for Business Leaders and City Officials to a New Central Business*. Chapel Hill: University of North Carolina, Institute of Government, 1961.

Malley, Frank H. *Location and Function of Urban Freeways: Post-War Patterns of City Growth*. New York: American Transit Association, 1946.

Mandelker, Daniel R. *Green Belts and Urban Growth*. Madison: University of Wisconsin Press, 1962.

Marks, Harold. "Subdividing for Traffic Safety." Unpublished paper. Los Angeles County Road Department, Ninth Annual California Street and Highway Conference, University of California, Berkeley, CA, 1957.

McClintock, Miller. *Short Count Traffic Surveys and Their Application to Highway Design*. Chicago: Portland Cement Association, 1935.

McKaye, Benton, and Mumford, Lewis. "Townless Highways for the Motorist." *Harper's*, August, 1931.

Mitchell, R. B., and Rapkin, C. *Urban Traffic: A Function of Land Use*. New York: Columbia University Institute, Urban Land Use and Housing Studies, 1954.

Mott, Seward H., and Hayden, Buford. "Providing for Automotive Services in Urban Land Development." *Traffic Quarterly*, 1953.

Mott, Seward H., and Wehrly, Max S. *Shopping Center: An Analysis*. Washington: Technical Bulletin No. 11, Urban Land Institute, 1949.

Moulton, Harold G. *The American Transportation Problem*. Washington, D.C.: The Brookings Institution, 1933.

Muncy, D. A. "Land for Industry." *Harvard Business Review*, March, 1954.

Murphy, Raymond E., Vance, J. D. Jr., and Epstein, Bart J. *Central Business District Studies*. Worcester: Clark University, 1955.

Nader, Ralph. "Politics of Land: Report on Land Use in California." New York: Ralph Nader's Study Group, Robert Z. Fellmuth, Project Director, 1973.

National Association of Real Estate Boards. *Blueprint for Neighborhood Conservation*. Washington, D.C.: The Build America Better Council, 1943.

National Resources Planning Board. *Human Conservation*. Washington, D.C.: U.S. Government Printing Office, 1938.

———. *Transportation and National Policy*. Washington, D.C.: U.S. Government Printing Office, 1943.

National Committee on Urban Transportation. *Better Transportation for Your City: A Guide to the Factual Development of Urban Transportation Plans*. Chicago: Public Administration Service, 1958.

National Federation of Settlements and Neighborhood Centers. "Neighborhood

Goals in a Rapidly Changing World." Unpublished paper. Action Research Workshop held at Arden House, Harriman, N.Y., 1958.

National Recreation Association. "Play Space in New Neighborhoods." A Committee Report on Standards of Outdoor Recreation Areas in Housing Developments. New York: 1939.

National Resources Board. "Recreation Use of Land in the United States, Vol. IX." Report of Land Planning Committee, Washington, D.C., 1938.

Neff, Edgar R. *Planned Shopping Centers vs. Neighborhood Shopping Areas. Marketing Series No. 3, Business Research Center,* Syracuse: College of Business Administration, Syracuse University, 1955.

Nelson, Richard Lawrence. *The Selection of Retail Location.* New York: F. W. Dodge, 1958.

Nelting, Orin F., and Opperman, Paul. *The Parking Problem in Central Business Districts.* Chicago: Public Administration Service, 1938.

Office of Planning Research. *Housing Element.* Sacramento: California State Planning Law, 1980.

Owen, Wilfred. *The Accessible City.* Washington, D.C.: The Brookings Institution, 1972.

———. *Cities in the Motor Age.* New York: Viking Press, 1959.

Pennsylvania State University College of Agriculture. "The Economic and Social Impact of Highways: A Progress Summary of the Monroeville Case Study." Agricultural Experiment Station, University Park, PA, Progress Report 219, 1960.

Perry, Clarence. *The Neighborhood Unit, Vol. 7: Neighborhood and Community Planning.* New York: Regional Survey of New York and Its Environs, 1929.

Peterson, John Eric. *Airports for Jets.* Chicago: American Society of Planning Officials, 1959.

Pfouts, Ralph W. *The Techniques of Urban Economic Analysis.* West Trenton: Chandler-Davis Publishing Co., 1960.

Rannels, John. *The Core of the City: A Pilot Study of Changing Land Uses in Central Business Districts.* New York: Columbia University Press, 1956.

Rasmussen, Steen Eiler. "Neighborhood Planning." *Town Planning Review,* January, 1957.

Ratcliff, Richard U. *Urban Land Economics.* New York: McGraw-Hill, 1949.

Renne, R. L. *Land Economics, rev. ed.,* New York: Harper & Row, 1958.

Roterus, Victor. "The Economic Background for Local Planning." In *Proceedings, Annual Meeting of American Society of Planning Officials,* Chicago, 1946.

Saarinen, Eliel. *The City: Its Growth, Its Decay, Its Future.* New York: Reinhold Publishers, 1943.

Sacramento Energy Commission. *Solar Access: A Guidebook for California Communities.* Sacramento: 1980.

Segoe, Ladislas. *Local Planning Administration, 1st ed.* Chicago: International City Managers' Association, 1941.

Sharp, Thomas. *The Anatomy of the Village.* Harmondsworth, Middlesex: Penguin Books, 1946.

Shoup, Donald C., and Pickrell, Don H. *Free Parking as a Transportation Problem.* Washington: U.S. Department of Transportation Office of University Research, 1980.

Siegel, Shirley. *The Law of Open Space.* New York: Regional Plan Association, 1960.

Smith, Paul E. *Shopping Centers: Planning and Management.* New York: National Retail Dry Goods Association, 1956.

Smith, Larry. "Space for the CBD's Functions." *Journal of the American Insti-tute of Planners,* February, 1961.

Smith, Wilbur S., and LeCraw, Charles S. "Parking." *Traffic Quarterly,* Decem-ber, 1946.

Snow, William Brewster. *The Highway and the Landscape.* New Brunswick: Rutgers University Press, 1959.

Spengler, Edwin H. *Land Values in New York in Relation to Transit Facilities.* New York: Columbia University Press, 1930.

Statistical Abstracts, Washington D.C.: U.S. Bureau of the Census, 1984.

Stein, Clarence, and Bauer, Catherine. "Store Buildings and Neighborhood Shopping Centers." *Architectural Record,* February, 1934.

Stonorov, Oscar, and Kahn, Louis I. *You and Your Neighborhood.* New York: Revere Copper and Brass, Inc., 1944.

Sutherland, Robert L., and Woodward, Julian L. *Introductory Sociology.* New York: J. B. Lippincott, 1937.

Technical Committee on Industrial Classification. *Standard Industrial Classifi-cation Manual.* Office of Statistical Standards, Superintendent of Documents, U.S. Government Printing Office, Washington, D.C. 1957.

Thompson, Richard Grant. *A Study of Shopping Centers.* Berkeley: Real Estate Research Program, Institute of Business and Economic Research, University of California, 1961.

Transit Research Foundation of Los Angeles, Inc. *City and Suburban Travel, Issue 2X,* Los Angeles, 1960.

Tratman, E. E. R. "Unification of Railway Passenger Terminals." *Engineering News-Record,* February 14, 1927.

Tuner, D. L. "The Fundamentals of Transit Planning for Cities." In *Proceedings, 14th National Conference on City Planning,* 1922.

United States Census Report. Washington D.C.: Department of Commerce, Bu-reau of the Census, 1980.

United States Bureau of Public Roads. *Parking Guide for Cities.* Washington, D.C., 1956.

United States Chamber of Commerce. *The Community Industrial Development Survey.* Department of Manufacture, Washington, D.C., 1959.

United States Congress. *Control of Advertising on Interstate Highways.* Wash-ington D.C.: Hearings, Senate Committee on Public Works. March 10, 1958.

―――. *The Impact of Suburban Shopping Centers on Independent Retailers: A report.* Senate Select Committee on Small Business, 86th Congress, Senate Report No. 1016. January 5, 1960.

United States Department of Commerce. *Data Sources for Plant Location Anal-ysis.* Business and Defense Services Administration, Office of Area Develop-ment, Superintendent of Documents, U.S. Government Printing Office. Washington, D.C., 1959.

―――. *Federal Laws, Regulations, and Other Material Relating to Highways.* Bureau of Public Roads, August, 1960.

―――. *General Location of National System of Interstate Highways.* Superin-tendent of Documents, U.S. Government Printing Office, Washington, D.C., 1955.

―――. *Highway Transportation Criteria in Zoning Law and Police Power and Planning for Arterial Streets.* Bureau of Public Roads, Washington, D.C., 1958.

―――. *National Airport Plan for 1958.* Superintendent of Documents, U.S. Government Printing Office, Washington, D.C., 1958.

―――. *Parking Guides for Cities.* Bureau of Public Roads, Superintendent of

Documents. U.S. Government Printing Office, Washington, D.C., 1956.
United States Federal Aviation Agency. *Small Airports.* Washington, D.C.: January, 1959.
United States Small Business Administration. *Basic Information Sources on Downtown Shopping Districts.* Washington, D.C., December, 1955.
Urban Land Institute. *Automobile Parking in Central Business Districts:* Technical Bulletin No. 6. Washington, D.C.: 1946.
————. *Community Builders Handbook: Executive Edition.* Washington, D.C.: 1960.
————. *Conservation and Rehabilitation of Major Shopping Districts:* Technical Bulletin No. 22. Washington, D.C. 1954.
————. *Industrial Districts Restudied:* An Analysis of Characteristics: Technical Bulletin No. 41. Washington, D.C. 1961.
————. *New Approaches to Residential Land Development: Technical Bulletin No. 40.* Washington, D.C.: 1961.
————. *A Re-examination of the Shopping Center Market:* Technical Bulletin No. 33. Washington, D.C.: 1958.
————. *Securing Open Space for Urban America:* Technical Bulletin No. 36. Washington, D.C.: 1959.
————. *Shopping Centers Restudied, Part One: Emerging Patterns.* Washington, D.C.: 1957.
Vernon, R. *The Changing Economic Function of the Central City.* New York: Committee on Economic Development, 1959.
Villanueva, Marcel. *Planning Neighborhood Shopping Centers.* New York: National Committee on Housing, Inc., 1945.
Voorhees, A. M., ed. "Land Use and Traffic Models." *Journal of The American Institute of Planners.* May, 1959.
Wagner, Hulse. *The Economic Effects of Bypass Highways on Selected Kansas Communities.* Lawrence: Center for Research in Business, University of Kansas, 1961.
Weir, L. H. *Parks: A Manual of Municipal and County Parks.* New York: A. S. Barnes Co., 1928.
Weiss, Shirley F. *The Central Business District in Transition.* City and Regional Planning Studies Research Paper No. 1, Department of City and Regional Planning, University of North Carolina, 1957.
Welch, Kenneth C. *Regional Shopping Centers.* Grand Rapids: City Planning Commission, 1948.
Whitten, Robert, and Adams, Thomas. *Neighborhoods of Small Homes: Economic Density of Low-Cost Housing in America and England.* Cambridge: Harvard University Press, 1931.
Williams, Richard L. "When the Earth is Stretched too Far." *Smithsonian Magazine,* April/July, 1983.
Williams, Wayne R. *Recreation Places.* New York: Reinhold Publishing, 1958.
Wilson, Leonard U. "Precedent-Setting Swap in Vermont." *Journal of the American Institute of Architects,* March, 1974.
Wingo, Lowdon, Jr. *Transportation and Urban Land.* Washington, D.C.: Resources for the Future, Inc., 1961.
Wood, Elizabeth. *A New Look at the Balanced Neighborhood: A Study and Recommendations.* New York: Citizens' Housing and Planning Council of New York City, 1961.
————. *The Balanced Neighborhood.* New York: Citizens' Housing and Planning Council of New York City, 1960.

————. *The Small Hard Core*. New York: Citizens' Housing and Planning Council of New York City, 1957.

————. *Housing Design*. New York: Citizens' Housing and Planning Council of New York City, 1957.

Yeomans, Alfred. *City Residential Land Development*. Chicago: University of Chicago Press, 1916.

Yokley, E. C. *Zoning Law and Practice, Vols. 1 and 2*. Charlottesville: The Michie Co., 1958.

Part 5

Abrams, Charles. *Revolution in Land*. New York: Harper & Brothers, 1939.

Adams, Frederick J. *Density Standards for Multi-Family Residential Areas*. Cambridge: American Institute of Planners, 1943.

Alterman, Rachelle, and Hill, Morris. "Implementation of Urban Land Use Plans." *A.I.P. Journal*, July, 1978.

American City Planning Institute. "Control of Land Subdivision and Building Development." *City Planning*, July, 1928.

American Institute of Planners, California Chapter. *California Planning Commissioner Handbook*. Sacramento: 1954.

American Society of Planning Officials. *Exclusive Industrial and Commercial Zoning*. Planning Advisory Service Information Report No. 91. Chicago: 1956.

————. *The Restoration of Nonconforming Uses:* Planning Advisory Service Information Report No. 94. Chicago, 1957.

Bassett, Edward M. *Zoning*. New York: Russell Sage Foundation, 1940.

Chase, Stuart. "Zoning Comes to Town." *Readers Digest*, February, 1957.

Churchill, Henry. *Densities in New York City*. New York: Citizens' Housing Council of New York, 1944.

Colean, Miles L. *American Housing*. New York: Twentieth Century Fund, 1947.

————. *Renewing Our Cities*. New York: Twentieth Century Fund, 1953.

Comey, Arthur C. *Transition Zoning*. Cambridge: Harvard University Press, 1933.

Cornick, Philip H. *Premature Subdivision of Urban Areas in Selected Metropolitan Districts*. Albany: Division of State Planning, 1938.

————. *Premature Subdivision and Its Consequences*. New York: Institute of Public Administration, Columbia University, 1938.

Cullen, Gordon. *Townscape*. New York: Reinhold Publishing Corp., 1961.

Eckbo, Garrett. *Landscape for Living*. New York: F. W. Dodge Corp., 1950.

Fagin, H., and Weinberg, R. C., eds. *Planning and Community Appearance*. New York: New York Regional Plan Association, 1958.

Ford, George B. *Building Height, Bulk, and Form*. Cambridge: Harvard University Press, 1931.

Gibberd, Frederick. *Town Design, 3rd ed.* New York: Reinhold Publishing Corp., 1959.

Goldston, Eli, and Scheur, James H. "Zoning of Planned Residential Developments." *Harvard Law Review*, December, 1959.

Goodman, Percival and Paul. *Communitas*. Chicago: University of Chicago Press, 1947.

Haar, Charles M. and Hering, Barbara. "The Lower Gwynedd Township Case: Too Flexible Zoning or an Inflexible Judiciary?" *Harvard Law Review*, June, 1961.

Herrey, Hermann. "Comprehensive Planning for the City: Market and Dwelling Place, Part 1, Traffic Design." *Pencil Points,* April, 1944.

Higbee, Edward. *The Squeeze: Cities Without Space.* New York: William Morrow & Co., 1960.

Highway Research Board. *Parking Requirements in Zoning Ordinances:* Bulletin 99, Publication 347. Washington, D.C.: 1955.

———. *Zoning for Truck-Loading Facilities:* Bulletin 59, Publication 243. Washington, D.C.: 1952.

Housing and Home Finance Agency. *Suggested Land Subdivision Regulations.* Washington, D.C.: Division of Housing Research, 1952.

Housing and Urban Development Agency (HUD). *Community Development Block Grants,* 1979.

Hoyt, Homer. *One Hundred Years of Land Values in Chicago.* Chicago: University of Chicago Press, 1933.

———. *Structure and Growth of Residential Neighborhoods in American Cities.* Washington, D.C.: Federal Housing Administration, 1945.

Lautner, Harold W. *Subdivision Regulations: An Analysis of Land Subdivision.* Chicago: Public Administration Service, 1941.

Lovelace, Eldridge, and Weismantel, William L. "Density Zoning: Organic Zoning for Planned Residential Developments." *Urban Land Institute, Technical Bulletin No. 42,* July, 1961.

Lynch, Kevin. *The Image of the City.* Cambridge: Technology Press and Harvard University Press (Publication of the Joint Center for Urban Studies), 1960.

McHarg, Ian. *Design With Nature.* New York: Doubleday, 1971.

McHugh, K. S., Commissioner. "Local Planning and Zoning." State of New York, Department of Commerce, 1960.

Merriam, Robert E. *The Subdivision of Land: A Guide for Municipal Officials in the Regulation of Land Subdivision.* Chicago: American Society of Planning Officials, 1942.

Metzenbaum, James. *The Law of Zoning.* 3 vols. and supplement. New York: Baker, Voorhis, 1955, 1961.

Mills, Stephanie. "Need for Economic Planning. San Francisco: A People's Geography of the Next Frontier." *California Tomorrow,* Fall–Winter, 1982.

National Housing Agency. *A Checklist for the Review of Local Subdivision Controls.* Washington, D.C.: U.S. Government Printing Office, 1947.

Osborn, F. J. *Nothing Gained by High Density.* London: Town and County Planning Association, 1953.

Owings, Nathaniel. *The Spaces in Between: An Architect's Journey.* New York: Houghton Mifflin Co., 1973.

Perloff, Harvey S., ed. *Planning and the Urban Community.* Pittsburgh: University of Pittsburgh Press, 1961.

Ranes, Herman. "The Impact of Political Decision Making on Planning." Master's thesis, Division of the School of Architecture, Columbia University, 1959.

Redman, Albert E. *Steps to Secure Sound Zoning.* Columbus: National Industrial Zoning Committee, 1958.

Sanders, S. E., and Rabuck, A. J. *New City Patterns.* New York: Reinhold Publishing, 1946.

Santa Clara County Planning Department. *Exclusive Agricultural Zoning.* 1958.

Schulz, E. E. *Performance Standards in Zoning Ordinances.* Pittsburgh: Air Pollution Control Association, 1959.

Siegel, Shirley Adelson. *The Law of Open Space.* New York: Regional Planning Association, Inc., 1960.

Stewart, Lyle A. "Tax Increment Financing of Redevelopment." Unpublished paper, 1983.

Superintendent of Documents. *Suggested Land Subdivision Regulation.* Washington, D.C.: U.S. Government Printing Office, 1960.

Tax Reform Act of 1976, Washington, D.C. Reprint of Legislation. National Trust for Historic Preservation, 1984.

United States Chamber of Commerce. *Zoning and Civic Development.* Washington, D.C.: Construction and Civic Development Department, 1950.

United States Department of Agriculture. *Talks on Rural Zoning.* Washington, D.C.: U.S. Government Printing Office, 1960.

———. *To Hold This Soil.* Washington, D.C.: U.S. Government Printing Office, 1938.

———. *The Why and How of Rural Zoning:* Bulletin No. 196. Washington, D.C.: U.S. Government Printing Office, 1958.

Part 6

Abercrombie, Patrick. *Greater London Plan 1944.* London: His Majesty's Stationery Office, 1945.

Aronovici, C. *Community Building: Science, Technique, Art.* Garden City: Doubleday, 1956.

Bauer, Catherine. "Cities in Flux." *The American Scholar,* Winter, 1943–44.

Bernarde, Melvin A. *Our Precarious Habitat.* New York: W. W. Norton, 1970.

Bronson, William. *How to Kill a Golden State.* Garden City: Doubleday, 1968.

Cahn, Robert. *Where Do We Grow From Here?* Boston: Christian Science Publishing Society, 1973.

California Roadside Council, Inc. "More Attractive Communities for California." San Francisco: 1960.

Chamber of Commerce of the U.S. "Balanced Rebuilding of Cities." Statement Issued by the Construction and Civic Development Committee, Washington, D.C., 1937.

Chase, Stuart. *The Road We Are Travelling.* New York: The Twentieth Century Fund, 1942.

———. *For This We Fought.* New York: The Twentieth Century Fund, 1942.

Cheney, Charles. "Architectural Control of Private Property. *Proceedings, National Conference on City Planning,* Palos Verdes Estates, CA., 1927.

Collection ASCORAL. *Les Trois Etablissements Humains.* Paris: Denoel Publishers, 1945.

Comarc Design Systems, Inc. "Computer Graphics Planning Information System." San Francisco: Comarc, Inc., 1978.

Copenhagen Regional Planning Office. *Preliminary Outline Plan for the Copenhagen Metropolitan Region.* August, 1961.

Cornish, Edward. *Wisdom and Knowledge.* Washington, D.C.: World Future Society Assembly and Exposition, 1982.

Crane, Jacob. *Urban Planning—Illusion and Reality: A New Philosophy for Planned City Building.* New York: Vantage Press, 1973.

Creighton, Thomas H., ed. *Building for Modern Man.* Princeton: Princeton University Press, 1949.

Dash, Jacob. "A Regional Approach to Local Planning." Unpublished paper, presented at International Federation for Housing and Planning Conference, Jerusalem, 1980.

———, and Efart, Elisha. *The Israel Physical Master Plan*. Jerusalem: Ministry of the Interior Planning Department, 1964.

Dahinden, Justus. *Urban Structures for the Future*. New York: Praeger Publishers, 1972.

Dickinson., R.E. *City, Region and Regionalism*. New York: Grove Press, 1954.

Directive Committee on Regional Planning. *The Case for Regional Planning with Special Reference to New England*. New Haven: Yale University Press, 1947.

Downs, Roger M., and Stea, David. *Image and the Environment*. Chicago: Aldine Publishing, 1973.

Duff, A.C. *Britain's New Towns*. London: Pall Mall Press, 1961.

Englebert, Ernest A., ed. *The Nature and Control of Urban Dispersal*. California Chapter of the A.I.P., 1960.

Eisner, Simon. *Art in the Economic Life of the City—Locational Planning*. Los Angeles: Council for the Arts, 1979.

Fagin, H., and Weinberg, R.C., eds. *Planning and Community Appearance*. New York: New York Regional Plan Association, 1958.

Forshaw, J.H., and Abercrombie, Patrick. *County of London Plan*. London: Macmillan & Co., Ltd., 1943.

Freilich, Robert H., and Greis, David T. "Timing and Sequence Development." Unpublished draft, 1974.

Friedmann, John, and Alonso, William. *Regional Development and Planning*. Cambridge: M.I.T. Press, 1964.

Futterman, Robert A. *The Future of Our Cities*. New York: Doubleday & Co., 1961.

Golany, Gideon. "New Towns." *Cities, New York*. Cooper Hewitt Museum, 1982.

Goodman, Robert. *After the Planners*. New York: Simon and Schuster, 1972.

Gottman, Jean. *Megalopolis*. New York: The Twentieth Century Fund, 1961.

Greer, Guy. *Your City Tomorrow*. New York: Macmillan Publishing Co., 1947.

Gripaios, Peter. *Impact of New Towns on Central London*. Devon, England: 1981.

Gropius, Walter. *Rebuilding Our Communities*. Chicago: Paul Theobald, 1945.

Gruen, Victor. "The Emerging Urban Pattern." *Progressive Architecture*, July, 1959.

Guttenberg, Albert Z. "City Encounter and Desert Encounter: Two Sources of Regional Planning Thought." *AIP Journal*, October, 1978.

Hawley, Amos H. *The Changing Shape of Metropolitan America: Deconcentration Since 1920*. Glencoe: Free Press, 1956.

Hegemann, Werner, and Peets, Elbert. *Civic Art: The American Vitruvius*. New York: Architectural Book Publishing Co., 1922.

Heller, Alfred. *The California Tomorrow Plan*. Los Altos: William Kaufmann, Inc., 1972.

Herrey, Hermann, Herrey, Erna, and Pertzoff, Constantine. "An Organic Theory of City Planning." *Architectural Forum*, April, 1944.

Hiberseimer, Ludwig. *The New City*. Chicago: Paul Theobald, 1944.

———. *The Nature of Cities: Origin, Growth, and Decline; Pattern and Form: Planning Problems*. Chicago: Paul Theobald, 1955.

Honikman, Basil, ed. *Responding to Social Change*. Stroudsberg: Dowden, Hutchinson, and Ross, Inc., 1975.

HUD. "Environmental Assessments for Project Level Action." Washington, D.C.: 1974.

Houstoun, Lawrence O., Jr. "Saving Urban Charm." *Planning, The ASPO Magazine*, December, 1974.

Hughes, Michael. *The Letters of Lewis Mumford and Frederic J. Osborn.* New York: Praeger Publishing, 1972.

Huxley, Aldous. *On Living in a Revolution.* New York: Harper & Brothers, 1944.

Inter-County Regional Planning Commission. *Metropolitan Growth Plan, 1970–2000.* Denver: 1959.

Isard, Walter. *Location and Space-Economy.* New York: John Wiley & Sons, 1956.

Isard, Walter, and Coughlin, Robert E. *Municipal Costs and Revenues Resulting From Community Growth.* Boston: Federal Reserve Bank of Boston and American Institute of Planners, 1957.

Isserman, Andrew M. "The Location-Quotient Approach to Estimating Regional Economic Impacts." *AIP Journal,* January, 1977.

Jacobs, Jane. *The Death and Life of Great American Cities.* New York: Random House, 1961.

Justement, Louis. *New Cities for Old.* New York: McGraw-Hill, 1972.

Knecht, Robert W. "Coastal Zone Management Comes of Age." *Practicing Planner,* AIP, December, 1978.

Kuenzlen, Martin. *Playing Urban Games.* New York: George Braziller Inc., 1972.

Lewis, Harold MacLean. *Planning the Modern City, Vols. 1 and 2.* New York: John Wiley & Sons, 1949.

Lilienthal, David. *TVA: Democracy on the March.* New York: Harper & Brothers, 1944.

Lynch, Kevin. *The Image of the City.* Cambridge: Cambridge Technology Press and Harvard University Press (Publication of the Joint Center for Urban Studies), 1960.

McKaye, Benton. *The New Exploration: A Philosophy of Regional Planning.* New York: Harcourt, Brace, 1928.

McKenzie, R.D. *The Metropolitan Community.* New York: McGraw-Hill, 1933.

Meyerson, M., and Terret, B. "Metropolis Lost, Metropolis Regained." *American Academy of Political and Social Science Annual,* November, 1957.

Mitchell, Robert B. *Metropolitan Planning for Land Use and Transportation: A Study.* Philadelphia: University of Pennsylvania Press, 1961.

Mumford, Lewis. *The Urban Prospect.* New York: Harcourt, Brace & World, 1968.

Niering, William A. *Nature in the Metropolis.* New York: Regional Plan Association, 1960.

Northeastern Illinois Metropolitan Area Planning Commission. *Land Use Handbook: A Guide to Understanding Land Use Surveys.* Chicago: 1961.

Owen, W. *The Metropolitan Transportation Problem.* Washington, D.C.: Brookings Institution, 1956.

Packard, Walter E. *The Economic Implications of the Central Valley Project.* Los Angeles: Adcraft, 1942.

Perloff, Harvey S. "The Arts in the Economic Life of the City." Unpublished paper, National Endowment for the Arts, 1979–80.

Pfeiffer, John E. "Wall Art." *Smithsonian Magazine,* April, 1983.

Regional Survey of New York and Its Environs. New York: Russell Sage Foundation, 1927–31.
> Vol. I.   *Major Economic Factors in Metropolitan Growth and Arrangement.*
> Vol. II. *Population, Land Values and Government.*
> Vol. III. *Highway Traffic.*

Vol. IV. *Transit and Transportation.*
Vol. V. *Public Recreation.*
Vol. VI. *Buildings: Their Uses and the Spaces About Them.*
Vol. VII. *Neighborhood and Community Planning.*
Vol. VIII. *Physical Conditions and Public Services.*
Regional Plan, Vol. I, The Graphic Plan.
Regional Plan, Vol. II, The Building of the City.
Rodwin, Lloyd. *The British New Towns: Policy, Problems, and Implications.* Cambridge: Harvard University Press, 1956.
———. *The Future Metropolis.* New York: George Braziller, Inc., 1961.
Saarinen, Eliel. *The City: Its Growth, Its Decay, Its Future.* New York: Reinhold Publishing Corp., 1943.
Sanders, S.E., and Rabuck, A.J. *New City Patterns: The Analysis and a Technique for Urban Reintegration.* New York: Reinhold Publishing Corp, 1946.
Selois, Henry. *Henry Moore in America.* Los Angeles: Praeger Publishers, 1983.
Sive. Mary Robinson, ed. *Environmental Legislation.* New York: Environmental Information Center, 1976.
Soleri, Paolo. *Arcology: The City in the Image of Man.* Cambridge: M.I.T. Press, 1969.
Stephenson, Gordon. *New Town Policies in Great Britain: A Brief Description.* Liverpool: Department of Civic Planning, Liverpool University, 1948.
Stein, Clarence S. *Toward New Towns For America.* New York: Reinhold Publishing Corp., 1957.
Tulsa Metropolitan Area Planning Commission. *1975 Metropolitan Tulsa.* Tulsa: 1959.
Tunnard, C., and Reed, H.H. *American Skyline: The Growth and Form of Our Cities and Towns.* Boston: Houghton Mifflin, 1955.
United States Chamber of Commerce. *A Brighter Future for America's Cities.* Washington, D.C.: 1954.
United States Housing Authority. *Planning the Site.* Department of the Interior, Washington, D.C., 1939.
University of California International Urban Research Institute of International Studies. *The World's Metropolitan Areas.* Berkeley: University of California Press, 1960.
Wagner, Richard H. *Environment and Man.* New York: W.W. Norton, 1971.
Weiss, Shirley. *New Town Development in the United States.* New Towns Research Series, University of North Carolina, Center for Urban & Regional Studies, Chapel Hill: 1973.
Wenkam, Robert. *Hawaii.* Chicago: Rand McNally, 1972.
Wood, Samuel E., and Heller Alfred E. *California, Going, Going.* San Francisco: California Tomorrow, 1962.
Wolf, Peter. *The Future of the City.* New York: Watson-Guptill Publications, 1973.

INDEX

Page numbers in *italic* indicate illustrations.

629